D1569921

Drug Trafficking, Organized Crime,
and Violence in the Americas Today

UNIVERSITY PRESS OF FLORIDA

Florida A&M University, Tallahassee
Florida Atlantic University, Boca Raton
Florida Gulf Coast University, Ft. Myers
Florida International University, Miami
Florida State University, Tallahassee
New College of Florida, Sarasota
University of Central Florida, Orlando
University of Florida, Gainesville
University of North Florida, Jacksonville
University of South Florida, Tampa
University of West Florida, Pensacola

DRUG TRAFFICKING, ORGANIZED CRIME, AND VIOLENCE IN THE AMERICAS TODAY

Edited by

Bruce M. Bagley and Jonathan D. Rosen

University Press of Florida
Gainesville · Tallahassee · Tampa · Boca Raton
Pensacola · Orlando · Miami · Jacksonville · Ft. Myers · Sarasota

This book may be available in an electronic edition.

20 19 18 17 16 15   6 5 4 3 2 1

A record of cataloging-in-publication data is available from the Library of Congress.
ISBN 978-0-8130-6068-2

The University Press of Florida is the scholarly publishing agency for the State University
System of Florida, comprising Florida A&M University, Florida Atlantic University,
Florida Gulf Coast University, Florida International University, Florida State University,
New College of Florida, University of Central Florida, University of Florida, University of
North Florida, University of South Florida, and University of West Florida.

University Press of Florida
15 Northwest 15th Street
Gainesville, FL 32611-2079
http://www.upf.com

CONTENTS

FIGURES

TABLES

PREFACE

On the Study of Drug Trafficking and Organized Crime Networks in Latin America and the Caribbean in the Twenty-First Century

One cannot pick up the newspaper without reading a story about drug trafficking and organized crime and the extreme levels of violence associated with such activities. This volume is an effort to discuss the major recent trends in drug trafficking, organized crime, and violence in the Americas. The book is divided into three parts covering overall trends and themes, as well as country-specific analyses.

Overview

This book seeks to provide a clear picture of the state of organized crime and drug trafficking and their impact on the state at the outset of the twenty-first century. The goal of this work is to examine where we have been and where we are in the twenty-first century in the war on drugs. In other words, what have been the major trends of the twenty-first century? What is the future of the "war on drugs" in the United States, Central America, and South America?

We have organized the book both geographically and thematically. In terms of geography, we are particularly keen on examining drug trafficking and organized crime and their consequences in various subregions. Organized crime and drug trafficking have had different impacts on the internal dynamics of countries as well as on levels of security and democratic stability. The war on drugs has had major negative consequences for countries throughout the region, causing politicians and experts to question the U.S.-led war on drugs. In this volume, we develop a framework for understanding why so many people are questioning the direction of the U.S.-championed war on drugs throughout the region. The war on drugs has been very costly in terms of lives lost and money spent. Critics and skeptics throughout the Americas do not want the same results that have occurred since 1990, and countries throughout the region are not willing to continue to incur such large costs.

Volume Organization

This volume is divided into three major sections. Bruce M. Bagley begins the volume with "Drug Trafficking and Organized Crime in Latin America and the Caribbean in the Twenty-First Century." As the title indicates, Bagley examines the major trends of the twenty-first century and provides a critical analysis of the war on drugs. He examines the "balloon" effect and provides a thorough discussion of the shifting routes.

In "Coca, Cocaine, and Consumption," J. Bryan Page analyzes the major trends in cocaine use over time by invoking the use of anthropological research techniques. This chapter is followed by Yulia Vorobyeva's "Illegal Drugs as a National Security Threat: Securitization of Drugs in the U.S. Official Discourse," which analyzes the discourse and securitization of the war on drugs. Juan Gabriel Tokatlian's "The War on Drugs and the Role of SOUTHCOM" examines the increasing presence of the military and identifies the various tasks that the military have performed.

Adam Isacson follows with "Mission Creep: The U.S. Military's Counterdrug Role in the Americas." From 2000 to 2012, the United States allocated $13.9 billion in military assistance to countries throughout the Americas, and the overwhelming majority of the money, 83 percent, was allocated to help countries combat drug trafficking.[1] Isacson explores the blurring lines between the duties of the police and the military and discusses the role of mission creep and its impact on security in the region.

Rocío A. Rivera Barradas focuses on security challenges at the U.S.-Mexico border, and Bruce M. Bagley ends the section with "Drug-Control Policies in the United States: Patterns, Prevalence, and Problems of Drug Use in the United States." He provides extensive analysis of drug-control policies, identifying those that have worked and examining why some have been ineffective and have not achieved their goals.

Part II examines drug trafficking and organized crime in various regions throughout the Americas. Elvira María Restrepo begins the Colombia section by providing a historical analysis of the war on drugs in Colombia from 1970 to 2010. Arlene Tickner and Carolina Cepeda follow with the role of the illicit-drug industry in Colombia. Clyde McCoy and his coauthors, a group of renowned physicians and epidemiologists, conclude the section by providing a detailed analysis of the spread of HIV among drug users. Their chapter is based on an extensive research project conducted in Colombia in collaboration with the University of Miami and scholars located in Colombia. Marten W. Brienen and Jonathan D. Rosen discuss drug trafficking and organized crime in the Andean region, focusing on Bolivia and Peru; Alberto Lozano-Vázquez and Jorge Rebolledo Flores focus on the Mérida Initiative; Sigrid Arzt addresses police reform in Mexico; and Francisco Rojas Aravena, Lilian Bobea, and Marcelo Rocha e Silva Zorovich discuss organized crime in Central America, the Caribbean, and Brazil. Khatchik DerGhougassian and Glen Evans end the section with drug trafficking in Argentina.

Part III continues with various chapters analyzing different regions. Alberto Lozano-Vázquez and Jorge Rebolledo Flores examine the Mérida Initiative and empirically analyze the consequences and outcomes of such policies. This section also includes a chapter on police reform in Mexico by Sigrid Arzt, and one on the impact of organized crime and drug trafficking on democracy in Central America by Francisco Rojas Aravena. Lilian Bobea's chapter highlights the major trends in violence and organized crime in Central America, focusing on the Dominican Republic and Puerto Rico.

Part III examines the role regional and international institutions play in drug trafficking and organized crime. Betty Horwitz and Roberto Domínguez discuss the role of institutions and drug trafficking. Betty Horwitz's chapter analyzes the Inter-American Drug Abuse Control Commission, and Roberto Domínguez concludes the section with "The Strategies of the European Union against Drug Trafficking."

The Evolution of the U.S.-Led War on Drugs

In this work, we argue that the war on drugs has had several main stages, beginning in 1971, when Richard Nixon declared it. Interestingly, Nixon recognized that the United States also had to address the concept of demand, as drug traffickers will continue trafficking drugs as long as a market exists.[2]

Since Nixon's declaration of the war on drugs, U.S. foreign policy with regard to drug trafficking has focused on combating the supply of drugs. For Reagan, drug trafficking constituted a major security threat because other countries cultivated, produced, and trafficked drugs.[3]

In 1982, Ronald Reagan declared the modern phase of the war on drugs. With the collapse of the Berlin Wall and the dissolution of the Soviet Union, the United States became the sole superpower, or hegemon, in the international system. The end of the Cold War was a critical juncture because the war on drugs became the number one national security priority of the United States. This stage emphasizes the notion that drug trafficking and organized crime also represent a major problem for the internal stability and political dynamics of a country.[4] Criminal organizations have the potential to challenge and disrupt national security, political order, and stability. Colombia, for example, has a long history of organized criminal networks that have challenged the capacity of the state, as organized crime spread its tentacles into nearly every aspect of society. The large drug cartels in Colombia during the 1980s and beginning of the 1990s resulted in Colombia being characterized as a narco-state.[5]

The third stage, where we are now, reveals that the war on drugs has not produced positive results. This book will demonstrate empirically that the war on drugs has been ineffective and has not achieved its goals. U.S.-led efforts to combat drug trafficking have resulted in lost lives and institutions being corrupted and illegitimated. Today, leaders and critics in other countries are increasingly noting the decline of U.S. hegemony and questioning whether it is in their national interest to pursue such a costly strategy. In the current stage, the alternatives have not been consolidated nor have they resulted in the implementation of an alternative strategy; they have set in motion new discussions, however. As of 2014, the United States has been forced to address issues such as legalization and decriminalization and to examine the socioeconomic and institutional roots that have made Latin America prone to high levels of criminality, institutional decay and corruption, and widespread violence.

Notes

1. See "Grant U.S. Aid Listed by Program, All Programs, Entire Region, 2000–2012," Just the Facts, last modified April 27, 2012 (information now resides at Security Assistance Monitor, http://www.securityassistance.org/latin-america-and-caribbean/data/country/military/country/2000/2012/is_all/Latin%20America%20and%20the%20Caribbean); "Grant U.S. Aid Listed by Program, Counter-Narcotics Programs, Entire Region, 2000–2012," Just the Facts, last modified April 27, 2012 (information now resides at Security Assistance Monitor, http://justf.org/).

2. See chapter 6 in this volume.

3. Bruce M. Bagley, "The New Hundred Years War? U.S. National Security and the War on Drugs in Latin America," *Journal of Interamerican Studies and World Affairs* 30, no. 1 (Spring 1988):161–182; idem, "US Foreign Policy and the War on Drugs: Analysis of a Policy Failure," *Journal of Interamerican Studies and World Affairs* 30, nos. 2/3, Special Issue: Assessing the Americas' War on Drugs (Summer–Autumn 1988): 189–212.

4. Bruce M. Bagley and Juan G. Tokatlian, "Dope and Dogma: Explaining the Failure of U.S.–Latin American Drug Policies," in *The United States and Latin America in the 1990s: Beyond the Cold War*, ed. Jonathan Hartlyn, Lars Schoultz, and Augusto Varas (Chapel Hill: University of North Carolina Press, 1992).

5. For more on Colombia, see Russell Crandall, *Driven by Drugs: U.S. Policy toward Colombia* (Boulder, Colo.: Lynne Rienner, 2002), 193; Bagley, "U.S. Foreign Policy and the War on Drugs."

ACKNOWLEDGMENTS

We have gathered leading scholars and authors to contribute to this volume. In addition to being experts, the authors have a unique characteristic in common in that they have had connections to the International Studies Department at the University of Miami (UM). Some of the experts, for instance, received their doctorates at the University of Miami and worked with Bruce M. Bagley and other scholars on issues of organized crime and drug trafficking. After receiving their doctorates, these individuals have gone on to successful careers, many of them becoming leading academics and policy analysts in their respective countries. This list of former doctoral students includes Sigrid Arzt, Roberto Domínguez, Khatchik DerGhougassian, Betty Horwitz, Jonathan Rosen, and Arlene Tickner. These individuals all have made significant contributions to the literature on organized crime and drug trafficking in the Americas. While these University of Miami graduates are at different stages in their careers, all of them have an extensive publication history and are experts on their respective topics, and many of them live and teach in the countries being studied.

In addition to former doctoral students at the University of Miami, this volume has contributors who are faculty members or researchers at the University of Miami. The list of UM faculty includes the following: Bruce M. Bagley, Zelde Espinel, Clyde McCoy, Bryan Page, Elvira María Restrepo, and James M. Shultz. Each has made significant contributions in his or her respective field of research.

In addition, several chapters have been authored by friends of the department who have had a relationship with the University of Miami for many years, often collaborating on research projects. As well, a group of young scholars have been working on issues of drug trafficking and organized crime under the tutelage of Bruce M. Bagley. The friends of the department include Marten W. Brienen, Adam Isacson, Francisco Rojas Aravena, and Juan Gabriel Tokatlian.

In sum, the list of contributors includes senior professors and policy experts who have a plethora of publications and who continue to be productive researchers and explore new issues with regard to the war on drugs and its consequences. It also is important to note that continuity and integration exist between the authors because many of them have collaborated on previous projects.

We would like to thank the University Press of Florida (UPF) and its staff for this wonderful opportunity and for their hard work and dedication. The UPF team has played an integral role in the production and publication process and has improved the quality of the work. We would like to thank the reviewers of the manuscript for their extremely useful comments. Their insights helped us improve the quality of the manuscript a great deal.

We also would like to thank the contributors to this volume. This book would not have been possible without the hard work and dedication of the numerous authors.

We would like to thank our respective home institutions, the University of Miami, Coral Gables (Bruce M. Bagley), and the Universidad del Mar, Huatulco, Mexico (Jonathan D. Rosen). We appreciate the help and support of the staff and our colleagues at the Departments of International Studies at the aforementioned institutions.

A special thanks to Yulia Vorobyeva for her help translating several of the chapters from Spanish to English. Thanks also to Alí R. Bustamante, Nilda García, Hanna Kassab, and Rocío A. Rivera Barradas for their research assistance and help preparing the manuscript.

In addition, we appreciate the editorial assistance of Vanessa Rayan and Christa Minardi. A special thanks to our copy editor, Kathy Bork, who helped improve the quality of the manuscript a great deal. We are very grateful for her hard work and dedication.

Drug Trafficking and Organized Crime in Latin America and the Caribbean in the Twenty-First Century

Challenges to Democracy

BRUCE M. BAGLEY

What are the major trends that have characterized the evolution of illicit-drug trafficking and organized crime (organized criminal networks) in the Americas over the last quarter of a century?[1] Which have been the principal transformations or adaptations—economic, political, and organizational—that have taken place within the region's vast illegal-drug economy during the first decade of the twenty-first century? This chapter identifies eight key trends or patterns that typify the ongoing transformation of the drug trade and the organized criminal groups it had spawned as of mid-2011: (1) the increasing globalization of drug consumption; (2) the limited or "partial victories" and unintended consequences of the U.S.-led war on drugs, especially in the Andes; (3) the proliferation of areas of drug cultivation and of drug-smuggling routes throughout the hemisphere ("balloon" effects); (4) the dispersal and fragmentation of organized criminal groups or networks within countries and across subregions ("cockroach" effects); (5) the failure of political reform and state-building efforts (deinstitutionalization effects); (6) the ineffectiveness of regional and international drug-control policies (regulatory failures); (7) the inadequacies or failures of U.S. domestic drug- and crime-control policies (demand-control failures); and (8) the growth in support for harm reduction, decriminalization, and legalization policy alternatives (legalization debate).

The Globalization of Drug Consumption

Many Latin American political leaders have long argued that if the U.S. population did not consume such large quantities of illegal drugs—if there were not so many American drug addicts and users—then Latin American and Caribbean countries would not produce large quantities of illegal drugs like marijuana, cocaine, and heroin for export, and the region would not be plagued by the powerful and well-financed drug-trafficking organizations—often called cartels—that have sprung up throughout the hemisphere over the last twenty-five years.[2] It is certainly accurate to claim that the United States has been for decades, and remains today, the largest single consumer market for illicit drugs on the planet. Although there is no definitive estimate, the value of all illicit drugs sold annually in the United States may reach as high as U.S.$150 billion. Some $37 billion per year may be spent on cocaine alone.[3]

Nonetheless, illegal-drug use (and/or addiction) is not a uniquely "American disease," despite the title of David Musto's pioneering book on the origins of drug control in the United States.[4] Since 2000, the twenty-eight countries of the European Union (EU) have seen the number of cocaine users increase from 4.3 million to 4.75 million, which represents 30 percent of the worldwide consumption in cocaine. The Europeans are almost closing the gap with the approximately 5 million regular cocaine users found in the United States.[5] Indeed, levels of cocaine use in the United States have dropped steadily since the early 1990s while cocaine consumption in Europe exploded exponentially during the first decade of the twenty-first century. In fact, the number of cocaine users in the four European Free Trade Association (EFTA) and twenty-seven European Union countries doubled from 1998 through 2006.[6]

Moreover, the Europeans pay more than twice as much per gram, ounce, kilo, or metric ton as do American consumers. The United Nations Office on Drugs and Crime (UNODC) 2011 report estimates that the Americas combined consumed 63 percent of the 440 metric tons of cocaine available, while the European population consumed 29 percent of the world supply. However, cocaine consumption in the United States decreased by 40 percent from 1999 to 2009.[7]

The global heroin market is quite complicated in terms of the supply chain. Afghanistan leads the world in heroin production, producing 380 metric tons, or 83 percent. It has been estimated that Afghanistan produced 6,900 metric tons of opium in 2009 alone. The heroin from Afghanistan is trafficked to every major region of the world with the exception of Latin America. Myanmar produces 5 percent, while Mexico produces 9 percent of the heroin supply. The supply from Mexico is trafficked to the U.S. market. Colombia, on the other hand, accounts for only 1 metric ton, which is approximately 2 percent of the world's production.

In terms of consumption, the UNODC 2011 report estimates that Central and Western Europe consumed 70 metric tons of heroin in 2009. People residing in Eastern Europe consumed even more, approximately 73 metric tons in 2009. Over the last decade, the bulk of the heroin consumed in Europe has come from Afghanistan, whereas most of the heroin consumed in the United States comes from either Colombia or Mexico.[8] Cocaine, in contrast, is produced in only three countries of the Western Hemisphere: Colombia (45 percent of world supply), Peru (35–40 percent), and Bolivia (15–20 percent). Cocaine is trafficked from these three Andean countries to 174 countries around the globe.[9]

Cocaine consumption is not limited to advanced capitalist markets such as those of the United States and Europe.[10] Cocaine use in Latin America has also skyrocketed since 2000. Indeed, Latin American consumers were, in 2010, estimated to have absorbed some 200 metric tons of cocaine. Until 2009, Brazil was considered to be the world's second-largest market for cocaine, behind only the United States.[11]

In the 2011 World Drug report, the United Nations reported that Brazil had replaced Argentina as the second-biggest consumer of cocaine. The report estimated that Brazil had 900,000 cocaine users, which made it the number one consumer in South America. Cocaine use in Argentina was reported to be 2.6 percent, and 2.4 percent in Chile.[12]

Cocaine consumption rates are quite high in other regions of the world. In 2009, Africa had between 940,000 and 4.42 million cocaine users. During the same year, Asia had an estimated 400,000 cocaine users on the lower end and 2.3 million users on the higher end. Eastern and southeastern Europe had fewer cocaine users in 2009 (310,000 on the lower end and 660,000 on the upper end).[13]

The dramatic rise in European and South American cocaine consumption specifically has greatly expanded world market demand for this illicit Andean product since 2000. As a consequence, a pronounced trend toward

the proliferation of new global trafficking routes and the increased involvement of criminal trafficking networks originating outside the Andean subregion has become increasingly evident.

Partial Victories in the Andean War on Drugs

From the middle of the nineteenth century through the mid-1980s, Peru
and Bolivia were the two principal suppliers of both coca leaf and refined
cocaine to the U.S., European, and other world markets.[14] As of 1985, Peru
was producing roughly 65 percent of the world's supply of coca leaf, while
Bolivia was growing approximately 25 percent and Colombia around 10
percent.[15] With the "partial victories" achieved by the U.S.-led war on drugs
in the southern Andes during the late 1980s and early 1990s—specifically,
U.S.-financed crop-eradication programs in Bolivia's Chapare under President Víctor Paz Estenssoro after 1986 (Operation Blast Furnace) and Presidents Hugo Banzer and Jorge Quiroga from 1998 to 2002 (Plan Dignidad),
along with Peruvian president Alberto Fujimori's interruption of the "air
bridge" between the Alto Huallaga coca region in Peru and the clandestine
cocaine laboratories located in Colombia in the mid-1990s, coca cultivation
in the Andes rapidly shifted to Colombia in the mid- and late 1990s.[16] By
2000, Colombia was cultivating an estimated 90 percent of the world's coca
leaf while production in Peru and Bolivia had dwindled to historical lows.[17]

In the early 1990s, Colombia's U.S.-backed all-out war against drug lord
Pablo Escobar and the Medellín cartel during the César Gaviria administration led to Escobar's death on December 2, 1993, and the rapid dissolution of the Medellín cartel.[18] Plea bargaining in 1994–1995, during the Ernesto Samper administration, with the major drug lords of the Cali cartel,
specifically, the Rodríguez Orejuela brothers, catalyzed the dismantling of
the Cali cartel.[19]

While some large criminal trafficking networks (e.g., the Cartel del
Norte del Valle), continued to operate in Colombia in the late 1990s and
early 2000s, some 300 plus smaller drug-trafficking organizations (known
as *cartelitos*) surfaced to fill the vacuum left by the dismantling of the two
major cartels in the political economy of Colombia's still highly profitable
drug trade. By the late 1990s, basically as an unanticipated and unintended
consequence of the demise of the country's major cartels, Colombia's left-
wing Revolutionary Armed Forces of Colombia (Fuerzas Armadas Revolucionarias de Colombia, or FARC) guerrillas and right-wing United
Self-Defense Forces of Colombia (Autodefensas Unidas de Colombia, or

AUC) paramilitary militias took control of coca cultivation and processing throughout rural Colombia, precipitating increased drug-related violence between these two groups of armed illegal actors, each of which sought to eliminate the other and to consolidate its own territorial control over drug-cultivation regions and the peasant growers across the Colombian countryside.[20]

As a direct result, levels of drug-fueled violence in Colombia spiraled out of control in the late 1990s and early 2000s. Indeed, during much of the first decade of the 2000s, Colombia became one of the most dangerous and violent countries in the world. In July 2000, President Clinton and the U.S. government responded by backing the Andrés Pastrana administration in its war against runaway drug production and trafficking in Colombia via the adoption of Plan Colombia. In August 2002, the newly inaugurated government of Álvaro Uribe received additional drug war assistance from Washington and the George W. Bush administration in the wake of the 9/11 terrorist attacks on the United States. Supported by almost $8 billion in U.S. aid under Plan Colombia over the course of a decade, by 2010, President Uribe and his program of "democratic security" had managed to beat back the FARC guerrillas, demobilize many—if not all—of the country's paramilitary bands, and substantially reduce the country's astronomically high levels of drug-related violence.[21]

Despite the substantial achievements of Plan Colombia and the Uribe administration's democratic security policies, however, as of 2010, Colombia remained a principal source of coca leaf and refined cocaine in the Andes, and drug-related violence and criminality appeared to be once again on the rise. The 2011 UNODC Drug Report states that the area used for cultivating coca in Colombia decreased by an estimated 15 percent in 2010, leaving the country just slightly ahead of Peru as the world's largest coca leaf producer. In 2011, the area under cultivation in Colombia was estimated at 62,000 hectares. In comparison, 2009 statistics reported 73,000 hectares under cultivation.[22]

As an unintended consequence of the U.S.-backed war on drugs in Colombia, the locus of organized criminal involvement in cocaine trafficking gradually shifted northward from Colombia to Mexico. As the Uribe administration and the U.S.-backed Plan Colombia succeeded at least partially in Colombia in the war against cocaine traffickers, the major drug-trafficking networks in Mexico took advantage of the vacuum left in the drug trade to take control of cocaine-smuggling operations from Colombia into the United States. As a consequence, drug-related violence and criminality shifted northward into Mexican territory as various Mexican trafficking organizations vied for control over the highly lucrative smuggling trade from Colombia and the southern Andes into the large and profitable U.S. market.[23]

Thus, Mexico's current drug-related bloodbath is, in part, directly attributable to the partial victory in the war on drugs achieved in Colombia via Plan Colombia. If the U.S.-backed Mérida Initiative currently being implemented in Mexico achieves results similar to those of Plan Colombia, it will not halt drug trafficking or end organized crime in Mexico or the region. The most likely outcome is that it will drive both further underground in Mexico while pushing many smuggling activities and criminal network operations into neighboring countries such as Guatemala and Honduras and back to Colombia and the Andes. Indeed, evidence that some Mexican drug-trafficking operations (e.g., Sinaloa's Zetas) are moving from Mexico into Central America is already abundant.[24]

Proliferation of Areas of Cultivation and Smuggling Routes (the Balloon Effect)

The 2010 UNODC World Drug report indicates that Colombia successfully reduced the number of hectares under coca cultivation within its national territory in the second half of the 2000–2010 decade, and production had still not returned to pre-2000 levels. How large the reductions in Colombian coca cultivation since 2010 have actually been is a controversial topic, plagued by inadequate data, methodological problems, and major uncertainties regarding the extent of cultivation and yield levels.

Given similar caveats, coca cultivation in both Peru and Bolivia, after almost two decades of decline, appears once again to be expanding.[25] Most observers believe that, overall, coca leaf production and cocaine availability in the Andean region remain roughly on a par with 2000 levels and well above those of 1990 or 1995. Evidently, the balloon effect that allowed coca cultivation to shift north from Bolivia and Peru to Colombia in the 1990s continues to operate, as cultivation moved back into Peru and Bolivia from Colombia by 2010. Various observers have speculated about the possibility that the tropical variety of coca—known in Portuguese as *epadu*—might well balloon coca cultivation from its traditional growing areas on the eastern slopes of the Andes into Brazil and elsewhere in the Amazon basin in coming years, if ongoing or renewed eradication efforts prove successful in Colombia, Peru, and Bolivia.

The UNODC 2010 report registered a 10–20 percent decline in coca production in Colombia from 2008 to 2009.[26] But enthusiasm regarding such statistics should be tempered by realism. First, it is important to note that year-to-year variations are commonplace owing to climate factors and short-term disruptions; declines over several years are required to identify enduring trends. Second, the UNODC statistics are approximations along a range rather than firm data points; it is entirely possible that the 2010 UN report underestimates the real levels of production. Third, innovations in more productive hybrid plants, yields-per-hectare, and processing can produce higher levels of refined cocaine production than anticipated by the UN analysts. Finally, the ongoing decentralization and dispersion of cultivation in Colombia makes accurate mapping of the total numbers of hectares under cultivation a very problematic endeavor.[27]

Such caveats aside, the key reason that Colombia appears to have experienced a significant decline in coca production in 2008 and 2009 is that the Uribe government moved away from its almost exclusive (U.S.-backed) reliance on aerial spraying to a more effective mixture of spraying and manual eradication linked to comprehensive alternative development programs in key coca-growing areas such as La Macarena. As a consequence of the weakening of FARC control in vast stretches of rural Colombia and the partial demobilization of the paramilitary bands engaged in drug trafficking over the period 2002–2007, 2008–2009 marked the beginning of an important decline after at least three years of steady increases in total production. Sustaining this decline will certainly require that Colombia continue its manual eradication efforts and that it provide additional funds for well-designed and -executed alternative development programs in coca-growing areas throughout the country.[28]

Meanwhile, recent increases in coca cultivation in both Peru and Bolivia suggest that the focus of U.S. attention and resources on Colombia has led to the neglect of coca cultivation in those traditional coca-growing countries in the central Andes. To forestall a recurrence of the balloon effect—pushing cultivation out of one country only to have it reappear in others—the Obama administration will have to seek to reestablish a workable relation with the government of President Evo Morales in Bolivia and find effective ways to combat the resurgence of Shining Path (Sendero Luminoso) and coca cultivation in Peru. Failure to achieve more effective drug-control policies in both countries will likely result in a continuing shift of coca production back to Peru and Bolivia, thereby nullifying any real progress in reducing coca cultivation in Colombia over the medium term.[29]

In the 1980s, largely as a result of the formation of the U.S. government's South Florida Task Force in 1982—headed by then–vice president George H. W. Bush—the established Caribbean routes used by the Medellín and Cali cartels in the 1970s and early 1980s were essentially closed down by American law enforcement and military operations. They were quickly replaced over the mid- to late 1980s and early 1990s with new routes that used Panama and Central America, the Gulf of Mexico, and the Pacific corridor to reach Mexico and then cross from Mexico into the United States.[30] When the Mexican cartels took over from Medellín and Cali in the late 1990s, the Pacific corridor became the principal smuggling route northward from Colombia to the United States, although the Gulf route also remained active.[31]

Beginning on December 1, 2006, Mexican president Felipe Calderón, with Washington's active assistance beginning in 2008 via the Mérida Initiative, waged an intense military campaign against Mexico's major drug cartels.[32] Although not by any means successful in eliminating key drug-trafficking groups, Calderón's militarization of the drug war unquestionably made smuggling across the U.S.-Mexican border from Mexico more dangerous and expensive than in past years. As a result, some of the Mexican trafficking organizations have begun to move into Central America—especially Guatemala and Honduras—to take advantage of these much weaker states to conduct their smuggling operations.[33]

There is also abundant evidence indicating increased use of both Venezuelan and Ecuadoran territory by Colombian traffickers to replace the increasingly problematic Mexico routes. Venezuela is a jumping-off point for smuggling through the Caribbean to the East Coast of the United States or across the Atlantic through West Africa into Europe. Venezuela also is used for drug flights into Honduras or Guatemala, where the shipments are then transferred to trucks and transported by land across the Guatemalan-Mexican border northward to the United States.[34]

The balloon effects produced by the partial victories in the war on drugs in the Andes on both drug cultivation and drug-smuggling routes are evident. Over the past twenty-five years and more, the war on drugs conducted by the United States and its various Latin American and Caribbean allies has succeeded repeatedly in shifting coca cultivation from one area to another in the Andes and in forcing frequent changes in smuggling routes. But it has proven unable to disrupt seriously, much less stop permanently, either production or trafficking in the hemisphere. The traffickers' constant, successful adaptations to law enforcement measures designed to end their activities have led to the progressive contamination of more and more countries in the region by the drug trade and its attendant criminality and violence.[35]

Dispersal and Fragmentation of Criminal Drug Trafficking Organizations

The differential insertion of individual countries into the political economy of drug trafficking in the hemisphere has produced a variety of forms or types of intermediation between peasant growers of illicit crops and consumers. In Bolivia, the presence of peasant cooperatives in the countryside since the National Revolutionary Movement (Movimiento Nacional Revolucionario, or MNR) revolution of 1952 produced coca grower associations and generally inhibited the rise of either criminal organizations or guerrilla movements as intermediaries, although the Bolivian military itself has on various occasions fulfilled this role.[36] In Peru, the absence of strong grassroots associations among peasant growers opened the way for both elements of the country's military apparatus (led by intelligence chief Vladimiro Montesinos) and guerrilla organizations (Shining Path) to perform the role of intermediaries or traffickers.[37] In Colombia, the absence of both peasant organizations and military intermediaries paved the way for the rise of major criminal organizations such as the Medellín and Cali cartels to fill the void. The demise of the major cartels opened the way for illegal armed actors such as the FARC and the paramilitaries.[38] In Mexico and Central America, elements of the military and police sometimes performed the functions of intermediation in previous decades, but in the 1990s and 2000s, these countries began to follow the Colombian pattern of criminal intermediation owing to the absence of strong grower associations.[39]

In terms of criminal organizations or criminal trafficking networks, Colombia and Mexico provide the two most important examples since 1990. In Colombia, the rise and fall of the Medellín and Cali cartels (and, subsequently, the Norte del Valle cartel) vividly illustrate the perils and vulnerabilities of large, hierarchical criminal trafficking organizations, especially when they attempt to confront the state openly. Both major cartels in Colombia were hierarchically structured and proved to be vulnerable targets for Colombian and international law enforcement agencies. In the wake of Medellín and Cali, Colombia has witnessed a rapid fragmentation and dispersion of criminal networks, which has proven far more difficult for law enforcement authorities to track down and dismantle than were their larger and more notorious predecessors.[40]

Although there may be countertendencies leading to reconcentration among criminal trafficking organizations in Colombia today (e.g., the Rastrojos, the Águilas Negras), the basic lesson to emerge from Colombia appears to be that smaller criminal networks are less vulnerable to law enforcement and state repression. Colombia's emergent *bandas criminales* (BACRIM), the descendants of the now formally demobilized paramilitary groups that made up the AUC, represent a new generation of drug traffickers in Colombia. They differ from the "paras" in several important respects: (1) they tend to be much more deft and subtle in seeking political alliances inside the Colombian economic and political establishment, often hiding their political linkages through indirect contacts and "clean" candidates without records of paramilitary affiliations or ties in the past; (2) they focus on establishing political influence at the municipal and departmental (provincial) levels rather than the national level; (3) the locus of their activities includes not only Colombia's Caribbean coast but also the Pacific Southwest; and (4) they have expanded their economic interests beyond drug trafficking to include other illegal activities (land piracy, gold mining, timber) as well as legal enterprises. From the Colombian state's perspective, such organizations are, at least to date, far less threatening because they do not have the capacity to threaten state security directly.[41]

In Mexico, as in Colombia in the 1980s and early 1990s, cocaine profits appear to have energized the country's major criminal networks and unleashed a wave of violence among criminal organizations seeking to strengthen and consolidate their control of key smuggling routes. As of 2014, this struggle was still playing itself out in brutal and bloody fashion. Nonetheless, Mexico's criminal trafficking groups do appear to be gradually following the Colombian pattern of dispersion and fragmentation, although the evidence is not yet conclusive. In 2000, the Tijuana cartel (the Arrellano Félix family) and the Juárez cartel (the Carrillo Fuentes family) were the two largest and most dominant drug-trafficking organizations in Mexico. Since 2000, after the Vicente Fox administration first went after Tijuana and then Juárez, Mexico has seen the rise of at least five new major trafficking organizations and a host of smaller, lesser known groups: Sinaloa, Golfo, Familia Michoacana, Beltrán-Leyva, and Zetas.[42] This dis-

Table I.1. Proliferation of Mexican cartels, 2006–2010

2006	2007–2009	2010
Pacífico cartel	Pacífico cartel Beltrán-Leyva cartel	Pacífico cartel Pacífico Sur cartel Acapulco Independent cartel "La Barbie" cartel
Juárez cartel	Juárez cartel	Juárez cartel
Tijuana cartel	Tijuana cartel "El Teo" faction	Tijuana cartel "El Teo" faction
Golfo cartel	Golfo-Zetas cartel	Golfo cartel Zetas cartel
La Familia Michoacana	La Familia Michoacana	La Familia Michoacana La Resistencia
Milenio cartel	Milenio cartel	Jalisco cartel–Nueva Generación
6 organizations	8 organizations	12 organizations

Source: Developed by the author from information obtained in personal interviews, Mexico, 2011.

persion of criminal networks in Mexico may well represent the beginning of the kind of fragmentation observed in Colombia in the 1990s. If it does, the trend would be warmly welcomed by Mexican governing authorities because it would portend a considerable diminution in the capacity of organized criminal networks in Mexico to directly challenge state authority and national security (see table I.1).

A key reason that some analysts do not accept the fragmentation of organized crime thesis in contemporary Mexico relates directly to the emergence of a new criminal network model—the Sinaloa cartel. Unlike its predecessors and current rivals in Mexico, the Sinaloa cartel is less hierarchical and more federative (with hub and spokes) in its organizational structure. Its principal leader, Joaquín "El Chapo" Guzmán Loera, forged a new type of "federation" that gave greater autonomy (and profits) to affiliated groups. To date, Sinaloa, also known as the Federation, seems to be winning the war against its rivals, although its fight against the Zetas (a paramilitary-style organization) is proving to be prolonged, costly, and bloody. It is likely that the Sinaloa model will prove more sustainable—better for business—than other criminal trafficker organizational models in Mexico, but the jury is still out.[43]

The escalating urban gang wars in Medellín's Comuna 13 neighborhood exemplify the kinds of violent internecine conflicts taking place over many contested drug-trafficking areas and routes across the entire Latin American region (e.g., the states of Nuevo León, Chihuahua, Michoacán, and Tamaulipas in Mexico; the Pacific coast of Guatemala; the Valle de Cauca Department near Cali, Colombia; the municipality of Caucasia in Colombia; or the *favelas* of Rio de Janeiro in Brazil). In Medellín, literally scores of relatively small, competing drug gangs have generated a pattern of "disorganized" crime: rather than rationally doing what would be "good for business—keeping murder rates low and police attention to a minimum—the criminal world is in turmoil and in need of an arbitrator to re-establish authority."[44]

Like Mexico, where the splintering of authority has led to the creation of smaller but no less violent groups such as the Cartel de Acapulco and Mano con Ojos, Colombia's drug gangs are fighting to establish their place in the new criminal hierarchy in Medellín's poor and marginalized barrios, long ignored by both the central Colombian state in Bogotá and by Medellín's municipal government. Under former mayor (now governor of Antioquia) Sergio Fajardo, Medellín did see a significant decline in violence rates for several years—especially homicide statistics—via informal negotiations with the gangs, new mayoral initiatives to reduce gang violence (e.g., increased social services, expanded educational opportunities, jobs programs, new public recreational spaces for youth) and the demobilization of the nation's paramilitary groups in 2005 and beyond. The relative peace achieved by the Fajardo administration in Medellín and the successor mayoral administration of Alonso Salazar did, unfortunately, gradually give way to renewed violence in Medellín's Comuna 13 and other urban neighborhoods, where drug trafficking and BACRIM activity resurged in 2010 and 2011.

Medellín's Comuna 13 or Ciudad Juárez' Rivera del Bravo slums are perfect launching platforms for gang warfare. In such neighborhoods, drug traffickers have found readily accessible pools of new gang members and many potential drug consumers, as well as efficient corridors for smuggling drugs and arms. In Comuna 13, the violence is mainly about controlling the San Juan highway, which leads out of the city to northern Antioquia and Urabá on Colombia's northern Caribbean coast. The gangs that control the highway decide who and what enter and leave Medellín: drugs, guns, money. The armed group established by former Medellín capo Pablo Escobar, now known as "the Office," remains the largest and most powerful criminal network in Medellín, even though it has splintered into rival factions, and neither side has yet managed to achieve control over Comuna 13 and the San Juan transit route.[45]

The *maras* (youth gangs) in Central American countries such as Honduras and Guatemala, the Barrio Azteca prison gang in El Paso, Texas, and Juárez, Mexico, and the Comando Vermelho in Rio de Janeiro provide additional examples of the proliferation of gangs, or *pandillas*, that work and fight—often in close association with major cartels—along with the phenomenon of fragmentation and dispersion. In 2004, for example, the armed wing of the Juárez cartel—La Línea—started to attack the local police openly while employing the *cobro de piso* (right-of-way tax) to move drug shipments through Chihuahua. This was possible owing to the incorporation of former police officials from Juárez into the ranks of the cartel. Following the intromission of the Sinaloa cartel into Juárez in the mid-2000s, rising levels of violence and murder involving Los Aztecas, a gang affiliated with La Línea, against opposition gangs such as the Mexicles, the Artistas Asesinos (Artistic Assassins), and the Gente Nueva (New Youth) have been the order of the day in Juárez, the murder capital of Mexico.[46] By October 2005, there were also an estimated 17,000 gang members that belonged to Mara Salvatrucha, or MS-13, and the 18th Street gang operating in Ciudad Juárez.[47] While no recent statistics are available, anecdotal evidence indicates that the numbers of *maras* active in Juárez and Mexico more generally appear to have increased steadily to above 25,000.

As in the Colombian case during the 1980s and 1990s, paramilitary groups have also surfaced in recent years in Juárez, Monterrey, and other parts of Mexico in response to the cartels and affiliated gang violence. The appearance of these paramilitary bands highlights the weak law enforcement capacities of the Mexican government and its perceived inability to effectively confront and defeat the country's powerful drug-trafficking organizations.[48]

Under pressure from Mexican and U.S. law enforcement, Mexican trafficker organizations have, since the mid-2000s if not before, sought to move at least part of their smuggling operations from Mexico into neighboring countries. Guatemala and Honduras are currently targets for both the Sinaloa cartel and the Zetas.[49] The upsurge in drug-related violence in both of these Central American nations is closely related to these shifts in operational bases. This trend, observable throughout the hemisphere, is sometimes labeled the "cockroach" effect because it is reminiscent of the scurrying of cockroaches out of a dirty kitchen into other places to avoid detection after a light has been turned on. Closely linked to the balloon effect, the cockroach effect refers specifically to the displacement of criminal networks from one city, state, or region to another within a given country or from one country to another in search of safer havens and more pliable state authorities.

Failure of Political Reform or State Building (the Deinstitutionalization Effect)

States determine the form or type of organized crime that can operate and flourish within a given national territory. Criminal organizations, in contrast, do not determine the type of state, although they certainly can deter or inhibit political-reform efforts at all levels of a political system from local to national. Advanced capitalist democracies—from the United States to Europe to Japan—exhibit wide variations in the types of organized crime that they generate or tolerate. The United States, for example, has eliminated the Italian Mafia model and seen it replaced by fragmented and widely dispersed domestic criminal organizations, many affiliated with immigrant communities. Europe is characterized by a similar evolution of organized crime groups affiliated with immigrant populations. Japan, in contrast, coexists with the Yakuza, a more corporate-style criminal network. In China, state capitalism coexists with the Chinese triads and other criminal organizations. In Russia, the Putin government, in effect, has subordinated and incorporated various elements of the Russian Mafia as parastate organizations.[50]

In Colombia, the paramilitary organizations, deeply involved in drug trafficking, were linked directly to both state institutions and specific political parties. In Mexico, the formerly dominant Revolutionary Institutional Party (Partido Revolucionario Institucional, PRI) developed almost tributary relations with organized crime groups. When the PRI's almost seventy-one-year monopoly over political power was broken at the national level in 2000 by the victory of the National Action Party's (Partido Acción Nacional, PAN) presidential candidate, Vicente Fox, the old lines of tribute and bribery broke down as well and unleashed a wave of internecine violence among trafficking organizations as they struggled among themselves for control of cocaine transit through their country.[51]

Transitions from authoritarian regimes to more open and democratic forms of governance in Latin America, as in Russia and Eastern Europe, are particularly problematic, because the old, authoritarian institutional controls often collapse or are swept away but cannot be easily or quickly replaced by new, democratic forms of control, at least in the short term. Mexico is experiencing precisely such a transition. The old institutions—police, courts, prisons, intelligence agencies, parties, elections—no longer work. Indeed, they are manifestly corrupt and dysfunctional. Nevertheless, in practice, few new institutional mechanisms have arisen to replace them. Moreover, reform efforts can be, and often have been, stymied or derailed entirely by institutional corruption and criminal violence intended to limit or undermine state authority and the rule of law. There certainly were significant institutional reforms proposed or under way in Mexico at the end of the Felipe Calderón sexenio (2006–2012), but there is little question that such reforms have not come fast enough nor have they been deep enough to date to contain drug-trafficking organizations and related violence and corruption in Mexico.

Such observations do not constitute arguments against democratization. Rather, they highlight challenges and obstacles along the road to democratization that are frequently overlooked or ignored altogether. Democratic theorists have only recently begun to seriously examine the problems for democratic transitions that emanate from organized and entrenched criminal networks. In the countries of Latin America and the Caribbean, such neglect of institutional reform may well imperil both political stability and democracy itself. Rather than democratic consolidation, the consequence of ignoring organized crime and its corrosive effects may well be institutional decay or democratic deinstitutionalization. Countries emerging from internal armed conflicts are significantly more vulnerable, although such conflicts are not the only source of institutional weakness. Transitions from authoritarian to democratic political systems may also engender such institutional deficits even in the absence of prior prolonged internal conflict.

The Inflexibility and Ineffectiveness of Regional and International Drug-Control Policies (Regulatory Failures)

Reflecting the hegemonic influence of the United States over international drug policy during the post–World War II period, the United Nations Office on Drugs and Crime (UNODC) and the Organization of American States (OAS) have both faithfully reproduced the U.S. prohibitionist regime at the multilateral level. The UN's approach to drug control (like that of the OAS) severely limits the flexibility of responses at the level of the member state because it in effect rules out any possible experimentation with legalization or decriminalization. Both the UN and the OAS start from the assumption that all illicit drugs are "evil" and must be prohibited and suppressed.

In practice, the UN-OAS-U.S. unwaveringly prohibitionist strategy has dominated international discourse on drug control and prevented individual countries from experimenting with alternative approaches (or forced them to ignore or defy their UN treaty obligations regarding narcotics control).[52] For example, the UN, the OAS, and the United States have, in effect, systematically rejected Bolivian president Evo Morales' declared policy of fostering traditional and commercial uses of legally grown coca leaf while preventing its processing into cocaine in that country. It must, of course, be recognized that coca cultivation in Bolivia did rise significantly in subsequent years beyond the amount that was necessary to supply traditional or ceremonial purposes and even "legal" noncocaine uses. Similarly, both the U.S. government and the UN opposed the November 2010 California ballot initiative that sought (and failed) to legalize marijuana cultivation and commercialization in that state. It is entirely possible that, had Proposition 19 been approved by the state's voters, it would have run afoul of both federal statutes and America's UN treaty obligations.

In practice, the UN prohibitionist inclination has meant that there is little or no international backing for options other than the current war on drugs, no matter what collateral damage is incurred in the process. The ten-year UN review of international drug-control policies (1998–2008), predictably, concluded that the UN's current prohibitionist policies were the best and only real strategic option available moving forward and generated no significant alterations in international drug-control policies and practices, despite growing doubts and questioning among some member states and many independent analysts.[53]

The Failure of U.S. Drug Control Policies (Demand-Control Policies)

While the United States has managed to stabilize or even reduce demand for most illicit drugs at home, it most certainly has not eliminated American demand for illicit drugs or the profits associated with supplying the huge U.S. market. Demand control has routinely been underfunded by Washington while primary emphasis has almost automatically been accorded to expensive, but ultimately ineffective, supply-side control strategies. There have been some efforts since 2009 undertaken by the Obama administration and his drug czar, Gil Kerlikowske, to redress this long-standing imbalance in U.S. drug policy, although prevention and treatment remain woefully underfunded. Analysis of the reasons behind the U.S. insistence on supply- over demand-control strategies lies beyond the scope of this chapter.

The consequences of Washington's strategic choices are, however, obvious. Washington has demanded that the countries of the region follow its lead in the war on drugs and, as in previous years, upheld a formal "certification" process that often sanctions those nations that do not "fully cooperate." U.S. insistence on such a policy approach not only has led to overall failure in the war on drugs over the last twenty-five years plus, it also has been counterproductive for both U.S. and individual Latin American country interests. The price that Colombia has paid for its role in the war on drugs has been high in both blood and treasure. The price that Mexico is being asked to pay today is as high or higher. The high costs associated with failure have generated a reaction to the U.S. strategy both at home and abroad and produced a new debate over alternatives to American prohibitionist approaches such as harm reduction, decriminalization, and legalization.[54]

The Search for Alternatives: Debates over Legalization, Decriminalization, and Harm Reduction

Some Latin American analysts anticipated that the possible passage of California's Proposition 19 in November 2010, which sought to legalize the cultivation, distribution, and possession of marijuana in the state, would signal the beginning of the end of the U.S.-led war on drugs and allow Mexico and other countries in the region to move away from the prohibitionist strategy that has generated so much drug-related violence throughout Latin America and the Caribbean in recent years. Many Latin American political leaders, however, openly oppose the legalization of marijuana in California and stridently argue against the legalization or decriminalization of harder drugs in the United States and around the globe. In the end, Proposition 19 was defeated at the polls (52 percent against versus almost 48 percent in favor). Undeterred, proponents of marijuana legalization in California are likely to place another Prop 19–style initiative on the California ballot in November 2012 with the hope for a larger turnout among under-thirty voters during a presidential year.

Whether one favors marijuana legalization in California and beyond, there are many reasons to be skeptical of the real impact of marijuana legalization on drug trafficking and organized crime in California or any-where else. First, even if such an initiative is ultimately approved in some American states, there are likely to be federal government challenges that could delay implementation for years. Second, legalization of marijuana, if and when it ever occurs, will not address the issues—production, process-ing, trafficking, and distribution—raised by criminal activity, violence, and corruption spawned by traffic in harder drugs such as cocaine, heroin, and methamphetamine. Criminal gangs in Mexico and elsewhere in the hemi-sphere will most likely move away from marijuana to deeper involvement in the still-illegal drugs, and organized crime and drug-related violence will continue. In the long run, as the 2011 Global Commission on Drug Policy report argues, some combination of legalization and decriminalization of illicit drugs along with serious harm-reduction policies and programs worldwide may well offer the only realistic formula for reducing the profits that drive drug-related crime, violence, and corruption in Latin America and the Caribbean and around the globe, even if addiction rates go up, as they did with the end of Prohibition in the 1930s in the United States.

But in the short and medium run, Latin American and Caribbean coun-tries will have to address their own seriously flawed institutions by end-ing long-standing corrupt practices; undertaking police, judicial, prison, and other key institutional reforms; and ensuring greater electoral ac-countability. Such measures are essential for their future political stability, democratic consolidation, and national security and cannot wait for global decriminalization or legalization. Neither the legalization of marijuana nor the decriminalization of harder drugs will constitute panaceas for the resolution of the problems created by proliferating crime, corruption, and violence throughout the region, for they will not do away with the many other types of organized crime that operate with virtual impunity in Latin America and the Caribbean today.

Notes

1. This chapter was originally published by the Woodrow Wilson Center in 2012. See Bruce M. Bagley, *Drug Trafficking and Organized Crime in the Americas: Major Trends in the Twenty-First Century* (Washington, D.C.: Woodrow Wilson Center, 2012). Thanks to the Woodrow Wilson International Center for Scholars for permission to reprint this work.

2. Former presidents of Brazil, Colombia, and Mexico, Fernando Henrique Cardoso, César Gaviria, and Ernesto Zedillo, respectively, have highlighted the necessity for the United States and Europe to "design and implement policies leading to an effective reduc-

tion in their levels of drug consumption and, as a consequence, in the overall scope of the narcotics criminal activities" (Latin American Commission on Drugs and Democracy, *Drugs and Democracy: Toward a Paradigm Shift* [New York: Open Society Institute, 2008]), 7.

3. United Nations Office on Drugs and Crime (UNODC), *The Globalization of Crime: A Transnational Organized Crime Threat Assessment* (New York, 2010), 5–6; idem, *World Drug Report, 2011* (New York: UNODC, 2011), 8.

4. See David F. Musto, *The American Disease: Origins of Narcotics Control*, 3rd ed. (New York: Oxford University Press, 1999, first published in 1973 by Yale University Press).

5. UNODC, *World Drug Report, 2011*, 87, http://www.unodc.org/documents/data-and-analysis/WDR2011/World_Drug_Report_2011_ebook.pdf. Note that the 5 million users of cocaine in the United States are between the ages of fifteen and sixty-four.

6. Cocaine demand has been decreasing steadily in the United States since 1982, from an estimated 10.5 million users to some 5.3 million in 2008. Cocaine users in the twenty-eight European Union countries have, however, more than doubled in a decade, increasing from 2 million in 1998 to 4.1 million in 2008 (4.5 million in all of Europe); UNODC, *World Drug Report, 2010*, 16; idem, *The Globalization of Crime*, v–vi, 82. The consumption of cocaine in the United States decreased to 1.9 percent of the population in 2009 from 2.5 percent in 2006. See UNODC, *World Drug Report, 2011*, 93.

7. Despite overall declines in the total area of coca leaf cultivation in the Andes, cocaine production remained essentially stable from the mid-1990s through 2008, at approximately 800–1,100 metric tons per year. North America, including Canada, accounted for some 40 percent of worldwide cocaine consumption. The EU and the EFTA countries consumed more than 25 percent of the world's total. Together, these two regions accounted for more than 80 percent of the global cocaine market, estimated at U.S.$88 billion in 2008; see UNODC, *The Globalization of Crime*, 82. In 2008, the total value of worldwide cocaine and heroin markets combined was estimated at U.S.$153 billion; see UNODC, *World Drug Report, 2010*, 19; idem, *World Drug Report, 2011*, 119.

8. UNODC, *World Drug Report, 2011*, 71–73.

9. UNODC, *The Globalization of Crime*, 81–82.

10. Some 4.3–4.75 million people had used cocaine in Europe as of 2009; see UNODC, *World Drug Report, 2011*, 86.

11. South America was the third-largest consumer market for cocaine in the world in 2008, with some 2.4 million users. The bulk of South American consumption was concentrated in two countries of the Southern Cone, although there was evidence of rising cocaine use in virtually every country in the hemisphere. Given its population of nearly 200 million, Brazil had the largest number of users, at roughly 1 million. However, use was most intense in Argentina, where an estimated 2.6 percent of the adult population used cocaine in 2006—a statistic roughly similar to that of the United States; see UNODC, *The Globalization of Crime*, 82.

12. UNODC, *World Drug Report, 2011*, 91.

13. Ibid., 86.

14. Paul Gootenberg, *Andean Cocaine: The Making of a Global Drug* (Chapel Hill: University of North Carolina Press, 2008), 1–14, passim.

15. Bruce M. Bagley, "La conexión Colombia–México–Estados Unidos," in *Atlas de*

la seguridad y la defensa de México 2009, ed. Raúl Benítez Manaut, Abelardo Rodríguez Sumano, and Armando Rodríguez Luna (Mexico City: Colectivo de Análisis de la Seguridad con Democracia [CASEDE], 2009), 25; Patrick L. Clawson and Rensselaer W. Lee III, *The Andean Cocaine Industry* (New York: St. Martin's Griffin, 1998), 12–16.

16. After the Peru-Colombia air bridge, which transported paste, or base, from Peru's Alto Huallaga to Colombia by small airplanes, was disrupted by Peruvian president Fujimori's adoption of a shoot-down policy in 1993–1994, the subsequent termination of the cocaine flights out of Peru during the mid to late 1990s and the launching of Plan Dignidad in 1998 (with U.S. government funding) by the newly installed Banzer government in Bolivia shifted the epicenter of illegal coca cultivation from eastern Peru and Bolivia to southeastern Colombia. See Gootenberg, *Andean Cocaine*, 291–324; Clawson and Lee, *The Andean Cocaine Industry,* 16–21; Francisco E. Thoumi, *Illegal Drugs, Economy, and Society in the Andes* (Washington, D.C.: Woodrow Wilson Center Press and Johns Hopkins University Press, 2003), 7 and passim.

17. Bagley, "La conexión Colombia–México–Estados Unidos," 29; UNODC, *Coca Cultivation in the Andean Region: Survey of Bolivia, Colombia and Peru* (New York, 2006).

18. Steven Dudley, *Walking Ghosts: Murder and Guerrilla Politics in Colombia* (New York: Routledge, 2004), 195–198; Virginia Vallejo, *Amando a Pablo, odiando a Escobar* (Bogotá: Random House Mondadori, Nomos Impresores, 2007), 352–385.

19. By September 1996, after allegations that the Cali cartel had financed Ernesto Samper's presidential campaign surfaced in 1994, the Rodríguez Orejuela brothers and other major Cali cartel leaders were imprisoned in Colombia. See María Clemencia Ramírez Lemus, Kimberly Stanton, and John Walsh, "Colombia: A Vicious Circle of Drugs and War," in *Drugs and Democracy in Latin America: The Impact of U.S. Policy*, ed. Coletta A. Youngers and Eileen Rosin (Boulder, Colo.: Lynne Rienner, 2005); Camilo Chaparro, *Historia del cartel de Cali: El ajedrecista mueve sus fichas* (Bogotá: Intermedio Editores, 2005), 125–148; Fernando Rodríguez Mondragón and Antonio Sánchez, *El hijo del "ajedrecista"* (Bogotá: Editorial Oveja Negra, Quintero Editores, 2007), 169–173.

20. Bagley, "La conexión Colombia–México–Estados Unidos," 28–29.

21. On the paramilitary demobilization, see Elvira María Restrepo and Bruce M. Bagley, eds., *La desmovilización de los paramilitares en Colombia: Entre el escepticismo y la esperanza* (Bogotá: Editorial Universidad de los Andes, 2011). The Uribe government emphasized a counterinsurgency strategy in Plan Colombia, an important difference from the Pastrana government's original Plan Marshall. During 2002 and 2003, Uribe increased the number of combat troops and pursued constitutional reforms to expand military activities; see Ramírez Lemus et al., "Colombia," 111–112.

22. These numbers include small fields in the calculation; see UNODC, *World Drug Report, 2011*, 100–111; Adam Isacson, *Don't Call It a Model: On Plan Colombia's Tenth Anniversary, Claims of "Success" Don't Stand Up to Scrutiny* (Washington, D.C.: Washington Office on Latin America [WOLA], 2010).

23. Bagley, "La conexión Colombia–México–Estados Unidos," 31. The U.S. government estimated in 2011 that the Mexican cartels made U.S.$19 billion to $39 billion annually from the drug trade. Drug policy analyst Dr. Peter Reuter estimates Mexican cartel drug profits at the much lower figure of U.S.$7 billion per year for 2010. Even at Reuter's lower

estimate, the profits remain substantial and are certainly enough to spur the intense violence Mexican drug traffickers have exhibited in recent years.

24. The Northern Triangle countries of Central America—Guatemala, Honduras, and El Salvador—have been deeply affected by the shift. The intense drug-related violence presents serious challenges to governance; see UNODC, *World Drug Report, 2010,* 26.

25. From 2009 to 2010, the area under cultivation increased in Peru by 2 percent. In terms of hectares, the estimates for 2010 were 61,200. Cultivation has varied in Peru based on region. Some smaller regions located in the Amazon basin saw dramatic increases in 2010, as much as 90 percent, in terms of the area under cultivation. It is important to note that cocaine production in Peru has been increasing since 2005, according to the UNODC report. On the other hand, Colombia saw a decrease in production in 2010; the 2010 estimate for production was 350 metric tons. For more information, see UNODC, *World Drug Report, 2011,* 101. Between 2000 and 2009, coca cultivation increased by 38 percent and 112 percent in Peru and Bolivia, respectively; see UNODC, *World Drug Report, 2010,* 65. Coca cultivation is, in short, returning to countries where eradication policies damaged the reputation of the United States and its drug-control policies and incentivized peasant unrest; see Gootenberg, *Andean Cocaine,* 315.

26. According to a UN estimate, in 2008, Colombia produced 450 of the 865 metric tons of cocaine produced worldwide. U.S. government estimates of total cocaine production were higher, reaching 1,000 metric tons. Regarding cultivation, there was a decrease in hectares cultivated, from around 80,000 to 68,000 in 2008–2009 in Colombia, according to UNODC, *World Drug Report, 2010,* 66. Estimates of cocaine production per hectare of cultivated coca are quite unreliable.

27. For a historical discussion of the difficulties of quantifying cocaine production, see Gootenberg, *Andean Cocaine,* 325–336; for a discussion of the difficulties with the UNODC estimates, see Francisco E. Thoumi, "Debates recientes de la Organización de las Naciones Unidas acerca del Régimen Internacional de Drogas: Fundamentos, limitaciones e (im) posibles cambios," in *Drogas y prohibición: Una vieja guerra, un nuevo debate,* ed. Juan Gabriel Tokatlian (Buenos Aires: Libros del Zorzal, 2010), 27–56; Francisco E. Thoumi and Ernestine Jensema, "Drug Policies and the Funding of the United Nations Office on Drugs and Crime," in *Global Drug Policy: Building a New Framework* (New York: Senlis Council, 2003).

28. See Coletta A. Youngers and John M. Walsh, *Development First: A More Humane and Promising Approach to Reducing Cultivation of Crops for Illicit Markets* (Washington, D.C.: WOLA, 2010); Vanda Felbab-Brown, Joel M. Jutkowitz, Sergio Rivas, Ricardo Rocha, James T. Smith, Manuel Supervielle, and Cynthia Watson, "Assessment of the Implementation of the United States Government's Support for Plan Colombia's Illicit Crop Reduction Components," produced for review by the U.S. Agency for International Development (USAID), April 17, 2009; U.S. Government Accountability Office (GAO), "Plan Colombia: Drug Reduction Goals Were Not Fully Met, but Security Has Improved: U.S. Agencies Need More Detailed Plan for Reducing Assistance" (Washington, D.C., 2008); Adam Isacson and Abigail Poe, *After Plan Colombia: Evaluating "Integrated Action," The Next Phase of U.S. Assistance* (Washington, DC: Center for International Policy, 2009).

29. UNODC, *Coca Cultivation Survey June 2009* (New York, 2010). "If the current trend continues, Peru will soon overtake Colombia as the world's biggest coca producer—a no-

torious status that it has not had since the mid-1990s," said UNODC executive director, Antonio María Costa. Coca cultivation in Peru increased 6.8 percent in 2009—from 56,100 hectares in 2008 to 59,900. Cultivation of coca in Colombia, however, decreased in 2009 by 16 percent—from 81,000 hectares in 2008 to 68,000 hectares in 2009. Despite Colombia's apparent decline, overall coca cultivation in the Andean region decreased only 5.2 percent in 2009. According to the UNODC data, cultivation of coca in Bolivia barely changed between 2008 and 2009, increasing by only 400 hectares (about 1 percent—from 30,500 hectares in 2008 to 30,900 in 2009). This UNODC report contradicted the U.S. estimate for Bolivia, which showed a 9.4 percent increase in cultivation between 2008 and 2009, and a 2009 cultivation estimate that was 4,100 hectares higher than the UNODC's estimate. See *Just the Facts: A Civilian's Guide to U.S. Defense and Security Assistance to Latin America and the Caribbean*, June 23, 2010, http://justf.org.

30. Bagley, "La conexión Colombia–México–Estados Unidos"; Peter Dale Scott and Jonathan Marshall, *Cocaine Politics: Drugs, Armies and the CIA in Central America* (Berkeley: University of California Press, 1998), 186–192.

31. This displacement is also confirmed by the fact that Mexican criminal organizations have increased their activities in the United States. By 2008, these organizations were present in 230 U.S. cities, while three years before they were present in only 100. Moreover, the Colombian groups controlled the illicit cocaine and heroin distribution in only 40 cities, mostly in the northeast; see UNODC, *World Drug Report, 2010*, p. 79.

32. On Calderón's military strategy and the Mérida Initiative, see Rafael Velázquez Flores and Juan Pablo Prado Lallande, *La Iniciativa Mérida: ¿Nuevo paradigma de cooperación entre México y Estados Unidos en seguridad?* (Mexico City: Universidad Nacional Autónoma de México [UNAM], 2009); Raúl Benítez Manaut, ed., *Crimen organizado e Iniciativa Mérida en las relaciones México–Estados Unidos* (Mexico City: CASEDE, 2010); David A. Shirk, *The Drug War in Mexico: Confronting a Threat,* Council Special Report no. 60 (New York: Council on Foreign Relations, March 2011).

33. Bagley, "La conexión Colombia–México–Estados Unidos"; Douglas Farah, "Organized Crime in El Salvador: The Homegrown and Transnational Dimensions," in *Organized Crime in Central America*, ed. Cynthia J. Arnson and Eric Olson (Washington, D.C.: Woodrow Wilson Center, Latin American Program, 2011); International Crisis Group, "Learning to Walk without a Crutch: An Assessment of the International Commission against Impunity in Guatemala," *Latin America Report* no. 36 (May 31, 2011), 3; Steven S. Dudley, "Drug Trafficking Organizations in Central America: Transportistas, Mexican Cartels and Maras," in *Organized Crime in Central America*, ed. Cynthia J. Arnson and Eric Olson (Washington, D.C.: Woodrow Wilson Center, Latin American Program, 2011).

34. Between 2006 and 2008, over half the detected maritime shipments of cocaine to Europe came from the Bolivarian Republic of Venezuela. Ecuador has also been affected by an increase in transit trafficking, and both countries are experiencing increasing problems with violence; see UNODC, *World Drug Report, 2010*, 30.

35. Randall C. Archibald and Damien Cave, "Drug Wars Push Deeper into Central America," *New York Times*, March 2, 2011.

36. In Bolivia, coca-growing peasants joined in unions, which helped maintain the struggle for their recognition in national politics relatively peaceful; see Gootenberg, *Andean Cocaine*, 313.

37. In Peru, the eradication policy caused discontent and rejection by the peasants and favored the growth of the Shining Path. Thus, the guerrillas took control of particular areas, forcing local authorities to resign and flee while the guerrilla leadership demanded payments for processing and transporting the drug. Intense eradication actions without economic alternatives made people join the guerrillas; see Mariano Valderrama and Hugo Cabieses, "Questionable Alliances in the War on Drugs: Peru and the United States," in *The Political Economy of the Drug Industry: Latin America and the International System*, ed. Menno Vellinga (Gainesville: University Press of Florida, 2004), 60–61.

38. This collapse of Colombia's two major cartels opened the way for new actors to assume expanded roles in the drug industry, particularly paramilitary and guerrilla organizations that use the illegal drugs to fund their activities: Francisco E. Thoumi, "Illegal Drugs in Colombia: From Illegal Economic Boom to Social Crisis," in *The Political Economy of the Drug Industry*, ed. Menno Vellinga (Gainesville: University Press of Florida, 2004), 76.

39. Francisco E. Thoumi, "Illegal Drugs in Colombia," 159–264; Kevin Healy, "Coca, the State and the Peasantry in Bolivia," in *Assessing America's War on Drugs*, ed. Bruce M. Bagley, Special Issue, *Journal of Interamerican Studies and World Affairs* 30, nos. 2 and 3 (Summer/Fall 1988): 105–126; International Crisis Group, "Coca, Drugs and Social Protest in Bolivia and Peru," *Latin American Report* no. 12, March 3, 2005, http://www.crisisgroup.org/en/regions/latin-america-caribbean/andes/bolivia/012-coca-drugs-and-social-protest-in-bolivia-and-peru.aspx.

40. Juan Carlos Garzón, *Mafia & Co.: The Criminal Networks in Mexico, Brazil and Colombia* (Washington, D.C.: Woodrow Wilson Center, Latin American Program, 2008); Luis Jorge Garay-Salamanca, Eduardo Salcedo-Albarán, and Isaac De León-Beltrán, *Illicit Networks Reconfiguring States: Social Network Analysis of Colombian and Mexican Cases* (Bogotá: Método Foundation, 2010).

41. Elyssa Pachico, "The New Political Face of Colombia's Drug Gangs," InSight, http://www.insightcrime.org/component/content/article?id=1743:the-new-political-face-of-colombias-drug-gangs.

42. Luis Astorga Almanza, *Seguridad, traficantes y militares: El poder y la sombra* (Mexico City: Tusquets, 2007); Luis Astorga Almanza and David A. Shirk, "Drug Trafficking Organizations and Counter-Drug Strategies in the U.S.-Mexican Context," in *Shared Responsibility: U.S.-Mexico Policy Options for Confronting Organized Crime*, ed. Eric L. Olson, David A. Shirk, and Andrew D. Selee (Washington, D.C.: Mexico Institute, Woodrow Wilson Center, 2010). From 1995 onward, several Mexican cartels became progressively more involved in cocaine traffic out of Colombia. The Tijuana and Juárez cartels started to fight for control of cocaine-smuggling routes across Mexico and cross-border plazas into the United States in the vacuum left by the collapse of the major Colombian cartels. Only after 2000, however, did Mexico experience the rise and participation of newer cartels such as Sinaloa, Golfo, and the Zetas; see Bruce M. Bagley and Aline Hernández, "Crimen organizado en México y sus vínculos con Estados Unidos," in *Seguridad regional en América Latina y el Caribe: Anuario 2010*, ed. Hans Mathieu and Catalina Niño Guarnizo (Bogotá: Friedrich Ebert Stiftung, 2010), 332–333.

43. Carlos Antonio Flores Pérez, *El estado en crisis: Crimen organizado y política. Desafíos para la consolidación democrática* (Mexico City: Centro de Investigaciones y Es-

tudios Superiores en Antropología Social [CIESAS], 2009), 137–228; Jorge Chabat, "El estado y el crimen organizado transnacional: Amenaza global, respuestas nacionales," IS-TOR: Revista de Historia Internacional 9, no. 42 (Autumn 2010): 3–14; Phil Williams, "El crimen organizado y la violencia en México," ISTOR: Revista de Historia Internacional 9, no. 42 (Autumn 2010): 15–40.

44. Elyssa Pachico, "Investigation: Medellín's Turbulent Comuna 13," InSight, May 2011.

45. Ibid.

46. Patricia Dávila, "La disputa por Ciudad Juárez," in El México narco, ed. Rafael Rodríguez Castañeda (Mexico City: Planeta, 2010); Charles Bowden, Ciudad Juárez and the Global Economy's Killing Fields (New York: Nation Books, 2010).

47. Agnes Gereben Schaefer, Benjamin Bahney, and K. Jack Riley, Security in Mexico: Implications for U.S. Policy Options (Santa Monica, Calif.: RAND Corporation, 2009).

48. See http://www.elpasotimes.com/newupdated/ci_17627581; also George W. Grayson, Mexico's Struggle with "Drugs and Thugs," Headline Series, no. 331 (New York: Foreign Policy Association, Winter 2009); Hal Brands, Mexico's Narco-Insurgency and U.S. Counterdrug Policy (Carlisle, Penn.: Strategic Studies Institute, U.S. Army War College, 2009).

49. On March 11, 2011, Honduran officials reported that they had for the first time dismantled a cocaine lab that belonged to the Zetas. This highlights the location-changing activities of the Zetas due to the pressure they are feeling elsewhere; see Stratfor Analysis, March 22, 2010.

50. Bruce M. Bagley, "Globalization and Transnational Organized Crime: The Russian Mafia in Latin America and the Caribbean," in The Political Economy of the Drug Industry: Latin America and the International System, ed. Menno Vellinga (Gainesville: University Press of Florida, 2004), 261–296.

51. Bagley and Hernández, "Crimen organizado en México," 332.

52. Thoumi, "Debates recientes de la Organización de las Naciones Unidas," 27–56; Global Commission on Drug Policy, War on Drugs: Report of the Global Commission on Drug Policy, June 2011, http://www.globalcommissionondrugs.org/Report.

53. Rafael Pardo, "Introducción: Hacia un nuevo pensamiento sobre drogas. Nueve anomalías sobre el paradigma convencional y dos propuestas de nuevos caminos," in Drogas y prohibición: Una vieja guerra, un nuevo debate, ed. Juan Gabriel Tokatlian (Buenos Aires: Libros del Zorzal, 2010), 13–26.

54. Bruce M. Bagley and Juan Gabriel Tokatlian, "Dope and Dogma: Explaining the Failure of U.S.–Latin American Drug Policies," in Neighborly Adversaries: Readings in U.S.–Latin American Relations, ed. Michael LaRosa and Frank O. Mora (New York: Rowman & Littlefield, 2007), 219–234; Bruce M. Bagley, "Políticas de control de drogas ilícitas en Estados Unidos: ¿Qué funciona y qué no funciona?" in La guerra contra las drogas en el mundo andino: Hacia un cambio de paradigma, ed. Juan Gabriel Tokatlian (Buenos Aires: Libros del Zorzal, 2009), 283–296; idem, "The New Hundred Years War?"

I

U.S. DRUG POLICIES AT HOME AND ABROAD

1

Coca, Cocaine, and Consumption

Trends and Antitrends

J. BRYAN PAGE

Imagine a European traveler in the late eighteenth or early nineteenth century visiting the Andes for the first time and feeling the oppressive lack of oxygen in the Altiplano of Bolivia and Peru, then noticing the apparent ease with which the local people strode long distances and carried heavy burdens in that region's thin atmosphere. Curiosity would naturally lead to questioning these people about how they were able to perform these feats of endurance under such difficult conditions. If the tourist were able to make himself or herself well enough understood so that the query elicited an answer, that answer inevitably would have been, "The coca helps me do it." These kinds of encounters led certain Europeans to explore in various ways the potential uses of coca leaf in order to share with the rest of the world its putative benefits of energy and stamina.

Indigenous Natives and Cocaine Consumption

The story of how the indigenous natives of the Andes, speakers of languages such as Aymara, Quechua, Jaquaru, and Jaquimara, started to consume the coca leaf and discovered its benefits is of course lost in the depths of South American prehistory, probably about 8,000 years ago. The first clear evidence of coca consumption appeared in what is now called the Nanchoc Valley on the western slopes of the Andes in what is now Peru[1] reporting presence of botanically identifiable coca leaf and evidence of people baking rocks to obtain mineral lime, the accompaniment to coca chewing. The presence of humans in that biodiverse region, in which highly variable altitudes combined with proximity to the Equator to generate varied microclimates made possible the series of accidents that led to the development of coca chewing. Much of the evidence found in the other parts of the archaeological record is inferential in nature, citing pottery with cheek bulges from Valdivia sites in Ecuador dated at about 1500 BCE,[2] and stone sculpture in Tiwanaku sites.[3] Presence in burial sites of lime containers and leaf pouches dates back as far as 2000 BCE.[4]

Although the materials were present in the sites or their consumption was implied, botanical characterization of the leaf material and clear evidence that the leaf was being chewed remained sketchy. The evidence became somewhat more convincing by 100 CE, with representations of people holding small bunches of leaves or having one protruding cheek (indicating the presence of the mass of coca leaves held in the cheek) and having a *llipta*, the small container of quicklime and ash used to enhance the coca. The Mochica pottery tradition (100–800 CE) has profuse examples of coca's importance in the lives of people under Moche rule.[5] Solid chemical evidence, based on radioimmunoassays of 3,000-year-old mummies found in the Atacama Desert of northern Chile,[6] indicates the presence of cocaine and its principal metabolite, benzoylecgonine, in trace amounts in the mummies' hair.

The sites mentioned above range from Ecuador to Chile, indicating widespread presence of coca throughout the Andean countries, and their accumulated evidence indicates that chewing the coca leaves was the mode of ingestion used throughout this region. When the Spanish arrived in the early sixteenth century, coca was consumed in the whole Andean region, often by people living at altitudes in excess of 3,000 meters.

The original conquistadores and Spanish colonial authorities developed ambivalent attitudes toward the indigenous consumption of coca. On one side, they regarded it as a nasty, disgusting behavior that they suspected was used in place of eating. On the other, their newfound slaves would not work unless they provided coca for them, and, because the dispensing of coca elicited more work from the native Andean people, the conquistadores took measures to assure supplies. The colonial authorities therefore supported the production of coca leaf, regarding it as a necessary evil in the interest of running labor-intensive industries such as mining.[7] These attitudes about coca consumption essentially quashed any inquiry into why chewing the coca leaf had a positive impact on the productivity of workers.

Recognizing the potential value of consuming some form of coca required unprejudiced eyes observing the Peruvian and Bolivian peasants as they took in stride the challenges of their harsh, bleak surroundings. Although the colonial Spanish valued coca as a means of controlling a conscripted labor force, they never imagined themselves or their fellow Europeans consuming some form of the plant.

Europeans and Cocaine

Other Europeans of a more scientific inclination, however, came to value aspects of coca that could be construed as beneficial. One of a family of French botanists, Joseph Jussieu, collected plant specimens throughout Bolivia and Peru, noting local uses and effects.[8] He almost lost his life in a river crossing as he attempted to reach the coca-producing region called the Yungas, but he succeeded in sending specimens to the Museum of Natural History in Paris.

Captain Don Antonio d'Ulloa, on an expedition in 1745 to explore botanical features of South America, commented about coca as follows: "This herb is so nutritious and invigorating that the Indians labor whole days without anything else, and on the want of it they find a decay in their strength. They also add that it preserves the teeth sound and fortifies the stomach."[9] The question of coca as a replacement for food will receive further attention in the discussion below, but the overall positive assessment of coca's properties was among the first of several scientific opinions on the leaf's value.

Subsequent commentary sometimes mixed the colonial ambivalence with wonder at the stamina of the coca chewers. One colonial personage, Dr. Don Hipólito Unanue, in 1791 wrote an account of the siege of La Paz, in which the garrison was able to hold out in part because of the coca that was available.[10]

As European travelers and scientists observed and commented on the properties of the coca leaf, the accumulation of foreign opinion became overwhelmingly positive, as in this excerpt, written in 1838, from the writings of Swiss naturalist Von Tschudi: "Setting aside all extravagant and visionary notions on the subject, I am clearly of the opinion that moderate use of Coca is not merely innocuous, but that it may even be very conducive to health. In support of this conclusion, I may refer to numerous examples of longevity among Indians, who, almost from the age of boyhood, have been in the habit of masticating Coca three times a day, and who in the course of their lives have consumed no less than two thousand seven hundred pounds if at the age of one hundred and thirty, and they commenced masticating at ten years—one ounce a day, yet nevertheless, enjoy perfect health."[11]

This kind of discourse became increasingly common as more interested parties traveled to South America and saw for themselves the stamina and resistance of native Andean people. By the time Mortimer wrote the following introductory words in 1900, not only had the vast majority of the discourse about the coca leaf been positive, but European chemists had thoroughly pursued the task of finding which of the plant's component alkaloids accounted for these salubrious effects. "In this locality—and among this wild profusion, grows a beautiful shrub, the leaves of which in shape somewhat resemble those of the orange tree, but in color are of a much paler green, having that exquisite translucence of the most delicate fern. The properties of this plant more nearly approach that ideal source of endurance than is known to exist in any other known substance."[12]

Mortimer's extensive treatise on the virtues of coca asserts that the chewing of the coca leaf has a positive influence on respiration, muscle strength, digestion, heart endurance, and mood. He provides as evidence the fact that Europeans and white North Americans conducted experiments with nonindigenous people to ascertain the universality of these qualities.[13]

The isolation of cocaine, which is attributed to Albert Niemann, took place between 1859 and 1860,[14] and was the product of laboratory activity aimed at identifying the most pharmacologically active ingredient in the coca leaf. Shortly thereafter, additional studies attributed to William Lossen resulted in cocaine's commodification through making the alkaloid water-soluble by adding a hydrochloride radical.[15]

Mid-nineteenth-century chemists focused their attention on the coca leaf because they thought that coca and its derivatives would have medicinal value in a rapidly expanding market for patent medicines. The first thing on the market to have cocaine in it, however, did not use the newly generated water-soluble preparation, but rather it took advantage of the ability of cocaine to dissolve in alcohol, imparting about 6 milligrams of cocaine per ounce of wine. Angelo Mariani, its inventor, released that preparation amid extravagant publicity to the world market in 1863, and he had great commercial success.[16]

Coca Derivatives and Medicine

By the mid-1880s, coca and its derivatives, lacing patent medicines and gaining popularity as a local anesthetic for facial surgery, were ubiquitous in the world's apothecaries. Coca had also attracted the attention of the medical community, as it struggled with diseases of the mind. Sigmund

Freud, as a young physician, published a treatise entitled "Über Coca" (On coca) extolling its virtues as a treatment for morphine addiction.[17] In what Davenport-Hines characterizes as a shameful exercise in professional expediency, self-promotion, and duplicitous behavior, Freud prescribed a regimen of cocaine doses to a patient who was addicted to morphine, and the patient died of cocaine toxicity. Freud eventually recanted his assertions but never admitted any error in judgment or procedure.

Other physicians were equally enthusiastic about the possibilities of cocaine, adding it to treatment regimens for everything from muscle weakness to voice quality.[18] At this point in the history of cocaine, the enthusiasm for its medicinal powers became tempered by realization of its power to seduce.[19] The consumers of the scores of elixirs that contained dissolved cocaine, predominantly white non-Hispanic housewives in the U.S. East and Midwest, began to encounter trouble related to their use of these elixirs.[20] Journalistic accounts of these women's experiences with cocaine-laced patent medicines warned of accelerating use, which resulted in personal and financial ruin.[21]

Physicians in the United States and Scotland warned that cocaine's combination of pleasurable intoxication and short duration of acute effects constituted a potential for disastrous patterns of use. Even as Mortimer was writing his adulatory book on coca,[22] the negative news about cocaine's effects was accumulating, eventually leading to the first decline of cocaine use in the United States, which, according to Morgan,[23] occurred fewer than ten years after its introduction as a commodity, by the late 1880s. Musto, on the other hand, characterized the entire period from 1883 through the 1920s as the "first American cocaine epidemic."[24]

In one sense, both were correct. Once introduced to the consuming public, cocaine would inevitably have developed an avid following, but as its use spread and intensified, downturns in use occurred, the first in the late 1880s and the last in the 1920s. The latter downturn can be attributed in part to Food and Drug Administration (FDA) regulations that forbade inclusion of cocaine in any patent medicines in 1904, and the influence of the Harrison Narcotics Act of 1914.

Cocaine's intrinsic seductiveness is worth mentioning at this point in the discussion. Its impact on the pleasure centers of the brain is so powerful that, even though withdrawal from cocaine use is not nearly as aversive as withdrawal from heroin or alcohol, users are strongly motivated to come back for more. In fact, recent research indicates that the reinforcement power of cocaine becomes stronger after periods of continuous use.[25] On urban streets, the word often used for cocaine is "girl," and this is meant to denote the drug's seductive properties.

In my own research, I have asked study participants what their first tastes of the drugs that they use were like. Overwhelmingly, the responses have been positive when describing the first cocaine experience, but not so with other drugs, legal or illegal. About 70 percent of my respondents in the study of drug use among Cubans in Miami,[26] for example, told me that they had a desirable "high" the first time they used cocaine. In contrast, about 40 percent of those who used marijuana reported a desirable high on their first experience. The other 60 percent reported either not feeling anything or having a negative reaction. Tobacco cigarettes had even less endorsement of first effects than marijuana, with reports of coughing and not much high. Apparently, the only drug that even comes close to cocaine in reinforcement power is heroin, but first-time users of heroin often report nausea and vomiting, something cocaine users never report.

With this principle of cocaine's seductiveness in mind, coupled with its relative ease of administration (drunk in a tonic or snorted in powder form), it is easy to understand how a wave of cocaine use might wash across a population of people seeking a good time. These facts would also help explain the difficulties in dislodging cocaine use in a population in which it had become normative. Nevertheless, cocaine use has diminished repeatedly since the drug's introduction in 1884, only to return repeatedly to previously high levels.

The propensity of cocaine users to accelerate use came under the scrutiny of Chitwood and Morningstar in the early 1980s. They noted that under conditions of high accessibility, cocaine users tended to accelerate their consumption patterns.[27] As consumption accelerated, Morningstar and Chitwood also noted behaviors such as covering their residence windows with aluminum foil and having large handguns in the house among cocaine dealers who also consumed. Because the acute intoxicated state for cocaine has a maximum duration of twenty minutes (with smoked cocaine, bazuco, freebase, or crack lasting three to five minutes), and because the "crash," or descent from the intoxicated state, is accompanied by dysphoria, cocaine users tend to pursue their next dose energetically.

This energy translates into something that I have observed repeatedly in users after doses of either injected cocaine or crack. In Miami and elsewhere, this phenomenon is called "tweaking," and I first heard about it while working out of a street-side office in Little Havana.[28] A person who tweaks during the period of acute cocaine high diligently searches through rug pile, clothing, or any flat surface for whatever fragment of powdery-looking substance they can find. If they find anything during this process, they will attempt to consume it, but it appears they do not really expect to find more cocaine. They just seem to enjoy the process of riffling through shag carpet or dirty clothes as their personal diversion during their three to twenty minutes of cocaine high. When asked about their tweaking, the study participants replied that it took the edge off the crash to think there might be some free cocaine nearby. Behaviors like this testify to the powerful impact of cocaine, and tweaking seems the logical analogue to the "personal favors" described by Carlson and Siegal and Siegal et al.,[29] such as the offer of crack in exchange for a wide variety of services and behaviors, including sexual and demeaning "favors."

Despite the fact that after 1914 cocaine would never again be a legal drug in the United States, it was just beginning a cycle of decline and resurgence that cycled several more times over the twentieth century. That cycle had a debatable relationship to the stringency of the laws against its consumption, trafficking, and production. Musto points out that between the end of Prohibition and the 1960s,[30] cocaine had all but disappeared from public awareness of drugs due to the effect of the Harrison Act and the FDA regulations, the end of Prohibition, the Great Depression, World War II, and postwar public attitudes.

Close examination of the discourse on cocaine during the twentieth century, however, draws attention to cocaine's accumulation of ill repute. Eventually, it seems, the primary users of cocaine learned, either through their own experience or that of their peers, that in circumstances of high availability and frequent use, personal use careens out of control, and that the out-of-control user expends personal treasure at an alarming rate, alienating interpersonal assets and social capital along the way.

Trends in Cocaine Usage

It did not take very long for a second ascension of cocaine use to begin—only about ten years (Musto's analysis notwithstanding), during the height of Prohibition. In this case, the popularity of cocaine depended in part on the fact that consumers of alcohol were forced to resort to illegal sources for that drug of choice. Cocaine had already been illegal for five years, but the "flaming youth" who sought new experiences in the jazz neighborhoods of New York, Chicago, and Los Angeles were not opposed to taking stimulants with their alcohol and hot music. Evidence of cocaine's circulation in the Roaring Twenties social scene can be found in song lyrics of the era, for example, from "Daddy Get Your Baby Out of Jail": "Daddy put my diamonds in to soak. Buy me just another shot of coke." Cole Porter's 1934 musical "Anything Goes"—"I get no kick from cocaine"—acknowledges a drug that circulated among sophisticates during the late 1920s and early 1930s. The arrival of the Great Depression in 1929 eventually curtailed the use of cocaine because of its expense, coupled with the likelihood of users' financial depletion. Again, users "hit bottom" (i.e., exhausted their resources) and concluded on their own that cocaine use was not a good idea. But in this case the U.S. economy was shrinking, which made personal finances especially vulnerable and subject to abrupt decline. Repeal of the Eighteenth Amendment in 1933 made alcohol legal again, essentially breaking down the marketing mechanisms that had brought illegal alcohol and illegal cocaine to consumers through similar smuggling channels.

Cocaine use in the United States had a down cycle after 1933 that lasted about three decades. Between 1933 and 1941, the effects of the Great Depression kept the demand down. World War II made procurement difficult, and the country in effect did not emerge from the Depression until after the war. Rationing made most commodities difficult to obtain, and the illegal ones were less important to most consumers than gasoline, nylons, tires, and chocolate bars. Exotic commodities like cocaine had far less importance in the wartime black markets than the mundane commodities that dominated them.

After the war, the population segment that could afford to consume cocaine moved away from city centers in favor of the suburbs, essentially breaking up potential networks of urban consumers, the backbone of drug-consuming networks in the United States. The xenophobia that gripped North America during the 1950s in the form of McCarthyism also played a part in North Americans of that era choosing not to use illegal drugs. Any appearance of straying from the precepts of conventional lifeways was viewed with great suspicion. David Musto sums up the absence of cocaine from public discourse in the 1950s this way: "By the time I was in medical school in the late 1950s, cocaine was described to medical students as a drug that used to be a problem in the United States. It was news to us."[31]

Gradual emergence from the thrall of McCarthyism showed some of its first signs in the form of the "Beat Generation" of the late 1950s. Participants in that cultural context, often called "beatniks," began to question the way of life that had emerged in postwar North America, including the ongoing prohibition of certain drugs. There is little historical evidence that the beatniks embraced any kind of illegal-drug use other than marijuana, but their questioning of Middle America's drug policies set in motion a process of questioning authority on drug issues that once again opened discussion of the laws against drug use. This process first opened the door to further contesting the laws against marijuana possession, consumption, and trafficking. Then it brought attention to drugs that at the time were considered experimental, such as LSD and DMT, and finally it led to the reexamination of laws against other drugs that had also been banned by law, including cocaine.

Cocaine did not reemerge as a widely consumed drug until the early 1970s, and its rise corresponded with an era of permissiveness and sexual experimentation as exemplified in the lifestyles of movie stars and rock musicians. The release of the blaxploitation film *Superfly* in 1972 signaled the emergence of cocaine as a drug of ambivalence—high fashion and sex versus addiction and crime. Curtis Mayfield's songs on the film's sound-track declare, "I'm your pusher man," but also "Fred is dead." As it became increasingly familiar through the popular media, cocaine use represented one way in which ordinary people could emulate the pleasure-seeking lives that they perceived their idols to lead. The pervasiveness of cocaine in Hollywood and the recording industry attracted frequent commentary on the part of tabloid writers and gossip columnists.

One compelling demonstration of this frequency can be found in Google's array of utilities. Using powerful search technology and the fact that much of the world's literature is digitized, Google has developed a utility called Ngram that samples 4 percent of the books written in English and calculates the proportion in which authors have used specific words or phrases.[32] The word "cocaine," as figure 1.1 indicates, began to appear in 1883, and its usage increased dramatically over the next decade and a half, dropping off slightly and then rising to a plateau that was maintained for the next twenty-five years, thereafter dropping on a soft decline until the 1960s, then rising in the 1970s on a meteoric trajectory to a peak in 2000, then a fairly sharp decline.

It is tempting to overinterpret these results, but the analysis has several limitations: (1) the random sample of books in English includes a high proportion of fiction; (2) how authors use the word "cocaine" may vary widely in terms of human behavior, descriptive license, metaphoric usage, and so forth; (3) usage of the drug and use of the word may be related to each other, but the nature of that relationship remains to be discovered; and (4) the gross numbers of books sampled at each time period are much smaller

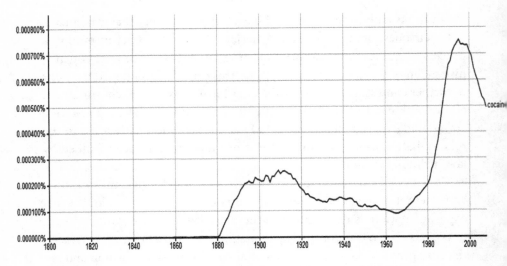

Figure 1.1. Use of the word "cocaine" between 1800 and the present (charted using Google Ngram, https://books.google.com/ngrams/).

in the early time periods than in the later ones. Nevertheless, as a reflection of what has occurred in the public discourse on drugs, it is clear that the word "cocaine" has had some fluctuations.

As the cocaine trend of the 1970s progressed, a celebrity would occasionally appear in the media as the latest to succumb to the drug's thrall. By the late 1970s, freebasing cocaine emerged among wealthy users. This practice involved using a series of highly volatile washes to separate the pure cocaine base from the hydrochloride radical, yielding a tiny quantity of smokeable cocaine base. Because the material used to complete this process is highly volatile and flammable, it is very dangerous, as Richard Pryor's famous accident, in which he narrowly escaped self-immolation, demonstrated.

By the beginning of the 1980s, cocaine was on the verge of another downward trend, just as it had sagged in the 1890s and the 1920s. People were ruining their lives by using cocaine, and word was getting around. Consumption of cocaine was beginning a downward trend by 1982, and it looked like yet another upward trend was about to succumb to the weight of its own bad reputation.

Events in the cocaine-producing lands of South America demand attention here, because the smoked form of cocaine does not have to be as astronomically expensive as the form of freebase practiced by the very rich. In the mid-1970s, a pattern of cocaine smoking emerged among urban youth in Peru, Colombia, and Bolivia that was relatively cheap and very habituating. The coca paste that results when large quantities of mashed coca leaves are placed in a lipid bath (gasoline or kerosene), agitated, and then the lipid solvent is drained off and sulfuric acid added is about 45 percent pure cocaine. That product can be smoked, and it produces a ferocious rush of pleasure for the smoker. Reports by Jerí, Sánchez, del Pozo, and Fernández tell of young men in Peru who began smoking this paste or base and kept smoking until they had no more money, no job, and no place to live.[33] These reports gave the United States a preview of what the next rise in cocaine use would be like, but drug researchers did not really pay attention. Jerí went as far as to conduct experiments in which he snipped out parts of the mid-brain to counteract the powerful allure of this form of cocaine for addicts. This strategy did not stop users from craving coca paste.

Back in the United States, powder cocaine was about to have a downturn in 1983. Experienced users were giving it up, and it had a bad reputation with most of them. The elite users had found out for themselves that they had been navigating a minefield of fiscal, family, and emotional hazards. In the chronically marginalized neighborhood of South Central Los Angeles, however, a new cocaine product called "ready rock" was being produced by adding cocaine hydrochloride to baking soda and water and cooking the mixture in a pan. The resulting pieces of a preparation that usually looked like white roofing gravel could be sold for between $5.00 and $10.00. When smoked, they made a cracking sound as the fumes released a small amount of vaporized cocaine base to be inhaled avidly by the user. The cocaine base afforded the user the same kind of ferocious, pleasurable rush experienced by the rich freebase smoker.

This development halted the downturn of cocaine use in the United States, opening access to cocaine's pleasures to a whole new segment of the population—poor folks living in the inner city. Crack spread rapidly throughout the cities of the United States, and it caused a major hiccup in cyclical fluctuations of cocaine use seen at other times in the twentieth century. The emergence of crack cocaine led to a new rise in overall cocaine use that lasted about seven years.

Although crack use in the United States probably ceased its epidemic trajectory by the early 1990s, it has become clear that cocaine use no longer fluctuates as it did in the late nineteenth and early twentieth centuries. The Community Epidemiology Work Group, comprising people who monitor trends of drug consumption and its impact in major U.S. cities, has repeatedly shown that cocaine has continued to appear as the primary drug among people asking to receive treatment for problems with drug use and among people seeking help for drug-related problems in hospital emergency rooms. Twenty-one sentinel communities plus a border work group reported yearly on the trends in their respective locations, using the sources of data at their disposal to describe the contours of drug use. This array varied somewhat by location, but it usually included reports from registered centers for treatment of drug abuse, hospital emergency rooms, medical examiners' offices, whatever school or community survey might have been conducted in the location, and, in some cases, ethnographic study results. Inspection of individual city reports between 1980 and the present indicates that fluctuations in the frequency of cocaine-related presentations at treatment centers and emergency rooms have been minor.[34] Since 1990, these numbers have remained essentially flat, with five-figure orders of magnitude in most cities.

Throughout the history of attempts to monitor illegal-drug use in the United States, the interpretation of these kinds of data has been difficult. Regardless of the source, with the possible exception of the ethnographies, inferences about the epidemiological meaning of treatment requests or emergency room presentations have given analysts only information about people who selected themselves to seek help. Therefore, those people cannot with any rigor be thought to represent the larger population of drug users. Rather, they can be seen as reflecting the gross size of treatment needs and the rate at which people have emergency-worthy trouble with their drugs of choice. These kinds of figures cannot tell us how many drug users go through adult careers of drug consumption without feeling the need for treatment or emergency help, yet we can be fairly certain that the population of adult drug users includes large numbers of people who avoid treatment or emergency room visits.[35]

Similarly, national surveys on drug use have become hodgepodges of heuristic research methods that, in asking randomly selected respondents to describe their personal drug use to perfect strangers with clipboards, have little hope of deriving accurate, reliable, valid information from their inquiries. The Substance Abuse and Mental Health Services Administration (SAMHSA), currently saddled with conducting the survey, has continued to expand the sample size in an effort to assure that some of the rarer behaviors, such as use of crack cocaine after 1995, can still be captured. Oversampling of key urban areas is one of the other expedient measures taken by SAMHSA.

These strategies to capture rare behaviors have had a bloating effect on the National Survey on Drug Use in Households (NSDUH),[36] which now collects about 85,000 interviews, a number between 50 and 100 times the sample sizes used by the likes of Harris and Gallup to study voting preferences or detergent choices nationwide in the United States. Table 1.1 arrays estimates of the numbers of cocaine users in the United States, based on responses to items in the NSDUH and its predecessor, the National Household Survey on Drug Abuse (NHSDA). In terms of proportions of the U.S. population, these estimates have fluctuated slightly since 1979, mostly holding steady for all years between 1979 and 2008, with users never exceeding 15 percent, users in the past year at around 2 percent, and users in the past month under 1 percent of the U.S. population. We may never know how close to the truth these estimates are, because they represent data from self-reports of personal consumption of illegal drugs. The estimates can, however, demonstrate that, regardless of the public perception that cocaine is fashionable or out of fashion, it is possible for a flawed method to find similar proportions of cocaine users year after year. The actual numbers might not be at all accurate, but the method succeeds in finding substantial numbers of people willing to report cocaine use.

These indicators mean that cocaine use in the United States may have become normative for some subsets of the population, so that media reports no longer have influence on the willingness or unwillingness of people in the United States to use cocaine in some form. Those who use cocaine may not be very numerous, although I expect most data sources to underestimate these numbers. Nevertheless, it is clear that they represent a demand for treatment and emergency care that cannot be ignored.

The story of cocaine begins, as all drugs' stories, with an accident. In the case of cocaine, the accident occurred eight millennia ago and led to the establishment of coca-chewing patterns among South American indigenous people. The nonaccident involved the efforts of botanists and chemists to extract the pharmacological essence of the coca leaf for the good of humanity and to attempt to earn a profit from a new commodity.

As often happens when the chemists tinker with plant-derived drugs, the result had unintended consequences. These consequences became recognizable after a time, but by that time, it was too late to prevent further consequences. Cocaine's seductiveness and its tendency to engender patterns of accelerated use made the drug difficult to dislodge from the pharmacopoeia. Despite its vicissitudinous history in the late nineteenth and early twentieth centuries, cocaine became embedded in the repertoire of

Table 1.1. Trends in cocaine use among those 12 and older, 1979–2008

Year	No. Pop. 12 and older	Ever used No.	Ever used % of population	Used in past year No.	Used in past year % of population	Used in past month No.	Used in past month % of population
1979	180,343,000	15,541,000	8.6	8,608,000	4.8	4,743,000	2.6
1982	186,440,000	21,756,000	11.7	10,458,000	5.6	4,491,000	2.4
1985	192,605,000	21,495,000	11.2	9,839,000	5.1	5,686,000	3.0
1988	198,347,000	21,058,000	10.6	7,151,000	3.6	3,140,000	1.6
1991	202,859,000	23,271,000	11.5	5,284,000	2.6	2,032,000	1.0
1992	205,713,000	22,482,000	10.9	4,332,000	2.1	1,402,000	0.7
1993	207,199,000	23,369,000	11.3	3,947,000	1.9	1,404,000	0.7
1994	209,411,000	21,821,000	10.4	3,664,000	1.7	1,382,000	0.7
1995	211,532,000	21,700,000	10.3	3,664,000	1.7	1,453,000	0.7
1996	214,047,000	22,130,000	10.3	4,033,000	1.9	1,749,000	0.8
1997	216,206,000	22,597,000	10.5	4,169,000	1.9	1,505,000	0.7
1998	218,445,000	23,089,000	10.6	3,811,000	1.7	1,750,000	0.8
1999	221,123,000	25,406,000	11.5	3,742,000	1.7	1,552,000	0.7
2000	223,280,000	24,896,000	11.2	3,328,000	1.5	1,213,000	0.5
2001	225,636,000	27,788,000	12.3	4,186,000	1.9	1,676,000	0.7
2002	235,143,000	33,910,000	14.4	5,902,000	2.5	2,020,000	0.9
2003	237,682,000	34,891,000	14.7	5,908,000	2.5	2,281,000	1.0
2004	240,515,000	34,153,000	14.2	5,658,000	2.4	2,021,000	0.8
2005	243,220,000	33,673,000	13.8	5,523,000	2.3	2,397,000	1.0
2006	246,022,000	35,298,000	14.3	6,069,000	2.5	2,421,000	1.0
2007	247,845,000	35,882,000	14.5	5,738,000	2.3	2,075,000	0.8
2008	249,815,000	36,773,000	14.7	5,255,000	2.1	1,855,000	0.7

Source: National Survey on Drug Use in Households and Health and National Household Survey on Drug Abuse, "Multiple Years Trends in Cocaine Use among

illegal-drug use as practiced in North America. Admittedly flawed sources of data on cocaine use indicate that North America is not making much progress in abating the demand for cocaine in its population of cocaine users (see table 1.1).

Notes

1. Tom D. Dillehay, Jack Rossen, Donald Ugent, Anathasios Karathanasis, Víctor Vásquez, and Patricia J. Netherly, "Early Holocene Coca Chewing in Northern Peru," *Antiquity* 84 (2010): 939.

2. For examples of these ceramics, explore the pages of Julie Jones, *Rituals of Euphoria: Coca in South America* (New York: Museum of Primitive Art, 1974).

3. Evidence of coca use in an impressive pre-Columbian site appears in José Berenguer Rodríguez, *Tiwanaku: Señores de Lago Sagrado* (Santiago: Museo Chileno de Arte Precolombino, 2000).

4. In sites not closely associated with Andean civilizations, evidence appears in coastal Peru; see Frederic Engel, "Early Sites on the Peruvian Coast," *Southwestern Journal of Anthropology* 1, no. 3 (1957): 54–68. More evidence appears in idem, "A Preceramic Settlement in the Central Coast of Peru: Asia," *Transactions of the American Philosophical Society*, n.s., 53, pt. 3 (1963). A wide regional view of the plant's migration appears in T. Plowman, "The Origin, Evolution, and Diffusion of Coca, *Erythroxylum* spp., in South and Central America," in *Pre-Columbian Plant Migration. Papers Presented at the Pre-Columbian Plant Migration Symposium, 44th International Congress of Americanists, Manchester, England*, ed. D. Stone (Cambridge: Harvard University Press, 1984).

5. Christopher B. Donnan, *Moche Art and Iconography* (Los Angeles: UCLA Latin American Center, University of California, 1976) presents examples of Moche art.

6. Use of hair analysis proves ingestion of coca in the south central Andes; see Mario Rivera et al., "Antiquity of Coca-Leaf Chewing in the South Central Andes: A 3,000 Year Archaeological Record of Coca-Leaf Chewing from Northern Chile," *Journal of Psychoactive Drugs* 37, no. 4 (2005): 455.

7. William E. Carter, *Coca en Bolivia* (La Paz: Librería Editorial "Juventud," 1986), 72.

8. W. Golden Mortimer, *History of Coca: "The Divine Plant" of the Incas*, Fitz Hugh Memorial Library ed. (San Francisco: And/Or Press, 1974), 166.

9. Ibid., 167.

10. Ibid., 168.

11. Ibid., 171–172.

12. Ibid., 6.

13. Ibid., 169–177.

14. Paul Gootenberg, *Andean Cocaine: The Making of a Global Drug* (Chapel Hill: University of North Carolina Press, 2008), 22; Mortimer, *History of Coca*, 296; Augusto Pérez Gómez, *Cocaína: Surgimiento y evolución de un mito* (Bogotá: Catálogo Científico, 1987), 32.

15. Gootenberg, *Andean Cocaine*, 23; Mortimer, *History of Coca*, 298.

16. Richard Davenport-Hines, *The Pursuit of Oblivion: A Global History of Narcotics* (New York: W. W. Norton, 2002), 132.

17. Ibid., 157–158.

18. Ibid., 159; Gootenberg, *Andean Cocaine*, 23–24; H. Wayne Morgan, *Drugs in America: A Social History 1800–1980* (Syracuse, N.Y.: Syracuse University Press, 1981), 19; Mortimer, *History of Coca*, 423–427; Pérez Gómez, *Cocaína*, 36–37.

19. Morgan, *Drugs in America*, 91.

20. David F. Musto, "America's First Cocaine Epidemic," in *The American Drug Scene*, ed. James E. Inciardi and Karen McElrath (Los Angeles: Roxbury, 2004), 226.

21. Morgan, *Drugs in America*, 92; Musto, "America's First Cocaine Epidemic," 227.

22. Mortimer, *History of Coca*.

23. Morgan, *Drugs in America*, 91.

24. Musto, "America's First Cocaine Epidemic," 225.

25. Felicity J. Miles, Barry J. Everitt, Jeffrey W. Dalley, and Anthony Dickinson, "Conditioned Activity and Instrumental Reinforcement Following Long-Term Oral Consumption of Cocaine by Rats," *Behavioral Neuroscience* 118, no. 6 (2004): 1331–1339.

26. J. Bryan Page, "Streetside Drug Use among Cuban Drug Users in Miami, Florida," in *Drug Use in Hispanic Communities*, ed. Ronald Glick and Joan Moore (New Brunswick, N.J.: Rutgers University Press, 1990), 169–191.

27. Dale D. Chitwood and Patricia C. Morningstar, "Factors Which Differentiate Cocaine Users in Treatment from Nontreatment Users," *International Journal of the Addictions* 20, no. 3 (1985): 449–459; Patricia J. Morningstar and Dale D. Chitwood, "Cocaine User Subculture," *Proceedings of the Symposium on Cocaine* (New York: Narcotic and Drug Research, Inc., and New York State Division of Substance Abuse Services, 1982).

28. I describe this research in Page, "Streetside Drug Use," 169–191.

29. Robert G. Carlson and Harvey A. Siegal, "The Crack Life: An Ethnographic Overview of Crack Use and Sexual Behavior among African Americans in a Midwest Metropolitan City," *Journal of Psychoactive Drugs* 23, no. 1 (1991): 11–20; Harvey A. Siegal, R. S. Falck, Jichuan Wang, and Robert G. Carlson, "Crack-Cocaine Users as Victims of Physical Attack," *Journal of the National Medical Association* 92, no. 2 (2000): 76–82.

30. Musto, "America's First Cocaine Epidemic," 229.

31. Ibid., 229.

32. Ngram Viewer, Google, Inc., 2012, http://books.google.com/ngrams.

33. F. Raúl Jerí, C. C. Sánchez, T. del Pozo, and M. Fernández, "The Syndrome of Coca Paste," *Journal of Psychedelic Drugs* 10 (1978): 361–369.

34. "Meeting Reports," Community Epidemiology Work Group (CEWG), accessed May 25, 2012, http://www.drugabuse.gov/about-nida/organization/workgroups-interest-groups-consortia/community-epidemiology-work-group-cewg.

35. CEWG, *Assessing Drug Abuse within and across Communities*, 2nd ed. (Rockville, Md.: National Institute on Drug Abuse, 2006).

36. "National Survey on Drug Use and Health & National Household Survey on Drug Abuse, Multiple Years Trends in Cocaine Use among Those 12 and Older (1979–2008)," *National Survey on Drug Use and Health*, SAMHSA, accessed May 28, 2012, http://www.briancbennett.com/charts/nsduh/cocaine.htm.

2

Illegal Drugs as a National Security Threat

Securitization of Drugs in the U.S. Official Discourse

YULIA VOROBYEVA

The issue of drugs has been present in the U.S. public discourse since the beginning of the twentieth century. However, for the past three decades, drugs have been presented by U.S. officials as a threat to national security. This process of securitization has had important policy implications, especially for Latin American countries, due to their record of exploiting the illegal-drug industry and supplying drugs to the U.S. market.

This chapter examines the official claim that drugs are one of the major threats to U.S. national security. It attempts to trace the securitization process and identify its mechanisms by analyzing the dynamics of the official U.S. rhetoric on drug trafficking in Latin America. Since the state shapes its foreign policy in response to threats posed by the international security environment, looking at how it perceives a threat helps us understand many foreign policy decisions that have profound implications for other countries.

Diachronic analysis based on observed changes at particular moments enables one to trace the development of a phenomenon. In other words, by analyzing crucial moments in the period under discussion, one can see how the U.S. official discourse on drugs evolved over time. Several critical moments since the beginning of the twentieth century demonstrate the securitization of drugs. This chapter focuses on a relatively recent period, starting with 1989. This year marks the unprecedented rise in importance of the Latin American drug problem for the United States, as illustrated by the Andean Regional Initiative. Plan Colombia represents one U.S. effort to reduce the supply of drugs through military and law enforcement means.

The terrorist attacks on 9/11 mark a shift in the official U.S. rhetoric on drugs by merging it with the threat of terrorism. The Mérida Initiative addresses the rising concern over the role of Mexico as a major drug-transit and -producing country and presents the U.S. view of possible solutions. Finally, Proposition 19, or the California Initiative, of 2010 suggests a possibility of desecuritization.

This chapter looks at selected governmental documents, official speeches, and press conferences in order to analyze the official position of the government regarding illicit drugs. The success or failure of securitization can be measured by specific policy outcomes such as spending and personnel deployment. Opinion polls represent an additional source of data that measure public perceptions of drugs. Using these conceptual tools, the analysis shows an increasing securitization of drugs as part of U.S. foreign policy toward Latin America. In sum, this chapter seeks to trace how an issue becomes securitized by analyzing authoritative statements made by key actors.

Securitization: A Conceptual Framework

Securitization is defined as the process of presenting an issue as a threat to national security whether the threat exists in reality or not.[1] This process occurs through discourse, when the securitizing actor speaks on behalf of the object to be secured (the referent object). When the referent object is the state, the government is usually entitled to act on its own behalf and has a right to speak on behalf of the nation. An issue becomes successfully securitized only when it is presented by the securitizing actor as a threat and when the audience is persuaded that the threat exists. As a result, the securitizing actor is allowed to break rules that otherwise would be observed and to resort to extraordinary measures to confront the threat. That is, state officials are allowed to resort to military means to deal with the securitized issue. Thus, securitization theory views the audience as an important agent that "empowers" the securitizing actor to adopt emergency measures.[2]

Although language is an essential component of a discourse, there are other aspects that any discourse analysis should include.[3] For example, the power of securitizing discourse depends on the securitizing actor's power position and relationship with the audience, the relative validity of statements, and the discursive strategy. In other words, besides a purely linguistic component, the discourse analysis is built around such sociological aspects as audience, power relations, context, and practices.[4]

The described framework is used here to analyze the U.S. official discourse of the "war on drugs." The first level of discourse analysis examines the actors that participate in the securitization process. As mentioned earlier, in order for a securitization act to succeed, the audience must be convinced by securitizing claims and support proposed solutions. In a democratic setting, for example, the constituency can be seen as empowering the audience because it may approve or reject the securitizing actor's views through election mechanisms. State bureaucratic structures are also common empowering agents because they often provide formal support of a securitizing act. For example, some bills proposed by the executive branch have to be approved by the legislative branch in order to be adopted.

Second, the power relationship between the securitizing actor and the audience determines the success of securitization. The securitizing actor manages to convince the audience as long as he or she has power over it; however, this power is partly granted by the audience itself through the mechanism of representation. In this sense, audience and securitizing actors are mutually constituted.[5] Because the government has a monopoly on the legitimate use of force, it can impose its policy on the citizens. But at the same time, it requires the consent of the citizens, which can be obtained through discourse. International consent may also be required in order to implement foreign policy.[6]

The next level of discourse analysis focuses on acts that constitute the securitization process. They include language, practices and tools, and outcome policies. The linguistic aspect of discourse is represented by a coherent rhetoric repetitively reproduced by the securitizing actor. This rhetoric includes a number of linguistic devices and is characterized by hybridity and intertextuality.[7] In other words, it draws upon other myths and narratives already known to the society. Contemporary U.S. antidrug policy discourse, for example, is rooted in the myth of drugs as evil. This myth was created at the beginning of the twentieth century, when the colonial powers initiated efforts to create the international drug-control regime. Drugs were demonized; that is, they acquired a new meaning, a connotation that previously had not existed: drugs are feared for their addictive power; they are believed to destroy the moral fabric of society and are associated with crime and moral degradation. Richard Nixon's declaration of the war on drugs appealed to parents by emphasizing their damaging effect on youth.[8]

Another level of the analysis focuses on security practices—policy tools utilized to deal with the issue identified as a threat.[9] Balzacq distinguishes two such tools: regulatory tools, which involve norms; and capacity tools, which involve training.[10] The drugs-securitization process has involved extensive training assistance by the United States to the Latin American military, police, and judicial institutions. Regulatory instruments include various institutionalized norms and rules established during the U.S.-led war on drugs.

The last level of discourse analysis is the context in which securitization takes place.[11] The success of securitization depends on a "perceptive environment," that is, whether it takes place in the critical moment when the audience is becoming more vulnerable to the threat. Another contextual factor that determines the success of securitization is the previously constructed cultural meaning, or the image of the issue to be securitized (the referent subject) adopted by society.[12] Thus, the relationship to an external reality conditions the success of a security statement.[13]

In sum, there can be singled out four main components of securitization on which this process rests: (1) actors (which includes the securitizing actor and the audience); (2) the referent object; (3) acts (meaning language and security practices); and (4) context (includes the perceptive environment and the power relations between actors). As Buzan et al. note, "Securitization studies aims to gain an increasing understanding of who securitizes, on what issues (threats), for whom (referent objects), why, with what results, and . . . under what conditions."[14] Based on these conceptual tools, this chapter analyzes five case studies that represent critical moments in the evolution of the U.S. antidrug discourse.

From the Andean Initiative to Proposition 19

To understand the context of the discourse on drugs, the historical background of the view of drugs as a security problem should be pointed out. Drugs came under public scrutiny at the beginning of the twentieth century as a result of British and U.S. moral entrepreneurs' efforts to draw attention to their detrimental effects on health.[15] Throughout the century, most states joined to combat drug trafficking and drug use. The United States has traditionally been at the head of the global drug-prohibition regime by actively promoting its stance on drugs as a threat to public health within international institutions and by exercising pressure on other states.[16] Over time, however, the rhetoric of public health shifted toward the rhetoric of national security.

Domestically, the use of drugs was first restricted at the federal level in 1914 by the Harrison Act. In 1971, President Richard Nixon declared a war on drugs, defining them as "public enemy No. 1" and calling for enhanced government control at the state and federal levels to deal with increasing drug use in the country. Before 1973, this function was shared by a number of state agencies and departments; in 1973, the Nixon administration established a single unified antinarcotics command by creating the Drug Enforcement Administration (DEA). In the 1980s, epidemics of crack use (smokeable cocaine) swept U.S. cities, providing justification for a further government campaign against drugs. The year 1986 can be considered as the beginning of the U.S. securitization of drugs, as President Ronald Reagan declared drug trafficking a national security threat that required a decisive response.

The next stage of the war on drugs took place in 1988 with the creation of the Office of National Drug Control Policy (ONDCP), also known as the "drug czar" office.[17]

On the international front, the United States had been pressuring the Andean countries since the 1970s to gain control of their flourishing drug trade. However, these efforts were not producing any positive results; the availability of drugs as well as the demand for them in the U.S. market was rising. By the end of the 1980s, Colombian drug-trafficking organizations (DTOs) had become so powerful that they could exercise violence against high-level politicians.

The 1990s witnessed an increase in U.S. antidrug assistance to Latin American drug-producing and drug-trafficking countries. Moreover, the end of the Cold War prompted a shift in security imperatives; if before 1991 the main national security threat stemmed from the spread of communism, now it was organized crime that captured the attention and resources of the United States.

The post–Cold War era has been characterized by the integration of U.S. security and law enforcement institutions, reflecting the malleability of the concept of security.[18] The terrorist attacks on September 11, 2001, accelerated this process.[19] As David Musto shows, narcotics control since its origin has been heavily politicized.[20] The following analysis is an attempt to trace this process in its critical moments from 1989 up to 2010.

George H. W. Bush's Andean Regional Initiative, 1989

The Andean countries of Colombia, Peru, and Bolivia are the world's largest producers of cocaine, most of which is exported to the United States. The United States had been providing some antidrug assistance to these countries since the early 1970s, but the continuing rise of DTOs, especially in Colombia, and the growth in cocaine consumption in the United States during the 1980s prompted the U.S. government to pay more attention to the region. The 1980s in Colombia were marked by the violent activities of two powerful cartels, the Medellín cartel and the Cali cartel, which posed a serious security threat to the Colombian state.[21] Their violent campaign against politicians and judges culminated with the assassination of presidential candidate Luis Carlos Galán in 1989. This event triggered emergency security measures imposed by President Virgilio Barco.

Due to geographical proximity and regional security concerns, the growing power of Colombian drug traffickers led to large-scale assistance to the Colombian government by the United States. In response to the security crisis in Colombia, the Bush administration launched a national strategy to combat illegal drugs. The *National Drug Control Strategy 1989*, an annual report prepared by the ONDCP, states in the introduction that "most Americans remain firmly convinced that drugs represent the gravest present threat to our national well-being."[22] One of the components of the strategy was the Andean Initiative, a multiyear tactic of allocating funds to curb drug production at the source in the Andean region. This approach represented a shift from interdiction to fighting drugs where they were cultivated. The Andean Initiative marks the beginning of greater U.S. involvement in the drug-control policies of Latin America.

The text of the Andean Initiative explicitly locates the referent subject abroad: "The source of the most dangerous drugs threatening our nation is principally international."[23] It states further: "While most international threats are potential, the damage and violence caused by the drug trade are actual and pervasive,"[24] thus prioritizing drug trafficking over other international threats. The document represents an official position of the government on the issue of drugs and the proposed way of dealing with it.

After the document was adopted, the government's approach was disseminated through the mass media to a broad audience. It can be argued that the text of the document appealed to the entire nation. The document stresses that as the category of drug users comprises the "elite," the middle class, and the poor,[25] the "problem" of drugs is "national in scope and size."[26] In terms of the relationship between actors, the securitizing actor (the government) placed itself in a higher power position as it was responsible for protecting the audience: "government has a solemn obligation to keep those Americans . . . safe and secure from the poison of drug trafficking and drug use."[27]

Since it was appealing to the generic public, the government sought moral rather than formal support through this document. There was an underlying process of construction of social identity at work, as this discourse tried to activate the language of collective interest: every citizen belongs to a bigger social group called a nation. The government, in turn, also appealed to its identity as protector of society. The entire nation in this case was the referent object threatened by the referent subject, drugs.

George H. W. Bush's speech on CNN on September 5, 1989, was a tool complementing the document and was designed to secure public consent. The speech was directed to "the American people," that is, to the nation. In the first paragraph Bush stated: "All of us agree that the gravest domestic threat facing our nation today is drugs."[28] By using the pronoun "us" he identified himself with the rest of the nation—a homogeneous entity that unanimously agreed with the utterance. The president utilized the mass media as a heuristic device to provide supporting evidence and to help construct shared meanings: "Turn on the evening news, or pick up the morning paper and you'll see what some Americans know just by stepping out their front door: Our most serious problem today is cocaine, and in particular, crack."[29]

Indeed, the years of the "crack boom" in the United States witnessed extensive media coverage of drug use and drug-related violence as well as mounting public concern. In 1990, for example, 37 percent of Americans considered drugs the top national problem (compared to 6 percent in 1987 and 23 percent in 1989).[30] Thus, it can be argued that the audience had been convinced by the securitizing actor.

The next level of analysis includes discursive practices such as linguistic devices designed to persuade the audience. For example, the use of metaphors is a common tool in securitization discourses. In the ONDCP strategy, drugs and drug use are repeatedly referred to as "epidemics," "poison," "evil," and a "plague," thus placing the issue in the semantic field of "disease." The logical tool for dealing with this type of issue would be treatment and other public health practices. However, presenting drugs as a threat to national security and often linked to other criminal activities is a stronger component of the discourse. Hence, to combat this "threat," military and law enforcement tools were utilized. The National Drug Control Strategy was itself part of security practice as it was a powerful tool of setting the agenda. Through these linguistic and nonlinguistic devices, the securitizing actor, in this case, the Bush administration, had to convince the audience of the need for the proposed policies.

At the domestic level, an implicit goal of the document was to legitimize the toughening of federal, state, and local drug-enforcement laws. For example, the Financial Crimes Enforcement Network (FinCEN), an agency designated to combat drug-related money laundering, was created in 1990. Institutional mobilization also can be evidenced by the fact that the Central Intelligence Agency (CIA) and the Department of Defense (DOD) joined the state institutional tools for combating the threat.

During the U.S.-led war on drugs, U.S. law enforcement agencies have obtained access to the international arena by leading operations in foreign territories.[31] International mobilization of U.S. personnel can be illustrated by Washington's decision to establish firebases for the DEA's agents in Peru as well as by leasing an air base from the Ecuadoran government to monitor parts of the Andean region.[32]

In terms of mobilization of funds, throughout the first Bush presidency, spending on antidrug activities in the Andean region increased dramatically, from U.S.$270 million to $600 million in FY1991–1992; compare this to the Reagan administration's $5 million budget.[33]

The U.S. military intervention in Panama in December 1989 was also an "emergency measure" aimed at fighting drug trafficking. In this case, the securitization of drugs was needed to justify the violation of sovereignty of another state. As the allocation of funds and personnel in most cases requires congressional approval, this mobilization of state resources illustrates the success of the administration in convincing the legislative branch of the rightness of its position.

Increased military involvement indicates that drug control was not exclusively in the law enforcement sphere anymore. Since the function of the military is to protect the state, the militarization of drug control is another indicator of a threat rising to the status of national security issue. It is important to point out that the Andean strategy was developed a year after the drug czar office was created, another crucial moment in the U.S. history of drug prohibition. Accordingly, the Andean program can also be viewed as the result of a broader securitization context and evidence that the war on drugs discourse had been successful.

Plan Colombia, 1999–2000

The U.S. Andean regional initiative cannot be understood without paying special attention to the Colombian conflict and its implications for U.S. antidrug policy. The issue of drugs has been gaining increasing importance in the U.S.-Colombian relationship since the early 1970s. However, it was in the early 1980s, in the context of Reagan's international war on drugs, that the United States took an especially tough stance in its antidrug policies in the Andean region. U.S.-Colombian relations became characterized by "narcotization"; that is, all aspects of U.S. involvement in Colombia were driven by drug-control policy.[34] The militarization of these policies began with the Andean Initiative and escalated through the 1990s.[35]

Although by the mid-1990s, joint U.S.-Colombian antidrug efforts managed to dismantle both major cartels, it was a "partial success" as it resulted in the proliferation of smaller DTOs rather than in curtailing drug trade and violence.[36] Moreover, since the 1960s, Colombia has been besieged by a number of leftist guerrillas such as the Revolutionary Armed Forces of Colombia (Fuerzas Armadas Revolucionarias de Colombia, FARC) and the National Liberation Army (Ejército de Liberación Nacional, ELN) and rightist paramilitary groups such as the United Self-Defense Forces of Colombia (Autodefensas Unidas de Colombia, AUC). In the mid-1990s, these insurgents became increasingly involved in illegal-drug trade. By the end of the 1990s, coca cultivation and production in Colombia had skyrocketed, and the U.S. government recognized the need to change its approach to drug-control policies in the country.

In 1999, Colombian president Andrés Pastrana announced a six-year U.S.$7.5 billion aid package, known as Plan Colombia, aimed at resolving the Colombian drug and security crisis. The U.S. government was to provide $1.3 billion, a major part of which constituted military assistance. The discourse used by the White House and the State Department to convince the U.S. Congress of the need for such a drastic budget increase emphasized the importance of Plan Colombia for U.S. national security.[37]

The urgency effect of discourse is created by such utterances as "an urgently needed package," "vital efforts,"[38] or "immediate and significant action is necessary."[39] The U.S. discourse constantly presents drug trafficking as a threat to democracy as well as a cause of corruption. Citing ONDCP director Barry McCaffrey, "rapidly expanding cocaine and heroin production in Colombia constitutes a threat to U.S. national security and the well-being of our citizens."[40] This discourse focuses on the U.S. national interest. President Clinton argued that "strengthening stability and democracy in Colombia, and fighting the drug trade there, is in [the United States'] fundamental national interest."[41] McCaffrey, by the same token, called Plan Colombia "a matter of critical importance to U.S. interests."[42] He placed heavy emphasis on the foreign roots of the U.S. problem; the main purpose of U.S. aid to Colombia was to stop the drug flow into U.S. territory. In other words, a domestic problem was claimed to have an external origin. Thus the pattern of focusing on the supply side to solve drug-related problems continued. The first success of this case of securitization can be seen in the bipartisan support received by Clinton in Congress.[43]

If Congress provides formal support for the securitizing actor, the general public is mostly a source of moral support. A study of public opinion published in March 2001 shows that stopping the importation of illegal drugs was considered potentially the "most effective" strategy that the government could adopt to control drug use.[44] That is, the source of threat was viewed as external by most people, which confirms the success of securitization. The survey also shows that most Americans (74 percent) viewed the war on drugs as a failure while still giving priority to interdiction and law enforcement strategies. This finding suggests that the government had succeeded in securitizing drugs and promoting a tough approach to this "threat." The almost complete sense of futility, in turn, reinforced the perceptive environment that would facilitate further construction of the threat by the government.

The link between guerrilla groups and drug-trafficking organizations, which was still seen as "a relatively recent phenomenon,"[45] took shape in the Plan Colombia discourse. The border between the two actors began to blur. However, in the U.S. discourse, armed groups had not yet been completely securitized. The Clinton administration supported the attempt at peace negotiations with the FARC initiated by Pastrana. Likewise, the official U.S. discourse stressed that the proposed aid package was strictly for antinarcotic efforts, in spite of the guerrillas' growing ties to illegal drugs.[46] Some critics, however, accuse McCaffrey of disguising his interest in fighting Colombian guerrillas with counterdrug rhetoric.[47] As Russell Crandall points out, the emphasis on antinarcotic efforts was meant to overcome the U.S. Congress' opposition and to justify a need for much harsher antidrug policy.[48]

Clinton's presidency was guided by the liberal view of the world rooted in the notion of globalization and interdependence.[49] His general approach to foreign policy was focused on a neoliberal economy and peace building. In this vein, he was advocating for shared responsibility with Colombia: "the fight against drugs is our joint responsibility. It must unite us, not divide us."[50] Official Clinton discourse claimed two main purposes of the aid to Colombia: drug interdiction and democratic development of the country. President Clinton made constant reference to both components of the strategy. In other words, the official U.S. rhetoric gave no priority to either aspect of the plan; in theory, it was an attempt at a balanced approach.

Although the initial draft of Plan Colombia by President Pastrana proposed a "comprehensive national reconstruction plan," the approved version of the document (virtually imposed by the United States) focused primarily on military assistance.[51] In the end, the biggest proportion of funds (U.S.$600 million) was assigned to military training and equipment.[52] According to the Annual Report of Foreign Military Training, the United States was planning to train 5,086 members of the Colombian police and military during 2000, a significant increase from the 2,476 trained in 1999.[53] Thus, the adoption of Plan Colombia was a key moment in U.S. international drug-control strategy, since it signaled greater militarization of the strategy. Provided with a total of U.S.$1.3 billion by the United States, Colombia became the third-largest recipient of U.S. foreign aid, after Israel and Egypt. Between fiscal years 2000 and 2008, the United States provided over $6 billion in military and nonmilitary assistance to Colombia.[54]

The explosive increase in funds directed at the fight against drug trafficking in Colombia illustrates a successful securitization case in which the Clinton administration was able to convince Congress of the need for emergency measures. This success was a result of presenting drug trafficking in Colombia as a direct threat to U.S. national security. But besides the speech act factor, the context of an ongoing security crisis in Colombia contributed significantly to the support received by the securitizing actor. The appeal to the language of national security threat thus legitimated the extraordinary measures undertaken by the U.S. government.

September 11, 2001

The year 2001 represents a radical change in U.S. foreign policy. First of all, George W. Bush assuming office led to a new political course based on unilateral and preventive use of U.S. military force.[55] As Zbigniew Brzezinski describes it, Bush's foreign policy reflected his view of the United States as the only superpower capable of fighting evil without taking into account its allies' views.[56] The crucial factor in the development of militarized U.S. foreign policy was the events of September 11, 2001. The terrorist attacks in New York City triggered the creation of a new security environment by providing the rationale to carry out Bush's "revolution" in foreign policy. As a result, the "war on terrorism" became the dominant political narrative. The vehicle for the construction of this new agenda was political discourse that presented terrorism as a threat to people's lives, well-being, and freedom.[57]

What were the implications of this new course for U.S. international drug policy? In the context of this change, links between drug trafficking and terrorism were dealt with in a new way: the war on drugs became part of the war on terrorism.[58] The two issues were merged and embedded into a wider sphere of national and international security, while antidrug policies were on the agenda as long as they contributed to the more important cause of the global war on terror. This can be seen in congressional testimony by Steven W. Casteel of the DEA in 2003 that states that after September 11, "for the DEA, investigating the link between drugs and terrorism has taken on renewed importance."[59] A Bureau of International Narcotics and Law Enforcement Affairs (INL) representative similarly stressed his agency's contribution to the war on terrorism through its counternarcotics activities.[60]

The impact of the events of September 11 could be also perceived in the development of Plan Colombia. After the terrorist attacks, the focus of the initiative shifted from drugs to counterinsurgency.[61] Colombian president Álvaro Uribe used the U.S. focus on the war on terror and securitized drug trafficking by linking it to the country's insurgent/"terrorist" groups. As a result, in contrast to Congress' initial emphasis on directing U.S. aid exclusively to counternarcotics efforts, the new agenda erased the line between Colombian guerrilla groups and drug traffickers.[62] The terms "narco-guerrilla" and "narco-terrorism" were appearing more frequently in the official discourse.

It is important to note that in the wake of the terrorist attacks in 2001, public opinion polls showed high support for Bush's policies (90 percent in 2001 and 70 percent in 2002). As of October 2001, 93 percent of Americans considered protection against terrorist attacks the top foreign policy priority for the United States (as compared to 80 percent in a pre-9/11 poll), while combating international drug trafficking lost 9 percent compared to August 2001 (from 64 percent in September 2001, before 9/11, to 55 percent in October).[63] The data demonstrate that the drugs-securitization process would receive more support if antidrug policies were subordinated to antiterrorism efforts.

Within the new security agenda, FinCEN broadened its scope to deal with terrorist-related money laundering.[64] There was also a sharp increase in the number of extraditions of drug traffickers from Colombia to the United States (from 13 in 2000 to 134 in 2005). The policy outcomes evidence that the context of the war on terror created a sense of urgency in dealing with the threat and provided a perceptive environment for the successful securitization of illegal drugs by both the Uribe administration and the U.S. government.

Mérida Initiative, 2007

Mexico became the main point of transit for Andean cocaine in the late 1980s, after the previously used routes through the Caribbean were brought under control by the South Florida Task Force.[65] The importance of Mexican DTOs further increased in the 1990s, when the major Colombian cartels were dismantled. The beginning of the twenty-first century was marked in Mexico by the transition of power from the Revolutionary Institutional Party (Partido Revolucionario Institucional, PRI) which had ruled the country for seventy-one years) to the National Action Party (Partido Acción Nacional, PAN). The new government, headed by Vicente Fox (2000–2006), began a large-scale crackdown on the major cartels with U.S. assistance of $397 million in the FY2000–FY2006 period.[66]

In 2006, shortly after assuming the presidency, Felipe Calderón declared a war on drugs throughout Mexico, making drug trafficking the top priority of his administration. His administration focused on the tough approach to drug trafficking by pouring significant resources into military and law enforcement action against drug cartels. This approach received wide support from the U.S. government; at the Mérida Summit in March 2007, Presidents George W. Bush and Calderón emphasized the threat presented by drug-trafficking organizations to both governments and agreed on the development of the Mérida Initiative, a multiyear "security cooperation initiative with Mexico and the countries of Central America in order to combat the threats of drug trafficking, transnational crime, and terrorism in the Western Hemisphere."[67] The official U.S. discourse recognized the role of the demand for drugs among American consumers by framing the new agreement within the notion of "shared responsibility."[68] It stressed a new level of cooperation, or a "new strategic partnership" in the "spirit of renewed collaboration."[69]

Despite this apparent shift away from viewing drugs as an exclusively external threat, the language implemented in the official discourse of the initiative conforms to the previously established patterns of threat construction. For example, each of the first six sentences of the Joint Statement on the Mérida Initiative contains the term "threat."[70] Moreover, it can be argued that Mexico itself had been securitized by the U.S. government. According to the International Narcotics Control Strategy Report of 2007, "Mexico is a major transit and source country for illicit drugs reaching the United States"[71]; by the same token, the Department of Justice argued that the "Mexican DTOs represent the greatest organized crime threat to the United States."[72]

Drug trafficking and drug-related violence were also presented as a threat to the national security of both countries, which made these issues transnational: "Transnational criminal activity," including drug trafficking, represents a "threat to the lives and well-being of U.S. and Mexican citizens."[73] Thus, now drug trafficking was constructed not only as a threat to U.S. national security but also as a transnational threat.

The discourse followed the securitization pattern. For example, the first paragraph of the bill approved by Congress in FY2008 states, "The drug crisis facing the United States remains a significant national security threat."[74] Likewise, a DEA representative blamed the illicit-drug trade for most socioeconomic problems, claiming that it was "responsible for the corruption of public officials and institutions, diminished respect for the rule of law and the loss of confidence in government institutions, undermining democratic governance and eroding political stability."[75]

According to a governmental report, "the Mérida Initiative brings a shift in both scale and scope to U.S. assistance to the region, particularly Mexico," referring to the significant increase in funds assigned to Mexico's counterdrug law enforcement efforts. U.S. funding increased from about $57 million in the 2000–2006 period to $400 million in FY2008.[76] In FY2009, the U.S. government appropriated $720 million to fund the Mérida Initiative in Mexico.[77]

However, more resources were directed to supply-side strategies. The allocation of money shows the prevailing focus of the initiative on law enforcement and military equipment. For example, for FY2008, $350 million was designated for military assistance and $120 million for law enforcement, compared to $73.5 million to be spent on judicial reform and institution-building activities.[78] This suggests that the initiative was an expansion of previous policies rather than a "shift," as it continued the militarization of Mexico's war on drugs.

The Washington Office on Latin America (WOLA) is one of the numerous critics of the heavy military assistance provided by the plan. WOLA believed that long-term progress could not be achieved through these measures.[79] WOLA's critique represents a rival discourse to the dominant official rhetoric. It is important to note that the INL has a Myth vs. Fact section about the Mérida Initiative on its web page. The "myths" section comprises the common critiques of the program, thereby suppressing rival discourses by labeling them as myths. The "facts" section supports the official rhetoric, emphasizing "shared responsibility" and a comprehensive approach.

Although actual spending for the Mérida activities developed extremely slowly because of the intricate bureaucracy, additional measures taken by the U.S. State Department suggest the perceived urgency of fund allocation. For example, in order to expedite the contribution of five Bell helicopters to Mexico, high-ranking State Department officials collaborated directly with the Department of Defense (which manages the implementation of the program) and were able to complete the transfer in eight months instead of the usual two years.[80] The Mérida Initiative also required mobilization of additional U.S. personnel: the U.S. Embassy in Mexico, for example, added staff specifically to handle initiative-related issues.[81]

The issue of international drug trafficking regained ground in 2004 compared with the aftermath of the terrorist attacks in 2001. According to a 2004 opinion poll, 63 percent of Americans believed that combating international drug trafficking should be a top foreign policy priority, compared to 55 percent in 2001.[82] However, as of 2010, according to opinion polls, only 5 percent of respondents closely followed the drug violence in Mexico in the news and it accounted for as little as 1 percent of news coverage.[83] This low public interest stands in contrast to the late 1980s and early 1990s, when opinion polls showed drugs receiving massive media attention. The data suggest a trend of waning public support for the securitization process. This possibility is examined in the next section.

Proposition 19

Despite all the "extraordinary measures" adopted by the U.S. government to tackle the "threat" of drug trafficking, the results have been far from positive. Drug cultivation, production, and transit have constantly ballooned from one Latin American country to another as a result of partially successful antidrug efforts in some countries.[84] Corruption, crime, and violence fueled by illegal drugs are on the rise in many Latin American countries. Central America has proved to be especially vulnerable as a result of Mexico's war on drugs. The overall availability of illegal drugs in the U.S. market is increasing,[85] and in spite of considerable reduction in consumption of marijuana and cocaine since the 1970s, overall drug use in the United States rose over the 2002–2010 period.[86]

The perceived failure of the war on drugs has led to the fragmentation of the official U.S. discourse as rival discourses have grown more powerful. A growing number of voices from within and outside the U.S. have been criticizing its prohibitionist approach to drugs. On the domestic level, the challenge to this approach began with the legalization of marijuana for medical purposes. In 1996, California became the first state to pass a medical marijuana bill that removed state-level criminal penalties on the use of the plant with a physician's recommendation. By 2014, almost half of the states (23 out of 50) and Washington, D.C., allowed for some use of marijuana for medical purposes. In 2010, California again went one step further by presenting a ballot initiative to legalize commercial marijuana-related activities. The proposition was defeated, albeit by a narrow margin (53.8% to 46.2%).[87] However, in 2012, the reformers in Washington state and Colorado succeeded in getting marijuana legalized for recreational use.[88]

The voting on the Colorado and Washington state initiative took place in the context of rethinking the whole prohibitionist strategy of drug control, both internationally and domestically. Those initiatives can be seen as part of the growing alternative discourse of desecuritization. Based on the theoretical framework, it can be suggested that, domestically, the securitization of drugs has not been successful, as Colorado's and Washington's voters were not convinced by the securitizing actor (the federal government) of the need to confront the threat through law enforcement strategies. The outcome of these referenda is an indicator of the relative success achieved by the alternative discourse of desecuritization.

Since any issue can be placed on any spectrum, ranging from the non-politicized to the securitized, drug-related issues may be desecuritized or even more securitized. The strategy of desecuritization deserves a separate study, but some observations can be made here.

First of all, the starting point of this process must be official speech acts. Since securitization itself starts with a speech act aimed at convincing the audience, desecuritization should follow the same model. As the dominant, or hegemonic, discourse of securitization is produced by certain actors in a certain social context, this assumption must be applied in analyzing the strategy of desecuritization.

The problem of a potentially counterhegemonic discourse is precisely one of the components of securitization theory: relations of power. Securitization theory argues that one of the conditions for a discourse to succeed is the credibility of the securitizing actor provided by his or her high position in the hierarchy of power. Until now, desecuritizing efforts have usually stemmed from academic circles, nongovernmental organizations, journalists, human rights activists, and former presidents.[89] Moreover, some of the sitting Latin American presidents, such as Otto Pérez Molina of Guatemala and Juan Manuel Santos of Colombia, have expressed their acceptance of the drug decriminalization debate.[90]

This has not brought the hegemonic discourse down yet, since at the international level the power position of the United States is much higher than that of Latin America. According to an Inter-American Dialogue report, "Latin Americans know that, given the size of the U.S. drug market and Washington's dominant role in shaping international antidrug policies, no initiative to revise global strategies and put new approaches in place can succeed without U.S. support and leadership."[91]

What is crucial, then, is a reframing of the issue as a matter of public health rather than one of national security. After the issue is reformulated by the government of the United States in official speech acts, it should be followed by specific policies, such as reducing resources and personnel involved in the war on drugs. These policies, in turn, should create a favorable context for further desecuritization.

However, there is a major caveat in reframing the threat. Discourse and actors are mutually constructed: on the one hand, speech acts are produced by actors, and thus actors have agency over their discourses; on the other hand, discourse, as a repetitive and institutionalized practice, constructs the actors, thereby reducing their ability to change it.[92]

Conclusion

Textual analysis of governmental documents and formal speeches shows consistency in the U.S. official discourse on international antidrug policy. Since drugs were first presented as a threat to public health at the beginning of the twentieth century, there has been a constant process of building and reinforcing this meaning. Since the beginning of the modern stage of the war on drugs during the Nixon administration, the referent object (the object to be secured) has been broadening.

The evolution of securitization has been a gradual process of constructing a belief that drugs represent a threat to U.S. society and, by the same token, to U.S. national security, even though most members of society do not consume them. At the international level, this process is reflected in the prioritization of drug-related issues in U.S. foreign policy. Moreover, in the wake of the events of September 11, 2001, there has been a tendency to escalate the securitization of drugs that has reached the point when previously separate issues of drugs and terrorism have converged into a single security framework.

Textual analysis also shows that the official discourse has been moving toward greater recognition of drugs as a threat whose source is partly domestic. This is illustrated by the rhetoric of "shared responsibility." However, analysis of policy outcomes demonstrates that the allocation of military resources and personnel to the war on drugs has been steadily increasing. Thus, we are witnessing success in the securitization process. The context that has facilitated this process constitutes normative beliefs about drugs associated with evil, illegality, and threat. These beliefs were constructed in U.S. society throughout the twentieth century and were reinforced by harsh policies and accompanying discourse.

All policies generated by the securitization discourse, in turn, contribute to further securitization as they represent institutionalized and routinized practices. They can thus be seen both as a result of the discourse and as a constituent part of the context in which the next discourse is based. The evidence supports the argument that the securitization of drugs in U.S. foreign policy has been taking place since the end of the 1980s.

The political and economic asymmetry between the United States and the Latin American states allows the former to exercise a significant influence on the latter in terms of their security agendas. Hence, the securitization of drugs in the U.S. official discourse has led to hardline policies abroad while imposing the securitized agenda on other countries. Many of them have been mobilizing funds and military personnel under pressure from the United States. In other words, the drug policies of Latin America have become subordinated to the U.S. vision of its domestic problem. The battle against drugs is often linked to other issues and, in many cases, conditions cooperation between the United States and Latin America in other areas.

Nevertheless, as the last case study shows, there has been an increase in alternative discourses. The outcome of the California vote implies that current antidrug policies are losing ground. Since the new voices have emerged within the official environment itself, there is a suggestion that there has been a fragmentation of the official discourse that may result in its breakdown. Drugs, still largely presented as a threat to national security, soon may be undergoing a process of desecuritization.

Notes

1. The securitization framework is part of the broader constructivist paradigm. The constructivist approach to international relations, developed in the 1980s, emphasizes concepts such as power, identities, and interests, which are constituted primarily of shared, or "intersubjective," ideas rather than given by nature. In other words, the behavior of actors is determined by the ideas that are formed through the actors' constant social interaction. An important implication of this perspective is that the perception of an existential threat is socially constructed and varies from state to state. See Alexander Wendt, *Social Theory of International Politics* (Cambridge: Cambridge University Press, 1999).

2. The concept of securitization was first developed by Barry Buzan, Ole Wæver, and Jaap de Wilde, who define it as a process of interpreting an issue as an existential threat and establishing this view at the intersubjective level. In the vein of constructivism, the authors argue that, theoretically, any issue can be placed on any of three possible agendas: nonpoliticized, politicized, and securitized. The nonpoliticized end of the spectrum means that "the state does not deal with [the issue]"; at the politicized level, "the issue is part of public policy"; the securitized level implies that "the issue is presented as an existential threat"; see Barry Buzan, Ole Wæver, and Jaap de Wilde, *Security: A New Framework for Analysis* (Boulder, Colo.: Lynne Rienner, 1998), 23–24. Accordingly, any issue can be securitized—or desecuritized—regardless of the existence of a real threat. See Buzan et al., *Security*, for more details.

3. Securitization theorists emphasize the active role of language. Ole Wæver, for example, states that by pronouncing an utterance, "something is done"; see "Securitization and Desecuritization," in *On Security*, ed. Ronnie Lipzchutz (New York: Columbia University Press, 1998), 55. Jef Huysmans views language not simply as a communication tool but as a "defining force" that can "prioritize questions and mobilize people"; see "Defining Social Constructivism in Security Studies: The Normative Dilemma of Writing Security," *Alternatives* 27 (2002): 45, 59. Buzan et al. view securitization as a speech act, which implies that just by using language in a correct way, it is possible to persuade an audience that a threat exists.

4. Thierry Balzacq, "A Theory of Securitization: Origins, Core Assumptions, and Variants," in *Securitization Theory: How Security Problems Emerge and Dissolve*, ed. Thierry Balzacq (London: Routledge, 2011), 25.

5. Ibid., 2

6. See Adrián Bonilla, "Teoría de las relaciones internacionales como discurso político: El caso de la guerra de las drogas" XVI Latin American Studies Association Congress, Washington, DC, April 1991.

7. Richard Jackson, *Writing the War on Terrorism: Language, Politics and Counter-Terrorism* (Manchester: Manchester University Press, 2005), 154.

8. Routinization and institutionalization of this discourse through domestic and international norms have created a dominant narrative; thus, the perception of drugs as a threat has been naturalized, that is, has become a norm.

9. Balzacq, "A Theory of Securitization," 15.

10. Ibid., 17.

11. Thierry Balzacq, "Enquiries into Methods: A New Framework for Securitization Analysis," in *Securitization Theory: How Security Problems Emerge and Dissolve*, ed. Thierry Balzacq (London: Routledge, 2011), 36–37.

12. Balzacq, "A Theory of Securitization," 13–14.

13. Thierry Balzacq, "The Three Faces of Securitization: Political Agency, Audience and Context," *European Journal of International Relations* 11, no. 2 (2005): 182.

14. Buzan et al., *Security*, 32.

15. David Musto, *The American Disease: Origins of Narcotic Control*, 3rd ed. (New York: Oxford University Press, 1999); Peter Andreas and Ethan Nadelmann, *Policing the Globe: Criminalization and Crime Control in International Relations* (Oxford: Oxford University Press, 2006).

16. Andreas and Nadelmann, *Policing the Globe*.

17. Musto, *The American Disease*.

18. Andreas and Nadelmann, *Policing the Globe*, 158.

19. Ibid., 236.

20. Musto, *The American Disease*, 294.

21. Bruce M. Bagley, "Drug Trafficking, Political Violence and U.S. Policy in Colombia in the 1990s," *Mama Coca*, January 5, 2001, accessed February 28, 2012, http://www.mamacoca.org/junio2001/bagley_drugs_and_violence_en.htm.

22. Office of National Drug Control Policy (ONDCP), *National Drug Control Strategy 1989* (Washington, D.C., 1989), 1.

23. Ibid., 61.

24. Ibid.

25. Ibid., 3.

26. Ibid., 4.

27. Ibid., 9.

28. George H. W. Bush, "Text of President's Speech on National Drug Control Strategy," *New York Times*, September 6, 1989, accessed May 8, 2011, http://www.nytimes.com/1989/09/06/us/text-of-president-s-speech-on-national-drug-control-strategy.html?src=pm.

29. Ibid.

30. Pew Research Center for the People and the Press, "Interdiction and Incarceration Still Top Remedies," People-press.org, March 21, 2001, http://www.people-press.org/2001/03/21/interdiction-and-incarceration-still-top-remedies/.

31. Andreas and Nadelmann, *Policing the Globe*.

32. Bruce M. Bagley, "After San Antonio," in *Drug Trafficking in the Americas*, ed. Bruce M. Bagley and William Walker III (New Brunswick, N.J.: Transaction Publishers, 1995), 64.

33. Sayaka Fukumi, *Cocaine Trafficking in Latin America: EU and US Policy Responses* (Abingdon, U.K.: Ashgate, 2008), 14.

34. Russell Crandall, *Driven by Drugs: U.S. Policy toward Colombia* (Boulder, Colo.: Lynne Rienner, 2002).

35. Ibid.

36. Bagley, "Drug Trafficking, Political Violence."

37. During the administration of Ernesto Samper, the United States "decertified" Colombia by significantly limiting aid after discovering links between the Colombian government and drug-trafficking organizations.

38. William Clinton, "President William Clinton, Statement on Aid to Colombia," *Le Monde Diplomatique*, January 11, 2000, accessed May 5, 2011, http://www.monde-diploma tique.fr/cahier/ameriquelatine/clinton11012000en.

39. Barry R. McCaffrey, "Statement of Director Barry R. McCaffrey. Announcement of Emergency and Increased Funding Proposal for Colombia and the Andean Region," *Le Monde Diplomatique*, January 11, 2000, accessed May 5, 2011, http://www.monde-diploma tique.fr/cahier/ameriquelatine/caffrey11012000en.

40. Ibid.

41. Clinton, "President William Clinton."

42. McCaffrey, "Statement of Director Barry R. McCaffrey."

43. This support, however, was not achieved immediately. In late 1999, the U.S. Congress rejected Clinton's bill, which proposed $1.6 billion over FY 2000 and FY 2001. This initial attempt can be seen as an example of failed securitization.

44. Respondents favoring this strategy compared to "arresting drug sellers" (19 percent), "educating Americans" (15 percent), "providing treatment" (10 percent), "arresting drug users" (4 percent); see Pew Research Center, "74% Say Drug War Being Lost."

45. McCaffrey, "Statement of Director Barry R. McCaffrey."

46. U.S. Department of State, ONDCP Director's Visit to Colombia, E.O. 12958, declassified 07/27/09.

47. Justin Delacour, "Plan Colombia: Rhetoric, Reality, and the Press," *Social Justice Magazine* 27, no. 4 (2000), accessed May 5, 2011, http://www.thirdworldtraveler.com/ South_America/PlanColombia_Rhetoric.html; Alexander Cockburn, "McCaffrey's Wars," *The Albion Monitor*, May 30, 2000, accessed May 5, 2011, http://www.albionmonitor. com/0006a/copyright/ac-mccaffreycolombia.html.

48. Crandall, *Driven by Drugs*, 149.

49. Zbigniew Brzezinski, *Second Chance: Three Presidents and the Crisis of American Superpower* (New York: Basic Books, 2007).

50. "The President's News Conference with President Andres Pastrana of Colombia," American Presidency Project, Presidency.ucsb.edu, October 28, 1998, accessed May 7, 2011, http://www.presidency.ucsb.edu/ws/index.php?pid=55165#ixzz1LiYygoSP.

51. Marc Cooper, "Plan Colombia: Wrong Issue, Wrong Enemy, Wrong Country," *The Nation* 272, no. 11 (2001): 14.

52. U.S. Embassy, Bogotá, "Temas bilaterales: Asistencia estadounidense al Plan Co-

lombia," Spanish.bogota.usembassy.gov, March 7, 2000, accessed May 5, 2011, http://span ish.bogota.usembassy.gov/pcolombia004.html.

53. U.S. Department of State and U.S. Department of Defense, *Foreign Military Training and DoD Engagement Activities of Interest in Fiscal Years 1999 and 2000, Volume I*, Washington, DC, March 1, 2000, accessed May 6, 2011, http://www.state.gov/1997-2001-NOP DFS/global/arms/fmtrain/toc.html.

54. U.S. Government Accountability Office (GAO), "Plan Colombia: Drug Reduction Goals Were Not Fully Met, but Security Has Improved: U.S. Agencies Need More Detailed Plans for Reducing Assistance, GAO-09-71 (Washington, DC, 2008).

55. Ivo Daalder and James M. Lindsay, *America Unbound: The Bush Revolution in Foreign Policy* (Washington, D.C.: Brookings Institution Press, 2003), 13–14.

56. Brzezinski, *Second Chance,* 136.

57. Jackson, *Writing the War on Terrorism,* 1.

58. Andreas and Nadelmann, *Policing the Globe,* 197.

59. Steven W. Casteel, "Narco-Terrorism: International Drug Trafficking and Terrorism—a Dangerous Mix," statement of Steven W. Casteel, assistant administrator for intelligence, before the Senate Committee on the Judiciary, May 20, 2003, accessed May 5, 2011, http://iipdigital.usembassy.gov/st/english/texttrans/2003/05/20030520162125retropc4.883 975e-02.html#axzz3GXNrAtPe.

60. House Subcommittee on Western Hemisphere Affairs of the Committee on International Relations, *The Western Hemisphere's Response to the September 11, 2001 Terrorist Attack on the United States*, 107th Cong., 1st sess., October 10, 2001, 34.

61. Crandall, *Driven by Drugs,* 6.

62. Sebastián Chaskel, "U.S. Foreign Policy towards Latin America's Oldest Guerrilla Group," FRIDE, July 4, 2008, accessed May 5, 2011, http://www.fride.org/publication/456/ us-foreign-policy-towards-latin-america%27s-oldest-guerrilla-group.

63. Pew Research Center for the People and the Press and Council on Foreign Relations, "America's New Internationalist Point of View," People-press.org, 2001b, http://www. people-press.org/2001/10/24/americas-new-internationalist-point-of-view/.

64. Andreas and Nadelmann, *Policing the Globe,* 195.

65. Bruce M. Bagley, *The Colombian–Mexican–U.S. Connection: Drug Trafficking, Organized Crime and Violence* (Coral Gables: University of Miami, 2009).

66. C. R. Seelke, L. S. Wyler, and J. S. Beittel, *Latin America and the Caribbean: Illicit Drug Trafficking and U.S. Counterdrug Programs* (Washington, D.C.: Congressional Research Service, 2011).

67. Council on Foreign Relations (CFR), "Joint Statement on the Merida Initiative," Cfr.org, Essential Documents, October 22, 2007, accessed May 5, 2011, http://www.cfr.org/ mexico/joint-statement-merida-initiative/p14603.

68. See "The President's News Conference with President Felipe de Jesus Calderon Hinojosa in Merida," American Presidency Project, Presidency.ucsb.edu, March 14, 2007, accessed May 8, 2011, http://www.presidency.ucsb.edu/ws/index.php?pid=24587#ixzz1 LudWoAcB.

69. U.S. Consulate General, Guadalajara, Mexico, "Joint Statement of the Merida Initiative," December 19, 2008, accessed May 5, 2011, http://guadalajara.usconsulate.gov/an-nouncements/announcements/joint-statement-of-the-merida-initiative.html.

70. See CFR, "Joint Statement on the Merida Initiative."

71. U.S. Department of State, *International Narcotics Control Strategy Report* (Washington, D.C.: Bureau for International Narcotics and Law Enforcement Affairs, 2007), 167.

72. National Drug Intelligence Center (NDIC), *National Drug Threat Assessment, 2009* (Washington, D.C.: U.S. Department of Justice, 2009), iii.

73. CFR, "Joint Statement on the Merida Initiative."

74. U.S. Congress, *Merida Initiative to Combat Illicit Narcotics and Reduce Organized Crime Authorization Act of 2008*, HR 6028 EH, 110th Cong., 2nd sess., June 10, 2008, 4.

75. Anthony P. Placido, "The U.S. Government's Domestic Obligations under the Merida Initiative," Chief of Intelligence, Drug Enforcement Administration, U.S. Department of Justice, before the House Foreign Affairs Committee Subcommittee on the Western Hemisphere, Washington, DC, February 7, 2008, accessed May 1, 2011, http://www.justice.gov/archive/olp/illegal_drugs.htm.

76. GAO, *Status of Funds for the Mérida Initiative*, GAO-10-253R (Washington, D.C., December 3, 2009), accessed May 2, 2011, 1, http://www.gao.gov/new.items/d10253r.pdf.

77. Ibid., 8.

78. U.S. Congress, *Merida Initiative.* The actual allocation of funds, however, was quite slow: according to State Department data, by September 2009, only $24.2 million (2 percent) had been paid out of $112 million planned (See GAO, *Status of Funds*, 7).

79. WOLA, "Military Aid Reflects Skewed Mérida Priorities; WOLA Urges More Civilian Security Aid," May 14, 2008, accessed May 5, 2011, http://www.wola.org/news/military_aid_reflects_skewed_merida_priorities_wola_urges_more_civilian_security_aid.

80. GAO, *Status of Funds,* 12.

81. Ibid., 14.

82. Pew Research Center for the People and the Press and Council on Foreign Relations, "Foreign Policy Attitudes Now Driven by 9/11 and Iraq," People-press.org, 2004, http://www.people-press.org/2001/10/24/americas-new-internationalist-point-of-view/.

83. Pew Research Center for the People and the Press, "Few Have Heard a Lot about GOP's 'Pledge to America': Elections Dominate Coverage, Not Public Interest," *People-press.org,* 2010.

84. Bagley, "The Colombian–Mexican–U.S. Connection."

85. NDIC, *National Drug Threat Assessment 2011* (Washington, D.C.: U.S. Department of Justice, 2011).

86. SAMHSA, *Results from the 2010 National Survey on Drug Use and Health: Summary of National Findings* (Rockville, Md.: U.S. Department of Health and Human Services, 2011).

87. California Secretary of State, "Regulate, Control and Tax Cannabis Act of 2010," sos.ca.gov, 2010, accessed May 5, 2011, http://cdn.sos.ca.gov/vig2010/general/pdf/english/text-proposed-laws.pdf#prop19.

88. For well-grounded arguments against Proposition 19, see Beau Kilmer et al., "Reducing Drug Trafficking Revenues and Violence in Mexico: Would Legalizing Marijuana in California Help?" The study shows that legalizing marijuana in California would not affect drug revenues of Mexican DTOs to any significant extent; neither would it reduce levels of violence in Mexico (Santa Monica, Calif.: RAND, 2010).

89. In 2009, the Latin American Commission on Drugs and Democracy, which included

former presidents of Brazil, Colombia, and Mexico, issued a statement called "Drugs and Democracy: Toward a Paradigm Shift," a critical assessment of the war on drugs, http://www.opensocietyfoundations.org/publications/drugs-and-democracy-toward-paradigm-shift.

90. G. Ramsey, "UN Report Enforces Orthodox Drug Strategy," Insightcrime.org, March 1, 2012, accessed March 3, 2012, http://www.insightcrime.org/news-analysis/un-report-enforces-orthodox-drug-strategy.

91. Peter Hakim, *Rethinking U.S. Drug Policy* (Oxford: Beckley Foundation, 2011), 5.

92. See Coletta A. Youngers, "The Obama Administration's Drug Control Policy on Auto-Pilot," IDPC Briefing Paper, April 2011.

3

The War on Drugs and the Role of SOUTHCOM

JUAN GABRIEL TOKATLIAN

The "war on drugs"[1] has never been a metaphor,[2] not even when President Richard Nixon declared it in 1971,[3] after the rise of heroin and marijuana consumption in the United States and during the upsurge of their production in Turkey and Mexico, respectively. The war on drugs can be characterized as a prohibitionist campaign that seeks to suppress, predominantly by harsh repressive measures, the phenomenon of drugs at each of its stages.[4] In essence, this prohibitionist agenda seeks to create a drug-free society. This implies the elimination of cultivation, production, processing, trafficking, distribution, commercialization, financing, selling, and consumption of a number of psychoactive substances that have been declared illegal.[5]

Conceptually, the dynamics of this war have been sustained by an unbalanced combination of punishment (for instance, extended criminalization) and compensation (for example, crop-substitution programs), have sought a global scope (it transcends the United States), and have pretended to be integral (namely, to cover the entire production chain of the drug business). However, in practice, the war on drugs has been concentrated in the periphery (Latin America, among other places) and has focused on combating the supply of narcotics. This "war" can best be characterized as essentially coercive.[6]

This war has failed and has persistently peaked in its manifestation in Latin America—with Mexico presenting today a uniquely complex and alarming case[7]—and has relied on a U.S. actor, the U.S. Southern Command (SOUTHCOM), whose role has been central but scarcely evaluated.[8] The purpose of this chapter is to explore the nature of the fight against drugs in Latin America, to highlight how the interpretive mistakes of the past are repeated in the Mexican case, and to underline the way SOUTHCOM has played a key role in the deployment and continuity of the war on drugs.

Mirando a Latinoamérica: A Glance into Latin America

Latin America adapted this crusade a long time ago. Although the United States played a decisive role in the process of imposing the war on drugs in the region, the intensity and depth this war has achieved there is a matter of shared responsibility: pressure (and even blackmail) from Washington has been a necessary but not sufficient condition; Latin America has embraced the prohibitionist paradigm and has not yet abandoned it. Regardless of the degree of the region's adoption of and commitment to the war on drugs, the war on drugs' suppositions and parameters have influenced the strategy applied in the area.

This strategy is based on the following components: (1) as long as it has been accepted, either tacitly or explicitly, that the phenomenon of drugs stems from supply, the governments' actions are directed primarily at dismantling the centers of production, processing, and shipment of the illegal psychoactive substances; (2) for this phenomenon to be perceived as a security problem rather than a health issue,[9] the emphasis in counterdrug efforts is placed on active participation not only by the police but also by the armed forces;[10] and (3) since it is assumed that the fight against drugs requires special attention, any alternatives to the "iron fist" (*mano dura*) approach were not considered for a while.

This has resulted in a series of specific public policies: (1) the eradication of illicit crops; (2) the dismantling of drug-trafficking organizations; (3) the militarization of the war on drugs;[11] (4) the criminalization of the entire internal chain related to the drug business; (5) the extradition of nationals—especially to the United States; and (6) the rejection, until the early 2010s, of any initiative that favored drug legalization.[12]

The results of crop eradication can be characterized as ineffective, damaging, and even paradoxical.[13] The policy has been ineffective because drug traffickers' power has not been affected nor have the socioeconomic conditions in the areas within the scope of this strategy been improved.[14] In addition, the quality, availability, and price of drugs have not been affected. The policy has created a vicious cycle in that the clearing of forests as a result of illicit crop cultivation, pressures due to forced eradication of plantations, use of aerial and manual spraying with chemicals, disarticulation of a subsistence peasant economy, violent persecution of the poor rural population (peasants and indigenous people), absence of alternative marketable crops, the sporadic and usually repressive presence of the state, the displacement of illicit crops to other areas, and the beginning of the cycle have culminated in a situation in which the incentives to continue illicit cultivation are reinforced.[15] Thus, the drug business in Latin America has become more profitable, virulent, and expansive.

The paradoxical nature of the crop-eradication program stems from the fact that it has led, in some cases, to greater mobilization and political and social strengthening of internal groups, traditionally less resourceful and powerful. In other cases, these policies have facilitated the growth of armed groups, for example, the *cocalero* (coca grower) movement in Bolivia, which actively organized itself during the 1980s based on its rejection of the forced eradication of illicit crops.[16] In the case of Colombia, Washington's counter-drug policies—including chemical eradication of illicit crops—prompted the strengthening of the Revolutionary Armed Forces of Colombia (Fuerzas Armadas Revolucionarias de Colombia, FARC).[17] Washington's insistence on eradication in spite of meager results contributed, to some degree, to the election of Evo Morales in Bolivia (2005–2012)[18] and to the FARC's persistent influence in some geographical areas.[19]

Parallel to these policies, the dismantling of drug-trafficking organizations was constituted on an important pillar of Latin American public policy. The persecution of "drug lords" was generally a marginal practice in the 1970s and erratic during the 1980s, but has moved to the forefront since the 1990s. The crackdown on prominent drug lords was implemented in an especially decisive manner in some countries, such as Colombia in the 1990s and Mexico in the first decade of the twenty-first century.[20] This involved tactics that ranged from imprisonment and death to internal trials and extradition dependent on governmental request.

The multiple effects of this policy in terms of violence and corruption are quite telling. The attempt to break up the drug-trafficking business has exacerbated two phenomena: drugs usually do not create sociopolitical conflict and institutional erosion but instead expand and perpetrate them; and, from the business point of view, the results of the dismantlement of drug trafficking have been mediocre. The confluence of factors such as increasing transnational criminal contacts, a stable high level of drug consumption in the United States, Europe (the fastest-growing market in recent years), and South America (the third-largest consumer in the world today),[21] displacement of marijuana by cocaine at the hemispheric level, social deterioration at the regional level, and state-level weakness have resulted in, for example, the attractiveness of the Caribbean basin for the expansion of drug trafficking.

Meanwhile, the rise of juvenile delinquency in the Caribbean and of organized crime in Central America have had negative social, political, economic, and institutional effects in the region.[22] The latest, most dramatic example is Mexico. The death toll related to drug-related violence was between 70,000 and 120,000 during the six-year mandate of President Felipe Calderón (2006–2012).[23]

In addition, the militarization of the fight against drugs became, with few exceptions (Argentina, Chile, and Uruguay), the norm in Latin America. What started as episodic and temporary participation in tasks that competed with the mandate of police or special security forces eventually evolved into a permanent mission for the armed forces. In the 1980s, the war on drugs turned into a national security issue for both the United States and several Latin American countries, thus making the militarization of counterdrug efforts irresistible. Since then, the difference between police and military activities has been erased. After 9/11 and in the wake of the so-called new threats (the alleged amalgam of evils such as international terrorism, organized crime, drug trafficking, and the proliferation of weapons of mass destruction by private actors, among others), Washington no longer differentiates between internal security and external defense and expects regional militaries to transform into *"crime fighters."*[24]

Likewise, the "securitization" of the drug issue has facilitated the militarization of antidrug efforts, and, most recently, this militarization has contributed to the privatization of security.[25] The most telling case of this phenomenon in Latin America is Colombia. Indeed, U.S. companies such as DynCorp operate in this country as Department of State subcontractors and as part of Plan Colombia. Moreover, Juan Manuel Santos, then minister of defense (July 2006–May 2009), confirmed hiring retired Israeli military personnel for the purpose of identifying and capturing top-ranking FARC members.[26] This example, then, represents an armed conflict of a particular kind: narcotized, internationalized, and privatized.[27]

In all cases in the region in which militarization of the war on drugs has occurred, the results have been unfortunate in institutional terms and unproductive in terms of fighting the drug business.[28] Military participation in counterdrug policies has had a negative effect on civil-military relations, human rights abuses, and corruption levels.[29] The military corps' direct and active role in eradication, interdiction, persecution, and dismantling missions has not resulted in promising progress toward elimination, or even reduction, of the drug phenomenon.

At certain points in time, depending on the country of interest, far-reaching victories attributed to the repressive use of military force have been announced, but some years later, in the context of multiplied fronts in the fight against drugs, one can see the Pyrrhic nature of these victories by comparing the historical and the existing situations. The military as corporation has become addicted to the war on drugs: it feeds on internal and external resources, gains influence domestically, and receives validation from the United States. Concomitantly, Latin American countries, as a whole, have criminalized different stages of the drug business' internal chain.

One aspect that has gained attention and generated certain expectations is measures taken against laundering drug profits. Although the effectiveness of this policy is subject to doubt, its significance has increased due to its use by terrorist groups. The governments of insular Caribbean states, for example, have endeavored to implement a hard-line stance against money laundering under heavy pressure from the Organization for Economic Cooperation and Development (OECD). However, the combination of factors such as the most rigorous implementation of anti-money-laundering measures, the drop in regional tourism, U.S. pressure for the adoption of the most drastic counterterrorist policies, and the progressing corruption and destabilizing impact of globalization have placed the Caribbean in turmoil that is hard to manage and endure.

South American states also have adopted the strictest measures against money laundering, but achievements have been discouraging. An evaluation of national reports presented to the South American Financial Action Task Force (Grupo de Acción Financiera de Sudamérica)—an intergovernmental organization designed to "combat money-laundering and terrorism financing"—shows that the countries of South America, with the exception of Colombia, have a poor record of confiscations, arrests, and convictions. Governments have assumed responsibility for confronting money laundering but, as happens in other regions, the results have been insignificant.

In addition, extradition has been an important pillar of counterdrug policy. This practice was expected to both relieve the load of and reinforce the judicial system, somewhat weakened by the surge in drug trafficking; to lead to greater effectiveness in the dismantling of the drug trade through judicial collaboration; and to discourage more people from entering the business. Moreover, the effective use of this mechanism was to imply the positive effect of reducing availability, elevating the price, and reducing the purity of illicit narcotics in the areas with the highest demand.

The extradition mechanism has had ambiguous results. The countries that have actively implemented it—for example, Colombia, Mexico, and the Dominican Republic—have significantly improved their relationship with the United States. However, the specific effects on the drug phenomenon have been less significant: drug traffickers have not been demotivated (there is always someone to step in for the extradited, the imprisoned, or the eliminated); performance in the justice system has not improved (except in a symbolic way); and the impact on demand (availability, price, and purity) has been very slight. Moreover, countries like Colombia, which has extradited several hundred nationals to the United States, are reassessing their extradition policy to the United States because of increasingly lenient sentences.[30]

Finally, public policy defined in terms of opposition—rejection of the legalization of drugs—exists in Latin America. Voices critical of the prohibition of drugs have been emerging in different countries. However, most governments reject alternative strategies despite the fact that many Latin American leaders admit publicly and privately the strikingly rising price of the prohibitionist regime for the state and the need to reconsider the current approach. The U.S. shadow has been looming large in this issue. Notwithstanding, there is a growing sense that after thousands of deaths and billions of dollars wasted, Latin America, by the early part of this century, is reaching a consensus on the narcotics issue: the war on drugs is unwinnable.

Mexico: The New "Basket Case"

In May 1997, a high-level Mexican-U.S. contact group issued the U.S.-Mexico Bi-national Drug Threat Assessment, a voluminous and surprising report on the drug issue in Mexico. It argued that Mexican drug traffickers had "not managed to reflect their economic power in a political equivalent." It also pointed out that "they lack[ed] infrastructure and organization capability necessary to exercise operations at the international scale independently." Finally, it asserted that "unlike other countries' organizations that know and base their operations in the authentic context, a Mexican criminal organization can hardly adapt to foreign cultural schemes with the same easiness."[31]

In February 2009, director of national intelligence Dennis Blair ranked Mexico first (followed by Colombia, Venezuela, Cuba, and Bolivia) in the "arc of instability" of Latin America because of spreading organized crime in the country and its impact on U.S. interests. In September 2010, Secretary of State Hillary Clinton asserted that Mexico, due to its monumental problems with drug trafficking, was "Colombianizing."[32] Mexico "is look-ing more and more like Colombia looked twenty years ago," she stated.[33] In February 2011, undersecretary of the army Joseph W. Westphal asserted even more boldly and categorically that "drug trafficking cartels of Mexico are a form of insurgency and potentially could take control of the Mexican government."[34]

The question is obvious: How is it possible that just a decade ago Mexi-can drug traffickers were still perceived as harmless gangs and now they are viewed as an insurrectional force? In other words, is it true that in the 1990s, Mexico was only slightly bothered by simple narco-gangsters and today it is challenged by powerful narco-rebels? In a way, the assertions of the late 1990s and current statements are consistent with three typical U.S. strategies concerning drugs and a historical constant in its stance toward Latin America.

The strategy of denial is resilient; that is, the levels and characteristics of such a complex and dynamic phenomenon as illegal-drug business are ignored, manipulated, or underestimated. In the late twentieth century, Washington considered Colombia the exclusive "problematic case" on the continent in terms of drug trafficking. Accordingly, the United States de-ployed unusually coercive diplomacy toward one of the most loyal and least anti-U.S. countries in the region. Colombia was subject to a decertifica-tion process for its alleged lack of collaboration with the United States in counternarcotics efforts, while Colombian president Ernesto Samper had his U.S. visa revoked.[35] The result—beyond arguably unintended conse-quences—was the erosion of the political regime's legitimacy in Colombia, institutional fragility, and exacerbation of internal conflict.

The balance sheet of events in Colombia in the second half of the 1990s presents two clear winners: various armed groups advanced significantly in terms of territorial expansion, regional influence, and material enrich-ment; the U.S.-imposed interference eventually became more extended and accepted. Colombia's unarmed civil society and the ambiguous state ended up more vulnerable and weakened.

Colombia continued to be an easy target in the counterdrug fight while Mexico, by the time already the epicenter of important mafia groupings, was neither questioned nor bothered. Fortunately for Mexico, at least tem-porarily, the United States had clear strategic interests concerning its im-mediate neighbor. The North American Free Trade Agreement (NAFTA) had been recently ratified, and various U.S domestic actors prevented excessive pressure on the Mexican government. Counterdrug bureaucracies in Washington employed various tactics in order to portray the U.S.-Mexican collaboration as a successful example. In addition, Washington presented the drug business in Mexico as relatively less worrying. However, years later, Mexico would shift from a "showcase" to a "basket case."

The United States usually resorts to a strategy of exaggerating the issue of drugs; that is, it magnifies the phenomenon in order to justify and impose the war on drugs on others. It should be clear that rhetoric plays a crucial role in this strategy—maybe a greater one than in the negation strategy—and the exaggeration is manifested on multiple fronts of U.S. foreign policy. For example, as a rule, officials use synthetic descriptions to create a perceived threat—even if those descriptions are erroneous. A "Hitler" (Saddam Hussein, Hugo Chávez) appears from time to time; a situation is approaching a "holocaust" (in Haiti or Libya); a country (Latin American, Asian, or African) is moving toward "Libanization" or "Balkanization" (meaning fragmentation and polarization). It is frequently argued that "appeasement" (in the Middle East or Southeast Asia) and emboldening "tyrants" (who rule only on the periphery) must be avoided, that a new "axis of evil" (like the USSR and its closest satellites) must be urgently contained, or that the "domino effect" of a certain phenomenon must be reversed by any means necessary (as if countries transmitted their problems to their neighbors by osmosis, and the United States would ultimately be affected).

Placing Mexico in the "arc of instability," the idea of Mexican "Colombianization," and the claim that there is an insurgency linked to drug trafficking that soon will make the Mexican government more stable and less legitimate, represent high-ranking U.S. officials' discourse that corroborates the continual use of exaggeration. This, in turn, reveals alarming ignorance. It seems like neither Blair nor Clinton nor Westphal realized that each country had drug trafficking in a form that corresponded to its particular historical, social, and political experience. The form and logistics of the evolution and expansion of drug trafficking in Mexico and Colombia, for example, differ. The birth and rise of the first powerful cartels in Colombia, a rather fragmented society, with the traditional elites watching impassively in a geospatial environment of high regional diversification, took place in the context of a proverbial weakening of the state. In the Mexican case, drug cartels emerged, to a high degree, with federal and state-level consent from a state centralized and monopolized for decades by the Institutional Revolutionary Party (Partido Revolucionario Institucional, PRI) (and its support groups), a state showing superficial signs of strength but in fact hugely fragile because of rampant corruption, highly inefficient police forces, the paralysis of the justice system, a disoriented establishment, and Washington's tacit consent.

The development of drug trafficking in both countries reached dramatic dimensions, but with peculiarities.[36] Paradoxically, in both cases, the state's lack of protection—referring to the absence or breakdown of the state, directly or indirectly, in the phenomenon of drugs—triggered uncontrolled virulence among organized crime groups and against the state. In Colombia, two clear mutations were observed: big cartels transformed into so-called boutique cartels, or *cartelitos*, while drug lords became warlords. Organized crime in Mexico also began to show signs of adaptation by consolidating its territorial presence, expanding external links—to the United States, where drug consumption remained constant, and to Europe, where demand was growing—and reinforcing gangster behavior.[37]

Clinton and Westphal failed, at the time, to understand that drug trafficking had the capacity to adapt and forge new strategic alliances. While the United States was obsessed with Colombian drug lords, Mexican drug traffickers seized the opportunity and expanded their control over the drug trade. Neither Clinton nor Westphal learned the lesson from Colombia that could be of use in Mexico: if more resources were not directed to democratic institutionality and improvement of social policy, crime associated with drugs would persist, political systems would degrade, and the drug subculture would be exacerbated. In addition, the former secretary of state, Hillary Clinton, in particular, was confused about the solution to the Mexico situation.

In terms of counterdrug efforts—not in terms of its counterinsurgency component—Plan Colombia has been a failure.[38] And in its institutional dimension—that is, the recovery of state sovereignty—Plan Colombia has resulted in limited and contradictory results: the FARC has lost significant territorial control and influence, but the paramilitaries have maximized expansion, penetration, and territorial and political control. It is wrong to insist that Plan Mérida for Mexico, very similar to Plan Colombia, is a viable and necessary alternative. It is worth noting that the United States channeled U.S.$11,913,624,614 in counternarcotics aid during the 2000–2011 period ($9,159,336,162 for law enforcement and military assistance and $2,754,288,452 for socioeconomic assistance) as part of Plan Colombia, the Andean Initiative, Plan Mérida, the Caribbean Basin Security Initiative, and the Central America Regional Security Initiative:[39] in a decade, Washington fueled a futile and disastrous war on drugs in most Latin American and Caribbean countries.

Finally, the United States resorts to the strategy of "stigmatization," which aims at discrediting (and weakening) a country and presents the "other" as somebody who affects Washington's vital interests and must be disciplined. Since 2010, many U.S. politicians, military representatives, journalists, and experts have claimed that Mexico is on the threshold of being a "failed state." To be sure, the concern with failed states is not new in the United States' international strategy. The official stance is that there are three gaps between a formal state and an empirical one: a legitimacy gap, a capacity gap, and a sovereignty gap. Failed states lack legitimacy, do not have at their disposal the attributes and strategies necessary to confront the challenges facing them, and have less territorial control than consolidated states do. This convergence has created a relative consensus: a failed state results from the combination of an incapacity to govern (the result of the lack of resources and ability) and the absence of political will. This prompts the ultimate collapse of the state.

The alleged lack of capacity and will led to the argument that the solution must come from abroad. The political correlate of this conclusion is that a potential or actual failed state requires an exogenous alternative in order to recover. Essentially, from the Washington decision makers' point of view, a failed state is not necessarily hostile and quarrelsome, but rather, inept and indolent, which makes it ungovernable. The disturbance resulting from a failed state type is a source of problems, particularly when terrorist actors are present. Consequently, failed states became a threat to national security and Washington's global interests. Thus, this subordinate and troublesome state must be stabilized so that it does not trigger major problems.

It is evident, however, that the stigmatization strategy has not solved the drug problem. Two distinct but notable examples support this assertion. Both Colombia, for many years the world's major cocaine producer, and Afghanistan, the world's major heroin producer, were classified as failed states at some point and received, with significant differences and to different degrees, generous U.S. assistance, including the deployment of U.S. forces. Nevertheless, both countries witnessed the proliferation of the lucrative drug trade, the rise of criminal groups linked to drug production, and failed state consolidation.

The drug-trafficking problem in Mexico will not vanish by labeling the country a failed state. A more bellicose presence, which includes more security aid, U.S. drone flights over Mexican territory, and the eventual creation of binational military squadrons, will not solve the problems in

Mexico. The tendency to think in terms of external solutions, through direct or indirect intervention, does not lead to greater or better statehood. No quick fix or magic bullet exists that will solve the drug phenomenon.

Bringing the United States Back In

In order to better understand Latin America's submissive subordination to the war on drugs logic, it is necessary to bring the United States back in.[40] The initial deployment of the counterdrug crusade during the Nixon administration followed decisions by civilians, reflected the simplistic notion of prompt solutions, was carried out within the national security framework, was backed by public opinion that demanded the government "do something" about the increase in drug use and abuse, and received wide support from the legislative branch and both Republicans and Democrats. By the late 1970s, the State Department was encouraging greater participation of the armed forces in the fight against drugs in some countries, particularly in Colombia. Thus, for example, in 1978, 10,000 Colombian soldiers launched Operación Fulminante in Guajira and the Atlantic coast in order to halt marijuana production and trafficking. Despite the operation's failure (only small traffickers were affected), the State Department insisted on a confrontation mechanism and on the nationalization of militarized strategy across all of Colombia.

U.S. military forces remained reluctant to get involved in counterdrug activities abroad until the early 1980s; in fact, according to the Posse Comitatus Act of 1878, they could not be used for domestic law enforcement. Thus, in 1981, the Defense Department did not receive any funds for drug interdiction. However, during the Reagan presidency, civilians' bellicosity intensified. The White House and Congress agreed on a prohibitionist offensive. The administration established the South Florida Task Force, which evolved into the National Narcotics Border Interdiction System in 1983 under the management of then vice president George H. W. Bush.

The growing role of the military in the war on drugs gained momentum starting in the mid-1980s, before the end of the Cold War. Public Law 97-86 amended the Posse Comitatus Act by authorizing "indirect" participation of the armed forces in counterdrug activities. In April 1986, Reagan signed Presidential Decision Directive 221, which declared drugs an existing threat to U.S. national security and expanded the role the military played in the fight against drugs. Three months later, on July 15, Washington sent a military combat unit (part of the 193rd Infantry Brigade stationed in Panama), accompanied by six Black Hawk helicopters, to Bolivia as part of Operation Blast Furnace in order to locate and destroy cocaine laboratories.

If, from Harry Truman to Ronald Reagan, neither the executive branch nor the legislative wanted to appear soft on communism, in the late 1980s, nobody wanted to be labeled soft on the war on drugs. In this framework, in September 1989, then secretary of defense Richard Cheney declared that the war on drugs was turning into a high-priority national security mission. This implied that the military would assume leadership in two tasks: detecting and monitoring drug flows into the United States, and providing assistance to counterdrug agencies such as the Drug Enforcement Administration (DEA) and the Department of State. Five commands were to be in charge of these tasks: the U.S. Atlantic Command, the Southern Command, the Pacific Command, the North American Air Defense Command, and the U.S. Forces Command.

Three months later—on December 20—Washington ordered the invasion of Panama as part of Operation Just Cause (with the participation of 57,684 U.S. military personnel). President Manuel A. Noriega was deposed, captured, and sent to the United States to face trial for drug trafficking.

In this context, SOUTHCOM—then headquartered in Panama—was gaining importance in the war on drugs. Beginning in 1990, SOUTHCOM requested and received—via Operation Coronet Nighthawk—an increase in aerial capacity to detect and intercept potential drug flights. When the Panama-based Howard Base was closed, SOUTHCOM moved to the Hato Rey Base in Curaçao. In addition, a vast number of radars were deployed in the Caribbean and the Andean region (especially in Colombia, Ecuador, and Peru).

From November 1990 to October 1993, SOUTHCOM was headed by General George A. Joulwan, who was convinced of the need to protect military corporate interests in the post–Cold War context and ready to expand the U.S. armed forces' counterdrug mission. Besides Joulwan's personality and convictions, three facts reinforced SOUTHCOM's relevance in the war on drugs. First, after the Pentagon's inspector general concluded in a July 1991 report that the five commands had not been effective in the fight against drugs, the Department of Defense pointed out in a September 1993 report that only the Atlantic Command and the Southern Command would continue counterdrug missions. Second, the 1992 drug-interdiction budget—that is, the portion corresponding to the Department of Defense—reached U.S.$1 billion. The Atlantic Command continued receiving significant resources after the Cold War, and SOUTHCOM found an important financing "niche" through its visible participation in the war on drugs. Finally, specific legislation and important official documents began to elevate the significance of the war on drugs. On the one hand, the National Defense Authorization Act approved in November 1990 supported the eventual formation of a multilateral counterdrug strike force. On the other hand, the National Security Strategy issued in August 1991 identified the control of drug flows entering the United States as one of its seven main objectives. Likewise, the U.S. Army Field Manual 100-5 Operations—considered the cornerstone of the U.S. Army—that was published in June 1993 determined that the fight against drugs was becoming a form of "operations other than war"—the new term for what was called low-intensity conflict in the 1980s. Eventually, this term was abandoned, but not so the counterdrug tasks conceived as a form of low-intensity conflict.

Consequently, since the mid-1990s, SOUTHCOM has played a central role in the U.S. counterdrug strategy concerning Latin America. Successive commanders have been gradually securing and expanding the Southern Command's role in the war on drugs to include budget increases, more bases and radar, and fewer limitations from the Pentagon and the Department of State. Moreover, together with SOUTHCOM headquarters in Miami, other military units have provided their services and served as key means for the external projection of SOUTHCOM's force: the U.S. Army South (from Fort Sam Houston, Texas); the Twelfth Air Force (from Davis-Monthan Air Force Base, Arizona); Naval Forces Southern Command (at Mayport Naval Base, Florida); Marine Corps Forces South (Florida); Special Operations Command South (Florida); Joint Task Force Bravo (Soto Cano Air Base, Honduras); Joint Task Force Guantánamo (Guantánamo Bay, Cuba); and the Joint Interagency Task-Force South (Florida).

The events that transpired on 9/11 further facilitated the relative influence of SOUTHCOM in Miami. While Washington's attention and resources were focused on the war on terrorism and on Asia, SOUTHCOM increased its influence on U.S. foreign policy and defense concerning Latin America and guaranteed funding through a deadly image of the narco-terrorists who, presumably, were spreading through the region. In addition, under General James T. Hill's management (2002–2004), so-called radical populism was classified by SOUTHCOM as a severe hemispheric threat.

The 2007 SOUTHCOM report—*U.S. Southern Command Strategy 2016: Partnership for the Americas*—is relevant in this framework.[41] The document represents the most ambitious strategic plan developed by a U.S.

official agency in regard to the region in years. It excluded not only multi-lateral instruments (such as the Inter-American Treaty of Reciprocal Assistance and the Inter-American Defense Board) and organizations (for instance, the Organization of American States and the United Nations) but also domestic political institutions of hemispheric scope (such as the Department of State, the Department of Justice, and Treasury). SOUTHCOM was autonomously proclaiming its power in the region.

The SOUTHCOM mission and vision seemed excessive. The organization claimed to be the leader of existing agencies in guaranteeing "security, stability and prosperity in the Americas." Besides the usual tasks of response to danger to the United States, SOUTHCOM was assigned additional missions, such as managing and supporting voluntary regional and global coalitions as well as identifying "alternative nations to accept immigrants" and providing installations to confront the problem of mass migration. In terms of fostering prosperity, missions were aimed at developing training programs in the "internal security" field; increasing the number of so-called cooperative security locations; supporting a joint military unit initiative in Central America "to carry out stabilization operations" in this subregion; collaborating with Latin American countries in the development of "national security strategies"; and improving the definition of the Department of Defense's role in "the political and socio-economic development processes" in the region. In this sense, the redeployment of the Fourth Fleet (which had operated from 1943 to 1950) under the command of Admiral Joseph D. Kernan since July 1, 2008, fits into the context of the increasing projection of U.S. military power in the region and of the inflation of tasks assigned to the military after 9/11.

The 2009 agreement between Washington and Bogotá, which ultimately was declared ineffective, was intended to allow U.S. troops to use Colombian bases. This initiative can be located within the above-mentioned tendency, but with additional components.

As details were revealed, the qualitative shift implied in the Colombian-U.S. compromise became evident. In essence, the agreement was presented in Bogotá as a necessary continuation of and complement to the fight against drugs and terrorism; in Washington it was presented as a substitute for the base in Manta, Ecuador, due to be vacated the same year, as a site for "contingency operations, logistics and training," and as a bridge to expand the contact between SOUTHCOM and the recently created African Command, according to the Pentagon's language.[42] Thus, although Bogotá had one perspective on the use of its bases, Washington had another. The former put forward local arguments, the latter advanced global ones; the former focused on the counterdrug struggle; the latter envisioned potential operations of a wider strategic scope.

Even though the results of an increased role for SOUTHCOM in the war on drugs have been mediocre, a larger task for the Miami Command was expanded: countering transnational organized crime, more directly, in the Caribbean basin.[43] Each year, higher records of seizure of tons of cocaine and marijuana and grams of heroin have only meant short-term success with insignificant effects on the overall drug business in the United States and Latin America. Not surprisingly, and to a large extent due to the conspicuous fiasco, even military analysts recognize that after four decades of an ongoing failed strategy, Washington's militarized international drug policy is more a sign of insanity.[44]

Coda

According to the 2013 UN World Drug Report,[45] between 167 and 315 million people (fifteen to sixty-four years old) have used an illicit drug. Among them, the "problem drug users" account for 39 million—0.9 percent of the people aged fifteen to sixty-four or 0.54 percent of the current total world population. Even though worldwide the number of very challenging drug consumers is small, the war on drugs, with its emphasis on the control of supply has not ebbed. It is worth mentioning that a new longitudinal analysis shows that "despite increasing investments in enforcement-based supply reduction efforts aimed at disrupting global drug supply, illegal-drug prices have generally decreased while drug purity has generally increased since 1990."[46] In addition, the UN Office on Drugs and Crime asserts that the estimated amount of money laundered annually oscillates between 2 percent and 5 percent of global GDP, that is, around U.S.$800 billion to $2 trillion.

Notwithstanding, drug-money laundering is difficult to tackle and suppress. For example, according to the DEA, "Americans spend approximately U.S.$65 billion per year on illegal drugs [with] only approximately U.S.$1 billion seized per year, domestically, by all Federal agencies combined."[47] Somehow, the U.S. example epitomizes the limits of confiscation as an effective tool for curtailing drug-related money laundering.[48] Growing coercion does not seem to be the best alternative for dealing with the appetite for drugs. It that sense, it may be recalled that thirty-three countries have, according to Harm Reduction International, capital drug laws: six with high application rates of the death penalty and seven with low application practices.[49] Tougher policies not only have not solved the drug dilemma, they have harmed the poor, the unemployed, and minorities even more, aggravating existing inequality.[50] Basically, high rates of incarceration and harsh sentencing have not attained the objective of a drug-free society among countries from the north or the south or among western and eastern states.

The war on drugs has been disastrous for the world in general and for Latin America in particular.[51] In spite of poor and frustrating results, the region does not seem to be ready to modify the current prohibitionist strategy. After more than thirty-five years of a mistaken logic fostered and regionally justified by U.S. social and political actors, the counterdrug crusade tends to be perceived and accepted as a normal feature of U.S.–Latin America narco-diplomacy. The "war" started by civilians has been assumed by the military, some directing (from the United States), others fighting (in Latin America). The U.S. military sectors—especially SOUTHCOM—have been assuming the leadership of the fight against drugs. Miami has filled the role Washington once played but has now relegated. As a result, the leverage of a command usually inferior in capabilities, power, and impact has grown.

Within this framework, we are witnessing a new dimension of the war on drugs. Now it behooves the Southern Command to expand its zone of influence, and the military in general continues to be imperturbable regarding the U.S. global primacy strategy outlined at the beginning of the post–Cold War period and essentially unchanged.

Notes

1. Thanks to Yulia Vorobyeva for translating this work into English.

2. As Hans T. van der Veen had asserted, "the War on Drugs is not a mere metaphor but a reality of wide-scale organized violence" ("The War on Drugs in the Creation of a New World [Dis]Order," in *Shadow Globalization, Ethnic Conflict and New Wars: A Political Economy of Intra-state War*, ed. Bietrich Jung [New York: Routledge, 2003], 94).

3. Ted Galen Carpenter, *Bad Neighbor Policy: Washington's Futile War on Drugs in Latin America* (New York: Palgrave Macmillan, 2003), 1–18.

4. For more on the history of drug prohibition, see David F. Musto, *The American Disease: Origins of Narcotics Control*, 3rd ed. (New York: Oxford University Press, 1999).

5. The war on drugs, according to Ron Chepesiuk, "used to describe the efforts of governments around the world to enforce the drug laws of their countries. Many government leaders believe that, in order to deal effectively with the negative consequences of drug trafficking and drug abuse, the problem of illicit drugs must be dealt with as if the countries were at war. . . . As in a real war, large numbers of drug dealers, users, and abusers are treated as enemies of the state. The laws are changed to provide severe penalties and

those convicted are often imprisoned for long stretches of time . . . As in war, civil liberties are given a lower priority in order to achieve the military objective . . . Some observers of the War on Drugs say the metaphor leads to an 'us against them' climate and feeds the illusion that illegal-drug trafficking and drug use can be stopped and that 'victory' can be achieved" (*The War on Drugs: An International Encyclopedia* [Santa Barbara, Calif.: ABC-Clio, 1999]), 261–262.

6. For more on the drug war in Latin America, see Brian Loveman, ed., *Addicted to Failure: U.S. Security Policy in Latin America and the Andean Region* (Lanham, Md.: Rowman & Littlefield, 2006); Coletta A. Youngers and Eileen Rosin, eds., *Drugs and Democracy in Latin America: The Impact of U.S. Policy* (Boulder, Colo.: Lynne Rienner, 2005); Carpenter, *Bad Neighbor Policy*.

7. Bruce M. Bagley and Betty Horwitz, *The International Relations of Latin America* (New York: Routledge, forthcoming); Clare Ribando Seelke and Kristin M. Finklea, *U.S.-Mexican Security Cooperation: The Mérida Initiative and Beyond* (Washington, D.C.: Congressional Research Service, 2013); Bruce M. Bagley, "Seminario de seguridad," YouTube video, 1:53:10, from a seminar conducted at El Colegio de la Frontera Norte, Mexico, on July 8, 2010, posted July 9, 2010, http://www.youtube.com/watch?v=sMeqNJzWXCo.

8. An attempt to include an evaluation of the role of the U.S. Southern Command in Latin America's war on drugs in the context of a broader war on terror can be found in R. Guy Emerson, "Radical Neglect? The War on Terror and Latin America," *Latin American Politics and Society* 52, no. 1 (2010): 33–62.

9. People for many years have been calling for drugs to be treated as a health issue as opposed to a security issue. See Ethan Nadelmann, "Addicted to Failure," *Foreign Policy*, no. 137 (July–August 2003): 94–95; Peter R. Andreas, Eva C. Bertram, Morris J. Blachman, and Kenneth E. Sharpe, "Dead-End Drug Wars," *Foreign Policy* 85 (1991–1992): 106–128; Peter Andreas, "Free Market Reform and Drug Market Prohibition: U.S. Policies at Cross-Purposes in Latin America," *Third World Quarterly* 16, no. 1 (1995): 75–88.

10. See chapter 4 in this volume.

11. Ibid. For a critical analysis of the concept of militarization, see Bruce M. Bagley, *Myths of Militarization: The Role of the Military in the War on Drugs in the Americas* (Coral Gables, Fla.: North-South Center, 1991).

12. Since 2010, the most important phenomenon has been the role and impact of Latin America on the continentwide and global debates on illicit drugs. Certain key characteristics should be underlined. First, the new Latin American tone and talk on drug matters are not the expression of a region that has abdicated its commitments to the resolution of the drug issue but the pronouncement of a region that has suffered the tragic consequences of a strategy that has failed to deal with illegal substances. Second, the position of important Latin American leaders on the drug question is realistic because most presidents in a majority of countries are witnessing a significant shift in society: the old "balloon" effect—mainly based on the changing nature of cultivation, production, processing patterns across nations, and geographies—is being superseded by a sort of Zeppelin effect by which transnational organizations—basically intertwining local narco-warlords, national drug barons, and global money-laundering tycoons—are rising to a point of generating a Pax Mafiosa in certain urban and rural areas. Third, there is a growing, de facto, loose epistemic community of voices critical of drug prohibition in which government-level and non-state-level actors are gaining visibility in the Americas and worldwide while si-

multaneously broadening and deepening the quality of the public discourse on the merits of alternative, nonconventional drug experimentation proposals. Fourth, the antiprohibitionist initiatives emanating from the region are similar in their nature but different in their motivation. For example, some highly pro-U.S. governments, such as the Mexican, Colombian, and Guatemalan, are inclined to promote regulatory regimes for drugs in order to fight more effectively other forms of organized crime and existing armed ideological challenges. Other countries, like Uruguay, are more concerned with domestic human rights, health issues, and youth violence when advancing the legalization of marijuana. Thus, a realpolitik perspective and a liberal approach coexist among those who are looking for regulatory options to deal with the drug phenomenon. And fifth, notwithstanding a more open outward-oriented debate on drugs in the area, most countries are still addicted to severe punishment as reflected in domestic legislation; that ambiguity may produce some costs in the near future in Latin America if there is a significant gap between deeds and words, both internally and internationally.

13. María Clemencia Ramírez Lemus, Kimberly Stanton, and John Walsh, "Colombia: A Vicious Circle of Drugs and War," in *Drugs and Democracy in Latin America: The Impact of U.S. Policy*, ed. Coletta A. Youngers and Eileen Rosin (Boulder, Colo.: Lynne Rienner, 2005), 61–98. For more on the consequences of aerial spraying, see Transnational Institute, "Ecuador: 'Collateral Damage' from Aerial Spraying on the Northern Border," *Drugs and Democracy*, December 1, 2003, http://www.tni.org/article/ecuador-collateral-damage-aerial-spraying-northern-border; Asociación Inter-Americana para la Defensa del Ambiente, "Letter to Colombian President Uribe Requesting No Aerial Spraying in National Parks," June 27, 2005, http://www.aida-americas.org/en/lettertoUribe.

14. See David Mansfield, "Assessing Supply-Side Policy and Practice: Eradication and Alternative Development," Working Paper, Global Commission on Drug Policies, January 2011, http://www.globalcommissionondrugs.org/wp-content/themes/gcdp_v1/pdf/Global_Com_David_Mansfield.pdf; Rocío Moreno-Sánchez, David S. Kraybill, and Stanley R. Thompson, "An Economic Analysis of Coca Eradication Policy in Colombia," paper presented at the AAEA Annual Meeting, July 28–31, 2002, Long Beach, Calif., http://ageconsearch.umn.edu/bitstream/19833/1/sp02mo07.pdf.

15. Francisco E. Thoumi, *Illegal Drugs, Economy, and Society in the Andes* (Washington, D.C.: Woodrow Wilson Center Press, 2003); Coletta A. Youngers and John M. Walsh, *Development First: A More Humane and Promising Approach to Reducing Cultivation of Crops for Illicit Markets* (Washington, D.C.: Washington Office on Latin America (WOLA), 2010).

16. See Ursula Durand Ochoa, "Coca, Contention and Identity: The Political Empowerment of the Cocaleros in Bolivia and Peru," PhD dissertation, London School of Economics and Political Science, 2012.

17. For more on Colombia, see Russell Crandall, *Driven by Drugs: U.S. Policy toward Colombia* (Boulder, Colo.: Lynne Rienner, 2002); Adam Isacson, *Plan Colombia—Six Years Later: Report of a CIP Staff Visit to Putumayo and Medellín, Colombia* (Washington, D.C.: Center for International Policy, 2006).

18. For more on Bolivia, see chapter 10 in this volume.

19. See Marc Peceny and Michael Durnan, "The FARC's Best Friend: U.S. Antidrug Policies and the Deepening of Colombia's Civil War in the 1990s," *Latin American Politics and Society* 48, no. 2 (2006): 95–116.

20. Bruce M. Bagley, "Drug Trafficking, Political Violence and U.S. Policy in Colombia in the 1990s," *Mama Coca*, January 5, 2001, accessed February 28, 2012, http://www.mama coca.org/junio2001/bagley_drugs_and_violence_en.htm.

21. For more on consumption and general trends, see the introduction; United Nations Office on Drugs and Crime (UNODC), *World Drug Report, 2011* (New York:, 2011).

22. For more on Central America, see chapter 14.

23. See Mark Karlin, "Fueled by War on Drugs, Mexican Death Toll Could Exceed 120,000 As Calderon Ends Six-Year Reign," Truthout report, November 28, 2012, http://truth-out.org/news/item/13001-calderon-reign-ends-with-six-year-mexican-death-toll-near-120000%20.

24. See Kristin Roberts, "U.S. Sees Latin American Armies as Crime Fighters," Reuters, October 3, 2007, http://www.reuters.com/article/2007/10/03/us-usa-latinamerica-military-idUSN0321503920071003; emphasis mine.

25. See chapter 4 in this volume; Adam Isacson, "Extending the War on Terrorism to Colombia: A Bad Idea Whose Time Has Come," *Foreign Policy in Focus*, February 6, 2002, http://fpif.org/extending_the_war_on_terrorism_to_colombia_a_bad_idea_whose_time_has_come/.

26. See "De Tel Aviv a Tolemaida," *Semana*, August 4, 2007.

27. See Kristen McCallion, "War for Sale! Battlefield Contractors in Latin America and the 'Corporatization' of America's War on Drugs," *University of Miami Inter-American Law Review* 36, nos. 2/3 (2005): 317–353.

28. See Juan Gabriel Tokatlian, "The War on Drugs: Time to Demilitarise," *Open Democracy*, August 10, 2011, http://www.opendemocracy.net/juan-gabriel-tokatlian/war-on-drugs-time-to-demilitarise; idem, "The Only Winner in the 'War on Drugs,'" *Guardian*, December 2, 2010, http://www.theguardian.com/commentisfree/cifamerica/2010/dec/01/us-military-colombia.

29. See Sven Peterke, "Urban Insurgency, 'Drug War,' and International Humanitarian Law: The Case of Rio de Janeiro," *International Humanitarian Legal Studies* 1, no. 1 (2010): 165–181.

30. See Geoffrey Ramsey, "Colombia to Reassess Policy of Extraditing Drug Traffickers to the United States," *Christian Science Monitor*, April 9, 2012; "Para los 'narcos' la extradición a EE.UU. ahora es atractiva," *El Espectador*, March 19, 2013.

31. It is worth noting that the report contains astonishing errors. For example, it is argued on page 84 that Amado Carrillo Fuentes (alias "Señor de los Cielos") "is the most powerful Colombian drug-trafficker." Carrillo Fuentes was born in Sinaloa, Mexico, in December 1955 and died in Mexico City in July 1997; see Estudio-Diagnóstico Conjunto, *México y Estados Unidos ante el problema de las drogas* (Mexico City: Secretaría de Relaciones Exteriores, 1997).

32. For more on the Colombianization of Mexico, see "¿México se está colombianizando?" YouTube video, 6:11, from a Código news broadcast, posted by "Código," July 25, 2010, https://www.youtube.com/watch?v=sTqYxBo7KuU.

33. Penny Starr, "Hillary Clinton Compares Mexican Drug Violence to Colombia's, But No Call for Securing Border," *CNS News*, September 8, 2010.

34. "U.S. and Mexico Clash over Narco-Insurgency," Justice in Mexico Project, February 9, 2011, https://justiceinmexico.wordpress.com/2011/02/09/.

35. Marc W. Chernick, *Colombia's "War on Drugs" vs. the United States' "War on Drugs"* (Washington, D.C.: WOLA, 1991), 11. See also Crandall, *Driven by Drugs*.

36. For more on drug trafficking in Mexico, see Peter Watt and Roberto Zepeda, *Drug War Mexico: Politics, Neoliberalism and Violence in the New Narcoeconomy* (London: Zed Books, 2012).

37. For more on the fragmentation, see the introduction in this volume; Juan Carlos Garzón, *Mafia & Co.: The Criminal Networks in Mexico, Brazil and Colombia* (Washington, D.C.: Woodrow Wilson Center, Latin American Program, 2008).

38. Jonathan D. Rosen, "Plan Colombia and Beyond: Pastrana to Santos (2000 to 2012)," Open Access Dissertations, Paper 880, 2012, http://scholarlyrepository.miami.edu/oa_dissertations/880.

39. See "Grant U.S. Aid Listed by Country, All Programs, Entire Region," Just the Facts, (information now resides at Security Assistance Monitor, http://justf.org/); http://fas.org/sgp/crs/row/RL32250.pdf.

40. See Juan Gabriel Tokatlian, "La guerra antidrogas y el Comando Sur: Una combinación delicada," *Foreign Affairs Latinoamérica* 10, no. 1 (2010): 43–50.

41. Southern Command, *United States Southern Command Strategy 2016: Partnership for the Americas* (Miami, 2007).

42. Nadja Drost, "A Heightened U.S. Military Presence in Colombia?" in Global Post, June 4, 2009, http://www.globalpost.com/dispatch/colombia/090530/military-base.

43. Southern Command, "Countering Transnational Organized Crime," http://www.southcom.mil/ourmissions/Pages/Countering%20Transnational%20Organized%20Crime.aspx.

44. See Lieutenant Colonel Michael F. Walther, "Insanity: Four Decades of U. S. Counterdrug Strategy," *Carlisle Papers* (December 2012).

45. See UNODC, *World Drug Report, 2013* (New York, 2013).

46. Dan Werb et al., "The Temporal Relationship between Drug Supply Indicators: An Audit of International Government Surveillance Systems," *BMJ Open* 3, no. 9 (2013), http://bmjopen.bmj.com/content/3/9/e003077.full.pdf+html.

47. DEA, "DEA Programs: Money Laundering," http://www.justice.gov/dea/ops/money.shtml.

48. As R. T. Naylor has asserted, "to the extent that the demand for drugs is 'inelastic,' any hike in laundering costs will be merely passed to the consumer. The effect, on balance, will be to take more income from consumers and transfer it to the criminal entrepreneurs. Just as anti-drug enforcement acts as a price-support program to raise the income of successful dealers, anti-money laundering measures might do the same for criminal money managers" ("Wash-out: A Critique of Follow-the-Money Methods in Crime Control Policy," *Crime, Law and Social Change* 32, no. 1 [1999]: 1–58).

49. See Patrick Gallahue et al., *The Death Penalty for Drug Offences: Global Overview 2012. Tipping the Scales for Abolition* (London: Harm Reduction International, 2012). China, Iran, Vietnam, Saudi Arabia, Singapore, and Malaysia are states that have high application of capital drug laws.

50. See April Shaw, James Egan, and Morag Gillespie, *Drugs and Poverty: A Literature Review* (Glasgow: Scottish Drugs Forum, 2007), http://www.dldocs.stir.ac.uk/documents/drugpovertylitrev.pdf.

51. See Loveman, *Addicted to Failure*; Carpenter, *Bad Neighbor Policy*.

4

Mission Creep

The U.S. Military's Counterdrug Role in the Americas

ADAM ISACSON

Since 2000, Latin America's militaries and police forces received levels of U.S. assistance that, even after adjusting for inflation, approached those of some of the hardest-fought years of the Cold War. Unlike the 1960s or the 1980s, though, nobody was warning about the Communist menace near U.S. borders. While terrorism was a constant concern in official rhetoric, Latin America and the Caribbean were not an important battleground in the post–September 11 context.

Instead, the set of threats, and the set of government programs used to fund the military-aid strategy to address them, has largely been illegal drugs–related. Between 2000 and 2012, the United States provided $13.9 billion in military assistance to Latin America and the Caribbean. Of that amount, 83 percent—about $11.6 billion—went through programs created specifically to help other countries limit the supply of drugs coming into the United States.[1]

Counterdrug Aid and Internal Military Roles

The "drug war," which is evolving into a larger battle against organized-crime groups that finance themselves with drug proceeds, has made it possible for the U.S. government to maintain the close military-to-military relationships forged during the Cold War, a period when many generals served as heads of government. Antidrug aid has also made it possible to help armed forces continue to play internal security roles, which implies direct contact with the civilian population. Today, as illegal-drug trafficking corridors have proliferated, and as the trade's profits have supported ever more violent organized crime syndicates, calls to involve militaries further in traditional "police" roles are increasing, especially in Mexico, Central America, the Andes, and the Caribbean. And with counterdrug programs paying the bill, the U.S. government has stood ready to help.

The turn to militaries to patrol the streets, to staff checkpoints, to carry out searches and seizures, and to arrest and interrogate suspects is a step backward for the region. A key characteristic of the past thirty years' transitions to democracy has been the removal of soldiers from tasks that would have them in constant daily contact with the population. Many countries' police forces were moved from defense to public security or interior ministries, with civilian chiefs and separate police academies.

These reforms were based on a growing recognition that militaries and police are fundamentally different in character, and that a thriving democracy must not blend them. Militaries are primarily tasked with defending a country's territorial sovereignty from external threats, though they are often called on to address internal emergencies like insurgencies. They are trained to defeat an enemy with overwhelming violence, using all resources at their disposal, and (with the exception of some elite intelligence units) are not trained to investigate crimes and criminal networks or to develop relationships with the population. In fact, their members usually live separately from the population, in barracks. A military must be respectful of international humanitarian law, but not necessarily the due process and similar protections afforded to civilians in most modern democracies.

Police are primarily tasked with protecting a country's civilian population by enforcing its internal laws. They are trained to serve the population using the least force necessary. They are charged with investigating crimes and, according to rules of evidence, building cases against the members of criminal networks. In so doing, they are encouraged to develop close relationships with communities. When off duty, police usually live in or near the communities they serve.

This is a distinction that the United States maintains rigorously at home. The Posse Comitatus statute, which dates to the 1870s, prohibits the use of soldiers for internal policing missions except under extraordinary circumstances and at the orders of the president. These exceptions, such as the 1992 Los Angeles riots, the National Guard presence at airport security checkpoints after the September 11 attacks, or the streets of New Orleans after Hurricane Katrina in 2005, are very brief, considered highly unusual, and closely supervised.[2]

The United States has not been so judicious in the military roles it has encouraged within Latin America. The Cold War mandate to roll back

Communist influence in the Americas made assistance to authoritarian military regimes' internal repressive apparatus an important element of U.S. policy. Notorious examples include 1960s and 1970s assistance to military juntas in the Southern Cone, through both military-aid programs and the U.S. Agency for International Development's Office of Public Safety, or the 1980s increase in support for militaries, and military-run police forces, in Central America. Human rights groups have extensively documented the excesses committed by U.S.-aided forces during this period. It is less frequently noted that, through its Cold War support for militaries, the U.S. government was helping the region's militaries play roles that the U.S. military would never be allowed to play at home.

Exit Cold War, Enter Drug War

Two decades ago, just as the Soviet threat faded, the drug war grew in importance among U.S. priorities in Latin America. The years 1989 and 1990, just as the Berlin Wall was falling, were the only two years in which the Gallup organization ever registered "drugs" as the number-one response to its regular open-ended question, "What is the most important problem facing the nation?"[3]

Amid the Cold War's end and the region's transition to democracy, U.S. military assistance began to fall—though not to end—in countries, like El Salvador or Chile, that were not seen as important drug source or transit countries. Where the illegal-drug trade was thriving, however, the United States turned to militaries to help fight this new "threat." In the words of the commander of the U.S. Southern Command at the time, General Maxwell Thurman, the drug war was "the only war we've got."[4]

At the time, the threat was most visibly embodied by the Medellín and Cali cartels, vertically integrated organizations sourcing their product in Peru and Bolivia and working with partners in Mexico and the Caribbean to ship it to the networks they controlled within the United States. The first big ramping up of counterdrug military aid came during the administration of George H. W. Bush, which viewed the big cartels as the chief target.

With the first Bush administration's Andean Initiative, the United States encouraged militaries to take on the counterdrug mission in earnest for the first time. The 1990–1993 aid package provided aircraft, equipment, weapons, and training to the militaries and police forces of Colombia, Peru, and Bolivia. The Peruvian armed forces under autocratic president Alberto Fujimori were happy to oblige, while in Bolivia the armed forces generally took a supporting role. Colombia's armed forces began to play more of a counterdrug role for the first time, though they turned down much equipment, preferring to stick with their traditional mission of fighting what at the time seemed like remnants of Communist guerrilla groups.[5] The hunt for the Medellín cartel's Pablo Escobar and the Cali cartel's Rodríguez Orejuela brothers was led by Colombia's national police and its partners in U.S. military, law enforcement, and intelligence agencies. Colombia's military played a relatively minor supporting role.

Section 1004

The Andean Initiative was born at the same time that the U.S. Defense Department gained important new authority. With the 1989 National Defense Authorization Act, the U.S. Congress added a new section to Title 10 of the U.S. Code. Section 124 made the U.S. military the "single lead agency" for interdicting drugs both overseas and within U.S. borders.

It was not clear, though, whether Section 124 meant that the Defense Department could use its massive budget to give weapons, training, and other aid to foreign militaries and police. Since the 1961 Foreign Assistance Act put U.S. diplomats in charge of foreign military aid programs, the Defense Department had not been a source of equipment and weapons for foreign militaries. A provision in the 1991 National Defense Authorization Act—Section 1004—made a big exception to that, allowing the defense budget to provide several kinds of military aid, as long as the mission was counterdrug.

The defense budget does not provide the biggest, most lethal equipment; items like helicopters still have to go through aid programs in the foreign assistance process, which are managed by the U.S. State Department and overseen by the congressional Foreign Affairs Committees. But the Defense Department may now use its counterdrug budget to provide, without diplomatic involvement, a long list of other items, among them, base construction, intelligence, equipment upgrades, and, especially, training.

Today, the Defense Department's Section 1004 authority is the second-largest military assistance program for the Americas, leaving way behind the nondrug military programs employed during the Cold War. The program is the number-one source of funding for training Latin American militaries and police, training 73,000 personnel—43 percent of the total for all programs—between 2000 and 2010.[6] In numerous cases, training has been carried out by U.S. Special Forces teams, which teach skills with applications well beyond counterdrug efforts, among them, light infantry skills, small-unit tactics, helicopter operations, marksmanship, and intelligence analysis. At times, Special Forces teams train foreign police units, blurring the line between military and police almost completely.

The 1990s

The Clinton administration did not continue the Andean Initiative. It focused on working with the Colombian police to kill fugitive drug lord Pablo Escobar and hunt down the Cali cartel's Rodríguez Orejuela brothers. Beyond these efforts, though, in its initial years, the new administration briefly reduced counterdrug military and police aid as drug czar Lee Brown sought to place more emphasis on reducing domestic demand for drugs.[7]

In Colombia, assistance—especially military assistance—dropped sharply after the 1994 election of scandal-tarred president Ernesto Samper. With Colombia's national police, however, the Clinton administration quietly began, at first on a pilot basis, implementing an aerial herbicide fumigation program to eradicate coca crops.

The brief period of reduced aid ended quickly. Drug war military assistance began to pick up again after Clinton's Democratic Party lost control of Congress in the 1994 elections. The recently retired head of Southern Command, General Barry McCaffrey, became the next drug czar, a big signal of a turn in policy. McCaffrey brought dozens of military personnel into the drug czar's office and focused heavily on reducing supplies in the Americas. At the same time, with the air forces and police forces of Colombia and Peru, the administration rolled out an "air bridge denial" program that aimed to interdict aircraft smuggling drugs.

Even as the country's president was denied a U.S. visa, meanwhile, Colombia's national police developed close relationships with top congressional Republicans, who began sounding the alarm about the Revolutionary Armed Forces of Colombia (Fuerzas Armadas Revolucionarias de Colombia, FARC) guerrillas, who, fueled by coca cultivation, grew rapidly after 1993. Though police aid and the fumigation program grew steadily, however, the Colombian military's reluctance to take on the counterdrug mission kept it from receiving much aid through counterdrug aid programs, and Colombia's legal "decertification," due to President Samper's alleged acceptance of Cali cartel campaign donations, prevented the Clinton administration from providing nondrug military aid.

With Mexico, where transshipment of drugs increased rapidly during the 1990s, the Ernesto Zedillo administration was open to more counter-drug cooperation and supported using the military to assist interdiction. The Clinton administration responded with a large shipment of old helicopters for Mexico's army and supported the training of thousands of Special Forces Airmobile Groups (Grupos Aeromóviles de Fuerzas Especiales, GAFE). The training occurred on U.S. soil, mainly at Fort Bragg, North Carolina, because of Mexican sensitivities, including a legal ban on U.S. trainers carrying weapons inside Mexico.

It was also during this period that the Clinton administration broadened the Defense Department's counterdrug military aid authority by letting it use its budget to beef up the riverine capabilities of Colombia's and Peru's navies. The program begun for two countries in the 1998 National Defense Authorization Act has since not only been renewed, but is also now a general (not solely riverine) antidrug military aid program authorized for thirty-five countries—even though, like all Defense Department assistance programs, its performance has never been officially, publicly evaluated.

Plan Colombia

It was in Colombia after 1997, as President Samper left office, where the Clinton administration's antidrug military aid accelerated most sharply. Officials like General McCaffrey began viewing Colombia with extreme concern. The disappearance of the Medellín and Cali cartels had had no effect on cocaine supplies, but it opened up a vacuum that Colombia's guerrillas and paramilitaries were filling rapidly. With the big cartels' multinational capacity gone, coca came to be grown principally in Colombia, the same country where it had been processed into cocaine. Profits from the trade swelled the coffers of the FARC guerrillas and the United Self-Defense Forces of Colombia (Autodefensas Unidas de Colombia, AUC) paramilitaries, which both more than quadrupled in size during the 1990s. By the end of the decade, the FARC had cleared the authorities out of dozens of municipalities and had made road travel very dangerous, while the paramilitaries, aided and abetted by the security forces, were shocking the world with a wave of bloody massacres throughout the countryside.

The solution promoted by McCaffrey and others in 1998–1999 was familiar: aid the Colombian armed forces, but at levels of generosity not seen since the peak of the Cold War (which was aid to Central America in the mid-1980s). In a mid-1999 memo to the rest of the cabinet, General Mc-Caffrey proposed a billion-dollar program to help Colombia regain control

Table 4.1. Highlights of U.S. aid to Colombia, 2000–2011

- At least 95 UH-60 and UN-1N helicopters
- Aerial herbicide fumigation of 3.5 million acres
- Training of over 75,000 soldiers and police
- Numerous cargo planes and patrol boats
- Creation of a new counternarcotics brigade in Colombian army and riverine brigade in Colombian navy
- Advice, intelligence, and logistical support for oil pipeline protection program, Plan Patriota military offensives, National Territorial Consolidation Plan

Source: Compiled by the author based on data from U.S. Department of State, *2009 End-Use Monitoring Report: South America (Asunción through Caracas)*, Bureau of International Narcotics and Law Enforcement Affairs, September 1, 2010, http://www.state.gov/j/inl/rls/rpt/eum/2009/147218.htm#bogota; idem, *International Narcotics Control Strategy Reports (INCSR)*, http://www.state.gov/j/inl/rls/nrcrpt/; idem, *Foreign Military Training and DoD Engagement Activities of Interest*, Bureau of Political-Military Affairs Reports, http://www.state.gov/t/pm/rls/rpt/fmtrpt/; Center for International Policy's Colombia Program, State Department Report to Congress, July 27, 2000, https://web.archive.org/web/20050104234112/http://ciponline.org/colombia/080102.htm; U.S. Senate Caucus on International Narcotics Control, Hearing on U.S. Policy in the Andean Region, Washington, DC, September 17, 2002, http://www.cfr.org/latin-america-and-the-caribbean/hearing-us-policy-andean-region/p5071; and Center for International Policy's Colombia Program, Department of State Report to Congress on Caño Limón Pipeline, December 2002, https://web.archive.org/web/20050105012721/http://ciponline.org/colombia/02120001.htm.

of, and allow expanded fumigation to go ahead in, the guerrilla-run coca-growing areas in the country's far south.[8] McCaffrey and the State Department's Thomas Pickering traveled to Bogotá and told President Andrés Pastrana that the U.S. government was prepared to offer a big aid package, but that it must be a contribution to a larger plan, with the Colombian government's authorship and resources. Plan Colombia, the framework that would guide U.S. cooperation with Colombia and the Andes for nearly a decade, was born. In January 2000, the Clinton administration proposed, and in June 2000 the Republican Congress approved, a U.S.$1.3 billion aid package for Colombia and its neighbors, of which U.S.$860 million—three-quarters of it military and police aid—went directly to the "Push into Southern Colombia" outlined in McCaffrey's 1999 memo (see table 4.1).

Plan Colombia was the first time that the United States began significantly aiding Colombia's military, as opposed to its police, for a counter-drug mission. At the time—before the 9/11 attacks and after the searing experiences of Vietnam and El Salvador—enthusiasm for a big new U.S.-

supported counterinsurgency mission was low. Clinton administration officials promised skeptics, including numerous legislators in its own party, that the aid package would not "cross the line" between counternarcotics and counterinsurgency. A key safeguard was the budget categories chosen: nearly all of the military assistance in the Plan Colombia package went through counterdrug aid accounts that legally could not be used for other purposes.

This is not to say that U.S.-trained Colombian military personnel were not fighting guerrillas with U.S.-donated equipment in the early years of Plan Colombia. To do so, though, required that they be carrying out a mission with a counterdrug nexus, such as establishing security conditions on the ground for fumigation aircraft, a frequent mission of the Colombian Army's Counternarcotics Brigade (Brigada Contra el Narcotráfico).

The original 2000 Plan Colombia aid package included smaller amounts of military assistance for the counterdrug missions of several of Colombia's neighbors. Ecuador got U.S.$12 million to help its army improve security near the Colombian border. Peru got U.S.$32 million.[9] Even Hugo Chávez' young government in Venezuela got U.S.$3.5 million for its Technical Judicial Police and National Guard.[10]

The Focus Shifts

By 2001, fumigation had expanded into the southern department of Putumayo. The U.S.-aided Counternarcotics Brigade was operating from bases located minutes away from the headquarters of paramilitary groups, which at the time were massacring hundreds in nearby Putumayo towns. Most Plan Colombia military equipment had yet to be delivered; the same slowness of purchasing and manufacturing would bedevil proponents of military aid to Mexico a decade later. The new Bush administration was undergoing a slow-moving "review" of policy toward Colombia, as neoconservative officials pushed to "cross the line" and allow Colombia's armed forces to use their counterdrug aid to fight guerrillas.[11]

The September 11, 2001, attacks and the advent of a "global war on terror" made this shift politically possible. It also made the counterdrug mission far less of a priority. Where before U.S. officials looked at Colombia and saw cocaine traffickers and coca fields, after September 11, they looked at Colombia and saw three groups on the State Department's list of foreign terrorist organizations, which happened to fund themselves partially through the coca and cocaine trade.

By mid-2002, after Colombians elected Álvaro Uribe to step up the war against the guerrillas, the U.S. Congress approved a Bush administration request to allow Colombia's armed forces to use all their counterdrug aid, past and present, to fight the FARC, the National Liberation Army (Ejército de Liberación Nacional, ELN), and the AUC. While Plan Colombia's foreseen counterdrug activities would increase—an incredible 171,600 hectares of Colombia would be fumigated in 2006—the post-2000 initiatives that would receive the most resources were not counterdrug programs.[12] Aid would instead go to help the security forces protect an oil pipeline; to encourage reforms of the forces' mobility, intelligence, and ability to operate jointly; for a major, sustained antiguerrilla offensive in the FARC's heartland (Plan Patriota); and, after 2006, for the National Territorial Consolidation Plan, or Consolidation, a "clear, hold and build" counterinsurgency effort carried out in several zones. In 2008–2009, as the Bush and Obama administrations negotiated a deal for U.S. military use of Colombian bases—later struck down by Colombia's Constitutional Court—the threats most frequently cited to justify the arrangement were illegal armed groups in Colombia's conflict and the possible scenario (since reduced) of conflict with Hugo Chávez' Venezuela.

Though not really a counterdrug strategy, Plan Patriota paved the way for increased fumigation and the capture of a mid-level FARC commander who was extradited to face drug-trafficking charges in the United States. But the Consolidation effort is especially noteworthy because it accompanied a mild shift in the United States' source-zone coca-eradication strategy. With U.S. support, troops were sent to specific zones noted for their violence, drug production and transshipment, and the near-total absence of the state. Once they established a security perimeter, according to the Consolidation plan's documents, the goal shifted to bringing in the non-military part of the state in an effort to win the local population's trust. This latter, civilian, part of the Consolidation has received backing from the U.S. Agency for International Development (USAID), making Consolidation a rare example of Southern Command and USAID coordination on the same program. As part of the effort to build the population's trust, fumigation in Consolidation zones was largely replaced by teams of manual coca eradicators and, in many (but certainly not all) cases, guarantees of food security and offers of development assistance to farmers whose coca was eradicated. With very rare exceptions, neither of these options was present during Plan Colombia's first years.

While the main stated goal of Consolidation has been to establish a full state presence in ungoverned zones, this goal has proven elusive. All such zones remain violent, with a strong presence of illegal armed groups, particularly outside of town centers. The military has taken on a host of noncombat roles (e.g., construction projects, leading community meetings, delivering food, and development aid) as civilian government agencies have been slow to arrive.

Consolidation did prove successful at attaining a subsidiary objective: reducing coca cultivation. In the La Macarena zone, one of the FARC's longest-held rearguards, manual eradication and economic assistance reduced coca cultivation by over 90 percent. The La Macarena program accounted for all of the reductions in coca growing that Colombia measured between 2004 and 2009.[13] Even as Consolidation struggled to reduce FARC influence in the La Macarena zone, the sharp drop in coca growing led Colombian and U.S. officials to hail its success. The zone is now a regular, albeit heavily guarded, stop on high-ranking Washington officials' visits to Colombia.

Unlike for Plan Colombia, U.S. aid for Consolidation included a big nonmilitary component that was placed at the center of the strategy, not awkwardly grafted on. Meanwhile, the post-2006 period saw a significant drop in fumigation, and in military assistance. By 2012, aid to Colombia from all U.S. accounts—once over 80 percent military and police assistance—was 45 percent nonmilitary, with big outlays for justice reform and the nonmilitary component of Consolidation.[14]

A big reason for this modest shift is the narrative that Colombia has been a "success" and thus does not require continued military aid infusions of U.S.$600 million per year. The post-2002 period saw a military offensive—which the Uribe government funded almost entirely from Colombia's treasury—that pushed guerrillas to marginal areas as well as a negotiation process that reduced and fragmented the paramilitary presence. The country's homicide rate has fallen by nearly 50 percent, and kidnappings have dropped from nearly 3,000 per year to around 300.[15]

Some credit for these and other security advances is owing to Plan Colombia, especially the provision of helicopters and U.S. advice, which improved logistics, intelligence, and management. However, much—somewhere between one-half and two-thirds—of U.S. military and police aid went to counterdrug programs that only began reducing cocaine supplies in the post-2007 period, ironically enough, after the fumigation program began to be cut back. The bulk of the credit goes to the Colombian government's multiplication of defense spending, fueled by the levying of new taxes, along with a near-doubling (using 2000 as the base year) of Colombia's security forces.[16] Colombia paid for this itself, along with the bulk of helicopter purchases (Colombia now has the world's third-largest Blackhawk fleet) and most attack aircraft purchases.[17] By the second half of the 2000–2010 decade, U.S. aid was equivalent to a tiny portion—less than a twentieth—of Colombia's defense budget.

The other reason for the modest shift in the United States' Colombia aid strategy was a political shift at home, encouraged by the Bush administration's debacle in Iraq. In November 2006, voters gave the Democratic Party majority control of both houses of Congress, propelling some of Plan Colombia's most prominent critics into legislative leadership positions. Military aid, both counterdrug and otherwise, began to drop, and economic aid programs, including support for Consolidation, increased.

Drugs or Organized Crime: Mexico and Central America

By the late 2000s, both before and after Barack Obama's election, it was plain that Latin America was not becoming a front in the "war on terror": the region showed a very scarce presence of terrorist groups with global reach likely to attack U.S. citizens on U.S. soil. As troops withdrew from Iraq and drew down in Afghanistan, counterinsurgency also began to lose momentum in U.S. policy circles, although in Colombia the Consolidation program continues on autopilot. Even as the post-2007 economic downturn has forced cuts in the worldwide aid budget, the war on drugs continues to account for most military assistance to the region. However, amid crime rates at their lowest point in generations in the United States, illegal-drug supplies are not viewed with the same urgency as before.

The sense of urgency, instead, has come from concern over the power of violent organized crime groups, which fund themselves largely but not entirely through the drug trade, in Mexico and Central America. If the 1990s' anticartel effort opened space for Colombia's guerrillas and paramilitaries to enter the drug trade, the antiguerrilla and paramilitary negotiation effort since 2000 has opened space for Mexico's criminal syndicates, whose lineage dates back to the pre-2000 authoritarian governments of the Institutional Revolutionary Party (Partido Revolucionario Institucional, PRI). Post-2000, a common view held that most cocaine en route to the United States ceased to be in Colombian criminal groups' hands once it left Colombia.[18] The most lucrative part of the trade—transshipment to the United States and the wholesale trade within the United States—fell to Mexican groups like the Sinaloa, Golfo, Zetas, Familia Michoacana, Beltrán-Leyva, Juárez, Tijuana, and smaller cartels.

As these groups' competition intensified in the post-PRI period, alarms began to sound in the United States about the violent activity of these so-called transnational criminal organizations (TCOs). Following his 2006 election, Mexican president Felipe Calderón launched an offensive against these violent groups that included a big increase in use of the Mexican armed forces for internal security. This was based on a belief that the country's federal, state, and local police forces were overwhelmed, outgunned, and—in many cases—thoroughly penetrated and corrupted by the criminal organizations. Instead, Mexico's secretive military, which had almost never before seen one of its members convicted for a human rights crime, was suddenly put on the front lines in contact with civilian populations. As the federal police slowly increased in size and even more slowly underwent reforms, the army and navy took over for police in several key jurisdictions, staffing roadblocks, carrying out searches, seizures and detentions, and maintaining a "dissuasive presence" in dangerous neighborhoods.

Calderón sought U.S. support for his offensive, breaking with predecessor Vicente Fox, whose 2000–2006 term saw a modest decrease in U.S. assistance and the end of Clinton-era programs like the GAFE training effort. At a March 2007 meeting in Mérida, Yucatán, Presidents Bush and Calderón formalized a three-year package of assistance for which the U.S. Congress began appropriating funds in 2008. The Mérida Initiative sharply increased U.S. aid to Mexico, which totaled $2.4 billion in the five years between 2008 and 2012, 70 percent of it for Mexico's military and police.[19] During those same five years, though, Colombia received U.S.$3.0 billion (63 percent of its military and police aid).[20]

The Mérida Initiative has been a smaller aid program than Plan Colombia, owing largely to Mexico's historical reluctance to host U.S. military personnel on its soil, including a constitutional ban on foreign personnel carrying weapons. Colombia's armed forces have sought close relationships with their U.S. counterparts at least since Colombia sent a contingent of troops to participate in the Korean War; over the past sixty years, the country has been the largest "feeder" of students to the U.S. Army School of the Americas and its successor.[21] However, Mexico's armed forces, especially its army, have long placed aggression from the country's northern neighbor high on their list of potential national security threats. While Mérida Initiative backers cite the great strides made in cooperation since 2008, distrust has still prevented aid from reaching Plan Colombia proportions. (Distrust, incidentally, is a two-way street: U.S. concerns about corruption in Mexico's security forces—mainly its police, but also its military—have limited intelligence sharing, joint operations, and similar efforts that require very close cooperation.)

The Mérida Initiative has also been less a military aid package than Plan Colombia. Most big-ticket military assistance to Mexico, like aircraft and helicopters, was front-loaded in 2008 and 2009. The Obama administration, with much input from U.S. ambassador to Mexico Carlos Pascual, sought to balance the "hard" assistance with an approach that Ambassador Pascual called "four pillars": strengthening security, strengthening justice, modernizing the border, and providing economic opportunity. With greatly increased funds for the second through fourth pillars, by 2012, U.S. aid to Mexico had become 55 percent nonmilitary, a proportion that nonmilitary aid to Colombia has never reached.

As of 2012, results of Calderón's offensive and the Mérida Initiative are still being awaited. The post-2006 period has been marked by a horrific increase in violence, with the number of drug trade–related homicides since Calderón's inauguration estimated to be over 50,000.[22] The military and police offensive against cartels has brought the capture or death of many top organized crime figures. The resulting disequilibrium and power vacuums in Mexico's underworld, along with profound weaknesses in governance and justice, have intensified brutal competition for drug routes and "microtrafficking" in Mexico's cities. They have also prodded criminal organizations to diversify beyond drugs into migrant smuggling, kidnapping, extortion, and other crimes against the population. While 2011 and 2012 crime statistics indicate that violence may be coming down from peak levels, it is still not clear whether this is owing to security policies or to a temporary realignment of criminal groups' dominion.

The Mérida Initiative included a modest outlay of assistance, most of it police and naval aid, to Central American states, particularly the three Northern Triangle countries (Guatemala, El Salvador, and Honduras). Since the middle of the 2000–2010 decade, the isthmus has become the transshipment point for an overwhelming majority of cocaine transiting from the Andes to the United States and has also seen a greater presence of violent Mexican organized crime groups.

This, along with the burgeoning presence of youth gangs in cities and prisons, has made the Northern Triangle countries the most violent in the world, measured in homicide rates. Leaders have responded by sending the armed forces back into the streets to a degree not seen since the 1980s civil war years. This disturbs many who viewed the military's return to the barracks as a major achievement of the region's 1990s peace processes—an achievement that witnessed a major setback with a 2009 military coup that removed an elected president in Honduras. However, the near-collapse of corrupt, poorly trained police forces, especially in Guatemala and Honduras, has left a vacuum that elected civilian leaders are pushing militaries to fill.

These leaders have been appealing to the United States for aid, both to reform police forces and, as happened in Mexico, to support ongoing military deployments for internal security. The Obama administration, with a reduced budget hit by economic crisis, has been willing to support police reform but—with the exception of maritime aid for navies and border-security aid for armies—has moved more slowly toward increased military aid. U.S. aid to Central America, both military and nonmilitary, has remained modest by Cold War, Plan Colombia, and even Mérida Initiative standards. The Obama administration's Central America Regional Security Initiative (CARSI) is providing the region with about $100 million per year in assistance that runs roughly according to the Mérida Initiative's four-pillars framework (minus the twenty-first-century border pillar). Nonetheless, in part for lack of other viable security institutions to aid, as of 2014, the Obama administration was giving ever more serious consideration to increasing aid to Central American militaries that were being tasked with citizen security or policing functions.

Most military and police aid in the Mérida and CARSI programs flows through counterdrug accounts in the U.S. foreign aid and defense budgets. Still, though the criminal groups generating insecurity in Mexico and Central America are responsible for most drugs transshipped to the United States, officials only occasionally use drug war rhetoric to sell these programs to the U.S. Congress. In 2000, Plan Colombia was sold principally as a program to step up drug-crop eradication and cocaine interdiction while avoiding involvement in Colombia's larger conflict with illegal armed groups. Ten years later, Mérida and CARSI were portrayed more as efforts to weaken criminal groups and improve public safety than as antidrug programs. While officials cite drug trafficking as a reason that these criminal groups pose a threat to U.S. interests, they rarely promise that Mérida and CARSI will actually make a significant dent in illegal-drug supplies within the United States.

The shift in rhetoric away from drug war and toward citizen security reflects concerns in the United States, where drug use is lower than it was twenty years ago, and in the region, where the violence and corruption associated with drug trafficking has always been a greater concern than the damage done by drug use. It also is owing to a policy shift in the Obama administration, which has formally abandoned the term "war on drugs," preferring to discuss the threat of organized crime "trafficking" defined more broadly, or "citizen security" in general. Meanwhile, the U.S. conservatives who most vocally backed drug war aid in the 1980s and 1990s today express more vocal concerns about the influence of leaders like Venezuela's Hugo Chávez, Bolivia's Evo Morales, Ecuador's Rafael Correa, or Nicaragua's Daniel Ortega. However, with the exception of Venezuela and Cuba, all "Bolivarian" and left-leaning governments in the Americas receive U.S. military and/or police aid for drug eradication and interdiction.

U.S. Aid and Internal Military Roles Today

Even as the center of gravity shifts from the drug war toward citizen security, U.S. encouragement of internal military roles remains a central issue. When elected civilian leaders in the region propose deploying the military into the streets to fight drug-funded gangs or organized crime, U.S. officials are, on balance, willing to make contributions from counterdrug aid accounts. U.S. military assistance programs in Latin America, then, still encourage militaries to take on internal security roles that would be inappropriate or, more likely, illegal in the United States and most other industrialized Western democracies.

Today, the U.S. government's use of counterdrug aid accounts to encourage internal military roles takes three main forms in the Americas: the Consolidation program and other antiguerrilla campaign plans in Colombia; the military component of the Mérida Initiative in Mexico; and the response to elected leaders' requests for anticrime military aid in Central America's Northern Triangle, especially for border and coastal security. The end-state goal of Consolidation is to make the Colombian armed forces' role unnecessary in the zones designated for building up a civilian state presence. After about five years of operation, though, civilian state agencies were still very slow to enter the territorial Consolidation zones, and security conditions remained challenging. U.S.-supported soldiers continued to play a host of unorthodox roles, including building roads and other infrastructure, coordinating community development meetings, and providing basic public security. Though Consolidation purports to do the opposite, so far, at least, the program has only helped to cement in place the military's predominant governance role.

The Mérida Initiative has steadily become less military-heavy since the program's initial rollout of expensive big-ticket items for Mexico's armed forces, such as helicopters and scanning equipment. The Initiative's other pillars—including assistance to police and investigators, the judiciary, border agents, and urban youth—have taken increasing precedence among U.S. priorities and resources. Four years into the Mérida Initiative, U.S. relations with Mexico's army were closer than ever before, but still far more distant and distrustful than they were with longtime aid recipients like Colombia or El Salvador. The armed force with which the United States has worked most closely during the Mérida period is Mexico's navy, especially on antikingpin operations that require extensive intelligence sharing. U.S. counterdrug aid nonetheless contributes to both forces' expanded internal role, both through military assistance and through the Bush and Obama administrations' full-throated praise for Mexico's decision to escalate the military's internal role.

In Central America's Northern Triangle, a remilitarization of internal security is rapidly gaining momentum. Guatemala's government has announced plans to increase the size of the army and to build new bases while declaring periodic states of emergency to combat criminal groups in specific zones. Honduras has passed new laws to formalize the military's crime-fighting role. El Salvador has placed recently retired military personnel in charge of its public security ministry and its National Civilian Police (Policía Nacional Civil, PNC), itself a product of post–civil war "civilianizing" reforms. All three countries' elected presidents are asking the U.S. government to provide increased equipment, training, and other support for military units on anticrime missions.

These requests, and a general sense of alarm about Central America, have led Obama administration officials to some internal debate and soul-searching. Unlike with Colombia and Mexico, there is a sense that Northern Triangle militaries have only a small advantage over police forces in terms of either capacity or lack of corruption. Thus, many perceive the likely security benefit of aiding militaries to do police work as not worth the institutional risks. "The militarization of the police mission" must be avoided, said assistant secretary of state for international narcotics affairs William Brownfield during a March 2012 visit to El Salvador. Any use of military personnel to fight organized crime, Brownfield explained, must be "very limited, very brief, and only in order to respond to an incredibly clear and concrete situation."[23]

Other officials, however, argue that "we in the United States need to avoid the impulse to project our systems on other countries. Sometimes there are other countries that might use the military in a different way than we would use the military, and that is not inherently improper, you know, in their system," said Brownfield's counterpart at the Pentagon, deputy assistant secretary of defense for counter-narcotics William Wechsler, at a March 2012 Senate hearing.[24] The desire to make military assistance for internal security more palatable also underlies hawks' efforts to re-label Mexican organized crime groups as "insurgents" or "terrorists," as well as U.S. Special Operations Forces' definition of their own overseas role as running along "the spectrum of conflict that straddles law enforcement and traditional armed conflict."[25]

Even as debate continues, though, as of this writing (mid-2012) the Obama administration is gradually increasing aid to the militaries of the Northern Triangle, in response to requests from the various presidents. The increase is small by Cold War or Plan Colombia standards so far, amounting to less than $10 million in additional annual aid to each military. It flows through the Defense Department's budget and, to a lesser extent, through the Central America Regional Security Initiative, a $120 million-per-year package of security and institution-building programs managed by the State Department's narcotics bureau and USAID.

The Way Forward

The halting but steadily growing support for Central American militaries' internal role raises a central question: How can the U.S. government support friendly countries' public security goals—and reduce the harm, such as drug flows, of these nations' insecurity to U.S. interests—without militarizing? Obviously, the quick answer is simply, "Don't militarize"; say no to any request to aid militaries' anticrime role.

This answer gets little traction even with many generally sympathetic officials and legislators, however, who feel that a categorical refusal to support militaries leaves recipient countries with no short-term U.S. response in situations where no other institutional option exists, citizen public security capacity has collapsed, and elected leaders are pleading for help. Assistance to build functioning police and judicial systems is important, the common response goes, but it takes years to work, and the security crisis demands a response right now. (It is worth noting that this "short-term crisis" argument is an old one: officials raised this same objection throughout the drug war, when they opted for military assistance over aid to civilian institutions that by now would have matured and consolidated.)

The hard fact, however, is that nothing is going to work in the short term. Soldiers, if they avoid corruption by criminal groups, may provide a dissuasive presence in the immediate vicinity of areas where they are temporarily deployed, and thus make some of the population feel safer. But they are unlikely to bring down violent crime rates in a sustained way, especially if no serious, well-resourced effort is under way to build the institutions that will replace them.

Anything that will ultimately bring down violence rates, make the population feel safer, and erode organized crime's power is going to take time to build. The resource that is lacking is not military firepower; it is state personnel with skills that traditional military training does not offer. These include community policing: developing trusting relations with citizens and identifying natural leaders, allies, and information sources. Also needed is "smart" policing: keeping careful records of crime "hotspots" that require intensified resources and focusing first on the illegal actors who generate the most violence. Even more important is investigative capacity: doing detective work, documenting criminal networks, and building strong cases following rules of evidence (and respecting due process) in order to guarantee successful prosecutions of the worst generators of insecurity. Militaries, trained to defeat enemies, are not at all adept at these skills.

Nor can militaries substitute for the lack of a functioning justice system. Judges, prosecutors, investigators, and witnesses need protection, equipment, transportation, computers, crime labs, and training. They need to see their overwhelming caseloads reduced. Prison systems, meanwhile, need to be funded and made humane.

Without bottom-up efforts to improve justice, soldiers will be just as demoralized as police already are at the sight of arrested criminals being set free and corrupt or abusive colleagues going unpunished. Without strong improvements to the justice system, any increased public security effort will occur in a climate of impunity, which guarantees more abuses.

Before acceding to a president's entreaties to aid the creation of an internal security role for the military, U.S. officials must be able to answer yes to the following questions:

- Is the military's internal-security role temporary? Does it have an end date?
- Following the foreseen military drawdown, is there a credible plan to have in place functioning police, justice, and prison systems?
- Is this plan clearly going to have sufficient domestic funding and elite political support?
- Is the U.S. government truly committed to helping the recipient country build its security and justice apparatus? Will this commitment be sustained and not abandoned in favor of more "urgent" priorities elsewhere if violence appears to decline?

If officials cannot unequivocally answer yes to all four of these questions, which lay out some very low expectations, any military aid for internal security will yield frustrating results. Not only will the U.S. government find itself "shoveling water" in the fight against violence, it will be doing so in a way that risks increased human rights violations.

In order to commit to such an institution-building assistance program for the security, justice, and oversight apparatus, though, the U.S. government must change the way it goes about this business. A first step is to stop measuring progress principally in tons of drugs eradicated or interdicted; focusing simply on antidrug results focuses only on one set of symptoms of a much deeper disorder.

Second, and even more important, the U.S. government must develop a real capacity to assist civilian police forces and justice systems to protect and serve populations. Right now, no such capacity exists. Law enforcement support falls mainly to the State Department's Bureau of International Narcotics and Law Enforcement Affairs, known as INL—but right now the "IN" in the Bureau's budget gets, by a multiple, far more resources than the "L." The Justice Department has a small role in police assistance and a large role in judicial reform assistance; these need to be evaluated, improved, and expanded. Meanwhile, Section 660 of the Foreign Assistance Act, added in 1974 after revelations of grantees' human rights abuses, prohibits much U.S. aid to foreign police forces.

The result of all this is that the agency that faces the fewest restrictions on its police aid programs is the U.S. military, which can use its budget to train police for counterdrug, counterterror and, in some countries, simply "train and equip" purposes. Because defense is far more politically popular than foreign aid, meanwhile, the U.S. military has far more budget and "surge capacity" to help foreign police than do agencies like INL or USAID. In a time of shrinking budgets, this is even truer than before.

The U.S. government needs to change this political calculus and build up a civilian capability to help foreign civilian police forces protect and serve populations, investigate organized crime networks, and immediately punish human rights abuse or corruption within their ranks. This capability must go hand in hand with a far larger effort to help partner countries build their judicial systems. Creating these capacities would require an increase in the annual State Department foreign operations budget. In a time of budget flattening, this increase would probably have to come from tiny cuts to the behemoth defense budget. That is the clear policy signpost for U.S. support of internal security efforts in the Americas.

The *political* way out is far less clear. Enormous obstacles are presented by a congressional committee system that favors defense over foreign aid and by the ease of applying the "drug war" label, which, though obviously outdated, appears to respond more immediately to U.S. citizens' concerns than does violence or insecurity in faraway lands.

Ultimately, breaking with the pattern of the Cold War and drug war and ceasing to encourage internal military roles that we would not adopt at home will require unusual political courage. But Latin America's long-term security and governance needs, and the importance of preserving the gains of the region's recent transitions to democracy, leave no other option.

Notes

1. These programs are the State Department's international narcotics control and law enforcement account and the Defense Department's counterdrug budget, which under authority first given in Section 1004 of the 1991 Defense Authorization Law, allow the Pentagon to provide some types of military and police aid to fight drug trafficking. See "Grant U.S. Aid Listed by Program, All Programs, Entire Region, 2000–2012," Just the Facts, last modified April 27, 2012, http://justf.org/All_Grants_Program?year1=2000&year2=2012& subregion=Entire+Region&x=57&y=6 (information now resides at Security Assistance Monitor, http://www.securityassistance.org/latin-america-and-caribbean/data/country/military/country/2000/2012/is_all/Latin%20America%20and%20the%20Caribbean).

2. For a fuller discussion, see George Withers, Lucila Santos, and Adam Isacson, *Preach What You Practice: The Separation of Military and Police Roles in the Americas* (Washington, D.C.: WOLA, 2010), http://www.wola.org/publications/preach_what_you_practice _the_separation_of_police_and_military_roles_in_the_americas.

3. Frank Newport, "Terrorism and Economy Seen as Top Problems Facing Country

Today, but Neither Dominates," Gallup, last modified March 20, 2002, http://www.gallup.com/poll/5500/terrorism-economy-seen-top-problems-facing-country-today.aspx.

4. Charles Call, *Clear and Present Dangers: The U.S. Military and the War on Drugs in the Andes* (Washington, D.C.: WOLA, 1997), 37.

5. Robin Kirk, *More Terrible Than Death: Massacres, Drugs and America's War in Colombia* (New York: Public Affairs, 2003), 188.

6. See State Department foreign military training reports aggregated and cited at "U.S. Military and Police Trainees Listed by Program, All Programs, Entire Region, 2000–2010," Just the Facts, last modified April 27, 2012, (information now resides at Security Assistance Monitor, http://justf.org/).

7. Benjamin Wallace-Wells, "How America Lost the War on Drugs," *Rolling Stone*, last updated March 24, 2011, http://www.rollingstone.com/politics/news/how-america-lost-the-war-on-drugs-20110324.

8. Barry McCaffrey, "White House Office of National Drug Control Policy Discussion Paper: Western Hemisphere Counterdrug Program Enhancements," Center for International Policy's Colombia Program, last modified March 20, 2000, https://web.archive.org/web/20131007142152/http://www.ciponline.org/old/colombia/00071301.htm.

9. "Conference Report 106-701," Congressional Record—House, last modified June 29, 2000, https://web.archive.org/web/20130228002218/http://www.ciponline.org/old/colombia/confrept.pdf.

10. "State Department Report to Congress, July 27, 2000," Center for International Policy's Colombia Program, last modified August 3, 2000, https://web.archive.org/web/20050104234112/http://ciponline.org/colombia/080102.htm.

11. For "review," see www.defense.gov/Transcripts/Transcript.aspx?Transcript ID=1598. For "cross the line," a term that was used frequently, see www.nytimes.com/2002/02/06/world/administration-shifts-focus-on-colombia-aid.html.

12. *2012 International Narcotics Control Strategy Report* (Washington, D.C.: U.S. Department of State, March 2012), http://www.state.gov/j/inl/rls/nrcrpt/2012/index.htm.

13. Sergio Jaramillo, *National Consolidation Policy* (Bogotá: Office of the President, 2010), 25.

14. "U.S. Aid to Colombia, All Programs, 2008–2013," Just the Facts, last modified April 27, 2012, (information now resides at Security Assistance Monitor, http://justf.org/).

15. Juan Carlos Pinzón Bueno, *Logros de la política integral de seguridad y defensa para la prosperidad* (Bogotá: Ministerio de Defensa Nacional, 2012), http://www.mindefensa.gov.co/irj/go/km/docs/Mindefensa/Documentos/descargas/estudios%20sectoriales/info_estadistica/Logros_Sector_Defensa.pdf.

16. International Institute for Strategic Studies, *The Military Balance 2001–2002* (Oxford: Oxford University Press), 2001; Pinzón Bueno, *Logros de la política integral*.

17. Sikorsky Aerospace Services, "Sikorsky Aerospace Services Provides In-Country BLACK HAWK Maintenance Team for Colombian Army," PR Newswire, last updated April 13, 2011, http://www.sikorsky.com/pages/AboutSikorsky/PressreleaseDetails.aspx?pressreleaseid=267.

18. See, for instance, "Reporting on the Front Lines of Mexico's Drug War," NPR Books, last modified October 26, 2011, http://www.npr.org/2011/10/26/141659461/reporting-on-the-front-lines-of-mexicos-drug-war.

19. "U.S. Aid to Mexico, All Programs, 2008–2012," Just the Facts, last modified April 27, 2012, (information now resides at Security Assistance Monitor, http://justf.org/).

20. "U.S. Aid to Colombia, All Programs, 2008–2012," Just the Facts, last modified April 27, 2012, (information now resides at Security Assistance Monitor, http://justf.org/).

21. "SOA Grads," SOA Watch, last modified April 27, 2012, http://www.soaw.org/about-the-soawhinsec/soawhinsec-grads; "Training Provided at Western Hemisphere Institute for Security Cooperation, Fort Benning, Georgia, Entire Region, 1996–2013," Just the Facts, last modified April 27, 2012, (information now resides at Security Assistance Monitor, http://justf.org/).

22. Rachel Donadio and Karla Zabludovsky, "At Mass in Mexico, Pope Urges Humility and Trust," *New York Times,* last modified March 25, 2012, http://www.nytimes.com/2012/03/26/world/americas/at-mass-in-mexico-pope-urges-humility.html.

23. Agence France-Presse, "U.S. Anti-Drug Official Will Propose Concrete Plans to Central America," *Diálogo: Forum of the Americas,* last modified March 19, 2012, http://www.dialogo-americas.com/en_GB/articles/rmisa/features/regional_news/2012/03/19/feature-ex-2978.

24. U.S. Congress, Senate, Committee on Armed Services, Subcommittee on Emerging Threats and Capabilities, *Hearing to Receive Testimony on the Department of Defense's Role in the Implementation of the National Strategy for Counterterrorism and the National Strategy to Combat Transnational Organized Crime in Review of the Defense Authorization Request for Fiscal Year 2013 and the Future Years Defense Program,* 112th Cong., 2nd sess., March 27, 2012.

25. "SOF Bias for Action and SOCSOUTH's Pragmatism," Institute for Defense and Government Advancement, last modified March 22, 2012, http://www.idga.org/unconventional-warfare/articles/sof-bias-for-action-and-socsouth-s-pragmatism/.

5

Security Challenges at the U.S.-Mexican Border

Understanding the Security Threats to State and Local Governments

ROCÍO A. RIVERA BARRADAS

> The violence in Mexico is not only an international threat. It is a homeland security issue in which all Americans have a stake . . . Threats to the United States come from every part of the globe, and the security situation of our next-door neighbor deserves our utmost attention.
>
> Janet Napolitano, secretary of homeland security, March 25, 2009

Security is an interdependent issue in the U.S.-Mexican bilateral relationship. The definition of Mexico's security "depends and will continue to depend largely on the United States' vision of its own national security and the place Mexico holds on its agenda."[1] Moreover, if the concept of national security is socially constructed, one should analyze the perceptions, expectations, meanings, interests, and moral values placed at the center in the security agenda of both countries in a particular time.[2] The meaning of security has changed over time in Mexico and the United States, thus having an impact also on the definition of security. Yet how Mexicans perceive their own security threats also has implications for the national security of the United States.

The threat that the United States confronts is the recent and increasing activity of drug-trafficking organizations on American soil. Seven cartels control the flow of drugs on the southern border: Tijuana, Golfo, Zetas, Juárez, Sinaloa, Beltrán-Leyva, and Michoacana. Drug-related crimes such as kidnapping and human smuggling and the presence of street and prison gangs have been increased in cities like Phoenix, Arizona, Birmingham, Alabama, and Atlanta, Georgia.[3] This shows that the activity of cartels does not stop at the border; there are cells operating in over 200 U.S. cities.[4]

In the National Southwest Border Counternarcotics Strategy (NSBCS) released by the Office of National Drug Control Policy in 2011, the U.S. government admits that due to the high levels of violence, the United States, particularly the four border states, faces security challenges. The strategy includes the concept of "Strong Communities," which emphasizes the development of strong and resilient communities on both sides of the border that can resist criminal organizations.

This strategy is an important step toward acceptance that the border region presents a particular threat for both countries. Even though the Mérida Initiative represents an approach of shared responsibility, it is not accurate to focus resources only in one country. Therefore, the Strong Communities idea "directs Federal agencies to provide border communities with enhanced prevention and drug treatment assistance in this region that has borne the brunt of the consequences of the drug trade."[5]

Following the framework proposed by Buzan, Wæver, and de Wilde,[6] this phenomenon could be analyzed by studying analytical levels, sectors, actors, threats, and referent objects. This chapter suggests that analysis should be at the level of the U.S.-Mexican border as a subregion and therefore, of the interaction between the state and local governments on each side of the border. This approach is supported by the Strong Communities concept delineated in the 2011 NSBCS.

The sectors in this approach include the military, political, societal, economic, and environmental. The strategy against organized crime in both the United States and Mexico includes the participation of the military force and the police. This is best shown by the fact that up to 1,200 U.S. National Guard members are currently deployed in the four border states and engaged in civilian law enforcement activities and security on the southwestern border.[7] In 2008, President Felipe Calderón deployed 7,532 soldiers in Ciudad Juárez as part of the program "Todos somos Juárez. Rescatemos la Ciudad" (We are Juárez. Save the city).[8]

In the political sector, local and state governments, especially in Mexico, are vulnerable to the threats of drug-trafficking organizations. The local security authorities as well as the municipal presidents have been the principal targets of the cartels, which presents a threat to local government.

The societal sector has been emphasized by the 2011 NSBCS. The well-being of the Mexicans and Americans in the border communities has become one of the main objectives in the development of U.S. national security strategy. This strategy was developed as part of the meetings identified as "Beyond Mérida" that took place between the U.S. and Mexican governments on March 23, 2010.[9] In the economic sector, the trade between the two countries could be vulnerable to the threat imposed by the drug-trafficking organizations. On the financial side, money laundering related to drug trafficking represents one of the main targets of the U.S. and Mexican governments.

The threats at the border targeted by the 2011 NSBCS are drug-related crime and public safety challenges, such as gang violence, home invasions, robberies, kidnappings, and the significant dangers associated with methamphetamine manufacturing. This new strategy is important because it presents not only the United States as a country but also the border communities as the referent objects of security. This is particularly important because the United States and Mexico have started to realize that they must focus on spatial and local cooperation, which the current approach to combating drug trafficking has demonstrated to be inadequate and insufficient.

Federal, state, and local governments have been the most proactive actors in addressing the securitization of the U.S.-Mexican border. It should be noted that the threats identified at the border are related not only to drug trafficking, but also to illegal immigration. The militarization of the border has responded to these two issues, but mainly to the latter.

In the case of the federal government, former secretary of homeland security Janet Napolitano, who had lengthy experience with the U.S.-Mexico border, stated in testimony regarding the drug-related violence that

> America has several roles to play: First, we *must provide assistance* to the Mexican government in its efforts to defeat the drug cartels and thereby suppress the flare-up of violence in Mexico. Second, *we must take action on our side of the border* to cripple smuggling enterprises. Third, we *must guard against and prepare for the possible spillover of violence into the United States.*

> Another reason combating cartel violence on the Mexican side of the border is *critical* is that many *Americans and Mexicans* who live in border communities cross back and forth regularly—to work, to shop, or to visit family. *Fear of the violence* occurring in Mexican border cities has reduced crossings that are important to the lives of Americans and to the economic health of American border communities. The dynamic of the border region makes violence on one side of the border a pressing concern on both sides. *The transnational nature of this threat clearly makes addressing the violence in Mexico a top priority in securing the United States.*

The partnership of state, local, and tribal law enforcement in the border *region is essential to securing our nation against the threat of cartel
violence.* They have significant roles to play both in *addressing the
current violence and preparing for scenarios where violence in Mexico
could further strain the United States.*[10]

Moreover, the governors of the border states have been vigorously demanding the support of the federal authorities. In 2009, the governor of Texas,
Rick Perry, requested that the Obama administration provide 1,000 additional national guard troops at the border.[11] In a speech delivered on August
9, 2010, Governor Perry emphasized the urgent involvement of the federal
government in enforcing security at the U.S.-Mexican border:

> The growing crisis along our southern border, cannot be overlooked
> any longer. Bottom line, an **unsecured U.S./Mexico border is a seri-
> ous national security threat, menacing the safety and security of
> our citizens, and the federal government is obligated to secure it.**
>
> Unfortunately, Washington has been an abject failure in this area,
> leaving our border **vulnerable** to exploitation, and **our citizens ex-
> posed to grave danger.** Washington's lackadaisical efforts have left
> the door open to a cadre of criminal organizations, including trans-
> national gangs, who readily engage in brazen violence, in pursuit of
> their sordid interests.
>
> Our **citizens deserve the best possible effort to protect them** from
> this advancing network of criminal gangs, including well-trained of-
> ficers on patrol, with cutting edge technology that gives them an edge,
> and the national resolve to stop these murderous cartels from extend-
> ing their reach into U.S. territory.
>
> With the help of the Legislature, Texas has invested more than **$230
> million in border security efforts** over the past two legislative ses-
> sions, filling gaps left by insufficient federal action. That money **has
> funded additional personnel**, helped pay overtime, and **purchased
> state-of-the-art technology**, to improve our communications and
> rapid response.[12]

Through speech acts and the relocation of funds and personnel to a particular issue, the actors are able to securitize an issue. The speech above
is an example on how an actor—the government—presents an issue—

migration, drug trafficking—as a threat to a referent object—the individuals living at the border.

As pointed out by some scholars, one of the deficiencies in the Mérida Initiative is that more money must be provided to state and local governments. The problem is that in Mexico, the state and local police are not well equipped and -trained to confront public safety issues. The federal police represent only 10 percent of Mexico's total police force, making state- and local-level authorities more responsible for facing organized crime.[13] In this sense, "the safety of Mexico's citizens (and of the U.S.-Mexican border) will depend on reforming and professionalizing local and state police."[14]

Another weakness of the Mérida Initiative is its narrow approach to military and law enforcement strategies to combat drug-trafficking organizations. Therefore, more attention should be paid to the demand for drugs and the money and gun flows from the United States to Mexico.[15] Local authorities have been demanding that the federal government take responsibility on this issue. As stated by Clint McDonald, sheriff of Terrell County, Texas, the spillover effects are dealt with principally by local jurisdictions along the U.S.-Mexican border:

> Spillover effects are the direct results of Mexican violence that *influ-ence U.S. citizens living in communities along the border.* For example, Mexican gangs fighting to control territory around the frontier village of El Porvenir, in Chihuahua, have threatened for almost a year to kill its residents. To escape the violence, nearly the entire village eventually relocated to Texas border communities—without, of course, being screened or processed. The results include schoolchildren fearing for their safety as their Mexican schoolmates talk of violence and murder, school buses "tailed" by armed private security guards and criminals relocating to the United States with their families and conducting their operations from this country. *The single greatest spillover effect: U.S. citizens living in fear.*[16]

This constitutes a demand to find a different strategy to deal with this phenomenon. A more comprehensive security strategy at the border should be delineated in order to effectively stop the spillover effects. The demand for a different approach arises from the failure of the so-called war on drugs at the border. It could be described as a cat-and-mouse game between law enforcement agencies and drug cartels. Even if the agencies increase personnel and resources, with more budget and technological advances, the drug cartels have demonstrated that they are flexible and extremely adaptable.[17]

The sectors in which drug-trafficking activities occur relate to a threat to a referent object. The nature of the threat varies across sectors and levels of analysis. The violence along the U.S.-Mexican border as a consequence of drug-trafficking activity is positioned in the military sector, where the referent object is the state. In the political sector, sovereignty and the governing authority are threatened by drug-trafficking organizations. In the societal sector, collectivities of individuals (such as border communities) are at risk. Finally, in the economic sector, one can argue that these organizations erode the free trade between Mexico and the United States because authorities have to check containers and vehicles, slowing down trade flow. The spillover effects of the violence and drug-related activities at the U.S.-Mexican border represent a threat to the state (the United States and Mexico), to state and local authorities, for the community and individuals, and, to a lesser degree, to the economic and trade regime.[18]

The Cases of Texas and Chihuahua

For the border states and, particularly, border cities in the United States and Mexico that have constant interaction, security issues are a priority. These are the first to confront the threats from the drug-trafficking organizations.

The Texas Department of Public Safety's Texas Fusion Center Intelligence and Counterterrorism Units released *The Texas Gang Threat Assessment 2010* on September 1, 2010, which identifies transnational gangs, prison gangs, street gangs, and outlaw motorcycle gangs as the most significant organized threat to the State of Texas.[19] It has been argued that Mexican cartels need the support of a network of gangs in the United States in order to conduct their smuggling and trafficking activities. "Gangs recruit new members in our prisons and our schools and routinely engage in murder, kidnapping, aggravated assault, robbery, auto theft, burglary, drug trafficking, weapons trafficking, prostitution, human trafficking and money laundering."[20] Therefore, it is expected that the scope and degree of gang violence in the major urban areas in Texas will increase.[21]

The report thus identifies in Tier 1 the gangs that are considered to pose the greatest threat on a statewide scale: the Mexican Mafia, Tango Blast, Texas Syndicate, and Barrio Azteca. There are twenty other gangs included in Tiers 2 and 3. In total, the Department of Public Safety identifies twenty-four gangs as posing a real and important threat to the State of Texas. McAllen, Laredo, and El Paso have been identified as the border counties with highest gang activity.[22]

The El Paso City Council released in spring 2010 a manifesto in support of Ciudad Juárez, in which the city urgently demanded efforts from the United States to change its strategy for dealing with the violence in Mexico:

> We can no longer afford to deny the overwhelming role that U.S. consumption of drugs plays in fueling the violence in Juárez and elsewhere in Mexico, or ignore that illicit cash and arms flows from the United States into Mexico play a direct and powerful role in sustaining the cartels and in the massive killing of people in our neighboring city.
>
> It is time to recognize that the U.S. 40-year War on Drugs has been a dismal social, economic and policy failure. It has not achieved any of its goals and narco-related violence along the U.S.-Mexico border is raging at unprecedented levels with no end in sight. We join many prominent Americans, including ex-U.S. secretaries of state George Shultz and James Baker, U.S. Nobel Prize–winning economist Milton Friedman, ex-presidents of Mexico Vicente Fox and Ernesto Zedillo, ex-president of Colombia César Gaviria, and ex-president of Brazil Fernando Enrique [sic] Cardoso in calling for a comprehensive revamping of the failed War on Drugs waged by the United States and other countries.[23]

These initiatives show that border communities have suffered the unintended consequences of the current strategy to combat drug trafficking in the region. Due to the ineffective results, they are demanding a shift in the paradigm.

In the case of Chihuahua, in March 2008, Mexican president Felipe Calderón launched Operativo Conjunto Chihuahua in an attempt to recapture Ciudad Juárez from the criminal organizations. His main strategy was to send over 2,000 soldiers to the border city and to assume control of the local police.[24] In addition, in February 2010, the United States developed a pilot program with Mexico in the border cities of Ciudad Juárez and El Paso in order to decrease the high levels of violence. This program was established to provide training, equipment, and intelligence and also includes training local and state police.[25]

Even though this cooperation represents a further stage in the bilateral relationship of the two countries, it has not been enough. The strategy should be more comprehensive and include social aspects, drug treatment, and attempts to decrease drug consumption. It has been a good step in recognizing that the border communities should be included in any strategy, but as stated by Stephen Clarkson, "what is security for some is insecurity for others," and that is exactly what is happening with the United States and Mexico. The North American border is seen as a site of contradictions because in the name of national security, it "actually generates considerable insecurity for both the nation itself and its two bordering countries."[26]

Juárez faces two main threats: the violence generated by the war among the Golfo, Zetas, Pacífico, and Juárez cartels; and the fears raised by the human rights violations of the military and police.[27] Even though El Paso and Ciudad Juárez—"Border Communities"—have been identified as referent objects in the new strategy, the emphasis on the supply side and not on the demand for drugs continues because of inertia and bureaucratic and political interests. It seems that the Obama administration cannot do much due to domestic limitations. The U.S. government and Congress continue with what Peter Andreas argues—"stupid policies, can be smart politics"[28]—or what Daniel Wirls calls "irrational security,"[29] because even though these policies do not accomplish the objectives established, they generate political and electoral profits.[30]

Cooperation and Potential Conflict Areas

Due to the threat posed by drug-trafficking organizations on both sides of the border, the United States and Mexico have found some areas of cooperation. In July 2011, the Obama administration published new federal regulations concerning arms trafficking on the southern border. The new regulations require gun shop owners in Arizona, Texas, California, and New Mexico to inform the authorities within five days whenever someone buys a weapon such as an AK-47 or a semiautomatic rifle that uses ammunition larger than .22 caliber.[31]

The flow of weapons to Mexico has been one of the key issues addressed by the security strategy. Mexico blames the United States for allowing the cartels to acquire weapons that are prohibited in Mexico except for the military sector. The Mexican authorities are thus weakened with respect to the cartels, resulting in skyrocketing violence.[32] Even though the Obama administration has taken an important step toward stopping arms trafficking to Mexico, powerful lobbying groups such as the National Rifle Association (NRA) are trying to get the regulations overturned.

Another area of cooperation is cross-border missions in which the Mexican police carry out drug raids inside the United States. The U.S. Drug Enforcement Administration (DEA) provides intelligence information to its Mexican counterpart in order to stage the operations more effectively. Moreover, U.S. participation has also widened in operations related to the surveillance of drug-production facilities with the use of predator drones and unmanned aerial vehicles. In addition, Mexico has agreed to allow a team of DEA and CIA agents and retired American military to conduct intelligence operations on a Mexican military base.[33]

The confirmation of a new U.S. ambassador to Mexico, Earl Anthony Wayne, on August 3, 2011, troubled some people in the Mexican government.[34] The career of this professional U.S. diplomat in Afghanistan was viewed as a sign of how Washington sees Mexico and the strategy that has to be pursued. The approach used by the United States in Iraq and Afghanistan is an obstacle and what Mexico fears most regarding U.S. involvement in combating drug trafficking and organized crime.[35]

Some analysts see the Mexican government as a buffer between the drug cartels and the U.S. government. They argue that the corruption at all three levels of the Mexican government, the economic benefits that derive from the drug trade, and the sovereignty issues between the two countries allow drug-trafficking organizations to operate freely along the border.[36]

Another issue that has generated some friction is money laundering. Mexico has criticized its neighbor for allowing the drug cartels to launder money through the U.S. banking system. Drug-trafficking gangs launder an estimated U.S.$36 billion each year through U.S. banks. The Wachovia case illustrates this problem. The bank allowed U.S.$420 billion to pass through its accounts unmonitored. It was later found that the funds belonged to the Sinaloa cartel.[37]

Conclusion

The securitization process in the U.S.-Mexican relationship has shifted to the border region. As we can see in the 2011 NSBCS, the referent object is the "border community," taking into consideration the high level of activity and interaction among cities and regions at the border.

The most interesting aspect of this strategy is that the consumption problem has been the main issue addressed by programs in border communities. Because they are suffering the consequences of the current strategy, which openly confronts organized crime, these communities have joined the clamor for a change in this strategy. El Paso's City Council, for example, has demanded a shift in the way the United States conducts the war on drugs. The council recognizes that this strategy has failed and that a new one, focused on the demand side, is necessary in order to save border cities like El Paso and Ciudad Juárez.

Interestingly, these communities, the referent objects, should be protected so they can survive," and they are demanding a new approach. Perhaps the "desecuritization" process could start at the border with health programs, which are emphasized in the 2011 NSBCS.

Two of the three actors (the federal and the state government) are pursuing and will continue to support strategies focused on military and law enforcement aspects. As noted in speeches by Janet Napolitano and Rick Perry, sending more national guardsmen to the border will continue. Unfortunately, this constitutes "irrational security," according to Daniel Wirls, because this policy will not bring the wanted solution. But because it appeals to political candidates, members of Congress, and the public, officers will continue to support it.

The regional security dynamic that Mexico and the United States are confronting today needs to redefine the concept of sovereignty. Just as during the NAFTA negotiations this term was constructed to privilege "economic sovereignty" in Mexico, the same could be done now. It is true that Mexico needs to strengthen its law enforcement institutions, but both countries need to face this threat jointly, which has become a major concern for the region.[38]

The problem with bilateral cooperation in security issues is the approach. Terms such as "narco-terrorism" should be avoided because they allow the intervention of bureaucracies and agencies that concentrate on counterterrorism. The approach in Afghanistan and Iraq cannot be used in Mexico. The drug cartels are employing terrorist tactics, but they do not have a political agenda that seeks to eliminate the government.[39]

Notes

1. Lorenzo Meyer, "Prologue," in *Mexico: In Search of Security*, ed. Bruce M. Bagley and Sergio Aguayo (Coral Gables, Fla.: North-South Center, University of Miami, 1993), vi.

2. Bruce M. Bagley, Sergio Aguayo Quezada, and Jeffrey Stark, "Introduction: In Search of Security," in Bagley, *Mexico: In Search of Security*, 11.

3. Jerry Brewer, "'Spillover' Violence Ranges beyond the U.S.-Mexico Border," Mexidata.info, March 22, 2010, http://mexidata.info/id2593.html.

4. Office of National Drug Control Policy (ONDCP), *National Southwest Border*

Counternarcotics Strategy 2011 (Washington, D.C.: Executive Office of the President of the United States, 2011), 25.

5. Ibid., ii.

6. Barry Buzan, Ole Wæver, and Jaap de Wilde, *Security: A New Framework for Analysis* (Boulder, Colo.: Lynne Rienner, 1998), 5. The levels of analysis are locations in which outcomes as well as sources take place. The five levels are the international system, international subsystems, international units, international subunits, and individual.

7. Army Staff Sergeant Jim Greenhill, "National Guard 'Hugely Beneficial' to Southwest Border Mission," National Guard Bureau, 2010, http://multibriefs.com/briefs/ROA/ROA122110.php.

8. Maureen Meyer, *Abused and Afraid in Ciudad Juarez: An Analysis of Human Rights Violations by the Military in Mexico* (Washington, D.C.: Washington Office on Latin America (WOLA), 2010).

9. ONDCP, *National Southwest Border Counternarcotics Strategy 2011*, ii.

10. "Testimony of Secretary Janet Napolitano before Senate Homeland Security and Governmental Affairs Committee," Southern Border Violence: Homeland Security Threats, Vulnerabilities, and Responsibilities, March 25, 2009, http://www.dhs.gov/ynews/testimony/testimony_1237993537881.shtm, emphasis added.

11. Stephanie Condon, "Rick Perry Asks Obama for 1,000 More Border Troops in Texas," CBS News, August 9, 2010, http://www.cbsnews.com/8301-503544_162-20013096-503544.html.

12. Rick Perry, "Warning Signs along Border Must be Heeded by Washington" (speech, Austin, Texas, August 9, 2010), Office of Governor Rick Perry, http://governor.state.tx.us/news/press-release/14989/, emphasis added.

13. Eduardo Guerrero-Gutiérrez, *Security, Drugs and Violence in Mexico: A Survey*, 7th North America Forum (Mexico City: Lantia Consultores, 2011), 20.

14. Shannon O'Neil, "Moving beyond Merida in U.S.-Mexico Security Cooperation" (statement prepared for the Hearing on U.S.-Mexico Security Cooperation: Next Steps for the Merida Initiative before the Committee on Foreign Affairs: Subcommittee on the Western Hemisphere; and Committee on Homeland Security: Subcommittee on Border, Maritime, and Global Counterterrorism, United States House of Representatives, 111th Cong., 2nd Sess., Thursday, May 27, 2010).

15. Ibid.

16. Clint McDonald, "Danger on the U.S.-Mexico Border," *Washington Post*, March 31, 2011, http://www.washingtonpost.com/opinions/danger-on-the-us-mexico-border/2011/03/30/AFQp4KCC_story.html, emphasis added.

17. Tony Payan, "The Drug War and the U.S.-Mexico Border: The State of Affairs," *South Atlantic Quarterly* 105, no. 4 (Fall 2006): 869–870.

18. Analysis based on figure 8.1, "Securitization at Different Levels of Analysis," in Buzan et al., *Security*, 165.

19. Texas Department of Public Safety, *Texas Gang Threat Assessment 2010*, September 1, 2010, 7, http://montgomerytx.countymonitor.com/files/2010/10/TxGngThrtAssessment2010.pdf.

20. Ibid., 3.

21. Ibid., 7.

22. Ibid.

23. El Paso City Council, *A Manifesto in Support of Ciudad Juárez and Its Efforts to Reduce the Violence Related to Drug Trafficking*, spring 2010, http://archive.maryknollogc.org/documents/CJ_Manifesto-2010-MAY-021.pdf, emphasis added.

24. M. Meyer, *Abused and Afraid in Ciudad Juárez*.

25. José María Ramos, "Gestión de la seguridad en la frontera norte e Iniciativa Mérida," in *Migración y seguridad: Nuevo desafío en México*, ed. Natalia Armijo Canto (Mexico City: Colectivo de Análisis de la Seguridad con Democracia [CASEDE], 2011), 84.

26. Stephen Clarkson, "Continental Borders and National Security: A Logical Diagnosis," in *National Solutions to Trans-Border Problems? The Governance of Security and Risk in a Post-NAFTA North America*, ed. Isidro Morales (Farnham, U.K.: Ashgate, 2011), 113.

27. Raúl Benítez Manaut, "México 2010: Crimen organizado, seguridad nacional y geopolítica," in *Crimen organizado e Iniciativa Mérida en las relaciones México–Estados Unidos*, ed. Raúl Benítez Manaut (Mexico City: CASEDE, 2010), 25.

28. Peter Andreas, *Border Games: Policing the U.S.-Mexico Divide* (Ithaca, N.Y.: Cornell University Press, 2000), 148.

29. Daniel Wirls, *Irrational Security: The Politics of Defense from Reagan to Obama* (Baltimore: Johns Hopkins University Press, 2010).

30. Patricia Escamilla Hamm, "La lucha contra el crimen organizado en Estados Unidos: Alcances y límites para la frontera," in *Crimen organizado e Iniciativa Mérida en las relaciones México–Estados Unidos*, ed. Raúl Benítez Manaut (Mexico City: CASEDE, 2010), 141.

31. Charlie Savage, "N.R.A. Sues Over Bulk Gun Sales Rule," *New York Times*, August 3, 2011.

32. Arindrajit Dube, Oeindrila Dube, and Omar García-Ponce, "Cross-Border Spillover: U.S. Gun Laws and Violence in Mexico," *American Political Science Review* 107, no. 3 (August 2013): 397–417.

33. Mark Mazzetti and Ginger Thompson, "U.S. Widens Role in Mexican Fight," *New York Times*, August 25, 2011, http://www.nytimes.com/2011/08/26/world/americas/26drugs.html?scp=1&sq=cross-border%20missions&st=cse.

34. Genaro Lozano, "Anthony Wayne, un alto diplomático de EU para la embajada de México," CNN Mexico, May 30, 2011, http://mexico.cnn.com/nacional/2011/05/30/anthony-wayne-un-alto-diplomatico-de-eu-para-la-embajada-de-mexico.

35. Mazzetti and Thompson, "U.S. Widens Role."

36. Scott Stewart, "The Buffer between Mexican Cartels and the U.S. Government," *STRATFOR*, August 17, 2011, http://www.stratfor.com/weekly/20110817-buffer-between-mexican-cartels-and-us-government#axzz3GS72XAnf.

37. Hannah Stone, "U.S. Targets Bank in Mexico Money Laundering Crackdown," InSight Crime, May 10, 2011, http://www.insightcrime.org/news-analysis/us-targets-bank-in-mexico-money-laundering-crackdown.

38. For a discussion of Mexican nationalism and neoliberalism, see Gavin O'Toole, "A New Nationalism for a New Era: The Political Ideology of Mexican Neoliberalism," *Bulletin of Latin American Research* 22, no. 3 (July 2003): 269–290; Stephen D. Morris, "Reforming the Nation: Mexican Nationalism in Context," *Journal of Latin American Studies* 31, no. 2 (May 1999): 363–397.

39. Arturo Sarukhan, "Choose Labels Carefully," *Dallas Morning News*, April 11, 2011.

6

Drug-Control Policies in the United States

Patterns, Prevalence, and Problems of Drug Use in the United States

BRUCE M. BAGLEY

The Bush administration (2001–2009) claimed that it was "winning" America's decades-long war on drugs.[1] Reports from the Office of National Drug Control Policy (ONDCP) and the State Department pointed to record seizures of cocaine and crop eradication in Colombia and disruption of criminal smuggling networks in Colombia and Mexico as signs of progress. "Overseas counter drug efforts have slowly constricted the pipeline that brings cocaine to the United States," the ONDCP stated in the 2006 National Drug Control Strategy report.[2] Similar pronouncements about progress in the drug war have been issued repeatedly by virtually every U.S. government since the Nixon administration, which in 1973 claimed the United States had "turned the corner" on addiction and drug use. In 1990, then-U.S. drug czar William Bennett said that the United States was on the "road to victory" regarding drug abuse.[3] According to the 2009 National Drug Control Strategy report released at the end of George W. Bush's tenure in the White House, "From community coalitions to international partnerships, we pursued a balanced strategy that emphasized stopping initiation, reducing drug abuse and addiction, and disrupting drug markets."[4]

The United States is still the world's most lucrative market for illicit drugs, however, as well as "the leading producer and exporter of marijuana, crack cocaine, and methamphetamine."[5] Moreover, illicit drugs—including marijuana, cocaine, heroin, and methamphetamine and synthetic drugs such as ecstasy—are more readily available, more pure, and cheaper in the United States than anywhere else in the world.[6]

In fact, while there has been some decline in overall drug use in the United States in recent years, especially among teenagers (from 11.6 percent in 2002 to 9.3 percent in 2008), the long-term trend is not positive.[7] If the analysis is broadened back to 1992, when the rate of teen illicit-drug use was just 5.3 percent, it is clear that although use has declined somewhat since 2008, teen drug use in the United States is still substantially higher than it was in the early 1990s.[8]

About 20.1 million Americans, or 8 percent of the population over the age of twelve, currently use some illicit drug.[9] Nonetheless, American rates of drug use are not exceptionally high in comparison with those of other advanced capitalist countries. This is a much lower rate of drug usage than, for example, that registered in Great Britain and similar to that of Spain. By a considerable margin, the number in the United States—as in Europe—is highest among older teenagers and young adults in their early twenties, peaking at about 40 percent using within the past twelve months for high school seniors. Most Americans who do try drugs use them only a few times and then quit. The "typical" continuing American user is usually a marijuana smoker who generally ceases to use drugs at some point during his mid- to late twenties.[10]

What such general survey data do not capture well are the negative be-havior patterns that often accompany drug usage and translate into the high social costs of drug-related crime, health issues, early mortality, and productivity losses. These drug-related problems tend to be worse in the United States than they are in most other affluent nations because of the high numbers of U.S. consumers who are dependent on highly addictive and expensive drugs such as cocaine (in particular, crack), heroin, and methamphetamine, as opposed to marijuana. Marijuana is by far the most widely used illicit drug in the United States, but it accounts for only about 10 percent of the adverse social costs associated with illegal-drug use, in large part because marijuana is relatively cheap, and its "distribution and purchase engender relatively little crime or violence."[11]

The compulsive use of relatively expensive and highly addictive drugs in the United States is the legacy of the four major drug "epidemics" that have swept the country since the 1960s. The term "drug epidemic" is employed here to underscore the fact that drug use is a learned behavior, "transmitted from one person to another."[12] Indeed, the available evidence unequivo-cally indicates that friends or family members who use drugs, rather than aggressive drug "pushers" or dealers, are primarily responsible for initi-ating new users into their first drug experience. Rates of initiation in a given area increase sharply as new and highly contagious users of a drug introduce it to friends and peers, for whom drug use is then reinforced by its consequences, the way it changes how a user feels, thinks, or behaves.[13] Long-term heroin, cocaine, and crack addicts are not especially contagious, as they are often socially isolated from new users because they reveal the negative consequences of addiction.[14] In the subsequent stage of a drug epidemic, usually within a decade or less, "initiation declines rapidly as the susceptible population shrinks," either because there are fewer nonusers or because the drug's reputation is tarnished as a result of knowledge of the adverse consequences associated with prolonged use. In this third stage, the number of dependent users stabilizes and then gradually declines.[15]

The first modern drug epidemic in the United States involved heroin. It developed rapidly in the late 1960s, mainly in a few big cities and most heavily among poor black and Hispanic inner-city minority communities. American soldiers returning from Vietnam, where heroin was widely available, were apparently a contributing factor in the heroin epidemic as well. The annual number of new heroin users in the United States peaked in the early 1970s, dropped by some 50 percent by the end of the decade, and remained low until the mid-1990s, when a new heroin epidemic began. For many users, the first epidemic proved highly lethal; for those who survived, addiction was long-lasting, severely detrimental to their health, and an almost insurmountable impediment to productive employment.[16] Heroin use in affluent nations has stabilized since 2000.[17]

Powder cocaine was the source of America's second drug epidemic. This epidemic lasted longer and peaked more sharply than the prior heroin epidemic. Broadly spread across racial and class lines, cocaine initiation peaked in the early 1980s and then fell sharply, by almost 80 percent, at the end of the decade. "Dependence always lags behind initiation, and cocaine use became more prevalent in the mid-1980s as the pool of those who had experimented with the drug expanded. The number of dependent users peaked around 1988 and declined only moderately through the 1990s" and early 2000s.[18] The United States remains the world's largest consumer of cocaine in absolute terms, used at least once by 5.7 million people in 2007, although cocaine abuse has declined in recent years.[19]

The third epidemic involved the use of crack (a smokeable form of cocaine). While clearly connected to the powder cocaine epidemic, the crack epidemic was more concentrated among minorities in inner-city communities. The epidemic's starting point varied by city. In Los Angeles and New York, for example, it began around 1982; in Chicago, it began in 1988. Nonetheless, in every American city during the 1980s where the crack epidemic hit, initiation seems to have peaked within about two years and to have again left a population with a chronic and devastating problem of addiction.

The fourth important drug epidemic to strike the United States involved methamphetamine use. This epidemic gradually spread across the United States from west to east during the 1900s and by the early 2000s had affected two-thirds of the country, mainly in areas where cocaine use was less common. It had already peaked and stabilized on the West Coast by the time rapid spread began in the Mississippi and Ohio River valleys in the mid-1990s.[20] In 2007, the availability of methamphetamine appeared to be declining due to decreased traffic from Mexico. There was a shortage of the drug in 2007 and continuing through early 2008, according to the National Drug Intelligence Center (NDIC), evidenced by higher drug prices and lower purity levels. The same study noted decreasing prices and increasing purity in 2008, which NDIC claims occurred when availability of the drug began to stabilize or even rise as a result of increased domestic production.[21]

There have been other epidemics (for example, ecstasy use), but heroin, cocaine (including crack), and methamphetamine probably account for some 90 percent of the social costs associated with illegal-drug use in the United States since 1960. It is important to note that the steep declines in cocaine and heroin street prices in the United States since the late 1970s have not triggered new epidemics involving these drugs. "Initiation goes up when prices go down, but once a drug has acquired a bad reputation, it does not seem prone to a renewed explosion or contagious spread in use," even if prices stay low.[22] Information about the negative consequences of use of a particular drug is a significant protective factor against new explosions, at least for a number of years.

Twenty-Five Years of U.S. Drug-Control Policies: An American Balance Sheet

The U.S. government spends billions of dollars every year on drug control. The ONDCP federal drug control budget grew by $4.2 billion, or 39 percent, from 2002 to 2009.[23] The ONDCP's reported figures, however, do not reflect all costs associated with drug control—such as the expense of federal drug prosecutions and prisoner incarcerations—that most analysts believe should be included. Leaving such costs out in effect permits Washington to claim today that U.S. antidrug policies roughly balance supply-reduction policies (mostly enforcement) and demand-reduction policies (mostly prevention and treatment). Inclusion of federal government prosecutorial and prison-related costs does, however, increase the annual U.S. federal antidrug budget to approximately $17 billion. State and local governments in the United States spend even more, so the total costs of the U.S. war on drugs have probably exceeded $40 billion annually in recent years.[24] A study by Columbia University's National Center on Addiction and Substance Abuse, which factored in other costs such as health care, calculated a much higher cost for the year 2005.[25] "The center found that federal, state and local governments spent some $467.7 billion on substance abuse–related costs, including health care, justice systems and family court, child welfare and homelessness." The total spent by all levels of the U.S. government in waging the war on drugs over the last twenty-five years is rapidly approaching the astronomical sum of a trillion dollars.[26]

Which kinds of drug-control programs work, if any do? Which programs are the most cost-effective and which are the least? The following discussion reviews the principal elements or aspects of U.S. drug policies with primary emphasis on demand control within the United States. To establish the context for this evaluation of American demand-control strategies, however, it is necessary to begin the review with a brief overview and analysis of U.S. supply-side control programs, including eradication and interdiction.

Supply-Side Control and Interdiction Programs

Most U.S. antidrug programs focus on enforcing American drug laws, predominantly against drug dealers or traffickers. Interestingly, a similar emphasis is also commonly found in the antidrug campaigns of countries with less prohibitionist and punitive policy approaches to drug issues, including the Netherlands. While eradication and crop-substitution programs in source countries outside the U.S. territorial boundaries, especially in the Andean republics of Colombia, Peru, and Bolivia, receive the lion's share of media coverage, in fact they account for a relatively limited share of the U.S. federal government's drug budget—approximately $1 billion per year in 2006.[27] Interdiction efforts—the seizure of drug shipments and the arrest of drug "mules," or couriers, on the way into the United States—receive substantially more funds—$3.8 billion per year in 2009.[28]

In practice, neither source-country eradication and crop-substitution programs nor interdiction efforts have demonstrated over the past twenty-five years any real capacity to bring about more than transitory reductions in drug consumption in the United States (or Europe, for that matter).[29] Nor have they succeeded in reducing the drug supply. For example, efforts to eradicate coca production in Colombia, under a program called Plan Colombia, have been unequivocally unsuccessful. "State Department figures show that the U.S.-sponsored aerial drug eradication program, the cornerstone of Plan Colombia, is not discouraging Colombian peasants from growing coca, the plant used to produce cocaine. In fact, they are growing more coca than ever. Attempted coca production in Colombia—defined as eradicated plus uneradicated coca—has surged 36 percent since 2000."[30] Such policies concentrate on disrupting the initial phases of the production and distribution chains, during which illicit drugs are still relatively cheap and easily replaced because there are plenty of land, labor, and alternative routes available to allow for trafficker adaptations to state-directed antidrug policies and tactics. In effect, such disruptions cause marginal increases in the costs of cultivation, refining, and smuggling of illicit drugs, but do not make drug production and trafficking sufficiently less profitable to discourage the transnational criminal organizations involved in it.[31]

Law Enforcement and Incarceration

After over forty years of the war on drugs, the United States now incarcerates its citizens at a rate that is nearly five times the world average. Prior to the war on drugs, the American incarceration rate was similar to that of other countries.[32] The bulk of all U.S. drug-control resources go into the enforcement of America's prohibitionist drug laws. Between 1980 and 1990, dependent drug use and violent drug-marketing and -trafficking organizations expanded rapidly while the number of drug-related incarcerations rose by 210,000.[33] Between 1990 and 2000, drug-related problems began to ease, but drug imprisonments increased by another 200,000. Since 2000, drug arrests and incarcerations have continued to rise in the United States despite further declines in rates of drug use, drug addiction, and drug-related violent crime. The total U.S. prison population currently stands at some 2.3 million inmates, with approximately one quarter of these jailed for some sort of drug-related (mostly nonviolent) offenses.[34] This is a 1100 percent increase from the 40,000 people incarcerated for a drug offense in 1980.[35]

The basic justification for aggressive punishment of drug-related crimes is that high rates of incarceration will reduce drug use and associated problems. The theory is that tough enforcement raises the risks of drug trafficking and, thus, will lead some traffickers to drop out of the business and prompt the remainder to demand higher prices for taking higher risks. In this logic, the price of illicit drugs should go up accordingly.[36] In fact, however, the general price trends since 1980 have gone in the opposite direction.[37] Of course, it is possible that prices might have fallen even further had it not been for the massive expansion in U.S. drug-law enforcement, as many U.S. drug officials have tended to argue. Nonetheless, even granting this counterfactual hypothesis, in light of the huge costs involved in incarcerating so many Americans for drug-related nonviolent crimes (between U.S.$30,000 and $40,000 per inmate per year, depending on the state where they are imprisoned), it is abundantly clear to most analysts that expanded incarceration has not been a cost-effective policy for controlling drug use in the United States.

Moreover, there is absolutely no clear evidence to support the idea that tougher enforcement has made illicit drugs harder for Americans to obtain. According to the 2008 Monitoring the Future survey, conducted by the University of Michigan, 83 percent of high school seniors believed marijuana was not difficult to obtain, and 42 percent of high school seniors believed cocaine would not be hard to obtain. The perceived availability of most drugs has declined overall in the past thirty-nine years, except for cocaine and heroin, which are moderately higher in perceived availability than they were in 1975.[38] Depending on the set of years selected for trend analysis, one could get a completely different picture of how successful the war on drugs has been in reducing the availability of drugs to America's youth.

Why then, in the face of overwhelming evidence that heavy emphasis on law enforcement, especially imprisonment of nonviolent drug offenders, does not work well and is not cost-effective have U.S. federal government authorities consistently pursued such a policy strategy? Any adequate explanation of this policy puzzle requires the analyst to delve into the "intermestic" dynamics of drug policymaking in the contemporary United States. Summarized briefly, at least three levels of explanation inevitably come into play. First, it is obvious that there is a high degree of "path dependency" present in U.S. drug policy; that is, decisions made in the past clearly shape present policy and make modifications or deviations from the current prohibitionist and punitive strategy and tactics difficult, if not impossible, in American governmental decision-making circles. While quite possibly valid, the path-dependency explanation nonetheless in effect begs the questions of why the U.S. government got started down this particular path in the first place and why it is so hard to change now, in the face of considerable empirical evidence that current policy is not succeeding in the goal of preventing or substantially reducing drug use and abuse in American society. A first approximation to a more comprehensive explanation involves understanding the "puritan" and religious backdrop to American rejection of drug use. The United States remains a highly religious society. All Protestant sects, especially the born-again Christian evangelical groups, the Catholics, the Jews, and the Muslims, unanimously condemn and reject drug use. Their moral condemnation of drugs weighs heavily against changes away from the currently dominant policy approach rooted in prohibition and punishment.

Second, the past almost five decades of cyclical drug epidemics have strongly reinforced middle America's religiously based rejection of drugs. Middle-class voting patterns in American politics have continually reflected and reinforced rigidly prohibitionist attitudes and policy preferences among the majority of U.S. voters. In short, middle-class parents in the United States fear that their children will be caught up in the next U.S. drug epidemic and so they use their vote to support prohibitionist policies in the hope that their families can be insulated from such dangers.

Third and finally, the institutional-electoral arrangements in the American political system, in which the entirety of the U.S. House of Representatives (435 members) must stand for election (or reelection) every two years, makes experimentation with alternatives to current prohibitionist and punitive policies all but impossible. Any member of Congress who publicly calls for nonpunitive policies is virtually guaranteed to lose the next election, thereby truncating any real possibility of obtaining and incorporating policy feedback into the congressional policy-making process. The fact that one-third of the U.S. Senate (100 members, each serving a six-year term) must stand for reelection is similarly, although slightly less, limiting. The end result is that drug-policy innovation at the federal or national level in the United States is virtually frozen in place and largely impervious to empirically based evaluations that conclude that current policies are not working.

In contrast, drug policy at the state level of government in the United States is presently far more inclined toward innovation. This is due largely to the fact that the states, rather than the federal government, must bear most of the administrative burdens and costs of executing current federal antidrug laws, such as imprisonment. The upshot is that states like California, New York, and Florida have begun to experiment with harm-reduction rather than more punitive policies, especially with regard to youthful and nonviolent offenders. The relatively new youth drug courts that have emerged in several states since 2000 or so and California's Proposition 36 (imposing treatment rather than jail time for nonviolent drug crimes) seem to promise drug-policy reform at the state rather than the national level in coming years. Some of these newer state programs are discussed briefly in the following section.

Prevention and Education

RAND Corporation studies of prevention programs in the United States have found that these programs are at least twelve times more cost-effective per dollar spent than supply-side or interdiction programs in reducing drug use among American primary and secondary school students. Despite that positive finding, however, it is nonetheless true that the most widely used prevention programs in American schools (e.g., the DARE program) have never been proven in empirical evaluations to have significant, long-term impacts on lowering drug use among American youth. Indeed, even the most sophisticated model prevention programs appear to produce only modest and largely temporary reductions in drug use among adolescents who tend to dissipate by the end of secondary school or soon after high school graduation.

Given that most such school-based prevention programs involve only some thirty or so contact hours with students, it is not surprising that they are relatively ineffective in countering the pro–drug use effects of ongoing socialization with relatives, friends, and peers, movies, and television that are known to stimulate initiation. Even when the inherent limitations of such programs are recognized, however, the budgetary costs per pupil involved in classroom prevention programs are so reduced that they still appear to be modestly cost-effective. A 2002 study by the RAND Corporation found that the best estimate of social costs saved per participant in a school-based prevention program was $840, greatly exceeding the program cost of $150 per participant.[39]

To improve the overall effectiveness of school-based prevention programs, many experts argue that it is necessary that they begin very early in primary school and continue throughout secondary school, that they be dynamic and interactive rather than simply preachy and passive, and that the number of contact hours be increased substantially. In addition, many experts maintain that such programs should be extended beyond high school as continuing public education programs for young adults.

Such beyond-school recommendations in favor of continuing drug-prevention education notwithstanding, in practice, media-centered antidrug campaigns have never been shown through empirical research to have any effect on American patterns of drug use. Data-based assessments of mass media campaigns against drug use are, of course, inherently difficult and problematic, because it is virtually impossible to isolate a control group unaffected by other factors against which the impacts of such campaigns might be measured accurately. Even so, the evaluations of mass media campaigns that have been done (e.g., the Westat and the Annenberg School of Communications studies of the U.S. federal government's expensive and widely viewed antidrug television campaign) indicate that such advertising efforts have no discernable effects whatsoever on drug use in America.[40] According to Westat, "There is little evidence of direct favorable Campaign effects on youth, either for the Marijuana and Early Intervention Initiatives, or for the Campaign as a whole."[41]

In light of what is known about past cycles of drug epidemics in the United States, especially with regard to the dynamics of initiation, stabilization, and gradual decline in use, there is little question that information about the negative consequences of drug abuse is of fundamental importance to effective reduction of drug use in American society. Armed with that knowledge and awareness, it would seem that permanent, widely distributed, public information campaigns (not the expensive, high-profile, thirty-second TV spot advertisements apparently preferred by U.S. authorities) might be more effective over time. Reaching diverse ethnic, racial, age, and class groupings with appropriate antidrug messages tailored to communicate accurate, factual information to specific segments of the American population (in a language and vocabulary they will understand and relate to) promises, at the very least, to shorten the time frame of future drug-epidemic cycles in the United States (and probably in other countries too). Given that the learning curve of each succeeding generation (or subgeneration) of new drug users poses different and complex problems of effective communication, antidrug campaigns must not only be permanent and ongoing, but they must also be constantly updated and modified to deal with new drugs and patterns of youth drug use.

Treatment and Rehabilitation

Treatment programs have been subjected to extensive, data-based evaluations since at least the 1990s in the United States. In 2008, for example, some 2.3 million American drug users underwent treatment at a specialty facility (hospital inpatient, drug or alcohol rehabilitation, or mental health center).[42] Federal government expenditures on such treatment programs totaled $2.4 billion, and the fifty state-level governments spent at least as much for an overall treatment budget of almost $6 billion. American heroin addicts usually receive methadone (a synthetic heroin substitute). All other drug users in treatment programs in the United States get some form of counseling. The majority of drug users in such programs quit the program before finishing treatment. Among the minority who do complete their treatment programs, more than half relapse into drug usage within five years.

Nonetheless, drug-treatment programs are consistently evaluated as cost-effective because most who enter such programs, especially for heroin or cocaine use, are serious criminal offenders. At least while they are enrolled in treatment, their rates of drug use tend to decline, along with their proclivity to engage in criminal activities. These crime-reduction benefits of treatment programs help the communities in which they are located as well as the patients themselves.[43]

In view of the positive, cost-effective results of treatment programs, it is confounding to observe that there is only limited availability of treatment programs in the United States. In 2008, an estimated 7.6 million persons had needed treatment for an illicit-drug use problem within the past year. Of these, 1.2 million received treatment at a specialty treatment facility. Therefore, 6.4 million persons needed treatment but did not receive it. Note that of the 6.4 million, only 400,000 perceived a need for treatment, and only 25 percent (99,000) of those who perceived a need for treatment made an effort to obtain it. In cases where those who made an effort to get treatment did not actually get it, the most often reported reasons were no health coverage and could not afford the cost (37.4 percent) and not ready to stop using (29.3 percent).[44]

Even more perplexing and worrisome, between 2002 and 2009, the federal budget for drug control grew by 39 percent (to $4.2 billion), but 90 percent of this amount was used for supply-reduction programs, while only 10 percent was allocated to demand reduction. According to John Carnevale, "the ONDCP implemented a federal drug control budget that was at odds with its goal of reducing drug use," a contradiction which he calls "the budget-policy mismatch."[45] The federal budget for drug control continues to grow, while the proportion of spending for demand reduction continues to shrink, from 44.9 percent of FY 2002 spending to 35.1 percent of FY 2009 spending. Interdiction expenditures alone increased the most, to the tune of $1.9 billion (a 100.5 percent increase since 2002) and composed 25 percent of the total federal drug budget for FY 2009.[46] The drug budget continues to shift to supply-side strategies, despite evidence that such programs have little promise in reducing drug consumption in the United States.[47]

Drug treatment as an alternative to incarceration has become a standard response, more talked about than actually implemented. Drug courts that use judges to persuade and legally compel drug offenders to enter and remain in treatment programs offer some promise of greater compliance, but they offer only modest and incremental solutions because the screening criteria for entering such programs are restrictive and often exclude violent and repeat offenders. Proposition 36 in California changed state law so that most of those arrested on drug-possession charges (not trafficking) for the first or second time would not be incarcerated (but rather sent to treatment). It has achieved some success, particularly in reducing the number of drug offenders sent to jail without a parallel rise in crime rates.

Such programs deal only with the least serious, nonviolent offenders and, thus, address only a limited spectrum of drug-related crimes. Furthermore, the Proposition 36 program may need reform, based on a study conducted by UCLA that found that more than a quarter of those sentenced never show up for treatment, and almost half never complete the required rehabilitation.[48]

Some analysts in the United States presently advocate shorter sentences and the imposition of what has been termed "coerced abstinence" from drugs via drug testing imposed and monitored by the courts once drug offenders are released from prison on parole. Immediate sanctions, including revocation of conditional-release status (and thus, incarceration or reincarceration), would result whenever a probationer or parolee tested positive in such programs.[49] However, if these programs were expanded significantly, it might be both difficult and expensive to administer and to monitor.

In conclusion, former president Richard Nixon (1969–1974), who began the war on drugs, said that demand was the driver of the drug industry and "when drug traffic in narcotics is no longer profitable, the traffic will cease."[50] Over 50 percent of the federal drug-control budget was dedicated to treatment and prevention programs in both 1970 and 1975. This basic philosophy was discarded somewhere along the way. Beginning in the 1980s, when Ronald Reagan took office, the nation's drug-control policy prioritized law enforcement above all else, and in 1985, Reagan's antidrug budget dedicated just 28 percent to prevention and treatment.[51]

Experts and analysts in the field tend to believe that the war on drugs has been grossly ineffective to date, and at the end of 2008, approximately 75 percent of Americans believed that the war on drugs was "failing."[52] Furthermore, the budget numbers are heavily tilted toward enforcement and supply-side initiatives. According to John Carnevale, "There was a complete mismatch [in the George W. Bush administration] between the rhetoric of the strategy, which emphasized treatment, and the budget. The long-run answer is for the U.S. to curb its demand or appetite for illicit drugs."[53]

The Obama administration, signaling a departure from the previous administration, said that it will shift drug policy toward a more treatment-based approach, with its selection of Seattle police chief R. Gil Kerlikowske as its new "drug czar" (in office May 7, 2009–March 7, 2014). Kerlikowske believes that reducing the drug trade is "largely dependent on our ability to reduce demand for them—and that starts with our youth."[54] "The choice of drug czar and the emphasis on alternative drug courts, announced by Vice President Biden, signal a sharp departure from Bush administration policies, gravitating away from cutting the supply of illicit drugs from foreign countries and toward curbing drug use in communities across the United States."[55]

In recent years, many policymakers and members of the public are increasingly recognizing the value of treatment over incarceration as an appropriate response to substance abuse.[56] Others are moving toward a less criminal justice–based approach as well, evident in the recent decriminalization of drugs in countries such as Mexico and Portugal. Given the multitude of issues the current administration is dealing with, it is unclear that America will attempt to aggressively tackle the illicit-drug trade in the near future. However, as Ethan Nadelmann of the Drug Policy Alliance has said, "The analogy we have is this is like turning around an ocean liner. What's important is the damn thing is beginning to turn."[57]

The current U.S. government drug policy priorities are similar to those that prevailed during the Reagan administration (1981–1989), when the key strategy was to limit the drug supply. No matter how the FY 2008 federal drug budget is interpreted, Gil Kerlikowske continued to emphasize interdiction and international programs to control supply and deal with the nation's drug problems. Nonetheless, no federal drug budget, from either party, can afford to ignore the overwhelming body of research that shows that only a balanced approach between supply- and demand-reduction programs will have any real effect on America's drug consumption patterns and the attendant societal costs.

Notes

1. This chapter is a revised and updated version of a work published originally in Spanish. See Bruce M. Bagley, "Políticas de control de drogas ilícitas en Estados Unidos: ¿Qué funciona y qué no funciona?" in *La guerra contra las drogas en el mundo andino: Hacia un cambio de paradigma*, ed. Juan Gabriel Tokatlian (Buenos Aires: Libros de Zorzal, 2009), 283–296.

2. The White House, *National Drug Control Strategy 2006* (Washington, D.C.: Office of National Drug Control Policy [ONDCP], 2006), 19, https://www.ncjrs.gov/pdffiles1/ondcp/212940.pdf.

3. Elaine Shannon, "The War on Drugs: A Losing Battle," *Time*, December 3, 1990, http://content.time.com/time/magazine/article/0,9171,971813,00.html.

4. The White House, *National Drug Control Strategy 2009* (Washington, D.C.: ONDCP, 2009), http://www.whitehouse.gov/sites/default/files/ondcp/policy-and-research/2009 ndcs.pdf.

5. Frank Shanty and Patit Paban Mishra, "Introduction," in *Organized Crime: From Trafficking to Terrorism*, ed. Frank Shanty and Patit Paban Mishra (Santa Barbara, Calif.: ABC-CLIO, 2005), xvii.

6. Nicholas D. Kristof, "Drugs Won the War," *New York Times*, June 13, 2009.

7. U.S. Department of Health and Human Services, *National Survey on Drug Use and Health 2008* (Rockville, Md.: SAMHSA, 2009), 1.

8. U.S. Department of Health and Human Services, *National Household Survey on Drug Abuse 2001* (Rockville, Md.: SAMHSA); idem, *National Survey on Drug Use and Health 2008* (Rockville, Md.: SAMHSA, 2002).

9. Data are for illicit-drug usage in the month prior to the survey interview, from page 15, U.S. Department of Health and Human Services, *National Household Survey on Drug Abuse 2008*. Estimates of illicit-drug usage include the following categories of drugs: marijuana, cocaine, heroin, hallucinogens, and inhalants, and the nonmedical use of prescription-type pain relievers, tranquilizers, stimulants, and sedatives. The sampled population does not include the homeless (unless they were in a shelter), active-duty military personnel, or residents of institutional group quarters (correctional facilities, nursing homes, mental institutions, and long-term-care hospitals) and therefore may underestimate the prevalence of illicit-drug usage in the United States.

10. Jonathan P. Caulkins and Peter Reuter, "Reorienting U.S. Drug Policy," *Issues in Science and Technology Online* 23, no. 1 (2006), http://www.issues.org/23.1/caulkins.html.

11. Ibid.

12. Ibid.

13. Ibid.; Kathleen M. Carroll, *A Cognitive-Behavioral Approach: Treating Cocaine Addiction,* Therapy Manuals for Drug Abuse: Manual 1 (Washington, D.C.: National Institute on Drug Abuse, 1998), http://archives.drugabuse.gov/TXManuals/CBT/CBT1.html.

14. Caulkins and Reuter, "Reorienting U.S. Drug Policy," 79.

15. Ibid.

16. Ibid.

17. Peter Reuter, "Ten Years after the United Nations General Assembly Special Session (UNGASS): Assessing Drug Problems, Policies and Reform Proposals," *Addiction* 104, no. 4 (2009): 510–517.

18. Caulkins and Reuter, "Reorienting U.S. Drug Policy"; Jonathan P. Caulkins, Peter Reuter, Martin Y. Iguchi, and James Chiesa, *How Goes the "War on Drugs"?: An Assessment of U.S. Drug Problems and Policy* (Santa Monica, Calif.: RAND, 2005).

19. UNODC, *World Drug Report, 2008* (New York, 2009).

20. Caulkins and Reuter, "Reorienting U.S. Drug Policy."

21. U.S. Department of Justice, *National Drug Threat Assessment 2009* (Johnstown, Penn.: National Drug Intelligence Center [NDIC], 2008).

22. Caulkins and Reuter, "Reorienting U.S. Drug Policy," 3.

23. John Carnevale, "The Continued Standstill in Reducing Illicit Drug Use," policy brief (Gaithersburg, Md.: Carnevale Associates, 2009), http://www.carnevaleassociates.com/drug_policy_budget_mismatch-_2009.pdf.

24. Caulkins and Reuter, "Reorienting U.S. Drug Policy."

25. "Report: Government Not Spending Much on Drug Prevention," CNN, May 28, 2009, http://www.cnn.com/2009/HEALTH/05/28/addiction.costs/.

26. Kristof, "Drugs Won the War."

27. Caulkins and Reuter, "Reorienting U.S. Drug Policy."

28. The White House, *National Drug Control Strategy: FY 2009 Budget Summary* (2008), 11, http://www.whitehouse.gov/sites/default/files/ondcp/policy-and-research/fy09budget_0.pdf.

29. Caulkins and Reuter, "Reorienting U.S. Drug Policy."

30. Adam Isacson and John Myers, "Plan Colombia's Drug Eradication Program Misses the Mark," Americas Program, International Relations Center (IRC), July 18, 2005, http://archive.today/rbbSH.

31. Ibid.

32. Kristof, "Drugs Won the War."

33. Caulkins and Reuter, "Reorienting U.S. Drug Policy."

34. Adam Liptak, "Inmate Count in U.S. Dwarfs Other Nations," *New York Times,* April 23, 2008; Peter Lupsha, "Transnational Narco-Corruption and Narco Investment: A Focus on Mexico," *Transnational Organized Crime Journal* 1, no. 1 (1995): 84–101.

35. Mark Mauer, *The Changing Racial Dynamics of the War on Drugs* (Washington, D.C.: The Sentencing Project, 2009), http://www.sentencingproject.org/doc/dp_raceanddrugs.pdf.

36. Caulkins and Reuter, "Reorienting U.S. Drug Policy."

37. Ibid.; Caulkins et al., *How Goes the "War on Drugs"?*

38. Lloyd Johnston, Patrick O'Malley, Jerald Bachman, and John Schulenberg, *Monitor-*

ing the Future: National Results on Adolescent Drug Use. Overview of Key Findings, 2008, NIH Publication no. 09-7401 (Bethesda, Md.: National Institute on Drug Abuse, 2009), 73.

39. Jonathan P. Caulkins, Rosalie Liccardo Pacula, Susan M. Paddock, and James Chiesa, *School-Based Drug Prevention: What Kind of Drug Use Does It Prevent?* (Santa Monica, Calif.: RAND, 2002), 32.

40. Caulkins and Reuter, "Reorienting U.S. Drug Policy."

41. Robert Orwin et al., *Evaluation of the National Youth Anti-Drug Media Campaign: 2004 Report of Findings* (Rockville, Md.: Westat, 2006), vii, http://archives.drugabuse.gov/initiatives/westat/NSPY2004Report/Vol1/Report.pdf.

42. U.S. Department of Health and Human Services, *National Survey on Drug Use, 2008*. In 2011, the statistics had not changed.

43. Caulkins and Reuter, "Reorienting U.S. Drug Policy."

44. U.S. Department of Health and Human Services, *National Survey on Drug Use, 2008* 85–86, http://books.google.com.mx/books?id=TOjeaoMoWG4C&pg=PA85&lpg=PA85&dq=29.3+not+ready+to+stop+drug+use&source=bl&ots=ajfA2WO7W2&sig=mlAnpkNTELdbLQdaBxacJdFTB9w&hl=en&sa=X&ei=F7dCVKKZMqfuiALWhICICg&ved=0CBsQ6AEwAA#v=onepage&q=29.3%20not%20ready%20to%20stop%20drug%20use&f=false. For the percentage who did not have health coverage, see http://www.justicepolicy.org/images/upload/08_01_rep_drugtx_ac-ps.pdf.

45. Http://www.carnevaleassociates.com/drug-policy-budget-missmatch.

46. Carnevale, "The Continued Standstill."

47. Caulkins and Reuter, "Reorienting U.S. Drug Policy."

48. Associated Press, "UCLA Study: Calif. Drug Treatment Program Is Flawed," *Contra Costa Times*, April 2, 2007, http://www.contracostatimes.com/search/ci_5575319.

49. Mark A. R. Kleiman, "Coerced Abstinence: A Neo-Paternalist Drug Policy Initiative," in *The New Paternalism: Supervisory Approaches to Poverty*, ed. Lawrence Mead (Washington, D.C.: Brookings Institution Press, 1997).

50. Alfonso Cuéllar, "America's Forgotten War," *Washington Post*, October 29, 2008.

51. "Does Treatment Work?" *PBS Frontline*, Drug Wars, http://www.pbs.org/wgbh/pages/frontline/shows/drugs/buyers/doitwork.html.

52. Inter-American Dialogue, "Public Views Clash with U.S. Policy on Cuba, Immigration, and Drugs," Zogby/Inter-American Dialogue Survey, October 2, 2008, http://www.thedialogue.org/zogbyinteramericandialoguesurveyseptember2008.

53. Carrie Johnson and Amy Goldstein, "Choice of Drug Czar Indicates Focus on Treatment, Not Jail," *Washington Post*, March 12, 2009.

54. Brian Montopoli, "Biden Introduces Drug Czar Nominee," *CBS News*, March 11, 2009, http://www.cbsnews.com/blogs/2009/03/11/politics/politicalhotsheet/entry4859510.shtml.

55. Johnson and Goldstein, "Choice of Drug Czar."

56. Cuéllar, "America's Forgotten War."

57. Gary Fields, "White House Czar Calls for End to 'War on Drugs,'" *Wall Street Journal*, May 14, 2009, http://online.wsj.com/article/SB124225891527617397.html.

II

DRUG TRAFFICKING AND
ORGANIZED CRIME

Country and Regional Analyses

7

Colombia and Its Wars against Drug Trafficking, 1970–2010

ELVIRA MARÍA RESTREPO

Colombia did not have a state policy against drug trafficking until the first administration of Álvaro Uribe (2002–2006).[1] The country witnessed important victories against drug traffickers as a result of Plan Colombia (PC), which was instituted during the Andrés Pastrana (1998–2002) and Bill Clinton (1993–2001) administrations. Despite these achievements, the production of illicit drugs has not been reduced, nor has their price been altered in consuming countries around the world.[2] However, such victories constitute an important change in Colombia, particularly with regard to its security and institutionality. In this respect, Colombia's wars against drug trafficking provide important lessons for other states that are struggling with the phenomenon, such as Mexico.

This chapter seeks to analyze the judicial, legal, and institutional aspects of the different "wars" against drug trafficking in Colombia beginning in the 1970s. The first section discusses the period between 1970 and 2000, which culminates with the failure of the Caguan peace negotiations with the Revolutionary Armed Forces of Colombia (Fuerzas Armadas Revolucionarias de Colombia, or FARC).[3] This period is characterized by the confluence of politics that oscillated between repressive solutions and negotiations on behalf of the different administrations. These types of fluctuations are common to governments characterized by weak institutions and limited state capacity and are exacerbated by assassinations and negotiations between the state and the drug cartels.

The second section briefly analyzes the complexity of the violence in Colombia, where drug trafficking has served as a catalyst for the prolonged armed conflict, and aims to highlight some important characteristics of the state. The final section examines the period between 2002 and the end of the Álvaro Uribe administration (2010). This section provides a detailed examination of PC, the Democratic Security Policy (Política de Seguridad Democrática, PSD), and the demobilization of the paramilitaries in relation to the fight against drug trafficking.

This chapter begins with the assumption that the reforms that occurred in Colombia with the 1991 Constitution—the restructuring of the armed forces during the Pastrana administration and of the PSD and PC during the first and second Uribe administrations—were crucial to strengthening Colombia's institutions. As a result of these reforms and policies, Colombia experienced the return of the rule of law. Moreover, it was also possible to dramatically reduce the insecurity and violence that characterized the country in the 1980s and 1990s. Paradoxically, Colombia's gains in security and the reduction of violence have directly or indirectly contributed to the rise of violence in most of the rest of the region, which has made drug trafficking even harder to control.

Between Carrots and Sticks: A Colombian Solution to Drug Trafficking (1970–2000)

This section provides a historical analysis of the institutional, legal, and judicial aspects that impacted drug trafficking during this period. For organizational purposes, this section will be divided into four stages. The first stage begins in the 1970s, when Colombia began to witness the introduction of marijuana on the Atlantic coast. At this stage, it is safe to say, drug trafficking was seen as a marginal and localized issue, not as a national security problem. As a result, it was treated as a criminal issue to be dealt with by the police and the judiciary. At the time, there was no special criminal statute against drug trafficking; not until 1986 did Colombia adopt Law 30 of 1986, based on the 1961 United Nations Single Convention on Narcotic Drugs.

The local nature of the drug problem was such that until the end of the 1980s, the United States did not focus on the faults and challenges of the Extradition Treaty, which Colombia and the United States finally signed in 1979,[4] after two years of negotiations.[5] During this time, it was clear that the Colombian drug traffickers did not have enough power to react to the implementation of the Extradition Treaty. However, this changed over time, as illustrated by their famous slogan: "Preferimos una tumba en Colombia que una cárcel en los Estados Unidos" (We prefer a burial in Colombia to a prison in the United States).

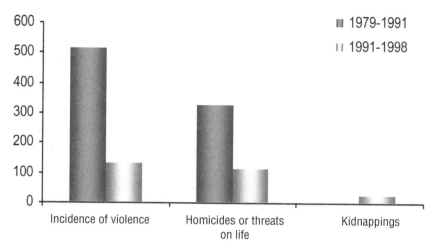

Figure 7.1. Violence against judges, 1979–1998. The figures for 1979–1991 include unaggregated data on violence against judges and lawyers. Statistics regarding the kidnapping of judges during this period do not exist (Elvira María Restrepo, *The Colombian Criminal Justice in Crisis: Fear and Distrust* [New York: Palgrave Macmillan, 2003]).

The period between 1980 and 1988 constitutes the second stage and can be characterized as a period dominated by erratic state policies that fluctuated between repression and negotiation. This period marks the beginning of the alliance between drug traffickers and paramilitaries, which initially materialized with the creation of Death to Kidnappers (Muerte a Secuestradores, MAS) in 1981.[6] These two organizations cooperated in criminal activities after their fortuitous alliance through MAS, a short-lived association designed by the Ochoa brothers (members of the Medellín cartel) in order to combat the kidnapping by the FARC of their cousin Marta Ochoa.

During this stage, drug traffickers established direct linkages to and involvement with the political and judicial systems. In the political realm, they penetrated parts of the state, representing a stark contrast to the guerrillas in that the Colombian drug traffickers always wanted to be part of the state, not to defeat it. In regard to the judicial realm, judges and clerks witnessed levels of violence and intimidation that had never been seen in the nation's history.[7] Statistics reveal that between 1979 and 1991, more than 100 judges were assassinated, including eleven of the twelve magistrates of the Supreme Court of Justice in the infamous Palace of Justice siege (toma del Palacio de Justicia) by the M-19 guerrillas in alliance with the Medellín cartel in November 1985 (see figure 7.1).[8]

Additional data from a representative survey taken in 1997 reveal that 70 percent of all judges were affected by the homicide of a relative or friend between 1992 and 1997, compared to 60 percent of the population in violent zones and 40 percent of the general population.[9] The judicial system at all levels was paralyzed, and the Extradition Treaty between Colombia and the United States was declared unconstitutional by the Supreme Court of Justice. The weakness of the state was such that the ministers of defense and justice, General Álvaro Camacho Leiva and Justice Felio Andrade, publicly suggested that judges arm themselves.[10]

The paralysis and inaction of the judiciary during this stage is evident. During this period, it could not convict a single drug trafficker. This generated great distrust of the judicial system, which had had a certain degree of legitimacy during the 1970s.

This second stage is also when the first assassinations of judges and high-ranking officers occurred. One of the most symbolic was that of the acting minister of justice, Rodrigo Lara Bonilla, in 1984. As a response to each such assassination, the government ordered the enactment of siege laws, using extradition or the threat of extradition to restore its weakened authority. In addition, several negotiations (some "secret") occurred between politicians and drug traffickers during this period. This second stage also witnessed the consolidation of both the Medellín and the Cali cartels.

The third stage occurred between 1988 and 1991 and is characterized by the proliferation of "narco-terrorism." During this short period, Colombia witnessed increased assassinations of high-ranking public figures, the most scandalous being that of presidential candidate Luis Carlos Galán in 1989 and the infamous Rochela massacre of a group of judicial officials investigating a paramilitary group.[11] At this stage, the alliance between right-wing paramilitaries and drug traffickers was consolidated. The judicial system, however, remained paralyzed, and judges were prone to intimidation.

In response to the assassinations of important individuals and increases in terrorist attacks against institutions and public places, President Virgilio Barco (1986–1990) reestablished extraditions to the United States by decree.[12] In contrast, the Supreme Court, for the second time, declared the Extradition Treaty between the United States and Colombia unconstitutional.

In Colombia, wide sectors of the public perceived extradition as being imposed by the United States. Some saw it as a threat to the country's sovereignty, and others, such as drug traffickers, rejected it, appealing to a sort of nationalism. During this period, approximately twenty Colombian drug traffickers were extradited to the United States.

In the political realm, neither the Colombian Congress nor the political parties wanted to approve a referendum to discuss the subject of extradition. Moreover, Congress and the political parties did not want to discuss the reforms proposed by President Barco; these reforms were not instituted until the following administration, when the Asamblea Nacional Constituyente enacted the 1991 Constitution.[13] President Barco, therefore, felt compelled to adopt repressive measures granting the police greater power to arrest, to raid, and to suspend habeas corpus.[14] The few extraditions that occurred during the Barco administration increased the levels of violence during an already violent period, unleashing, for the first time ever, a wave of terrorist attacks against civilians and state institutions.

The fourth stage analyzed in this chapter dates from 1991 to 2000 and comprises the administrations of César Gaviria, Ernesto Samper, and the first two years of Andrés Pastrana's term. This period can be characterized by a mixture of "sticks and carrots" offered to the drug traffickers. Some of the sticks were the creation of the Attorney General's Office (Fiscalía General de la Nación), in charge of criminal investigations,[15] and its special unit to combat money laundering (Decreto 2790/1990); the existence of Faceless Justice (Justicia sin Rostro) from 1991 to 1999;[16] the enactment of the law of Extinción de Dominio (expiration of ownership) (Law 333 of 1996) to recover for the state the licit and illicit goods of drug traffickers;[17] and the assassination of Pablo Escobar by the Bloque Búsqueda in a cooperative operation by Colombian forces,[18] the U.S. Drug Enforcement Administration (DEA), and People persecuted by Pablo Escobar (Perseguidos por Pablo Escobar, PEPE).[19] Such efforts ultimately led to the destruction of the Medellín cartel. During this period, Colombia also witnessed the implementation of other stick strategies, such as the air bridge denial strategy. This strategy sought to neutralize flights and boats between the producer countries of coca leaves (Bolivia and Peru) and the processors (Colombia) in order to halt the transport of illegal drugs between the Andean countries.

Some of these methods resulted in successes in the fight against drug trafficking. Despite its arbitrary character and its relative inefficiency in the adjudication of cases, the Justicia sin Rostro initiative resulted in decreases in deaths and less intimidation of judges.[20] In addition, it is quite possible that this initiative helped decrease judicial corruption in a system that was virtually paralyzed during the previous decade.[21] Without a doubt, Justicia sin Rostro empowered attorneys to investigate and prosecute powerful drug traffickers and organized crime. At the same time, the politics of the air bridge denial strategy,[22] the concrete results of which are difficult to measure, had a significant impact on the reduction of coca cultivation in Peru and Bolivia. Nevertheless, these partial victories resulted in what scholars and policy experts refer to as the "balloon" effect.[23] Bruce M. Bagley argues that in the case of Colombia the collapse of the Cali and Medellín cartels in the 1990s created a vacuum filled by the creation of smaller "*cartelitos.*"

In contrast, there are two carrots from this fourth period: first, the constitutional prohibition of extradition of Colombian nationals (as noted earlier, this is historically the only instrument feared by Colombian drug bosses); second, the Policy of Compliance with the System of Justice (Política de Sometimiento a la Justicia, PSJ), a form of American-style plea bargaining that led to the surrender of the feared leaders of the Medellín cartel,[24] Pablo Escobar and the Ochoa brothers. Despite the weaknesses of the PSJ, in particular, the luxurious reclusive conditions Escobar enjoyed in his club-style jail, La Catedral, it prompted the beginning of the end of the Medellín cartel. The assassination of Pablo Escobar and his main allies by the Bloque de Búsqueda, the DEA, and the obscure collaboration of the PEPEs completed the annihilation of the cartel. The controversial participation of the PEPEs illustrates the decisive support that existed regarding the destruction of the Medellín cartel.[25]

The results of the fight against drug trafficking in the fourth stage are ambiguous, particularly regarding extradition, which was prohibited between 1991 and 1997 and eventually restored at the end of this phase. This ambivalence was exploited by those subject to extradition and influenced the writing of the controversial Code of Penal Procedure of 1997 (Código de Procedimiento Penal, CPP). The CPP was designed in consultation with lawyers of the Cali cartel, who managed to ensure that the extradition of the cartel's members was almost impossible. Additionally, the Ernesto Samper (1994–1998) administration, tainted by allegations of receiving campaign money from the Cali cartel, was forced to persecute and prosecute cartel members in order to govern the country. As a result, the Bloque de Búsqueda was revived, and such efforts eventually led to the capture of the Rodríguez Orejuela brothers and other members of the Cali cartel.[26]

The Cali cartel was perceived as less violent than the Medellín cartel, as many of its members participated in corrupt practices rather than using violent tactics. As noted previously, lawyers of the Cali cartel influenced the drafting of the CPP in 1997, which also made minimal prison sentences (e.g., six to seven years for the Rodríguez Orejuela brothers) possible in Colombia. Contrary to expectations, the role of the Colombian justice system was more relevant in the initial weakening of the Medellín than the Cali cartel, despite the fact that the Medellín cartel paralyzed the justice system in the 1980s.

The demise of the major cartels in Colombia generated immense benefits for the country. First, Colombia experienced a general reduction of violence, mainly in numbers of homicides and other violent crimes. Second, although the magnitude is difficult to measure, the reduction of the cartels' ability to corrupt the justice system and intimidate individuals working in this arena represents a positive advancement for the rule of law. Nevertheless, the destruction of the cartels did not reduce the production, processing, and distribution of drugs, according to most empirical studies. Instead, quantity, price, and purity remained intact in the international market.[27]

In the short term, the destruction of the large cartels fragmented the business to the point of undermining its power as a hierarchical and monolithic structure. By disintegrating and disarming these actors, drug traffickers' capacity to interfere in U.S. interests such as extradition, or to challenge Colombia's governability, ceased. It is important to recognize that the dismantling of the cartels represented a major victory for the traditionally weak Colombian state. However, the victory against the major cartels was short-lived, as the vacuum created by the collapse of the cartels enabled the FARC and the paramilitaries to increase their power over drug trafficking. As discussed below, the paramilitaries evolved into a Mafia-like organization whose power extended far beyond the power of the former cartels, as witnessed during the demobilization process between 2003 and 2006.[28]

From the Violence of the Cartels to the Penetration of the State

Before analyzing the major period in the war on drugs in Colombia, from 2000 to 2010, it is important to highlight factors that make the situation in Colombia unique. It is necessary to recognize that the country also has a long history of internal armed conflict between leftist guerrillas and right-wing paramilitaries. Without a doubt, drug trafficking accelerated the expansion of the armed conflict, which was initially triggered by marginalized guerrilla organizations.[29]

As a direct consequence of these armed actors and of drug trafficking,[30] Colombia had the highest homicide rate in the region in 1991 (80 per 100,000 inhabitants). In addition, it has experienced thousands of massacres and ranks second for internally displaced people (IDP) in the world. Colombia also had the largest number (until recently) of extortive kidnappings in the world (approximately 5,000 at its peak in 2001 versus double-digit estimates in 2010). According to *País Libre*, in 2013, there were 24 extortive kidnappings in Colombia.

The fight of the Colombian state against drug trafficking has occurred in a context in which at least three types of actors participate: guerrillas (mainly the FARC, which currently drives a good portion of drug trafficking in its zones of influence, but also the National Liberation Army [Ejército de Liberación Nacional, ELN]); the paramilitaries (many demobilized between 2003 and 2006, but since the mid-1990s operating as an Italian-style mafia with strong control of drug trafficking and legal political and economic activities in their zones of influence); and an army that has been strengthened and professionalized since the end of the 1990s and that is capable of conducting this war in more favorable conditions than its opponents.

Given the new correlation of forces and their clear geographical division, the violence of the drug traffickers has gradually been replaced by the capture of the state, led initially by the paramilitaries, then its remnants, the *bandas criminales* (BACRIM),[31] and drug traffickers. All these actors have to some extent been supported or financed by politicians and landed elites. Rapidly, these "new illegal elites" have systematically penetrated virtually all public institutions and many private entities.[32] This phenomenon, which began at the local level in the 1990s, has extended into the 2000s despite the demobilization of the paramilitaries via the Law of Justice and Peace (Ley de Justicia y Paz, LJP), Law 975 of 2005, which is the legal framework regulating the paramilitaries' demobilization and reintegration into society. In Colombia, drug trafficking has financed internal conflict and the different actors since the 1980s. Drugs have fueled the five decades–long conflict that has produced in Colombia extreme levels of violence, terrorism, and widespread corruption.

The Uribe Administration (2002–2010) and the PSD

The failure of the Pastrana administration's peace negotiations with the FARC in 2001 caused Colombians to alter their electoral and policy preferences as they focused on new ways to end the armed conflict. In 2002, after the failed negotiations under Pastrana, Álvaro Uribe received overwhelming support and assumed power.[33]

Many administrations in Colombia have utilized national security doctrines as important parts of their programs since the National Front (Frente Nacional, 1958–1970). However, these security agendas never ended in dictatorships, as in some other countries in the region. Nonetheless, Colombians witnessed restrictions on their civil liberties and severe human rights violations that challenged the country's democratic tradition.[34]

From the beginning of his first administration, President Uribe proposed a policy known as the Democratic Defense and Security Program in order to combat terrorist threats, illicit-drug business, illicit finances, weapons, ammunitions and explosives, drug trafficking, kidnappings, extortion, and homicide.[35] In short, Uribe's democratic security policy, the PSD, can be described as having a major military focus and a poor political component:

> This state policy considers the necessity of its ground rules being applied by the armed forces, the ministries, and other government agencies. These are the subjects that classically direct a policy of this type. Nevertheless, it also considers the justice apparatus a specific recipient. The policy of "democratic defense and security" establishes the creation of interinstitutional support structures that facilitate the work of judicial authorities in such a way that the armed forces, the investigative agencies, and the judicial authorities work "with a team philosophy and not in a hierarchical relationship." Hence the operations carried out to regain and maintain control of territory should be accompanied by the "successful judicialization of those responsible."[36]

Like any repressive method of imposing order, Uribe's policies proposed that "where territorial control is weak, emphasis will be placed on the actions of the armed forces, and where territorial control is not threatened . . . judicial organizations will take the initiative."[37]

Some jurists believe that this method "seriously threatens judicial independence and autonomy, since it challenges the judges and investigators to attain common goals with the armed forces, weakening their own functions."[38] While such repressive tactics could consolidate gains in the short term, in the long run, they could exacerbate the problems.

According to Alfredo Rangel, the merit of the PSD is that it placed security at the center of the national political agenda and positioned it as a long-term goal.[39] The PSD also substantially improved the situation and perception of internal security. As a result, President Uribe recorded an approval rating of 80 percent. Under Uribe, Colombia witnessed decreases in the number of homicides, kidnappings,[40] massacres, IDPs, and captures of populations and saw reduced economic sabotage by the guerrillas. In addition to the aforementioned growth in security, the increasingly positive perception of security in Colombia facilitated economic growth.

Despite these positive outcomes, several underlying issues remained. First, the issue of border security became quite important, particularly after Colombia violated Ecuador's sovereignty and crossed into Ecuador in order to capture Raúl Reyes, one of the major leaders of the FARC. The second problem was the production of coca. Despite aggressive fumigation during the first and second Uribe administrations, as a direct product of Plan Colombia, the hectares of coca cultivated remained the same and production was intact.[41] In fact, Colombia is the only country in the world that permits aerial spraying of drug-producing crops.

Third, this aggressive fumigation created huge health and environmental issues for Colombians. The social and political costs are also immense: most Colombians from areas where aerial fumigation occurs have no other contact with the state than through aerial spraying. Thus, the state is perceived as the enemy while the illegal actors that defend the illicit crops become their natural allies.

Fourth, the PSD created great controversy due to the abuses that occurred from the mass detentions or the extrajudicial executions conducted during both Uribe administrations. The pressures to obtain "positive" detentions or "enemy" casualties, as required by the PSD, resulted in human rights abuses for an important number of innocent civilians.[42] Even though the scope of these unjust detentions is still unknown, it is quite troubling that many of these measures limited civil liberties and created potential justification for abuse by the Fuerza Pública (Public Force). In essence, mandating the army to police without obtaining arrest warrants or asserting control after the fact is equivalent to putting the state in a situation similar to that of the illegal actors. These arrangements delegitimize the state's legal actions against illegal groups and deter international cooperation and support.

Even more troublesome, there have been hundreds of extrajudicial executions of innocent civilians committed by members of the army, mainly in order to inflate the number of conflict-related deaths and create public perception favorable to the state (known in Colombia as the "false positives" scandal).[43] Such violence is a direct product of the PSD, which granted concrete incentives to militaries and police that detained or killed members of the FARC. These types of policies inevitably led to increases in the number of human rights abuses. Only one year after the implementation of the PSD, nongovernmental organizations such as the International Crisis Group (ICG) were strongly criticizing the military component of the PSD:

Sending a message that the security forces would be more successful if less constrained by the state's human rights obligations is dangerous and, as history has often shown, counterproductive. The bulk of the conflict, including the increased number of clashes resulting from Uribe's more aggressive security policy, has taken place in rural Colombia. The absence of any coherent rural development policy constitutes perhaps the most serious threat to the potential effectiveness of the DSP [PSD]. Making lasting gains against the insurgents will be difficult, if not impossible, unless rural communities see clear and immediate benefits in the government campaign. A comprehensive policy aimed at reducing poverty in the countryside, investing in social programs, and establishing the rule of law is a necessary complement to the military components of the DSP; its absence makes the military task more difficult.[44]

A fifth problem, mainly related to the inherent risks of the excessive militarization of the PSD, is the privatization of Colombian security, which itself is a by-product of the war against drugs. As Juan Gabriel Tokatlian argues, the privatization of security in Colombia is very clear:

In effect, U.S. companies like DynCorp act as State Department subcontractors and as part of PC from Washington. Only recently, the minister of defense, Juan Manuel Santos, confirmed the contracting of retired Israeli military to work in the identification and capture of FARC leaders.

He continues:

The dangers of the failure to effectively regulate and control this terrain have been eloquently expressed in the 2002 report of the British House of Commons about the "Private Military Companies" (PMCs): generally, PMCs are not accountable to anyone, usurp the sovereignty of weaker nations traversed by armed conflicts; they are involved in the economic exploitation of the countries in which they intervene; they have a manifest interest—especially for profit—in the perpetuation of these conflicts; they convert into clandestine arms of the government from which they originate and generate immense moral problems like the legitimization of paid assassination (killing for money) instead of the fight for a just cause. In the last decades the advancement of the PMCs has accompanied the growth of what traditionally has been deemed "low intensity conflicts" known today as military operations other than war.[45]

Finally, a sixth problem of the PSD is the slow reestablishment of the rule of law in locations formerly controlled by the paramilitaries and the guerrillas. Moreover, Uribe's PSD failed to bring economic and social alternatives to the recently recovered regions. In sum, Uribe's PSD failed to address the underlying issues fueling the conflict.[46]

Plan Colombia and the FARC

It is important to clarify that there were at least two versions of PC. The first originated during the Pastrana administration (1998–2002)[47] and coincides with the attempted peace negotiations between the FARC and the Colombian government.[48] This first version of Plan Colombia assumed that a negotiated peace with the FARC could facilitate the programs designed for counternarcotic purposes (e.g., manual crop eradication by the guerrillas, economic aid to peasants to create viable alternatives to cultivating coca leaves, or alternative development). In other words, Pastrana did not believe that it was necessary to combat drug cultivation, production, and trafficking by repressive or military means.

President Clinton and his administration disagreed fundamentally with the formulation of this first Plan Colombia and the original policy proposed by Pastrana.[49] The final version focused on the military component. It assigned 80 percent of the resources to the military and the police in order to help these forces combat illicit-drug production. A mere 20 percent of the money devoted to PC was divided among the following key issue areas: strengthening justice, human rights, and economic recovery. According to some analysts, "the debate [about PC] in the US Congress reflected the interests, tendencies and priorities of each of the representatives and senators, more than a careful understanding of the Colombian conflict."[50] Consequently, the Europeans refused to support PC and instead provided aid for nonmilitary projects.

In essence, PC is a set of legal provisions and funds from the U.S. government, executed by various agencies to combat drug trafficking and terrorism in Colombia.[51] Some suggest that PC also existed because the United States desired to assist Colombia in recovering its ability to govern effectively and to improve relations, which had deteriorated during the Samper administration. In this respect, "PC attempted to revert the deterioration of the political situation in Colombia."[52] Irrespective of this opinion, the

United States' main priority toward Colombia since the mid-1980s has been combating narcotics, and PC was designed to assist in the U.S.-led war on drugs in Colombia. Paraphrasing Marco Palacios, Plan Colombia is Washington's answer, as part of its global security policy, to the consolidation of drug trafficking and the globalization of the narcotics market and of organized crime, particularly in illicit weapons and money.[53]

PC went from being an instrument of peace, with emphasis on carrots (support of the peace process with the FARC, alternative development, and manual eradication of coca leaves) to a war plan, with stick components. More important, the new PC coincided perfectly with Álvaro Uribe's PSD.

Additionally, a fundamental shift occurred in the goals of PC after the events of 9/11 and the Bush administration's declaration of a global war on terrorism. President Uribe convinced President Bush of the need to support Colombia's fight against what he called the "narco-guerrillas." As a result, on August 2, 2002, PC explicitly authorized the use of resources to combat illegal armed groups that also participated in drug trafficking, that is, the FARC. The reorientation of PC coincided with Uribe's belief that there was no armed conflict and that drug trafficking was the major source of revenue for FARC terrorists and drug traffickers. In short, this authorization signified that PC resources would help finance both the war on drugs and the Colombian war against the guerrillas, since the paramilitaries had embarked on a peace process, as shown below.

After the law passed on August 2, 2002, the United States provided Colombia with resources to protect pipelines in the country and supported the construction of monitoring posts in rural areas as well as strategic support for Colombia's Plan Patriota.[54] Given the United States' involvement in the counterinsurgent war, the U.S. Congress placed a limit on troops, allowing a maximum of 600 U.S. troops and 800 contractors to operate in Colombia. As mentioned before, all of this contributed to the privatization of security and, in the long term, to the prolongation and degradation of the conflict.

Independently of Plan Colombia's being a plan to fight drugs, its support of and compatibility with the PSD, together with the professionalization of the Colombian military after the Pastrana administration, has forced many members of the FARC to retreat or to demobilize (approximately 24,000 members had done so by 2011). Many have also been imprisoned or killed (most members of the FARC Secretariat). In sum, PC was quite effective in the military gains made in Colombia against the FARC, certainly more so than in reducing the number of illegal drugs in the country, as originally proposed.

The Impact of the Demobilization of the Paramilitaries
on Drug Trafficking

The demobilization of the paramilitaries was a product of a strategy of the
Uribe administration, not related to the PSD, that had a major impact on
drug trafficking. While the final outcome of the process oscillates between
skepticism and hope,[55] the demobilization of the paramilitaries transformed drug trafficking in both Colombia and the region.

President Uribe initiated talks with the heads of the United Self-Defense
Forces of Colombia (Autodefensas Unidas de Colombia, AUC) paramilitaries when he took office.[56] The initial negotiations, between 2002 and 2003,
culminated in an agreement by which the paramilitaries would demobilize
and turn in their illicit goods. This proposal was rejected by activists and
human rights organizations, both nationally and internationally, as well as
by some members of Congress and the judiciary. Between 2003 and 2006,
all these actors successfully fought the simple rendition of the paramilitaries in exchange for impunity. The magnitude of the crimes against humanity perpetrated by the paramilitaries and the quantity of victims (counted
in the millions) made impunity a moral impossibility.

As a result of the overwhelming opposition, the impunity project of the
Uribe administration culminated when Congress managed to pass a law
known as the LJP (and the modifications introduced by the Constitutional
Court in 2006), which allowed the victims a dignified exit and at the same
time was acceptable to the murderous, yet still-undefeated paramilitaries.
The LJP created the tools necessary for the demobilization of the paramilitaries and other armed actors under a framework of transitional justice.[57]

While the LJP is a statute with everything necessary to demobilize, dis-
arm, and reintegrate illegal combatants,[58] no legal instrument, however
well designed, is capable of dealing with an illegal armed actor that simultaneously has political, Mafia, and drug-trafficking characteristics. In fact,
the LJP expressly stipulates that drug traffickers cannot take refuge in the
numerous benefits of the LJP. In the Colombian context, the latter precept
is impossible to apply. It is public knowledge that the paramilitaries overtly
operated as drug traffickers long before Carlos Castaño's (the main leader
of the AUC) open "confession" in 2001.[59]

Of even more concern than the paramilitaries' involvement in drug trafficking were their linkages with the political class and some of the economic elites. From its inception, the paramilitaries were closely linked with
landowners and cattle ranchers, the local political elites, and sectors of the

military and the police in some regions. The paramilitaries later developed connections with national politicians and public officials and with both private national and international entrepreneurs (multinationals). This "new" reality, known as "*parapolítica*," which put the paramilitaries and the Italian Mafia in the same light, came to the public's attention in 2006 thanks to the investigations resulting from the LJP. Tokatlian describes the *parapolítica* thus:

> The actual scandal of the "*parapolítica*"—the revelation of a shady and criminal network of ties between armed groups from the right and its historical links with the drug business, the landowning sectors, segments of the ruling class at the local level, members of the national political elite, and numerous officials from the armed forces—expresses the third episode in which the ascendance and consolidation of a new criminal social class is made evident. Faced with the dilemma of containing it or allowing to be co-opted by it, the Colombian state chose, on prior occasions, a particular combination of selective repression, partial control, and tactical coexistence. It's good to remember that the United States had a tactical tolerance or the implied consent of the paramilitary phenomenon, followed by frustrations, threats, and blows by Washington.[60]

The Uribe administration's negotiations with the paramilitaries were a necessity. His administration mastered a Machiavellian ploy. No one had attempted to demobilize these actors since the mid-1990s.

Despite the abyss that separates the initial negotiations between the paramilitaries and the Uribe government from the current LJP process, both are the product of a negotiated process, a situation that distinguishes the LJP from most policies adopted by Uribe against other illegal armed actors. The process, however imperfect, led to the greatest accomplishment vis-à-vis negotiations between the state and paramilitaries: the dismantling of an Italian-style mafia in the making.[61] At its zenith, the AUC represented a type of mafia confederation of drug traffickers and legal elites that not only controlled a great slice of drug trafficking in Colombia, but also was capable of penetrating the state at different levels. Its clear links with legal private business and multinationals, while harder to prosecute, are also indisputable today.[62]

Consequently, specific achievements and failures since the demobilization of the paramilitaries between 2003 and 2006 are products of Uribe's initial plan. This includes the gradual implementation of the LJP and later developments such as the Law of Victims and Restitution of Land (Ley de Víctimas y de Restitución de Tierras, Law 1448 of 2011).[63] The most controversial failure or achievement, depending on how you look at it,[64] was the May 2008 extradition of fourteen AUC bosses to the United States on drug-trafficking charges.[65] The Uribe administration then extradited many more. The primacy given by Uribe to the interests of the United States, or to his own, in extraditing the bosses of the AUC on drug-trafficking charges generated severe criticism for considerations that the truth of the bosses of the paramilitary project had been extradited to the United States, denying the thousands of victims in Colombia their right to the truth.

Numerous reasons were invoked to explain the real reasons behind the extraditions, including the fear that the paramilitary bosses would reveal alliances with Uribe's party and the incapacity of the Colombian judicial system to keep such individuals in prison. Whatever the truth, the reality is that the leaderless paramilitaries then fragmented into three groups. The first group comprises some of the 32,000 officially demobilized paramilitaries, mainly the foot soldiers who are part of the government's Reinsertion Program.[66] The second group emerged from the middle-ranking paramilitaries, who never demobilized or reorganized after the official demobilization. The third group comprises criminals of diverse origin who united in drug trafficking and took advantage of the vacuum left by the extinct AUC. The government classifies the last two groups as BACRIMs in order to separate them from the conflict and treat them as criminals.

In sum, the exit negotiated by the Uribe administration with one of the largest illegal actors in the conflict, although inadequate against drug trafficking, did remove a powerful mafia-like organization and a military actor capable of challenging the state not just by its indiscriminate use of violence, but also by the capture of state institutions. As a result, the drug business was again fragmented and subjected to "balloon" and "cockroach" effects throughout the region.[67] The new fragmentation gives the Colombian state greater governance and in some way allows it to concentrate on recovering its monopoly over force (via security and the rule of law) while removing the mafia-style organizations that had become embedded in the nation's institutions. Meanwhile, the Colombian government has recently initiated a new peace process with the FARC.

Some Obvious Conclusions: The Failure of Plan Colombia and of the U.S.-Led Repressive War on Drugs in the Region

As discussed above, most experts and empirical studies clearly reveal that despite the amount of resources invested (in accordance with PC) to reduce the production of illicit drugs, the policy has not been effective.[68] The ICG, like hundreds of other experts, has recognized the ineffectiveness of the repressive Colombian and U.S.-sponsored efforts against illicit drugs: "Despite UNODC and U.S. praise for Colombia's commitment to fighting production and trafficking in the past decade—record aerial and manual eradication levels, impressive cocaine seizure numbers, interception of imported precursor chemicals, destruction of processing laboratories and action against drug traffickers and armed groups—Colombia remains the world's major cocaine producing country; its 610 tons in 2006 are 62 per cent of the global total."[69] In fact, U.S.-led repressive policies against illicit drugs have been divisive with respect to the politics and degree of support within the countries involved. The absence of cooperation and integrated coordination among all the producer, exporter, transient, and consumer countries is one of the main results of this divide. This lack of cooperation and unity has allowed organized crime to grow and become more transnational. Indeed, the ICG claims that "insufficient international cooperation and coordination—in particular between the U.S. and Europe—has worked to the advantage of the drug networks. Displaying great resourcefulness, the drug trafficking organizations exploit the policy divide between the U.S. and the EU and some member states over how best to define and conduct counter-drug strategies and which aspects of cocaine supply and demand reduction efforts should be given priority. Since there is no shared vision of the problem and how to address it, a concerted response to address transnational crime does not exist."[70]

In contrast to the state's lack of coordination against the drug-trafficking industry, there has been a slow but steady transnational "integration" of drug traffickers, even at the risk of losing control of the traffic, as is the case between Mexico and Colombia. While one cannot speak of transnational organizations in the region, since most criminal organizations in Mexico, Central America, and Colombia are fragmented, the constant integration and adaptation of producers and traffickers is often superior to that of the governments of the countries where these operate. Moreover, political instability and the generalized absence of a monopoly of force in many Latin

American countries and the still-unresolved Colombian conflict are all fertile terrain for the future prosperity of drug trafficking in the region.

In short, the war against drugs led by the United States cannot be won, even with huge resources, high levels of military training, and strong political commitment, as the case of Colombia clearly shows. There is plenty of serious evidence-based literature that documents the failure of both the war on drugs and the U.S. security policy in the Andean region, as the provocative title of Brian Loveman's *Addicted to Failure* graphically depicts. Drug traffickers remain at large and have become more difficult than ever to control, particularly because, unlike in the 1980s and 1990s, most countries in the region are now deeply involved.

Notes

1. Thanks to Alí R. Bustamante for translating this article from Spanish to English.

2. Almost all the recent empirical studies show that the quantity and price of cocaine have remained stable since 2000, confirming what many call the failure of the war against illegal drugs.

3. The FARC is the oldest Marxist guerrilla organization in Colombia and counts the most years fighting on the entire American continent.

4. Such was the irrelevancy of drug trafficking in Colombia during this period that the money from this "bonanza marimbera" was easily legalized through the so-called *ventanilla siniestra* (sinister window) of the Banco de la República (the Colombian central bank).

5. A detailed explanation of the treaty's major issues can be found in Elvira María Restrepo, *Colombian Criminal Justice in Crisis: Fear and Distrust* (New York: Palgrave Macmillan, 2003).

6. For a detailed analysis of the origins of the paramilitaries and MAS, see Elvira María Restrepo, Nicolas Velásquez, and Grant Cohen, "The Colombian Paramilitary Project: Buried in Public Opinion" (forthcoming).

7. See a recap of this period in Restrepo, *Colombian Criminal Justice in Crisis*.

8. The Palace of Justice siege also shows the drug traffickers' capacity to ally with their worst enemies to guarantee their own ends, that is, to destroy the extradition files that contained evidence against them.

9. María Mercedes Cuellar, *Colombia: Un proyecto inconcluso* (Bogotá: Editorial Taurus, 2000). During the 1990s, the violence against judges passed relatively unnoticed until the *parapolítica* scandal in 2008. Headlines in the major newspapers then began to talk about the issue openly: "628 judges have been threatened in the past 5 years, and Bogotá is the city with more intimidations." See *El Tiempo*, March 23, 2008.

10. M. Cuellar, *Colombia*.

11. Grupo de Memoria Histórica, *La Rochela: Memorias de un crimen contra la justicia* (Bogotá: Editorial Tauros, 2010).

12. Extradition to the United States is the only instrument that deters Colombian drug traffickers and organized criminals.

13. The 1991 Constitution, which governs Colombia, was adopted during the César Gaviria administration (1990–1994), but many of its fundamental reforms were conceived during the Virgilio Barco administration (1986–1990).

14. Interestingly, Barco enacted approximately twenty decrees that granted wider powers than those in the Antiterrorist statute proposed (and rejected) years later, during the first Álvaro Uribe administration (2002–2006).

15. In Colombia, in contrast to the rest of the region, the adversarial system was introduced in two stages. The first stage occurred in 1991 with the creation of the Fiscalía, a prosecutorial agency that preserves judicial powers such as ordering arrests and searches. The second stage occurred in 2004, when an adversarial system akin to that of the United States was adopted.

16. Justicia sin Rostro created a group of anonymous prosecutors and judges with jurisdiction over crimes of great social impact such as drug trafficking, terrorism, and kidnapping. The idea was to protect the judges from threats and intimidation and to expedite criminal procedures. For this second purpose, due process was limited by allowing secret witnesses, diminished procedural guarantees or due process, and the negotiation of penalties (a sort of plea bargaining).

17. Legal technicalities and practical problems inhibited the expropriation of drug traffickers' property and goods as allowed by Law 333 of 1996. Until 1999, only one conviction had been enforced while many others awaited judgment. See Colombia, Fiscalía, "Informe de gestión" (1998–1999), 150. See Ley 333 de 1996 (diciembre 19) por la cual se establecen las normas de extinción de dominio sobre los bienes adquiridos en forma ilícita, http:// www.mindefensa.gov.co/irj/go/km/docs/Mindefensa/Documentos/descargas/Sobre_el_ Ministerio/fondelibertad/ley_333_1996.pdf.

18. The Bloque Búsqueda was an elite force composed of the police and the Colombian military, members of the U.S. Special Forces informally trained by Delta Force, and the PEPEs. The Bloque de Búsqueda managed to kill the feared Pablo Escobar in December 1993.

19. The PEPEs were personalities on the fringes of the law who had outstanding accounts with Escobar. Among them were members of the Cali cartel and paramilitaries like the Castaño brothers, the latter members of the Medellín cartel. By December 1993, the PEPEs were responsible for the murder or execution of more than sixty members of the Medellín cartel.

20. For the reader who is interested in comparing Justicia sin Rostro to the ordinary criminal justice system, see Gabriel Eduardo Nemogá, La Justicia sin Rostro (Bogotá: Unijus, Universidad Nacional, 1996), 35–55.

21. For more on this, see Restrepo, Colombian Criminal Justice in Crisis.

22. This policy was suspended after Peruvian authorities shot down a plane that was transporting U.S. missionaries, killing a mother and her son in 2001. The United States reestablished the program but this time only in Colombia, where the Uribe administration authorized attacking planes suspected of carrying drugs.

23. The balloon effect is an often-cited criticism of US drug policy. It draws an analogy between efforts to eradicate the production of illegal drugs in South America and what

happens to the air inside of a latex balloon when it is squeezed: the air moves but does not disappear; pressure applied in one area pushes the air into an area of less resistance. See Bruce M. Bagley, *Drug Trafficking and Organized Crime in the Americas: Major Trends in the Twenty-First Century* (Washington, D.C.: Woodrow Wilson Center, 2012).

24. The PSJ (Law 81 of 1993 and its statutory decrees) was enacted during the Gaviria administration with the purpose of lowering the penalties for the leaders of the Cali cartel who were still free at the time and those for other drug traffickers in return for their surrender and further cooperation with the system of justice.

25. Natalia Morales and Santiago La Rotta, *Los Pepes: Desde Pablo Escobar hasta don Berna, Macaco y don Mario* (Bogotá: Editorial Planeta, 2009).

26. After being captured, they were extradited to the United States in 2006. Today, having negotiated with the United States, they are convicted and imprisoned. They also paid a large fine to Colombia to protect their children from future charges under the U.S. justice system.

27. Alejandro Gaviria and Daniel Mejía, eds., *Política antidrogas en Colombia: Éxitos, fracaso y extravíos* (Bogotá: Ediciones Uniandes, 2011).

28. Elvira María Restrepo and Bruce M. Bagley, eds., *La desmovilización de los paramilitares en Colombia: Entre la esperanza y el escepticismo* (Bogotá: Ediciones Uniandes, 2011).

29. Marco Palacios, *Plan Colombia: ¿Anti-drogas o contrainsurgencia?* Cátedra Corona Series (Bogotá: Universidad de los Andes, Facultad de Administración, 2007).

30. Fabio Sánchez, ed., *Las cuentas de la violencia: Ensayos económicos sobre el conflicto y el crimen en Colombia* (Bogotá: Editorial Norma, 2007).

31. BACRIM is the official name given to the remnants of the paramilitaries that did not demobilize in 2003–2006 or that rearmed after the demobilization.

32. Claudia López, ed., *Y refundaron la patria: De cómo mafiosos y políticos reconfiguraron el estado colombiano* (Bogotá: Corporación Nuevo Arco Iris, 2010).

33. Palacios, *Plan Colombia*.

34. Gustavo Gallón, *Quince años de estado de sitio en Colombia: 1958–1978* (Bogotá: Librería y Editorial América, 1979).

35. Colombia, Presidencia de la República, Ministerio de Defensa Nacional, Imprenta Nacional, Bogotá, 2003, no. 66.

36. Ibid.; all translations are mine unless otherwise noted.

37. Ibid., no. 17.

38. Rodrigo Uprimny, "Un marco teórico de reflexión sobre los riesgos de las medidas antiterroristas en Colombia," Estado de derecho, de justicia, January 30, 2006, accessed January 10, 2012, http://www.dejusticia.org/#/actividad/176.

39. Alfredo Rangel, *Sostenibilidad de la seguridad democrática* (Bogotá: Editorial Kimpres, 2005), 51–52.

40. It is important to note that some of these favorable indicators for improvements in security, particularly regarding kidnappings, occurred before the implementation of the PSD.

41. Gaviria and Mejía, eds., *Política antidrogas*.

42. The arrests were based on "preventive detention," declared constitutional by the Constitutional Court's decision C-024 of 1994, in which the court opened the possibility that the police could preventively detain individuals without an arrest warrant.

43. Michael Evans, "The Truth about Triple A: U.S. document Implicates Current, Former Colombian Army Commanders in Terror Operation," *National Security Archive Electronic Briefing Book*, no. 223 (Washington, D.C.: National Security Archive, 2007).

44. International Crisis Group, "Colombia: President Uribe's Democratic Security Policy," *Latin America Report*, no. 6 (Bogotá, November 2003).

45. Juan Gabriel Tokatlian, "La construcción de un 'estado fallido' en la política mundial: El caso de las relaciones entre Estados Unidos y Colombia," *Análisis Político* 21, no. 64 (September/December 2008).

46. Lilian Yaffe claims that between 1995 and 2009, the intensity of the conflict in Colombia, as measured by the number of attacks initiated by the illegal actors, decreased in (1) departments located in the center of the country, (2) departments where poverty decreased, (3) departments where the number of illegal actors decreased, and (4) departments where institutional presence (measured as effective arrests) was stronger. Her methodology used PSD as her independent variable.

47. According to Palacios, in 1998, the Clinton and Pastrana administrations agreed that the fight against drug trafficking and the fight against the guerrilla insurgency should be separated; see *Plan Colombia*. In October of 1998, before his first presidential visit to Washington, Pastrana publicly denarcotized the bilateral relationship; see "Pastrana denarcotized the peace," *El Espectador*, October 19, 1998, 1–3, 23.

48. The 1999–2002 Caguan peace process with the FARC originated when the Colombian state unilaterally yielded to this group the clearing of a demilitarized zone, the *zona de despeje*, the size of Switzerland, in the south of the country, for further peace conversations. As we know now, it ended in colossal failure after almost three years of conversations in which the FARC grew militarily and used the *zona de despeje* as a depository for kidnapped individuals, stolen weapons, and illicit drugs.

49. To compare the original vision of Pastrana's Plan Colombia with PC as is known today, see "Bases 1998–2002: Cambio para construir la paz," Plan Nacional de Desarrollo (Bogotá: Departamento Nacional de Planeación, 1998); U.S. Embassy, Bogotá, Colombia, "U.S. Support for PC," February 2001.

50. Marc Chernik, *Acuerdo posible: Solución negociada al conflicto armado colombiano* (Bogotá: Ediciones Aurora, 2008), 134.

51. The U.S. government expenditures attributable to PC from July 2000 to 2012 exceeded $7 billion.

52. Andrés López Restrepo, "Narcotráfico, ilegalidad y conflicto en Colombia," in *Nuestra guerra sin nombre*, ed. Francisco Gutiérrez (Bogotá: Editorial Norma, 2007), 430.

53. Palacios, *Plan Colombia*.

54. Plan Patriota was a large-scale Colombian military offensive in territories controlled by the guerrillas in the south of Colombia.

55. Restrepo and Bagley, *La desmovilización*.

56. AUC is the umbrella organization of the paramilitaries, which allegedly represented 90 percent of the members of the existing right-wing groups at the time of the negotiations.

57. Elvira María Restrepo, "Transitional Justice without a Compass: Paramilitary Demobilization in Colombia," in *After Oppression: Transitional Justice in Latin America and Eastern Europe*, ed. Veselin Popovski and Monica Serrano (New York: United Nations University Press, 2012).

58. Authorities in the field of transitional justice claim that the LJP in Colombia passes the proportionality test and follows the accepted principles of international law; see Kai Ambos, "The Legal Framework of Transitional Justice," in *Building a Future on Peace and Justice*, ed. Kai Ambos, Judith Large, and Marieke Wierda (New York: Springer, 2009), 52.

59. Mauricio Aranguren, *Mi confesión: Carlos Castaño revela sus secretos* (Bogotá: Editorial La Oveja Negra, 2001).

60. Juan Gabriel Tokatlian, "Colombia: ¿La última oportunidad?" *El Tiempo*, June 6, 2007, accessed March 15, 2012, http://www.derechos.org/nizkor/colombia/doc/tokatlian. html.

61. The use of the term "mafia" is inspired by Diego Gambetta; see *The Sicilian Mafia: A Business of Private Protection* (Cambridge: Harvard University Press, 1996). The paramilitaries, unlike the Medellín and Cali cartels, penetrated most state institutions and obtained the unconditional support of a great number of politicians, public officials, and private entrepreneurs who allowed them to function not just amidst other illegal actors, but in the field of perfectly legal business. The extent of the latter, for obvious reasons, has been more difficult to uncover fully.

62. For updated information on the results of the paramilitary process, see www.verdad abierta.com; http://www.fiscalia.gov.co/jyp/.

63. See Law 1448 of 2011 in http://www.secretariasenado.gov.co/senado/basedoc/ ley/2011/ley_1448_2011.html.

64. The extradition of the AUC leaders was a failure for the millions of victims who suffered massive violations of their human rights at the hands of the paramilitaries. The heads of the AUC were extradited to the United States without negotiations between Colombian and U.S. authorities on the specific conditions for their future collaboration in reconstructing the truth or for pending judicial processes in Colombia.

65. Gerardo Reyes, "La nave del olvido," in *La desmovilización de los paramilitares en Colombia: Entre la esperanza y el escepticismo*, ed. Elvira María Restrepo and Bruce M. Bagley (Bogotá: Ediciones Uniandes, 2011).

66. See http://www.reintegracion.gov.co/en. The Reinsertion Program has been replaced by the Consejería para el Desarrollo.

67. This terminology and its meaning are the subject of Bruce M. Bagley, *Drug Trafficking in the Americas* (Washington, D.C.: Woodrow Wilson Center, 2002).

68. See Daniel Mejía and Pascual Restrepo, "The War on Illegal Drug Production and Trafficking: An Economic Evaluation of Plan Colombia," seminar, Tufts University, December 8, 2008, http://ase.tufts.edu/econ/events/seminars/2008-2009/mejia.pdf; Daniel Mejía and Alejandro Gaviria, *El libro blanco de la droga* (Bogotá: Ediciones Uniandes, 2011); Adam Isacson, "El PC: Consecuencias no deseadas," *Foreign Affairs* 8, no. 1 (2008).

69. International Crisis Group, "Latin America's Drugs I: Losing the Fight," *Latin America Report*, no. 25 (March 14, 2008).

70. Ibid.

8

Illicit Drugs in the Colombia-U.S. Relationship

Review and Prospects

ARLENE B. TICKNER AND CAROLINA CEPEDA

After ten years and more than U.S.$7 billion invested,[1] Plan Colombia (PC) is considered a successful model of bilateral cooperation. Although it was initially set as an expanded and improved version of antidrug cooperation agreements between Bogotá and Washington that had existed since the 1980s, in practice, PC has worked—especially since the completion of the peace process with the Revolutionary Armed Forces of Colombia (Fuerzas Armadas Revolucionarias de Colombia, FARC) in 2002—as a counterinsurgency strategy and a mechanism for strengthening the state, within which the "war on drugs" has been a priority.

Although there is a consensus among advocates and opponents of PC that since 2000 Colombia has undergone a major transformation in terms of its internal security climate, less clear is its achievement on the issue of illicit drugs. The reduction in coca cultivation and coca's productive potential in the country, after gradual increases since 2004, has led to claims that Colombia is winning the war on drugs, which is also considered critical to winning the "war on terror," given the links between Colombian armed groups and drug trafficking. In contrast, the fact that the total number of illicit crops in 2008 was comparable to 1999 levels, according to U.S. statistics, in addition to PC's marginal effects on the availability, price, and purity of cocaine on U.S. streets, and its "collateral" effects—including the "balloon" effect[2]—have been identified as compelling evidence of its failure.

While the Uribe government insisted on maintaining a policy of zero tolerance of all forms of illicit drugs, including coca (and poppy) crops, and their personal use, the trend in the United States has been different. Fourteen states and the District of Columbia have legalized medical marijuana, and a growing number of people believe that drugs should be regulated and taxed as are alcohol and tobacco.[3] The economic crisis has highlighted the costs of punitive policies: the U.S. prison population has increased 400 percent since 1980, and U.S. courts are filled with minor possession cases. Although the issue of illicit drugs is still highly dependent on bureaucratic inertia in Washington, there are indications that both the administration of Barack Obama and Congress have begun to reevaluate official policy that has resisted fundamental changes for nearly forty years. Among the Obama administration's efforts was the appointment of Gil Kerlikowske as antidrug czar. He called for an end to the war on drugs and a change from strategies such as the eradication of illicit crops in countries like Colombia and Afghanistan. A bill was introduced by Congressman Eliot Engel to review antidrug policy in the Western Hemisphere.

The fact that the tenth anniversary of PC coincided with a change of government in Colombia and a climate of relative evaluation and openness in the United States provided the opportunity to explore bilateral relations retrospectively and to propose possible future scenarios. The discussion that we will develop further emphasizes mainly illicit drugs, and only secondarily touches on other implications of PC, such as counterinsurgency and the strengthening of the public force, considering that these have been equally or more important from the perspective of the Colombian government.

In the first section of the chapter, we identify the basic assumptions that have accompanied the war on drugs. Although these have been analyzed by other authors,[4] it is important to place the war on drugs' origins within the complementary trends of "American exceptionalism" and securitization in order to understand the kind of policies the United States has historically adopted to combat illicit drugs and the obstacles to the modification of these policies.

The second part briefly reviews the evolution of Colombian-U.S. relations in the period between the governments of Andrés Pastrana and Álvaro Uribe. Although bilateral relations have been "narcotized" from the 1980s, we explore the period preceding Plan Colombia to demonstrate how and why it underwent a transformation whose most significant result was the extension of the bilateral agenda and thus greater U.S. involvement in the country's internal conflict.

In addition, we provide an overall assessment of the antidrug strategies of both countries and "unexpected" consequences that have been detected.[5] While it is difficult to separate the analysis of the war on drugs from other objectives of bilateral cooperation, the fact that it has occupied such an important place in PC merits its focal position.

Finally, we discuss the debates regarding drugs that have taken place recently in the United States, which must be kept in mind in order to understand the present course of bilateral relations and future scenarios. The chapter concludes with recommendations.

The War on Drugs: Principles and Assumptions

The interpretation of illicit drugs as a "threat" and a "danger" has a long history in the political and social realms of the United States. It was not until 1971 that President Richard Nixon declared that they constituted "public enemy number one," against which it was necessary to wage a "war"—an interpretation that was radicalized during the administration of Ronald Reagan. From the beginning of the twentieth century, U.S. policy has been based on two distinct but complementary assumptions: on the one hand, drugs are morally wrong; on the other, they represent a security threat.

Among the features that have determined American exceptionalism, moralism, derived mainly from the Protestant work ethic, plays a prominent role in the national and international politics of the United States.[6] The religious origin of attitudes in the United States toward issues such as drugs, sexuality, crime, and punishment largely explains the nature of the public debate on drugs.[7] In addition to its representation as an "evil" against which the United States has a moral duty to act, drug consumption has been understood historically as a depraved behavior that is outside the limits of "normal" society.[8] Hence the issue of illicit drugs, and the policies that have been developed to combat them, have been based on the assumption that this problem has its origins outside the United States, in producing countries, and inside the country, among undesirable social groups, typically racial and ethnic minorities.[9] The fact that drugs are interpreted as a universal evil that threatens moral purity also exerts a restraining influence on public debate. This leads to the use of rigid and dichotomous terms (good/evil, prohibition/legalization), but a number of studies from multiple disciplines suggesting that the war on drugs has not worked tend to be ignored and delegitimized because they do not have a central moral imperative that accompanies the problem.

Seemingly opposite the moralism pole, the drug policy of the United States also relies on the identification of illicit drugs as a threat to security.

The concept of securitization emphasizes the importance of discourse employed by states to justify policy.[10] In particular, using speech, state actors produce specific readings of various public issues that are not the product of objective assessments but of a set of historical, political, social, and cultural factors.[11] In the case of security, when a specific topic is named as a threat or is securitized, the act of naming itself produces important political effects.[12] By declaring that "x" is a security threat, representatives of the state are allowed to call for emergency measures and are given the right to use any strategy needed to combat it, including the use of force. Consequently, securitization enables the state to monopolize the handling of certain problems while taking them from the public sphere, where they could be subject to the dynamics of democratic debate and consideration of policy alternatives.

Taken together, the religiosity that accompanies the understanding of the drug phenomenon as well as its securitization explains the longevity of current policies. What is commonly known as the punitive or prohibitionist paradigm provides a specific interpretation of illegal drugs—"they are bad and have to be ended"—the source of the problem—"drugs are very cheap and easy to get"—and possible solutions—"punishment, coercion, and prohibition."[13] With this, the paradigm sets the limits within which the debate on the subject can take place as well as the policies to be adopted. These consist of a combination of interdiction, eradication, combating drug trafficking organizations in producer countries, and criminalization and imprisonment within the United States to address the problem of demand, with a reduced emphasis on treatment and education. "If the war against supply seeks to discourage consumption by increasing the economic cost of drug use, the war against consumers seeks to increase the risk associated with consumption by imposing punitive measures."[14] Given drugs' identification as a security threat, the war on drugs also presupposes a significant military component, the cession of the right of society to express its opinion on the handling of the issue, and the "collateral damage" present in the formulation of policies to combat the phenomenon.

Apart from the aforementioned factors, political and bureaucratic inertia in Washington reinforces opposition to change despite the growing recognition that the war on drugs has been a failure. Although a growing number of Americans believe that the current policy does not work, only a small percentage believes that the punitive paradigm needs to change, except in the case of marijuana.[15] Therefore, the political risk associated with the formulation of alternative strategies is high, especially in the case of the House of Representatives, which is elected every two years.[16] The high level of bureaucratic institutionalization that was created after decades of implementing the same policy constitutes an additional obstacle.

Terrorization of the War on Drugs

The terrorist attacks of September 11, 2001, altered the war on drugs. The global "war on terrorism" was a new strategy for securitization on the part of the United States that linked within a single analytical framework a set of global threats, including illegal trafficking of drugs and weapons and weapons of mass destruction. The nexus between terrorism and drugs, symbolized by a new concept—"narco-terrorism"[17]—made it possible to tie together the securitization of these two issues.[18] Additionally, as happened in the case of drugs, terrorism began to be seen through a moralist lens, as evidenced by such terms such as "axis of evil," "zero tolerance," and "infinite justice" used when talking about this new threat.

The terrorization of the war on drugs has significant implications for drug policy in the United States and in Colombia, where termination of the negotiation process with the Revolutionary Armed Forces of Colombia (Fuerzas Armadas Revolucionarias de Colombia, FARC) by President Andrés Pastrana led to this group's identification as a terrorist actor.[19] As discussed in the next section, the Colombian government's insertion of the internal conflict into the global war on terrorism affected the bilateral relations between Colombia and the United States by expanding their main axes. Prior to September 11, U.S. interest in Colombia revolved around drug production and trafficking. This, however, changed after the events of September 11, and the relationship between Colombia and the United States also became focused on the strengthening of the coercive apparatus of the Colombian state through the use of counterinsurgency tactics.

Colombia–United States: The Drug Relationship

Since the mid-1980s, bilateral relations have had drugs at their center as a result of the expansion of drug-trafficking organizations in Colombia, as well as the growing concern in the United States with illegal-drug use and the crime associated with it.[20] The Andean Initiative, introduced by the first Bush administration in 1989 at the end of the Cold War, gave Colombia a certain place on the agenda of U.S. foreign policy in terms of drug trafficking. Since then, the conduct of the war on drugs in Colombia has relied heavily on the U.S. approach to the problem.[21]

The role of drugs in bilateral relations underwent a major transformation after the government of Ernesto Samper, mostly due to the mutation of the political economy of drug trafficking in the country and its growing synergy with the armed conflict.[22] When Samper took office in 1994, the division of labor for the cocaine trade was such that Peru and Bolivia produced most of the raw material (coca paste) and the Colombian cartels processed and exported it. This production structure changed in the mid-1990s to the extent that coca crops began to move to Colombia, largely as a result of successful eradication and interdiction campaigns in Peru and Bolivia and the breakdown of the air bridge between these countries and Colombia. Accordingly, between 1996 and 1998, coca production in Colombia increased by about 50 percent,[23] which established the country as the largest producer of coca in the world. In addition, more than 50 percent of coca cultivation was in Putumayo, a department controlled by the FARC.

On the other hand, the dismantling of the Cali and Medellín cartels in mid-decade created a power vacuum that was filled not only by the mini-cartels but also by illegal armed actors, particularly the paramilitaries and the FARC. In both cases, participation in various links in the chain of production provided a crucial source of income that enabled their territorial expansion.

When Andrés Pastrana was elected president in June 1998, Colombia supplied 90 percent of the cocaine entering the United States and much of the heroin sold on the U.S. East Coast. Pastrana therefore inherited a country on the verge of collapse: "a convergence of destabilizing factors, including drugs, illegal armed groups, weak public security, government corruption, increasing violence and a severe economic recession, pointed to the dramatic loss of state authority."[24] For the incoming government, a "Marshall Plan" for Colombia—which put forward the idea of the country's reconstruction by means of international cooperation—was crucial for achieving peace. The struggle against drug trafficking was one of the plan's objectives. In the first version of what would be Plan Colombia, in October 1998, alternative development was identified as the first of six goals in addition to (1) reducing supply (eradication occupied a very secondary place); (2) the strengthening of justice; (3) reduction in demand; (4) environmental protection; and (5) international cooperation. Meanwhile, during various visits to the White House the same year, the Colombian president sought to convince his counterpart, Bill Clinton, that the end of armed conflict was a necessary prerequisite to a more effective attack on the drug trade.[25]

Despite efforts to distance itself from the U.S. interpretation of the problem, it was clear to the Pastrana government that the success or failure of its "diplomacy for peace" depended largely on U.S. support—given the lack of commitment on the part of other international donors—and that Washington's interest in Colombia remained centered on the war on drugs.[26] Therefore, Pastrana sought to ensure U.S. involvement by calling for its support.[27] The Plan Colombia version that was presented in the United States incorporated a wide range of issues that were considered important—including economic recovery, reform of the justice system, development, and human rights—in a strategy in which illegal drugs played a central role.[28]

Although in its original understanding PC was proposed as a policy that would complement the peace process with the FARC, it ended up being overdetermined by the military component and the problem of illicit crops in the south, where the presence of the FARC made it difficult for the national police to carry out counternarcotic activities. Consequently, the first package of U.S. aid—the largest source of external funding for PC—$1.6 million in 2000 and 2001, allocated 80 percent for the army and, to a lesser extent, the police and provided for the supply of helicopters, training of counternarcotics battalions, and military support for eradication and interdiction activities.

Despite this, it would be a mistake to perceive Plan Colombia simply as more of the same in the war on drugs. The argument made by the Pastrana government in the "Plan for Peace, Prosperity and the Strengthening of the State" was that illicit drugs constituted a threat to national security because they fueled armed conflict, and the state was too weak to face the problem by itself. The weakness of the state was associated with a lack of monopoly over the national territory and the use of force, preventing, among other things, the effective implementation of antidrug policies by the national police in areas of the south that were controlled by the guerrillas and where coca was cultivated. Thus, from the Colombian perspective, PC served a dual function: to strengthen the state by improving its military capabilities, and to isolate the FARC from one of its main sources of income in southern Colombia, specifically, in Putumayo, where the size of crops had been growing exponentially.[29]

Regardless of the benefits of PC as antidrug strategy—an issue we will explore in the next section—it managed to satisfy the interests of the two countries, which were not necessarily the same: in the case of the United States, to demonstrate its determination in the war against drugs; and in the case of Colombia, to ensure the support of Washington in strengthening the army and to begin cutting down the FARC's territorial control in the coca zones. However, to the extent that the terms of bilateral discussions began to change with PC, the main U.S. objective in Colombia—to reduce the amount of narcotics that could enter the country—was limited to strengthening the Colombian state and the stabilization of the country.[30]

The terrorist attacks of September 11, 2001, and the shift in U.S. foreign policy once more impacted bilateral relations. Besides the FARC, the National Liberation Army (Ejército de Liberación Nacional, ELN) and the United Self-Defense Forces of Colombia (Autodefensas Unidas de Colombia, AUC) were placed on the U.S. State Department's list of terrorist organizations, and the war on drugs became, to a great extent, attached to the global war on terrorism, especially in cases where the two phenomena converged. While some U.S. officials began referring to the Colombian case as "narco-terrorism," it was not until February 20, 2002, when President Pastrana made the decision to end the peace process with the FARC, that the Colombian government welcomed that description.[31] Later, Pastrana began spreading the idea that the Colombian conflict was the greatest terrorist threat in the Western Hemisphere, which placed the country firmly onto the new map of U.S. priorities.[32]

An almost immediate effect of the change in the language used in both countries was the lifting of restrictions associated with the use of U.S. military aid received through Plan Colombia. In March 2002, President George W. Bush asked Congress for authorization to use military aid in the fight against terrorism, which completely erased the tenuous distinction between antidrug activities and counterinsurgency that Washington had sought to preserve.

This trend continued and deepened after the election of Álvaro Uribe in May 2002. From the beginning, the backbone of Uribe's government was to define and implement security policy, with the war against illegal armed groups and drug trafficking as its two axes. Despite the marked differences between the Pastrana and Uribe governments—especially the emphasis of the first on peace and the statement by the second that there was no armed conflict in Colombia—the Democratic Security Policy (Política de Seguridad Democrática, PSD) started with a similar interpretation of the Colombian crisis as it was formulated by the Pastrana government in its drafting of Plan Colombia together with the United States, namely, that the weakness of the Colombian state created conditions that permitted growth of armed groups and drug trafficking, and that an essential condition to ensure the rule of law and to strengthen democratic authority was the reinforcement of the state's control over its national territory.[33]

Convergence of problem identification, as well as of some of the policies needed to address it—especially the professionalization and modernization of the armed forces, initiated under Pastrana—helped preserve a significant degree of continuity in the relationship between Colombia and the United States.[34] As far as Washington considered itself a vital partner in the implementation of the PSD, the main objective of Colombian foreign policy became the fostering of "special" bilateral relations and expansion of the U.S. role in Colombia's internal conflict.[35] The Uribe government's toughening of the discourse against drugs and terrorism facilitated this process by creating a greater rapprochement between the perspectives, strategies, and goals of the two countries than had existed during the Pastrana administration.

With regard to drugs, for Pastrana, they basically constituted a means to ensure the collaboration of Washington in strengthening the state and thus creating conditions for peace; for Uribe, the "war against narco-terrorism" became one of the main purposes of his government, both within and outside the country.[36] This was a different interpretation of the crisis in Colombia and the role played by drug trafficking, expressed repeatedly by President Uribe: "Colombia still suffers from violence because of illicit drugs." Thus, if there were no drugs, there would be no terrorism.[37] Vigorous implementation of a policy of zero tolerance against all manifestations of the drug problem, including consumption, can be attributed primarily to this change of focus. The toughening of the war on drugs was reflected, among other things, in the Uribe government's lifting of all restrictions on aerial fumigation of illicit crops, the exponential increase in the fumigated areas, the increase in seizures of coca paste and cocaine and destruction of laboratories, and the rise in the number of extraditions of Colombian nationals to the United States, as discussed in the next section.

The beginning of Plan Patriota in 2003, with the objective of increasing the offensive capability of the armed forces, led to a deeper level of military cooperation between Colombia and the United States. This period coincided with the first of three phases of the strategy to consolidate the PSD, designed in collaboration with the U.S. government and consisting of (1) clearing different areas of the national territory of the FARC in order to establish control of the state; (2) stabilizing controlled areas with the permanent presence of a public force; and (3) consolidating the state presence through a comprehensive action plan that coordinated military and counterinsurgency efforts and the war on drugs, with civil activities, including economic development and the administration of justice.[38] Beginning in 2006, this strategy was fully adopted by the Uribe government in the creation of the Center for Coordination of Integrated Action (Centro de Coordinación de Acción Integral, CCAI), followed by the implementation of comprehensive consolidation plans in various regional centers, including Macarena and Montes de María.[39]

As discussed below, one of the lessons learned from past implementation of the doctrine of integral action in Colombia—especially for the U.S. Agency for International Development (USAID), which administers funds for alternative development—and suggested changes in the approach of the United States, is that the traditional emphasis on the eradication of illicit crops should be replaced by a more flexible policy.[40] This trend is further reinforced by transformations in U.S. aid to Colombia since 2008, consisting of cuts in military assistance, mainly for fumigation, and increases for activities such as alternative development and judicial reform.

Review of the War on Drugs in Bilateral Relations

Several analyses have been made about the achievements and failures of Plan Colombia.[41] While most of them emphasize both safety and drugs, they provide input on assessment of the war on drugs in bilateral Colombian-U.S. relations.[42] It is important to consider the different objectives of both countries in the field of illicit drugs and to analyze available statistics. The United States' main goal has been to minimize the amount of cocaine coming into the country by affecting its purity and price to reduce consumption (which is also discouraged by punitive policies); Colombia has sought to reduce production to lessen the sources of financing of illegal armed groups. Given that the nature of drug trafficking makes it difficult to collect accurate data on prices, profits, and levels of purity and that the two entities that collect statistics on drugs—the government of the United States and the United Nations Office on Drugs and Crime (UNODC)—use different methodologies and measurement tools, we refer where possible to the data of both sources.[43]

Colombia

Colombia, particularly during the two governments of Álvaro Uribe, had as its main focus in the war on drugs the policy of zero tolerance of cocaine production, which includes the reduction of coca leaf crops, the dismantling of laboratories, the seizure of coca paste, cocaine and chemical precursors, and extradition. However, as noted, the Uribe interest in accommodation to and cooperation with the U.S. military in counterinsurgency activities was equal or greater. While PC helped to improve internal security in Colombia, there is consensus that its achievements in reducing cultivation and production of cocaine are relatively far from the proposed goals.[44]

Between 1999 and 2008, there was an overall decline in coca cultivation in Colombia, although there is no consensus in the U.S. State Department reports and UNODC on its magnitude.[45] According to the State Department, the number of cultivated hectares in 2008 (119,000) was almost equal to 1999's level (122,500), the year prior to the implementation of Plan Colombia. In contrast, UNODC statistics suggest that in the 1999–2008 period, coca crops were cut in half, from 160,100 to 81,000 hectares. Regardless of the discrepancy between the figures,[46] both sources show a pendulum trend of ups and downs in coca crops, the increases being more pronounced for the State Department. For both the State Department and UNODC, there is no reciprocation between the rates of reduction in illicit crops and the exponential increase in eradication efforts adopted since 2000. Crops have decreased much more slowly than the increase in their eradication—since 2006, eradication exceeds two or three times the total of cultivated areas—while there are also periods during which illicit crops grew despite substantial increases in eradication efforts. This suggests not only a high capacity for adaptation by growers and the industry in general, but the limited effectiveness of eradication as a predominant strategy to combat drugs.[47]

Since 2005, aerial fumigation of illicit crops has been supplemented with manual eradication, which grew steadily to a peak level in 2008, when 95,620 of 229,117 hectares of coca were eradicated manually. This manual-eradication peak coincided with the first reduction in the total crop area reported by the United States since 2003, which led to the declaration that this was a more effective strategy than aerial fumigation. However, according to the operating balance of the Narcotics Division of Colombia's national police, manual eradication in 2009 fell to 60,557 from a total of 165,329 hectares, not only because it is a more costly and slower method,[48] but because cuts in the assistance provided by the United States have mainly affected the eradication effort.

Felbab-Brown et al. identify three factors that have allowed the recovery of coca in Colombia after the initial successes in its reduction between 2001 and 2003: (1) strategies such as the use of stronger plants, increased crop density, reduction in the territory planted in coca, and techniques that allow farmers and drug traffickers to minimize the effects of fumigation; (2) structural barriers to viable licit alternatives for growers and former growers; and (3) the Uribe government's policy of zero tolerance of illicit crops, which denied government support for those areas of the country where there were still coca crops.[49] This and other analyses conducted by Acevedo, Bewley-Taylor, and Youngers of the International Crisis Group point to the need to formulate a new approach to address the structural causes of coca cultivation, along with integration and synchronization of all elements of antidrug policy.[50]

Although the number of hectares planted in coca in Colombia has decreased (from slightly below to almost half of the total hectares cultivated, according to the State Department and UNODC, respectively), this has not translated into a proportional reduction in potential cocaine production or its availability on the streets of the United States. The data suggest that there has been a reduction in cocaine potential since 2000; however, there is neither a direct nor a constant relationship between the decrease in coca crops and cocaine potential. According to the U.S. government, although between 1998 and 2008 illicit crops declined by only 2.8 percent, potential cocaine production fell by 44.3 percent. In contrast, UNODC claims that the reduction in crops was greater than potential cocaine production, 49.4 and 36.8 percent, respectively.

The asymmetrical relationship between the reduction of crops and potential cocaine production suggests that technological innovations in the drug industry allow the production of more cocaine with less coca leaf.[51] However, the difference between State Department and UNODC figures indicates that there is no consensus on this point. While the UNODC reported 81,000 hectares of coca in Colombia in 2008, compared to 119,000 reported by the State Department, the potential cocaine production was higher for the UNODC than for the State Department, 430 tons compared with just 295. This means the UNODC believes that coca leaf productivity in Colombia is higher than State Department estimates. Meanwhile, in both cases, the reciprocation between crops and cocaine potential is highly variable over time. Between 2001 and 2002, both sources determined that both crops and cocaine potential had fallen, while between 2006 and 2007, coca cultivation increased but production potential decreased.[52]

The data also indicate that cocaine seizures have increased steadily in Colombia, suffering a slight decline in 2006. The most effective actions are seen in the case of the destruction of coca and cocaine base labs, which increased from 347 labs destroyed in 2000 to 1,751 in 2008. There is a trend in seizures that the number of tons of cocaine seized, especially in 2008 (119 tons), tends to approach potential cocaine production (295 tons); thus there should not be much cocaine in Colombia.[53]

Another cornerstone of drug policy in Colombia, especially during the two governments of Álvaro Uribe, is extradition. According to Colombia's Drug Observatory (National Narcotics Directorate, Dirección Nacional de Estupefacientes, DNE), since its reestablishment in 1997, 913 Colombian citizens—including 13 paramilitary leaders—have been extradited to the United States, 849 during the period 2002–2009. This suggests that extradition was no longer an exceptional practice and became instead an everyday deterrent that played a central role in the policy of zero tolerance.

While this strategy immediately removes certain bosses and mid-level leaders from business, the places they occupy in the chain of production are filled quickly as the conditions that make drug trafficking possible are not altered.[54] Similarly, the extradition of paramilitary leaders has had a negative impact on the processes of truth, justice, and adjustment that bring the country and demobilized groups together.[55]

The United States

The main U.S. objective in the war on drugs has been to prevent the entrance of large quantities of cocaine into the country through strategies such as interdiction and eradication, which are intended to affect the drug's availability, price, and purity.[56] Between 2002 and 2006, there was a clear trend toward decreasing or maintaining the price and increase in purity of cocaine, which contradicts the results expected from the war on drugs.[57] By the first half of 2008, this trend had reversed slightly, since, according to data from the National Drug Intelligence Center (NDIC), purity decreased from 63 percent in 2007 to 56 percent, while there was a minimal increase in the price of U.S.$121.00 to $124.00 per gram. On the other hand, it turned out that in 2007 a significant shortage of cocaine in thirty-six major U.S. markets had no visible impact on prices (which should have increased), purity (which should have decreased), or retail distribution.[58] This suggests that blocking the entry of cocaine, by either the increase in seizures or decreases in production, has no direct or immediate effect on purity or prices.[59] Despite this, with the data for 2007 and 2008, it was assumed, with considerable optimism on the part of the Bush administration, that a slight increase in price and a decrease in purity were evidence of the success of the interdiction and eradication policies.

This supposed achievement was questioned by various U.S. organizations, which claimed that it was a passing stage in the cocaine market, similar to other cycles—for example, 1999–2001—which in no way contradicted the clear trend of declining prices and increased purity.[60] These fluctuations can be interpreted as moments of cyclic rearrangement of the structure of drug trafficking, which after being hit, quickly adapts, reorganizes, and provides continuity to business.

In the United States, cocaine consumption behavior does not follow punitive paradigm predictions. Even with increased availability on U.S. streets of lower-priced cocaine, there have been no significant increases in its overall consumption in recent years; this suggests that there is no direct relationship between the availability and the demand for or consumption of cocaine. In fact, 2008 and 2009 NDIC reports suggest that cocaine use has remained stable since 2005, despite lower prices and higher purity.

The problem of consumption has been handled through prevention and treatment programs, but mainly through the persecution and imprisonment of distributors, dealers, and consumers. The punitive component has been problematic for several reasons, including strictness of punishment, high levels of incarceration, increased financial costs for the prison system, and racial bias in the scale of incarceration.[61] To compare the amount invested in education and prevention and the spending on incarceration for drug-related crimes—in 2006, U.S.$12.3 million was spent for the maintenance of prisoners incarcerated for drug-related crimes versus $4.6 million for education during 2008.[62] This provides evidence of a strong imbalance that invites us to reflect on a new outline for drug policy that tends to balance spending in favor of education and prevention.

Collateral Effects

Overall assessments of the war on drugs in bilateral relationships agree that the great achievements of Plan Colombia are not in the reduction of coca crops and cocaine production in Colombia or in U.S. consumption but in

increased security, the weakening of illegal armed groups, the modernization of justice, and the reduction of poppy cultivation, whose demeanor has
been different from cocaine.[63] Besides failing to effectively combat drugs,
such policies have been extremely expensive. Mejía and Restrepo, for example, encountered a deficient relationship between the resources invested
in Plan Colombia by the governments of Colombia and the United States
and its results in terms of crop reduction, potential production, and price
of cocaine.[64]

The fight against drugs in Colombia has also negatively impacted coca
crops and cocaine production in the other two producing countries, Peru
and Bolivia, which have shown increases since 2008 as a result of the "balloon" effect.[65] In the Andean region, coca crops as a whole suffered slight
reductions between 1999 and 2008, although U.S. State Department figures
suggest that they remained almost the same. However, as far as potential
cocaine production is concerned, UNODC information suggests that there
has been only a slight decrease in the potential production of cocaine during the same period, from 925 to 845 tons.

Other identified "collateral" damage relates to the environment, human
rights and democracy, and violence. The environmental, economic, political, and social effects of eradication by fumigation include damage to
vegetation, human health, animals, and water quality,[66] loss or reduction
of legal crops, population displacement in fumigated areas, and intensification of armed conflict.[67] The militarization of antidrug policy has produced
a negative effect on human rights and democracy.[68]

Even on the issue of security, where the consensus on the positive impact
of PC is greater, the correlation between U.S. cooperation and improvement of public safety in Colombia is unclear. In particular, the success of
the comprehensive strategy currently being implemented depends on what
public safety refers to.[69]

Internal Debate in the United States: Gradual Learning?

Since the 1990s, the prohibitionist paradigm has begun to weaken in the
United States, a process in which the decriminalization of marijuana consumption, its legalization for medical purposes, and opposition to prison
policies have played a central role. The use of medical marijuana has been
legalized in twenty-three states and the District of Columbia. In 2009,
Senator Jim Webb (D-Va) introduced a bill to reform the criminal justice
system,[70] and the Obama administration has abandoned George W. Bush's

policy of prosecuting marijuana users in states where medical use is legal or consumption has been decriminalized.

There are signs that this trend may deepen, among them the appointment of former chief of the Seattle Police Department Gil Kerlikowske (in office until March 2014) as drug czar and the changes in antidrug policy in countries like Afghanistan and Colombia.[71] In May 2009, the new drug czar called for ending the war on drugs,[72] whose invocation has played a key role in the securitization of the fight against drugs. This was interpreted as a change in the lens through which the Obama administration perceived the problem. In particular, it suggested that, rather than a threat to security, the drug phenomenon should be treated as a public health issue in which treatment and harm reduction should take priority over incarceration. The fact that the deputy director of the Office of National Drug Control Policy (ONDCP), A. Thomas McLellan (in office until 2012), is a pioneer in addiction and rehabilitation research supports this hypothesis. As a result of this, it is expected that ONDCP priorities will begin to change as has been confirmed by Kerlikowske himself.[73]

Moreover, the transformation of the public debate in the United States on the drug issue has begun to take its toll on Congress, which has been characterized by its inertia in addressing this problem. Congressman Eliot Engel (D-N.Y.) has promoted the Western Hemisphere Drug Policy Commission Act of 2009, whose purpose is to review and assess U.S. antidrug policy, especially in the Western Hemisphere, and propose alternatives for improving existing policy.[74]

Besides the looming changes regarding the general guidelines of U.S. drug policy in Afghanistan and Colombia, the Obama administration has demonstrated a great willingness to learn from the mistakes of the policies implemented so far and to develop an alternative strategy. In Afghanistan, which Felbab-Brown identifies as the test case for new U.S. antidrug policy,[75] there has been a break with the conventional reading of narco-terrorism—which argues that the main objective of a dual war against drugs and terrorism is to eliminate the income sources for armed groups—in favor of prioritizing public safety and an alternative approach to poppy eradication. This supports the argument that the lack of security in various areas of Afghanistan is the reason for the cultivation of poppy crops, and not vice versa.[76] Consequently, the U.S. military no longer participates in or sponsors eradication efforts in Afghanistan.[77]

In the case of Colombia, USAID has argued that the Uribe government's policy of zero tolerance of coca constrained the state's ability to work with local communities and bring about the transition to a legal economy.[78] It has therefore emphasized the need to make current policy more flexible and to change the approach to one in which the eradication of coca is replaced by greater concern with the establishment of the state's institutional presence and economic opportunities other than coca cultivation. Similarly, Stepanova suggests that armed conflict and drug trafficking should not be viewed as purely military problems that can be solved simultaneously, but as long-term phenomena that must be addressed as a part of comprehensive strategies for building democratic states, such as development and integration of marginalized populations and geographic areas.[79]

Recommendations

The growing consensus among various governmental and societal sectors in Colombia and the United States that the war on drugs has failed opens substantial political space for its reformulation. As noted, the securitization of drugs, especially in categories such as "narco-terrorism," has resulted in the militarization of the war on drugs in countries like Colombia while preventing a more open public discussion by establishing a false dichotomy between policy alternatives such as legalization versus prohibition or suppression versus permissiveness. By insisting on this dichotomy, the Uribe government took Colombia farther from the United States (and Europe, but not necessarily with other countries) and lost the opportunity to play a leading role in bilateral discussions on illegal drugs.

Currently, there are conditions in place for the country to take a lead in this discussion. Not only will it bring together a long and extensive experience on the subject, but also it will provide the moral authority to begin a frank discussion of the war on drugs on the hemispheric level.[80] As we have argued, the debate in the United States also has been relaxed, among other reasons, because of the high economic and social costs associated with the current policy.[81] The opening in October 2010 of a high-profile dialogue on human rights, democracy and good governance, energy, and science and technology between Colombia and the United States to restate the terms of bilateral interaction and broaden the agenda can be utilized to drive a parallel binational discussion on drug policy.[82]

This situation is very different from that analyzed by the Colombia–United States Commission in the late 1990s, created with the goal of analyzing the state of bilateral relations, in which drugs occupy a prominent place. More than a decade after the publication of its findings,[83] it is interesting to note that although most of the proposals were never implemented by the two governments, they remain central components of any alternative approach to the problem of illicit drugs: ongoing evaluation of drug legislation to establish its efficacy; objective analysis of the costs and benefits of fumigation policies; greater attention to links in the chain different from cultivation and distribution; systematic following of the debate on drugs in consuming countries; and rejection of a military orientation as a solution to the problem.

Given the analysis throughout this chapter and the current political situation, we conclude with the following recommendations:

1. Taking advantage of current conditions, Colombia should prompt a comprehensive review, involving representative sectors of both countries and of others most affected by drug trafficking, such as Mexico and Brazil, of the role that drugs have played in hemispheric and bilateral relations as well as the costs, results, and adverse effects of their securitization. While the UN Security Council is not an appropriate place for this discussion—because it would reinforce the undesirable perceived relationship between drugs and security—the seat held by Colombia can be used positively to raise the issue with other member states.

2. Colombia needs to diversify its current diplomatic strategy toward the United States, which focuses on the relationship between Bogotá and Washington, with a goal of opening dialogue with states that have adopted policies other than prohibition and criminalization, learning from their experiences, and creating strategic alliances with them, in particular, in their dialogue with the legislative branch. Such rapprochement should include local governments in the areas of Colombia most affected by drug trafficking.

3. Similarly, the Colombian government should encourage discussion with nongovernmental organizations and academic institutions dedicated to research on the effects of the ban, both in Colombia and the United States, in order to have more objective elements of analysis when considering alternative strategies in the fight against drugs.

4. Following the recommendation of USAID and the experience of the coalition in Afghanistan, the governments of Colombia and the United States should channel more resources toward alternative development strategies and nonmilitary strengthening of the

state, which may be more effective. To make such strategies self-sustaining in the long term, it is essential that they be the product of negotiation and consensus building with local governments and affected communities, from identifying the problem that needs to be solved to the design and implementation of policy.

5. The Colombian government must realize that while there is a significant interdependence between illicit drugs and armed conflict, the fact that drug trafficking does not depend exclusively on conflict, and vice versa, requires the adoption of different policies to address each of them, not only its tangible effects but also its root causes. Also, given that the militarization of the war on drugs can worsen the human rights situation in the country, any new strategy to combat drug trafficking should incorporate an explicit proposal for overcoming this dissonance.

Notes

1. An earlier version of this chapter was published in Spanish: Arlene Tickner and Carolina Cepeda, "Las drogas ilícitas en la relación Colombia–Estados Unidos: Balance y perspectivas," in *Política antidroga en Colombia: Éxitos, fracasos y extravíos*, ed. Alejandro Gaviria Uribe and Daniel Mejía Londoño (Bogotá: Uniandes, 2011), 205–234. We would like to thank Uniandes for giving us permission to republish this article. Thanks also to Yulia Vorobyeva for translating this document into English.

2. The balloon effect refers to the tendency of illicit crop cultivation and other stages in drug production, such as traffic, to move to other areas in response to local control campaigns.

3. Various surveys of public opinion, including Zogby, Gallup, and the Pew Research Center for the People and the Press, suggest that around 75 percent of the people living in the United States favor the sale and use of marijuana for medicinal purposes, while between 40 and 50 percent believe that consumption should be legalized completely.

4. See Bruce M. Bagley and Juan G. Tokatlian, "Dope and Dogma: Explaining the Failure of U.S.–Latin American Drug Policies," in *The United States and Latin America in the 1990s: Beyond the Cold War*, ed. Jonathan Hartlyn, Lars Schoulz, and Augusto Varas (Chapel Hill: University of North Carolina Press, 1992), 214–234; Juan Gabriel Tokatlian, *Drugs, Dilemmas and Dogmas* (Bogotá: TM Editores, CIS, 2009); Peter Zirnite, *Reluctant Recruits: The U.S. Military and the War on Drugs* (Washington, D.C.: Washington Office on Latin America [WOLA], 1997).

5. For a more detailed analysis of the main indicators of the illicit-drugs phenomenon in Colombia, see chapter 3 of this volume.

6. David Campbell, *Writing Security* (Minneapolis: University of Minnesota Press, 1992); David Bewley-Taylor, Chris Hallam, and Rob Allen, *The Incarceration of Drug Offenders: An Overview.* (Oxford: Beckley Foundation Drug Policy Program, 2009).

7. Further discussion can be found in Seymour Martin Lipset, *American Exceptionalism: A Double-Edged Sword* (New York: W. W. Norton, 2007); Peter H. Schuck and James Q. Wilson, eds., *Understanding America: The Anatomy of an Exceptional Nation* (New York: Public Affairs/Perseus Books, 2008).

8. Sheila Kennedy, *God and Country: America in Red and Blue* (Waco, Tex.: Baylor University Press, 2007), 178–181.

9. David R. Bewley-Taylor, *The United States and International Drug Control* (New York: Continuum, 2001), 6.

10. Campbell, *Writing Security*, 169–189.

11. Ole Wæver, "Securitization and Desecuritization," in *On Security*, ed. Ronnie D. Lipschutz (New York: Columbia University Press, 1995), 46–86.

12. Ronnie D. Lipschutz, "On Security," in *On Security*, ed. Ronnie D. Lipschutz (New York: Columbia University Press, 1995), 1–23.

13. Wæver, "Securitization and Desecuritization," 46–86.

14. Eva Bertman, Morris Blachman, Kenneth Sharpe, and Peter Andreas, *Drug War Politics: The Price of Denial* (Los Angeles: University of California Press, 1996).

15. Bagley and Tokatlian, "Dope and Dogma," 214–234.

16. Moisés Naím, "Wasted," *Foreign Policy*, April 15, 2009, http://foreignpolicy.com/2009/09/30/wasted/.

17. This risk is not limited to the legislature, as evidenced during the Clinton administration. After a thorough review of drug policy, Clinton introduced significant changes to the policy, which had to be reversed due to congressional pressure.

18. See, for example, the testimony of Rand Beers, assistant secretary for narcotics affairs, "Narco-Terror: The Worldwide Connection between Drugs and Terror," presented to the U.S. Senate, March 13, 2002.

19. Barry Buzan, "Will the 'Global War on Terrorism' be the New Cold War?" *International Affairs* 82, no. 6 (2006): 1101–1118.

20. While the FARC, as well as the ELN and the AUC, were classified as terrorist organizations before February 20, 2002, to that point, the Colombian government refused to use the term in its public references to these armed groups.

21. Russell Crandall, *Driven by Drugs: U.S. Policy toward Colombia* (Boulder, Colo.: Lynne Rienner, 2002); Juan Gabriel Tokatlian, *Drogas, dilemas y dogmas* (Bogotá: TM Editores, CEI, 1995).

22. Despite this, the violence waged by drug cartels in the late 1980s to prevent his extradition led to President Gaviria designing a different strategy, whose main focus was the policy of surrender to the Colombian justice system. However, with the escape of Pablo Escobar from La Catedral jail, the U.S. government lobbied for the country to return to its orthodox antidrug policy. See Tatiana Matthiesen, *Political Art of Reconciling: The Drug Issue in Relations between Colombia and the United States, 1986–1994* (Bogotá: FESCOL-CEREC-Fedesarrollo, 2000).

23. For further analysis of the Samper period, see Juan Gabriel Tokatlian, "The Debate over Drug Legalization in Colombia, President Samper and the United States," *Latin American Research Review* 35, no. 1 (2000): 37–83; Arlene B. Tickner, "U.S. Foreign Policy in Colombia: Bizarre Side-Effects of the 'War on Drugs,'" in *Democracy, Human Rights*

and Peace in Colombia, ed. Gustavo Gallón and Christopher Welna (Notre Dame, Ind.: University of Notre Dame Press, 2007), 309–352.

24. U.S. Government Accountability Office (GAO). 2008. Plan Colombia, GAO-9-71 (Washington, D.C., October 2010).

25. Peter DeShazo, Johanna Mendelson, and Phillip McLean, "Countering Threats to Security and Stability in a Failing State: Lessons from Colombia," Americas Program, Center for Strategic and International Studies (CSIS), no. 6 (2009).

26. Tickner, "U.S. Foreign Policy in Colombia."

27. For a more detailed discussion of the origins of Plan Colombia, see Cynthia J. Arnson and Arlene B. Tickner, "Colombia and the United States: Strategic Partners or Uncertain Allies?" in *Contemporary U.S.–Latin American Relations: Cooperation or Conflict in the Twenty-First Century?* ed. Jorge I. Domínguez and Rafael Fernández de Castro (New York: Routledge, 2010), 164–196.

28. Personal interview with Jaime Ruiz, former director of the National Planning Department, Bogotá, June 4, 2009.

29. Colombia, Office of the President, "Plan Colombia: Plan for Peace, Prosperity and the Strengthening of the State" (Bogotá, 1999), 9.

30. Ibid.

31. Ben Wallace-Wells, "How America Lost the War on Drugs," *Rolling Stone*, December 13, 2007, http://www.rollingstone.com/politics/news/how-america-lost-the-war-on-drugs-20110324; Arnson and Tickner, "Colombia and the United States," 164–196.

32. In a televised address, Pastrana said that "no one can doubt that, between politics and terrorism, FARC opted for terrorism."

33. Luis Alberto Moreno, "Aiding Colombia's War on Terrorism," *New York Times*, May 3, 2002.

34. Colombia, Office of the President and Ministry of National Defense, "Defense Policy and Democratic Security," 2003, 12, http://www.mindefensa.gov.co.

35. Arlene B. Tickner and Rodrigo Pardo, "En busca de aliados para la 'seguridad democrática': La política exterior del primer año de la administración Uribe," *Colombia Internacional* 56–57 (2002): 64–81.

36. Sandra Borda Guzmán, "La internacionalización del conflicto armado después del 11 de septiembre," *Colombia Internacional* 65 (2007): 66–89.

37. Álvaro Uribe's speech before the UN General Assembly, September 24, 2008.

38. The "doctrine of integral action" reflects current U.S. military thinking on counterinsurgency operations, which emphasizes the importance of coordinating these activities with antinarcotics action and the civil presence of the state, as in securing engagement with the civilian population. See Gabriel Marcella, *Affairs of State: The Interagency and National Security* (Washington, D.C.: Strategic Studies Institute, U.S. Army War College, 2008), 433–436.

39. Colombia, Ministry of National Defense, "Policy for the Consolidation of Democratic Security Policy (CSDP)" (Bogotá, 2007).

40. USAID, "Lessons Learned from the Integrated Consolidation Plan for La Macarena (PCIM)," working paper, 2009.

41. Since the 1990s, there have been a number of analyses of the prohibitionist model

and its main deficiencies as applied by the United States and reproduced in producing countries such as Colombia. See Patrick Clawson and Rensselaer W. Lee III, *The Andean Cocaine Industry* (New York: St. Martin's, 1996); Bertman et al., *Drug War Politics*; Francisco Thoumi et al., *Drogas ilícitas en Colombia: Su impacto económico, político y social* (Bogotá: UNDP, DNE, and Editorial Planeta, 1997); Tokatlian, *Drogas, dilemas y dogmas*; USAID, "Lessons Learned."

42. GAO. 2008. Plan Colombia; David R. Bewley-Taylor, Chris Hallam, and Rob Allen, "Incarceration of Drug Offenders," in *Drugs and Democracy in Latin America: The Impact of U.S. Policy*, ed. Coletta Youngers and Eileen Rosin (Buenos Aires: Byblos, 2005); Daniel Mejía and Pascual Restrepo, *The War on Illegal Drug Production and Trafficking: An Economic Evaluation of Plan Colombia* (Bogotá: Uniandes Editions, 2008).

43. Statistics on illicit drugs are published annually and may be consulted in the following reports: U.S. Department of State, International Narcotics Control Strategy Report; UNODC, *Colombia Coca Cultivation Survey*; and idem, *World Drug Report*. See also Francisco Thoumi, "Las drogas ilegales, el fracaso de la política antinarcóticos y la necesidad de reformas institucionales en Colombia," in *La guerra contra las drogas en el mundo andino: Hacia un cambio de paradigma*, ed. Juan Gabriel Tokatlian (Buenos Aires: Libros del Zorzal, 2009), 51–123; Daniel Mejía and Carlos Posada, "Cocaine Production and Trafficking: What Do We Know?" in *Innocent Bystander: Developing Countries and the War on Drugs*, ed. World Bank (New York: Palgrave Macmillan, 2010), 253–300.

44. GAO. 2008. Plan Colombia; Beatriz Acevedo, Dave Bewley-Taylor, and Coletta Youngers, *Ten Years of Plan Colombia: An Analytical Assessment* (Washington, D.C.: Center for Strategic and International Studies [CSIS], 2008); Adam Isacson and Abigail Poe, *After Plan Colombia: Evaluating "Integrated Action," The Next Phase of U.S. Assistance* (Washington, D.C.: Center for International Policy, 2009).

45. According to UNODC, in 2009, coca leaf crops in Colombia decreased from 81,000 to 68,000 hectares. However, as happened between 2007 and 2008, a significant portion of this reduction was due to drought, not the eradication policy. See chapter 1 in this volume.

46. See Thoumi, "Las drogas ilegales"; Mejía and Posada, "Cocaine Production and Trafficking."

47. Ibid.

48. According to the U.S. Bureau of Narcotics, manual eradication of 1,000 hectares of coca takes an average of two months, while the same area can be fumigated in a day, although this does not mean total eradication of the fumigated plants (personal interview, Bogotá, January 6, 2009).

49. Vanda Felbab-Brown, Joel M. Jutkowitz, Sergio Rivas, Ricardo Rocha, James T. Smith, Manuel Supervielle, and Cynthia Watson, *Assessment of the Implementation of the United States Government's Support for Plan Colombia's Illicit Crop Reduction Components* (Washington, D.C.: Management Systems International–USAID, 2009).

50. Bewley-Taylor et al., *The Incarceration of Drug Offenders*; International Crisis Group, "La droga en América Latina I: Perdiendo la lucha," *Informe sobre América Latina* 25 (2008).

51. Mejía and Restrepo, *The War on Illegal Drugs*.

52. The reduction in productivity is attributed in part to the intensification of perfusion, which has reduced the average age of the crop.

53. Double counting of seizures—which are recorded simultaneously as a paste and base and as cocaine hydrochloride—may partly explain this trend.

54. Vanda Felbab-Brown, *Shooting Up: Counterinsurgency and the War on Drugs* (Washington, D.C.: Brookings Institution Press, 2010).

55. Overuse of this instrument was challenged in 2009 by the Colombian Supreme Court, which rejected several requests for extradition based on the argument that crimes against humanity superseded drug trafficking.

56. National Drug Intelligence Center (NDIC), *National Drug Threat Assessment 2007* (Washington, D.C.: U.S. Department of Justice, 2008); idem, *National Drug Threat Assessment 2008* (Washington, D.C.: U.S. Department of Justice, 2009).

57. Between 1997 and 2007, similarly, the price of heroin fell by 30 percent. See Crandall, *Driven by Drugs*; Ekaterina Stepanova, "El negocio de las drogas ilíticas y los conflictos armados: Alcances y límites de sus vínculos," in *Drogas y prohibición: Una vieja guerra, un nuevo debate*, ed. Juan Gabriel Tokatlian (Buenos Aires: Libros del Zorzal, 2010), 313–343; Acevedo et al., *Ten Years of Plan Colombia*.

58. NDIC, *National Drug Threat Assessment 2008*; idem, *National Drug Threat Assessment 2009*.

59. In contrast, the fact that since 2004 there has been an increase in consumption in Europe can explain the periods of scarcity in the U.S. market.

60. John M. Walsh, *Lowering Expectations: Supply Control and the Resilient Cocaine Market* (Washington, D.C.: WOLA, 2009), 2.

61. International Crisis Group (ICG), *Latin American Drugs II*; Bewley-Taylor, *The United States and International Drug Control*.

62. ICG, *Latin American Drugs I*; idem, *Latin American Drugs II*.

63. Acevedo et al., *Ten Years of Plan Colombia*; Felbab-Brown et al., *Assessment of the Implementation*; DeShazo et al., "Countering Threats to Security."

64. Mejía and Restrepo, *The War on Illegal Drug Production*.

65. Coca crops have also been scattered and fragmented as a result of the balloon effect. Between 1999 and 2008, they increased from twelve departments to twenty-four (DNE).

66. It is worth noting that the environmental effects of cocaine production are equally negative.

67. Tomás León Sicard et al., *Observaciones al "Estudio de los efectos en el Programa de Erradicación de Cultivos Ilícitos mediante la aspersión con el herbicida glifosato y de los cultivos ilícitos en la salud humana y en el medio ambiente* (Bogotá: Instituto de Estudios Ambientales, Universidad Nacional de Colombia, 2005); Clawson and Lee, *The Andean Cocaine Industry*.

68. Coletta A. Youngers and Eileen Rosin, eds., *Drugs and Democracy in Latin America: The Impact of U.S. Policy* (Buenos Aires: Biblos, 2005).

69. Isacson and Poe, *Evaluating "Integrated Action."*

70. With only 5 percent of the world's population, the United States has 25 percent of its population in prison, 20 percent of whom are incarcerated because of nonviolent crimes related to drugs.

71. Although Proposition 19, which proposed full legalization of marijuana in California, was not approved in the election on November 2, 2010, it marks an important milestone in the public debate on the subject.

72. Gary Fields, "White House Czar Calls for an End to the War on Drugs," *Wall Street Journal*, May 19, 2009, http://online.wsj.com/article/SB124225891527617397.html.

73. Gil Kerlikowske, "Remarks at the Release of the 2009 World Drug Report," June 24, 2009.

74. It is too early to identify the true impact this revision may have on U.S. policy. The law that will set it in motion still has not been ratified by the Senate, while Republican control of the House of Representatives after the elections of November 2, 2010, may have repercussions on further toughening, at least rhetorically, of laws against illegal drugs. See U.S. House of Representatives, *Act to Establish the Western Hemisphere Drug Policy*, 111th Cong., 1st sess., December 9, 2009.

75. Felbab-Brown, *Shooting Up*, 178.

76. Rod Nordland, "U.S. Turns a Blind Eye to Opium in Afghan Town," *New York Times*, March 20, 2010, http://www.nytimes.com/2010/03/21/world/asia/21marja.html.

77. This policy has not been without controversy. In particular, Russia, the largest consumer of heroin in the world, has accused the United States and NATO of being tolerant of poppy farmers in Afghanistan.

78. USAID, "Lessons Learned."

79. Stepanova, "El negocio de las drogas ilícitas," 313–343.

80. In this regard, see Commission on Drugs and Democracy in Latin America (2009), http://www.opensocietyfoundations.org/sites/default/files/democracy_20090218.pdf.

81. Additionally, the violence associated with drug cartels in Mexico has created a favorable climate for considering alternative strategies, especially in border areas.

82. Regardless of the controversy surrounding the agreement with the United States to use seven military bases in Colombia in mid-2009 (which did not take effect because of a Constitutional Court ruling), it suggests that despite the differences that have existed between the two countries on issues such as human rights, "false positives," and free trade agreements, Colombia is considered an important ally, which implies its potential influence.

83. Comisión Colombia–Estados Unidos, *Informe de la Comisión* (Bogotá: Tercer Mundo Editores, 1998).

9

Escalating Heroin Consumption and the Spread of HIV in Colombia

An Emerging Public Health Threat

CLYDE MCCOY, DANIEL H. CICCARONE, ZELDE ESPINEL BEN-AMY,
JEANENE MCCOY BENGOA, OSCAR BERNAL, DUANE C. MCBRIDE,
AND JAMES M. SHULTZ

In May 2012, at the 51st Session of the Inter-American Drug Abuse Control Commission (CICAD) of the Organization of American States (OAS), convened in Washington, D.C., "prevention of the spread of heroin consumption" was identified as an urgent hemispheric priority. The introduction of opium poppy cultivation and heroin production into Colombia in the 1980s had rapidly transformed the drug trade throughout the Americas. Colombian drug-trafficking organizations (DTOs), together with their compatriots in Mexico, have become the dominant heroin suppliers to the United States, rapidly usurping market share from traditional opium/heroin sources in Southeast and Southwest Asia by driving down prices while providing higher-quality heroin.[1]

Opium poppy cultivation was first detected in Colombia around 2000, signaling the diversification of the illicit-drug crop (continuing to grow coca plants while devoting a smaller proportional acreage to opium poppies).[2] Colombian heroin exports, renowned for high quality and low price, have become very lucrative, particularly with the United States as the primary customer. Heroin supply exceeds demand worldwide, and in Colombia, some "export-quality" heroin remains in the country and is consumed domestically.[3] Currently, Colombia is facing a growing internal threat as substance abuse of all types has reached alarming levels within the adolescent and young adult population. Most worrisome is the rising number of youthful heroin users (HUs) inside Colombia, where the average age of heroin initiation is eighteen.

This quantum transformation of the drug-use landscape within Colombia was highlighted on April 19, 2012, when Justice Minister Juan Carlos Esguerra commented unequivocally that Colombia had transitioned in recent years from being a "producer country to a consumer."[4] He made these comments at a Colombian Senate forum, "Antidrug Policy within an International Security Framework." Referencing the rising rates of drug use in youth, the minister added emphatically, "It is indisputable that there are concerns in Colombia over the advancement of drug addiction in schools and universities."[5] In the same forum, similar sentiments were voiced by health and social protection minister Beatriz Londoño Soto regarding the need to address all forms of substance use and abuse. She too reserved special comment for the rising trend in heroin use among youth.[6]

In short order, heroin use inside Colombia has developed into a national public health emergency, setting in motion escalating epidemics of heroin consumption, injection, and heroin use–associated HIV transmission. According to Minister Londoño, "The consumption of heroin is starting to increase in cities like Cúcuta, Medellín, Bogotá, and regions such as the Coffee Region [Zona Cafetera] and the municipality of Santander de Quilichao in the Department of Cauca."[7] She described how the proliferation in heroin addiction threatened to potentiate epidemics of HIV and hepatitis B.

Minister Londoño's comments had been anticipated by national and international drug-abuse researchers who had been monitoring these emerging drug-use patterns. For example, during the July 12–16, 2010, International Seminar on Drugs and HIV in Colombia, drug-abuse subject matter experts were convened to define the nexus of substance use and HIV risks facing Colombia as trends in both noninjection and injection drug use evolved. In that forum, a key theme of our invited presentation was summarized with the phrases, "Where there is heroin, there is injection; where there is injection, there is infection."[8]

Point of View

Much of the U.S. literature on the international drug trade is posed rather ethnocentrically from the American perspective. Considering the totality of international patterns of drug production and consumption, of supply and demand, this U.S.-centric point of view is distinctly skewed. Given that the United States is the major consumer nation of illicit substances in the world, and therefore, necessarily, a major economic driver for the international drug trade, it is not surprising that it tends to examine the "supplier" nations from a threat perspective and a militant vantage point. Colombia, indeed, is the hemisphere's primary source for cocaine and, along with Mexico, a leading source for heroin.

Cognizant of these realities, in this chapter, we will attempt to present the Colombian story from a more balanced perspective. While acknowledging the notorious drug-supplier role in which Colombia is traditionally cast and routinely stereotyped, we focus primarily on the challenges that Colombia faces when dealing with the emergent patterns of drug consumption within its borders, particularly focusing on heroin.

Opium in the Kingdom of Coca

Colombia has been one of the world's primary source nations for coca and cocaine. Yet despite its stereotypic global identity as the source nation for cocaine, its first major export drug to reach the international market was marijuana, during the 1960s. Colombian marijuana exports to the United States surged in the 1970s, when Mexican marijuana was targeted for crop eradication and drug interdiction.[9] Success with marijuana smuggling led to coca trafficking along the same routes, particularly those transiting the Caribbean.

Historically, communal chewing of coca dates back thousands of years. In the Andean region of the Americas, circa the 1400s, coca was regarded by the Inca as being of divine origin and reserved for special classes. Large-scale cocaine trade gained momentum in the 1970s, as ample supplies of coca leaf and coca paste in the Andean nations (Bolivia, Peru, and Colombia) coincided with strong demand for cocaine in the United States. Colombia ascended to preeminence in the cocaine trade by assuming the intermediary and most profitable roles of processing raw coca into cocaine and devising systems for shipping cocaine undetected across U.S. borders.[10]

Colombia's success as one of two major cocaine suppliers to the United States pivots on its geographic proximity to the United States, which is the number one consumer of drugs in the world, the establishment and maintenance of robust drug supply routes, and remarkable ingenuity in cloaking drug products during transport. Colombian cocaine traverses America's seemingly porous borders with ease despite the proliferation and deployment of massive law enforcement patrolling U.S. borders. Periodically, U.S. drug interdiction efforts achieve stunning successes: seizures of large caches of drugs, captures of high-profile Colombian drug operatives, even drone strikes to assassinate guerrilla leaders. Through the multibillion dollar Plan Colombia, the United States has outfitted Colombia's military with sophisticated technology, trained units in all-terrain tactics, and equipped Colombian law enforcement with cutting-edge intelligence-gathering capabilities. Yet despite this formidable assemblage of personnel and equipment operating in service to the "war on drugs," most Colombian cocaine (and, more recently, heroin) exported to the United States reaches the end users on the streets of America; in exchange, laundered money flows back.

Based on his review of U.S. government documents, Ciccarone attributes the astonishing rise in Colombian cocaine exports,[11] particularly during the 1980s, to the fortuitous actions of the Colombian drug cartels stepping up cocaine trade while U.S. drug policy was preoccupied with drugs from Mexico and fending off the most "dangerous" drugs, such as heroin, coming from the other side of the globe.[12] While the focus of U.S. drug enforcement was distracted by neighboring Mexico, Colombian cartels thrived and cocaine exports catapulted. The 1980s became the epoch of the Medellín and Cali cartels and the flagrant, frenetic use of cocaine that was caricatured and immortalized in the *Miami Vice* television series.

However, with the killing of drug kingpin Pablo Escobar (of the Medellín cartel) in 1993 and the capture, extradition, and incarceration of leaders from both the Medellín and Cali cartels in the 1990s, control of the cocaine trade fragmented into smaller factions for survival and expediency.[13] As control of drug production shifted away from the ribald, in-your-face antics of the giant cartels (portrayed in the exile art of Fernando Botero) and toward smaller, diffuse organizations, the cultivation of the opium poppy took on increasing attraction.

Cicarrone surmises that the United States' blunt force attack on the cocaine trade may actually have been instrumental in promoting diversification to opium poppy.[14] Ironically, the full-bore onslaught to disrupt the cocaine supply may have incentivized the metamorphosis to heroin production. The first report of poppy cultivation in Colombia dates from 1986, but only after the demise of the cartels did the heroin trade gain traction. Compared with cocaine, heroin has a much higher price-to-weight (or price-to-volume) ratio.[15] Stated simply, higher profits can be derived from heroin with nominal hectares of poppy under cultivation as compared with coca. In addition, to achieve the same profitability as cocaine, heroin requires much smaller volumes and less weight of drug product to be transshipped to drug consumers.

Furthermore, both left-wing guerrilla (Revolutionary Armed Forces of Colombia—Fuerzas Armadas Revolucionarias de Colombia, FARC; National Liberation Army—Ejército de Liberación Nacional, ELN) and right-wing paramilitary forces began to take a more active role in the drug trade in the areas they controlled. By their very nature, these armed actors are nimble, mobile, and clandestine. Growing poppy afforded economies of scale. Compared to cocaine, less acreage and fewer workers are necessary. Small, well-hidden plots escape detection while generating substantial profits.

Transforming World Heroin Sources

The latter decades of the twentieth century and first decade of the twenty-first witnessed heroin sourced to the world from geographically dispersed areas. Patterns of heroin supply have been remarkably fluid and dynamic. Within Southeast Asia, the Golden Triangle is the major area of opium cultivation, consisting of remote mountainous regions in northern Myanmar (Burma), Thailand, and Laos. These inaccessible locales are ideal for sustaining the illicit enterprise of cultivating poppy and producing heroin, but they necessitate transshipment of the heroin product overland through the Yunnan Province of China to reach global markets.[16]

As a historical note, for centuries, China was the world center for the opium trade, relying heavily on opium originating in India.[17] Beginning in the sixteenth century and extending until the Communist takeover in 1949, opium abuse was highly prevalent in China, with an estimated 200 million victims. The opium era ended abruptly and, for decades under the harsh sanctions of Communist rule, drug use virtually vanished in China. The "reopening" of China also ushered in illicit-drug imports, including heroin from the Golden Triangle. In China, some of the heroin moving through the Yunnan Province was detoured into local drug markets created by an expanding hidden population of HUs. HUs rapidly transitioned from "chasing the dragon" (inhaling heated heroin) to injection, and rates of injection drug use (IDU)–related HIV spiked upward.[18]

In the mid-1980s, the Golden Triangle supplied 55 percent of heroin consumed worldwide,[19] including 19 percent of the U.S. market.[20] Shortly thereafter, Southwest Asia heroin (from Afghanistan, Pakistan, and Iran) supplanted portions of the markets formerly serviced by the Golden Triangle. From the mid-1980s to 1990, Southwest Asia heroin supplied approximately half of the U.S. heroin trade.

A hemisphere away, in the Americas, Mexico had only been a minor global supplier of heroin in the early 1980s, but due to its shared border with the United States, Mexico became the source of one-third of heroin coming to America by 1986.[21] The emergence of Colombian heroin into the U.S. market during the 1990s tipped the balance of power and fundamentally rearranged North American hemispheric patterns of heroin importation.[22] By 2000, almost 90 percent of retail heroin in the United States came from Colombia (48 percent) and Mexico (39 percent).[23] And by 2007, the Colombia/Mexico market share had reached 98 percent while the Asian share had shrunk to only 2 percent.[24]

Despite the oligopolization of the U.S. heroin market by Colombia and Mexico, prices for heroin fell precipitously. Ciccarone describes the paradox of a "global heroin glut" bringing purity up and price down even as control of heroin sources for heroin supplied to the United States became centralized in Latin America.[25]

Drugs and Colombian Culture

Long-term, Colombian culture has been saturated with drugs—but not drug abuse. Drug crops have been cultivated throughout the last three millennia or longer. With the availability of chemical solvents in recent decades, drug crops (coca and *amapola*) could be synthesized into physically compact, high-potency cocaine and heroin derivatives for transport and export. Even so, high rates of drug consumption have not been reported in Colombia. While Colombia has been the primary cocaine supplier to the world, the lifetime prevalence of cocaine use inside the country has hovered at only 4 percent—one quarter the rate in the United States. Lifetime prevalence of heroin use is less than 1 percent.[26] Indeed, opiate use has been uncommon throughout all of Latin America until recent times.[27] Thus, the public health consequences of drug abuse per se have not yet impacted the Colombian population.

This does not mean that Colombia has not experienced repercussions from the drug trade. Drugs fund the proliferation of armed actors, including guerrillas, paramilitaries, mafias, and common criminals. By providing the economic engine for these warring factions, drugs have played both direct and indirect roles in decades of human rights violations. Colombian citizens have endured extortion from competing militants, displacement, disappearance, kidnappings, assassinations, massacres, and forced recruitment into armed groups. These armed conflicts, dating from the period known as "La Violencia" (commencing in 1948), have resulted in at least

200,000 deaths and pervasive historical trauma. In fact, Colombia has the highest number of internally displaced persons (IDPs) of any nation.

Despite the extraordinary loss of life and livelihood through population-wide systemic violence, with all perpetrators drawing financial sustenance from the drug trade, nevertheless, Colombia had been seemingly spared from major health and disease consequences of drug abuse per se. Two recent, intersecting, trends threaten to destabilize this situation: first, rates of substance use, including polysubstance use, are rising among youth; second, heroin use is proliferating inside Colombian cities. With regard to heroin, Colombia is breaking from the previously established pattern of supplier nations; in other words, it is no longer "abstaining."

Colombia: Heroin on the Horizon

The recent introduction of opium poppy cultivation in Colombia and Mexico has resulted in spreading epidemics of heroin consumption, heroin injection, and heroin use–associated HIV transmission. As noted, prevention of the spread of heroin consumption throughout the Americas was identified as an urgent hemispheric priority during the 51st Session of CICAD. Presentations on this theme were given by the CICAD commissioner from Mexico and a high-ranking official from the Colombian Ministry of Health and Social Protection. Both of these opium-cultivating, heroin-producing nations are vulnerable to surges in consumption within their borders, and this has already been documented inside Colombia.

Just three weeks prior to the OAS/CICAD convocation, the Colombian government sounded the alarm in an April 19, 2012, forum where the results of a nationwide school-based survey of more than 92,000 students[28] were juxtaposed against data from two cross-sectional studies of IDUs[29] regarding drug and sexual-risk behaviors for HIV infection. Comments from the ministers of justice and health were presented in the opening paragraphs of this chapter.[30]

The substrate for heroin use is a new generation of youthful substance users. The national survey of 92,000 students ages eleven to eighteen indicated that one-third drank alcohol, one-quarter smoked tobacco, one-fifth used energy drinks, and one-eighth used illicit drugs.[31] In five of Colombia's thirty-two departments, rates are even higher, with one-in-five students using illicit drugs (marijuana and cocaine are the most commonly mentioned).

Since heroin use is reported by less than 1 percent of students, why the national concern? The answer cannot be found in the school survey. Many youthful heroin users are not in school, and the upper age on the survey (eighteen) is actually the mean age when adolescents begin to experiment with heroin. Two contemporaneous surveys of IDUs supply the missing link.[32] Studies of IDUs—primarily HUs—in Medellín and Pereira[33] and in Cúcuta[34] found that half were in the eighteen to twenty-four age range. This is an extremely young population of HUs already transitioning to injection. Most of these IDUs "graduated" to injection of heroin after a period of using a variety of noninjection drugs.

To illustrate this point, consider data on IDUs in Medellín, capital of the Department of Antioquia and Colombia's second-largest city, and Pereira, capital of the Department of Risaralda in Colombia's famed coffee region.[35] Using a sophisticated respondent-driven sampling approach for developing a representative sample of these hidden and hard-to-reach populations, Ministry of Health and CES University researchers sampled 237 IDUs in Medellín and 297 in Pereira. The following data are presented as percentage of Medellín sample/percentage of Pereira sample. IDUs are very young (ages eighteen to twenty-four: 53.8 percent/60.5 percent; ages eighteen to thirty-four: 95.1 percent/89.5 percent), predominantly male (94.4 percent/92.4 percent), single (82.4 percent/83.2 percent), and low socioeconomic status (70.4 percent/81.7 percent).

In the thirty days immediately prior to initiation of drug injection, study participants reported (noninjection) use of the following drugs: pure heroin (54.7 percent/77.7 percent), mixture of heroin and cocaine (34.3 percent/18.3 percent), mixture of heroin with other drugs (32.0 percent/37.0 percent), pure cocaine (66.1 percent/77.7 percent), marijuana (90.8 percent/86.5 percent), benzodiazapines (40.2 percent/29.5 percent), basuco (20.3 percent/39.7 percent), and alcohol (65.0 percent/57.2 percent).

These data proffer a set of interrelated inferences: (1) noninjection use of substances typically precedes initiation of drug injection; (2) most IDUs have previously used both licit and illicit substances; and (3) most IDUs experimented with noninjection use of heroin before transitioning to injection of heroin. This is where the school study becomes very important.[36] Although most students ages eleven to eighteen who participated in the study had not experimented with heroin prior to completing the survey, large proportions had experimented with the "gateway" drugs that tend to predict later use of "harder" drugs.[37] The large, youthful, substance-using population profiled in the survey will soon advance to the age range where heroin experimentation and regular use are more common.

The Medellín/Pereira study of IDUs also provides evidence that IDUs/ HUs are polysubstance users.[38] The following data are presented as percentage of Medellín sample/percentage of Pereira sample. Recall that all study participants were current IDUs and they reported the following rates of *past-year* use of other substances: cigarettes (85.1 percent/93.1 percent), alcohol (70.9 percent/68.9 percent), alcohol to the point of intoxication (56.2 percent/48.0 percent), marijuana (88.7 percent/87.5 percent), cocaine (81.7 percent/46.5 percent), rohypnol (74.7 percent/51.2 percent), basuco (22.9 percent/50.5 percent), and inhalants (25.9 percent/14.1 percent).

Where There Is Injection, There Is Infection

We previously presented in Bogotá on a mainstream theme from our four decades of research on IDUs that began even before HIV was known or crack cocaine was introduced. We were able to explore and document the nexus of drug use and sexual risks for HIV infection.[39] Having followed cohorts of thousands of IDUs over time we can say the following plainly: (1) where there is heroin, there will be injection; and (2) where there is injection, there will be infection (with HIV, hepatitis B, hepatitis C, and other blood-borne pathogens). This was the focus of our presentation in 2010 at the International Seminar on Drugs and HIV in Bogotá.[40]

This has now come full circle. The Colombian research reports have found rates of HIV infection in IDUs in Pereira of 2.0 percent; Medellín, 3.8 percent; and Cúcuta (capital of the Department of Norte de Santander), 9.0 percent[41]—sufficiently high to sustain an HIV epidemic indefinitely. Colombia is on the verge of a major drug-related overlay to their ongoing national HIV epidemic.

Four Epidemiological Factors and Points for Potential Intervention

The driving force behind the brewing drug-associated HIV epidemic in Colombia comes from four compounding contributors: (1) increasing prevalence of heroin use; (2) ongoing transition from inhalation to injection of heroin; (3) significant drug use/sexual HIV risks among drug users; and (4) increasing HIV/HCV infection among drug users.

Increasing Prevalence of Heroin Use

The 2008 Colombian National Household Survey on Drug Use estimated that 37,800 persons had tried heroin,[42] but the authors concluded that this figure was an underestimate due to the clandestine nature of heroin use, the increasing demand for treatment of heroin addiction, the rising rate of heroin overdose deaths in Bogotá and Medellín, and the fact that the people most at risk for heroin use were underrepresented in the household survey.

As highlighted by the minister of health in April 2012, heroin use is well established in Colombia's three largest cities (Bogotá, Medellín, Cali), capital cities in the coffee region (Armenia, Pereira, and possibly Manizales), along the Venezuelan frontier (Cúcuta), in resort cities along the Atlantic Coast (e.g., Cartagena de Indias), and in areas where opium poppy (*amapola*) is cultivated (e.g., Santander de Quilichao in the Department of Cauca). Accelerating the adoption of the heroin habit is the availability of high-quality heroin at very low prices. Added to this is the purposeful initiation of adolescent youth into heroin use through the inducement of "free" samples in places such as Santander de Quilichao. Further research is required because this is one of the first reports internationally of the use of heroin as the initial drug of abuse, in contrast to the usual progression through a series of gatekeeper drugs (cigarettes, alcohol, marijuana) prior to experimentation with harder illicit drugs such as heroin.[43]

Ongoing Transition from Inhalation to Injection

Injection use of heroin elevates risks for morbidity and mortality associated directly with heroin injection and with transmission of HIV, HCV, and other blood-borne infections.[44] Initially, Colombian HUs tended to inhale heroin (inhaling the aerosol smoke plume from heroin powder heated in soda cans—described as "chino," "dragon," or "aluminio") due to several factors: (1) easy access to heroin; (2) high purity; (3) low price; (4) needle aversion; and (5) stigma associated with injection drug use. Injection is now progressively replacing inhalation due to a reverse set of factors: (1) intentional dilution of heroin purity; (2) increasing price; (3) availability of needles and syringes at low cost without prescription at local pharmacies; (4) conserving drug doses (one inhalation dose is equivalent to eight to ten injection doses); and (5) the strong, dependable "high" achieved through injection. The best current approximation is that 20–40 percent of Colombian HUs are injecting heroin (Inés Elvira Mejía Motta, consultant to the Colombian Ministry of Health, personal communication, May 2012).

Significant Drug Use and Sexual Risks among Drug Users

Along with injection, the practice of sharing needles is common; for example, as early as 2003, 47 percent of Bogotá IDUs reported sharing needles.[45]

The rate of needle sharing varies by geography; in 2010–2011, 12 percent of Pereira IDUs reported sharing needles during the last injection event, while for Medellín, sharing was reported by 20 percent, and in Cúcuta, 40 percent. Additional insights can be gained by examining the snapshot provided in the results of a recent study of IDUs in Medellín and Pereira where 90 percent of IDUs injected one to four times daily and the remainder, five to nine times daily. While injecting, 38 percent had shared their "works" (syringes, cookers, cottons, rinse waters, etc.) with someone else in the past six months. IDUs justified sharing equipment based on being careful in selecting injection partners and believing that cleaning works with water made them safe. Half of Medellín IDUs (52.3 percent) and one-third of Pereira IDUs (35.0 percent) got money, drugs, or material things through the sale of drugs, needles/syringes, or payment for injecting others.

The majority of IDUs reported having vaginal or anal sex with a regular partner in the past six months, and greater than 40 percent reported having sex with a casual partner. With regular sexual partners, almost half of the IDUs reported "never" using condoms (49 percent) while "always" using condoms was reported by only one in five. With casual partners, condom use was more common. About 15 percent of IDUs reported receiving money or drugs for sex, and about 15 percent reported paying money or giving drugs in exchange for sex. Moreover, 39 percent reported "never" using condoms when having intercourse with sex workers.

Increasing HIV/HCV Infection Rates among Drug Users

Some Colombian IDUs who inject heroin, or heroin in combination with other drugs, have already progressed to HIV infection. HIV seroprevalence in Bogotá IDUs was just 1 percent in 2003. By 2010–2011, HIV infection rates had increased to 2.0 percent in Pereira, 3.8 percent in Medellín, and 9.0 percent in Cúcuta. This contrasts with mature epidemics elsewhere, including 30 percent HIV seroprevalence rates among South Florida IDUs in our studies,[46] so the prognosis for Colombia is for rapidly rising rates of HIV infection among IDUs.

The Critical Moment for Intervention

Each of the four contributing factors represents a potential point for intervention along the risk continuum. The heroin-associated HIV epidemic in Colombia is already in process, but there may be a brief window of time available to intervene.

Intervening on Rising Rates of Heroin Use

The good news is that (1) most youth are not using illicit drugs, (2) most youth who are using illicit drugs have not experimented with heroin, and (3) most youth are accessible through the neighborhoods and communities, including schools. Effective school-based drug-prevention programs can be adapted for use in Colombia. Education needs to be coupled with referral to science-based substance-abuse treatment for youth who are identified as having alcohol and/or drug-related problem behaviors or addiction. Other evidence-based community programs can be adopted for the specific cultural environments of Colombia. These can operate as a first line of defense against the escalation of heroin use.

Preventing the Transition from Inhalation to Injection Use of Heroin

Most Colombian HUs are not yet IDUs. But the window of opportunity is vanishingly brief, as we learned in China in the 1990s. We were among the few international investigators who directly observed the rapid reemergence of drug abuse and the early phases of the drug-related HIV/AIDS epidemic when China reopened after the era of Communist control (when proscription of drug use was enforced with the death penalty). With drug use came heroin, and with heroin came the almost-immediate transition from inhalation (chasing the dragon) to injection. HIV rates among Chinese IDUs surged. Intervention was not implemented early enough, and the Chinese HIV epidemic continues to spread among IDUs. In contrast, Colombia has a brief moment of intervention potential while 60–80 percent of HUs are not yet IDUs.

At least three basic methods have proven to be successful for reducing high-risk drug use behaviors: (1) behavioral risk reduction programs; (2) drug treatment; and (3) access to sterile injection equipment.[47] Different strategies are available for acquiring or sterilizing injection equipment that could be introduced in Colombia, including low-cost bleach disinfection.[48] Drug-treatment programs are financially inaccessible to drug users with limited resources,[49] and the scientific rigor of these programs is highly variable throughout Colombia. Adaptation of evidence-based behavioral interventions, such as the National Institute on Drug Abuse (NIDA) Standard,[50] represents a viable option for reducing the transition from inhalation to injection.[51]

Intervening on Drug Use and Sexual Risks of Heroin Users

HUs and IDUs have two behavioral avenues of risk for infection: unsafe drug use (sharing needles, syringes, and other injection paraphernalia), and unsafe sexual behaviors (interrelated with the drug use itself).[52] We have been evaluating the effectiveness of behavioral intervention programs with drug users since the mid-1980s, culminating with our recent randomized community-based trial, which demonstrated that these programs are effective for reducing both drug and sexual risk relative to HIV.[53] Developing evidence-based behavioral interventions tailored to the HUs in Colombia may successfully decrease both drug use and sexual risks.

Preventing the Increase of HIV/HCV Infections among Heroin Users

Here there is a prime opportunity to intervene and thwart a rising epidemic. Even in Cúcuta, where the seroprevalence rate among IDUs is now 9 percent, an estimated 60 percent of HUs have not progressed to drug injection, so the strategies to prevent HIV infection are applicable. Some of the same evidence-based interventions that have proven effective for reducing drug use and sexual risk will also dampen the rise in seroprevalence of HIV/HCV and other blood-borne pathogens.[54]

For those HUs and IDUs already infected, NIDA recommends the approach of Seek, Test, Treat, and Retain as the best-practices approach to providing optimal HIV care to seropositives while simultaneously intervening to prevent serial transmission of HIV infection to their sexual and drug-sharing partners. This represents an additional line of defense along the risk continuum and focuses on the subset of drug-using HIV seropositives.

In conclusion, Colombia may present the best opportunity of any country for exploring the scientific answers to the complex interrelationships among production, distribution, and consumption of heroin. It also presents the opportunity to determine whether the seemingly relentless progression from nonuse of heroin, to noninjection use of heroin, to injection use of heroin (with its attendant risks for HIV transmission) can be slowed or halted. Evidence-based scientific interventions must address prevention, intervention, and treatment for at-risk, drug-addicted, and HIV-infected individuals. Critically needed for comprehensive programming in Colombia are culturally adapted, population-based, ecologically grounded public health and policy measures targeting drug and HIV risk behaviors across multiple spheres of influence and designed for delivery at individual, school, community, and population levels.

Notes

1. Daniel Ciccarone, George J. Unick, and Allison Kraus, "Impact of South American Heroin on the U.S. Heroin Market 1993–2004," *International Journal of Drug Policy* 20, no. 5 (2009): 392–401.

2. Daniel Ciccarone, "Heroin in Brown, Black and White: Structural Factors and Medical Consequences in the U.S. Heroin Market," *International Journal of Drug Policy* 20, no. 3 (2009): 277–282.

3. Daniel Ciccarone, "The Political Economy of Heroin: Regional Markets, Practices and Consequences," *International Journal of Drug Policy* 17, no. 5 (2005): 289–290.

4. Mark Hall, "Drug Use on the Rise in Colombia's Cities," Colombia Reports, April 19, 2012, http://colombiareports.com/colombia-news/news/23563-drug-use-on-the-rise-in-colombias-cities-govt.html; Colombia, Ministerio de Salud y Protección Social, *Boletín de Prensa* no. 070, 2012: "Cuando hablamos de consumo de sustancias psicoactivas no podemos centrar el debate en las ilegales," last modified April 19, 2012, http://www.min salud.gov.co/Paginas/%E2%80%9CCuando%20hablamos%20de%20consumo%20de% 20sustancias%20psicoactivas.aspx.

5. Colombia, Ministerio de Salud y Protección Social, *Estudio de prevalencia de VIH y comportamientos de riesgo asociados en usuarios de droga por vía inyectada (UDI) en Medellín y Pereira*, Investigación del Ministerio de Protección Social realizada por la Universidad CES en el marco del convenio con la Oficina de las Naciones Unidas contra la Droga y el Delito (New York: United Nations Office on Drugs and Crime [UNODC], 2012).

6. Colombia, Ministerio de Salud y Protección Social, *Boletín de Prensa* no. 070;" Colombia, Ministerio de Salud y Protección Social, *El consumo de heroína en Cúcuta, una realidad visible, evaluación rápida de situación del consumo de heroína y seroprevalencia de VIH en los municipios de Cúcuta y Pamplona para el desarrollo del plan de respuesta rápido en heroína del departamento de Norte de Santander* (2012).

7. Hall, "Drug Use on the Rise."

8. Clyde B. McCoy and James M. Shultz, "Culturas diferentes, problemas similares: Experiencias del estudio del consumo de heroína en los Estados Unidos y China," paper presented at the Seminario Internacional: Drogas y VIH en Colombia, Bogotá, July 12, 2010.

9. Ciccarone, "Heroin in Brown, Black and White;" María Celia Toro, "The Internationalization of Police: The DEA in Mexico," *Journal of American History* 86, no. 2 (1999): 623–640; Francisco Thoumi, "Illegal Drugs in Colombia: From Illegal Economic Boom to Social Crisis," *Annals of the American Academy of Political and Social Science* 582, no. 1 (2002): 102–116; U.S. Drug Enforcement Administration (DEA), *Drug Enforcement Administration: A Tradition of Excellence 1973–2003* (Washington, D.C.: U.S. Department of Justice, DEA, 2005).

10. Ciccarone, "Heroin in Brown, Black and White"; DEA, *Coca Cultivation and Cocaine Processing: An Overview* (Washington, D.C., 1993); UNODC, *Crime Prevention: Global Illicit Drug Trends 1999* (New York: United Nations Publications, 1999).

11. Ciccarone, "Heroin in Brown, Black and White."

12. DEA, *Drug Enforcement Administration*; U.S. Domestic Council Drug Abuse Task Force, *White Paper on Drug Abuse, September 1975: A Report to the President from the Domestic Council Drug Abuse Task Force* (Washington, D.C., 1975).

13. Ciccarone, "Heroin in Brown, Black and White."

14. Ibid.

15. UNODC, *Crime Prevention*; DEA, "Colombian Heroin a Major Threat: Almost One Third of Heroin Seized in the United States Originates in South America," news release, June 21, 1995.

16. Clyde B. McCoy, Shenghan Lai, Lisa R. Metsch, Xue-ren Wang, Cong Li, Ming Yang, and Li Yulong, "No Pain No Gain: Establishing the Kunming, China Drug Rehabilitation Center," *Journal of Drug Issues* 27, no. 1 (1997): 73–85.

17. Jack Beeching, *The Chinese Opium Wars* (New York: Harcourt Brace Jovanovich, 1975); C. Suwanwela and V. Poshyachinda, "Drug Abuse in Asia," *Bulletin on Narcotics* 38, nos. 1–2 (1986): 41–53.

18. McCoy et al., "No Pain No Gain."

19. UNODC, *Crime Prevention*.

20. National Narcotics Intelligence Consumers Committee (NNICC), *NNICC Report 1991: The Supply of Illicit Drugs to the United States* (Arlington, Va., NNICC, 1992).

21. Ciccarone et al., "Impact of South American Heroin"; President's Commission on Organized Crime, *America's Habit: Drug Abuse, Drug Trafficking, and Organized Crime, Report to the President and the Attorney General* (Washington, D.C.:, 1986).

22. Ciccarone et al., "Impact of South American Heroin."

23. DEA, *Domestic Monitor Program 1999–2000* (Washington, D.C.: Domestic Strategic Unit, Domestic Intelligence Section, Office of Domestic Intelligence, 2002).

24. DEA, *2006 Domestic Monitor Program* (Washington, DC: Domestic Strategic Intelligence Unit, Special Strategic Intelligence Section, 2007).

25. Ciccarone, "Heroin in Brown, Black and White."

26. Gobierno Nacional de la República de Colombia, *Estudio nacional de consumo de drogas en Colombia,* data from the 2008 National Household Survey on Drug Use (Bogotá: Ministerio del Interior y de Justicia, Ministerio de la Protección Social, and Dirección Nacional de Estupefacientes, 2009).

27. UNODC, *World Drug Report, 2011* (New York, 2011).

28. Gobierno Nacional de la República de Colombia, *Estudio nacional de consumo de sustancias psicoactivas en población escolar.* (Bogotá: UNODC, 2011).

29. Colombia, Ministerio de Salud y Protección Social, *Estudio de prevalencia de VIH y comportamiento de riesgo asociados, en usarios de drogas por vía inyectada (UDI) en Medellín y Pereira* (Bogotá, March 29, 2011), http://observatoriovihycarceles.org/es/vih-drogas/drogas-y-vih-drogas-menu.raw?task=download&fid=635; idem, *El consumo de heroína en Cúcuta.*

30. Hall, "Drug Use on the Rise"; Colombia, Ministerio de Salud y Protección Social, *Boletín de Prensa* no. 070; Sarah Kinosian, "Drug Use High among Colombian Students," *Colombia Reports*, April 27, 2012, http://colombiareports.com/colombia-news/news/23755-colombia-becoming-drug-consuming-nation-report-.html.

31. Gobierno Nacional de la República de Colombia, *Estudio nacional de consumo de sustancias psicoactivas.*

32. Colombia, Ministerio de Salud y Protección Social, *Estudio de prevalencia de VIH*; idem, *El consumo de heroína en Cúcuta.*

33. Colombia, Ministerio de Salud y Protección Social, *Estudio de prevalencia de VIH.*

34. Colombia, Ministerio de Salud y Protección Social, *El consumo de heroína en Cúcuta.*

35. Colombia, Ministerio de Salud y Protección Social, *Estudio de Prevalencia de VIH.*

36. Gobierno Nacional de la República de Colombia, *Estudio nacional de consumo de sustancias psicoactivas.*

37. Clyde B. McCoy, "Global Research Opportunities: Conducting Drug Abuse & HIV Research (Spectrum of Risks)," University of Miami, May–June 2007.

38. Colombia, Ministerio de Salud y Protección Social, *Estudio de prevalencia de VIH.*

39. Clyde B. McCoy, Lisa R. Metsch, James A. Inciardi, Robert S. Anwyl, Judith Wingerd, and Keith Bletzer, "Sex, Drugs, and the Spread of HIV/AIDS in Belle Glade, Florida," *Medical Anthropology Quarterly* 10, no. 1 (1996): 83–93; Clyde B. McCoy, Lisa R. Metsch, Fernando Collado-Mesa, Kristopher L. Arheart, Sarah E. Messiah, Dolores Katz, and Paul Shapshak, "The Prevalence of Human Immunodeficiency Virus Type 1 and Hepatitis C Virus among Injection Drug Users Who Use High Risk Inner-City Locales in Miami, Florida," *Memórias do Instituto Oswaldo Cruz,* Rio de Janeiro 99, no. 8 (2004): 789–793; Clyde B. McCoy, Shenghan Lai, Lisa R. Metsch, Sarah E. Messiah, and Wei Zhao, "Injection Drug Use and Crack Cocaine Smoking: Independent and Dual Risk Behaviors for HIV Infection," *Annals of Epidemiology* 14 (2004): 535–542; Clyde B. McCoy and Duane McBride, "HIV Research within the Global Context: Introduction to the Special Issue," *Journal of Urban Health* 82, no. 3 (2005): 2–4; Clyde B. McCoy and Frank Rodríguez, "Global Overview of Injecting Drug Use and HIV Infection," *Lancet* 365 (2005): 1008–1009.

40. McCoy and Shultz, "Culturas diferentes."

41. Colombia, Ministerio de Salud y Protección Social, *Estudio de prevalencia de VIH;* idem, *El consumo de heroína en Cúcuta.*

42. Gobierno Nacional de la República de Colombia, *Estudio nacional de consumo de drogas.*

43. Shenghan Lai, Hong Lai, John Bryan Page, and Clyde B. McCoy, "The Association between Cigarette Smoking and Drug Abuse in the United States," *Journal of Addictive Diseases* 19, no. 4 (2000): 11–24; McCoy and McBride, "HIV Research."

44. McCoy, Lai et al., "Injection Drug Use."

45. Anna Maria Bueno Ramírez, Zelde Espinel, Inez E. Mejía Motta, D. Ojeda Visbal, J. C. Varon Forero, Clyde B. McCoy, and James M. Shultz, "Colombia: Nexus of Armed Conflict, Heroin, and HIV," CPDD Annual Meeting, Palm Springs, California, June 2012, http://www.cpdd.vcu.edu/Pages/Meetings/Meetings_PDFs/2012Programbook.pdf.

46. McCoy, Lai et al., "Injection Drug Use."

47. Brian R. Edlin, Kathleen L. Irwin, Sairus Faruque, Clyde B. McCoy, Carl Word, Yolanda Serrano, James A. Inciardi, Benjamin P. Bowser, Robert F. Schilling, Scott D. Holmberg, and the Multicenter Crack Cocaine and HIV Infection Study Team, "Intersecting Epidemics—Crack Cocaine Use and HIV Infection among Inner-City Young Adults," *New England Journal of Medicine* 331, no. 21 (1994): 1422–1427; Lisa R. Metsch, Virginia V. McCoy, Clyde B. McCoy, Christine Miles, Brian R. Edlin, and Margaret Pereyra, "Use of Health Care Services by Women Who Use Crack Cocaine," *Women and Health* 30, no. 1 (2000): 37–53.

48. Duane C. McBride and Clyde B. McCoy, "The Drugs-Crime Relationship: An Analytical Framework," *Prison Journal* 73, nos. 3–4 (1993): 257–278; Paul Shapshak, Clyde

B. McCoy, Jim E. Rivers, Dale D. Chitwood, Deborah C. Mash, Norman L. Weatherby, James A. Inciardi, S. M. Shah, and B. S. Brown, "Inactivation of Human Immunodeficiency Virus-1 at Short Time Intervals Using Undiluted Bleach," *Journal of Acquired Immune Deficiency Syndromes and Human Retrovirology* 6, no. 2 (1993): 218–219; James A. Inciardi, Duane C. McBride, Clyde B. McCoy, Hilary L. Surratt, and C. A. Saum, "Violence, Street Crime, and the Drug Legalization Debate: A Perspective and Commentary on the U.S. Experience," *Studies on Crime and Crime Prevention* 4, no. 1 (1994): 105–118; Paul Shapshak, Clyde B. McCoy, S. M. Shah, John B. Page, Jim E. Rivers, Norman L. Weatherby, Dale D. Chitwood, and Deborah C. Mash, "Preliminary Laboratory Studies of Inactivation of HIV-1 in Needles and Syringes Containing Infected Blood Using Undiluted Household Bleach," *Journal of Acquired Immune Deficiency Syndromes and Human Retrovirology* 7, no. 7 (1994): 754–759; K. S. Sridhar, W. A. Raub, Norman L. Weatherby, Lisa R. Metsch, H. L. Surratt, James A. Inciardi, Robert C. Duncan, Robert S. Anwyl, and Clyde B. McCoy, "Possible Role of Marijuana Smoking as a Carcinogen in the Development of Lung Cancer at a Young Age," *Journal of Psychoactive Drugs* 26, no. 3 (1994): 285–288; Clyde B. McCoy and James A. Inciardi, *Sex, Drugs, and the Continuing Spread of AIDS* (Los Angeles: Roxbury, 1995); Clyde B. McCoy, Lisa R. Metsch, and James A. Inciardi, eds., *Intervening with Drug Involved Youth* (Thousand Oaks, Calif.: Sage Publications, 1996); Dale D. Chitwood, D. K. Griffin, Mary Comerford, John B. Page, Edward J. Trapido, Shenghan Lai, and Clyde B. McCoy, "HIV Risk Factors among Seroincident Injection Drug Users: A Case Control Study," *American Journal of Public Health* 85, no. 11 (1995): 1538–1542; Dale D. Chitwood, Duane C. McBride, Lisa R. Metsch, Mary Comerford, and Clyde B. McCoy, "A Comparison of the Need for Health Care Utilization of Health Care by Injection Drug Users, Other Chronic Drug Users, and Non-Drug Users," *American Behavioral Scientist* 41, no. 8 (1998): 1107–1122; Dale D. Chitwood, John B. Page, Mary Comerford, James A. Inciardi, Clyde B. McCoy, Edward J. Trapido, and Shenghan Lai, "The Donation and Sale of Blood by Intravenous Drug Users," *American Journal of Public Health* 81, no. 5 (1991): 631–633.

49. Lisa R. Metsch, Clyde B. McCoy, Virginia H. McCoy, James M. Shultz, Shenghan Lai, Norman L. Weatherby et al., "HIV-related Risk Behaviors and Seropositivity among Homeless Drug-Abusing Women in Miami, Florida," *Journal of Psychoactive Drugs* 27, no. 4 (1995): 435–446; Virginia H. McCoy, Clyde B. McCoy, Shenghan Lai, Norman L. Weatherby, and Sarah Messiah, "Behavior Changes among Crack-Using Rural and Urban Women," *Substance Use and Misuse* 34, nos. 4–5 (1999): 667–684.

50. Dale D. Chitwood, James Inciardi, Duane McBride, Clyde B. McCoy, Virginia H. McCoy, and Edward J. Trapido, *A Community Approach to AIDS Intervention: Exploring the Miami Outreach Project for Injecting Drug Users and Other High Risk Groups* (Westport, Conn.: Greenwood Press, 1991).

51. Clyde B. McCoy, Victor De Gruttola, Lisa R. Metsch, and Mary Comerford, "A Comparison of the Efficacy of Two Interventions to Reduce HIV Risk Behaviors among Drug Users," *AIDS and Behavior* 15, no. 8 (2011): 1707–1714.

52. Clyde B. McCoy, Dale D. Chitwood, Elizabeth L. Khoury, and Christine E. Miles, "The Implementation of an Experimental Research Design in the Evaluation of an Intervention to Prevent AIDS among IV Drug Users," *Journal of Drug Issues* 20, no. 2 (1990): 213–219; Clyde B. McCoy and Elizabeth L. Khoury, "Drug Use and the Risk of AIDS," *American Behavioral Scientist* 33, no. 4 (1990): 419–431; D. Simpson, L. Camacho, K. Vogts-

berger, M. Williams, R. Stephens, and A. Jones, "Reducing AIDS Risks through Community Outreach for Drug Injectors," *Psychology of Addictive Behaviors* 8 (1994): 86–101; Kathleen J. Sikkema, Jeffery J. Koob, Victoria C. Cargill, Jeffery A. Kelly, Laurie L. Desiderato, Roger A. Roffman, Ann D. Norman, Michelle Shabazz, Crystal Copeland, and Richard A. Winett, "Levels and Predictors of HIV Risk Behavior among Women in Low-Income Public Housing Developments," *Public Health Reports* 110 (1995): 707–713; Clyde B. McCoy, Lisa R. Metsch, Virginia H. McCoy, and Shenghan Lai, "A Gender Comparison of HIV and Drug Use across the Rural-Urban Continuum," *Population Research and Policy Review* 189, nos. 1–2 (1999): 71–87; Clyde B. McCoy, Lisa R. Metsch, Virginia H. McCoy, and Norman L. Weatherby, "HIV Seroprevalence across the Rural/Urban Continuum," *Substance Use and Misuse* 34, nos. 4–5 (1999): 595–615; Richard A. Crosby, William L. Yarber, and Beth Meyerson, "Prevention Strategies Other Than Male Condoms Employed by Low-Income Women to Prevent HIV Infection," *Public Health Nursing* 17, no. 1 (2000): 53–60; Sheila T. Murphy, Lynn Carol Miller, Jan Moore, and Leslie F. Clark, "Preaching to the Choir: Preference for Female Controlled Methods of HIV and Sexually Transmitted Disease Prevention," *American Journal of Public Health* 90, no. 7 (2000): 1135–1137.

53. Dale D. Chitwood, James A. Inciardi, Clyde B. McCoy, Duane C. McBride, Mary Comerford, Edward J. Trapido, and Virginia H. McCoy, "HIV Seropositivity Rates among Needles from Shooting Galleries in South Florida," *American Journal of Public Health* 80, no. 2 (1990): 150–152; McCoy and Khoury, "Drug Use and the Risk of AIDS"; Chitwood, Griffin et al., "HIV Risk Factors"; Clyde B. McCoy, Edward J. Trapido, Nancy Lewis, and Elizabeth L. Khoury, "Belle Glade: HIV and Drug Use in a Rural Environment, Community-Based AIDS Prevention," *Proceedings of the First Annual NADR National Meeting* (Washington, D.C.: Government Printing Office, 1991), 295–308; Clyde B. McCoy, Jim E. Rivers, and Elizabeth L. Khoury, "The Role of Epidemiologic and Demographic Data in Substance Abuse Research and Interventions," *Proceedings of the Community Epidemiology Work Group (CEWG) Meetings* (Washington, D.C.: Government Printing Office, 1992), 475–479; Clyde B. McCoy, Elizabeth L. Khoury, and Robert S. Anwyl, "Facilitating HIV-Related Behavioral Change among Latinos in South Florida," technical review cosponsored by National Institute of Mental Health (NIMH) and National Institute on Drug Abuse (NIDA) (Washington, D.C.: Government Printing Office, 1992); McCoy and Inciardi, *Sex, Drugs*; Veronica H. Accornero, James C. Anthony, Connie E. Morrow, Lihua Xue, Elana Mansoor, Arnise L. Johnson, Clyde B. McCoy, and Emmalee S. Bandstra, "Estimated Effects of Prenatal Cocaine Exposure on Examiner-Rated Behavior at Age 7 Years," *Neurotoxicology and Teratology* 33 (2011): 370–378; McCoy, De Gruttola et al., "A Comparison of the Efficacy of Two Interventions."

54. McCoy, Rivers et al., "The Role of Epidemiologic and Demographic Data"; Richard C. Stephens, Dwayne D. Simpson, Susan L. Coyle, Clyde B. McCoy, and the National AIDS Research Consortium, "Comparative Effectiveness of NADR Interventions," in *Handbook on Risk of AIDS, Injection Drug Users and Sexual Partners*, ed. B. S. Brown and G. M. Beschner (Westport, Conn.: Greenwood Press, 1993).

10

Bolivian Drug Policy under the Morales Administration

MARTEN W. BRIENEN

The ascent of Evo Morales to the Bolivian presidency has been regarded alternately as a long-overdue moment of indigenous political ascendancy in a country in which a small elite of *criollos* and *mestizos* has long dominated the indigenous majority or as a left-wing takeover in one of the three major producers of cocaine by a man who not only has championed the right of Bolivian farmers to grow the plant from which cocaine is derived—*erythroxylum coca*[1]—but who is himself a farmer of this raw material.[2] Depending on whom we ask, his electoral victory in 2005 constituted either a triumph for indigenous rights and anti-imperialism[3] or a transfer of power to narco-interests.[4] In the context of such diametrically opposed opinions with regard to the significance of Morales' presidency, it is difficult to stake out a position anywhere between these extremes. Of course, Morales' anti-American rhetoric and his public embrace of self-proclaimed enemies of the United States and its foreign policy, such as Fidel Castro, Rafael Correa, and Hugo Chávez, as well as his strong opposition to U.S. drug policies in the Americas have made it very difficult to regard him as anything other than part of the wave of leftist populism sweeping Latin America since 2000.[5] It is not surprising, therefore, that the United States has been rather hostile to Morales, while members of leftist movements around the globe have welcomed him as something akin to the Messiah of indigenous rights and political lefts.[6]

The U.S. opposition to Morales' regime—and indeed to his political and nonpolitical activities prior to his election—was predictable, given that U.S. involvement in Bolivian politics and society since the 1980s has been focused almost exclusively on the role of that country in the production of *e. coca* and its highly addictive derivatives.[7] Morales' rise to prominence was built primarily on his role as leader of the *cocalero* movement and his ongoing efforts to resist U.S. drug enforcement policies in Bolivia.[8] He has denounced the abuses that occurred as a result of efforts to eradicate *e. coca* from the Chapare region and has argued that the implementation of eradication efforts was nothing less than a direct assault on Bolivian sovereignty and indeed on indigenous traditions themselves.[9] In fact, when it comes to resistance to U.S. drug-enforcement efforts in Bolivia, Morales represents the primary antagonist, with the now proven ability to garner sufficient popular support to oust the main allies of the United States in Bolivia. Morales was front and center in the public protests that resulted in the ouster of Gonzalo Sánchez de Lozada in 2003 and of Carlos Mesa Gisbert in 2005.[10]

Moreover, a number of the steps Morales has taken during his tenure as president of the Plurinational Republic of Bolivia—itself a result of constitutional changes he advocated—appear to give credence to the notion that he is an enemy of the U.S.-led "war on drugs" as well as an enemy of U.S. economic interests in the region. The most important indicators of his apparent unwillingness to cooperate with the United States on the eradication of so-called *coca excedentaria*[11] were the expulsion of the U.S. Drug Enforcement Administration (DEA) in 2008 and the withdrawal of Bolivia from the 1961 United Nations Single Convention on Narcotic Drugs as of January 1, 2012,[12] due to the rejection of Bolivian proposals to remove Article 49 of that convention, which states that coca leaf chewing must be abolished.[13]

In reality, and in contrast to the ease with which U.S. representatives continue to paint Morales as a drug trafficker or narco-president,[14] Morales' role has been much more complex. On the one hand, the notion that his presidency would result in a handover of the machinery of the republic to narco-interests, as had been the dire prediction of U.S. officials—as well as some of their European colleagues—is incorrect: the distinction of having established a true Bolivian narco-state goes to the military juntas of the late 1970s and early 1980s rather than to the current administration.[15] On the other hand, Morales' fortunes have rested firmly on his role as representative of the *cocaleros*, and given his experience in the sector, it is inconceivable that he would not fundamentally recognize that a significant proportion of the produce grown by his core constituency ultimately serves the illicit-drug industry.[16]

It is this duality that can help us understand the particularly difficult position Morales occupies. While his mantra that "*coca no es cocaína*" is certainly true in and of itself in the same way that barley is not scotch,[17] and while it is likewise true that coca has many traditional uses in Bolivian society that deserve to be recognized as both culturally significant and harmless, it is also true that Bolivia is a major manufacturer of cocaine for the regional market. In addition, the country's relations with its regional allies depend on the Bolivian state's willingness to effectively address the manufacture and trafficking of illicit substances, cocaine first among them.

Given that he came to power because of his role as representative of the *cocaleros*—whose resistance to U.S. intervention through the DEA and related agencies operating in Bolivia gave him the sheen of anti-Americanism that made him popular among a much broader leftist constituency—his most immediate loyalty is to the *cocaleros* and their interests. It should be noted that he has maintained his position as leader of the *federaciones especiales* (the *cocalero* union of the Chapare) even as he serves as president of the republic. At the same time, international politics require that he address drug trafficking, especially given that some of his natural allies, such as Rousseff's Brazil, are the primary targets of Bolivian trafficking. Indeed, Bolivian cocaine in effect serves a regional market and remains largely absent from the North American market, which continues to be supplied primarily by Colombia and Peru. Brazil's growing economy has been accompanied by growth in the consumption of cocaine, meaning that for all the anti-American slant of the *cocalero* movement, it is Brazil that is increasingly unhappy with Bolivia's inability to effectively control drug trafficking.

It is important to move beyond the polarized view of Morales and his tenure as president and to look more rationally at his policies, as he has been required to very carefully balance quite contradictory national and personal interests. In this chapter, I will examine Morales' drug-related policies in the context of this very complex issue. In order to do this, I will provide a brief overview of the role of U.S. drug enforcement in Bolivian politics and society and the relationship between the war on drugs in the Bolivian theater and the rise of Evo Morales. I will then provide an analysis of the evolution of Bolivian drug policy during Morales' tenure as president.

U.S. Drug Enforcement in the Bolivian Theater until *Coca Cero*

Bolivia has always been a producer of *e. coca*.[18] For most of the country's history, this particular fact has been politically unimportant, the practice of coca chewing largely being the object of disdain among the country's upper classes,[19] an excuse for taxation among more practically inclined statesmen, and an accepted part of daily routine for a significant portion of the rest of the population.[20] Indeed, even after the invention of cocaine in 1860,[21] Bolivia exported relatively little coca and even then largely to its neighbors.[22] The plant remained of little interest domestically throughout much of the twentieth century. The failure of Bolivian coca exports to thrive even as cocaine became a popular drug in the late nineteenth and early twentieth centuries was due to the fact that cheaper supplies of the drug were made available by European manufacturers—primarily German, Swiss, and Dutch—who had established plantations in Nigeria, Ceylon, and the Dutch East Indies, the last having become the world's foremost producer of both coca and cocaine by 1910.[23] Bolivia, meanwhile, was to remain of note throughout most of the nineteenth and twentieth centuries as an exporter of minerals rather than of agricultural produce, licit or otherwise.

While the precise causes for the rapid increase in the abuse of cocaine in the United States during the 1960s and 1970s are outside the scope of this chapter, it is important to note that the drug did become increasingly popular during that time frame, overtaking heroin in 1970 and becoming ever more popular thereafter.[24] Indeed, it has been argued that it was precisely the war on drugs declared by President Nixon in 1971, which mainly targeted marijuana and heroin, that helped speed along the growing popularity of cocaine. It was regarded as somewhat harmless, witness Peter Bourne's 1974 description of cocaine as "not physically addicting [and] acutely pleasurable."[25] Limited attention to the drug on the part of the United States thus allowed the still relatively small market to become increasingly sophisticated as emerging criminal networks—above all, the infamous cartels of Medellín and Cali—seized on the tremendous profits that were theirs for the taking and slowly constructed highly complex organizations capable of producing ever-increasing amounts of cocaine and of bringing it to the consumer in the United States and, to some extent, Europe. This increased complexity allowed for increases in production, resulting in an increasing supply, which then drove down prices to make the drug available to a broader public.

This increased demand coupled with the establishment of highly sophisticated criminal networks capable of manufacturing cocaine in large quantities and trafficking it into the emerging market of the United States, permanently and irrevocably changed the nature of *e. coca* cultivation in Bolivia. Moreover, this change in consumer patterns in the United States coincided with the collapse of the Bolivian mining industry, ensuring a steady flow of former miners into the burgeoning Chapare region,[26] which had, somewhat ironically, been prepared for a massive influx of migrants by the United States Agency for International Development (USAID). The agency had been instrumental in the construction of a road that would open up the region to development[27]—and very successfully so, one might add—thus creating the perfect circumstances for aspiring and developing criminal networks. They could operate in an environment that lacked a clear state presence, was wild enough to allow hidden laboratories and air-strips,[28] and was clearly very well apportioned for the successful cultivation of e. coca by recently laid off miners who enjoyed the steady profits and ease of cultivation. Little to no experience is required to successfully grow the plant, which is in effect impossible to kill through neglect and which produces up to four harvests per year.

As a result of this convergence of factors, Bolivian production of e. coca expanded from an estimated 34,000 acres in 1977 to around 143,000 acres by 1983, making the country the world's second-largest exporter of coca.[29] The farmers of e. coca knew perfectly well which market they served,[30] but due to the fast-growing demand, no other crop could compete. It is impor-tant to note that in many ways, the emergence of cocaine and crack cocaine as drugs of choice in the North American and European markets signaled the first time Bolivian smallholders could produce a crop that actually al-lowed them to compete on the global market and that guaranteed an escape from the deepest depths of poverty.

While the Reagan administration relaunched the U.S. war on drugs in 1982 in part in response to the growing popularity of cocaine, a turning point occurred when crack cocaine entered the U.S. market in 1984. This form of cocaine not only could be smoked, but it was also cheap and be-came readily available in cities in the United States. The result of the ap-pearance of crack cocaine on the U.S. market can only be described as a moral panic, seized upon by the Reagan and Bush administrations for clear political gain.[31] The shift from cocaine as an elite drug to crack cocaine as the inexpensive drug of choice for the masses had a lasting effect on atti-tudes toward illicit drugs in the United States. Public opinion in the United States not only rapidly shifted to regard mind-altering substances as inher-ently evil but indeed went one step further: attitudes in the United States shifted definitively from considering that the abuse of illicit drugs might be a consequence of pervasive social ills to being the root cause of them.

The reaction to this moral panic was both swift and severe. Not only did the United States embark on policies to ensure that no abuser of illicit substances—whether reformed or not—would ever again be a productive member of society, but it shifted its foreign policy to include a very heightened alertness to any issue that might be construed as related to the issue of drugs and drug abuse in the United States.

It was the outbreak of the crack cocaine–related moral panic in the United States in the mid-1980s that resulted in renewed U.S. attention to Bolivian production of *e. coca* and that would ultimately change the relationship between the two countries in a fundamental way. Whereas U.S. interests in Bolivia had always been dominated by the latter's exports of strategic minerals, the collapse of large-scale tin mining accompanied by a shift in U.S. policies concerning the production and consumption of illicit drugs toward "control at the source" meant that Bolivia was fast becoming a primary target for U.S. drug policy.[32]

Given that Bolivia itself was suffering from severe economic problems and desperately needed economic assistance—which it would receive from the International Monetary Fund, the World Bank, and the United States— the state was vulnerable to outside pressures, all the while realizing that the revenues from illicit coca were crucial to the country's economy.[33] The United States was thus able to pressure the Bolivian government into undertaking several efforts throughout the 1980s to combat the scourge of cocaine: in 1983, it created the Mobile Rural Patrol Unit (Unidad Móvil de Patrullaje Rural, UMOPAR), which was tasked with combating the trafficking of cocaine and which was materially supported and trained by the United States under a 1984 treaty.[34] UMOPAR was followed by the creation of the Special Force against Drug Trafficking (Fuerza Especial de Lucha Contra el Narcotráfico, FELCN) in 1987, and this special force, too, was funded, trained, and overseen directly by the United States, in particular, the DEA and the U.S. Embassy in La Paz. Indeed, UMOPAR was incorporated into the FELCN as a special branch of the DEA.[35]

The most significant effort undertaken in the late 1980s, however, was the promulgation in 1988 of the infamous Law 1008, which regulated the cultivation of *e. coca* and the sale of coca itself and in effect made coca a controlled substance. The law did not, however, ban coca outright, but rather established a legal limit for the amount of land that could be dedicated to cultivation (30,000 acres) and declared the Chapare a zone of illegal cultivation, the Yungas east of La Paz now being the only zone where *e. coca* could be grown legally. The law further established a special branch of the judiciary to deal with drug-related crime, as well as a process for the eradication of what became known as *coca excedentaria*, that is, coca grown beyond the legal limits. With aid provided by the United States through USAID, *coca excedentaria* was to be gradually replaced with other crops so that over time none would be produced other than the amount established by law to meet domestic demand for traditional uses.[36]

Although the law did virtually nothing to stem the flow of cocaine or indeed to reduce the amount of coca produced in Bolivia—production actually peaked at nearly 125,000 acres in 1990 and remained relatively stable at around 110,000 acres throughout most of the decade[37]—it did prompt widespread resentment. Under the law's provisions, *cocaleros* and others involved in the production of coca and cocaine were subject to harsh treatment in secretive judicial processes that did not bother with even the pretense of due process. Moreover, many Bolivians regarded the law as little more than a simple imposition by the United States and therewith as a direct affront to national sovereignty. The lofty promises of alternative development were not a particularly resounding success, mostly because, as the country was traversing the devastating effects of economic readjustment in the aftermath of Paz Estenssoro's "shock therapy" and its attendant unemployment, there simply was no alternative crop that could possibly compete with *e. coca* and ensure smallholders a semblance of economic stability.[38] Inevitably, then, attempts to enforce the eradication of *e. coca* met with significant resistance on the part of *cocaleros*, who were organized into *sindicatos* (syndicates)—often named after former mining camps, indicating the level of continuity in political organization that came with the migration of miners to the Chapare to seek their fortunes.

Eradication of *coca excedentaria* as required by law, then, remained a politically unattractive option for successive Bolivian governments throughout the 1990s. Gonzalo Sánchez de Lozada, during his campaign for the presidency in 1993, attempted to capitalize on popular discontent by proclaiming that "*coca no es cocaína*" and suggesting that he would be willing to "fix" the immensely unpopular Law 1008.[39] Pressure from the Clinton administration soon saw to it that he corrected his course and embarked on yet another half-hearted effort to eradicate *e. coca* from the Chapare. He managed to destroy a paltry 2,500 acres in 1994 and maintained a pace that more or less coincided with the speed with which the crop was replaced to produce a very stable crop.[40]

The first real effort to eradicate all *coca excedentaria* came with the election of former dictator Hugo Banzer Suárez in 1997. Whereas his predecessors had rather unwillingly embraced U.S. policies on coca and had acted on that pressure only inasmuch as they needed to in order to retain the support of the U.S. government (but preferably without causing enough discontent to make their political fortunes uncertain at home), Banzer and his vice president—Jorge Tuto Quiroga—wholeheartedly embraced the effort to once and for all rid Bolivia of *coca excedentaria*. The effort would be presented to the Bolivian public in 1998 as Plan Dignidad, which called for *coca cero* (zero coca) by 2002, meaning the complete eradication of all *e. coca* grown beyond the 30,000 acres permitted in the Yungas.[41]

With heavy support from the United States, the Banzer administration attempted to reach its goal through a militarization of the Chapare, using UMOPAR and FELCN troops as well as the newly created (1998) Expeditionary Task Force (Fuerza de Tarea Expedicionaria, FTE), which consisted of military, police, and civilian personnel and was supported and trained by the United States. The FTE embarked on an absolutely merciless campaign in the Chapare, burning and slashing its way through the livelihoods of impoverished *cocaleros* and converting the region into one of open conflict between government forces—with a heavy helping of quite visible U.S. assistance—and the self-defense committees (*comités de autodefensa*) through which the *cocaleros* sought to halt the process. Scores of *cocaleros* died, but in late 2000, President Banzer declared that he had reached his goal—only to withdraw that claim soon after, after it became clear that a few thousand acres had survived the onslaught.[42] *Coca excedentaria* had been reduced to a historic low of just 5,000 acres.

A Perfect Storm

On the one hand, the efforts to eradicate *coca excedentaria* as defined by Law 1008 were successful in the sense that the total production of *e. coca* in Bolivia was reduced significantly. Indeed, between the mid-1980s and the early twenty-first century, the importance of Bolivia as a supplier to the United States dropped precipitously from around 15 percent of available cocaine in the United States to virtually nothing. On the other hand, as has been widely noted, neither the price nor the availability of cocaine appear to have been affected at all, and global consumption has continued to rise, especially regionally and in Europe.[43] The blame for this is the infamous "balloon" effect, whereby reduction in output in one area (either regionally or nationally) is compensated for by an increase in another region.[44] In the 1990s, that increase took place largely in Colombia, where total output reached precipitous levels within just a few years and very quickly overtook both Peru and Bolivia and the most important producers of *e. coca*.[45]

In terms of stemming the flow of cocaine into the United States, then, Plan Dignidad had no effect. The militarization of the Chapare, on the other hand, was to have a very lasting effect on the shape of Bolivian politics. The most immediate consequence was five years of very serious political upheaval marked by the fall of two successive regimes. Protests against eradication were not, of course, new—such protests by the *cocaleros* had taken place during the 1980s—but they had taken on a rather different shape during the Banzer regime. The exceptional levels of violence coupled with the fact that this violence was being committed against poor former miners, who squarely blamed international interference for their plight to begin with, especially by agents sent by the United States in the form of USAID and the DEA created a rather different atmosphere.

It should be noted that to many common Bolivians—in fact, to a majority of Bolivians who do not form part of the elite—coca is a regular part of daily life, and perhaps it is in prevailing attitudes toward this plant that we can most easily draw a distinction between the elites and the popular majority: to the former, coca is a vice to be extirpated, whereas to the latter, coca is what regular people do. Both agree that the very notion that coca is as dangerous as cocaine is insulting and just plain wrongheaded.

This struggle over eradication, especially given the involvement of U.S. agents, thus became a struggle between foreigners and elites, on the one side, and the common man, on the other, thereby allowing the process of eradication to become the point where leftist activism and *cocalero* interests converged. *Cocalero* activism thus became synonymous with anti-imperialism and the struggle against the very foreign interests who had earlier imposed "shock therapy" and all manner of subsequent hardships upon the Bolivian people. Coca itself became nothing less than the symbol of Bolivian sovereignty.

It was this convergence of interests and the emergence of the *cocalero* movement as the spear point of anti-imperialism that propelled Evo Morales into the political forefront in a manner that would have been unthinkable a decade earlier. Morales was himself a *cocalero* and had become actively involved in the *sindicatos* during the early 1980s, becoming the youngest director of a *sindicato* in 1984. He very quickly rose through the ranks to become, in 1991, the joint representative of the six special federations (*federaciones especiales*) that together represent the *cocaleros* of the

Chapare.[46] He was thus the public face of the *cocalero* movement through-out the 1990s, gaining sufficient credibility and visibility to be elected to Congress in 1997 as the Movement for Socialism (Movimiento al Social-ismo, MAS) representative for the Chapare and Carrasco.

The MAS had been adopted as the political arm of the movement that year in a compromise of sorts. Throughout the 1990s, it was clear to the *cocaleros* that they needed a political arm, and to this end the Political In-strument for the Sovereignty of the Peoples (Instrumento Político para la Soberanía de los Pueblos, IPSP) had been created, but due to legal techni-calities, the IPSP could not register for elections, thus necessitating a move to adopt an already registered but nonfunctioning party. That party was MAS, and thus the MAS/IPSP was born as the political vehicle for the *co-calero* movement headed by Morales.[47]

Since the very nature of the struggle in the Chapare was one of com-peting worldviews—one in which coca was equal to cocaine and one in which coca was part of indigenous traditions—Morales had been able to rally not only the support of leftists, whose objections were rooted primar-ily in the imposition of Law 1008 by U.S. capitalists and the presence of U.S. agents on Bolivian soil, but also that of the indigenous peoples, who constituted the majority of the Bolivian population.[48] Not only was Morales one of them—born to Aymara-speaking parents and fluent in Quechua to boot[49]—but he fought for their right to engage in traditional practices and against the deeply insulting notion that their *hoja sagrada* (holy leaf) was somehow a drug. That is to say, the struggle for the rights of the *co-caleros* had become simultaneously a struggle against imperialism, against capitalism, against the arrogant impositions of the United States, and for indigenous rights.[50] From leader of the *cocaleros*, Morales had become the champion of the oppressed. It was U.S. drug-interdiction efforts that had managed to transform him from a single-issue *cocalero* representative into the anti-imperialist icon who could successfully unite *cocaleros* and other farmers, factory workers and indigenous merchants, and leftist intellectuals under a single anti-imperialist, pro-indigenous banner.

It was under this anti-imperialist and decidedly nationalist banner that Morales became the public face of protest against the notion of exporting the country's recently discovered natural gas deposits through Chile and managed to bring down two legitimate governments in quick succession. The first was that of Gonzalo Sánchez de Lozada in 2003,[51] who had only narrowly defeated Morales in the 2002 presidential elections, and the sec-ond was that of Carlos Mesa Gisbert in 2005, who as vice president had succeeded Sánchez de Lozada and who declared the nation to be "ungovernable" upon his exit.[52] In the 2005 elections, Morales won a landslide victory with an unprecedented absolute majority.

Drug Policy under Morales

When U.S. officials look at Evo Morales, what they see is a man who not only farms *e. coca* but who has advocated for the right of Bolivians to cultivate the crop despite the fact that the majority of it is converted into cocaine, which is then sold to addicts worldwide. Indeed, what they see is an "illegal coca agitator" who appears hell-bent on protecting the interests of traffickers and dealers and whose electoral victory in 2005 represented a victory for narco-interests. Given that Morales has indeed spent much of his adult life championing the rights of those who cultivate a crop that everyone knows serves a sinister purpose and that he has made it a point to publicly denounce the United States for its foreign policy and to embrace the traditional enemies of the United States and its interests in Latin America, it is understandable that U.S. officials should look at him rather unenthusiastically. There can be no better evidence for this profound dislike of Morales and everything he stands for—insofar as U.S. officials have been able to decode exactly *what* he stands for—than the particularly dire warnings uttered by U.S. representatives to Bolivia during the election cycles in which Morales sought public office.[53]

Indeed, Morales has made a series of policy decisions and public statements that on the surface would appear to vindicate the U.S. position on his tenure: he has not only publicly embraced Hugo Chávez, Rafael Correa, Daniel Ortega, Fidel Castro, and Mahmoud Ahmadinejad as kindred spirits,[54] but he has also enacted land reform,[55] made a fellow *cocalero* his drug czar, joined the Bolivarian Alliance for Our America (Alianza Bolivariana para Nuestra América, ALBA) as a very active member, nationalized hydrocarbons,[56] expelled USAID from the Chapare, expelled the DEA from Bolivia, helped rewrite the Constitution and thus created the Plurinational Republic of Bolivia, declared himself a socialist and anti-imperialist, smuggled coca to international meetings in order to make a point,[57] denounced the United States at every conceivable turn, and withdrawn from the 1961 Single Convention on Narcotic Drugs.[58] Taken at face value, one might almost think that he cares little for the United States and its policies, drug-related or otherwise.

To take these things at face value, however, is to fall into the same trap that has made it impossible for U.S. officials to recognize what Morales stands for. What they have failed to grasp so fundamentally is that to Morales, and indeed to the majority of Bolivians, coca is a traditional product whereas cocaine is a different beast altogether. They are no more the same than potatoes and vodka, and to farm *e. coca* is to engage in an activity that has been both normal and acceptable for thousands of years: "*coca no es cocaína*" is not a slogan; it is a very deeply held belief. Moreover, what U.S. officials have failed to grasp is that their efforts to "go to the source" in the fight against illicit drugs and the damage they do are not regarded as a reasonable response to a social problem, but rather as an imperial imposition that mercilessly sacrifices the livelihoods of the poor and oppressed in Bolivia rather than resolving the issue of addiction at home.[59] Eradication is not regarded as one step in the war on drugs—and Bolivians tend to hold very negative opinions of illicit drugs and their abusers—but as a frontal assault on tradition, sovereignty, and human dignity. The level of misunderstanding between the two positions is so absolute that it has blinded U.S. officials to the very simple fact that Morales' defense of coca does not mean that he favors cocaine.

In much the same vein, it would be a mistake to view the 2008 expulsion of the DEA from Bolivia—along with U.S. ambassador Greenberg and USAID from the Chapare in that same year and for the same reasons—as evidence of a surrender to "narco-terrorism."[60] Not only was the DEA accused of plotting to overthrow the Morales regime[61]—the evidence admittedly being very scant, the idea itself nevertheless perfectly plausible—but it was also the single most unpopular U.S. agency in the country, its agents associated with violent repression, torture, and other human rights violations. Its very presence was widely regarded as an affront to Bolivian sovereignty as well as a threat to political stability. Given Morales' position as president of the *federaciones especiales*—a position he still holds—and his history of directly confronting DEA agents, the agency's ejection from Bolivian soil was entirely predictable and ultimately inevitable; a failure to do so would have irreparably damaged Morales' credibility among his core constituency. More important, there is an argument to be made that this action was not only reasonable but, ultimately, not altogether very important to drug interdiction and eradication efforts. The agency had been equally present and active during all those years when cultivation was on the rise and not just during the implementation of Plan Dignidad; in terms of the effectiveness of drug-interdiction efforts, it does not seem to matter all that much whether the DEA has boots on the ground. That said, the expulsion of the DEA did not constitute the end of cooperation with U.S. agencies on drug interdiction and *e. coca* eradication efforts, the Bolivian government remaining perfectly happy to call on U.S. support in its fight against illegal drugs.[62]

What has in effect characterized the Morales administration's position on coca and its illicit derivatives has been the now oft cited notion that coca is not an illicit drug and that drug-interdiction efforts should be focused on those substances that are, alternately using phrases such as "*¡Coca Sí! ¡Cocaína No!*" and "*Cero Cocaína*" instead of Hugo Banzer's "*Cero Coca.*"[63] Contrary to what one might have expected given Morales' history as a *cocalero* organizer,[64] this has not meant the abandonment of efforts to eradicate *coca excedentaria*, nor has it meant the abolition of Law 1008, which has remained in full effect throughout Morales' tenure. The Morales administration's approach, however, has been to pursue eradication as a voluntary effort whereby *cocaleros* and their *sindicatos* agree to reduce the amount of *e. coca* grown to meet a yearly target, in return for assistance from the state and the right to maintain one *cato* (0.4 acre) of *e. coca* even in the Chapare, effectively ending the wholesale ban on the crop in that region—an approach that had been the result of a compromise reached by Carlos Mesa Gisbert in 2004 in response to widespread protest against eradication.[65] Social control through the *sindicatos* is supposed to guarantee that overproduction is slowly eliminated, the process having been renamed "rationalization" in place of the tainted "eradication."[66] For now, the strategy appears to be working about as well as the more violent eradication efforts of the 1990s. While there has been an increase in the total acreage dedicated to *e. coca* cultivation, it has been minimal. According to the United Nations Office on Drugs and Crime (UNODC), from 2004 to 2010, the total acreage grew from 68,500 to 76,600, the majority of the growth being located in areas outside of the Chapare, where the voluntary regime of rationalization appears to be effective in reducing total acreage.[67]

When we look at what the policy of rationalization means in effect, it is important to underscore that the abandonment of forced eradication in the Yungas and Chapare regions—it is still practiced in areas where cultivation is prohibited, leading at times to violent confrontations[68]—should not be looked at as a mere surrender to the interests of the *cocaleros* by one of their own but rather as an acknowledgment of the fact that the earlier goal of *coca cero* was unattainable. Despite lovely rhetoric touting the benefits of coffee and other options, alternative development is not a viable model due to the fact that no crop can compete with *e. coca* when it comes to ease of cultivation, pest resistance, and profitability.[69] The dire poverty that still afflicts a sizable proportion of Bolivians guarantees that coca production will continue unabated, as it has even in the face of violent repression.

The importance of *e. coca* in mind, a new alternative chosen by the Morales administration has been an attempt to combat the flow of coca into laboratories where it is converted into its addictive derivatives. The administration is seeking alternative uses and arguing vociferously for the creation of new licit markets. The theory is that by diverting coca to nondestructive uses while controlling the total output, the ultimate goal of combating the manufacture of cocaine may be achieved without denying *cocaleros* their most important source of income, and it is in this light that Morales has sought to end the illegal status of coca prescribed by the 1961 Single Convention on Narcotic Drugs and to convince neighboring countries, as well as some overseas, to permit the importation and consumption of coca for tea, toothpaste, and other harmless products. Indeed, the strategy has met with limited success as the European Union is considering such proposals, and Bolivia has found some support from Uruguay for the notion that coca should be accessible as a commodity on world markets.[70]

In short, Morales' tenure has certainly not been a disaster for efforts to control the production and trafficking of illicit drugs, as had been the dire prediction. That is not to say that he is not faced with a very serious problem. Voluntary rationalization has been somewhat successful in preventing significant growth in the cultivation of *e. coca*, but the same fundamental problems that his predecessors faced remain unaltered: there is no viable alternative to *e. coca* for the tens of thousands of Bolivian smallholders who now supply an important market.[71]

Moreover, there may be trouble on the horizon. While consumption of cocaine in the United States has been on the decline, the European, African, and regional markets have been expanding at an impressive clip. This is especially true for Brazil, where cocaine abuse has been on the rise along with the country's economic fortunes. One of the results has been an increase in the price of coca and its derivatives on the Bolivian market,[72] which means that the appeal of the crop is on the rise. Without a viable alternative to *e. coca*, we may well be on the verge of a renewed increase in production that voluntary eradication seems unlikely to be able to halt. Indeed, it may be reasonable to assume that the depressed prices for coca since 2000 have been in part responsible for the lack of significant growth, but as Plan Colombia is reducing the ability of Colombian farmers to supply the market while consumption of cocaine and related illicit drugs is on the rise globally, it seems optimistic to assume that Bolivian *cocaleros* will neglect to take advantage of the economic opportunities that are bound to present themselves in the near future.

A First-Rate Balancing Act

As Will Reisinger puts it, "[*But*] *for* the U.S. war on drugs, neither Morales nor his socialist political party would hold power in Bolivia today."[73] Indeed, U.S. policies on coca and its unwillingness to take social and cultural sensitivities into consideration (the United States has repeatedly insisted on astoundingly harsh treatment of *cocaleros* in its zeal to resolve what is ultimately a U.S. domestic problem) have damaged the country's credibility so severely that the mere pronouncement that Bolivians should not vote for a particular candidate is almost good enough to guarantee that candidate's electoral victory. Given the history of U.S. involvement in Bolivian drug policy, the United States has maneuvered itself into a position where a return of its agents to Bolivia—even under the most favorable of circumstances—would be political suicide for the politicians involved in brokering such a deal. The result of its arrogant impositions, of course, has been that the United States now in effect has no influence on Bolivian policymaking and little hope of gaining such influence in the near future.

At the same time, Morales' ability to thumb his nose at the United States and to choose his own path in the formulation of drug policy has largely been the result of historical happenstance. The pliability of his predecessors had, after all, been largely the result of economic necessity:[74] the very shaky foundations of the Bolivian economy during the 1980s and 1990s meant that the country was very heavily dependent on U.S. assistance, which came with strings attached. Gonzalo Sánchez de Lozada, for example, made it quite clear that he was never personally a proponent of the harsh policies he was forced to enact in order to retain the assistance upon which his government depended.[75] Morales came to power under a markedly different set of economic circumstances, the Bolivian economy increasingly flush with cash from natural gas, while his friends—the late Hugo Chávez in particular—have proven to be quite generous.

While Bolivia's newfound hydrocarbon wealth and moneyed regional friends may have immunized the Morales administration to a large extent against the type of economic pressure that the United States applied so successfully on his predecessors, cocaine is not an issue that concerns only the United States. On the contrary, as noted earlier, Bolivia is not a supplier to the United States but rather to the regional market and markets in Africa and Europe. In the case of Brazil, the sharp increase in the consumption of illicit derivatives of *coca* has meant an increase in the Brazilian state's interest in the manufacture and trafficking of cocaine.

This puts Morales in a decidedly difficult position. On the one hand, he was not only elected very specifically as the leader of the *cocalero* movement but remains the president of the *federaciones* and answers to a base with a very particular interest in the matter of *coca excedentaria*. On the other hand, he is also a statesman who needs to collaborate with regional allies on issues that concern them while remaining mindful of the fact that he is still vulnerable to accusations that would paint his tenure as one marked by a surrender to narco-interests. That is to say, he must remain vigilant not to be seen as friendly to narco-interests, given not only foreign interests but also the fact that Bolivian popular opinion on cocaine is markedly different from its opinion on coca.

In that sense, the expulsion of the DEA was tantamount to a promise that Bolivia could manage the issue of drug trafficking without the aid of the United States and its financial and material resources. A failure to deliver on that promise would permanently damage Morales' reputation and bolster the U.S. argument that Morales, given his background, is not serious about illicit drugs. A substantial increase in cocaine manufacture and export would undermine his "*coca no es cocaína*" stance, making the constant hammering on the traditional and cultural importance of coca a rather less convincing plea internationally and undermining efforts to find new markets for licit coca. Moreover, a failure to stem the flow of cocaine and related products into neighboring countries would put Morales in the unenviable position of having to choose between going it alone in a likely losing battle against drug lords or calling in the cavalry. The latter option would mean a serious loss of face and, likely very significantly, upset his base; he is, after all, still the leader of the *cocalero* union, and that is an uncomfortable place from which to call on the United States to lend a helping hand in controlling the drug trade. In one sense, Morales is lucky in that he will likely not have to deal with the consequences: term limits will keep him from having to face the music.

In sum, this chapter has discussed the role of *e. coca* cultivation in Bolivia in the context of Bolivian policy with regard to the manufacture and export of illicit substances. As a result of various "partial victories" in the Andean region, *e. coca* cultivation shifted from Peru and Bolivia to Colombia.[76] As of 2013, Bolivia and Peru were experiencing an increase in coca cultivation as a result of the U.S.-led efforts in Colombia, particularly Plan Colombia.[77] The balloon effect continues today, and, therefore, it is difficult for any one country to declare victory in the war on drugs when in reality coca production and trafficking has shifted back to Bolivia and Peru.[78] In that sense, eradication has remained relatively meaningless as it masks the movement of production from one country to another, or indeed from one region to another.

Notes

1. The language with regard to this plant and its derivatives can at times be confusing. In this chapter, the plant shall be referred as *e. coca* whereas the dried leaf of the plant shall be referred to as coca.

2. Daniel Kurtz-Phelan, "'Coca Is Everything Here': Hard Truths about Bolivia's Drug War," *World Policy Journal* 22, no. 3 (2005): 104.

3. Benjamin Kohl, "Bolivia under Morales: A Work in Progress," *Latin American Perspectives* 37, no. 3 (2010): 119.

4. Kurtz-Phelan, "Coca Is Everything Here," 106. Indeed, prior to his election, the U.S. State Department described Morales as an "illegal coca agitator"; see Shira Gordon, "Bolivia: Beyond the Rhetoric," *Columbia Political Review* 7, no. 1 (2007).

5. Marten Brienen, "Interminable Revolution: Populism and Frustration in 20th Century Bolivia," *SAIS Review* 27, no. 1 (2007): 21–23; James Dunkerley, "Evo Morales, the 'Two Bolivias' and the Third Bolivian Revolution," *Journal of Latin American Studies* 39, no. 1 (2007): 139–144; Alan L. McPherson, *Anti-Americanism in Latin America and the Caribbean* (New York: Berghahn Books, 2008), 1–36; Kohl, "Bolivia under Morales," 117.

6. As Hugo Chávez would have it, "an emissary sent by God"; see Will Reisinger, "The Unintended Revolution: U.S Anti-Drug Policy and the Socialist Movement in Bolivia," *California Western International Law Journal* 39, no. 2 (2009): 280.

7. Solimar Santos, "Unintended Consequences of United States' Foreign Drug Policy in Bolivia," *University of Miami Inter-American Law Review* 33, no. 1 (2002): 129.

8. *Cocaleros* are farmers of *e. coca.*

9. Robert Lessmann, *Das neue Bolivien: Evo Morales und seine demokratische revolution* (Zurich: Rotpunkt Verlag, 2010), 179–181.

10. Brienen, "Interminable Revolution," 21–23.

11. *Coca excedentaria* is the legally established overproduction of *e. coca* as determined by Law 1008.

12. William Marcy, *The Politics of Cocaine: How U.S. Foreign Policy Has Created a Thriving Drug Industry in Central and South America* (Chicago: Chicago Review Press, 2010), 254.

13. Mattia Cabitza, "Bolivia to Withdraw from Drugs Convention over Coca Classification," *The Guardian*, June 23, 2011; Linda Farthing and Benjamin Kohl, "Social Control: Bolivia's New Approach to Coca Reduction," *Latin American Perspectives* 37, no. 4 (2010): 197–213.

14. Kurtz-Phelan, "Coca Is Everything Here," 106.

15. Bettina Schorr, "Von nützlichen feinden und verfehlter politik: Der drogenkrieg der USA in Bolivien," in *Bolivien: staatszerfall als kollateralschaden*, ed. Thomas Jäger (Wiesbaden: VS verlag für Sozialwissenschaften, 2009), 183.

16. Which is indeed likely also for the coca he himself has produced.

17. "*Coca no es cocaína*" is a phrase he borrowed from his predecessor, Gonzalo Sánchez de Lozada, who used it in 1993 as he was publicly contemplating putting an end to the efforts to eradicate *e. coca* from the Chapare region; see Schorr, "Von nützlichen feinden," 184.

18. Bolivia was, of course, founded in 1824, but *e. coca* has been cultivated in the Andean region for at least 4,000 years, as evidenced by the presence of coca in ancient burial sites. See Steven B. Karch, *A Brief History of Cocaine* (Boca Raton, Fla.: CRC Press, 2006), 11; Paul Gootenberg, *Andean Cocaine: The Making of a Global Drug* (Chapel Hill: University of North Carolina Press, 2008), 16.

19. Gootenberg, *Andean Cocaine*, 19–20.

20. Ibid.

21. Ibid., 22.

22. Some coca exports went to Germany in the late 1930s, due to its inability to access regular suppliers of the local anesthetic; see Marten Brienen, "The Liberal Crisis and Military Socialism in Bolivia, 1930–1939," MA thesis, University of Leiden, 1996, 62. Japan managed to supply itself through plantations and refineries in its colony of Taiwan (Karch, *A Brief History*, 102–103).

23. Karch, *A Brief History*, 91–102. Indeed, Gootenberg notes that Peruvian exports of coca dropped from a peak of around one million kilos around 1905 to roughly half that amount some five years later, entering a steep decline that would not be reversed until the cocaine boom that started in the last quarter of the twentieth century. It was of course precisely around that time that exports from the Dutch East Indies rose precipitously, reaching 1.5 million kilos in 1920 (*Andean Cocaine*, 63–66; see also Karch, *A Brief History*, 100–103).

24. Gootenberg, *Andean Cocaine*, 307.

25. As quoted in Karch, *A Brief History*, 163.

26. Jeffrey R. Webber, *From Rebellion to Reform in Bolivia: Class Struggle, Indigenous Liberation, and the Politics of Evo Morales* (Chicago: Haymarket Books, 2011), 57–59.

27. James Painter, *Bolivia and Coca: A Study in Dependency* (Boulder, Colo.: Lynn Rienner, 1994), 110; Kevin Healy, "The Boom within the Crisis: Some Recent Effects of Foreign Cocaine Markets on Bolivian Rural Society and Economy," in *Coca and Cocaine: Effects on People and Policy in Latin America*, ed. Deborah Pacini and Christine Franquemont (Cambridge: Cultural Survival and LASP, 1986), 102.

28. Healy, "The Boom within the Crisis," 111; Kurtz-Phelan, "Coca Is Everything Here," 105.

29. Healy, "The Boom within the Crisis," 112.

30. Kurtz-Phelan, "Coca Is Everything Here," 105.

31. Michelle Alexander, *The New Jim Crow: Mass Incarceration in the Age of Colorblindness* (New York: The New Press, 2010), 4–7.

32. Schorr, "Von nützlichen feinden," 180.

33. Washington Estellano, "From Populism to Coca Economy," *Latin American Perspectives* 21, no. 4 (1994): 39–40; Kenneth D. Lehman, *Bolivia and the United States: A Limited Partnership* (Athens: University of Georgia Press, 1999), 199.

34. The unit is also referred to as the Unidad Móvil Policial para Áreas Rurales (Mobile Police Unit for Rural Areas); see Schorr, "Von nützlichen feinden," 183. Also see Painter, *Bolivia and Coca*, 80–81.

35. Kathryn Ledebur, "Bolivia: Clear Consequences," in *Drugs and Democracy in Latin America: The Impact of U.S. Policy*, ed. Coletta Youngers and Eileen Rosin (Boulder, Colo.: Lynne Rienner, 2005), 151–155.

36. Lehman, *Bolivia and the United States*, 202; Reisinger, "The Unintended Revolution," 257–259.

37. United Nations Office on Drugs and Crime (UNODC), *World Drug Report, 2006* (New York, 2006), 81.

38. Santos, "Unintended Consequences," 136–138.

39. Lehman, *Bolivia and the United States*, 210–211.

40. Ibid., 210–212.

41. Reisinger, "The Unintended Revolution," 259–262; Schorr, "Von nützlichen feinden," 184–185; Ledebur, "Bolivia," 154–157.

42. Schorr, "Von nützlichen feinden," 85; Reisinger, "The Unintended Revolution," 267–268.

43. The street price for cocaine in the United States dropped from an average of $278.00 per gram in 1990 to $195.00 per gram in 2000 and would continue to fall, to $169.00 per gram in 2010 (inflation-adjusted for 2010 dollars); see UNODC, *World Drug Report, 2012* (New York, 2012).

44. Kurtz-Phelan, "Coca Is Everything Here," 103.

45. UNODC, *World Drug Report, 2012*, 35.

46. The organization of the *sindicatos, centrales,* and *federaciones* is purely hierarchical: most *sindicatos* exist at the village or community level. The roughly 800 *sindicatos* of the Chapare are governed by 40 *centrales*, which in turn answer to six *federaciones especiales*. At the top of the hierarchy sits the *coordinadora*, which is currently presided over by Morales (Lessmann, *Das neue Bolivien*, 129–130).

47. Webber, *From Rebellion to Reform*, 60.

48. Reisinger, "The Unintended Revolution," 271–280.

49. Ibid., 275. It should be noted that few other sources claim that he speaks Quechua, although it seems likely that he does, given that he spent much of his adult life among Quechua-speaking farmers in the Chapare. His political and ideological adversary, Felipe Quispe, made a big deal out of the fact that Morales speaks neither Quechua nor Aymara fluently; see Martin Sivak, *Evo Morales: The Extraordinary Rise of the First Indigenous President of Bolivia* (London: Palgrave Macmillan, 2010), 167.

50. Reisinger, "The Unintended Revolution," 276–278.

51. Pilar Domingo, "Evo Morales, the MAS, and a Revolution in the Making," in *Governance after Neoliberalism in Latin America*, ed. Jean Grugel and Pía Riggirozzi (New York: Palgrave Macmillan, 2009), 118–123.

52. Robert Barr, "Bolivia: Another Uncompleted Revolution," *Latin American Politics and Society* 47, no. 3 (2005): 73.

53. Kurtz-Phelan, "Coca Is Everything Here," 104.

54. Brienen, "Interminable Revolution," 21–22.

55. Lessmann, *Das neue Bolivien*, 156–158.

56. Dunkerley, "Evo Morales," 134; Kohl, "Bolivia under Morales," 117.

57. Reisinger, "The Unintended Revolution," 280.

58. Bolivia withdrew only temporarily, to allow the country to add a signing statement officially disagreeing with the illegal status of coca.

59. Reisinger, "The Unintended Revolution," 278–280.

60. Kathryn Ledebur and Coletta Youngers, "Balancing Act: Bolivia's Drug Control Advances and Challenges," *WOLA*, unnumbered, May 2008.

61. Marcy, *The Politics of Cocaine*, 254.

62. Lessmann, *Das neue Bolivien*, 184; Rory Carrell, "Bolivia Accepts Financial Aid Offer from U.S. to Monitor Coca Eradication," *The Guardian*, April 20, 2011.

63. Schorr, "Von den nützlichen feinden," 186.

64. Or indeed if one had listened to the various U.S. officials who argued that Morales' electoral victory would mean the end of efforts to control illicit substances in Bolivia.

65. Lessmann, *Das neue Bolivien*, 182–187.

66. Schorr, "Von den nützlichen feinden," 187; Farthing and Kohl, "Social Control," 197–213.

67. UNODC, *World Drug Report, 2012*, 35.

68. Farthing and Kohl, "Social Control," 207–208.

69. Kurtz-Phelan, "Coca Is Everything Here," 108–109.

70. Farthing and Kohl, "Social Control," 208–209.

71. Kurtz-Phelan, "Coca Is Everything Here," 108–109.

72. UNODC, *World Drug Report, 2012*, 30–35.

73. Reisinger, "The Unintended Revolution," 280.

74. With the very notable exception of Hugo Banzer, who appears to have relished the opportunity to rain down violence upon the poor—just like in the good old days.

75. Lehman, *Bolivia and the United States*, 210–211.

76. See the preface in this volume.

77. UNODC, *World Drug Report, 2011* (New York, 2011).

78. Ibid.

11

The Vicious Cycle

The Resurgence of Drug Production and Drug Trafficking in Peru

MARTEN W. BRIENEN AND JONATHAN D. ROSEN

Peru has an extensive history of coca cultivation and drug trafficking and, therefore, has been a target of the over forty year U.S.-led "war on drugs." Indeed, the country is considered to be of particular importance as one of the three major producers of coca. At the height of the "crack cocaine moral panic" of the 1980s, Peru was the leading coca cultivator in the world, producing an estimated 65 percent of the world's supply.[1] With a mixture of support and pressure from a succession of U.S. administrations, Peru has witnessed what might be considered "partial successes" in the war on drugs, as U.S.-backed efforts to reduce or eliminate coca cultivation resulted in a shift of production to Colombia. Peru, however, continues to face many challenges with regard to coca cultivation, the manufacture of cocaine, and the trafficking of both, especially in light of active guerrilla movements that look to these activities as primary sources of revenue to support their efforts.[2]

This chapter will examine Peru's role in the drug-trafficking sector and the challenges the country will face in the twenty-first century. Our argument is that Peru confronts many security dilemmas, particularly with the rising guerrilla movements and linkages to international criminal organizations such as the Mexican cartels. This chapter will answer the following questions: What are the major challenges that Peru faces in the second decade of the twenty-first century? What have been the consequences for Peru of U.S.-led efforts, such as Plan Colombia, in the Andean region? What security challenges does Peru face that could impact social, political, and economic stability within the country as well as security in the Andean region? And, finally, what linkages do criminal and guerrilla organizations in Peru have today with other actors, particularly in other countries like Mexico?

A Brief History of Coca in Peru

Virtually all coca is currently cultivated in just three countries in the world:[3] Bolivia, Colombia, and Peru. It is clearly a misconception that coca itself (*erythroxylum coca*) is the same as cocaine or that the only use of coca is as an ingredient used to manufacture cocaine.[4] In fact, coca has been cultivated in the Andean region for over four thousand years, and it has been clearly established that ancient Andean peoples used the leaf ceremonially, medicinally, and as a part of their diet.[5] Indeed, the chewing of coca remains commonplace and accepted practice among indigenous peoples of the Bolivian and Peruvian highlands, where some of its physiological effects—increasing oxygen uptake and reducing hunger—are especially desirable.[6] More recently, coca has been used to produce products like candies, tea, toothpaste, and a variety of other products, not to mention that it was originally an ingredient in Coca-Cola. Perhaps most important, coca plays a key role in various Peruvian rituals and cultural practices.

Enrique Obando has argued that coca never constituted a major problem for Peru and the other Andean countries until a process was discovered to use the leaf to manufacture cocaine:

> Coca was never a problem in the Andes. But modern science processed it into cocaine and turned it into a powerful drug. Even then it was sold openly in pharmacies and drugstores for years. It was only at the end of the 1970s that cocaine became a real problem, thanks to the considerable increase in drug use in the United States and Western Europe. Suddenly, Peruvian farmers' traditional coca harvests were being brought to foreigners at very high prices. In a farming economy marked by extreme poverty, it was a godsend for traditional crops to bring such high prices. Naturally, farmers began to plant more and more coca until, over time, they realized it was not profitable to grow anything else.[7]

Indeed, the process by which cocaine is extracted from coca leaf is hardly new, having been invented in 1860,[8] and as cocaine became an increasingly popular product throughout Europe and the United States in the form of medicinal tonics, cocaine-infused wines, and other such products—Sigmund Freud famously praised the drug in his so-called cocaine papers in the mid-1880s[9]—increased demand was met with Peruvian production, until European and Asian powers shifted cultivation to their holdings in Africa and East Asia.[10] The result of this shift was a reduction of Peruvian production by about half.[11] Demand, of course, fell sharply as a result of the first cocaine-related moral panic of the 1910s, which led to prohibition of the drug through the Harrison Act of 1914.[12]

Cocaine made its resurgence in the United States in the 1960s and 1970s, for reasons that are outside the scope of this chapter. It overtook heroin as the drug of choice by 1970, and its popularity continued to increase after that, in part due to its reputation as a comparatively harmless drug.[13] Indeed, while President Nixon declared the war on drugs in 1971, his focus was mainly on the evils of marijuana and heroin, and it has been argued that increased suppression of supplies of those substances aided in the rapidly increasing demand for cocaine, which had been described by Peter Bourne—deputy of Nixon's Special Action Office of Drug Abuse Prevention—in 1974 as "not physically addicting [and] acutely pleasurable."[14]

While the 1970s marked a continued uptick in the consumption of cocaine in Europe and the United States, it was not yet regarded as a focal point in the war on drugs, allowing Peruvian and Bolivian production of coca leaf to soar to never-before-seen heights. A lack of attention to the substance by enforcement agencies in countries where consumption was concentrated allowed the market to become increasingly sophisticated. Emerging criminal networks—including the cartels of Medellín and Cali—seized on the tremendous opportunities for profit and consequently developed more and more into highly complex organizations capable of producing and trafficking ever larger amounts of cocaine. This increased trafficking, of course, resulted in marked increases in production and supply, which in turn depressed prices and thus increased the appeal of the drug among a much broader public.[15]

The situation changed dramatically with the introduction of crack cocaine in the 1980s, during the Ronald Reagan presidency. Crack cocaine is different from powdered cocaine in several respects: it is generally smoked in a pipe, while powdered cocaine is snorted through the nose; more important, it is much cheaper than cocaine, leading to its widespread popularity among lower-income individuals in America's inner cities. Reagan was very concerned about drug abuse in American society, and the appearance of crack fundamentally altered the political mathematics surrounding the, at the time, decade-old war on drugs. Reagan witnessed the devastation wrought by the crack boom in the inner cities of New York and Los Angeles as well as the accompanying moral panic and viewed drugs as an evil that required immediate and far-reaching action. Only then did he embrace the war on drugs that his predecessor had declared in 1971, but he did so with incomparable zeal. Moreover, unlike Nixon, who had argued strenuously that the drug problem should be tackled by addressing demand, Reagan shifted the rhetoric to a heavily supply side–oriented approach.[16]

U.S. Drug Policy toward Peru in the 1980s

It is interesting to note, in this light, that while cocaine had been around for a century by the time of the second great cocaine-induced moral panic that gripped the nation, and coca leaf had been cultivated for thousands of years in the Andean highlands, where consumption of coca leaf remains legal—both in Peru and Bolivia—and widespread, it was the apparent crack epidemic of Reagan's presidency that prompted an approach that would directly and devastatingly affect Peruvian politics and society. Since Peru cultivated an estimated 65 percent of the world's coca supply, the Reagan administration argued that in order to protect the American people from the scourge of crack cocaine, something must be done to halt Peruvian cultivation of coca, and it did not shy away from heavy-handed tactics to coerce the Peruvian government into action. It should be noted that Peru's exceptionally vulnerable position—due to its transition from dictatorship to democracy and the widespread economic malaise that resulted from the debt crisis that affected many Latin American countries during the 1980s—made it exceptionally difficult for the country to resist pressure applied by the United States.

As a result of U.S. pressure, the Peruvian government implemented a familiar three-pronged approach, consisting of enforcement and interdiction, eradication, and crop substitution. Enforcement was to be handled by the national police, the eradication of existing crops would be handled by the newly created Special Project for the Control and Reduction of Coca Cultivation in the Alto Huallaga (Proyecto Especial de Control y Reducción del Cultivo de la Coca en el Huallaga, CORAH),[17] and crop substitution would be pursued by the Upper Huallaga Special Project (Proyecto Especial Alto Huallaga, PEAH).[18] The theory was, of course, that through gentle persuasion—eradication and the threat of arrest—*cocaleros* of the Huallaga valley could be persuaded to trade in their coca crops for more acceptable ones, such as coffee and a variety of other tropical produce. CO-

RAH was launched first, and the second phase (PEAH) was launched in 1982.

In their initial incarnation, the eradication efforts of CORAH were intended to be carried out by employing people locally to manually uproot the crop, which in retrospect seems woefully naïve. Indeed, even if the manual eradication were effective and farmers chose not to replant coca—both of which were hardly very likely—the initiative was doomed by the logistics of the effort, as it was simply not reasonable to expect that such vast quantities of fields spread out through the entire Huallaga valley and up the slopes could be manually removed by underpaid and unenthusiastic laborers. Obando has commented on the effort: "Thirty men, working by hand, could eradicate 1 hectare of coca per day; working very intensively, they might eradicate 2. That is an average of 1.5 hectares. From 1983 to 1985 CORAH eradicated only 8,666 hectares with the assistance of 450 workers, while it had committed to eradicate 15,000 hectares. At that rate it would have taken sixty-nine years to eradicate the 200,000 hectares of coca that existed at the time, provided not one more hectare was planted."[19]

The program, predictably, failed to achieve its goals and appears not to have had much of an impact of any kind on Peru's productive capacity, a fact clearly noted by policymakers in Washington. In its search for a more effective way to eradicate the crop from the Peruvian highlands, the U.S. government embraced the notion of aerial spraying, that is, chemical eradication through aerially applied herbicides. Despite widespread concern about potential ecological damage, the U.S. government has consistently contended that such efforts do not harm human beings or, indeed, protected species that inhabit the region. However, aerial spraying initiatives carried out in Colombia have not been effective and have been clearly harmful.[20] Not only have the aerial spraying initiatives not worked but the program has been counterproductive, destroying the environment throughout Colombia. The major problem with aerial spraying is that spray drift occurs as a result of wind and causes the herbicides to miss their intended target and enter the water or kill legitimate crops.

Many people in Colombia became outraged as a result of the aerial spraying program, which is illegal in all other countries in the region. During Álvaro Uribe's presidency (2002–2010), a Colombian court ruled that the aerial spraying initiatives were unconstitutional because they violated every Colombian's basic constitutional right to a healthful living environment. President Uribe, however, ignored the ruling and continued the aerial spraying initiatives.[21] The practice was abandoned in Peru very early on and has not been a part of counternarcotics efforts in Peru in this century.

Why Coca Eradication Is Ineffective

In 1985, Washington spent $4 million on eradication efforts, but by 1989, the amount spent had more than doubled, to $10 million.[22] Despite spending millions of dollars trying to eradicate coca from Peru, it continued to be planted—and replanted—rendering eradication programs completely ineffective and neatly replicating similar experiences in both Colombia and Bolivia.[23] The reason for the failure of this strategy is the same throughout the region and is rooted in issues of development and economics. In effect, this particular crop—leaving aside discussions regarding the desirability of its derivatives—offers farmers several rather compelling incentives. Most important, coca is a very resilient and hardy crop that grows easily throughout the region—and indeed elsewhere. It is disease- and pest-resistant and requires very little detailed care. Moreover, it produces up to four harvests per year, thus allowing farmers a steady income rather than a seasonal one. Since the leaf is dried and then primarily used to produce derivatives through a chemical process, transportation poses few problems. The end product, of course, has a great shelf life. Last, coca is by far the most profitable crop and one of relatively few that allow a farmer with a limited amount of land to lead a life of relatively high quality. These characteristics set it apart from alternatives touted by development organizations and agencies such as PEAH or its American partner, the United States Agency for International Development (USAID). In the more remote regions of the Huallaga valley, substitute crops such as oranges and bananas stand virtually no chance of making it to market intact due to underdeveloped infrastructure, devaluing the produce at the point of sale.[24] Market prices for export crops such as coffee are notoriously fickle, and the plants themselves much more demanding than coca. In effect, notwithstanding the efforts of PEAH and like-minded organizations, there is no true economically viable substitute.

Given the dire state of infrastructure in the region, then, coca is in effect the only viable crop for export that farmers can reliably grow in order to produce income to supplement the subsistence farming that further marks the economic realities of the region. In circumstances of terrible poverty, coca allows farmers a means to generate income that enables them to feed and clothe their families. David Scott Palmer states that "one basic problem was that coca production was the major, often the sole, source of income for almost all of the approximate 300,000 farmers in the Upper Huallaga Valley (UHV). Buyers usually paid for the crop in cash right at the farm or nearby."[25] The choice to grow coca, then, is ultimately a rational one and clearly the result of simple market forces.

Under these circumstances, regardless of sustained efforts by regional and national authorities to halt the cultivation of coca, even with the financial and material backing of the United States, such efforts are unlikely to be successful for anything but the short term so long as the economic well-being of farmers remains dependent on this one crop. The incentives are such that in areas where coca has been forcefully or voluntarily eradicated, it makes a quick comeback as soon as the agencies have moved on to new regions; in the meantime, production is shifted to other areas. This is what is referred to as the "balloon" effect, which is when production or trafficking "balloon out" to other regions when authorities focus on shutting down illicit activities in one region. The balloon effect has been observed time and again and can be proven empirically by looking at the trends of coca cultivation and drug trafficking and examining the shifts that have occurred. Since coca farming is generally an illegal business, coca farmers must be innovative and have continued to adapt to avoid detection by various means such as intermixing coca with other legal crops. This has been the case in Colombia, as coca farmers want to make it more difficult for airplanes to spot coca from the sky and spray the crops.[26]

Of course, the absence of governmental oversight in the illicit production of coca is a further boon in and of itself, since it sidesteps the inefficient and deeply problematic bureaucracy that regulates legal exports. At one point, growing crops legally for export required an astounding thirty-six bureaucratic steps.[27]

Guerrillas in Peru

A complicating factor of significant importance has been the existence in Peru of multiple groups of guerrillas bent on the overthrow of the national government, the most important being the Shining Path (Sendero Luminoso) and the Túpac Amaru Revolutionary Army (Movimiento Revolucionario Túpac Amaru), both of which continue to plague portions of the Peruvian countryside, although they are not nearly as influential as during the 1980s and 1990s.[28] Internationally, it was the Shining Path that garnered most attention, as it spread terror throughout the country and effectively controlled large portions of the interior for many years. Indeed, the threat to the state was such that by the late 1980s, more than half of the national territory was under a state of emergency, marked by the suspension of civil liberties and effective military control over more than half of the country's population.[29]

The advance of the Shining Path required significant economic resources, and it comes as little surprise that the movement displayed a clear interest in control of the Huallaga valley, where it could tax the production of coca, its derivatives, and exports to Colombia and other major processing centers. Moreover, the movement was able to tap into general discontent with government policies in this area, as government representatives were eradicating coca and thereby destroying the livelihoods of farmers. Indeed, it has been noted that after the capture of the enigmatic leader of the movement, Abimael Guzmán, the remnants of the movement—which is still active in parts of Peru—became much more focused on coca and cocaine. It was ideologically an easy sell, given that it meant funding the ongoing war against capitalism by in effect poisoning the capitalists themselves. Indeed, the Upper Huallaga has consistently remained one of the areas where Sendero has remained particularly active, and it has been argued that the movement has in effect gone the route of Colombian guerrillas and become more of a cocaine cartel than an ideological movement. Palmer argues that "by protecting the coca-growing peasants there from joint-Peruvian-U.S. government efforts to combat the drug trade, Sendero [Luminoso] believes it can gain additional support bases for its proposed New Democracy in Peru."[30]

The Fujimori Doctrine

The circumstances in which Alberto Fujimori was elected in 1990, then, were dire and marked by ongoing civil war, exceptional levels of violence, and pressure from the United States to more effectively tackle the issue of coca cultivation in Peru. While the struggle against insurrectionary movements was clearly Fujimori's primary concern, the role of coca and cocaine in funding these movements meant that this military struggle was inextricably linked to the goal of eradication. Successful removal of large coca plantations was considered essential to the survival of the state, and removal required a more sophisticated approach than had been embraced in earlier years. The Fujimori Doctrine emphasized the need to address the underlying socioeconomic issues and focus on alternative development.

The Fujimori administration recognized that a military solution to the problem of coca cultivation alone would not work, but that coca cultivators were rational people who would grow coca for the various aforementioned reasons and that any successful strategy would therefore need to address the economic and social needs underpinning the cultivation of coca.

This approach would require extensive crop-substitution programs—more similar to a hearts and minds campaign—than the more forceful approaches favored by Washington. As Adam Isacson discusses in chapter 4, the militarization of the war on drugs has been a consistent trend over time but has not yielded the desired results.[31] While the 1991 counternarcotics accord signed by both the U.S. and Peruvian governments focused on alternative development, it would be wrong to assume that this agreement failed to recognize the role of the military. Enrique Obando states, "Alternative development was an important piece of the 1991 counternarcotics agreement signed with the United States, but was not devoid of a military angle. Once implementation began, greater amounts of assistance went to the military than to alternative development."[32]

One particular goal in interdiction efforts was to enable the Peruvian authorities to stop aircraft flying between Peru and Colombia, where the coca was processed in laboratories and refined into cocaine to be trafficked by the notorious Medellín and Cali cartels. To achieve this, the U.S. government provided the Peruvians with radar to help track airplanes flying between the two countries and supplied aircraft, such as the P-3 and AWACS, which the Peruvians used to shut down the airspace and interdict shipments.[33] Led by Fujimori's efforts, the Peruvians witnessed great successes from interdiction efforts as the government eventually shut down the "air bridge" between Colombia and Peru.[34] It is important to note that Bolivia also witnessed "partial victories" as a result of the Bolivian government's efforts to eradicate coca cultivation.[35] Predictably, however, the end result of such victories in Peru and Bolivia was that coca cultivation began to shift to Colombia. As Bagley notes in chapter 1, by 2000, Colombia had become the leading coca cultivator in the world.[36]

This example is a classic example of the balloon effect. While these victories might appear to be major achievements for Peru and Bolivia, the reality is that the overall drug-trafficking scene and, indeed, the availability of cocaine in the United States, did not change. Said differently, while Peru and Bolivia may have had less coca being cultivated within their own borders during this period, the overall market for drugs did not change at all because the routes simply shifted to Colombia. It would be premature to praise such efforts and sing of victory in the U.S.-led war on drugs because coca continued to be produced, processed, and trafficked despite these efforts.

Therefore, it is important to look at the larger picture when analyzing the drug war as opposed to focusing on minor victories. Determining what constitutes a success or victory inevitably depends on the person and his or her definition of success.[37] Washington viewed the initiatives in Peru and Bolivia as important successes, but they actually constituted minor victories, demonstrating that the United States had won a minor battle but continued—and continues today—to lose the war on drugs.[38]

Plan Colombia and Its Impact on Coca Cultivation in Peru

In the 1990s, Colombia became the epicenter in the war on drugs as the country was the leading cultivator, producer, and trafficker of cocaine in the world. During this period, events in Colombia began to spiral out of control as the cartels earned large quantities of money from drug trafficking and other criminal activities and, in turn, used the money to bribe politicians, judges, and police officers and even assassinated presidential candidates.[39] Said differently, the Medellín and Cali cartels infiltrated nearly every aspect of society. President Andrés Pastrana developed an initiative known as Plan Colombia designed to help Colombia combat its problems and achieve peace with the guerrilla organizations trying to overthrow the government. Pastrana had a different version of Plan Colombia than the Clinton administration, desiring to focus on peace in Colombia, developmental issues, and, finally, drugs. The Clinton administration did not want to become involved in the internal dynamics in Colombia, fearing another Vietnam, and used the power and influence of the United States to reverse the formula and focus solely on drug trafficking.[40] The Clinton administration rewrote Plan Colombia, and President Clinton signed the initiative in the summer of 2000, after Congress approved the bill.[41]

Despite U.S.$8 billion spent on Plan Colombia from 2000 to 2012, the initiative failed to achieve its goals of reducing drug trafficking, production, and cultivation by 50 percent.[42] In fact, drug cultivation increased in some areas of rural Colombia by 27 percent.[43] While Plan Colombia had some partial successes in terms of increasing security in Colombia and combating guerrilla organizations, particularly the Revolutionary Armed Forces of Colombia (Fuerzas Armadas Revolucionarias de Colombia, FARC), Plan Colombia was an utter failure with regard to drugs and did not achieve its objectives. The end result of the initiatives in Colombia was to shift coca cultivation to Peru and Bolivia and the routes to Mexico.

This should come as no surprise, as history reveals that decades earlier cultivation shifted from Peru and Bolivia to Colombia as a result of operations and efforts discussed above. The simple fact is that Washington has failed to learn from history and continues to repeat the same mistakes over and over again, spending billions of dollars on the same failed strategies.[44]

What have been the consequences of Plan Colombia for Peru? Since 2005, the country has experienced a rapid increase in the levels of coca being produced within its borders. Peru recorded 48,200 hectares of coca in 2005, while the country witnessed an increase to 61,200 hectares by 2010, empirically demonstrating that coca cultivation has been on the rise in Peru as a result of efforts such as Plan Colombia.[45] As of 2012, Peru had surpassed Colombia as the leading producer of cocaine.[46] Therefore, despite all the previous efforts, Peru remains a key player in the drug trade.

The Toledo Government

The militarization efforts in Peru led to the defeat of Shining Path. In 2003, however, the president of Peru, Alejandro Toledo, declared the creation of a new strategy to address the linkages between drug trafficking and terrorism. The president's declaration of this new strategy was designed to reassure the Peruvian people, who had become concerned about the reemergence of remnants of Shining Path.[47] Isaías Rojas argues that the new strategy "also was directed at Washington," as the Bush administration was concerned with the rise of Shining Path and the potential security threats that could emerge.[48] Rojas explains the Peruvian government's message to Washington: "U.S. officials, placing regional policy in the context of September 11, had voiced concerns about the supposed reappearance of the Shining Path, saying it was a 'serious threat' that represented an 'immediate danger' to Peru, and urged the Peruvian government to 'increase its efforts to bring the narcoterrorists under control.'"[49]

Conclusion

This chapter has examined Peru's role in the drug trade. As of 1985, Peru was the number one coca cultivator in the world. The U.S.-financed efforts in Bolivia and Peru resulted in coca cultivation shifting to Colombia, which surpassed Peru and became the leading cultivator of coca leaves in the world by the year 2000.[50] Colombia became the major focus of the war on drugs and the U.S.-led initiatives to stop the supply of drugs coming from Colombia. Plan Colombia, in terms of drugs, did very little, as coca cultivation in rural parts of Colombia actually increased.[51]

Advocates of Plan Colombia argue that the initiative had major successes,[52] because Colombia is safer today than ever before, and, indeed, it shifted drug cultivation away from Colombia and back to Peru and Ecuador. This logic, however, is extremely flawed and shortsighted as it does not take into account the overall drug-trafficking dynamics in the region. It would be a grave mistake to assume that Plan Colombia constituted a success for Colombia because it shifted drug routes to Mexico and coca cultivation back to Peru and Bolivia.

Peru has many major challenges today, particularly a resurgent Shining Path, which has not quite been eliminated and retains a presence in the Upper Huallaga region. Given the history of the movement, it is not surprising that its continued existence—though clearly much weakened—remains a cause for concern, even if the movement no longer represents a direct threat to the security of the state. Perhaps most troubling are the linkages between Shining Path and the Mexican cartels. The Mexican cartels are very powerful and dangerous due to the large profits that they earn from drug trafficking. The presence of the Mexican cartels in Peru has the potential to result in much more violence as drug traffickers battle for control of routes and territory. One simply has to look to Mexico to see the results of the drug war and competition among the cartels for power and control. The streets in places like Ciudad Juárez have flowed with blood as cartels try to intimidate other actors and defeat their rivals.[53] Therefore, the existence of the Mexican cartels in Peru is quite dangerous from a security standpoint. The Mexican cartels also are problematic because they can increase the levels of corruption and bribery within the country and undermine democracy in Peru.

Therefore, it appears as though the situation in Peru will only continue to worsen. In fact, some people have argued that Peru is on the verge of becoming a narco-state as a result of the high levels of drug activity within the country. Sonia Medina, the chief prosecutor of drug-related crimes in Peru, has declared, "We are moving toward becoming a narco-state."[54]

Peru, in essence, is one of the latest victims of the U.S.-led war on drugs.[55] It is time that Washington learns from its failures and recognizes that the balloon effect is real and will continue as long as government authorities clamp down on a region. The simple fact is that Washington has failed to address the underlying causes of the war on drugs and implements the same strategies time and time again.[56] For Peru—as well as the other countries in Latin America—less money should be spent militarizing the war on drugs and more should be allocated to addressing the underlying issues. Clearly, the United States has not done enough about reducing the demand for drugs. As Bagley points out in the introduction, the countries in Latin America would still have a drug problem even if all the "gringos" to the north did not consume such large quantities of drugs. Latin American countries, in general, must address rising demand and allocate more money to treatment and rehabilitation.[57]

The U.S.-led war on drugs in Peru as well as other countries in the region has focused too much energy on supply and not enough effort on strengthening or consolidating democracy. In addition, more resources must be allocated to strengthening institutions, combating corruption, and impunity. These changes do not happen overnight, but they are more effective in the long term because it is difficult for democracy to consolidate when drug traffickers and organized criminals can bribe politicians, judges, and police officers and infiltrate every aspect of government and society.

Notes

1. See the introduction, this volume.

2. Ibid.

3. See Deborah Pacini and Christine Franquemont, eds., *Coca and Cocaine: Effects on People and Policy in Latin America*, Cultural Survival Report no. 23 (Cambridge: Cornell University, 1986).

4. Francisco E. Thoumi, *Illegal Drugs, Economy and Society in the Andes* (Baltimore: The Johns Hopkins University Press, 2003).

5. Enrique Obando, "U.S. Policy toward Peru: At Odds for Twenty Years," in *Addicted to Failure: U.S. Security Policy in Latin America and the Andean Region*, ed. Brian Loveman (Lanham, Md.: Rowman & Littlefield, 2006), 169; William G. Mortimer, "The Divine Plant of the Incas," in *The Coca Leaf and Cocaine Papers*, ed. George Andrews and David Solomon (New York: Harcourt Brace Jovanovich, 1975). See also Roderick Burchard, "Coca y trueque de alimentos," in *Reciprocidad e intercambio en los Andes peruanos*, ed. Giorgio Alberti and Enrique Mayer (Lima: Instituto de Estudios Peruanos, 1974); Steven B. Karch, *A Brief History of Cocaine* (Boca Raton, Fla.: CRC Press, 2006), 11; Paul Gootenberg, *Andean Cocaine: The Making of a Global Drug* (Chapel Hill: University of North Carolina Press, 2008), 16.

6. Ralph Bolton, "Andean Coca Chewing: A Metabolic Perspective," *American Anthropologist* 78, no. 3 (1976): 630–634.

7. Ibid., 170; Gootenberg, *Andean Cocaine*.

8. Gootenberg, *Andean Cocaine*, 19–20. The drug did not, however, become popular until after it was shown by Merck that it could be used as a topical anesthetic in 1886.

9. Ibid., 23.

10. Karch, *A Brief History*, 91–102.

11. Ibid., 100–103; Gootenberg, *Andean Cocaine*, 63–66.

12. Tim Madge, *White Mischief: A Cultural History of Cocaine* (Edinburgh: Mainstream Publishing, 2001), 106.

13. Gootenberg, *Andean Cocaine*, 307.

14. As quoted in Karch, *A Brief History*, 163

15. See chapter 6 in this volume; Alfonso Cuéllar, "America's Forgotten War," *Washington Post*, October 29, 2008.

16. Ted Galen Carpenter, *Bad Neighbor Policy: Washington's Futile War on Drugs in Latin America* (New York: Palgrave Macmillan, 2003).

17. Obando, "U.S. Policy toward Peru," 171.

18. Ibid., 171; Cynthia McClintock, "The War on Drugs: The Peruvian Case," *Journal of Interamerican Studies and World Affairs* 3, nos. 2–3 (Summer/Fall 1988): 127–142.

19. See Obando, "U.S. Policy toward Peru," 171; José Barsallo Burga and Eduardo Gordillo Tordolla, *Drogas, responsabilidad compartida* (Lima: J. C. Editores, 1988).

20. For more on the war on drugs in Colombia, specifically, Plan Colombia, see Russell Crandall, *Driven by Drugs: U.S. Policy toward Colombia* (Boulder, Colo.: Lynne Rienner, 2002); María Clemencia Ramírez Lemus, Kimberly Stanton, and John Walsh, "Colombia: A Vicious Circle of Drugs and War," in *Drugs and Democracy in Latin America: The Impact of U.S. Policy*, ed. Coletta A. Youngers and Eileen Rosin (Boulder, Colo.: Lynne Rienner, 2005); Eduardo Pizarro and Pilar Gaitán, "Plan Colombia and the Andean Regional Initiative: Lights and Shadows," in *Addicted to Failure: U.S. Security Policy in Latin America and the Andean Region*, ed. Brian Loveman (Lanham, Md.: Rowman & Littlefield, 2006).

21. Ramírez Lemus et al., "Colombia," 61–98, 121.

22. David Scott Palmer, "Peru, Drugs, and Shining Path," in *Drug Trafficking in the Americas*, ed. Bruce M. Bagley and William O. Walker III (Coral Gables, Fla.: University of Miami, 1996), 181; David Scott Palmer, "United States–Peru Relations in the 1990s: Asymmetry and Its Consequences," in *Latin American and Caribbean Contemporary Record: 1989–1990*, vol. 9, ed. Eduardo Gamarra and James Malloy (New York: Holmes and Meier, 1992).

23. Obando, "U.S. Policy toward Peru," 171. In chapter 10 in this volume, Marten Brienen discusses the role of coca and the failures of eradication in Bolivia.

24. Thoumi, *Illegal Drugs*; Jamie Malamud-Goti, *Smoke and Mirrors: The Paradox of Drug Wars* (Boulder, Colo.: Westview Press, 1992); Scott B. MacDonald, *Dancing on a Volcano: The Latin American Drug Trade* (New York: Praeger, 1988).

25. David Scott Palmer, "Peru, Drugs, and Shining Path," in *Drug Trafficking in the Americas*, ed. Bruce M. Bagley and William Walker (Coral Gables: North-South Center Press, 1996), 181. Palmer notes that this estimate was by the U.S. government.

26. Coletta A. Youngers and John M. Walsh, *Development First: A More Humane and Promising Approach to Reducing Cultivation of Crops for Illicit Markets* (Washington, D.C.: Washington Office on Latin America [WOLA], 2010); Ramírez Lemus et al., "Colombia," 61–98.

27. Obando, "U.S. Policy toward Peru," 176.

28. Palmer, "Peru, Drugs, and Shining Path," 182.

29. See Tom Marks, "Making Revolution with Shining Path," in *The Shining Path of Peru,* ed. David Scott Palmer (New York: St. Martin's Press, 1992).

30. Palmer, "Peru, Drugs, and Shining Path," 183.

31. See chapter 4 in this volume.

32. Obando, "U.S. Policy toward Peru," 180.

33. Ibid., 182.

34. See introduction in this volume.

35. Ibid.

36. Ibid.

37. This is a constructivist issue. For more on constructivism, see Barry Buzan, Ole Wæver, and Jaap de Wilde, *Security: A New Framework for Analysis* (Boulder, Colo.: Lynne Rienner, 1998); Alexander Wendt, *Social Theory of International Politics* (Cambridge: Cambridge University Press, 1999).

38. See Bruce M. Bagley, "Bruce M. Bagley on the War on Drugs," YouTube video, 14:09, interview with Canadian television, posted by *The Agenda* with Steve Paikin, February 23, 2010, http://www.youtube.com/watch?v=WwGZtFyaVyo.

39. Rensselaer W. Lee III, *The White Labyrinth: Cocaine and Political Power* (New Brunswick, N.J.: Transaction Publishers, 1989); Crandall, *Driven by Drugs.*

40. This is realist logic. For more on realism, see Kenneth N. Waltz, *Theory of International Politics,* 2nd ed. (Long Grove, Ill.: Waveland Press, 2010); Christopher Layne, *The Peace of Illusions: American Grand Strategy from 1940 to Present* (Ithaca, N.Y.: Cornell University Press, 2006), 290; John J. Mearsheimer, *The Tragedy of Great Power Politics* (New York: W. W. Norton, 2001).

41. Crandall, *Driven by Drugs.*

42. U.S Government Accountability Office (GAO), "Plan Colombia: Drug Reduction Goals Were Not Fully Met, but Security Has Improved: U.S. Agencies Need More Detailed Plan for Reducing Assistance" (Washington, D.C., October 2008).

43. Simon Romero, "Coca Sustains War in Rural Colombia," *New York Times,* July 27, 2008; Adam Isacson, *Plan Colombia—Six Years Later: Report of a CIP Staff Visit to Putumayo and Medellin, Colombia* (Washington, D.C.: Center for International Policy, 2006), 1–19; Brian Loveman, ed., *Addicted to Failure: U.S. Security Policy in Latin America and the Andean Region,* 367, and chapter 2; *Colombia: Coca Cultivation Survey 2011* (New York: UNODC, 2011), 8–107; "Overall Picture of Coca Cultivation in Colombia Remains Stable—UN Agency," UN News Centre, July 25, 2012, accessed August 26, 2012, http://www.un.org/apps/news/story.asp?NewsID=42554&Cr=drugs&Crl=.

44. William Marcy, *The Politics of Cocaine: How U.S. Foreign Policy Has Created a Thriving Drug Industry in Central and South America* (Chicago: Chicago Review Press, 2010); Ethan Nadelmann, "Addicted to Failure," *Foreign Policy,* no. 137 (July–August 2003): 94; idem, "Ethan Nadelmann/Uso y prohibición de drogas," *Reforma* (November 19, 1999): 13; Peter Andreas, "Dead-End Drug Wars," *Foreign Policy,* no. 85 (Winter 1991–1992): 106–128; idem, "Free Market Reform and Drug Market Prohibition: U.S. Policies at Cross-Purposes in Latin America," *Third World Quarterly* 16, no. 1 (1995):75–88.

45. UNODC, *World Drug Report, 2012,* 21; Simon Romero, "Coca Production Makes

a Comeback in Peru," *New York Times,* June 13, 2010; UNODC, *World Drug Report, 2011* (New York, 2011).

46. See http://worldnews.nbcnews.com/_news/2012/07/31/13045253-us-peru-over takes-colombia-as-top-cocaine-producer?lite.

47. Isaías Rojas, "Peru: Drug Control Policy, Human Rights, and Democracy," in *Drugs and Democracy in Latin America,* ed. Coletta Youngers and Eileen Rosin (Boulder, Colo.: Lynne Rienner, 2005), 185.

48. Ibid.; "Toledo hace autocrítica y lanza ambicioso paquete de medidas," *La República,* July 29, 2003; "Narcoterrorismo está en fase inicial en Perú," *La República,* June 30, 2003; "Hay alianza entre Sendero y los narcotraficantes. Ministro de Defensa Loret de Mola: La postura oficial sobre el terrorismo," *La República,* July 6, 2003.

49. Rojas, "Peru," 185.

50. See introduction in this volume; UNODC, *Coca Cultivation in the Andean Region: Survey of Bolivia, Colombia and Peru* (New York, 2006).

51. Romero, "Coca Production."

52. Peter DeShazo, Tanya Primiani, and Phillip McLean, *Back from the Brink: Evaluating Progress in Colombia, 1999 to 2007* (Washington, D.C.: Center for Strategic and International Studies, 2007).

53. Charles Bowden, *Murder City: Ciudad Juárez and the Global Economy's New Killing Fields* (New York: Nation Books, 2010).

54. Sara Miller Llana, "Violent Cartel Culture Now Threatens Peru," *Christian Science Monitor,* April 3, 2007, http://www.csmonitor.com/2007/0403/p06s01-woam.html.

55. In an interview, Bruce M. Bagley argues that Mexico has become the latest victim. In this chapter, we argue that Peru, along with other countries, is the latest victim of the U.S.-led war on drugs. For his interview on Canadian television, see Bagley, "Bruce M. Bagley on the War on Drugs."

56. Bruce M. Bagley, "The New Hundred Years War? U.S. National Security and the War on Drugs in Latin America," *Journal of Interamerican Studies and World Affairs* 30, no. 1 (Spring 1988): 161–182; Bruce M. Bagley and Juan Gabriel Tokatlian, "Colombian Foreign Policy in the 1980s: The Search for Leverage," *Journal of Interamerican Studies and World Affairs* 27, no. 3 (Autumn 1985): 27–62; Bruce M. Bagley, "Seminario de seguridad," You-Tube video, 1:53:10, from a seminar conducted at El Colegio de la Frontera Norte, Mexico, on July 8, 2010, posted July 9, 2010, http://www.youtube.com/watch?v=sMeqNJzWXCo.

57. See the introduction in this volume; Bruce M. Bagley, "Tráfico de drogas y crimen organizado en América Latina y el Caribe en el siglo XXI: Retos de la democracia," You-Tube video, 37:41, from the Encuentro Internacional Drogas, Usos y Prevenciones, Quito, Ecuador, May 16–18,2012, http://www.youtube.com/watch?v=sLbYHUs7F5c.

12

In Search of the Mérida Initiative

From Antecedents to Practical Results

ALBERTO LOZANO-VÁZQUEZ AND JORGE REBOLLEDO FLORES

This chapter stems from the unclear nature of the Mérida Initiative (MI) in terms of its effectiveness and durability.[1] It also is a reflection of the need to study the MI since it represents—for better or worse—an alternative policy for combating transnational organized crime (TOC). The MI sought to obtain higher security levels in Mexico and focused on securing the border with the United States. During its implementation—October 2014—not much changed: violence was still manifested in several Mexican states and at various points on the U.S.-Mexican border, and the drug-trafficking business does not seem to have decreased, but rather remains despite the weakening of several cartels. In addition, Mexican institutions have not fully consolidated, corruption seems never-ending, and the decrease in cocaine consumption in the United States has not had a visible impact on violence or corruption generated as a result of drugs trafficked through Mexico. While challenges remain, the MI is an important instrument of cooperation between Mexico and the United States to fight the detrimental effects of drug trafficking and organized crime.

As a cooperative program between Mexico and the United States to counter organized crime, the MI has become a topic of study for some observers, military analysts, scholars, policymakers, and politicians and represents a relatively new form of bilateral cooperation between both countries. However, the nature of the bilateral relationship represented by the MI has been debated without much agreement: there is no consensus about its definition (as there is about other contested political issues, such as sovereignty, anarchy in the international system, or terrorism), and it is usually described in extreme terms as good or bad, useful or useless, paradigmatic or insignificant. Ultimately, perceptions about the MI differ a great deal depending on the actor: some people believe that Mexico was desperately in need of the MI to curb the increasing levels of violence, while others have been highly critical of the plan, characterizing it as imprecise and insufficient.

This chapter examines these ideas, seeks to identify what is being done well, and analyzes those aspects that need more deliberation and further improvement. The chapter is divided into three parts. The first part deals with general and diplomatic antecedents of the MI. General antecedents are divided into indirect and direct: indirect antecedents associate the MI with the traditional punitive mechanisms designed to combat drug trafficking during the twentieth century; direct antecedents stem from more recent political circumstances that contributed to its design and implementation. Diplomatic precedents analyze how the MI was the result of political maneuvers by both the president of Mexico, Felipe Calderón, and U.S. president George W. Bush. Both leaders were driven by rational incentives to create an initiative to combat drug trafficking and the increasing levels of violence in Mexico.

The second part of the chapter analyzes the traditional debate about whether the MI is paradigmatic or not. Using different perspectives, we can deduce that both answers are valid, depending on the perspective employed. These theoretical perspectives allow scholars to better understand the MI and the bilateral relationship between the United States and Mexico regarding drug trafficking.

The final part of this chapter assesses the results of the MI and is based on the four official pillars that support it.[2] This chapter, however, is limited to the evaluation of the MI and does not explore the implications for other countries indirectly involved in Central America and the Caribbean, specifically, the Dominican Republic and Haiti.

General Antecedents

The historical roots of the MI are related to the history of drug trafficking both in Mexico and throughout the Americas. On the one hand, scholars have recognized that marijuana (and even some opiate) cultivation and consumption shifted from being tolerated to criminalized activity in Mexico, mainly since 2000. On the other, scholars agree that the nature of drug trafficking has been not only a domestic issue, but also a transnational one. As Bruce M. Bagley notes in the introduction to this volume, drug production and trafficking routes have changed over time as a result of "partial victories" in the "war on drugs." Said differently, governments have focused on combating drug production and trafficking in one region or country while, in reality, the immediate effect is that routes shift to other countries.[3] This is what scholars refer to as the "balloon" effect. Colombia has been at the epicenter of the U.S.-led war on drugs for decades, but initiatives such as Plan Colombia have caused activity to shift to Mexico. According to Bagley, it is Mexico, not Colombia, that has become the latest victim of the war on drugs.[4] As a result of the efforts in Mexico, the drug routes are now shifting toward Central America and even back toward Colombia.[5] Therefore, the history and dynamics of production, trafficking, and consumption of drugs should be seen as transnational in nature.

Indirectly, the MI is linked to the criminalization of drugs, which extends back to the Shanghai Conference of 1909 and the Harrison Act of 1914. Both occurred during the twentieth century, resulting in the evolution of the idea that drug consumption is linked with crime.[6] Policies enacted in response to this approach are well known: the war on drugs, which President Nixon launched in 1971; its continuation by President Reagan in 1982; the polemic Operación Casablanca of 1998 against money laundering; and various other initiatives and counternarcotics strategies. In this sense, the fundamental motivations for the MI are not that different from the initiatives implemented in the 1970s, 1980s, and 1990s: to fight drug trafficking with the same prohibitionist logic. However, the case of the MI presents a wider vision and deeper levels of cooperation between Mexico and the United States, which are very different from exercises in the past.

More directly, the MI finds its antecedents in four contextual aspects: (1) the National Action Party (Partido Acción Nacional, PAN) winning the presidency of the Mexican republic at the beginning of the twenty-first century; (2) the subsequent weakness of the new democratic regime in Mexico as a consequence of the political shifts that in turn changed the relations of power that used to exist between drug traffickers and the authoritarian system of the Institutional Revolutionary Party (Partido Revolucionario Institucional, PRI);[7] (3) the strengthening and penetration of the drug-trafficking groups in many Mexican institutions; and (4) the context of U.S. security policies derived from the "war on terrorism."

In 2000, Vicente Fox Quezada assumed the presidency of Mexico in democratic elections. The executive transition represented a positive step for the state, but it also resulted in many challenges, particularly, weaker institutions. In practical terms, the transition to democracy in Mexico led to greater cooperation and improved bilateral relations between the United States and Mexico, as democracies tend to cooperate more.[8]

In the first years of the Fox administration, he confirmed this logic when he launched various initiatives designed to combat drug trafficking, which led to the successful capture and extradition of several drug lords in Mexico.[9] However, the major changes produced by the opposition of the president were limited by historical inertia as well as weak and corrupt institutions. Consequently, the Mexican political system evolved from an authoritarian centralized and nondemocratic system with democratic features,[10] but continued to suffer from lack of accountability and weak institutions. As Bagley notes, institutional change and democratic consolidation do not happen overnight; it is a rather extensive process.[11]

Almost in a parallel way, the terrorist attacks of September 11, 2001, fortified Fox's policies against drugs and, at the same time, strengthened the flow of goods and people on the U.S. border. The U.S.-Mexican border was fortified based on Washington's perception of the possibility that al-Qaeda terrorists could cross the border and penetrate the United States from Mexico.[12] Stricter border-control policies made it more difficult—at least for several months—to traffic drugs into the United States. Such policies resulted in excesses of marijuana and cocaine that could not be sold in the U.S. market by Mexican drug traffickers.[13] In the absence of a new strategy to combat drug trafficking, traffickers strengthened in power like never before.

There was a lot of speculation about organized crime as well as decreases in criminal activity during the Fox administration.[14] However, a closer look at the statistics during these years reveals an increase in the rate of violence.[15] During this period, the governor of Michoacán, Lázaro Cárdenas Batel (2001–2008), warned about the growth and empowerment of an organization dedicated to drug trafficking and extortion in his own state: La Familia Michoacana. Cárdenas Batel, the opposition governor at the time (a prominent member of the Party of the Democratic Revolution [Partido de la Revolución Democrática, PRD]) and a believer in many ideas that contradicted the PAN'S vision, asked the federal government to intervene in his state. This petition came in conjunction with a federal assessment that demonstrated that vast zones of the country were dominated by drug-trafficking groups empowered by the absence and inaction of the state.[16] This assessment led to Operación México Seguro. In the last year of the Fox administration, 2006, Michoacán became the first arena for the deployment of state resources to combat organized crime and drug trafficking.

President Felipe Calderón Hinojosa (2006–2012) continued the counternarcotics efforts when he won the presidency in 2006 by a narrow victory. Calderón embraced the idea that the main task of his government was to confront drug trafficking and organized crime. Eleven days after assuming power, he increased the national security budget by 24 percent and deployed 27,000 military and federal police to combat the cartels in eight Mexican states. Michoacán, his native state, was the first state to receive federal troops.[17]

Diplomatic Antecedents

President Calderón admits that he assumed power during a weak period of the Mexican state, which he describes as a terminally ill patient whose symptoms were visible in the violence perpetrated by drug cartels. According to him, Mexico was plagued by unacceptably high levels of corruption, organized crime, and violence.[18] In a paradoxical way, the unfinished Mexican transition promoted even higher levels of corruption as a result of the transition being based on the same clientelistic state of the past and absence of legality and the rule of law. Consequently, the failure of institutional strengthening led to battles to fill power vacuums generated by the absence of the state.[19] With Calderón facing such a severe state of affairs,[20] he recognized that the country needed assistance from its neighbor to the north—the United States—and any diplomatic initiative or device to cooperate with the United States—at that point necessary and urgent—had to take this complex context into account.

This explains why the MI cannot be characterized by traditional diplomatic origins. Instead, the main diplomatic creators were Presidents Bush and Calderón, when in March 2007 they met in Mérida, Yucatán, to plan a new scheme of cooperation that initially foresaw U.S.$1.4 billion in aid to Mexico distributed over three years. The way this new measure took shape is quite interesting for several reasons. For instance, based on historical precedents, we know that Mexico has never allowed or requested the presence or action of U.S. government agents within its national territory with the specific goal of assisting in the fight against drug trafficking. Despite this, the levels of violence in Mexico during 2007 created fertile soil for speculating that a new plan for cooperation with the United States was being designed. This eventually evolved into what was informally called Plan Mexico, which inevitably was associated and compared with Plan Colombia.[21]

The almost secret nature of the MI's original negotiations led to numerous warnings about the negative consequences of Plan Colombia and an assumption that similar effects would occur in Mexico with an additional direct impact on its national sovereignty.[22] The most visible opposition came from the Congresses of both countries. Since the MI was designed as a "program" and not as an "international treaty," parliamentary groups were excluded from original design and negotiations.[23] In Mexico, for example, most parliamentary groups opposed Bureau of Alcohol, Tobacco, Firearms, and Explosives agents being deployed in Mexico, reinforcing the historical trend of the rejection of U.S. actions in Mexico.[24] The exclusion of members of Congress from negotiations changed over time because of congressional pressures from both sides of the border.

Some of the antecedents of the MI are related to its association with Plan Colombia. It is important to note, however, that some differences exist between Plan Colombia and the MI, as Mexicans have always been wary of the presence of U.S. troops in Mexico. As a consequence, the U.S. military does not have a presence in Mexico under the MI.[25] In essence, the Bush administration and the proponents of Plan Colombia (see chapter 8 in this volume) argue that Plan Colombia should be a model for other countries experiencing drug trafficking and organized crime.[26] Adam Isacson argues the opposite.[27]

The concept of a model is quite troubling for several reasons. First, Mexico and Colombia are different countries with different problems. Colombia, for instance, has a long history of internal armed conflict while Mexico does not. This one-size-fits-all formula for combating drug trafficking fails to take into account the differences and nuances between different countries. In addition, despite expenditures of U.S.$8 billion,[28] Plan Colombia failed to achieve its goals in terms of drug trafficking and simply caused routes to shift from Colombia to Mexico and drug cultivation to shift back to Peru and Bolivia.[29]

At one point, 80 percent of the money for Plan Colombia was allocated for "hard components" such as aerial spraying and the military. As Adam Isacson's chapter in this volume demonstrates, the militarization of the war on drugs has been quite troubling.[30] First, it fails to address the underlying issues, such as institutional strengthening, democratic consolidation, and demand. Ultimately, the United States and Mexico failed to learn from the past and, in essence, implemented a Plan Colombia for Mexico, calling it initially Plan Mexico.[31]

So, despite some similarities with Plan Colombia, we will treat the MI as a different exercise in cooperation with the United States. The relationship between the United States and Mexico can be described as one of complex interdependence, as both countries share a long border and have many direct linkages.

Criminal activity in Mexico has spilled over the border and impacted security in the United States. President Bush recognized the need to help his southern neighbor combat the various organizations battling for the control of routes and territory, which would inevitably impact the situation within the United States.[32] In order to determine the origins of the MI, we can deduce that it was rational for both presidents to create it. In other words, it was a win-win game. While President Calderón would extend and institutionalize its domestic war against drug cartels with the United States, President Bush extended the militaristic approach of the war on terror to the Mexican border. At home, both presidents used the MI to legitimize their security policies under the concept of "shared responsibilities."

The designers of the MI—Calderón and Bush—are not in power anymore. President Barack Obama assumed office and vowed to continue his support for the MI. However, he reduced the number of resources for Mexico in his 2013 budget because of belt-tightening measures as he focused on domestic issues such as the economy. President Enrique Peña Nieto (2012–2018) has not shown great enthusiasm for continuing the initiatives adopted during the Bush administration. As a result, the future of the MI is uncertain.

The Mérida Initiative: Practical Results

The official version of the practical results of the MI was presented on April 29, 2011, during the third meeting of high-level officials from Mexico and the United States in Washington, D.C.[33] It highlights the following: (a) there have been higher levels of information sharing that have led to the capture of at least twenty-nine important TOC leaders; (b) the use of nonintrusive inspection mechanisms has increased, strengthening the surveillance capacities of the common border; (c) more than 8,500 federal police, 2,600 judicial officials, and 1,800 prison employees have received training; (d) the bilateral mechanisms against illegal transborder flows of money and money laundering have been strengthened; (e) there has been a transfer of eleven helicopters, which has increased the mobility of the Mexican armed forces; and (f) the Bilateral Implementation Office (BIO; Oficina Bilateral de Seguimiento, OBS), with personnel from both countries, was opened in order to monitor activities related to the MI.[34] Despite such valuable efforts, the results have been limited regarding combating TOC and drug traffickers in Mexico. Indeed, the MI never had the goal of eliminating drug trafficking and violence, as this task is nearly impossible.

As stated by Raúl Benítez Manaut, from Collective Security Analysis with Democracy (Colectivo de Análisis de la Seguridad con Democracia, CASEDE), for the MI to be successful, it must meet three basic requirements: (1) integrity (coercive and preventive actions); (2) symmetry (combating all drug cartels); and (3) respect for human rights (a crucial aspect of a democracy).[35] However, in order to avoid ambiguities, Benítez bases his analysis on the original four pillars, or objectives, on which the MI is based: (1) frontal attack on criminal organizations; (2) institutional strengthening; (3) border strengthening; and (4) strengthening of the social fabric and the culture of legality.[36]

Pillar 1: The Frontal Attack on Organized Crime

Pillar 1 is characterized by the use of coercive methods based on the deployment of force by the state against TOCs. The objective is twofold: to diminish the power of the TOC by capturing or killing the leaders of drug cartels; and to reduce the profits of drug trafficking. This pillar has had partial successes with the seizure of drugs and arms and, mainly, with the capture and killing of major leaders such as Arturo Beltrán-Leyva ("El Barbas") and Édgar Valdez Villareal (La Barbie) from the Beltrán Leyva cartel; Ezequiel Cárdenas Guillén (Tony Tormenta) of the Golfo cartel; Vicente Carrillo Leyva (El Vicentillo) of the Juárez cartel; and Ignacio Coronel Villareal (Nacho Coronel) of the Sinaloa cartel. However, the main critique of this pillar is that although the leaders of some cartels were killed and removed—which inevitably made other cartels stronger—the absence of leadership is filled by other members of the organization, which reinforces the thesis that the main problem of drug trafficking lies not in an individual's profile (leadership, personality, intelligence, etc.) but in structural features (economic incentives, rampant corruption, drug criminalization, etc.). Since the Calderón administration did not capture Joaquín "El Chapo" Guzmán, the president's strategy and the effectiveness of the MI were highly questioned, reinforcing the accusation that Calderón favored the Sinaloa cartel over other organizations.

The second objective, to reduce the profits from drug trafficking, shows even more limitations because, on the one hand, the drug market in Mexico (U.S.$25 billion per year) and in the United States ($150 billion per year) does not seem to decrease, but instead constantly generates the highest economic incentives to keep the business going.[37] On the other hand, tracking money-laundering activities is a very complicated process in which the Financial Intelligence Unit (Unidad de Inteligencia Financiera, a branch of the Mexican treasury that receives benefits from the MI) must be much more effective than it has been to this point in freezing illegal assets that allow drug cartels to buy weapons and bribe public servants.

Finally, the biggest criticism of this pillar is that it fit into Calderón's war on drugs strategy, which—besides increasing human rights violations by the military—had resulted in more than 47,000 deaths as of 2011 and more than 70,000 as of 2012,[38] including drug traffickers, forces of the state, and civilians.[39] This cannot be considered a success by any measure.

Pillar 2: Strengthening Institutions

This pillar is responsible for a crucial part of the war on TOC: the strengthening of institutions responsible for combating organized crime, violence, corruption, and injustice. Any country that says that it lives under the rule of law must have strong institutions with minimal corruption so that they can be effective in exercising justice and the rule of law. It therefore does not make sense in Mexico to declare a war on drug traffickers if the military, the police, the judiciary, and the intelligence systems do not function efficiently. The modernization and strengthening of institutions expected from the MI with constant training of officials from the Secretariat of Public Security (Secretaría de Seguridad Pública, SSP), the Mexican Attorney General (Procuraduría General de la República, PGR), the Secretariat for Civil Service (Secretaría de la Función Pública, SFP), and the penitentiary system is urgent and necessary but insufficient if "la cultura de la mordida" (the culture of bribery), deeply rooted in many public spheres, is not combated effectively. Training courses must address these general problems. At the moment, it is difficult to assess the results of this pillar, but not too much should be expected in the short term.

Parallel to the MI, if we highlight the structural nature of institutions, we can see that major reforms proposed by Calderón—and postponed by Congress—might have played a fundamental role in institutional strengthening, especially those reforms that suggested reforming the police forces, improving the judicial system, increasing the accountability of the states, and the reelection of state officials.

Pillar 3: Improving Border Conditions

Mexico and the United States are economically and politically interdependent (although asymmetrically so), and the shared border plays a major role in this bilateral independent relationship. Pillar 3 recognizes that the solution is not just to close the border—by building walls between both countries—but to create a competitive and secure border. The first requires mechanisms that make the legitimate transit of people, goods, and services faster and more efficient by installing modern equipment (provided by the MI) to interrupt illegal inflows of drugs, money, and arms. Security is clearly insufficient. The porous 2,000-mile border makes it difficult to achieve these objectives, especially with the necessary political coordination between the six Mexican and four U.S. states sharing the border.

Pillar 4: Strengthening of the Social Fabric and the Culture of Legality

The objectives of this pillar are as follows: the strengthening of social cohesion; individuals' integrative development; promotion of a culture of legality; and the transformation of perceptions about the real connection between drugs, crime, and violence. This pillar is the most difficult to evaluate because its connection with intangible values remains a crucial component for long-term social transformation. The automatic connection of this pillar with civic values, education, the culture of legality, and the generation of a consciousness of drug trafficking and corruption is of high importance for societal transformation. These results will be accessible in the medium and long terms when the children and youth who are now learning and absorbing these ideals through education modify ontologically their perceptions of the problem to form a society that sees things differently.

Pillar 4 emphasizes that it is necessary to combat drug trafficking with military force and also with education. An addict is not seen as a criminal but as an individual with a problem that requires medical and psychological help. More resources must be allocated for prevention, education, treatment, and rehabilitation, which are more effective than punitive measures and prohibitionist strategies.

It is worth pointing out that the major dilemma of this pillar is to challenge the attractiveness of drug trafficking to social sectors (both rich and poor) that have developed a tolerance or justification of crime, which results from a pervasive culture of delinquency, impunity, and corruption.[40]

Limitations of the MI

The practical effectiveness of the MI is limited by three factors: its temporary nature; the slow delivery or reduction of resources; and the lack of information about the MI itself. The medium- and long-term implications of pillars 2, 3, and 4 challenge the success of the MI because it has always been conceived as having a limited duration. The National Intelligence Council forecasts that by the year 2025, Latin America, especially some regions of the Caribbean and Central America, will still be one of the most violent and unsafe regions of the world due to the persistence of drug traffickers and increasing levels of drug consumption.[41] Paradoxically, the presence of cartels in Central America is possibly a result of the MI and Calderón's strategy, which resulted in the "balloon" and "cockroach" effects.[42] The cockroach effect occurs when a government attempts to eliminate or fragment organized crime, leading the criminal organizations to move into and operate in the weakest neighboring states. It is associated with the displacement of the Zetas to Honduras, Guatemala, and Costa Rica and the spread of the Sinaloa cartel to these countries as well as to Nicaragua and Panama.

The results of the MI also are impacted by the slow delivery and reduction of resources. The U.S. economic crisis of 2008 stalled the delivery of funds, and budgetary reductions made by President Obama in 2013 also affected results,[43] although reductions in resources are justified by the goal of strengthening institutions and not only the acquisition of military equipment. During times of crisis, it is normal for the U.S. Congress to become stricter with regard to the management of resources, especially since the United States has other foreign policy priorities.

The measurement of practical results is more difficult because of the lack of shared national security information between Mexico and the United States.[44] For example, although in 2009 the Secretariat of the Interior (Secretaría de Gobernación, SEGOB) and the Secretariat of Foreign Relations (Secretaría de Relaciones Exteriores) established a "mechanism of dialogue with civil society about the Mérida Initiative,"[45] important information is not disseminated in proportion to its relevance for the public and the federal government.

In the same vein, on August 31, 2010, Mexican authorities announced the opening of the Bilateral Implementation Office with headquarters in Mexico City, but the information provided by this office is exclusively for U.S. and Mexican technical representatives and officials. Though some secrecy is understandable, both governments could provide more clear, precise, and accurate information about the real impact of the MI.

Overall, the practical results of the MI are coming to fruition, but they are limited by factors that could seriously erode its success. Thus, the MI could become just another program with contextual and contemporary results but without any real and profound repercussions for the problem that it was designed to combat. Moreover, as of 2014, it remained unclear how the MI would address highly contested topics such as the use of drones in the border region and on Mexican soil. In addition, immigration reform and the renewed attempt to build a border wall will continue to be a highly contested and important issue for discussion.[46]

Practical Results of Demand Reduction and Mexican Consumption

For several decades, the governments of Mexico and the United States perceived and treated changes and developments in Mexican drug-trafficking organizations as merely an expanded challenge for local Mexican law enforcement. Such perceptions underlined the traditional reasoning that a strong police response in Mexico and stricter control on the Mexican-U.S. border would reduce or eliminate drug trafficking. Strategies rested on the assumption that containing the illegal supply of drugs from Mexico would make drugs in the black market more expensive and riskier to obtain. Thus, keeping drugs relatively scarce and expensive would restrict consumption in the U.S. market.[47] These bilateral law enforcement strategies, however, have created greater opportunities for profits and thus have attracted new actors into drug trafficking in Mexico.

In this sense, the strategy implemented by Calderón and the Mérida Initiative have failed. The profits offered by black market drugs have resulted in the multiplication of Mexican DTOs and the shifting of drug-trafficking routes. Instead of fragmenting and weakening the Mexican DTOs—which was the Mexican government's goal—Calderón's frontal assault, implemented through the MI, only fractionalized them. In the absence of a real demand-reduction strategy in the main market, the United States, profits are still high and are still a big incentive for smuggling drugs into that country.

As a consequence, the drug-trafficking scenario in Mexico, which was dominated for decades by four DTOs (Tijuana, Juárez, Golfo, and Sinaloa), was transformed. Mexico's drug-trafficking map now registers the presence of at least a dozen powerful and violent organizations, among them, the Zetas, the Beltrán-Leyva, La Familia Michoacana, and Los Templarios, which are cashing in and taking the profits of a high-demand drug market. These new organizations emerged from the large presence of the Mexican military in the effort to combat drug trafficking and the internal warfare to fill the vacuum among DTOs. In order to avoid law enforcement and retaliation from the dominant DTOs, the new organizations moved to places where drug trafficking was less powerful before and shifted their smuggling routes.

In the absence of drug-demand reduction in the United States and the strengthening of Mexico's institutions, law enforcement strategies have failed to keep street prices of key illicit substances stable and to reduce the number of drug offenders locked up in U.S. prisons since 1990.[48]

Furthermore, stable demand for methamphetamine in the U.S. market and the void caused by U.S. law enforcement's efforts to stop its production on American soil have presented Mexican DTOs with a new and profitable opportunity. According to the U.S. Government Accountability Office (GAO), "reported seizures along the U.S. border rose from about 500 kilograms in 2000 to highs of almost 2,900 kilograms in 2005 and about 2,700 kilograms in 2006."[49] It is estimated that nowadays Mexican TOCs introduce 80 percent of the meth consumed in the United States. It should be noted that Mexican TOCs became key players in the meth trade only after the number of local meth labs seized in the United States went down from 10,212 to 5,846 between 2003 and 2006.[50]

The inability of Washington to reduce the demand for drugs demonstrates that the United States has not been an effective partner in the war on drugs in Mexico. In addition, as of 2013, cocaine and marijuana consumption had also increased. In sum, the Mexican drug cartels will continue to traffic these substances as long as a market exists. Today, the major market remains Mexico's neighbor to the north: the United States.

As border control became stricter, Mexican DTOs grew in power and opened up local markets for cheap and very accessible drugs. It must be noted that during Felipe Calderón's administration, the data regarding drug consumption in Mexico were scattered, as if the Mexican government was trying to hide the rise in drug consumption in the country. For several years, and prior to the Calderón administration, the results of a long effort to measure the phenomenon were collected and made public in the

National Addiction Survey (Encuesta Nacional de Adicciones), conducted by the Secretariat of Health (Secretaría de Salud). It was only after Calderón left office that the results of such efforts became available once again. Through the last report we know now that drug consumption in Mexico during 2002 and 2008 grew, and it stabilized between 2008 and 2011.[51]

The official data signal marijuana and cocaine as the preferred drugs of Mexican consumers and disregard other highly addictive drugs like crack cocaine and ice (methamphetamine). Other accounts, however, point out that consumption of methamphetamine has increased rapidly and has been used by DTOs as a way to recruit and maintain labor and armed forces. Indeed, accounts of young *sicarios* (hired killers) coming in and going out of private rehabilitation centers only to feed DTOs pervade media reports. In sum, the MI has so far failed in reducing drug demand both in Mexico and the United States.

Conclusions

The antecedents of the MI responded to domestic (political alternations, weak democracy, and the empowerment of transnational organized crime) and international (the war on terror led by the United States) causes. By the end of 2012, however, neither of the creators of the MI—Bush and Calderón—were still in office. Therefore, the future of the MI depends on two factors: (1) whether the Obama administration continues to decrease resources designated for the initiative; and (2) whether the current president of Mexico, Peña Nieto, is willing to support and continue such policies.

In addition, the evaluation of practical results depends on which of the four pillars of the MI is analyzed. The first and hardest pillar, with its coercive measures, demonstrates partial success in the capture of drug lords and the weakening of some cartels.

The second pillar, strengthening institutions, shows that the training of officials from different areas (the SSP, the PGR, the SFP, the prison system, etc.) is under way but is experiencing only modest progress compared with the huge challenge of substantially improving the army, the police, and the judicial and intelligence systems.

The third pillar, with its emphasis on improving the border, has not resulted in effective results; on the contrary, it still has not achieved efficient control of illegal flows of money, arms, and drugs across the border.

Finally, it is still impossible to evaluate the fourth, the culturalist, pillar because its results will be visible only in the medium and long terms, especially with regard to building a culture of legality and social cohesion.

Notes

1. This chapter was translated by Yulia Vorobyeva.

2. We associate the nature of every pillar with a theoretical perspective, thereby creating a classification that enables researchers to examine and measure levels of success and failure.

3. See the introduction in this volume.

4. Bruce M. Bagley, "Tráfico de drogas y crimen organizado en América Latina y el Caribe en el siglo XXI: Retos de la democracia," YouTube video, 37:41, from the Encuentro Internacional Drogas, Usos y Prevenciones, Quito, Ecuador, May 16–18, 2012, http://www.youtube.com/watch?v=sLbYHUs7F5c. Bagley argues that Mexico has become the latest victim in the war on drugs; see "Bruce M. Bagley on the War on Drugs," YouTube video, 14:09, interview with Canadian television, posted by *The Agenda* with Steve Paikin, February 23, 2010, http://www.youtube.com/watch?v=WwGZtFyaVyo.

5. Bagley, "Tráfico de drogas."

6. An excellent account of the history of criminalization of drugs is found in Luis Astorga Almanza, "Drug Trafficking in Mexico: A First General Assessment," UNESCO, March 13, 2012, http://www.unesco.org/most/astorga.htm.

7. Links between drug trafficking and the Mexican political system are described in Luis Astorga Almanza, "Mexico: Drugs and Politics," in *The Political Economy of the Drug Industry: Latin America and the International System*, ed. Menno Vellinga, (Gainesville: University Press of Florida, 2004), 85–102.

8. Jorge Rebolledo and Alberto Lozano, "Iniciativa Mérida: ¿Viejo vino en botella nueva?" in *La Iniciativa Mérida: ¿Nuevo paradigma de cooperación entre México y Estados Unidos en seguridad?* ed. Rafael Velázquez and Juan Pablo Prado Lallande (Mexico City: Universidad Nacional Autónoma de México [UNAM]–Benemérita Universidad Autónoma de Puebla [BUAP], 2009), 160.

9. During 2001, Fox's administration launched an unprecedented offensive against criminal organizations in Mexico. As a result, leaders from the Arellano Félix cartel were captured. See Gretchen Peters, "U.S., Mexico Finally Drug-War Allies: President Vicente Fox's Unprecedented Cooperation with the U.S. Yields Big Blows to Latin Narcotraffickers," *Christian Science Monitor,* July 9, 2002, 1.

10. David C. Jordan calls this phenomenon "anocratic democracy"; see Max. G. Mainwaring, *A "New" Dynamic in the Western Hemisphere Security Environment: The Mexican Zetas and Other Private Armies* (Carlisle Barracks, Pa.: Strategic Studies Institute, 2009), 6.

11. Bruce M. Bagley, "Seminario de seguridad," YouTube video, 1:53:10, from a seminar conducted at El Colegio de la Frontera Norte, Mexico, on July 8, 2010, posted July 9, 2010, http://www.youtube.com/watch?v=sMeqNJzWXCo.

12. See Ramón J. Miró, *Organized Crime and Terrorist Activity in Mexico, 1999–2002* (Washington, D.C.: Library of Congress, 2003), 43–45.

254 · Alberto Lozano-Vázquez and Jorge Rebolledo Flores

13. See Secretaría de Salud–Consejo Nacional contra las Adicciones, *El consumo de drogas en México: Diagnóstico, tendencias y acciones* (Mexico City, 1999); Jesús Narváez, "Cada año aumenta más de 20% el consumo de drogas in México," *La Jornada*, January 19, 2006; Rebolledo and Lozano, "Iniciativa Mérida," 161.

14. See Rubén Aguilar V. and Jorge G. Castañeda, *La guerra fallida* (Mexico City: Punto de Lectura, 2009).

15. Regarding variations in violence levels, see Fernando Escalante, "Homicidios 2008–2009: La muerte tiene permiso," *Nexos*, Mexico City, January 2011, http://www.nexos.com.mx/?p=14089.

16. A detailed explanation of the evolution of drug trafficking and the increase of violence in Mexico during the Vicente Fox administration can be found in Laurie Freeman, *State of Siege: Drug-Related Violence and Corruption in Mexico. Unintended Consequences of the War on Drugs* (Washington, D.C.: Washington Office on Latin America, WOLA), 2006.

17. This attitude has been recognized and praised by the U.S. government. See U.S. Government Accountability Office (GAO), *U.S. Assistance Has Helped Mexican Counternarcotics Efforts, but Tons of Illicit Drugs Continue to Flow into the United States* (Washington, D.C., August 2007), 13–23.

18. The analysis of Felipe Calderón's discourse reveals that the drug-trafficking phenomenon is not clearly defined but frequently presented as a social cancer. See Miguel David Norzagaray López, "El narcotráfico en México desde el discurso oficial," Master's thesis, Facultad Latinoamericana de Ciencias Sociales [FLACSO], 2010), 224–228.

19. See Stephen D. Morris, *Political Corruption in Mexico* (Boulder, Colo.: Lynne Rienner, 2009), 21–22.

20. Some critics point out that the level of severity was fictitious. See Aguilar V. and Castañeda, *La guerra fallida*, 33–49.

21. John Bailey, "Plan Colombia and the Mérida Initiative: Policy Twins or Distant Cousins?" In *National Solutions to Trans-Border Problems: The Governance of Security and Risk in a Post-NAFTA North America*, ed. Isidro Morales (Burlington, Vt.: Ashgate, 2011), 149–160.

22. José Luis Piñeyro, "Plan ¿México?" *El Universal*, September 29, 2007.

23. Members of Mexico's Congress had knowledge of the negotiations on the Mérida Initiative as a result of the intervention of U.S. Representative Silvestre Reyes (D-TX), who unveiled the negotiations of the then called Plan Mexico during the XLVI Mexico–United States Interparliamentary Meeting, held in Austin, Texas, in May 2007; see Alejandro Chanona, "La Iniciativa Mérida y el Congreso Mexicano," in *La Iniciativa Mérida: ¿Nuevo paradigma de cooperación entre México y Estados Unidos en seguridad?* ed. Rafael Velázquez and Juan Pablo Prado Lallande (Mexico City: UNAM-BUAP, 2009), 59.

24. Ibid., 67.

25. For more on the differences between Plan Colombia and the MI, see Bailey, "Plan Colombia and the Mérida Initiative."

26. For more on Colombia, see the preface and chapters 7 and 8 in this volume.

27. Adam Isacson, *Don't Call It a Model: On Plan Colombia's Tenth Anniversary, Claims of "Success" Don't Stand Up to Scrutiny* (Washington, D.C.: WOLA, 2010).

28. See Bruce M. Bagley, introduction in this volume.

29. See Bruce M. Bagley, "Tráfico de drogas"; United Nations Office on Drugs and Crime (UNODC), *World Drug Report, 2011* (New York, 2011).

30. See chapter 4 in this volume.

31. Bailey, "Plan Colombia and the Mérida Initiative."

32. See Aguilar V. and Castañeda, *La guerra fallida*; Norzagaray López, "El narcotráfico en México."

33. Prior meetings were held in November 2008 and March 2010; see http://2006-2012. sre.gob.mx/images/stories/doctransparencia/rdc/2lbrean.pdf.

34. Ibid.

35. Raúl Benítez Manaut, ed., *Crimen organizado e Iniciativa Mérida en las relaciones México–Estados Unidos* (Mexico City: Colectivo de Análisis de la Seguridad con Democracia [CASEDE], 2010), 8.

36. "Iniciativa Mérida."

37. Bruce M. Bagley, "La conexión Colombia–México–Estados Unidos," in *Atlas de la seguridad y la defensa de México 2009*, ed. Raúl Benítez Manaut, Abelardo Rodríguez Sumano, and Armando Rodríguez Luna (Mexico City: CASADE), 25.

38. This number reflects the official account of Mexico's Office of the Attorney General (the Procuraduría General de la República, PGR). For a good picture of the recrudescence of violence in Mexico, see Eduardo Guerrero, "2011: La dispersión de la violencia," in *Nexos*, February 2012, http://www.nexos.com.mx/?p=14089.

39. Independent projections in February 2012 predicted that the death toll of the Calderón years would reach a "modest" 61,000, an estimated mean of 66,000, and 71,000 in the worst-case scenario. See Eduardo Guerrero, *Diario Milenio*, February 23, 2012.

40. A controversial and good example of increased tolerance took place in January 2012, when Mexican actress Kate del Castillo—who at the time was playing a leading role on a Mexican TV series about drug trafficking, *La reina del sur*—declared via Twitter that for her Chapo Guzmán had more credibility than the Mexican government. Del Castillo's tweet went viral and was the subject of heated discussion.

41. U.S. National Intelligence Council, *Global Trends 2025: A Transformed World* (Washington, D.C.: Government Printing Office, 2008), 15.

42. Bruce M. Bagley and Jorge Chabat coined and use this allegory as a way to illustrate how drug-trafficking organizations move around when facing pressure or are cornered by law enforcement (just as cockroaches do when one is trying to exterminate them).

43. The budget for the Mérida Initiative was U.S.$199 million with an additional $35 million as an economic support fund, for a total of $234 million, which was a reduction from 2012 levels.

44. John Bailey, "Tiempo fuera," *El Universal*, March 30, 2009.

45. "Iniciativa Mérida."

46. A critical view of how the MI addressed migration is found in Laura Carlsen, "A Primer on Plan Mexico," Americas Program, May 5, 2008, http://www.cipamericas.org/archives/1474.

47. See, for example, Karim Murji, *Policing Drugs* (Brookfield, Vt.: Ashgate, 1998), 12–24.

48. See Harold Pollack, "The Most Embarrassing Graph in American Drug Policy," *Washington Post*, May 29, 2013.

49. GAO, "U.S. Assistance."

50. José Luis León, "El tráfico de metanfetaminas: Asia–México–Estados Unidos," in *Atlas de la seguridad y la defensa de México 2012*, ed. Sergio Aguayo and Raúl Benítez, (Mexico City: CASEDE, 2013).

51. See Mexico, Secretaría de Salud, *Encuesta Nacional de Adicciones* (Mexico City, 2011).

13

Police Reform in Mexico

A Never-Ending Story

SIGRID ARZT

This chapter describes and analyzes police reform in Mexico since 1990. In terms of organization, this work first provides an extensive background section describing when the federal government began advocating for police reform. This advocacy represents a critical juncture that placed police reform at the center of the public debate in the 1990s. Next, this chapter examines the events that transpired during the transition from the Institutional Revolutionary Party (Partido Revolucionario Institucional, PRI) to the National Action Party (Partido Acción Nacional, PAN), headed by Vicente Fox. Finally, this work examines the policies of Felipe Calderón and his administration and how far police reform went, especially at the local level.

A quotation from Jorge Chabat provides an excellent starting point by framing the issues facing Mexico:

> Mexico is facing a serious security threat. During the last two decades the levels of insecurity at different levels have grown in a very substantial way. The reasons are several: the deterioration of Mexican police forces due to its political use and corruption, the development of nontraditional threats like drug trafficking and terrorism, and the process of globalization. An additional factor that explains this phenomenon is the process of political transition that Mexico is experiencing in which the old rules do not work anymore and the new rules are still in process of creation. Insecurity is present at several levels: it goes from the personal level (human security) to the national and international level (national, hemispheric and collective security).[1]

It is important to note that Mexico has a federalist political system and experienced a transition from an authoritarian regime characterized by centralized presidentialism, which began to unravel as a result of the forces of pluralism and the triumph of the opposition at the local-municipal level in the 1980s. The election of Vicente Fox as the president in 2000 signified the end of seventy-one years of PRI rule. The transition was accompanied by increases in political pluralism at the state and municipal levels and resulted in the dispersion of political power. In addition, criminal groups became more diverse, violent, sophisticated, and economically powerful. The organized criminal networks began operating on an international scale and started challenging the state and its monopoly on the use of force.

In fact, the ability of the PRI, the hegemonic political party, to control politics and crime became considerably more ineffective after 1997, at the height of political pluralism prior to the alternation of power at the presidential level. The transition was accompanied by an incremental political pluralism at the state and municipal levels and resulted in the dispersion of political power. In addition, criminal groups became more diverse, violent, sophisticated, and economically powerful. The organized criminal networks began operating on an international scale and started challenging the state and its monopoly on the use of force.

Instead, they started strengthening networks of local and state protection by bribing the police and local political *caciques*. In addition, organized criminal networks began recruiting such actors as soldiers for criminal organizations and employed them to work as the "eyes" of the criminal rings by alerting them of the deployment of police or military officials in the cities and rural areas.

Mexico has experienced rapid changes since 1990. In 1996, it had a population of about 92 million, of which some 65 million lived in urban areas, while 27 million lived in rural areas. There are some 50 cities that have more than 100,000 inhabitants. Of the 2,400 municipalities, 145 contain the largest percentages of the population.[2] A decade later, Mexico had more than 110 million inhabitants, and the population had doubled in the metropolitan areas, reaching 358 urban centers, according to the Secretariat of Social Development (Secretaría de Desarrollo Social [SEDESOL]).[3]

It is important to underline the point of departure when analyzing police reform and security. That is to say, security is a local matter. Public security is one of the responsibilities of the municipality according to Article 115 of the Mexican Constitution. It is within this legal framework that the municipalities have autonomy to plan, provide services, and develop the economic, political, and sociocultural activities of their population. It is also important to remember that officials at this level of government hold office for only three years with no reelection. Hence, the incentives to develop and implement long-run policies that address poverty and poor urban planning and that improve social cohesion or basic services are considerably rare.

In addition, Article 21 of the Mexican Constitution, enacted in 1994, states that it is the responsibility of the public prosecutor to head the investigation of crimes and to order the police to solve crimes. Public prosecutors faced constant tensions with the investigative police because the latter had no legal obligation to investigate or follow a case, unless ordered by the public prosecutor. This institutional arrangement between what the judicial police could and could not do in relation to what was ordered by the public prosecutor contributed considerably to the lack of professionalization of the police force in such basic matters as guarding a crime scene or talking to suspects and witnesses.[4] Today, the framework of police responsibility has changed, particularly at the federal level.

It is also important to underline that, according to the Constitution, the first responder to a criminal act or social disturbance is the local authority, the police. Today, the public demands that the federal government respond to any criminal activity, particularly if it is closely linked to drug trafficking. For example, in the mid-1990s, President Zedillo faced the first wave of kidnappings and violent crimes. It was in the midst of this crisis that the National Public Security Council (NPSC; Consejo Nacional de Seguridad Privada, CNSP) emerged as a response to demands for better coordination, alignment, and policies to mitigate the crime rates of that time. The NPSC comprised the thirty-two governors and a representative from an important federal ministry (such as the Ministry of Defense, the Navy, the Interior, or the Federal Preventive Police, FPP—Policía Federal Preventiva), who shared the responsibility of subsidizing public security activities. Eighty-six percent of the police force operates at the state and local levels, and yet these are the levels of government where less attention has been paid to professionalization, recruitment, protection, and buildup of institutional capacity. In fact, periodically, the federal government has had to intervene to provide help and ameliorate insecurity at the local level. In Chihuahua in 1997, for example, homicides and drug trafficking made Ernesto Zedillo deploy the military and seize control of portions of the state, municipal, and federal police.[5] Years later, President Calderón deployed a plan called Todos Somos Juárez (We Are All Juárez) after more than 8,000 homicides occurred in Mexico between 2008 and 2011, 5,000 in Juárez. During this period of severe insecurity and violent crisis, at least three changes of state governors occurred, and at least twice, changes took place at the municipal level. None of these candidates addressed security as a critical electoral issue.

It is safe to say that since 1990, under heightened levels of violence, particularly kidnapping, insecurity has not been an electoral topic in the competition for any of the three levels of government. Citizens in Mexico have not punished the authorities for the alarming levels of insecurity and kidnapping. Electoral triumphs have been driven by other issues that have more to do with the institutional capacity of the locally entrenched political parties, the lack of or weak opposition to, or issues of corruption and economics. In fact, no politician has lost an election or won one on the security ticket.

Public insecurity goes hand in hand with police reform. Yet reform has systematically faced many challenges, particularly the institutional incapacity of the municipal and state levels to plan and implement sound policies. The policies implemented can be classified as shortcuts and quick responses to specific situations. These policies, therefore, lack a long-term vision and fail to address various challenges faced by the police force, such as its relationship with the communities it serves and protects. Profound structural and institutional changes require political will and leadership, and state and municipal authorities have invested very little in this.

As mentioned before, municipal governments have no incentive or the human capacity to provide good and sound services. Even worse, they lack economic resources, given the deficient mechanism they have to collect money. In fact, they depend considerably on the annual redistribution of money from the federal budget. With the exception of the States of Mexico, Nuevo León, and Jalisco, the states remain considerably behind in collecting taxes and their own resources and continue to depend heavily on redistribution from the federal government. By the end of the 1990s, the Zedillo administration saw the need to deploy military forces to mitigate the levels of insecurity and to provide technical support to almost all the state attorneys general to respond to kidnappings. It was apparent that the local and state authorities had done little or nothing to recruit and develop a police force that could address crime in their states.

Under the so-called New Federalism, Zedillo promoted the creation, within the Ministry of the Interior (Secretaría de Gobernación), of the NCPS and the FPP, in an effort to support the other two levels of government. By the end of 1997, political plurality was increasing, and Nuevo

León, Guanajuato, Chihuahua, Baja California, and Querétaro were represented by the PAN; Mexico City was under a left-leaning government with the Revolutionary Democratic Party (Partido Revolucionario Democrático, PRD); the rest of the country was represented by the PRI. Yet the PRI lost its majority in Congress, resulting in the following composition: PRI, 38 percent; PAN, 25.85 percent; and PRD, 24.98 percent. This scenario clearly meant that the PRI would need to negotiate policies and that governors had to have political incentives to abide by these new policies.

Unfortunately, the potential for reform remained bleak, given the unwillingness of the Panista (PAN) authorities—and many other parties—to promote different policies. In addition to the fact that insecurity (on the discourse level) existed, it was not the policy over which citizens would decide their vote.[6] Hence, the central government's policies tended to address local crime and drugs. Yet the government faced many challenges, particularly as a result of the high levels of fragmentation, dispersion of police forces, asymmetries between the different actors, and the lack of technological, human, financial, and material resources.

In 1997, 1.49 million crimes were registered,[7] of which only 20 percent were investigated, 9 percent went before a judge, and 1 percent of the convicted were punished.[8] In order to meliorate the context of the late 1990s, institutional and legal reforms were put in place in an effort to improve coordination and to allocate specific resources from a federal fund for public security. In 1997, distribution of resources was based on a formula that provided no incentives to reform the police and justice system.

The federal budget provides for a specific distribution of federal resources for each state based on the Federal Fiscal Law, which states in Article 44 that the distribution of resources will incorporate the following criteria: (a) the number of inhabitants in the states and federal district; (b) the jail population; (c) the implementation of prevention programs to mitigate crime; (d) the issues identified in the National Public Security Program (Programa Nacional de Seguridad Pública): recruitment, professionalization, equipment, infrastructure, and technology.

The idea behind the creation of the National Public Security Council was to provide a framework for coordination and institutional capacity with the federal authorities so that the states could work on transforming their police forces, infrastructure, and institutional capacity. However, such changes never occurred. After decades, the reality is that governors and local authorities had no incentive or political will to alter the status quo.

Due to collusion or outright neglect, governors and local authorities have learned to safely decide when it is necessary for the federal government to intervene in their localities to address matters of insecurity. Zedillo was the first Mexican president to deploy the military to mitigate the levels of violence in the states, in this case, Chihuahua and Baja California. In fact, when President Zedillo began implementing such tactics during the second half of his six-year term, Congress—in the hands of the opposition—promoted a constitutional review about the use of the armed forces. Today, all political parties at the state level, regardless of ideology, have demanded the deployment of military forces to contain crime and violence. In fact, left-leaning parties like the PRD appointed a military man as chief of the state police during the six-year term of Governor Zeferino Torreblanca in Guerrero. The Federal District, in the hands of this same party, headed by Cuauhtémoc Cárdenas, also had military officers in charge of the security apparatus until they were accused of being involved in human rights violations. The PRI has also had military officers as state police chiefs in Veracruz, Quintana Roo, Hidalgo, Tamaulipas, and Nuevo León. The same has occurred with the PAN in states like Baja California and Chihuahua at the local level.

The use of the military has occurred cyclically to the incapacity of the local police to curtail crime and violence. The institutional capacity of the municipal and state police continues to face major challenges. In fact, the municipal police have become partners of the entrenched local organized crime groups, and the policies that need to be implemented in order to improve public security are obstructed by those who are supposed to protect the general population.

The complexities of the evolving organized crime groups and the dispersal of criminal activities demand considerable trust between society and the different police forces. In fact, because of the level of police corruption and the penetration of criminal groups, the military was deployed together with state and local authorities during the Zedillo administration to perform basic policing such as patrolling or specific police interventions. Unfortunately, this policy was insufficient because it was not accompanied by other critical policies, such as changing patterns of recruitment, improving and providing social benefits, guaranteeing a modest but good salary, and even recovering society's trust.

During the Fox administration, it was thought that by appointing military officers as police chiefs at the state and local levels, corruption would diminish and disciplinary standards could be put in place. However, long-term planning and structural transformation of the police force as a whole did not occur. Coordination and collaboration lasted while the sense of emergency was at its peak. Once the level of violence decreased, though, the authorities concentrated on other issues and, basically, abandoned the policies—such as vetting police officers, investing in infrastructure, professionalization, and improving salaries—that needed to be inserted in the security apparatus.

The logic that has dominated patterns of criminality is an incremental context of exacerbated violence and criminality. Governors demand help from the federal government, which deploys the military or the federal police, and once public attention shifts to other matters, the local authorities stop collaborating or even sharing intelligence information with the federal forces. The SNSP in 1995 reported that 335 municipalities had no police force at all.[9] At that time, 749 municipalities had a police force of between 1 and 10; 77 had between 1,001 and 5,000 police officers; 10 had between 5,001 and 13,100; the rest had more than 14,000. In that same year, only the Federal District and the States of Mexico, Jalisco, Nuevo León, and Veracruz had large numbers of police officers, some 70,000 total, of which 25,000 belonged to the Federal District.[10]

The number of local police officers in 1995 was estimated at approximately 400,000 agents; that number has not changed. According to a report presented to the NPSC in September 2011, the numbers are as follows: 397,664 police officers, of which 231,517 are state agents and 166,147 are municipal. Of those, the states with more than 10,000 police officers per 100,000 inhabitants are Baja California Sur (444 officers per 100,000 inhabitants); Federal District (1,061), Quintana Roo (521), State of Mexico (428), and Guerrero (406). States with fewer than 5,000 police officers per 100,000 inhabitants are Durango (239), Nuevo León (225), Puebla (218), Guanajuato (209), and Baja California (248). States with a force between 5,000 and 10,000 are Oaxaca (277), Jalisco (265), Chihuahua (263), Sonora (260), and Veracruz (256). In sum, there are an average of 354 police officers nationally for every 100,000 inhabitants.[11] In other words, 93 percent of the total force remains at the state and municipal levels.

Another aspect that is worth analyzing is salary. Low salaries with no social security have been a constant since the crisis exploded. In 1995, the average monthly salary of the 223,533 police officers was around U.S.$200. Add to this the fact that 55.6 percent had only a primary school education.[12] Only 24.7 percent had secondary school education, 13.7 percent had completed a bachelor's degree, and the rest had some type of schooling beyond primary school.[13] It is clear that these conditions imposed challenges on the recruitment, professionalization, and specialization of the police force that were never really addressed.

As a result of the Gutiérrez Rebollo crisis in 1997, when it was found that the nation's drug czar was in the pocket of the drug cartels, a general regulation was put in place to initiate a vetting process for every agent recruited. However, given that this vetting process was not mandatory, the polygraph exams, psychological tests, and examination of personal assets, medical history, and general knowledge about the applicant were applied differently in every state and even in every federal institution. The vetting of police officers and any personnel linked to security activities became mandatory nationwide only after the promulgation of the National General Public Security Law in January of 2009.[14]

In fact, in a five-year period, crime grew 13.2 percent annually, according to Mexico's General Accounting Office:[15] "73,803 crimes were reported by the year 2002, by 2007 the number was 137,289 crimes. The average rate of drug-related crimes for this period had an annual increase of 28.1."[16]

Even before changes in the party of the president, the public security apparatus was very precarious, abandoned and with few or no resources. Policies were merely reactions to specific circumstances; at no time were they meant as a long-term investment. In fact, one could argue that much of that line of policy implementation was also followed by the first democratically elected president, Vicente Fox.

Police Reform in the Context of a New Democratic Government (2000–2006)

The crisis of insecurity continued to increase, according to a Citizens Institute for Studies on Insecurity (Instituto Ciudadano de Estudios sobre la Inseguridad, ICESI) survey (see tables 13.1 and 13.2). After three years in office, President Fox presented the National Public Security Program 2000–2006. The document stated that in the year 2000, 14.3 crimes were committed for every 100,000 inhabitants, and of the thirty-two states, only thirteen were considered to have a high recurrence rate. The average crime rate was 14 to 49 percent for every 100,000 inhabitants in states like Baja California, Baja California Sur, Chihuahua, the Federal District, Jalisco, State of Mexico, Morelos, Nuevo León, Quintana Roo, Querétaro, San Luis Potosí, Tamaulipas, and Yucatán. According to the same source, the states with a crime rate between 10 and 13.9 crimes per 100,000 inhabitants were Aguascalientes, Coahuila, Guanajuato, Guerrero, Nayarit, Oaxaca, Puebla,

Table 13.1. Citizens Institute for Studies on Insecurity crime survey, 2008

Insecurity in Mexico	Location
85.9% of victims have been robbed	
Six of 10 citizens have been robbed	State of Mexico and Federal District
85% of robberies are perpetrated by people under age 36	National statistic
Five of every 10 aggressive acts involve firearms and 3 knives	
65% of crimes committed per 100,000 inhabitants	Occur in a public space (streets)
30% of crimes per 100,000 inhabitants	Occur at home

Source: Compiled by the author based on data from Instituto Ciudadano de Estudios sobre Inseguridad (ICESI), *Cuadernos del ICESI no. 1: ENSI-5 Quinta Encuesta Nacional sobre Inseguridad–Resultados* (Mexico City, 2008), http://drcureces.files.wordpress.com/2009/12/icesi-5a-encuesta-nacional-sobre-inseguridad.pdf.

Table 13.2. Citizens Institute for Studies on Insecurity crime survey, 2008

Sense of insecurity in Mexico
79% of victims did not file a police report; thus, every 21 crimes committed over 100 were not reported
59% of population feels unsafe at home
More than half of population feels unsafe on public transportation, in the street, on roads, in marketplaces, and on playgrounds
Citizens' trust in army (30%); in federal police (15%); in local police (7.8%), in public prosecutor (6.9%)

Source: Compiled by the author based on data from Instituto Ciudadano de Estudios sobre Inseguridad (ICESI), *Cuadernos del ICESI no. 1: ENSI-5 Quinta Encuesta Nacional sobre Inseguridad–Resultados* (Mexico City, 2008), http://drcureces.files.wordpress.com/2009/12/icesi-5a-encuesta-nacional-sobre-inseguridad.pdf.

Sonora, and Tabasco. The 10 remaining states had fewer than 10 crimes per 100,000 inhabitants: Campeche, Colima, Chiapas, Durango, Hidalgo, Michoacán, Sinaloa, Tlaxcala, Veracruz, and Zacatecas.[17] Even though the Fox administration created the Ministry of Public Security at the federal level in an effort to align and coordinate better with the other two levels of government, the final result was not achieved. At some level, the Fox administration continued to deploy the military in every crisis to reduce the rates of violence that cyclically affected states such as Chihuahua, Baja California, or Nuevo León.

By the year 2003, the level of organized crime's penetration and disorder of the state and local police was evident. The cartels recruited police escorts in order to establish law and order. In Nuevo Laredo, the murder of the police chief, who lasted only six hours after taking office, gives a picture of the level of incremental violence and the *"plata or plomo"* (silver or lead) drug cartel policy. After these incidents, federal police officers were deployed to investigate the murders and were ambushed by local police who were in the pocket (*en el bolsillo*) of a drug cartel. The incidents resulted in the arrest of 179 local police officers serving as escorts for Osiel Cárdenas Guillén.[18]

By June 2004, President Fox faced an outraged civil society. An estimated one million Mexicans took to the streets and demanded public security and police reform. Six months later, he launched México Seguro in order to improve coordination between local and state authorities and to help improve their ability to fight crime. With this strategy, Fox was trying to revamp the police force, but the governors and local authorities had no political will to change the situation and did not want to commit to implementing such a profound transformation.

México Seguro was an attempt to obtain peace among the different actors,[19] but it was, in the end, a palliative that was put in place to douse metaphorical fires. The federal police and the military were like firefighters driving from state to state, putting out fires by mitigating the levels of violence among criminal groups and against the population. It seems clear that this policy also hindered federal forces from improving their own condition, including their intelligence and operative capacity.

It is safe to say that the recurrent use of the military to contain crime and violence resulted in the local and state authorities postponing the institutional transformation of their police forces. The safety net cyclically provided by the federal authorities permitted the other two levels of government to delay any major changes in the institutional design and functions of the police force and its investigative duties.

This delay was also accompanied by demands from the local police, who protested the lack of social benefits, job security, decent salaries, and access to housing and credit. The deplorable conditions under which a large number of local and state police found themselves continues, as the authorities have done practically nothing to improve conditions.

Calderón and the Security Challenge (2006–2012)

By the time Calderón took office in 2006, there was a sense of lawlessness in the country. Civil society shared a complete sense of panic and did not trust the authorities or have confidence in the ability of the state to combat organized crime. During Fox's administration, almost 3,000 drug-related executions were carried out, of which around 10 percent were of police and military officials. During the six-month transition period prior to the end of the Fox administration, 1,427 drug-related executions occurred; during the same time period, homicides of citizens reached a total of 1,624.

The ability of organized criminal groups to intimidate and penetrate political structures threatened democracy in Mexico. It was clear to the Calderón administration that organized crime undermined political institutions and had developed a formidable presence in political parties, fundamentally impacting the fabric of society. The organized crime groups gave ample evidence of providing parallel security services and military equipment, which challenged the state and led to losses in its monopoly on the use of force (see tables 13.3 and 13.4).

By the end of the first year of the Calderón administration, the number of drug-related executions had reached 10,000. Of this number, almost 10 percent were of federal, state, and municipal police officers, soldiers, and marines. Mexican organized crime had taken a step forward in 2007, terrorizing people and communities. In 2007, in the border city of Ciudad Juárez, Chihuahua, there were 2,000 deaths in twelve months; over 500

Table 13.3. Citizens Institute for Studies on Insecurity crime survey, 2009

Insecurity in Mexico

70% of the population felt insecure during Calderón's tenure
79% did not report a crime
70% did not trust local police
90% of the crimes were robberies
Average of 19 homicides per 100,000 inhabitants

Source: Information compiled by the author based on the data from Instituto Ciudadano de Estudios sobre Inseguridad, *Cuadernos del ICESI no. 8: Victimización, incidencia y cifra negra: Análisis de la ENSI-6* (Mexico City, 2009), http://www.oas.org/dsp/documents/victim ization_surveys/mexico/mexico_analisis_ensi6.pdf.

Table 13.4. President Felipe Calderón Hinojosa's national strategy against organized crime, 2006–2012

Axis 1	Axis 2	Axis 3	Axis 4	Axis 5
Rule of law	Dismantling of criminal organizations	Strengthening of public institutions responsible for fight against organized crime	Prevention policies against crime and violence	Strengthening of international cooperation
Policy actions	**Policy actions**	**Policy actions**	**Policy actions**	**Policy actions**
Strengthen rule of law; guarantee public safety; launch joint operations	Weaken operations, logistics, and financial capacities of organized criminal groups; collect intelligence from power structures; process information to add value in regional, national, and international arenas; reduce impunity; extradite and incarcerate key leaders	Modernize Mexico's federal institutions; increase federal, state, municipal budgets; justice system and law enforcement reform; constitutional reform from inquisitor system to accusatory system (2008); combat organized crime and corruption	Social development policies; recover public space programs; safe schools programs; treatment centers; reconstruct social tissue; civic participation; recover public confidence in state	Mutual confidence, cooperation, and co-responsibility; key allies: U.S., Canada, Colombia; Mérida Initiative

Source: Table developed by author in her capacity as national security adviser to President Felipe Calderón.

encounters between law enforcement and military officials and criminal groups; and organized crime groups made use of mass media to send their messages. At the end of 2008, more than 100 "*narco mantas*" (public ads sending a message to the police, to politicians, and to the community) were placed in several states the same day. Finally, the traffickers had the equipment and capacity to use automatic weapons, hand grenades, and human shields indiscriminately.

In 2010, the Institutional and Social Survey showed the following results:[20]

- Three of every 10 persons say insecurity is the most important challenge faced by the nation, their state, and municipality
- Four in every 10 persons say alcohol consumption in the streets is the problem that seriously contributes to the insecurity issue
- On a scale of 1 to 10, the national average of trust in the police is 5.8; the state of Yucatán has the highest level, 7.1, and the State of Nuevo León the lowest, 4.7
- On a scale of 1 to 10, the fight against crime receives a 6; Yucatan has the highest score, 7.1; the State of Mexico fails, with a 5.5, and Mexico City has 5.4; Durango scored lowest, 4.8
- 60 percent of the people consider corruption and police collusion with organized crime the reason behind the lack of results
- The state and local police forces are perceived as the most corrupt
- Three of every 10 persons are afraid of being robbed
- Two of every 10 persons are afraid of a home invasion
- And 1 of every 10 persons is afraid of being kidnapped
- One in every 10 has been a victim of a crime during the past year; of those victims, 4 out of 10 were physically assaulted, 5 out of 10 called the police for help; the help provided by the police was graded at 5.6; almost 65 percent of those victims did not file a complaint with the public prosecutor.

These statistics demonstrate that despite all the effort and money invested in improving the capacity of the police and state security personnel, societal mistrust of the police force and judicial actors remained a key issue. President Calderón instructed the Secretariat of Public Security (Secretaría de Seguridad Pública) to develop a comprehensive police system that demanded the buildup of technological capabilities to exploit databases, train new intelligence personnel, and promote a police model that could be replicated at the other two levels of government.[21] The objectives were to guarantee job stability and equal opportunities for police agents, to consolidate an institutional framework, and to foster a sense of belonging to a corporation. It also meant a first-time-ever consistent investment in financial and infrastructural resources to build up a police force at the federal level.

In June 2008, Calderón promoted a constitutional amendment that established the bases for the selection, recruitment, evaluation, certification, and professionalization of the police force. The vetting process became compulsory, as did the homogenization of protocols, a ranking system,

Table 13.5. Federal resources directed to the states, Calderón administration

Year	Billions of pesos	State receiving most resources
2007	5,000,000,000	State of Mexico
2008	6,000,000,000	Federal District
2009	6,916,800,000	Veracruz
2010	6,916,800,000	Jalisco
2011		Chiapas
2012	7,373,650,500	
Total	37,891,550,500 (U.S.$261,320,379 × 14.5 pesos)	

Source: Secretariado Ejecutivo del Sistema de Seguridad Pública, "Fondo de Aportaciones en Materia de Seguridad Pública (FASP)," Diario Oficial, March 5, 2007, February 22, 2008, February 26, 2009, February 10, 2010, February 28, 2011, February 10, 2012.

police organization, a career path, and a clear distinction between police officers, public prosecutors, and crime scene investigators.[22] A few months later, the National Public Security Council approved the National Vetting Model for police and public prosecutors. The objective was to certify all personnel in the security sector at all three levels of government.

Two years later, President Calderón sent to Congress a new package of reforms for the organization and operation of the police forces in the country.[23] The proposal recognized that the municipal police represented 38 percent of the total national force, that less than half of the thirty-two states had police forces in every municipality.[24]

In the course of the Calderón administration, the federal resources to support and provide a coherent public policy for police reform meant a spillover of federal resources to the states (see table 13.5). Documents from the Public Security Municipal Subsidy (Subsidio para la Seguridad Municipal), distributed since the year 2008 among 190 municipalities and the 16 delegations in Mexico City, report that of the more than 30,000 police agents vetted by the Ministry of Public Security, only 40 percent were certified; the rest did not abide by the mandate to be certified or they simply did not pass the exams.

Between 1994 and 2009, local crime accounted for 95 percent of all the crime reported. Robbery remained the most harmful crime against individuals across the nation, and impunity offered to the perpetrators remained very high. The local police forces collapsed; they lacked concrete protocols, organization, and budgets. In addition, they lacked the proper equipment to respond to the crime challenges of their communities. In this context, building up local and state police was also a task under the leadership of President Calderón, and a number of cases became politicized and hence obstructed by the same authorities that were calling for help.

Despite Calderón's efforts, today, municipal police forces completely lack the basic skills to conduct their assignments. It has been documented that the educational level of the police force is very low: primary school, 68 percent; 2 percent, illiterate.

Finally, approximately 61 percent of municipal police forces earn U.S.$275 per month. The police have neither social recognition nor respect for their profession; in fact, many of them do not have job stability or the ability to take professional development courses and seminars. The recruiting mechanisms have not been reviewed since 2000, and although the Calderón administration inaugurated a specialized police institute, the capacity to teach, prepare, and graduate the number of police required lags far behind the need. In conjunction with this reality, criminal organizations have developed a good capacity to recruit young people for their activities.

The combination of the elements described above and crime and kidnapping rates peaked again in 2008 and pressed the National Public Security Council to take action. Police disorder, violence, and crime were high, especially in the wake of the kidnapping and killing by police of the son of a prominent entrepreneur, Alejandro Martí. This murder and the death of the daughter of another prominent elite figure, Nelson Vargas, forced the Calderón administration to design the National Accord for Security, Justice, and Legality (Acuerdo Nacional para la Seguridad, Justicia y Legalidad). The agreement set up a number of public policies, with specific commitments at the federal, state, and municipal levels. The agreement, therefore, was a reflection of the sense of urgency and the need to improve coordination and collaboration and to invest in equipment, recruitment, and training at the state and municipal levels. It was signed not only by political authorities, but also by prominent members of Congress, members of the media, the religious leadership, academics, and some nongovernmental organizations.

The agreement had specific deadlines for every policy. Some of the most important commitments were to create specialized vetting units so every police agent could be examined; to continue collecting data on police officers, their training, location, and skills; to collect information on why officers were removed from the police force and where they were, thereby keeping officials in other states from hiring them. The federal government invested in the National Police Database in which police from all levels of government have to be registered, including all their personal data. The demand for training and specialization strengthened the National Police Academy at San Luis Potosí, which provides mid-level police managers with the training necessary to allow them to supervise police activities.

Efforts by entities outside the state led to the implementation of social and preventive rather than punitive policies, leading to the creation of national programs for safe schools, prevention of drug addiction, and recovery of public spaces. Critics also demanded that a number of laws and regulations be standardized and that the military have clear legal limits on their policing activities, given the increasing number of human rights violations.

By the year 2010, a public discussion about the possibility of dissolving the municipal police became critical. In fact, President Calderón presented a reform dissolving the municipal police forces and, from what could be recovered from those forces, create a state-level police unit and improve the cooperation, coordination, and collaboration between the state and federal governments. Thus, instead of dealing with more than 2,000 police units, with totally diverse capabilities, resources, training, and tactics, thirty-two of the best police units would be grouped. By 2012, the initiative had not been even discussed in Congress. Numerous local authorities publicly opposed the initiative, claiming that it was unconstitutional. Lobbying and a lack of political will made it impossible to seriously debate the importance of this proposed new framework. Instead, it became highly politicized and was put to rest.

In the meantime, other states—Guerrero, Morelos, Durango, and Coahuila—demanded the intervention of the federal government. It took almost three years to approve the national vetting process and the same amount of time to agree on the application of specific vetting criteria for those police officers who were part of the antikidnapping units.[25]

Juan Miguel Alcántara, executive director of the National Security Council, in a public statement in November 2011 indicated that state and local authorities could strengthen local capacity and build up accreditation centers that would allow them to certify their law enforcement personnel. However, the truth is that most of the states have no interest in allocating these resources, and hence, it appears that the deadline for certifying all police officers by January 2012 is unattainable. According to the latest report issued by the National Public Security System 90 percent of the total police force has been vetted, yet the report fails to say how many passed the examination.[26]

Conclusion: Why Such Chronic Incapacity?

Chronic incapacity has three basic elements. First, the disorderliness with which police reform has been advanced is directly linked to the level of political commitment and cooperation governors are willing to invest. There is a clear correlation between the efforts of states facing an emergency and those that are not feeling the same pressure; the latter work on other issues. It is also clear that term limits (three or six years with no reelection), a lack of accountability, and the constant redesign of police and military strategies because there is no electoral cost undermine the political incentives for authorities to commit to police reform in the long term.

Second, implementing the policies of the National Accord puts considerable pressure on the governors that have links with drug-trafficking networks because that means breaking the chains of corruption and control that criminal organizations exercise over local and state police.

Third, even with all the investment in human resources, infrastructure, and technology, the truth is that there are areas that, even with immense resources, could not be covered in the near future because universities need to prepare criminologists, psychologists, and other professionals who view public security as a sector that provides opportunities to develop personally and professionally.

Today, criminal activities are highly complex, and officials clearly have been unprepared and unequipped to handle them. In addition, many officials are linked to those very criminal activities. The context of fragile or nonexistent police-judicial institutions in combination with weak law and order and high levels of impunity allows for rampant transnational crime (drugs/arms trafficking) and local organized crime (kidnappings).

As of 2014, we still saw a disarticulated response: police and military forces doing police work. The local and state authorities did not live up to their promises—with absolutely no electoral cost. President Peña Nieto has deployed military and federal police forces to curtail crime and kidnapping in Tamaulipas, the State of Mexico, and Michoacán, similarly to his predecessor's "firefighter's policy."

In sum, security and law enforcement remain high on the national agenda, but the implementation of the policies agreed on by the principal actors to transform institutions is moving very slowly and in nonstandardized ways. As of this writing, 67 percent of the organized crime–related executions occur in five states. In May of 2012, 49 persons were found dead on a road outside Monterrey, Nuevo León; in Tamaulipas, 14 people were found decapitated; in Durango, 300 bodies with signs of torture were found; and another 18 persons were found executed in Jalisco.

It is interesting that none of these events appear to have put heavy pressure on the presidential candidates—Josefina Vázquez Mota (PAN), Enrique Peña Nieto (PRI), and Andrés Manuel López Obrador (PRD)—to commit to continuing police reform. Reform continues to depend heavily on the political will of governors and local authorities to collaborate not only with federal institutions, but, more important, with local resources and to invest in their police forces. As long as the security issue does not challenge the electoral process, there are few incentives for the authorities to implement consistent, long-term policies such as those described above.[27]

When President Peña Nieto took office, he mandated a full restructuring of the federal security and law enforcement apparatus, dissolving the existing Secretariat of Public Security and concentrating human and financial resources under the Secretariat of the Interior. This institutional arrangement is not new; this is how President Zedillo operated. The military continues to be deployed to high crime areas, and a legal and normative framework for the operation of the military in police activities is still pending in Congress. Creating a professional police force to tackle crime will remain a daunting task.

Notes

1. In Jordi Diez, ed., *Canada and Mexico's Security in a Changing North America* (Kingston, Montreal: Queen's-McGill University Press, 2000).

2. Mexico, Secretaría de Gobernación, "Programa Nacional de Seguridad Pública 1995–2000," *Diario Oficial de Federación* 514, no. 14 (1996): 37.

3. Mexico, Secretaría de Desarrollo Social (SEDESOL), "Diagnóstico social 2009." I obtained this document while serving as national security adviser during the Calderón administration, 2009; see http://www.sedesol2009.sedesol.gob.mx/archivos/802567/file/Diagnostico_Habitat.pdf.

4. Ibid.; idem, "Decree Reform Article 21 Mexican Constitution," *Diario Oficial de la Federación*, December 31, 1994.

5. Sigrid Arzt, "Democracia, seguridad y militares en México," PhD dissertation, University of Miami, 2011, 196–228.

6. Personal interview with a Panista representative, Mexico City, 2009.

7. Mexico, Secretariado Ejecutivo del Sistema Nacional de Seguridad Pública (SNSP), "Denuncias ante agencias del Ministerio Público," dataset (Mexico City, 1997), http://www.secretariadoejecutivosnsp.gob.mx/work/models/SecretariadoEjecutivo/Resource/131/1/images/CIEISP1997.pdf.

8. Rafael Ch, Marien Rivera, "Números rojos del sistema penal," Centro de Inves-

tigación para el Desarrollo (CIDAC), October 11, 2011, http://www.cidac.org/esp/cont/publicaciones/N_meros_Rojos_del_Sistema_Penal.php.

9. Mexico, Secretaría de Gobernación, "Programa Nacional de Seguridad Pública."

10. Gobierno del Distrito Federal, "Programa de seguridad pública para el Distrito Federal 1995–2000," November 28, 1995, http://info4.juridicas.unam.mx/ijure/nrm/1/338/default.htm?s=is.

11. Mexico, Secretaría de Seguridad Pública, "The State of Mexican Police Force." I obtained this document while serving as national security adviser during the Calderón administration, 2011; see Analisis_Estado_de_Fuerza_21092011.pdf.

12. Mexico, Secretaría de Gobernación, "Programa Nacional de Seguridad Pública."

13. Mexico, Secretaría de Gobernación, "Datos de la Dirección General de Supervisión de los Servicios de Protección Ciudadana." I obtained this document while serving as national security adviser during the Calderón administration, 1994.

14. Ibid.; Mexico, Secretaría de Seguridad Pública, "Ley General del Sistema Nacional de Seguridad Pública," *Diario Oficial*, January 2, 2009.

15. Mexico, Auditoría Superior de la Federación, *Informe del resultado de la revisión y fiscalización superior de la cuenta pública 2009* (Mexico City: Chamber of Deputies, 2009), 532, http://www.asf.gob.mx/Trans/Informes/IR2009i/indice.htm.

16. Ibid.

17. Mexico, Secretaría de Seguridad Pública, "Programa Nacional de Seguridad Pública 2001–2006," *Diario Oficial de la Federación*, January 14, 2003, http://dof.gob.mx/nota_detalle.php?codigo=705848&fecha=14/01/2003.

18. Arzt, *Democracia,* 197–198.

19. Ibid., 199.

20. Mexico, Secretaría de Gobernación, *Resumen ejecutivo de resultados de las encuestas ciudadana e institucional sobre seguridad pública 2010* (Mexico City: Secretariado Ejecutivo del Sistema Nacional de Seguridad Pública, 2011), http://issuu.com/oaxacavisual/docs/resumen_ejecutivo_de_las_encuestas_2010.

21. Genaro García Luna, *The New Public Security Model for Mexico* (Mexico City: Litoprocess, 2011), 65–85.

22. Ibid., 74.

23. Mexico, Secretaría de Gobernación, Subsecretaría de Enlace Legislativo, proposed law on police reform, oficio no. SEL/300/577/10, October 6, 2010, http://sil.gobernacion.gob.mx/Archivos/Documentos/2010/10/asun_2686848_20101007_1286462603.pdf.

24. Ibid.

25. Mexico, Secretariado Ejecutivo del Sistema Nacional de Seguridad Pública, XXX Sesión del Consejo Nacional de Seguridad Pública, June 30, 2011, http://www.secretariadoejecutivosnsp.gob.mx/work/models/SecretariadoEjecutivo/Resource/341/1/images/08072011_acuerdos_formato_DOF.pdf.

26. See http://www.secretariadoejecutivosnsp.gob.mx/es/SecretariadoEjecutivo/Informe_de_Avances_Centro_Nacional_de_Certificacion_y_Acreditacion_Centros_de_Evaluacion_y_Control_de_Confianza__Evaluaciones_de_Control_de_Confianza, July 2014.

27. I want to thank Guillermo Vázquez del Mercado for gathering some of the statistical information.

14

Democracy, Security, and Organized Crime
in Central America

FRANCISCO ROJAS ARAVENA

Central America historically has presented structural backwardness in the political, economic, and social spheres, creating serious obstacles for its development and the welfare of the people. It is necessary to generate a joint vision that will tackle common issues in a coordinated manner and reach a national consensus in order to develop sound state policies in the most sensible and urgent areas. The aforementioned implies the need for structural reforms in different spheres:

- With regard to the political system, it is necessary to strengthen democratic institutions in order to obtain wider citizen participation, to reinforce the capacity of the political parties and the legislature, and to combat corruption.
- In the sphere of security, it is necessary to implement deep reforms with regard to the judicial and prison systems that would address in a comprehensive manner the issues of violence and insecurity.
- In terms of the international role, it is necessary to improve the capacity of different states and actors and their ability to cooperate in order to obtain the advantages offered by the globalized world and to create defense mechanisms against the dark side of globalization (i.e., organized crime and drug trafficking).

Addressing these challenges requires the development and coordination of policies that can help improve the ability of the state to govern and improve civic participation. Such changes will help improve democratic stability and the coexistence of states within the region. Central America has witnessed profound changes since the 1990s. The civil war resulted in the deaths of thousands of people in three states, and political instability spread across the rest of the Central and Latin American region.

Nearly twenty years after the signing of the Agreement on a Firm and Lasting Peace (Acuerdo de Paz Firme y Duradera), however, Central America has achieved consolidation as a region without armed conflict and has established electoral processes. In addition, the region has achieved major improvements with the consolidation of democracy. Despite advances in the social and economic spheres, high levels of exclusion, deprivation, conflict, and insecurity are challenges not only for the progress of the region but also for safeguarding against the return of instability, militarization, and the increasing presence of drug traffickers and organized criminal networks.

In terms of domestic development, countries in Central America have different levels of development that vary in different dimensions. Although they share many of the same problems, challenges, and threats, the degree or severity of these problems differs.

Violence and the Main Challenges for Democracy and Security in Central America

Postconflict social violence has been increasing and deeply impacting the societies of the region, which today are considered the most violent in the world. There are reportedly an average of 33.5 homicides per 100,000 inhabitants annually.[1] The World Bank points out that the total population of Central America is approximately the same as that of Spain; however, in 2006, Spain registered 336 murders (less than one per day), and Central America had 14,257 (almost 40 per day).[2] The numbers of murders in Central America are even higher than those during the civil war in Spain. In Guatemala, it is estimated that two out of five murders are related to drug trafficking.

According to the World Bank, such violence has a huge cost for development and economic growth. It also affects the investment climate and the allocation of scarce government resources, which have gone to improving the implementation of justice instead of promoting economic activity. The growing levels of criminality and violence that affect Central America could reduce the GDP of the region by 8 percent, according to the World Bank. For example, in El Salvador, administrative and public security expenses reached U.S.$500.1 million in 2009, compared to $387.6 million in

2005.[3] The World Bank calculates that a reduction by 10 percent in the levels of violence in the region with the highest homicide rates could improve the annual economic growth per capita up to 1 percent of GDP.[4] Due to its alarming indicators, public security in Central America has become a major priority on the political agenda.

The transnationalization phenomenon of the risks and threats and the consequences of illicit activity are quite evident in Central America. The region has witnessed human trafficking, drug trafficking, money laundering, and arms trafficking. Various other problems not only question the legitimacy of the state's monopoly on the use of force, but also demonstrate that failed zones exist in all big cities and certain rural areas. These zones lack the presence of the state, and illegal actors determine the rules. Naturally, criminal activities impact the rule of law, governability, and democratic stability. In addition, such activities reduce entrepreneurial capacity, hamper the activity of legitimate businesses, and discourage foreign direct investment throughout the region. The UN Report on Crime and Development in Central America highlights serious vulnerabilities that affect the number of incidents of crime, violence, delinquent activity, and insecurity. These issues negatively impact the development of the region, increase social inequality, and limit the functioning of the justice system and the rule of law.

It also is important to address the challenges inherent in postconflict societies and territories. These societies and states have the following characteristics, which foster organized crime in the region: (1) severely weakened institutions; (2) the hardships of economic recovery linked to the changing nature of globalization and accompanied by weak mechanisms of social cohesion; (3) lack of democratic legitimacy; (4) a debilitated political system with a lack of public support for political parties and high levels of distrust; (5) an inability to implement the rule of law; (6) low levels of police professionalism; and (7) the presence of high levels of corruption and impunity. In addition, it is important to consider socioeconomic, geographic, and environmental vulnerabilities. In fact, four out of the seven Central American countries are among the twenty most vulnerable countries in the world in terms of environmental security and natural disasters.

All of these factors erode and weaken the democratic state and the rule of law and provide the necessary conditions for drug trafficking and various other criminal activities to flourish. The following problems demonstrate the major challenges that countries face every day throughout the region. Implementing change is a daunting task because the results are not immediate. The nature of the challenges reaffirms the need for national and regional coordination in the context of transnational phenomena that worsen the situation of postconflict societies

The Emergence of Transnational Threats and Challenges

Transnational dimensions constitute important processes throughout the societies of Central and Latin America, and such challenges simultaneously affect more than one state. Such challenges and threats cannot be resolved within national territories as the states throughout the region do not possess the capacity to resolve them. Therefore, these challenges and threats require international cooperation. Even the hemispheric superpower cannot confront these new challenges and threats alone. In addition, it is worth noting that the challenges and threats stem from nonstate actors and agents, such as drug traffickers, which constitute transnational forces and are not confined to territories or boundaries. The main threats that afflict Central America represent a new type; they do not stem from interstate disputes anymore, although many of them remain latent and without effective solutions.

Narco-Activity

Drug trafficking is an example of the transnationalization of the threats. In more than fifteen years of drug trade, the dynamics as well as the routes of the drug trade have shifted to Central America, subsequently increasing narco-activity within the region. As a result, the region has shifted from being an area of transit between producing and consuming areas into zones where the cartels store drugs in large quantities. In addition, the complex trafficking operations are planned in the region, and the local production of marijuana and opium poppy has increased drastically. The use of different land, sea, and aerial routes has become more sophisticated and now implements resources and infrastructure that significantly exceed the security capacity of the state.

These processes have involved the local populations in all the stages of the illicit activities, permeating and eroding societies in Central America and resulting in higher levels of violence, more homicides, high levels of delinquency, and population displacement. The use of Central America as a transit zone for drug trafficking is fundamental and continues to increase over time. According to UN estimates, 88 percent of the cocaine enter-

Table 14.1. Consumption and seizures of cocaine in Central America

Country	% of cocaine users among total population, 2006 (estimated)	Tons of cocaine seized, 2004 (rounded)
Costa Rica	0.4	5
El Salvador	0.5	3
Guatemala	1.4	4
Honduras	0.9	4
Nicaragua	1.0	6
Panama	1.4	7

Source: UNODC, *Crime and Development in Central America: Caught in the Crossfire* (New York: United Nations Publications, 2007).

ing the United States is transported through Central America.[5] Despite increases in cocaine transited through the region, cocaine consumption there does not appear to have increased (see table 14.1). However, illegal activities have increased, such as contract killings, among other illicit activities. In addition, the drug-trafficking industry has penetrated other legitimate businesses such as fishing.

Drugs and drug trafficking continue to negatively impact the population throughout the region. In fact, 59 percent of Latin Americans indicate that drug trafficking and consumption occur in their community. For instance, seven out of every ten Costa Ricans in 2009 pointed out that drugs were sold or consumed in their neighborhoods, and nearly 59 percent of Latin Americans believed that their communities were more violent than a year earlier. The highest increase in crime perception occurs in Costa Rica (71 percent).[6] Drug-trafficking operations also have increased in various areas, such as Petén, Guatemala, the region between Honduras and Nicaragua, and Limón, Costa Rica, which are characterized by high levels of social and economic exclusion, the lack of state presence, high levels of poverty, and fragile social cohesion.[7] In sum, these areas can be classified as "failed states."

Despite multiple efforts to combat drug trafficking in the hemisphere, Central America has not received the necessary support and resources to effectively defeat it. On August 1, 2008, the regional Summit on the World Drug Problem occurred in Cartagena, Colombia, with the participation of the presidents of Mexico, El Salvador, Guatemala, Panama, the Dominican Republic, and Colombia as well as nineteen delegations from various Central American and Caribbean countries. During the summit, the presidents and delegates committed to specific and concrete measures: (1) to develop national drug task forces working in conjunction with the Inter-American Drug Task Force to reinforce the mechanisms of technical and institutional coordination and exchange between countries of the region; (2) to promote activities to recover and consolidate the fragile ecosystems affected by the cultivation of illicit crops.[8]

The Mérida Initiative was another policy designed to combat drug trafficking and promote cooperation and coordination. However, the resources directed to Central America (U.S.$65 million) were clearly insufficient. Nevertheless, as a result of the rising violence in Mexico, Hillary Clinton, the former U.S. secretary of state, expressed during a visit to Mexico in March 2010 that the initiative would be broadened and it would not only be focused on law enforcement and military measures but also on social problems in order to create a comprehensive strategy to combat drug trafficking.[9] During President Obama's visit to El Salvador, the U.S. government announced that it would contribute U.S.$200 million to assist Central America combat drug trafficking in the region. It could be argued that such initiatives represent the beginning of the shared responsibility of various actors involved in combating drug trafficking.

Human Trafficking

The region also confronts the issue of human trafficking as Central America has become the origin and destination of trafficked persons for the purpose of sexual activities or forced labor, according to the Trafficking in Persons Report issued by the U.S. State Department in 2009.[10] Due to its strategic location, the region serves as a transit point for individuals traversing the region illegally from Latin America as well as other continents with the main purpose of reaching the United States.[11] It is estimated that between 2000 and 2005, the number of individuals who illegally crossed the U.S.-Mexican border tripled.[12]

A high percentage of these individuals do not have legal documents, which makes them vulnerable to trafficking networks. Sexual tourism is a problem that impacts the region in various ways. According to the United Nations Development Programme (UNDP), between 35,000 and 50,000 underage Central Americans are forced to work in prostitution, and 20 percent of sexually exploited children of the region are exploited by foreigners and tourists.[13] As long as this migratory phenomenon from Latin America toward the United States and the European Union is not approached from a comprehensive perspective with reasonable solutions for all parties and from multiple dimensions, organized crime will inevitably continue to play a major role in human trafficking.[14]

The Trafficking of Arms

Another phenomenon which impacts Central America is the trafficking of small arms. El Salvador, Guatemala, and Honduras are among the thirteen countries that have higher levels of death by firearms.[15] Such increases in violence are accompanied by transnational organized crime.

Small arms are in high demand, and, therefore, their trafficking became a highly profitable business. According to the Action Network of Small Arms, it is estimated that there are 1.6 million small arms in Central America, of which only 500,000 are registered. While it is true that Latin America is the region with the highest number of deaths by firearms in situations not associated with armed conflicts, Central America is most affected by this phenomenon; 70 percent of the population of the region dies as a result of murder by firearm. The majority of the dead are youths living in the region. The disarmament of some of these countries following the armed conflict has proved ineffective and has provided space for underground arms trafficking. According to data collected by the military and law enforcement agencies, around two million unregistered small arms currently circulate in the market in Central America.

A comprehensive study organized by the Facultad Latinoamericana de Ciencias Sociales (FLACSO) notes six means for intervention that must be taken in order to address the situation:[16] (1) the creation of an adequate normative framework at both the national and the regional levels in which the ratification of international treaties results in the actual implementation of such agreements; (2) the strengthening of institutional capacity, resulting in better management and systematization of information and records; (3) improvement and updating of the implementation of commitments related to private security; (4) the formulation of national and regional public policies; (5) addressing local and regional problems; and, finally, (6) coordination of decisions among important actors.

Money Laundering

Money laundering is a significant problem for all countries of the region because many obstacles impede the measurement or estimation of such activities, and millions of dollars are inundating the region as a result. In

Table 14.2. Private security agents and police in Central America, by country

Country	Total private security personnel	Total police officers
Belize	N/A	1,324
Costa Rica	31,195	12,553
El Salvador	23,546	21,000
Guatemala	106,700	20,299
Honduras	60,000	8,887
Nicaragua	13,500	9,225
Panama	12,000	17,113

Source: UNDP, *Abrir espacios para la seguridad ciudadana y el desarrollo humano: Informe sobre desarrollo humano para América Central, IDHAC 2009–2010*, October, 2009, http://hdr.undp.org/sites/default/files/central_america_rhdr_2009-10_es.pdf.

Central America, money laundering is a thriving activity. Control of the activity has been limited due to the region's inability to enforce the rule of law and prosecute violators, corruption, and the lack of coordination between countries and multilateral entities.[17]

The Privatization of Security

It is important to highlight the increasing number of private security enterprises in the region. In some countries, the difference in the number of private security agents and public security agents is quite significant.[18] As a result, the business of private security has led to various debates. In some states, the state's monopoly over the use of force has come under doubt, which has led to the privatization of the issue of public security and is something that must be understood as a common good. Additionally, these businesses have become sources of illegal arms (see table 14.2).

The *Maras*: An Emerging Threat

The *maras*, a highly complex and important phenomenon, present a particular challenge related to social violence in Central America.[19] Currently, there are more than 900 gangs, or *maras*, in Central America, with 70,000 members between the ages of fifteen and thirty-four. Sadly, the majority of them eventually become victims of homicide. The rise of violence in countries such as Guatemala, Honduras, and El Salvador also should be linked to the *maras* and their operations.

The peace accords signed in Central America to end the armed conflict that some countries in the region experienced in the 1980s had important social effects besides the increase in illegal firearms and drug trafficking. One of the direct consequences was the incapacity of the political system to reintegrate people and families involved in the conflict back into society. The peace accords also failed to produce an effective national reconciliation and promote social cohesion.

Another social consequence is the emergence of youth gangs since the 1990s. These gangs are a partial product of the deportation of Central American youths from Los Angeles. The *maras* adopted a model of organization, objectives, and methods of action similar to that of the gangs located on the West Coast of the United States. These groups have developed in the context of fragmented societies where young people lack social networks that bring them together and give them a sense of belonging and hope.

The *maras* are the best example of how violence relates to exclusion and unemployment as well as to weak social and family cohesion. Exclusion and marginalization in both education and employment are incentives for the youth to join these organizations, which provide them with an identity and protection as well as values that the current political system and family cannot provide. The gangs have traditionally been analyzed as a local phenomenon of young people from the same neighborhood who established organizations in order to defend themselves against outsiders and to promote loyalty and solidarity. However, the gangs now reflect a transnational problem, meaning that these groups are related under a common international label, connected by strong group identity despite the fact that they are autonomous. There is no evidence of a hierarchically transnational structure; however, if a transnational hierarchy were formed, the phenomenon would become a severe threat to national security in the region.

In addition to the absence of mechanisms that would promote social cohesion and seek to end marginalization and exclusion, the challenges presented by U.S. deportation policies must be taken into account. In the case of the isthmus, the number of deported persons exceeded 7,600 annually in 2004 and 2005.[20] Deportation from the United States resulted in the return of many convicts to Central America who immigrated to the United States and have returned to their countries of origins after being arrested and imprisoned within the United States. Researchers accept claims that violence results from such policies. What is clear is that the home countries do not possess the economic resources to monitor the deportees. It

Table 14.3. Incarcerated population, Central America (absolute value)

Country	2007	2008	2009	2010	2011
Belize	1,086	1,114	1,114	—	—
Costa Rica	7,793	7,955	9,304	10,455	12,154
El Salvador	17,867	19,814	22,101	24,439	25,099
Guatemala	7,114	—	9,904	11,148	12,681
Honduras		10,809	—	11,846	11,879
Nicaragua	6,663	5,925	5,807	6,789	—
Panama	11,345	9,651	10,296	12,555	13,170

Source: Entity in charge of penal and/or judicial matters in each country; Belize: Observatorio Hemisférico de Seguridad de la OEA; Panama: Instituto Nacional de Estadística y Censo.

is crucial for the Central American governments to establish programs to reintegrate these persons into society.

The Militarized Response

The state tends to respond to such challenges in a military fashion, as the Northern Triangle countries have recognized: in Honduras, the Zero Tolerance, Operation Liberty, and Libertad Azul programs; in El Salvador, Mano Dura and Super Mano Dura; and Plan Escobar in Guatemala.[21] The reinstatement of capital punishment in Guatemala constitutes another major policy shift, and such laws have resulted in the United Nations' expressing concern about the violations of the Convention on the Rights of the Child. One result of these programs is that in one year—July 2003–July 2004—in El Salvador, 17,162 persons were arrested; 91 percent of the 15,618 cases were postponed, while 858 persons remained in judicial detention, representing 5 percent of the total number detained. In addition, 4 percent continued to wait for a trial.[22]

Finally, the tendency toward militarization and penalization of the different forms of social violence in Central America, not only regarding the *maras*, has resulted in some countries seeing increases in the number of prisoners. For example, in 2007, there were 181 prisoners per 1,000 inhabitants in Costa Rica, 174 prisoners per 1,000 in El Salvador, and 161 per 1,000 in Honduras (see table 14.3).[23]

The Destruction of Central America's Youth

The data show that homicides in the region are mainly a youth phenomenon, unlike in the rest of the world. The youth population accounts for
36.6 percent of the total number of homicides in Latin America, compared
to 16.1 percent in Africa, 12.0 percent in North America, 2.4 percent in
Asia, 1.6 percent in Oceania, and 12.0 percent in Europe. But these numbers
do not explain the demographic significance to the country. For example,
in a highly violent country such as El Salvador, where the national homicide rate in 2009 was 70 per 100,000 inhabitants, the homicide rate among
young males was 270 per 100,000 in the same year.[24] Similar trends can be
observed in other countries of the region. In all cases, when the number
of homicides of youth is considered, the figures rise to levels that could be
described as genocide.

Brazil faces a similar situation regarding the homicides of youths between fifteen and twenty-four. Colombia faces the same challenges and
daunting statistics. The risk of being a victim of a homicide in Latin America, in particular, in Central America, is linked to age. Thus, a comprehensive response to youth violence is needed. As Gomariz notes, the "adult
centric" solutions should be avoided and new solutions specific to this age
range should be developed.

Corruption in and Mistrust of Security Institutions

In addition to increases in drug trafficking, a parallel increase in corruption has occurred in countries throughout the region. In numerous cases,
state officials, police agents, and the judiciary have been involved in some
form of illegal activity, presenting many challenges for an already weak
institutional structure. This weakness results in higher levels of impunity,
the weakening of governability, and lower levels of state legitimacy. Central Americans' confidence in basic institutions such as the justice system
is quite low. In fact, the regional average in 2009 was 29 percent.[25] The
perception of corruption of public officials also is very high (the regional
average is 73.2 percent).[26] The relationship between this phenomenon and
violence is clear: citizen mistrust of government and high levels of corruption foment participation in organized crime.

In many instances, the defective security systems of the Central American nations is reflected not only in the mistrust of many of its institutions
but also in violations of human rights and impunity for the perpetrators. In

all countries of the region, more than 20 percent of imprisoned individuals are still awaiting sentencing. In countries such as Honduras, for example, this percentage reaches 79 percent, while in Guatemala and Panama, the levels reach 51 and 53 percent, respectively.[27]

With regard to impunity for the commission of a crime, it is important to highlight the International Commission against Impunity in Guatemala (Comisión Internacional contra la Impunidad, CICIG). The commission seeks to do the following: (a) identify illegal security forces and underground groups that violate the rights of Guatemalans; and (b) recommend to the state reforms and public policies to eradicate these illegal groups.

In mid-April 2010, the head of the CICIG, Carlos Castresana, declared that judges, prosecutors, politicians, members of Congress, and police were participating in the activities of the powerful mafias operating in Guatemala: "They are very powerful because they have the ability to impose their will on the state of law." Highly powerful elements, including magistrates, act within the judicial system. According to Castresana, these people "totally know what they are doing" as "they are groups that were operating 20 or 30 years ago in the context of armed conflict and now operate in order to gain profits. It is clear that they protect one another and cut corners when they feel pressure from the government."[28]

Looking to the Future

The situation in Central America requires measures to address the region's problems and improve development and human security. Central America requires substantive reforms in its political systems to foment citizen participation and the development of social policies aimed at addressing the needs of the half of the population that lives in poverty. All these require leadership and institutional improvements. There is a need to establish a national consensus to professionalize the civil service, to foment a culture of legality, to promote judicial and security sector reforms, and to professionalize the police and armed forces.

Such efforts reveal that no country can confront security challenges alone. A shared vision that allows countries to confront transnational and transborder threats is needed. In practice, this implies an integrated and comprehensive preventive strategy that covers all sectors. This strategy must combine policies designed to tackle individual and community risks and challenges. It must reinforce those policies with other policies designed to modify structural conditions that lead to delinquent and violent behavior, such as the quality and scope of education, job opportunities, and training, as well as judicial and police reforms. These policies must be of a binational, regional, subregional, and hemispheric nature in conjunction with specific local policies.

Central America has achieved some progress despite the aforementioned adverse conditions, for instance, consolidation of electoral democracies throughout the region. Central America cannot afford a reversal of achievements, because this would lead to international condemnation and isolation as well as regional and national political delegitimization. This, therefore, must be the starting point for rebuilding the state and confronting the challenges. In order to succeed, the willingness of the major political actors and civic organizations is needed.

Organized crime, violence, and public security have become more important on the social agenda. These issues demand better and more efficient responses by the states in the sphere of law and order. Thus, building integrated public policies must involve spheres (security, health, youth, social and economic issues) that also involve organized civil society, responsible media, and international cooperation. These kinds of policies must be understood from a holistic perspective and through the lens of human security. Human security is a useful approach for looking at the security of persons because it concerns nonmilitary threats that affect civilians and because these threats produce more victims than do military conflicts and wars.

During the almost two decades of using the human security approach to problem solving in Central America, its importance has fluctuated significantly. There have been moments when this view was considered highly relevant in the global system presented by the United Nations as well as in regional systems. At other times, it lost its presence and relevance. Currently, human security is a central and important issue in the United Nations' system. The Central American countries and Mexico have the potential to initiate and promote the perspective of human security.

The main debate around human security stems from the scope of the concept and the difficulties in operationalizing security. The strength of the concept of human security is its focus on people, cooperation, and multilateralism. However, it also has weaknesses with regard to the scope of action, on the one hand, and the introduction of security into the priorities of development, on the other. In this sense, the broadening of the concept of the securitization of development leads to certain reservations regarding increasing participation of the armed forces in public security missions.

Table 14.4. Homicides per 100,000 inhabitants, Latin America and the Caribbean, 2003–2008

Country	Homicides
Argentina	5.2
Bahamas	13.7
Barbados	8.7
Belize	34.3
Bolivia	10.6
Brazil	22.0
Chile	8.1
Colombia	38.8
Costa Rica	8.3
Dominican Republic	21.5
Ecuador	18.1
El Salvador	51.8
Guatemala	45.2
Honduras	60.9
Jamaica	59.5
Mexico	11.6
Nicaragua	13.0
Panama	13.3
Paraguay	12.2
Peru	3.2
Trinidad and Tobago	39.7
Suriname	13.7
Uruguay	5.8
Venezuela	52.0

Source: Adapted from UNDP, *Human Development Report 2010. 20th Anniversary Edition. The Real Wealth of Nations: Pathways to Human Development* (New York: Palgrave Macmillan, 2010).

Note: The data correspond to the last available year.

The Inter-American Democratic Charter is a public good in the Americas. It collects the demands presented by democratic societies in order to consolidate democratic processes and broaden the liberties granted to individuals. It also seeks to generate better conditions for satisfying the needs of the people. The concept of democratic security focuses on the individual as its objective, and the democratic charter is seen as the instrument for assuring democracy in the region. These two concepts, therefore, complement and reinforce each other. The effort to predict the Democratic Character in the future will project regional and hemispheric multilateralism and consolidate the public good in this sphere of security in the region (see tables 14.4, 14.5, and 14.6).[29]

Table 14.5. Comparative indicators for Central America

Country	Intentional homicide count per 100,000 population (2011)	Firearms-related homicides (2011) (%)	Perception of Corruption index (2013)	Gini index (2011)	Poverty (2011) (%)	Unemployment % (2011)	Youth Unemployment % (2011)
Belize	124	67	—	—	—	14.4	—
Costa Rica	474	63	53	0.515	24.8	7.7	16.6
El Salvador	4,371	70	38	0.441	47.5	6.6	12.2
Guatemala	5681	—	29	—	53.7	4.1	7.5
Honduras	7104	84	26	0.552	61.9	4.3	8.0
Nicaragua	738	—	28	—	—	6.3	11.9
Panama	759	76	35	0.531	25.3	4.5	12.5

Source: Prepared by the author with data from Global Study on Homicide, United Nations Office on Drugs and Crime, 2013; Transparency International, Corruption by Country, 2013; Programa Estado de la Nación, Compendio estadístico de Centroamérica; Organización Internacional del Trabajo, *Trabajo decente y juventud en América Latina: Políticas para la acción* (Lima: Oficina Regional para América Latina y el Caribe, 2013).

Table 14.6. Economic costs of crime and violence in Central America as a percentage of GDP

Type of cost	Guatemala	El Salvador	Honduras	Nicaragua	Costa Rica
Health-related	4.3	6.1	3.9	4.5	1.5
Institutional	1.0	1.5	2.6	1.6	1.0
Private security–related	1.5	1.8	1.9	2.3	0.7
Material (transfers)	0.8	1.4	1.2	1.5	0.4
% of total	7.7	10.8	9.6	10.0	3.6
Total (millions of U.S.$)	2,291	2,010	885	529	791

Source: World Bank, *Crime and Violence in Central America: A Development Challenge* (Washington D.C., 2011), 7.

Notes

1. La Red Centroamérica de Centros de Pensamiento e Incidencia (La Red), "Seguridad y crimen organizado transnacional: Una propuesta de acción para Centroamérica" (Guatemala City, 2011), 29.

2. World Bank, *Crime and Violence in Central America: A Development Challenge* (Washington, D.C., 2011).

3. La Red, "Seguridad," 26.

4. World Bank, *Crime and Violence.*

5. United Nations Office on Drugs and Crime (UNODC), *Crime and Development in Central America: Caught in the Crossfire* (New York, 2007).

6. Facultad Latinoamericana de Ciencias Sociales (FLACSO), Secretaría General/ IPSOS, *Estudio de opinión pública en Latinoamérica: Gobernabilidad y convivencia democrática en América Latina* (San José, C.R., 2009–2010).

7. Reina Rivera Joya, "Centroamérica: Dilemas de la seguridad y defensa regionales," in *Anuario 2009 de la seguridad regional en América Latina,* ed. Hans Mathieu and Paula Rodríguez (Bogotá: Fundación Friedrich Ebert Stiftung, 2009).

8. Regional Summit on the World Drug Problem, Security and Cooperation, *Action Plan* (Cartagena de Indias, Colombia, 2008); "Países que participaron en Cumbre Antidrogas impulsarán creación de observatorios nacionales de drogas," August 1, 2008, http:// historico.presidencia.gov.co/sp/2008/agosto/01/11012008.html; "Seis presidentes y un gran problema," BBC Mundo, August 2, 2008, http://news.bbc.co.uk/hi/spanish/news/.

9. "Se amplía la Iniciativa Mérida a temas sociales, informa Clinton," *La Jornada,* March 24, 2010, http://www.jornada.unam.mx/2010/03/24/politica/003n1pol.

10. U.S. Department of State, *Trafficking in Persons Report 2009* (Washington, D.C., 2009).

11. For more information on migration, see Jairo Hernández and Ana Cristina Lizano eds., *América Latina y la segunda administración Bush: Un debate sobre migración,* (FLACSO–Secretaría General, Juricentro, 2008, www.flacso.org.

12. La Red, "Seguridad," 30.

13. UNDP, *Abrir espacios para la seguridad ciudadana y el desarrollo humano: Informe sobre desarrollo humano para América Central, IDHAC 2009–2010* (New York, 2009).

14. Francisco Rojas Aravena, *El crimen organizado internacional: Una grave amenaza a la democracia en América Latina y el Caribe,* II Informe del Secretario General, FLACSO–Secretaría General, 2006, www.flacso.org.

15. Small Arms/Firearms Educational and Research Network, "Global Firearms Deaths," in *Armas pequeñas y livianas: Una amenaza a la seguridad hemisférica,* ed. Stella Sáenz Breckenridge, comp. Jairo Hernández and Luis Emilio Jiménez, FLACSO–Secretaría General, 2007, www.flacso.org.

16. Stella Sáenz Breckenridge, ed., *Armas pequeñas y livianas: Una amenaza a la seguridad hemisférica* (San José, C.R.: FLACSO–Secretaría General, 2007), 500.

17. La Red, "Seguridad," 37.

18. Gabriel Aguilera, "Enfrentar la violencia criminal con 'mano dura': Políticas de contención en C.A.," *Revista Pensamiento Iberoamericano,* no. 2 (Second Term, 2008).

19. The information about the *maras* is based mainly on Luis Guillermo Solís, coord., *Pandillas juveniles y gobernabilidad democrática en América Latina y el Caribe*, FLACSO–Secretaría General, Seminario Madrid, April 16–17, 2007.

20. PNUP, *Abrir espacios.*

21. Rivera Joya, "Centroamérica."

22. Eduardo Gamarra, "Antimaras Policies in El Salvador," paper presented at Strategic Opportunities: Charting New Approaches to Defense and Security Challenges in the Western Hemisphere International Conference, Miami, March 9–11, 2005.

23. PNUP, *Abrir espacios.*

24. Enrique Gomariz Moraga, "La devastación silenciosa: Jóvenes y violencia social en América Latina" (San José, C.R.: FLACSO, 2010).

25. The trust level in judicial institutions in 2009 was 30 percent in Costa Rica, 40 percent in El Salvador, 29 percent in Guatemala, 28 percent in Honduras, 18 percent in Panama, 21 percent in Nicaragua, and 38 percent in the Dominican Republic; see Consorcio Iberoamericano de Investigaciones de Mercadeo y Asesoramiento, *Barómetro iberoamericano de gobernabilidad 2009,* www.cimaiberoamerica.com.

26. By 2008, it was 68.9 percent in Nicaragua, 76.2 percent in Guatemala, 80.6 percent in Honduras, 64.4 percent in Costa Rica, 74.6 percent in Panama, 72.3 percent in El Salvador, and 75.7 percent in the Dominican Republic; see http://www.latinobarometro.org/docs/INFORME_LATINOBAROMETRO_2008.pdf.

27. UNDP, *Abrir espacios.*

28. Costa Rica, "Denuncia de Comisión contra Impunidad: Élites guatemaltecas integran mafias del país," Cable Acan-EFE, April 13, 2010.

29. This chapter is a translated and revised version of a chapter originally published in Spanish; see Francisco Rojas Aravena, "Seguridad y crimen organizado en Centroamérica," in *Elementos para la profundización de la democracia en Centroamérica*, ed. Cecilia Cortés, Daniel Zovatto, Irene Klinger, and Randall Arias (San José, C.R.: Fundación para la Paz y la Democracia, 2011), 79–97.

15

Seeking Out the State

Organized Crime, Violence, and Statetropism in the Caribbean

LILIAN BOBEA

Since 2000, the Caribbean region has ranked among the most violent in the world.[1] Countries in the region have suffered extreme levels of violence. In 2008, for instance, Jamaica had a homicide rate of 59 per 100,000 inhabitants, while Trinidad and Tobago had a rate of 42 per 100,000.[2] In 2011, despite a modest decrease, regional homicide rates were at least double that of the Americas as a whole (15.6 per 100,000). Some of the smallest nations—Saint Kitts and Nevis, Santa Lucia, and Guyana—have violent death rates three times the average of the region.[3] Consequently, their citizens' perception of security tends to be very low. By the year 2010, only 24.7 percent of Trinidadians declared that they felt secure in their country, followed by 35.7 percent of Jamaicans, 37.7 percent of people from Saint Lucia, and 42.7 percent of residents of Guyana.[4]

These levels of violence are considered to be associated with drug trafficking and other manifestations of organized crime.[5] Regional reports on Caribbean violence emphasize several key factors, from systemic ones, like poverty, economic inequality, and corruption, to institutional factors, such as diminished law enforcement capacity, poor intrastate cooperation, obsolete and inadequate legal frameworks, and the precarious integrity of the judicial and security systems. There are situational factors as well that promote organized criminal activities, among them, the establishment of networks, circuits, and routes for drug trafficking; human trafficking; weapons and merchandise smuggling; and firearms accessibility.[6]

Criminal gangs are an important catalyst as well.[7] Despite many studies of organized crime in the region, there still is only a limited understanding of how these criminal dynamics operate in local environments to create resistant, adaptable, and opportunistic criminal structures, niches, and opportunities.

Armed violence, especially related to drugs and gangs, has increased in nearly all Caribbean countries. In Jamaica and Trinidad and Tobago, for example, official statistics demonstrate that approximately 60 and 65 percent, respectively, of murders committed annually are related to drug trafficking.[8] Some of this criminal violence has been carried out by virulent gangs, which have defied the limits of the state's internal sovereignty in countries like Jamaica, Trinidad and Tobago, Barbados, Saint Lucia, and Belize, to the point of obliging regional governments to declare states of siege as a way of regaining spatial control over slums and garrisoned and marginalized urban areas.[9]

However, not all organized crime is violent. A myriad of loose configurations such as transnational networks, clusters, "offices," and individuals linked to private and public entities and national political elites have succeeded in establishing profitable and diversified criminal businesses by employing less-violent methods of co-optation. The absence of explicit violence in these scenarios could reflect how thoroughly the enforcement apparatus, judicial and security systems, financial institutions, and political parties have been penetrated by different types of organized criminal entities and dynamics.[10]

Some scholars argue that in order to understand the recurrence of chronic violence in the Caribbean (and elsewhere in Central America), it is important to analyze the shifting drug markets as opposed to concentrating solely on overall levels of illicit flows. As Bruce M. Bagley notes in this volume, "partial victories" in the "war on drugs" have led to shifting routes as well as the fragmentation of criminal networks into smaller units.[11] In the same vein, this chapter examines the reconfiguration and diversification of the organized crime-corporate complex and the impacts that these changes are having in several Caribbean states and societies.

The first part of this chapter identifies the main tendencies of organized crime and drug trafficking, focusing on the extreme levels of violence that have resulted from such activities: (1) the reemergence of the Caribbean as an important conduit for drugs, a niche for proliferating retail markets, and a hub for drug traffickers and associated illicit functions; (2) the systematic use of violence as a tool by multiple public and private actors, which has resulted in a condition of chronic, systemic, and institutionalized violence meant to intimidate, to control, and to eliminate competition in these societies;[12] (3) the social, political, and institutional embeddedness of complex criminality in Caribbean societies, which is based on the diversification of criminal agents and the intensification of organized crime enterprises; and (4) the formation and reinforcement of alternative social orders and the reorientation of complex criminality toward the state.

In approaching these issues from a broader Caribbean perspective, analysts must remember that the Caribbean archipelago has an extremely fragmented cartography, with twenty-eight countries and overseas territories of diverse size and political/jurisdictional status. In addition, more than 700 islands, cays, and territories are scattered across 1,063,000 square miles. There are significant differences among countries in the following areas: (a) economic development; (b) the capacity to implement comprehensive security policies; and (c) political and diplomatic coordination with other countries and regions (i.e., bilateral agreements or subregional entities such as CARICOM, IMPACS, RSS, and SICA).[13]

The second part of the chapter examines drug trafficking and organized crime in two Caribbean countries: Puerto Rico and the Dominican Republic. I briefly document one notorious criminal network that operated within and between both countries for more than a decade. The third section critically analyzes the multilevel policy currently in place.

The Reemergence of the Caribbean

In mid-2012, the U.S. House Homeland Security Subcommittee on Oversight, Investigations, and Management called a hearing on Caribbean security. The event, titled "U.S.-Caribbean Border: Open Road for Drug Traffickers and Terrorists," was certainly not the first sign of concern about the resurgence of drug trafficking and organized crime in this region, which currently transports 30 percent of the illegal drugs entering the United States.[14] A year earlier, in another public hearing before the Senate Foreign Relations Subcommittee on Western Hemisphere and Global Narcotics Affairs, Assistant Secretary of State William R. Brownfield called for a more holistic U.S. strategy in the hemisphere. His concerns were based on the outcomes of previous counterdrug initiatives. Brownfield argued that the United States focused on stopping drug trafficking and organized crime in Colombia during the 1980s and, in effect, ignored the role of the Caribbean as a transshipment route. Thus, as Bruce M. Bagley remarks, the "partial victories" in Colombia and in reinforcing the border with Mexico had unintended consequences for the Caribbean,[15] by bringing the region back as a conduit in a much more complex narco-cartography.[16]

Table 15.1. Drugs seized in the Dominican Republic, by type, 2002–2011

Year	Cocaine (kilos)	Crack (kilos)	Heroine (kilos)	Marijuana (kilos)	Marijuana plants	Hash (grams)	Noncontrolled substances
2002	1,101.90	5.50	115.50	1,696.00	4,122	7.10	142.40
2003	1,362.20	5.90	58.90	535.30	420	324.30	110.70
2004	2,235.40	7.30	68.90	529.60	476	—	93.10
2005	2,233.20	14.30	121.80	562.70	2,425	308.50	106.60
2006	5,091.80	13.50	257.60	429.20	175	1,360.90	244.70
2007	3,789.50	15.30	53.70	735.20	3,159	29.40	377.00
2008	2,698.40	14.50	120.30	378.30	3,649.	1.50	553.60
2009	4,655.70	15.00	38.60	1,405.30	23,906	20.50	1,127.80
2010	4,526.90	12.90	30.40	658.90	67	291.40	719.70
2011	6,715.40	10.30	42.00	851.20	15,319	—	398.50
Total	34,401.40	114.50	907.70	7,781.70	53,718	2,343.60	3,874.10

Source: National Counterdrug Directorate (Dirección Nacional de Control de Drogas), Dominican Republic, 2011.

Note: — means not available.

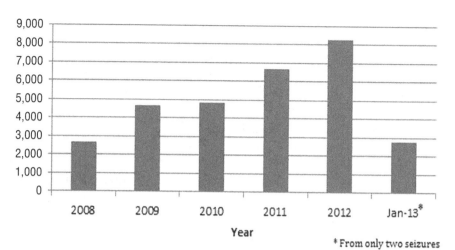

Figure 15.1. Dominican Republic cocaine seizures, 2008–2013 (Dominican National Counter-Drug Directorate and United Nations Office on Drugs and Crime, 2013).

In the same vein, Rodney G. Benson of the Intelligence Drug Enforcement Administration stressed that cocaine was the most prominent drug being transported across the region. In his view, the sale and consumption of drugs were increasing in places like Puerto Rico and the U.S. Virgin Islands and were also responsible for the growing levels of violence in such territories.[17] According to official sources, more than 165,000 metric tons of illegal drugs were seized in 2011 in the Caribbean and the Gulf of Mexico, representing an increase of 36 percent over a four-year period.[18] As table 15.1 shows, the contribution of the Dominican Republic to that amount was 34,401.40 metric tons (20.8 percent). The Dominican Republic, despite interdiction efforts and the shutting down of the air corridors in 2010, along with Puerto Rico remains a major transit point for South American cocaine to the United States and Europe, as figure 15.1 shows.

Organized criminal networks are creative and continue to use various methods of transportation—ranging from ferries to submersible torpedoes—to transport drugs. In fact, criminal networks have, paradoxically, become the main catalyst for connecting the politically, culturally, and linguistically fragmented Caribbean region.

Drug traffickers have started to search for alternative routes as a result of law enforcement's efforts to combat illegal activities on the north-south terrestrial frontier. This is a common side effect of the war on drugs, yet today, the narco-criminal networks tend to be more dispersed. For example, Dominican authorities discovered a cell of the Sinaloa cartel operating in the country, gathering logistical support, raw materials, and intermediaries. The authorities dismantled the organization in 2012.[19] Earlier, counternarcotics forces confirmed that important cadres of the Zetas in Hidalgo, a cell under the command of Joaquín "El Chapo" Guzmán, were operating throughout the Dominican Republic and Panama.

Law enforcement officials continued to witness increasing levels of cocaine shipments in the region. From 2005 to 2009, the Dominican Republic ranked as the third country in Latin America—after Brazil and Argentina—in terms of cocaine seized while being transported to Europe. Eighteen percent of the cocaine seized from the Dominican Republic was intended for Spain; the rest was being shipped to the United States. According to the U.S. Department of Defense, at least 19,500 of the approximately 39,000 kilos of cocaine exported annually from the Dominican Republic made their way to Puerto Rico since 2000.

For the officials of the European Union's Cooperation Programme between Latin America and the European Union on Drugs Policies (COPOLAD), by 2013, "the Dominican Republic continues to be the main command center for drug trafficking in the Caribbean region, with an increase since 2012 of 800 percent of the cocaine to the United States and Europe."[20] The main reasons cited are the lack of control and technology at the main ports. Powerful business groups oppose stricter inspections and controls in private Dominican ports, arguing that increased inspections will delay merchandise flow and, consequently, increase transaction costs. In addition, high levels of corruption and lack of accountability in the Dominican Republic have made the country a safe haven for drug traffickers.

The revitalization of Caribbean transshipment routes challenges any underestimation of the capacity of adaptation and resilience that criminal entities have shown, as well as the impacts they have had within the countries where they operate. Today, criminal agencies have become more difficult to apprehend due to their smaller size (see the introduction in this volume). According to the National Counterdrug Directorate (Dirección Nacional de Control de Drogas, DNCD), by 2011, around 25,040 individuals were arrested for violating drug consumption and commercialization laws in the Dominican Republic. The total number of arrestees between 2002 and 2011 was 136,453. This amount does not include the Dominicans repatriated from the United States facing drug charges. Such arrests, however, have not deterred high-profile criminal organizations from continuing to traffic drugs (among other things) through the Caribbean.

Authorities speculate that at least 70 percent of the drugs enter the United States, while the rest remain in the local markets of Puerto Rico and the Dominican Republic. As the governor of Puerto Rico explained to Congress, the cocaine supply that remains inland as payment in-kind during the transshipment process feeds a lucrative stateside market.[21] Market saturation leads to price dropping and greater internal demand, a circular mechanism that puts several intermediaries out of business while incentivizing violent competition among rivals for control of the local drug markets.

In terms of profits, it is estimated that every kilogram of cocaine costs U.S.$20,000 in Puerto Rico, approximately $35,000 in the United States, and $50,000 in Europe. Competitiveness and profitability are two major reasons for the resilience of the markets operating between the Dominican Republic and Puerto Rico. According to estimates made by economists at the University of Puerto Rico, drug trafficking generated U.S.$9 billion in 2011 and accounted for 20 percent of Puerto Rico's GDP.[22]

These facts contest the oversimplification of considering Caribbean nations as essentially "transit points." As several studies have revealed, more than 50 percent of the cocaine that passes through the Caribbean impacts several territories. Even though most of the profit remains in the consumption markets, the inflow and outflow of thousands of kilos of cocaine generate significant profits for some influential national economic and political actors.[23] They also create micromarkets based on low-paid informal employment at the national level, even as they generate violent competition and hypercorruption.

These trends reveal that nations do not have a singular role in the illicit international economy of drug trafficking. The mapping of trafficking and consumption tendencies makes it obvious that the location of Caribbean countries between the major drug-production zones (Colombia, Venezuela, Peru, and Bolivia) and the main consumer destinations (the United States and Europe) facilitates the movement of approximately two-thirds of the cocaine from the region to North America.[24]

Despite the location factor, and the increasing sale of narcotics in the region, the estimated level of drug consumption in the Caribbean remains quite low.[25] That does not negate the fact that drug trafficking and organized crime impact Caribbean societies in critical ways. As the Inter-American

Drug Abuse Control Commission (Comisión Interamericana para el Control del Abuso de Drogas, CICAD) reports, "drug use, as well as the social context in which that use occurs, are etiological factors in a wide range of other social phenomena."[26] One such phenomenon is the "normalization" of selling drugs as a complementary source of income by informally employed and socially deprived citizens.

Another collateral effect is that drug commercialization triggers violent competition among retail sellers. Local consumption would not be such a major issue if drug use were treated as a health-related and social problem rather than a criminal one. However, that paradigm change requires the transformation of the moral and juridical determinants around which policies currently gravitate, reframing them in terms of the social implications for citizens' well-being.

The relationship between drug trafficking and violence, as well as the former's impact in the institutional, political, social, and economic realms, constitutes a more complex dimension of organized crime. From the economic perspective, organized crime produces an inflow of money that competes with productive and licit capital and with the limited resources managed by public administrations. It is not clear how this illicit capital compensates for unmet developmental needs, public service vacuums, and the economic distortion created within unequal societies. However, illicit flows of capital translate to huge rewards for criminals, tainted bureaucrats, and corrupt business owners. In 2007, the United Nations Office on Drugs and Crime (UNODC) and the World Bank estimated those assets to be around U.S.$850 million, equivalent to 5.3 percent of the GDP for most of the Caribbean region and U.S.$650 million for Puerto Rico, representing approximately 1.4 percent of its GDP.[27]

On the deficit side of the ledger are the costs of crime. These numbers include private and public spending on security, restrictions on business expansion, health care–related expenses, and loss of productivity. In Jamaica, the cost of crime was estimated to be as high as 3.7 percent of GDP by 2003, while in the case of Trinidad and Tobago, the estimates were 1.6 percent of GDP during the same period.[28]

Criminality and Violence Threaten Caribbean States and Societies

Dominican Republic: From Transit Point to Destination Hub

With its 48,000 square kilometers, the Dominican Republic has become in the last decade a major locus for individuals involved in organized criminal activities. It has come to play a major role as a hub for storage of illicit drugs, facilitating logistics by providing precursor supplies and enabling places where small airplanes can land and ports from which unchecked containers carrying drugs can easily depart and private yachts can arrive, bringing money to be laundered through different channels.[29]

Some of the social impacts of the role of the country as a growing criminal agent are reflected in the official crime statistics. Beginning in 2000, lethal violence increased, first gradually and then sharply by 2004. This trend was accentuated at the beginning of the twenty-first century and reached its peak in 2004, which was an election year that produced a shift in governmental elites. From 2001 to 2004, the homicide rate jumped from 12.5 to 25.2 per 100,000 inhabitants; despite interannual fluctuations, by 2012, the death rate was the same as it was at its most critical moment of irruption, in 2004–2005.[30]

When compared with the rest of Latin America and the other Caribbean countries, whose homicide rate was registered on average as 15.5/100,000, the Dominican Republic occupied an intermediate position in terms of violent deaths in 2010.[31] This is also confirmed by the *Latinobarómetro 2010* report, which shows that the country ranked medium-high among those where at least 30 percent of the population had been victimized. The Dominican Republic is also included in the group of countries where the public considers delinquency and insecurity to be the two most serious problems.[32]

A major concern among policymakers and Dominican citizens is the consistency of this escalation, since none of the structural and circumstantial factors that provoked such tendencies have been resolved. From 2003 to 2013, official records of deaths related to drug activity in the Dominican Republic (mostly in primary and secondary cities) point to turf wars among competitors, settling scores, suspects killed by the police, and altercations while under the influence of drugs. In 2005, those killed in drug-related violence accounted for 3 percent of all violent deaths. By 2007, the percentage of victims of drug violence had risen to 21.3 percent, and to 22 percent by 2009. In the first eight months of 2008, drug-related homicides represented 21 percent of all homicides so far that year, that is, 311 homicides of a total of 1,423 violent deaths. That means that there were more people killed as a result of issues related to drugs than there were victims of robbery. However, the police murdered 408 people that year, which accounts for 28.6 percent of all violent deaths in 2008, surpassing the number of drug-related deaths.[33] Inconsistencies regarding police compilation and even categorization of crimes could actually hide an overlap between those killed in drug-related incidents and those murdered by the police.

Taking into account that complex criminality is a multidimensional phenomenon that involves overlapping levels of armed violence, criminality, and a diversified set of groups, all embedded in criminal and illicit activities, it is not possible to single out the main source of these homicides. To add more inaccuracy to the evaluation of the magnitude of organized crime in the region and its linkages with the social fabric and the political and economic realms, there are discrepancies in the gathering of statistical data across the Caribbean. Jamaica and Trinidad and Tobago are among the few countries that keep records on gang activities, whereas in the Dominican Republic there are no official data on gang activity, and information about drug violence and drug-related murders overlaps with other categories (fights or other) and is often inconsistently registered.

Data gathered by UNODC in 2011 on homicide rates and cocaine seizures suggest that there is a positive correlation between cocaine seizures and the homicide rate in selected countries. However, in the Dominican Republic, the correlation with the highest levels of cocaine seizure is negative; the pattern of homicides looks constant no matter how many drug shipments are interdicted. This pattern could also reflect a more complex scenario where violent competition is highly concentrated and controlled or where Dominican drug enterprise does not necessarily involve extreme violence if other sources of intimidation can be used.

On the other hand, while volume and routes of drug transit vary constantly in the subregion, patterns of violence reaffirm themselves locally through the diversification of criminal activities and actors, public and private. As part of the organized crime networks' repertoire of violent practices, kidnappings and *sicarios* (killers for hire) have become a serious matter in countries where they hardly existed before, especially in the Dominican Republic, Trinidad and Tobago, and Haiti.[34] These patterns could result from a process of negative adaptation to changes experienced within the illicit political economy of competitive drug trafficking and marketing.

The growing narcotics activity can also be cautiously calibrated from

Table 15.2. Arrests for drug-related crimes, Dominican Republic, 2002–2011

Year	No. arrested
2002	4,223
2003	4,372
2004	3,637
2005	3,868
2006	4,284
2007	18,392
2008	21,791
2009	24,635
2010	25,948
2011	25,303
Total	136,453

Source: National Counterdrug Directorate (Dirección Nacional de Control de Drogas), Dominican Republic, 2011.

the annual comparison of the number of people arrested, deported, and extradited, including not only nationals but also foreigners. Official data register a rising tendency in each category.

Table 15.2 shows the number of people arrested between 2002 and 2011 for violating Law 50–88, related to drug crimes. Regarding the former, the drastic increase in arrests in just one decade (2002–2011) is notable. The amount looks even more dramatic when compared with detentions during the 1980s and 1990s, when the Caribbean region played an even greater role as a transit zone. The total number of Dominicans arrested between 1988 and 1998 was a little more than 25,000.[35]

Changes in the volume of individuals prosecuted for drug-related crimes could be interpreted in several ways. One possible scenario suggests an improvement in the efficiency of enforcement, perhaps explained by a more consistent presence of U.S. forces, especially the Drug Enforcement Agency (DEA). Another possible explanation could be an expanded and diversified black market.[36]

Puerto Rico: "An Island Surrounded by Mirrors"

Like the Dominican Republic, Puerto Rico has witnessed a proliferation in violence and crime in recent years.[37] In 2011, Puerto Ricans living on the island (3.7 million inhabitants) witnessed violence levels similar to those in the Dominican Republic in 2004 and experienced the highest rate of violent deaths for the previous seven decades, including a 17 percent increase

Table 15.3. Crimes by type, San Juan, Puerto Rico, 2010–2011

| | December 1–December 31 | | | | Accumulated through December 31 | | | |
| 2011 | 2010 | Change | | Type of crime | 2011 | 2010 | Change | |
		No.	%				No.	%
937	859	78	9	Total type 1	11,125	9,933	1,192	12
147	191	(44)	-23	Violent crime	2,146	2,056	90	4
16	20	(4)	-20	Murder and homicide	232	205	27	13
1	0	1	NA	Forced violence	9	2	7	350
101	146	(45)	-31	Robbery	1,560	1,538	22	1
29	25	4	16	Aggravated violation	345	311	34	11
790	668	122	18	Crime against property	8,979	7,877	1,102	14
109	143	(34)	-24	Escalation	1,604	1,537	67	4
573	380	193	51	Illegal appropriation	5,954	4,792	1,162	24
108	145	(37)	-26	Larceny	1,421	1,548	(127)	-8

Source: State Police, Statistics Department, Puerto Rico.

in violent crime from 2007 to 2009.[38] Most of this violence was concentrated in the metropolitan area of San Juan (see table 15.3).

Despite the already high annual homicide rate of 19 per 100,000 registered between 1980 and 2005, by 2011, that average had escalated to 30.5 homicides per 100,000 inhabitants. These numbers are higher than those for Mexico (24 homicides per 100,000) and six times higher than for the rest of the United States. Compared with 2010, Puerto Rico experienced an increase of 15 percent in violent deaths in 2011.[39]

Authorities and the media attribute most of this violence to drug transactions and activities.[40] Table 15.4 shows that from a total of 894 homicides in 2009 in the thirteen municipalities on the island, 258 were in fact drug related. Nevertheless, there were 581 murdered people classified as "unknown," which could also be related to drugs.

This lethal violence affects mostly poor young males, placing Puerto Rico among the Latin American countries with the highest rates of youth homicide (see table 15.5). It also tends to concentrate in public housing developments located in the urban centers and around the modern highways

Table 15.4. Homicides by municipality, situation, and sex of decedent, Puerto Rico, 2009

Police area	No. of fights		No. of crimes of passion		No. of domestic violence and related deaths		No. of drug-related deaths		No. of robberies		No. of other		No. from unknown causes		Total no.
	Male	Female	Male	Female	Male	Female	Male	Female	Male	Female	Male	Female	Male	Female	
San Juan	1	0	0	0	0	1	65	0	0	0	2	0	110	8	187
Bayamón	0	0	0	0	0	3	50	1	4	1	3	1	93	3	159
Ponce	2	0	0	0	0	1	39	0	0	0	0	0	81	2	125
Carolina	2	0	0	0	0	4	27	2	0	0	1	0	88	1	125
Caguas	2	0	0	0	0	2	15	1	1	0	1	0	36	4	62
Fajardo	1	0	0	0	0	0	11	0	1	0	0	0	32	2	47
Arecibo	0	0	0	0	0	0	6	0	2	0	1	0	30	0	39
Humacao	2	0	0	1	0	0	20	0	0	0	0	0	30	0	53
Guayama	1	0	0	0	0	2	9	0	1	0	0	0	22	2	37
Mayagüez	3	0	0	0	0	1	4	0	0	0	0	0	16	0	24
Aguadilla	0	0	0	0	1	1	1	0	0	0	0	0	8	0	11
Aibonito	2	0	0	0	0	0	7	0	0	0	1	0	10	0	20
Utuado	0	0	0	0	0	1	0	0	1	0	0	0	2	1	5
Total deaths	16	0	0	1	1	16	254	4	10	1	9	1	558	23	894

Total for both sexes	Male	Female
894	848	46
% of total	95	5

Source: State Police, Department of Statistics, Puerto Rico.

Table 15.5. Homicides in Puerto Rico, by age and sex, November 30, 2012

Age of decedent	No. of homicides	Sex of decedent	
		Male	Female
<10 years	6	2	4
10–11 years	0	0	0
12–13 years	1	0	1
14–15 years	3	3	0
16–17 years	16	15	1
18–19 years	52	51	1
20–24 years	156	147	9
25–29 years	120	114	6
30–34 years	109	98	11
35–39 years	57	54	3
40–44 years	39	35	4
45–49 years	31	24	7
50–54 years	20	18	2
55–59 years	14	12	2
60–64 years	8	7	1
65+	17	13	4
Unknown	222	217	5
Total	871	810	61

Source: State police, Department of Statistics, Puerto Rico.

that circumnavigate metropolitan San Juan.[41] With a population of barely half a million, this municipality registered the highest density of crime and criminal groups in 2010, ranking number 26 among the top 50 most violent cities in Latin America and the Caribbean. On just one warm and bloody June weekend in 2010, twenty-five killings broke the record for violence in San Juan.[42] With the proliferation of mafia-style executions within or near Puerto Rico's public housing sites, many residents of the barrios recognize the toll that the increasing violence and insecurity has taken on their communities and are frustrated by the lack of effective government response.

Violence, crime, inequality, and poverty have segregated the metropolitan areas of Puerto Rico spatially, converting the territory into a garrison society. In San Juan, wealthy citizens live in apartment towers guarded by private security, doormen, cameras, and alarm systems. Private security guards are armed and hired to protect people. Shopping malls have a strong police presence. Middle-class families have followed the pattern of the rich by hiring private security to the extent they can afford.

Many public housing projects are also enclosed and gated. They often have a kiosk staffed by police officers at the entrance. Garrisoning of projects within the barrios is funded by the local government and is seen by some residents as a form of protection from criminal groups, which battle among themselves to expand their drug business from one project to another. However, most critical voices see this garrisoning pattern as an encapsulation mechanism promoted by the rich to separate them from their poor neighbors, who are seen as potential perpetrators and criminals.

It is not enough to assert that there is a correlation between this abrasive violence and organized criminal activities. As the devil is in the details, the most demanding task consists of explaining how such patterns work, and how resilient they are. This implies looking more carefully at the formal and informal public and private institutions. It also requires contextualizing the evolution of politics among political forces from conservative and populist to socialist, which all paved the path for the consolidation of a political caste whose leaders tend to transfer and delegate power to their cronies.

In Puerto Rico, violent actors have gradually become instrumental in the political system and sometimes affiliated with political parties. A study I conducted in 2012 on the municipality of San Juan makes it clear that the ubiquitous influence of the drug business cut across the Puerto Rican state and society and, most of all, the institutional sphere and the party system. To better explain these linkages, it is worth understanding the favorable structure of criminal opportunities for members of the elite. The political configuration allows elites to establish informal agreements with criminal gangs located mostly in *barriadas* (slums) and public housing settlements, but also with high-profile capos living in residential neighborhoods of the metropolitan area. In the last eight to ten years, Puerto Rico's violent and criminal gangs have had ties to several local candidates and political parties, a phenomenon that resembles to some degree the institutionalized links between Jamaican criminal gangs and political castes that can be traced back to the 1960s.

The nexus between narco-enterprise and Puerto Rican politicians was evident in the 2012 congressional and municipal elections. One of the most publicized cases was the dismantling of one of the strongest trafficking organizations operating between 2000–2012, headed by Christian ("Chemito") Soto Mujica, who is now in jail and was formally accused of drug trafficking. Chemito Soto is the son of the mayor of the district of Carolina, located in the northern part of the island. He is the brother of Senator Lornna Soto, whose personal chauffeur was also part of the criminal gang directed by her brother. This group was part of a network that distributed marijuana in Mexico, California, Florida, and inside Puerto Rico. At the time of his arrest, Chemito was actively running as a candidate for mayor of San Juan in the 2012 municipal elections.

Another former senator, Héctor Martínez, convicted on corruption charges, was a facilitator for a renowned drug trafficker, José "Coquito" López, killed in 2006. Coquito was a capo who controlled the whole drug market in Carolina, which remains a district dominated by gang and drug activity and continues to experience high levels of violence.[43] The "narco-legisladores," as those members of Congress involved in organized crime are known in Puerto Rico, represent a well-established institution; they facilitate political contacts, open and close doors, veto laws that favor more accountability, and use their political influence with other state powers.

Police Corruption in Puerto Rico

Constituting the second-largest police force in the United States after the New York Police Department, the 17,153 active members of the Puerto Rican Police (PRP) have been subject to serious criticism by the U.S. Justice Department (USJD). In a public report in 2011, the USJD stated that more PRP members had been involved in criminal activities than employees from any other public agency in the nation. According to the report, 1,709 officials were arrested between 2005 and 2010, again, the highest amount in any U.S. jurisdiction. In just one year (2010), the FBI conducted its biggest anticorruption operation within the PRP and apprehended eighty-nine agents on numerous charges, including possession of drugs and violation of the regulations on the use of their guns.[44]

Due to the loss of confidence in the state police, the U.S. government is gradually increasing its role in the area of citizen security. Even though the state police are the institution formally in charge of internal security, coordination between local and federal authorities is becoming more common on matters of drug trafficking and other organized crime activities. This liaison is intended to make the state police more professional, since among Puerto Rican citizens there is much talk of police corruption and lack of professionalism, while the DEA is not seen as corrupt and inefficient. However, the PRP resent being viewed as subordinate to the DEA, unleashing undeclared animosity and reluctance on the part of the state police to work with DEA personnel. Real efforts to change law enforcement institutions have to come from the rank and file of the DEA.

A Conceptual Framework: Transgressive Ecosystems and Statetropism as Contesting Social Orders

To better describe the rationale and impacts of organized crime across societies and states, I have coined two terms. The first is "transgressive ecosystems" (TEs), a sociospatial construct based on interactions of organized and opportunistic criminal and illicit actors and activities that establish symbiotic and functional relations as a way to negotiate power and benefits. TEs involve political, economic, cultural, and relational factors that interconnect licit and illegal, formal and informal institutions, activities, and actors, prompting instrumental violence in fragile urban environments. However, through TEs, benefits are also widely distributed.

TEs crystallize themselves territorially through exchanges and arrangements between unregulated private actors such as gang members, petty criminals, elected politicians, bureaucrats, police officers, and prosecutors. Every actor develops certain levels of adaptation as well as resilience.[45] For example, since drug dealers are the main producers of income in the barrios, and many gang members work for them, they become the main target of police extortion and harassment.

On the other hand, gangs, drug dealers, and their local networks also regulate the territory they share with the residents of marginalized barrios. This, in turn, forces ordinary people to behave differently with regard to criminality. People, with an understanding of the authority and representation they feel the actors have, learn to negotiate with the contesting actors. As remarked by a member of a focus group that I facilitated, "When the community plans to put in place some social or cultural activity we do tell the head of the *puntos* [drug-selling points]." She clarified: "But that doesn't mean that we are asking for their permission; we are just informing them in order to avoid any conflict or violent act on their part."[46]

To the degree to which those transgressing social orders purposely court and incorporate agents of the state, they propel "statetropism," a phenomenon similar to the heliotropic tendency shown by plants seeking sunlight. As a systemic pattern of behavior, statetropic criminality prefers a scenario in which civil servants at all levels come to terms with criminal actors and provide protection for their illicit activities.

At macrolevels, statetropic power brokers open doors and provide security for operations that generate profits while providing money and, in the Puerto Rican case, facilitating the political influence of public officials and political elites. From these interactions it follows that statetropism is a crucial condition for granting consistency and robustness to illicit flows, making it almost impossible for organized criminality to flourish without this orientation. As Peter Andreas points out, just as traffickers and terrorists depend on the state, some state functionaries depend on traffickers and terrorists.[47] These alliances have produced serious consequences by undermining any attempt to reform the state's security and justice agencies and, consequently, impeding the implementation of effective public policies.

TEs and statetropism draw on an expanding body of literature that analyzes structural and organizational changes, modalities of operation, and adaptations of criminal agencies to outside stimuli, like those generated by interdiction and disruption policies.[48] Most of this scholarly work has resulted in consensus about criminal entities' configurations that demystify well-established notions of vertically rigid structure, proposing instead the predominance of small, loose, kin- and friendship-based configurations that bolster trust. These sometimes-disconnected networks and nodes tend to be more functional and efficient, highly adaptable to the environment.

In a similar paradigmatic approach to transgressive ecosystems, the work of scholars on complexity theories emphasizes the study of actors sharing social systems and the impact of their relations on recomposing those systems.[49] Michael Kenney's work on competitive adaptation is relevant here since he remarks that in order to survive, competitors have to learn through interaction and the diffusion of reciprocal activities.[50]

However, as remarkable and relevant as this body of literature is to the understanding of typologies and constituencies of criminal agents, it says very little about their impact on transforming institutional arrangements in the context of becoming autonomous transgressive agents themselves.

Statetropism as an expression of criminal adaptation and its form varies according to the particularities of each state and society. Sometimes the state itself becomes the organizer of transgressive actions and alternative political and social orders by explicitly transferring functions and resources to nonstate actors. This is the case in Jamaica, Trinidad and Tobago, Puerto Rico, and Haiti, where street gangs and other criminal groups have become part of the political system, establishing clear alliances with political party members and state sectors. These officials, in turn, transfer welfare resources to holders of local power that help the government establish political control in garrisoned areas.

In the Dominican Republic, on the contrary, there is not a significant welfare or redistribution system in place, as in Puerto Rico or Jamaica.

There, the state has been absent as a provider of services and present largely in a repressive form. The absentee state has left open space for nonstate actors to assume statelike responsibilities. Beginning decades ago, nonviolent actors such as nongovernmental organizations (NGOs), the church, and community-based organizations assumed welfare functions. Over time, though, gangs have conquered those spaces and become recognized territorially not for being part of the system, as elsewhere, but for being excluded and prosecuted by the system. Within a context of overwhelming exclusion and almost nonexistent state resources, local criminal entities have constructed alternative social and political orders in the barrios.

The absence of institutionalized arrangements between gangs and political structures opened the door to a more informal and opportunistic type of alliance among actors, which became the peculiar form of statetropism in the Dominican Republic.[51] This process was accelerated by the complete lack of official mediation to reduce criminality and create employment opportunities in the poorest neighborhoods.[52]

As a result, a preexisting culture that favored nonstate actors created the preconditions for the rapid growth of transgressive ecosystems and statetropism (hypercorruption and criminal clientelism) in the Dominican Republic. These preconditions help explain why violent organized crime seemed to emerge so quickly starting in 2004 in the Dominican Republic, as demonstrated by the earlier review of crime statistics at the beginning of this chapter. The phenomenon of statetropism is taken as a given in the poor barrios of Santo Domingo, where there is a widespread certitude that the police are directly involved in illicit businesses, especially the business of drugs. It also explains the reluctance of residents to cooperate with the police. Residents commonly assume that any information they deliver to the police will filter back to the criminals, putting them in danger.

These examples show how statetropism works at the "retail" level and how these patterns stimulated the evolution of illicit and violent agencies at the micro and the macro levels through informal settlements and with agents of the police, the military, and the justice system. At the macro level, statetropic power brokers provide profitable business and political support to political elites and public officials in exchange for protection of their illicit activities. These trends create a simultaneous two-track scenario: at the highest level of political, economic, and administrative influence, a tendency toward concentration of criminal entities takes the form of well-connected criminal actors who rely on cooperation and dissuasive competition; at the street, or retail, level, fragmentation, diversification, and violent competition are more intense as petty sellers proliferate in a context of increasing risk and exposure.

From these interactions it follows that statetropism is a crucial condition for achieving the stability and predictability of illicit flows, making it almost impossible for large-scale criminals to succeed without this orientation. Clearly, such alliances work against attempts to improve and reform the country's security and justice systems.

The Composition of an Interstate Statetropic Network

One notorious case that links the Dominican Republic and Puerto Rico illustrates statetropism at the macro level. On September 18, 2009, Puerto Rican newspapers reported that infamous drug trafficker Ángel Ayala-Vázquez, a kind of antihero among criminal sectors and widely known as Angelo Millones and "El Buster," was arrested on the island. At the time of his arrest, Ayala-Vázquez was the main leader of an organization that had imported several thousand kilograms of narcotics to Puerto Rico since 1995.

Ayala-Vázquez' criminal network was an intrinsic part of a wheel-type supranetwork that contained at least two core groups located simultaneously in Puerto Rico and the Dominican Republic.[53] Both groups administered their own subnetworks, with peripheral nodes responsible for the execution of several tasks. They used what some scholars characterize as bounding, bridging, and linking as part of their strategy to spread horizontally and vertically within the Puerto Rican state and society. The organizational structure that facilitated the smuggling of drugs and money between the two countries did not require a very formal and verticalized arrangement, but that does not mean the absence of a hierarchical configuration that promoted social mobility from a low-level to a higher-ranking position in recognition of and thanks for an actor's efficiency and effectiveness.

The arrest of Angelo Millones nearly dismantled the whole network in Puerto Rico, at the time comprising sixty-five of his acolytes, who identified themselves as El Combo de los Setenta (the Group of Seventy) and El Combo Que No Se Deja (the Group That Does Not Allow). Their main operations were conducted in public housing on the periphery of Bayamón, in the José Celso Barbosa and Sierra Linda projects. Despite the fact that there have been distribution points in those places since the 1990s, it was only after 1995 that Angelo Millones' groups managed to control the whole operation in the area of Bayamón by buying points or extorting previous owners to sell at points controlled by Millones. By obligating other points' owners in the municipality to buy drugs from his network, Millones became the main cocaine supplier in the area.

Roles, Rules, and Routines

During its fourteen years of operation in Puerto Rico, the Ayala-Vázquez network used family and friends to diversify operations inside and outside of Puerto Rico. The fact that this was a loose network does not mean, however, that it lacked functional structure, primary among which was the structured context of corruption and impunity in which the network operated (see table 15.6).

Rules

Rules create cohesion in the absence of a formal vertical structure. Implicit and explicit rules apply to everybody in the organization. Few rules are kept as stringently as the one that Millones applied to himself when he was arrested in 2009 and sentenced to life in prison: not to cooperate with law enforcement.

Routines

The main objective of a routine is to keep business moving by circulating assets in order to reinvest. While keeping a low profile, drug traffickers try to safely diversify the mechanisms for making illegally obtained resources legal. As Angelo Millones' indictment indicates, he and his partners utilized their illicit assets to purchase winning tickets from legal winners of the Puerto Rico lottery to "legitimize" the money; they bought real estate in lower-, middle-, and high-class neighborhoods under the names of family members, friends, and colleagues. To improve their public image, they promoted musicians by paying for public concerts, the revenues from which were laundered. In just one year, from 2007 to 2008, the Millones network was able to bring 1,000 kilograms of cocaine into the United States. The jury estimated that his illicit business was worth U.S.$100 million.

Networking in the Dominican Republic

A year after the arrest of Angelo Millones and the disbanding of his network, a widely publicized enforcement operation broke up another crimi-

Table 15.6. Configuration of the Ayala Vázquez network

Role	Function
Leader	Ayala-Vázquez (Angelo Millones) and 2 close friends personally control and supervise in person drug-trafficking operations at distribution points. They purchase, cut, and distribute drugs to different points in Puerto Rico and overseas.
Supplier	Suppliers are responsible for purchasing and transporting wholesale narcotics to the leaders.
Administrator	Administrators supervise daily operations at the distribution points in different locations on the island.
Drug point owner	Point owners sometimes purchase by consignment the drugs to be sold at their points. They also lease the right to sell drugs in areas other than their own, but only with permission from the leaders.
Enforcer	Enforcers protect the leaders and other members of the organization while safeguarding merchandise and assets obtained from the drug business and related illicit activities. They are armed and use extortion and violence against those who infringe on business.
Runner	Runners occupy an important position in the network. Supervised by the leaders, their duties include packaging and providing material to the sellers and distributors at the points. They are also responsible for collecting money and for paying street sellers. They keep records of street inventory and refills. They also recruit street sellers and other runners.
Seller	Sellers distribute all types of drugs (heroin, cocaine, base cocaine, marijuana, oxycodone, and other synthetic drugs) and have to account for sales and revenue generated.
Facilitator	Facilitators are essentially money launderers. They make sure illicit money and other assets from the network are legitimized through formal and legal financial, economic, and commercial systems.
Lookout (*bakeador*)	Lookouts have a low ranking in the network. Their job is to alert sellers, runners, and customers of law enforcement or a rival organization in the sales area.

Source: Lilian Bobea, based on descriptions contained in the Angelo Millones indictment.

nal organization in Puerto Rico. In July 2010, José D. Figueroa Agosto, alias "Junior Cápsula," a renowned Puerto Rican capo, was arrested in the streets of San Juan. Figueroa Agosto was in fact the leader of a large criminal network, considered one of the biggest in the Caribbean, which was initially commanded by Ayala-Vázquez, before Figueroa Agosto became his partner by establishing his own related branch in the Dominican Republic in 1995. Both men were able to carry on their business between Puerto Rico and the Dominican Republic for more than a decade.

Figueroa Agosto moved to the Dominican Republic to avoid prosecution by the Puerto Rican authorities. There he started a criminal network that actively operated starting in 2000. Even though he was arrested on several occasions in the Dominican Republic, he was able to evade authorities. At his arrest in Puerto Rico, he was carrying several passes to sensitive security institutions, including the office of the police chief and the head of the counternarcotics office. They were determined to be official identification cards given to him by high-ranking officials in each institution. His arrest led to the exposure of a long list of public servants, officials, and entrepreneurs who were involved at different levels with several of Figueroa Agosto's businesses.

During the decade that the Puerto Rican capo was operating in the Dominican Republic, he established different drug-distribution cells in the poorest neighborhoods and in middle-class residential areas of the two main cities, Santo Domingo and Santiago. Figueroa Agosto's technique was to create criminal networks in which each node had a functional role that was kept separate and disconnected from the others. Cristián Almonte Peguero, apparently a successful architect and decorator, found ways to be introduced to high-class clients in social clubs, and selective circles helped him gain entry into Dominican society and protected him from his enemies. His use of "soft" power in both countries was countered by intimidation and extortion of and social pressure on community members and corrupt law enforcement. The network also used "straw" owners to launder money.[54]

The arrest of Figueroa Agosto in July 2010 closed a long cycle of impunity, high-level corruption, and interconnected statetropic criminality in both countries. The combined criminal networks of Angelo Millones and Figueroa Agosto allowed them to expand their criminal enterprise at different levels of the Puerto Rican and Dominican states and societies. Commenting on this enterprise, a DEA officer publicly declared, "Puerto Ricans and Dominicans [drug traffickers] have been successful in establishing a friendly criminal association to work together in the drug business. There is a nexus of reciprocity where they use the same routes, private yachts, and aircraft."[55]

The wheel-type network that Figueroa Agosto and El Buster managed together was a complex one. It had several peripheral spokes in both countries and established a network of alliances with Colombians, Venezuelans, Puerto Ricans, and Dominicans. In fact, this network opened a window of opportunity for several chains in both countries. In the words of the entering head of the DEA, Pedro J. Janer, "they function as a society, rather than a hierarchical structure."[56] That is to say, they were not megacartels; rather, they minimized risks and cost by going small, creating compact but efficient groups.

Gaining Ground: Alternative Social Orders in the Caribbean

At the detention of Angelo Millones, the U.S. attorney, Rosa Rodríguez-Vélez, publicly stressed, "The arrest of Ayala-Vázquez marks a significant victory in our war against drug traffickers, in Puerto Rico and the continental United States." She congratulated law enforcement and prosecutors, "who tirelessly worked night and day." She closed her remarks by asserting, "Puerto Rico is a safer place today."[57]

She, however, did not mention that the capture of El Buster was not a Puerto Rican achievement but a DEA and FBI success. Two years earlier, a report issued by the Civil Rights Division of the USJD highlighted that "the amount of crime and corruption involving PRPD officers further illustrates that PRPD is an agency in profound disrepair. From January 2005 to November 2010, there were more than 1,709 arrests of PRPD officers. The charges varied widely, from theft and simple assault to rape, drug trafficking, and murder."[58]

Conclusion: Policy Options for Weak States

This chapter's central point is that organized crime, drug trafficking, and the violent criminal systems they foster have brought Caribbean societies to a crossroads: either they turn toward a comprehensive strategic policy that breaks rooted cultures of clientelism, corruption, and impunity, or they continue recycling old patterns of negative adaptation and resilience.[59] Both paths have implications in terms of, first, the scale of economic resources they extract but also generate, and, second, the social and political costs they involve.

The consequences of accommodation to these trends by regional political and economic elites have long been discussed.[60] Indeed, the usually constrained Caribbean economies are thriving because of the illicit money pouring into the private and public sectors. What is a relatively new outcome is the impact that these trends have had in reshaping the social order, affecting the social fabric as well as the state's configuration. Almost without exception, the toll of crime has increased as a consequence of the proliferation of the risky and competitive street market for drugs, flourishing all over the region, from poor coastal shantytowns to slum neighborhoods in urban areas, where violence tends to concentrate. Usually, lower-level stakeholders are the target of the authorities, while major sources and flows of illicit capital remain untouched.

Regional strategies have had only a limited effect as organized criminal networks have fragmented and drug-trafficking routes have shifted and promoted the widespread diffusion of criminal actors throughout the region.[61] Bagley's work highlights the impact of policies such as interdiction and eradication on smuggling modalities and structures, making it even more difficult for law enforcement to have a consistent and perdurable impact on drug smuggling.

Three fundamental policy levels need to be taken into account when designing intervention strategies: (1) the macro (regional/national) level; (2) the micro (local) level; and (3) the level of intersection and articulation between these two. This distinction means that a policy that is designed to work at the macro level will have different implications at the micro local level, and it is critical to understand where and how they intersect and affect each other.

To be more effective, crime-prevention and -control policies need to depart from social, spatial, institutional, and organizational settings. A deeper understanding of the nexus between organized crime and the political and bureaucratic systems, in terms of the subjacent conditions, motivations, and opportunities that promote such a nexus, is also critical for developing more targeted policies against systemic statetropic corruption.

Again, these are dilemmas that force governmental and political elites to answer the question, Is there a real willingness to break up, once and for all, patterns of illicit accumulation, negligence, and denial, instead of continuing to perform the "crying game" before the international community?

These elites could obliterate the issue, but what seems to be an undeniable truth is that the phenomenon of complex (organized and disorganized) criminality is constantly changing, following a cost-benefit and modernization rationale that will always challenge the nature and precepts of public response and the established social order.[62]

Notes

1. United Nations Office on Drugs and Crime (UNDP), *Caribbean Human Development Report, Human Development and the Shift to Better Citizen Security 2012* (New York: United Nations Publications, 2012), 19; idem, *Global Study on Homicide* (Vienna, 2011), 22.

2. The homicide rate in 2010 for Jamaica was 52 per 100,000 inhabitants; for Trinidad and Tobago, 36 per 100,000. Characteristically, the highest homicide rates affected the metropolitan areas of Kingston, with 47.2 homicides per 100,000; San Juan, 52.60 homicides per 100,000; and the National District of Santo Domingo, with 36 per 100,000 inhabitants.

3. See United Nations Office on Drugs and Crime (UNODC), *Global Study on Homicide*. For the data on Kingston and San Juan, see the report issued by the Mexican NGO Seguridad, Justicia y Paz, "Consejo ciudadano para la seguridad pública y justicia penal," http://www.consejociudadanobcs.org/. A.C. Saint Kitts and Nevis show a rate of 38 per 100,000 inhabitants. This violence has an urban profile, with the highest homicide rates affecting mostly the metropolitan area of Kingston, with 47.2 homicides per 100,000.

4. UNDP, *Caribbean Human Development Report*, 19.

5. UNODC, *Global Study on Homicide*, 25; see also UNPD, *Caribbean Human Development Report*, 19.

6. Caribbean Community (CARICOM), *Crime and Security Report, 2002* (Trinidad and Tobago: Caribbean Community Task Force on Crime, 2002).

7. U.S. Department of Justice, National Drug Intelligence Center, *National Drug Threat Assessment 2010*, report no. 2010-Q0317-001 (Washington, D.C., 2010); UNDP, *Caribbean Human Development Report*, 65–89.

8. CARICOM, *Crime and Security Report, 2002*.

9. Ivelaw L. Griffith, "Drugs and Crime as Problems without Passports in the Caribbean: How Secure Is Security, and How Sovereign Is Sovereignty?" paper presented at the Thirteenth Annual Eric E. Williams Memorial Lecture, Florida International University, 2011, http://ufdc.ufl.edu/AA00007154/00001. See also UNDP, *Caribbean Human Development Report*, 76–77; Charles M. Katz, Edward R. Maguire, and David Choate, *A Cross-National Comparison of Gangs in the United States and Trinidad and Tobago, International Criminal Justice Review* 21, no. 3 (September 2011): 1–20, accessed March 11, 2012, http://icj.sagepub.com/content/21/3/243.abstract; Dorn Townsend, *No Other Life: Gangs, Guns and Governance in Trinidad and Tobago* (Geneva: Small Arms Survey, 2009).

10. See Lilian Bobea, "Organized and Disorganized Crime, Muertos Legales and Ilegales in the Caribbean," *ReVista* (Winter 2012): 56–58, http://revista.drclas.harvard.edu/book/organized-and-disorganized-crime; idem, *Violencia y seguridad democrática en*

República Dominicana (Santo Domingo: Facultad Latinoamericana de Ciencias Sociales [FLACSO], 2011).

11. See the introduction in this volume.

12. For more details, see Tani Mariela Adams, *Chronic Violence and Its Reproduction: Perverse Trends in Social Relations, Citizenship and Democracy in Latin America.* (Washington, D.C.: Woodrow Wilson Center , 2011), 10.

13. CARICOM is the Caribbean Community; IMPACS is the Implementation Agency for Crime and Security; RSS is the Regional Security System; and SICA is the Sistema e Integración Centroamericano (Central American Integration System).

14. See Rep. Michael McCaul, "U.S. Caribbean Border: An Open Road to Drug Traffickers and Terrorist," opening statement made before the Subcommittee on Oversight, Investigations, and Management, June 21, 2012, accessed July 2012, http://homeland.house. gov/sites/homeland.house.gov/files/06-21-12%20McCaul%20Open.pdf.

15. See Bruce M. Bagley, *Drug Trafficking and Organized Crime in the Americas: Major Trends in the Twenty-First Century* (Washington, D.C.: Woodrow Wilson Center, 2012).

16. This statement was made by Ambassador William R. Brownfield, assistant secretary of state for international narcotics and law enforcement affairs, before the Senate Foreign Relations Subcommittee on the Western Hemisphere, Peace Corps, and Global Narcotics Affairs, "The U.S.–Caribbean Shared Security Partnership: Responding to the Growth of Trafficking Narcotics in the Caribbean," Washington, D.C., December 15, 2011.

17. Rodney G. Benson, assistant administrator, chief of Intelligence Drug Enforcement Administration Subcommittee on the Western Hemisphere, Peace Corps, and Global Narcotics Affairs Committee on Foreign Relations United States Senate, "Next Steps on the Caribbean Shared Security Partnership," statement for the record, Washington, D.C., December 15, 2011, 2.

18. "Congress to Eye Caribbean Security," *CBS News*, June 1, 2012, http://homeland.house. gov/hearing/subcommittee-hearing-us-caribbean-border-open-road-drug-traffickers -and-terrorists.

19. Interview with General Mateo Rosado, head of the Dirección Nacional de Drogas (National Counterdrug Directorate of the Dominican Republic), Santo Domingo, January 11, 2013.

20. See COPOLAD, "Dominican Republic Is the Command Center for Drug Trafficking," January 23, 2013, accessed April 15, 2013, http://voxxi.com/2013/01/22/ dominican-republic-center-drug-traffic/.

21. Luis G. Fortuño, governor of Puerto Rico, before the U.S. House of Representatives Committee on Homeland Security Subcommittee on Oversight, Investigations and Management, Washington, D.C., June 21, 2012, http://homeland.house.gov/sites/homeland. house.gov/files/Testimony-Fortuño.pdf.

22. "Dominican Republic Emerges as Drug Trafficking Center of the Caribbean," January 23, 2013, http://www.voxxi.com/dominican-republic-center-drug-traffic/#ixzz2Io5IoUaw.

23. Michael Platzer with Flavio Mirella and Carlos Resa Nestares, "Illicit Drug Markets in the Caribbean: Analysis of Information on Drugs Flows through the Region," in *Caribbean Drugs: From Criminalization to Harm Reduction,* ed. Klein Axel, Marcus Day, and Anthony Harriott (London: Ian Randle Publishers and Zed Books, 2004), 194.

24. A study that projected a "best estimate" for consumption calculated around 15.6 million cocaine users in 2009 worldwide, that is, 0.35 percent of the population between fifteen and sixty-four years old. The researchers suggested that 5.7 million North Americans consume cocaine, making this the largest group of consumers, followed by Central Europeans (4.1 million) and South Americans, Central Americans, and inhabitants of the Caribbean (2.7 million).

25. United Nations Office on Drugs and Crime, *Global Study on Homicide*, 58. These data need to be taken with a grain of salt, though, since most of the information comes from official sources that lack consistency and even credibility. Despite that, hard-drug consumption is relevant in the small islands. According to the Inter-American Drug Abuse Control Commission, in 2010, Guyana showed lifetime use of 4.12 percent of cocaine, 3.86 of ecstasy, and 4.3 of crack cocaine; Jamaica, 3.1 of cocaine, 2.79 of ecstasy, and 1.63 of crack cocaine; Haiti, 2.69 of cocaine, 2.95 of ecstasy, and 2.65 of crack cocaine.

26. Dirección Nacional de Control de Drogas (DNCD), Dominican Republic Statistics (2002–2011).

27. UNODC and the Latin American and Caribbean Region of the World Bank, "Crime, Violence, and Development: Trends, Costs, and Policy Options in the Caribbean," Report no. 37820 (Washington, D.C., 2007).

28. See Anthony Harriott, *Police and Crime Control in Jamaica: Problems of Resolving Ex-Colonial Constabularies* (Kingston: University of the West Indies Press, 2000); Yvette Holder and Folade Mutota, "Guns and Criminality: A Case Study of Trinidad and Tobago," background paper prepared for the World Bank Study on Crime and Violence in the Caribbean (Washington, D.C., 2006).

29. According to the World Bank, around 1,000,300 containers leave Dominican ports every year; however, the current installed capacity to check every container is dramatically low; see World Bank, Container port traffic http://data.worldbank.org/indicator/IS.SHP. GOOD.TU. TEU = 20-foot equivalent units.

30. See the annual statistical reports of the Dominican Republic's Attorney General's Office (Procuraduría General de la República), www.procuraduria.gov.do; http://www. insightcrime.org/news-briefs/police-killings-dominican-republic (published 2013); http:// www.refworld.org/docid/50aa06522.html (2012 stats).

31. UNODC, *Global Study on Homicide*. See also Jana Morgan, Rosario Espinal, and Mitchell Seligson, *Cultura política de la democracia en República Dominicana: Hacia la igualdad de oportunidades* (Nashville, Tenn.: Vanderbilt University, Latin American Public Opinion Project (LAPOP), 2012), 100.

32. *Latinobarómetro 2010*, Chile, 2010, 15–16, www.latinobarometro.org.

33. See statistics from the Procuraduría General de la República Dominicana, annual report, "Razones de muertes violentas," 2006, 2007, and 2008, procuraduria.gov.do.

34. See UNODC and the World Bank, "Crime, Violence, and Development," 22–23.

35. Statistics from the National Counterdrug Directorate Office (Dirección Nacional de Control de Drogas), 2000.

36. We have to consider that by official estimates the amount of seized drugs represents barely 10 percent of the drugs that enter or pass through the country.

37. The expression "an island surrounded by mirrors" comes from Rosario Ferre in an interview with Julio Ortega in *Apropiaciones: Cultura y nueva escritura en Puerto Rico* (San Juan: Universidad de Puerto Rico, 1991).

38. Statistics from the Puerto Rican Police Department, http://www.policia.gobierno. pr; "Crime Statistics," FBI, http://www.fbi.gov/stats-services/crimestats.

39. Gretchen Sierra-Zorita, "As Violent Puerto Rican Drug Trade Seeps into Mainland U.S., Washington Must Act," *Christian Science Monitor*, February 16, 2012, http://www. csmonitor.com/Commentary/Opinion/2012/0216/As-violent-Puerto-Rican-drug-trade-seeps-into-mainland-US-Washington-must-act?nav=457639-csm_article-bottomRelated.

40. Jorge Rodríguez Beruff, "La seguridad en el Caribe en 2008: Huracanes, crimen, rusos y soft power," in *Seguridad regional en América Latina y el Caribe: Anuario 2009*, ed. Hans Mathieu and Paula Rodríguez (Bogotá: Friedrich Ebert Stiftung, 2009), 55. See also the testimony of Puerto Rican governor Luis A. Fortuño, http://homeland.house.gov/sites/ homeland.house.gov/files/Testimony-Fortuño.pdf.

41. In the municipality of San Juan, Puerto Rico, the homicide rate is 52.6 per 100,000. In the National District of Santo Domingo, Dominican Republic, the homicide rate is 36 per 100,000 inhabitants. According to the World Health Organization, by mid-2011, there were 250,000 homicides every year among youths ten to twenty-nine, representing 41 percent of the total number of homicides globally; see www.who.int/mediacentre/ factsheets/fs356/en.

42. Seguridad, Justicia y Paz, "Estudio comparativo de la incidencia de homicidios doloso en ciudades y jurisdicciones sub-nacionales de los países del mundo," 2010, http:// editor.pbsiar.com/upload/PDF/50_ciud_mas_violentas.pdf.

43. Javier Colón Dávila, "Narcos usan el aeropuerto y logran acceso a políticos; diez de los arrestos se realizaron en el mismo aeropuerto," *El Nuevo Día*, June 7, 2012, www. elnuevodia.com.

44. U.S. Department of Justice, Civil Rights Division, "Investigación de la policía de Puerto Rico," September 5, 2011, 16, http://www.justice.gov/crt/about/spl/documents/ prpd_letter_espanol.pdf.

45. Diane E. Davis, *Urban Resilience in Situations of Chronic Violence* (Boston: Massachusetts Institute of Technology and United States Agency for International Development (USAID), 2012), 37. Davis conceptualizes resilience as "individual or communities' capacities to resist against the perpetrators of violence through strategies that help them establish relatively autonomous control over the activities, spaces, and social or economic forces and conditions that comprise their daily lives."

46. Participant in a focus group in San Juan, Puerto Rico.

47. Peter Andreas, *Border Games: Policing the U.S.-Mexico Divide* (Ithaca, N.Y.: Cornell University Press, 2000).

48. See Peter Reuter and John Haaga, *The Organization of High-Level Drug Markets: An Exploratory Study* (Santa Monica, Calif.: RAND, 1889). See also Mary Layne, William Rhodes, and Caben Chester, *The Cost of Doing Business for Cocaine Smugglers* (Washington, D.C.: Abt Associates, 2000); Ivelaw Griffith, *Drugs and Security in the Caribbean: Sovereignty under Siege* (University Park: Pennsylvania State University Press, 1997); idem, "Drugs and Crime."

49. Among the most relevant are Michael Kenney, *From Pablo to Osama: Trafficking and Terrorist Networks, Government Bureaucracies and Competitive Adaptation* (University Park: Pennsylvania State University Press, 2007); Powell Walter, "Neither Market nor Hierarchy: Network Forms of Organization," in *Research in Organizational Behavior*, vol. 2, ed. Barry M. Staw and L. Cummings (Greenwich, Conn.: JAI, 1990), 295–336; James

G. March, Lee S. Sproull, and Michal Tamuz, "Learning from Samples of One or Fewer," *Organization Science* 2 (1991): 1–13.

50. Kenney, *From Pablo to Osama: Trafficking and Terrorist Networks, Government Bureaucracies, and Competitive Adaptation* (University Park: Penn State University Press, 2007); http://spectrum.ieee.org/telecom/security/the-truth-about-terroristsnet.

51. Regarding the issues of institutionalized informalities, see Gretchen Helmke and Steven Levitsky, "Informal Institutions and Comparative Politics: A Research Agenda," Working Paper no. 307 (Notre Dame, Ind.: Kellogg Institute for International Studies, 2003). Also see David Pion-Berlin, "Informal Civil-Military Relations in Latin America: Why Politicians and Soldiers Choose Unofficial Venues," *Armed Forces & Society*, SAGE, 2009, accessed June 16, 2010, http://afs.sagepub.com/cgi/content/abstract/36/3/526.

52. Regarding conflict-resolution initiatives, there are ongoing mediation experiences between local governments, police, and contesting actors such as the initiative developed by the municipality of Barcelona with youth associations and several truces experienced by the police in Chicago's and Boston's Operation Ceasefire.

53. Kenney, *From Pablo to Osama*, 31–32. According to Kenney, there are essentially two types of networks: wheel and chain. Wheel networks contain a core group that centralizes the management of the whole enterprise while the peripheral nodes execute the tasks. The cores are usually managed by veteran traffickers who possess capital, contacts, and know-how. Chain networks, on the other hand, are defined as "decentralized and self organizing [and] contain independent nodes that perform specific tasks and transact directly with other nodes without mediation and oversight by core groups."

54. U.S. District Court for the District of Puerto Rico, indictment *United States v. Jose Figueroa Agosto et al.*, November 15, 2010.

55. Limarys Suárez Torres, "Alianza caribeña de narcos," *El Nuevo Día*, Puerto Rico, February 9, 2012, www.elnuevodia.com.

56. Edward Fox, "Puerto Rico Increasing in Importance to Drug Traffickers: DEA," In SightCrime, May 22, 2012, accessed July 1, 2012, http://www.insightcrime.org/news-briefs/puerto-rico-increasing-in-importance-to-drug-traffickers-dea.

57. U.S. Department of Justice, "DEA Bust Puerto Rico's Top Drug Trafficker," September 22, 2009, http://www.justice.gov/dea/divisions/car/2009/carib092209p.html.

58. U.S. Department of Justice, Civil Rights Division, "Investigation of the Puerto Rico Police Department," (Washington, D.C., September 5, 2011), 7, http://www.nytimes.com/interactive/2011/09/08/us/08police-doc.html?ref=us&_r=0.

59. Ibid.

60. See Anthony Maingot, "Confronting Corruption in the Hemisphere: A Sociological Perspective," *Journal of Interamerican Studies and World Affairs* 36, no. 3, Special Issue, The Summit of the Americas—Issues to Consider (Autumn 1994): 49–74, accessed November 21, 2009, http://www.jstor.org/stable/166526.

61. See the introduction in this volume.

62. Here I subscribe to the sociological notion of social orders described by Ana Arjona as "a particular set of shared norms that regulate the interaction among members of a given community; see Ana Arjona, "National War, Multiple Local Orders: An Inquiry into the Unit of Analysis of War and Post-War Interventions," *Forum for International Criminal Justice and Conflict*, no. 2 (2008): 1–27.

16

The Power of Organized Crime in Brazil

From Public and Social Challenges to the Effectiveness of Reforms

MARCELO ROCHA E SILVA ZOROVICH

This chapter discusses organized crime and drug trafficking in Brazil, analyzing the underlying problems which help foment organized crime. In addition, this work highlights the interconnections between the borders in South America, the criminal powers in Brazilian prisons, and the role of organized criminal groups in the Brazilian slums. It also analyzes Brazil's institutional challenges as a result of the negative perception of and lack of confidence in institutions designed to combat organized crime (that is, the police and the judiciary). These institutions are known for their high levels of bureaucracy, ineffectiveness, and corruption. The chapter also underlines the proliferation of transnational criminal groups and their actions. Such activities are enabled by globalization and facilitated by the shrinkage of distance on a global scale through the emergence and thickening of social, economic, political, and technological connections.

In this respect, organized crime and drug trafficking in Brazil are fueled by the globalization of drug consumption and the internationalization of the trade routes. As a consequence, there is evidence of increasing levels of violence throughout the country. Organized crime and drug trafficking occur not only in major cities such as Rio de Janeiro and São Paulo, but also in small and medium-sized municipalities as it is fragmented into different types of illegal activities. This is also part of a complex picture of social and economic conditions increasingly favored by marginalization and the omission of the state.

An Alarming Scenario

There is a continual concern with some of the issues intrinsically related to the power of organized crime in Brazil, particularly the power of organized criminal groups and their extensive impact on Brazilian society. Because of the so-called balloon and cockroach effects, "the proliferation of areas of drug cultivation and of drug-smuggling routes throughout the hemisphere," and "the dispersion and fragmentation" of organized criminal groups across subregions, Brazil is inserted into the increasing globalization of drug consumption as part of the complex organized criminal networks.[1] Brazil is confronting organized crime and violence as a consequence of its lack of foresight in the past. For decades, the country has not succeeded in implementing a drug policy, nor has it been able to implement reforms to decrease corruption. Before 1998, Brazil did not have a national policy on drugs. According to Jorge Armando Félix, the former antidrug secretary,[2] the first antidrug measures were adopted by the United Nations General Assembly in 1998. Under Lula's government in 2003, some priorities were defined: (a) the centralization of efforts to integrate public sector policies and national antidrug policy; (b) decentralization at the municipal level allowing demand-reduction activities to be adapted to local realities; and (c) the strengthening of relationships with society and the scientific community.[3]

What has happened to these initiatives? Effectiveness and implementation have been part of the challenges faced by the Brazilian government, along with many other factors. Jorge Armando Félix,[4] Brazil's national antidrug secretary at the time, stated that "there was a government group that advised politicians on the wide-ranging legislative process that culminated in the Law on Drugs, sanctioned by the President in August 2006. This new law placed Brazil in the spotlight on both the national and international stage with the creation of a National System of Public Policies on Drugs, replacing a 30-year-old legislation that was out of touch with scientific advances and social transformation."[5]

Despite improvements, Brazil still faces major security challenges. In addition, a large drug market has been created and has developed rapidly. This market links "criminal elements of the society, among those with the lowest levels of purchasing power. These individuals are instrumentalised by organized crime networks, to the upper-middle classes, who represent the social base for drug consumption and carry enormous political responsibility over this critical issue."[6] This situation also impacts national security

Table 16.1. Expenditures on public security, Brazil and the United States, 2007–2009

Country	Expenditures as % of GDP		
	2007	2008	2009
Brazil	1.4	1.4	1.5
United States	2.1	2.2	2.3

Source: Anuário brasileiro de segurança pública, 5th ed., 2011, Brazilian Forum on Public Security, Ministry of Justice, Brasília.

and sovereignty. One of the main challenges for Brazil is to work effectively with institutions and governments to combat corruption. Brazilian citizens continue to be victims of violence as a result of organized criminal activities and a lack of action by law enforcement and the judicial system.

The country spent around U.S.$47.5 billion on public safety in 2010,[7] a figure that includes spending on civil defense. This amount represents an increase of 4.4 percent from 2009 and highlights a decrease in the rate of spending in this sector.[8] In addition, it corresponds to approximately 1.36 percent of GDP spent on public safety initiatives in 2010 alone. Table 16.1 indicates a three-year trend in Brazil and in the United States on public security expenditures.

The complexity of organized crime in Brazil has resulted in many social challenges as organized criminal actors cross borders and impact all levels of society. As a result of organized criminal activities, Brazil has witnessed increasing levels of violence. In addition, insecurity plagues civil society and is characterized by a framework of conflicts between the police and criminals, both of which often overlap.

According to Queiroz, organized crime nationwide has increasingly been supported by material, technical, and strategic resources and has required the adaptation of the police, the Brazilian justice system, and the Ministry of Justice to mobilize more effectively.[9] Major demographic changes occurred as a result of urbanization during the previous decades.[10] Beginning in the 1980s, the number of individuals murdered as a result of criminal activity caught the attention of authorities, and research indicates that over one million Brazilians have been murdered since that time.[11] These are civil war–level figures, concentrated in large urban centers. In response to such events, the federal government deployed troops to the Complexo do Alemão slum in Rio de Janeiro.

There are around 700 slums in Rio de Janeiro, with more than one million inhabitants. According to police data, drug traffickers operate in almost every slum in the city, including but not limited to Acari, Turano, Maré, Borel, Rocinha, Alemão, Mangueira, Manguinhos, Jacarezinho, Turano, Vigário Geral, and Providência.[12]

Organized criminal networks operate in other areas besides Rio de Janeiro. Levels of violence and criminality have skyrocketed as a result of drug trafficking and armed conflicts. During the first decade of the twenty-first century, the map of violence resulting from organized crime in Brazil also underwent fragmentations in small and medium-sized municipalities as well as other states across the country and across its borders.[13] This fact reflects industrialization and the restructuring of Brazilian manufacturing,[14] thus increasing the importance of regions outside the south-southeast axis.[15]

Another major issue in Brazilian society has been the weakness of public institutions, such as the police, which have been riddled with corruption. Members of the police force earn low salaries and are therefore tempted to accept bribes. Instances of police violence and corruption further contribute to the negative image of the police forces. According to a survey, almost half of all crime victims did not make a complaint to the police due to a general distrust of the institution. Another study, conducted by the Institute of Applied Economic Research (Instituto de Pesquisa Econômica Aplicada, IPEA),[16] reveals that 70 percent of the population does not trust the state police. Surveys also indicate that over 70 percent of eighteen-year-olds have very little trust or no trust in the military police, whereas approximately 66 percent of respondents have little confidence or do not rely on the civil police at all. Additionally, 51 percent have little confidence or do not rely on the federal police.[17]

Machado da Silva argues that crime is increasingly beyond social control and social policy objectives and institutions. Furthermore, according to Bandeira, the state police's investigative capacity is very poor, as "the training of its commanders has been influenced by military conceptions that emphasize the idea of repression" and not intelligent prevention.[18] As Soares notes, the "Brazilian police, as a rule, are inefficient at prevention and delimited repression, in investigation and in winning the indispensable confidence of the population."[19] Corruption and brutality are disturbingly commonplace. The police do not submit to rational management, evaluate their own performance, or allow monitoring of their actions. They are not organized to deal with the basic problems identified by defined priorities and goals that need to be confronted. They neither plan their activities nor correct their errors by analyzing the results of their initiatives.

A similar situation occurs in the Brazilian prison system, where a lack of preparation and overcrowding contribute to the power of militias. Organized criminal networks with defined hierarchies operate inside the prisons, and subcommands or cells operate outside the prisons. Furthermore, criminal networks rely on the bribery of officials, dirty money, and various other mechanisms to facilitate the trafficking of weapons, narcotics, and devices to allow the incarcerated to communicate with people outside the penitentiary system. Although some authors disagree about what defines organized crime in Brazil,[20] it appears that most agree on the activities that make organized crime different from ordinary crime, primarily drug trafficking, the formation of gangs, bank robbery, illicit activities, illegal gambling, clandestine actions, home invasions, kidnappings, money laundering, profiteering, use of violence, symbiosis with the state, the law of silence, monopoly control of territory, prison riots, and corruption.[21]

Global Consumption and Transnational Drug Trafficking

The proliferation of transnational criminal groups has a direct bearing on security. Such activities are enabled by globalization and facilitated by the shrinkage of distance on a global scale through the emergence and thickening of social, economic, political, and technological connections.[22] While crime has become global, crime control has remained largely state-based. Unquestionably, globalization has facilitated the transnational growth of illicit activities.[23] Global consumption transcends borders. Far from being uniquely in the American hemisphere or Europe, illicit-drug trafficking has invaded all continents to different degrees, and transnational organized crime has presented itself in different ways.

One example of transnational organized crime is the export of relatively small quantities of drugs by criminal organizations via Brazil's international airports.[24] According to Silva, drugs are exported in several forms often by one or more persons. Silva also explains that the export of large quantities of drugs by these criminal networks generally is by sea in either medium or large ships or by air. Silva's remarks demonstrate the following:[25]

(a) Two groups sponsor the trade of illicit drugs trafficked in small amounts in Brazil: the Nigerian mafia traffics drugs from Brazil (primarily cocaine). Research indicates that 10,000 Nigerians live in São Paulo. They have attempted to integrate into Brazilian society, "but really render any type of service to organized transnational networks, specifically by acquiring cocaine in the borders of Brazil," either by air or by land. In fact, "many Africans are really sent to Brazil to serve as mules for these multinational criminal organizations."[26] Other criminal transnational organizations, such as the Italian Mafia, deal with the illicit trafficking of small amounts of drugs by purchasing cocaine in neighboring countries. Simple measures are adopted for the export of the drug through international airports, and the drugs are transported in a distilled form by "mules," predominantly Europeans.[27]

(b) Brazil is known to be "a passageway for drugs, especially cocaine and heroin coming from Colombia, Peru and Bolivia, destined primarily to European and North-American consumer markets." In these cases, evidence exists that Brazilian criminal organizations have become responsible for the transportation, storage, packaging, and export of drugs, although these organizations are not the owners of these drugs. In addition, "plantation refining laboratories for cocaine [exist] in the Brazilian Amazon," where producers are able to hide in the sparsely populated areas of that region.[28]

(c) "The illicit traffic of firearms and the frontiers smugglers play a major role to arm the organized crime groups. They are supposed to exchange firearms for cocaine with terrorist groups from neighboring countries," in addition to investigations regarding the importation of illicit arms in the country through the ports of Santos and Rio de Janeiro.[29] There is evidence of the Russian Mafia, which has sponsored such activities in Latin America.[30]

(d) On the border with Paraguay, families have emerged to participate in the smuggling of illegal goods. These families have become more organized and have formed a structure akin to the one used by the American Mafia. Furthermore, they have begun to acquire political power and influence in certain regions of Paraguay, which leads them to expand their market. For instance, they participate in the trafficking of firearms because of the opportunity they have as buyers, as there are constant deliveries to the drug dealers in the slums of Rio de Janeiro.[31]

The Power of Borders

Brazil's size poses an increasingly important challenge to authorities supervising the flow of legal goods and fighting the trafficking of illegal goods.

The state does not have the capacity to effectively police a continent-sized country with over 16,000 kilometers of land borders. The Brazilian Federal Police, "a multi-mission agency with responsibilities ranging from investigating federal crimes and countering international drug trafficking to providing border control and immigration services,"[32] suffer from a severe shortage of agents. With fewer than 8,000 professionals, this organization is severely underresourced. The lack of professionals underscores the need for interagency cooperation in border security protection such as with the National Department of Public Safety (Secretaria Nacional de Segurança Pública), the Department of Federal Revenue (Secretaria da Receita Federal), the state police forces, and the armed forces.[33] The lack of professionalism also highlights the importance of state-level cooperation. In this sense, according to the International Narcotics Control Strategy Report,[34] "Brazil has signed bilateral narcotics control agreements with the U.S. and every country in the region." This is highly significant, as Brazil borders the three largest coca-cultivating countries in the world (Colombia, Bolivia, and Peru) as well as Paraguay, which is one of the largest producers of marijuana. Brazil and the United States are parties to a "mutual legal assistance treaty and a mutual assistance agreement on customs matters."[35]

These issues also impact security in Argentina and Paraguay. The tri-border area (TBA), including Foz do Iguaçu (Brazil), Puerto Iguazú (Argentina), and Ciudad del Este (Paraguay), is a prime location for organized criminal activities such as drug and weapon trafficking.[36] From there, merchandise, drugs, and weapons are transported to the states of Paraná and São Paulo and to other regions in Brazil.[37] In order to help combat organized crime, Brazil has also signed counternarcotics agreements with countries outside the Western Hemisphere, such as Japan, Italy, Spain, Portugal, and Lebanon and has formed alliances with the Organization of American States–Inter-American Drug Abuse Control Commission (Comisión Interamericana para el Control del Abuso de Drogas, OAS-CICAD), INTERPOL, and the United Nations Office on Drugs and Crime (UNODC).[38]

Illegal enterprises facilitate money laundering, tax evasion, counterfeiting of goods, police corruption, and immigration. The Brazilian government estimates that money laundering costs the country U.S.$12 billion per year. Social, economic, and geographical variables create a business environment conducive to transnational organized crime. Many of the illicit drugs, particularly cocaine and cannabis, enter the country across the border with Paraguay, thereby involving the Brazilian state in international trafficking from Bolivia, Colombia, and Peru.

The illegal products are then trafficked to consumers in Europe and the United States. Furthermore, the flow of cocaine goes via different routes, such as through Belém and other northern states, whose proximity allows access to Suriname and the Caribbean, or through the Amazon via Manaus.

The central axis of Brazil is no less important, as farms in Mato Grosso do Sul allow entry into the countryside of São Paulo, which includes the ports of Santos and Rio de Janeiro. These, in turn, distribute goods to criminal partners located in Africa. In 2009, Brazil was one of the most prominent transit countries for cocaine in the American hemisphere, especially in terms of shipments to Europe.[39]

The Paraguay–Rio de Janeiro–São Paulo axis has always been linked to trafficking of AK-47s and AR-15s to organized criminal networks located in the hills and slums[40] and in other parts of Brazil. These weapons are sometimes used in confrontations with police or by gangs as they fight for control. Land mines, antiaircraft weapons, machine guns, bazookas, and an extensive collection of automatic weapons have been found by the police. Rio de Janeiro's police helicopters have been shot at by drug dealers.[41] A civil war scenario has threatened both the police and civil society, which is exposed to constant shootouts.

The structural characteristics of drug trafficking in Brazil initially developed from the country's position as a transit country, not a producing or a consumer country. Transit-oriented activity helps organized criminal groups coordinate with both producing and consuming countries and, consequently, with large international cartels, such as those in the main centers of drug consumption and production. Brazilian drug dealers have adapted to market conditions, allowing them to establish effective ways to conduct business. Integration with other international drug-trafficking operations could lead to competition or rivalry with the large international cartels.

Filho and Vaz argue that the structure of drug trafficking in Brazil differs from that of other countries,[42] such as Colombia. They explain that the structure of drug trafficking in Brazil is linked to smuggling and institutional corruption. Organized criminal networks in Brazil have established connections with, especially, the Italian, Japanese, and Lebanese Mafias. Therefore, they have a solid command and operation structure but are less complex when compared to other organized criminal organizations and drug cartels.

The Strength of Organized Crime in the Brazilian Penitentiary System and Its Extension to Slums

According to Paixão, organized criminal groups date back to the 1970s and 1980s, with the inception of Falange Vermelha (Rio de Janeiro) and Serpentes (São Paulo).[43] In 1979, the Cândido Mendes Penal Institute (in Rio de Janeiro), a penitentiary built to house around 540 prisoners, housed over 1,200 men who struggled to survive as beggars in a veritable storehouse of the most criminal. It was known as the Devil's Cauldron because of the terror and bloodshed that occurred daily there.[44]

At that time, crimes related to bank robbery and drug trafficking required more efficient responses from law enforcement. Greater organizational capacity for handling these types of crimes resulted not only in economic gains, but also in prestige for some operating in the criminal world. This was one of the mechanisms that resulted in leaders forming criminal groups and demanding their own identity in the urban crime wave. Many crime bosses became stronger because they understood how to manipulate and monopolize the resources available in the prisons to accumulate wealth by participating in various illegal activities. Major studies indicate that the prison population comprises mostly persons with few personal resources. In other words, prisoners are susceptible to immediate influences and are quite vulnerable.[45]

The story of Comando Vermelho (Red Command) is one of the most remarkable stories of organized crime in Brazil. This organization began in a prison on Rio de Janeiro island known as Ilha Grande, the former Cândido Mendes Penal Institute, and operated with unprecedented control over the lives of many prisoners. Even behind bars, criminal networks controlled drug trafficking and other organized criminal activities on the streets.

As conceptualized by Amorim, some drug-trafficking revenue has been applied to improvements in the slums, including the construction of sewage systems.[46] Furthermore, drug traffickers have provided people living in the slums with security. In many cases, the slum residents have benefited from these initiatives, which may be related to the lack of social control by the authorities and the government.

Drug dealers use this strategy to gain the community's respect, although slum dwellers are often motivated by fear and coercion and are considered collaborators. The drug dealers' managers have been touted as ambassadors of crime or protectors of slum society. In many circumstances, groups involved in organized crime have a social impact, even providing basic public goods and services such as law and order, property-rights enforcement, dispute resolution, or basic forms of social security. In addition, "many such groups create livelihoods by connecting local drug producers with far-off consumers in global markets," demonstrating the weakness of state control and the state's failure to help poor citizens.[47]

Unfortunately, in Brazil's social reality, slums are characterized as communities without citizenship on the margins of society, which puts men, women, youth, children, and the elderly in the hands of this parallel power. Organized criminal networks have taken advantage of people living in poverty and started to control the slums. Most of the criticisms of police actions in the slums claim incompetence and lack of preparation for dealing with organized crime. However, it is important to note that the police face many tactical obstacles, such as the intricate design and construction that shape the slums and the organized military power, mainly weapons, accumulated by organized criminal networks.[48]

São Paulo is not an exception, as observed during the First Command of the Capital (Primeiro Comando da Capital, PCC) case. According to Lima, this organized crime group was formed around 1993, with its origins in the São Paulo state prison system.[49] PCC terrorized São Paulo in 2006 and used weapons against civilians and police authorities. More than 400 people were killed, and there were reports of riots that occurred in more than 70 prisons in the state. Driven by fear and insecurity, the city came to a halt.

This group's actions showed the power of organized crime and its impact on society. In the case of São Paulo, "the market is very fragmented, if compared to the highly organized cocaine-based one of Rio de Janeiro." There is, in this case, "an indefinite number of dealers and buyers, which results in strong competition. The city also has become the main route for international trafficking in Brazil, due to the proximity to the main harbor and the main international airport of the country."[50] These elements are crucial when analyzing drug trafficking in São Paulo.[51]

Slums and Organized Crime

These interconnections are part of a broader framework that sets up the structure of organized crime and its extensions, in the prisons as well as the slums. However, we cannot confirm the current number of slum dwellers involved in drug trafficking and organized crime. What we can say is that slums are part of national and international organized power

Table 16.2. Inhabitants of Brazil's slums, by municipality, population, and percentage of total, 2010–2011

Metropolitan region	No. of slum dwellers	Slum dwellers as % of total population
São Paulo	2,162,368	11.0
Rio de Janeiro	1,702,073	14.4
Belem	1,131,268	53.9
Salvador	931,662	26.1
Recife	852,700	23.2
Fortaleza	430,207	11.9
Grande São Luis	325,139	24.5
Manaus	315,415	15.0
Baixada Santista	297,191	17.9
Grande Teresina	154,386	13.4

Source: IBGE, "2010 Census: 11.4 Million Brazilians (6.0%) Live in Subnormal Agglomerates," Ibge.gov.br, December 21, 2011, http://censo2010.ibge.gov.br/en/noticias-censo?busca=1&id=3&idnoticia=2057&view=noticia.

relations. According to the Brazilian Institute of Geography and Statistics (Instituto Brasileiro de Geografia e Estatística, IBGE), Brazil has 11.4 million inhabitants living in slums, or 6 percent of the population (see table 16.2).[52] This survey indicates that the number of people living in slums has almost doubled since the early 1990s. In 1991, 4.48 million people lived in squatter settlements compared to 6.53 million in 2000. The metropolitan areas of São Paulo, Rio de Janeiro, and Belém together account for almost half (43.7 percent) of the total households considered irregular settlements. The slums' population profile, obtained by the IBGE, shows that the average age in these areas was 27.9 years in 2010, compared to 32.7 in the regular areas of the municipalities. A very young population—ranging from 6 or 7 to 14 years old—usually recruited by organized criminal groups, accounts for 28.3 percent of the total slum population. The average household density is higher in slums than in regular urban municipalities. This difference is more pronounced in the Southeast, South, and Midwest, but northern Brazil has the highest average household density in irregular settlements, for example, Amapá (4.5 people).[53]

Drastic inequalities, therefore, characterize the Brazilian system. Located primarily in metropolitan areas, slum dwellers are at a severe disadvantage compared with those who live in the "asphalt—decent conditions and infrastructure."[54] But they have some social indicators that are much better than those in small and medium-sized cities, especially in rural areas. Half of the Brazilian slum dwellers aged ten or older have a monthly income of up to 370 reais, equivalent to U.S.$200. In the slums, 8.4 percent of residents aged fifteen or older are illiterate.[55]

In terms of basic needs, one in four households in slums (27.5 percent) obtains energy illegally, and one in three (32.7 percent) has a poor-quality sewage system, as identified by the IBGE. The 2010 census data illustrate the precariousness of services in these areas. In urban areas of cities that have irregular slums, 11.5 percent have no regular access to energy, and 15 percent do not have adequate sewage. Slums are classified by IBGE as substandard clusters.

According to Zaluar and Alvito,[56] the attribution of the name *favela* seems to have several explanations. The most logical stems from the *favela*, a shrub common in the Northeast of Brazil where federal soldiers were fighting against a revolutionary movement aimed at keeping an autonomous community from central government control. This shrub was also found on the first hill to be occupied in Rio de Janeiro by those same soldiers, and the hill became known as Morro da Favela.[57] Today, the term *favela* refers to the slums built mostly along the hillsides of Rio de Janeiro and other Brazilian cities.

Carvalho and Hughet clearly explain the evolution of shantytowns by using the example of Rio de Janeiro. The first shantytown dates back to 1897 (Morro da Favela),[58] built to shelter men, women, and children who were not part of the republic's progressive project (see table 16.3).

People living in the slums suffer from prejudice and daily discrimination. Although many residents and workers do not participate in criminal activity, the association between living in a slum, crime, and drug trafficking is extended to all poor Brazilians. This association confuses poverty with crime, turning poor Brazilians into targets of inhumane treatment as victims of either traffickers or corrupt police officers.

Moreover, the fact that both aggressors and victims are mostly poor, the stereotype of the uneducated young black male stigmatizes an entire group of people. What happens in Brazil is seen as simultaneous separation and integration of the urban world of asphalt and the hills and slums and, ultimately, favors criminal organizations, which use the lack of a state presence to build themselves into a formidable power.[59] As a consequence, "organized crime subjected the *favela* communities to their economic and political interests and power, enforcing a kind of dictatorship, developing rules along with codes of conduct, and even tribunals held in the narrow alleyways of the *favelas*."[60] Sometimes honest citizens excluded from the

Table 16.3. Historical evolution of slums, Rio de Janeiro

Year	Key facts
1927	Eradication of *favelas*, regarded as the only way to eliminate slums, was "included in an official project aiming to remodel Rio de Janeiro"
1937	Elimination of the slums ("shantytowns"), called an "urban aberration," was again proposed
1945	"*Favelados*—(those who lived in the *favela*)—afraid of the threats of removal made several times by the public authorities in Rio, reacted for the first time, formulating a list of social rights regarding the infrastructure problems they faced"
1948	The first census of the *favelas* revealed that they were occupied by 7% of the city's population
1957	The Colligation of *Favela* Workers (Coligação dos Trabalhadores Favelados) was created to improve living conditions for people in poor communities
1968	To organize and oversee eradication of the *favelas*, the Coordination of the Habitation of Social Interest of the Metropolitan Area of Rio de Janeiro (Coordenação de Habitação de Interesse Social da Área Metropolitana do Grande Rio) was developed
1979	Promorar, a "habitation program that based its actions on basic sanitation, transference of property titles, and other important matters," was established by the military government. A registry of all *favelas* was made, and a "new municipal body was created to take care of their social development and the implementation of assistance services" within them
1991	A new census conducted by IBGE counted approximately 962,793 people living in Rio's *favelas*: in "forty-five years, the number of slum inhabitants had multiplied by seven"

Source: Clarissa Huguet and Ilona Szabó de Carvalho, "Violence in the Brazilian *Favelas* and the Role of the Police," *New Directions for Youth Development* 119 (2008): 93–109.

traditional systems may be included in parallel—often illegal—systems. This is what happens in slums, whose residents, excluded from the formal labor market and educational system, often end up included in the drug trade—the "parallel system."[61]

Slums are also viewed as a microcosm of the capitalist system, as a clear labor market works to achieve the highest positions in the hierarchy of organized crime. Young boys start as *fogueteiros*—using fireworks or kites to let people know that the police are coming. Then these boys become *vaporeiros*, drug distributors. They then become *novos soldados*, new soldiers, to defend the organization until they reach the next level, *gerentes de boca*—managers of a drug-distribution location. In sum, social marginalization leads to criminal marginalization. This hierarchical model provides the youth with a "feeling of power" and a "false perspective of career growth" derived from belonging to "a kind of organized group."[62]

As Barcellos' work suggests,[63] we must understand the relationships between the powerful and the oppressed as well as their relationships with the police in order to better understand the linkages and routes of organized crime in the slums. Barcellos describes the atrocities of the prison system and the various shapes of injustice and persecution.[64]

The map of violence and drug trafficking in the *favelas* has changed significantly, especially with the arrival of cocaine in the 1980s and the establishment and organization of drug factions. The emergence of cocaine in the retail drug market and its profitability were very critical to the establishment and development of the specific structure of armed groups and the high levels of violence associated with them.[65] In addition, with the emergence of the drug factions, a military structure was instituted either as a defense or because of invasions, and a division of labor was settled on for the preparation and sale of drugs. Dowdney highlights behavioral changes within the *favela* communities before the 1980s and their effects after the explosion of the drug business since 1990.[66] For Anjos, organized crime was born as a result of social exclusion.[67] Zaluar argues that traffickers who were born in slums are victims and are not responsible for trafficking in Brazil.[68] In Oliveira's opinion, the greatest contribution of Alba Zaluar is allowing researchers to conclude that, indeed, there is integration of poverty and drug trafficking, for example, in Cracolândia (Crackland) in downtown São Paulo.[69] This area has a high concentration of crack cocaine users, including children and adolescents. The highest rates, however, occur in Recife, Curitiba, and Vitória, which are also state capitals. Brazil needs to better implement the 2012 plan to deal with crack and other illicit drugs.[70]

Policy Recommendations

This chapter has examined some of the intrinsic aspects of organized crime in Brazil, its interconnections with the bordering countries of South America, and the criminal power in Brazilian prisons and its extension to the slums. It has also emphasized the challenges Brazil faces regarding the negative perception of and lack of confidence in institutions that are designed to address organized crime, such as the police and the judiciary. The discussion has underlined the proliferation of transnational crime groups and how Brazil has been inserted into the increasing globalization of drug consumption and international drug trade routes. As a result, these aspects contribute to the increasing levels of violence throughout the country, not only in the main capitals, but also in small and medium-sized municipalities. This is part of a complex situation that flourishes as a result of social and economic conditions that increasingly marginalize sectors of the population and because of the lack of a state presence.

The state needs to improve the quality of basic social services. Many segments of society lack access to quality education, public services, and employment, which makes them even more likely to work with organized crime in order to survive. The lack of basic services also triggers an alarming perspective with respect to the violence that affects civil society. In addition, it highlights the sheer power of the organized criminal networks and their ability to infiltrate and corrupt institutions.

Moreover, due to the proliferation of drug-smuggling routes as well as the fragmentation and dispersion of criminal groups in the hemisphere and the country (for example, the *maras*, or gangs, in some Central American countries; the Barrio Azteca prison gang in El Paso, Texas, and Juárez, Mexico; the Comando Vermelho in Rio de Janeiro;[71] or the PCC in São Paulo) or across subregions, policymakers must take action. Instead of watching this "epidemic" erode Brazilian society, the state should prioritize policies to prevent the proliferation and operation of organized criminal networks.

Intelligence services need more resources in order to combat organized crime. The police must be better equipped to fight drug dealers, who have an array of arsenals. The world has watched the battlefield of the slums in Rio de Janeiro, where the local police, sometimes supported by the national army, have had to invade areas controlled by drug traffickers in order to implement the so-called Police Pacification Units (Unidades de Polícia Pacificadora, UPPs).[72] This, however, is a long-term public management process and will not be resolved overnight.

Along with this scenario, if the same fragmented public security conditions prevail—inefficiency, corruption, violence, and racism—the overall situation cannot be significantly improved. It also is necessary to have more coordination between public leaders and other officials. As previously discussed, Brazil desperately needs to implement police reform, specifically in terms of training and psychological preparation. Society is tired of high levels of police corruption. Brazilians want freedom, security, and citizenship, values that need to be rescued from being swept away by criminal activity. As a result of the state's continuous failure to act, private security (at banks, shopping malls, houses, apartments, transport companies, and sporting events) has grown as a way to protect citizens and has become one of Brazil's most profitable businesses, reaching around U.S.$16 billion per year. Official statistics cite 2,000 private companies registered by the Ministry of Justice, which employ 600,000 professionals; the federal police and the state police have 500,000 agents.[73]

The historical character of Brazilian legislation is another fundamental aspect. The legislative definition of organized crime should be reviewed in accordance with social, economic, and technological changes observed not only in Brazilian society, but also in the structure of organized crime.

To some extent, the restructuring of the prison system, with its archaic structure, obsolete infrastructure, resource limitations, and endless corruption, is part of our policy recommendations. There is a lack of professionals prepared to deal with high-tech criminals inside and outside prison walls. As stated by the United Nations Office on Drugs and Crime, "organized crime takes advantage of new technologies and benefits brought by globalization to coordinate and lead their businesses from the most remote corners."[74] Few prisons are equipped with appropriate mechanisms for implementing security.

Our observations highlight some of the challenges and obstacles along the road to institutional reform to fight corruption and are frequently ignored. As emphasized by Bagley, "in the countries of Latin America and the Caribbean, the consequence of ignoring organized crime and its corrosive effects may well be institutional decay or democratic de-institutionalization."[75] In the case of Brazil, long-standing institutional weakness (and, in some cases, institutional decay) has enabled organized criminal networks to flourish. In order to successfully combat such networks, Brazil must strengthen the aforementioned institutions.

The phenomenon of globalization has resulted in ideal conditions for the rapid penetration and spread of transnational organized crime. It has opened new avenues for illicit activities, and not only dirty money but also political power influence organized crime's actions. Illicit global trafficking requires a combination of effective strategic actions by the government. In the case of Brazil, due to its physical size as well as "the large Amazon basin with its extensive river system, drug trafficking organizations can operate and elude law enforcement."[76]

According to the Brazilian minister of justice, José Eduardo Cardozo, "a new border control system was developed through the integration of Federal Government bodies—the Ministry of Justice, the Ministry of Defense, and other ministries, with State Governments and the strengthening of international relations with other countries."[77] The major goal of government policy is to strengthen this plan with better equipment and technology and to increase the number of law enforcement personnel on the borders.

Criminals bribe poorly paid civil, military, and state police. The situation also requires the recruitment of qualified federal police and customs agents. Nonetheless, the role and challenge of the state is to dismantle the corruption facilitated by the porous borders. The TBA is known for its lax immigration control so that anyone can easily obtain false documents from corrupt officials.[78] In addition to weapons and narcotics, a variety of counterfeit goods is trafficked between Paraguay and Brazil. Integration of South American policies is important so that all countries may play a meaningful role in combating criminal activities, for example, the dialogue between the UNODC and the Brazilian government to create a more relevant office in Brazil will play a bigger role in the formulation of public policies for all countries in the region.[79]

Ultimately, according to the 2011 UNODC report, Brazil represents one of the main markets for cocaine consumption, accounting for 33 percent of usage in South America, Central America, and the Caribbean.[80] A National Institute for Public Policy on Alcohol and Drugs study, coordinated by Ronaldo Laranjeira, reveals that, most likely, Brazil has become the largest crack market and the second-largest cocaine market in the world. Cocaine use has proliferated, and researchers' findings suggest that cocaine has become popular among the middle and lower-middle classes. Brazil's economic situation has contributed to this scenario, and the drugs' growing popularity reflects Brazil's role in the globalized narcotics trade market.[81]

The Latin America Commission on Drugs and Democracy proposes three main directives aimed at drug trafficking and consumption: (a) "treating drug users as a matter of public health"; (b) "reducing drug consumption through information, education and prevention"; and (c) "focusing repression on organized crime."[82] According to Mina Carakushansky, prevention is the policy that the Brazilian government should adopt to combat the spread of drugs in the country.[83]

Rousseff's government plans to invest a total of U.S.$4 billion in the Integrated Plan to Combat Crack and Other Drugs by 2014. The money will be invested in various integrated public policy plans and in various sectors such as health, education, social care, and public safety. Responsibility will be shared with states and municipalities that have committed to supporting these actions.[84]

In summary, policy should aim at prevention and providing treatment and rehabilitation for drug users and at combating drug trafficking and criminal organizations. Rehabilitation should be sustained by the following directives: (a) articulation in conjunction with areas of health and social care; (b) partnerships with states and municipalities to promote safe urban spaces; (c) strengthening intelligence and research on integration with state forces; (d) integrated intelligence between the federal police and the state police in addition to the reinforcement of the federal police and the federal highway police.[85]

Notes

1. See the introduction in this volume.

2. Jorge Armando Félix, "The Makings of Brazilian Drug Policy," in *New Approaches to Public Security and Drug Policy*, ed. International Council on Security and Development (Petrópolis, Brazil: Vozes, 2009), 21–24.

3. Ibid.

4. Ibid.

5. Ibid.

6. Ibid.

7. *Anuário brasileiro de segurança pública*, 5th ed. (Brazilian Forum of Public Security, Ministry of Justice, 2011).

8. Ibid.

9. Carlos Alberto Marchi de Queiroz, *Crime organizado no Brasil: Comentários à lei no. 9034/95. Aspectos policiais e judiciários, teoria e prática* (São Paulo: Esfera, 2005).

10. Milton Santos and Maria Laura Silveira, *O Brasil: Território e sociedade no início do século XXI*, 3rd ed. (Rio de Janeiro: Editora Record, 2001), 202.

11. Júlio Jacobo Waiselfisz, *Mapa da violência 2012: Os novos padrões da violência homicida no Brasil* (São Paulo: Instituto Sangari and Ministério da Justiça, 2011).

12. Michel Misse, "Crime organizado e crime comum no Rio de Janeiro: Diferenças e afinidades," *Revista Sociologia Política* 19, no. 40 (2011): 13–25.

13. C. C. Diniz and M. A Crocco, "Reestruturação econômica e impacto regional: O novo mapa da indústria brasileira," *Nova Economia* 6, no. 1 (1996): 77–103.

14. Ibid.

15. João Sabóia, "Desconcentração industrial no Brasil nos anos 90: Um enfoque regional," *Pesquisa e Planejamento Econômico* 30, no. 1 (2000): 69–116.

16. Instituto de Pesquisa Econômica Aplicada (IPEA), *Sistema de indicadores de percepção social: SIPS 2ª edição 2011/2012, Segurança Pública*, July 5, 2012, http://www.ipea.gov.br/portal/images/stories/PDFs/SIPS/120705_sips_segurancapublica.pdf.

17. A. Oliveira Júnior, "Dá para confiar nas polícias? Confiança e percepção da polícia no Brasil," *Revista Brasileira de Segurança Pública*, no. 9 (2011): 6–22.

18. Luiz Antonio Machado da Silva, "Sociabilidade violenta: por uma interpretação da criminalidade contemporânea no Brasil urbano," *Revista Sociedade e Estado* 19, no. 1, http://www.scielo.br/scielo.php?script=sci_arttext&pid=S0102-69922004000100004. See also Francisco Rojas Aravena and Luis Guillermo Solís Rivera, eds., *Organized Crime in Latin America and the Caribbean: Summary of Articles*, 1st ed. (San José, C.R.: Facultad Latinoamericana de Ciencias Sociales [FLACSO], 2009).

19. Luiz Eduardo Soares, "Public Security: Present and Future," *Estudos Avançados* 21, no. 56 (2007): 91–106.

20. Guaracy Mingardi, *O estado e o crime organizado* (São Paulo: IBCcrim, 1998); idem, "O que é crime organizado: Uma definição das ciências sociais," *Revista do Ilanud*, no. 8 (2008): 25–27.

21. Adriano Oliveira, "As peças e os mecanismos do crime organizado em sua atividade tráfico de drogas," *Revista de Ciências Sociais* 50, no. 4 (2007): 699–720.

22. Bruce M. Bagley, "Globalization and Transnational Organized Crime: The Russian Mafia in Latin America and the Caribbean," *Mama Coca*, October 31, 2001, http://www.mamacoca.org/feb2002/art_bagley_globalization_organized_crime_en.html.

23. Ibid.

24. Ruy Gomes Silva, "Effective Methods to Combat Transnational Organized Crime in Criminal Justice Processes," Resource Material Series, no. 58, United Nations Asia and Far East Institute for the Prevention of Crime and the Treatment of Offenders [UNAFEI], December 2001, http://www.unafei.or.jp/english/pages/PublicationsRMS.htm.

25. Ibid.

26. Ibid

27. Ibid.

28. Ibid.

29. Ibid.

30. See Bagley, "Globalization and Transnational Organized Crime."

31. Silva, "Effective Methods."

32. U.S. Department of State, *2012 International Narcotics Control Strategy Report, Volume I: Drug and Chemical Control*, Bureau for International Narcotics and Law Enforcement Affairs, March 2012, http://www.state.gov/documents/organization/187109.pdf.

33. Ibid.

34. Ibid.

35. Ibid.

36. Marcus Alan Fagner dos Santos Ferreira, "A guerra global contra o terrorismo na América Latina: A tríplice fronteira Argentina, Brasil e Paraguai como uma ameaça à segurança dos Estados Unidos," in *De Clinton a Obama: Políticas dos Estados Unidos para a América Latina,* org. Luis Fernando Ayerbe (São Paulo: Universidade Estadual Paulista [UNESP], 2009), 175–177.

37. Michael Lyman and Gary Potter, *Organized Crime*, 5th ed. (Upper Saddle River, N.J.: Prentice Hall, 2011).

38. U.S. Department of State, *2012 International Narcotics Control Strategy Report.*

39. Lyman and Potter, *Organized Crime.*

40. Misse, "Crime organizado."

41. Oliveira, "As peças."

42. Argemiro Procópio Filho and Alcides Costa Vaz, "O Brasil no contexto do narco-tráfico internacional," *Revista Brasileira de Política Internacional* 40, no. 1 (1997): 75–122.

43. Antonio Luis Paixão, *Recuperar ou punir? Como o estado trata o criminoso* (São Paulo: Cortez, 1987).

44. Regina Campos Lima, *A sociedade prisional e suas facções criminosas* (Londrina, Brazil: Edições Humanidades, 2003).

45. Sérgio Adorno and Fernando Salla, "Criminalidade organizada nas prisões e os ataques do PCC," *Revista Estudos Avançados* 21, no. 61 (2007): 7–29.

46. C. Amorim, *CV PCC: A irmandade do crime* (São Paulo: Record, 2003).

47. Ibid.

48. Lima, *A sociedade prisional.*

49. Ibid.

50. Guaracy Mingardi and Sandra Goulart, "Drug Trafficking in an Urban Area: The Case of São Paulo," in *Globalisation, Drugs and Criminalisation: Final Research Report on Brazil, China, India and Mexico,* ed. UNESCO/MOST and UNODCCP (Paris: UNESCO, 2002), 92–119.

51. Ibid.

52. IBGE, "2010 Census: 11.4 Million Brazilians (6.0%) Live in Subnormal Agglomer-ates," Ibge.gov.br, December 21, 2011, http://censo2010.ibge.gov.br/en/noticias-censo?busc a=1&id=3&idnoticia=2057&view=noticia.

53. Ibid.

54. Ibid.

55. Ibid.

56. A. Zaluar and M. Alvito, *Um século de favelas* (Rio de Janeiro: FGV, 2003).

57. Lícia Valadares, "Gênesa da favela carioca: A produção anterior às ciências sociais," *Revista Brasileira de Ciências Sociais* 15, no. 44 (2000): 5–34.

58. http://onlinelibrary.wiley.com/doi/10.1002/yd.275/abstract.

59. L. Dowdney, *Children of the Drug Trade: A Case Study of Children in Organized Armed Violence in Rio de Janeiro* (Rio de Janeiro: Viva Rio/ISER, 2003).

60. C. Huguet, "The Dictatorship of the Drug Traffic in the Slums of Rio de Janeiro vs. the International and National Human Rights Law," L.L.M dissertation, University of Utrecht, 2005.

61. Ibid.

62. Ibid.

63. Caco Barcellos, *Rota 66—A história da polícia que mata* (Rio de Janeiro: Editora Record, 2009).

64. Caco Barcellos, *Abusado—O dono do Morro Dona Marta* (Rio de Janeiro: Editora Record, 2005).

65. C. Amorim, *CV PCC: A irmandade do crime* (São Paulo: Record, 2003).

66. Dowdney, *Children of the Drug Trade*

67. Haroldo dos Anjos, *As raízes do crime organizado* (Florianópolis, Brazil: Instituto Brasileiro do Direito de Defesa, 2003).

68. Zaluar and Alvito, *Um século de favelas.*

69. Adriano Oliveira, "Tráfico de drogas, crime organizado, atores estatais e mercado

consumidor: Uma integração muito mais perversa," *Revista Espaço Acadêmico*, no. 42 (November 2004), http://www.espacoacademico.com.br/042/42res_oliveira.htm.

70. U.S. Department of State, *2012 International Narcotics Control Strategy*, http://www. state.gov/j/inl/rls/nrcrpt/2012/.

71. Bruce M. Bagley, *Drug Trafficking and Organized Crime in the Americas: Major Trends in the Twenty-First Century* (Washington, D.C.: Woodrow Wilson Center, Latin American Program, 2012).

72. Governo do Rio de Janeiro, "Conceito UPP: A polícia da paz," Secretaria de Segurança, accessed June 1, 2012, http://www.upprj.com/index.php/faq.

73. State of São Paulo, "O estatuto da segurança privada," July 30, 2012, http://www. defesanet.com.br/seguranca/noticia/7006/O-Estatuto-da-Seguranca-Privada.

74. United Nations Office on Drugs and Crime, "Uruguay y UNODC promueven discusión sobre la gestión de seguridad en el sistema penitenciario," UNODC.org, May 18, 2012, http://www.unodc.org/southerncone/en/frontpage/2012/05/18-uruguay-y-unodc-promueven-discusion-sobre-la-gestion-de-seguridad-en-el-sistema-penitenciario.html.

75. Bagley, *Drug Trafficking and Organized Crime*, 12, http://www.wilsoncenter.org/ sites/default/files/BB%20Final.pdf.

76. U.S. Department of State, *2012 International Narcotics Control Strategy*.

77. UNODC, interview with Brazilian minister of justice, José Eduardo Cardozo, March 13, 2012, http://www.unodc.org/southerncone/en/frontpage/2012/03/13-interview-jose-eduardo-cardozo.html.

78. Rex Hudson, *Terrorist and Organized Crime Groups in the Tri-Border Area (TBA) of South America*, Library of Congress, July 2003, http://www.loc.gov/rr/frd/pdf-files/TerrOrgCrime_TBA.pdf.

79. Ibid. See also http://ultimosegundo.ig.com.br/brasil/2012-09-05/brasil-e-o-maior-mercado-consumidor-de-crack-do-mundo-aponta-estudo.html.

80. UNODC, *World Drug Report, 2011* (New York, 2011).

81. Instituto Nacional de Ciência e Tecnologia para Políticas Públicas do Álcool e Outras Drogas (INPAD), accessed June 3, 2013, http://inpad.org.br/inpad/; http://www.ncbi. nlm.nih.gov/pubmed/21382116, accessed October 20, 2014.

82. Latin American Commission on Drugs and Democracy, *Drugs and Democracy: Toward a Paradigm Shift* (New York: Open Society Institute, 2008), http://www.plataforma democratica.org/Publicacoes/declaracao_ingles_site.pdf.

83. Comissão Brasileira sobre Drogas e Democracia, "Especialista defende política de prevenção contra drogas no Brasil," May 10, 2013, http://cbdd.org.br/pt/2013/05/10/ especialista-defende-politica-de-prevencao-contra-drogas-no-brasil/.

84. Brazil, "Programa Crack é possível vencer," http://www2.brasil.gov.br/crackepossive lvencer/programa.

85. Ibid.

17

Under (Loose) Control

Drug Trafficking in Argentina in Times of Paradigm Change

KHATCHIK DERGHOUGASSIAN AND GLEN EVANS

Argentina has become a leading country in the postprohibitionist debate toward a new paradigm[1] for the global antidrug regime.[2] Along with other Latin American countries, Argentina is now voicing doubts about the supposed virtues of the so-called war on drugs. It is emphasizing the need for a change in the dominant approach of repressive politics to better implement the principle of "shared responsibility" as it is framed in the document of the South American Council on the Global Problem of Drugs (Consejo Sudamericano sobre el Problema Mundial de las Drogas) of November 2011.[3] Moreover, Rafael Bielsa, the then head of the state agency in charge of the fight against drug trafficking and drug addiction–related problems since December 30, 2011, the Ministry for the Prevention of Drug Abuse and Drug Trafficking (Secretaría de Programación para la Prevención de la Drogadicción y la Lucha contra el Narcotráfico, SEDRONAR), criticized publicly the United Nations' Office on Drugs and Crime (UNODC) 2011 *World Drug Report*.[4] In that report, Argentina was the second major cocaine consumer in the Americas, after the United States, but the data used for the report dated from 2005.[5] According to Bielsa, cocaine consumption in Argentina had fallen to 0.9 percent among fifteen- to sixty-four-year-olds in the total population, which was within the regional average of consumption of 1 percent and was far less than the 2.6 percent claimed in the U.S. State Department and UN report. Furthermore, as the security minister argued, important increases in cocaine and marijuana seizures occurred in 2011 (6,306 and 92,615 kilos, respectively): "If more people die because of the war on drugs than consuming, then there you have empirical data," declared the head of SEDRONAR.[6]

The political controversy between Argentina and the United States concerning cooperation in antidrug policies with the end of Drug Enforcement Administration (DEA)–SEDRONAR joint operations in 2011 is only a small aspect of the highly complex issue of the drug problem in Argentina. Drug trafficking, in particular, refers to an activity involving multiple actors related to the production of primary materials, the processing or elaboration of the illicit substance, storage and transportation, distribution, sale and consumption, and money laundering.[7] Any effort to understand the phenomenon must examine the general characteristics of offer, demand, and the state's relationship with both.

This chapter proposes an analysis that will explore this threefold aspect of drug trafficking in Argentina to critically discuss the role that Argentina plays in the regional and international arena in terms of drug trafficking and consumption. Focusing on the threefold aspect of drug trafficking also reveals its "hybrid" nature, its impact on national and international security, and its role in spreading a new form of violence where the "other" is, in practice, unidentified, to be defined by the traditional "threat."[8] As a result of drug trafficking's hybrid nature, this chapter will adopt as a theoretical approach a combination of the illicit markets' perspective and the *problématique* of the phenomenon. In addition, this work will examine the structural approach used to study organized crime as an "industry of protection."[9]

The offer factor highlights the drug trafficking–organized crime nexus. It is well known that drug trafficking is the most lucrative business within the realm of organized crime; INTERPOL estimates the global production of cocaine and heroin at more than 800,000 kilos per year.[10] According to the UN's Human Development Report, in 1999, global drug trafficking represented 8 percent of the global trade.[11] The total volume of drug production and the large economic benefits that derive from its trade create incentives to perpetuate the interest of criminal organizations in every operation related to drug-trafficking activity.

It is important to underline that drug trafficking is not exclusive to organized crime; indeed, organized crime is the most efficient entity for this type of illicit business, but the offer side of the trifold aspect of drug trafficking also involves other factors. As for organized crime, not all criminal organizations are similar; however, when discussing the general characteristics of the phenomenon, scholars and analysts distinguish between organized crime (OC) and transnational organized crime (TOC). INTERPOL defines the former as groups with a corporate structure seeking to generate an income through illegal activities that often are based on fear and corruption.[12] The UN Vienna Convention against Organized Crime uses the same definition of OC but with some differences (considering, for instance, a group to be three or more people acting together over a period of time and expanding the concept in its second article). Specifically, the Vienna Convention's definition states that if the criminal activity involves more than one state, or when the preparation, planning, leadership, or control of same is undertaken in a state other than the one where it is committed, then the criminal activity is considered transnational.[13]

The offer factor in drug-trafficking activity involves all individuals and types of organizations that take part in any stage of the activity, from the production of primary materials to money laundering. Differentiating OC from TOC is often impossible. Conceptual abstractions are useful for rationalizing the phenomenon; however, the inherent dynamics of drug trafficking lead inevitably to a rapid diversification of each stage of the activity and, thus, make it complex. The diversity of the offer is such that there is a specific product for each consumer income level and also explains the high potential for territorial penetration of criminal groups.

The study of drug criminality cannot ignore the factor of "respected" citizens, the consumers, without whom the market cannot exist. Consumers make up the second element of our threefold analytical framework: the demand. Public demand for drugs generates "the incentives, the opportunities and the conditions for the emergence of different criminal modalities."[14] However, the border between the public demand for consumption and the victims of drug-related criminal activities is much more diffuse than in other criminal enterprises, such as prostitution. Among consumers one can identify those who participate in such activities from time to time and the addicts who constitute the core of the demand and, usually, are the victims of the dealers.

Next, it is important to consider the state's role in both offer and demand. Our point of departure, however, is prohibition, which makes the offer-and-demand dynamics illegal. Prohibition added to the resources that the state has for law enforcement purposes defines the margins of the risk that criminal organizations have to face when engaging in a specific activity. Prohibition also defines the price of the product or the service, as well as the profit that is expected. In Argentina, Law 17.818 (1968) and Law 19.303 (1971) establish, successively, a list of narcotics and another of psychotropic substances the circulation of which is not forbidden in the country but which needs to be under strict control. Decrees 722/91 and

299/10 provide further details about substances that could generate physical or psychological dependency as defined in the last paragraph of Article 77 of the Penal Code and whose use is subject to punishment measures set out in Law 23.737.

Successive international reports have considered Argentina a country of transit for Andean cocaine to markets in the United States and Europe. Nevertheless, there is convincing empirical evidence of increasing levels of consumption within the country, making it attractive also as an "emerging market." By the end of the first decade of the twenty-first century, drug-related violent episodes in the greater Buenos Aires metropolitan area, including the federal capital and suburban cities, were usually linked to disputes between local street dealers; however, they started to involve criminal elements from Colombian and Mexican cartels and revealed the increased importance that the Argentine pharmaceutical industry was gaining in the production of chemical precursors for cocaine production.

Following our threefold analytical framework, we offer, first, an analysis of what might be considered the "offer," or supply side, of drug trafficking in Argentina. Next, we focus on consumption, and, in the third section, we deal with state policies. Our conclusion brings together the results of our threefold analysis to rationalize the broader picture of drug trafficking in Argentina and to offer some preliminary reflections about future trends.

The Offer of Drugs: The Trademark of a "Transit" Country, the Importance of Chemical Precursors, and the Emerging "*Paco*" Industry

Since 1997, the first year the U.S. State Department published the *International Narcotics Control Strategy Report*,[15] Argentina has not been considered a major drug-producing country. In this first report, however, the authors mention that Argentina "faces a growing problem with illegal narcotics, both in domestic use and in the flow of drugs transiting its territory." In the following years, until 2011, the sections of the report dealing with Argentina use almost the same wording, stating that "Argentina is not a major drug producing country," but "remains a transit country for cocaine flowing from neighboring Bolivia, as well as for undetermined amounts moving in transit from Peru and Colombia" and for small amounts of Colombian heroin destined for the United States, primarily New York. In the 2009 report, Mexico is mentioned for the first time: "Argentina is . . . a source country for precursor chemicals, as well as a transshipment country for ephedrine being sent to Mexico." The impact of Mexico is repeated in the report the following year, but not in the 2011 report.

Within the offer variable, the State Department considered Argentina as a source of chemical precursors due to its advanced chemical production facilities; the concerns were higher in the 2006 report and remained high in the following ones, evolving into a tougher statement in 2011: "Argentina is one of South America's largest producers of precursor chemicals and remains a source of potassium permanganate."

While almost nonexistent in the reports, local production of cocaine is mentioned first in 2005, related to increased Colombian presence in the country, and considered a probable signal of "a new chapter in the global war on drugs, as Colombian narcotics traffickers search out alternative bases of operations and transit routes in response to the increased pressure of Plan Colombia." In 2007, "an increased number of small labs converting cocaine base to cocaine hydrochloride" was reported, and in the following years, "small labs" are repeatedly mentioned as part of the drug enterprise. According to the State Department, marijuana from neighboring Paraguay is the most consumed drug in Argentina; however, the 2011 report emphasizes the sharply rising demand for cocaine, claiming that "the country has the second largest internal cocaine market in South America after Brazil." Finally, though Argentina is not considered a major money-laundering center, money-laundering activity always appears as a "concern" in the reports.

The lack of the development of a drug industry in Argentina (with, perhaps, the exception of synthetic drugs such as amphetamines and ecstasy) is not surprising.[16] But drugs have been transiting through Argentina since the 1980s, when security forces started to report seizures of small quantities of cocaine from foreign visitors. The seizure of 600 kilos of cocaine on a ship transporting shrimp and another 700 kilos from another one upon its arrival in Philadelphia, both embarking from the Argentine city of Mar del Plata, revealed the seriousness of the problem of drugs leaving the country.[17] From this first reported important seizure, drug trafficking increased in Argentina to reach an average of one ton per day of cocaine destined to Europe and the United States by the end of the 1990s,[18] making Argentina a central transit point, especially after the pressure put on goods exported from Bolivia, Colombia, and Peru.[19]

With approximately 1,079 miles of border with Paraguay, an important source for marijuana production destined to Argentina, Brazil, and Chile, and around 467 miles with Bolivia, a major producer of cocaine hydrochloride, Argentina "naturally" would become interesting to drug traffickers. Drugs enter Argentina illegally across the borders mostly, but the use of small airplanes has become more frequent. In March 2000, Operation Vigía II registered thirty unidentified flights in three days landing in abandoned areas mostly in the northern provinces of Misiones and Corrientes.

Another indicator of drugs coming into Argentina is drug seizures by police and other security forces. Critics maintain that the serious deterioration of vigilance over Argentine airspace, especially after 2001 because of successive budget cuts, is the main cause of this situation, even though in 2004 the government decided to implement a plan for eleven new radar installations to cover all the national territory.[20]

Still another indicator of Argentina's position as a transit country for drugs destined to Europe and the United States is systematic police and other security forces' reports on seizures. The problem is a lack of shared criteria to use to define how to elaborate the central database of reliable statistics. Despite the creation of the National Directorate of Criminal Intelligence (Dirección Nacional de Inteligencia Criminal, DNIC) in 2001 as mandated by the National Intelligence Law (25.250), there is no systematic data collection, and implementation of the law faced political and bureaucratic obstacles.[21] Since the creation of the Ministry of Security in December 2010, an effort has been made to centralize the information of the Federal Police (Policía Federal Argentina, PFA), the National Gendarmerie (Gendarmería Nacional Argentina, GNA), the National Coast Guard (Prefectura Naval Argentina, PNA), and the Airport Security Police (Policía de Seguridad Aeroportuaria, PSA).

A critical analysis of information provided in 2009, 2010, and 2011 by these four security forces leads to three basic observations regarding the quality of the data. First, almost all seizures refer to marijuana and cocaine hydrochloride, which reached 52,018 and 3,957 kilos, respectively, in 2009 (see figure 17.1).

Second, the GNA was revealed to be the most competent security force in drug seizures: 32,561 kilos of marijuana and 3,163 kilos of cocaine in 2009. The PNA seized 19,407 kilos of marijuana and 40 kilos of cocaine, and the PSA seized 50 kilos of marijuana and 753 kilos of cocaine in the same year. The proportion of seizures was similar in 2010 and 2011 (see figure 17.2).

Third, the overall quantity of drug seizures, especially of cocaine (see figure 17.3) is much lower than hypothesized by the judiciary and other authorities and by private researchers. Even with the additional statistics

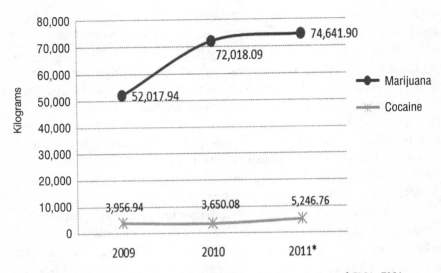

Figure 17.1. Marijuana and cocaine seizures during implementation of GNA, PNA, and PSA procedures, 2009–2011 (compiled by author from 2011 Argentine police force records).

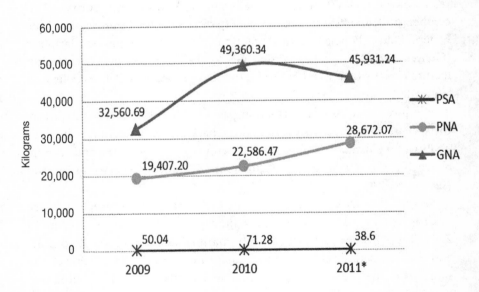

Figure 17.2. Marijuana seizures during implementation of GNA, PNA, and PSA procedures, 2009–2011 (compiled by author from 2011 Argentine police force records).

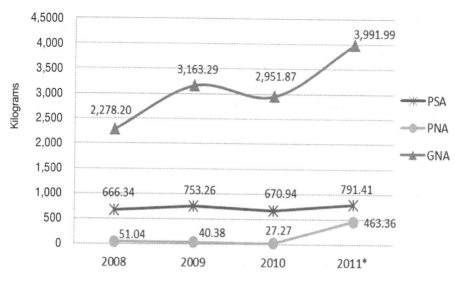

Figure 17.3. Cocaine seizures during implementation of GNA, PNA, and PSA procedures, 2008–2011 (compiled by author from 2011 Argentine police force records).

provided by the PFA between January and October of 2011, 5,759 kilos of cocaine were seized, much less than what was estimated to be transiting in the country per year in the 1990s.[22]

Concerning the offer variable, though Argentina lacks the climatic conditions of the Andean countries that would make it an important coca leaf producer, its developed chemical industry nevertheless provides many of the precursors needed to transform the coca leaf into cocaine. In other words, chemical precursors shift the drug flows to Argentina, usually on the Argentine-Bolivian border or toward Paraguay—the tri-border area to be triangulated later to Colombia and Mexico. The same procedure is observed concerning chemical precursors, such as ephedrine for ecstasy, needed for the production of synthetic drugs. Article 24 of Law 23.737 requires companies dealing with these kinds of products to report their activities annually to the National Register for Chemical Precursors (Registro Nacional de Precursores Químicos, RENPRE), which, in turn, provides police and security forces information about the destination of each shipment. Nevertheless, considering the annual budget of RENPRE and the number of personnel, it is easy to see why its usefulness for control is fairly limited. In fact, RENPRE has so far proven useful only for generating a list of companies that are dedicated to the production and commercialization of chemical precursors and for fixing the amount that each company is officially permitted to produce of a given product.

One of the hypotheses that police and security forces are considering maintains that the complications that the triangulation of chemical precursors generate added to the paperwork that the authorities impose on the companies for official permission for export might be leading to the proliferation of small laboratories where the coca leaf is processed. While the seizure of these laboratories, commonly known as "kitchens" (*cocinas*), is reported from time to time,[23] it is very difficult to prove this hypothesis. One of the indicators police and security forces deal with is the rise in consumption of the residual product known as "*pasta de base*" (PBC, cocaine base), or "*paco*," from the manufacture of cocaine in the metropolitan area of Greater Buenos Aires and the capital city. For instance, according to a study using official figures from SEDRONAR (2008) and UNODC (2009),[24] the percentage of high school students consuming *paco* was 0.5 in 2001 and 1.4 in 2007. One of the earliest studies on the proliferation of the kitchens maintains that government concern dates to 2000, but the number of kitchens started to show a sustained increase in 2002. Greater quantities of PBC circulating suggest a

> relocation of the cultivation-production-exportation circuit . . . the cocaine industry is modifying, and it is not the product ready for consuming and export that enters Argentina anymore; according to this hypothesis, it is basic cocaine that is currently imported from Bolivia and Peru to be manufactured into its final phase in clandestine laboratories in Argentina and to be distributed in the local market or exported to "attractive" international markets. The modality for local manufacture of cocaine allows that "intermediate products" (such as "*paco*") circulate in the neighboring locations of these laboratories and become a minor branch of the big cocaine business.[25]

Demand: Drug Consumption in Argentina

At first glance, drug consumption is on the rise in Argentina. As was the "transit country" trademark, "the second largest consumer country" in South America is now a major characteristic of Argentina. Numbers certainly are eloquent in this sense; there are objective indicators that Argentines were consuming more drugs in the first decade of the twenty-first century. However, discovering the reasons for this increase is far more complicated than reporting them.

Like crack in the United States in the 1980s, *paco* in post-2001 Argentina is the drug of the poor. It costs barely 10 percent of cocaine; it also causes more severe damage and is more rapidly addictive. It is not difficult, then, to understand why consumption rises in the poorest neighborhoods and consumers are teenagers, sometimes even children.

But when talking about the causal relationship between poverty and PBC consumption, prudence must be the rule. Individuals who are less wealthy do not consume PBC because they cannot afford cocaine; *paco* became popular mainly because of the relocation of the cultivation-production-export circuit mentioned in the previous section after the 2001–2002 social and economic crisis. "PBC did not get in because of poverty," notes a research paper on the *paco* market in the Southern Cone. "It gets in because there are laboratories, because without laboratories there would not be PBC; therefore, what appeared is the laboratory, and once it is installed it also finds a market for residual cocaine. It means that without laboratories there would not be *paco*; as for laboratories, they are not built to sell *paco*, but to manufacture cocaine."[26]

This leads us to focus on the impact of the 2001–2002 collapse of the economy. The widespread social crisis is probably a major explanatory factor when analyzing the relationship between PBC consumption and poverty. If laboratories were built in a country with no tradition of drug manufacturing, then the reason was that the conditions were there, especially a demand for jobs. Of course, laboratories also helped spread consumption; they almost created a market for *paco* following the logic of supply-side economics, but they primarily created jobs. Market-oriented reforms in the 1990s resulting from the Washington Consensus led not only to deindustrialization but also to a dramatic rise in unemployment and the marginalization of large sectors of the low-income population. The drug business became, first, a form of survival, and, later, generated true "socialization" of PBC in the poorest neighborhoods, where it became a family business.

In this sense, and very ironically, of course, the socialization of PBC signals the reindustrialization of the country, though no modernization is to be expected, nor would the sectors dedicated to the production and distribution of PBC see any upward movement in social mobilization, a higher standard of living, or brighter expectations for the future. Though certain mass media create an image of all-powerful drug dealers operating in the poorest neighborhoods of the Greater Buenos Aires metropolitan area, the bosses of the PBC business in marginal zones "are just the poor uncles of the business compared to those who run the exports and are related to big financial capitals."[27]

To understand whether the current stage of drug consumption in Argentina is responding to higher demand or not, it is important to examine the periodization of the phenomenon and look beyond statistics. The most interesting study of the historical evolution of massive consumption of drugs in Argentina is a document prepared within the context of the national politics of prevention education.[28] Five consecutive periods of consumption of different drugs were identified. As in the rest of the world, drug consumption started to be perceived as a problem by the mid-1960s, when marijuana was the most popular drug.

During the troubled 1965–1975 period, marijuana was associated with rebellious youth to such an extent that during a television show, the then minister of health and social action, José López Rega, and the U.S. ambassador in Argentina, Robert Hill, made public a bilateral agreement to fight drugs, maintaining that the primary consumers of drugs in Argentina were the guerrillas; therefore, the antidrug campaign would be an antiguerrilla campaign.

This linkage would be deepened during the 1976–1982 military dictatorship, when drugs became a social problem, and the consumer was profiled as a threat to security. Cocaine displaced marijuana as the "queen" of illicit drugs in 1983–1991, when the war on drugs appeared on the international and, particularly, the Latin American security agenda.

The once-criminal figure of the consumer was modified to a "sick person" with the return to democracy as a way to mark the distance from the repressive policies of the military government. It was also in this same period that the previously limited consumption of cocaine became massive and reached every level of society. Despite the "zero tolerance" policy that the Menem government declared in 1989, the 1992–2002 decade witnessed further expansion of drug consumption. Marijuana consumption became not only acceptable but even something to be expected in youth circles. A relationship between HIV/AIDS and drug consumption was revealed in 1998, when 41 percent of the people suffering from AIDS admitted having injected heroin, and synthetic and experimental drugs made their way into the circles of wealthier individuals. It also was a period during which drug consumption trends differed between the nouveau riche and the massive numbers of poor people: ecstasy, popper, ketamine, and powder amphetamine for the former, PBC, glue, and other cheap drugs for the latter.

The 2001–2002 crisis triggered a rise in all sorts of consumption and abuse, including of alcohol, cigarettes, and psychotropics, which generated the concept of "the medicating of everyday life."

The current period of drug consumption, starting in 2002, is characterized as "massification" (*masificación*), in which, for different reasons, the consumption of different sorts of drugs, both legal and illegal, is becoming widespread. The massification process does not mean that it is not possible to classify consumption and identify sectors of society for each; rather, it reflects a major acceptance of, if not tolerance for, the phenomenon. Thus, with respect to illegal drugs, the consequences of the strong social polarization of the 1990s also typifies consumption, with PBC becoming part of the marginalized neighborhoods' landscape, whereas more natural or synthetic, sophisticated drugs appear in the urban nightlife of the middle and upper classes as part of recreation. In both cases, however, there is also major access to illegal drugs, and in one way or another, drugs have become a "necessary" recreational consumer good, especially for young people.

From the historical perspective of drug consumption in Argentina, and inserted into the particular social, political, and cultural context of each period, the rise in demand after 2002 is not a unique phenomenon, but should be understood as a wider, almost global, trend in the history of drug consumption. This does not make drugs unproblematic in Argentina, nor does it imply that with the massification of consumption, drug-related violence is of less concern. It simply means that demand as a statistical number cannot, per se, explain changes in drug-trafficking trends in Argentina or the drop in drug-related violence. Thus, the following section deals with state policies concerning both consumption and the fight against trafficking; we leave our reflections on the most troublesome aspect of drugs—violence—for the conclusion, as we believe it is basically drug violence that should drive any normative judgment about drug trafficking.

State Policies: From Repression to Postprohibition and Persistent Failure

Argentina adopted a prohibitionist way of dealing with drug consumption in 1926, when the Legislature, responding to demands from the Federal Police, contemplated criminalization for the first time. The PFA had created its own Addiction Cabinet (Gabinete de Toxicomanía) in 1921.

In 1963, Argentina ratified the Single Convention on Narcotic Drugs of 1961, thereby moving toward a prohibitionist/repressive model. In 1968, personal consumption ceased to be a crime though the legislation against trafficking became tougher. The same year, some Argentine police officers traveled to the United States for special training on fighting drugs and trafficking.

A nationwide group of police forces was formed, and cooperation with international organizations began. In 1974, one year after the creation of the DEA in the United States, President Richard Nixon declared heroin the "non-economic number one public enemy." That same year in Argentina, Law 20.771 instituted a prison term from one to six years for any person who was caught possessing drugs, even if only for personal use. It was the toughest prohibitionist measure ever implemented in Argentina, as drugs became associated with subversion and, more specifically, the guerrillas.

The repressive/prohibitionist policy was expanded during the 1976–1983 dictatorship, and the Colavini sentence in 1978 demonstrates the depth of the repression. Ariel Colavini, who was arrested on the charge of possessing two marijuana cigarettes, was condemned to two years in prison because, as the court declared, "the use of drugs represents a danger for collective ethics."

With democracy restored in 1983, the drug user was identified as a sick person who needed help. State policies shifted from repression to prevention, and reforms were introduced in police structures to deal with drug problems. Citing Article 19 of the National Constitution, which protects private actions that do not harm public order, the Supreme Court in 1986 declared Law 20.771 unconstitutional.

In 1989, a new law, 23.737, reduced the sentence for drug possession to one month to two years and created SEDRONAR. Ten years later, in 1999, SEDRONAR released the first national statistics on drug consumption, revealing a total population of 600,000 using drugs, 200,000 of them on a regular basis. As a result of active mobilization of civil society organizations, Argentina started to move even farther away from prohibitionist policies with the first implementation of harm-reduction strategies in 2000. These strategies became increasingly important with the emergence of PBC in 2001 as the dominant drug in the most vulnerable sectors of the population.

The first National Conference on Drug Policies was held in 2003, opening public debate on the decriminalization of possession, the geopolitics of drugs, and the sociocultural context of drug use. In 2005, Law 26.052

federalized drug policies while still allowing each state to assume the responsibility for the investigation of smaller infractions, such as possession. One year later, a committee of scientists was created within the Ministry of Justice and Human Rights to propose legal reforms to deal with the issue of drugs.

A major step toward decriminalization was taken in 2009, when the Supreme Court, considering the Arriola case, declared unconstitutional the second paragraph of Law 23.737, which forbade possession of drugs for personal use. This opened the way to new legislation that excluded the persecution of drug users and the criminalization of poverty.[29]

This process explains Argentina's active international engagement with decriminalization as described at the beginning of this chapter. As in many countries, Argentina's drug policies started from a prohibitionist position and generated repressive measures during the 1976–1983 dictatorship, when the local variant of the war on drugs was tied to the rhetorical association of drug consumption and the guerrillas.

With the return of democracy, a long but firm postprohibition process started. Argentina never adhered to President Reagan's crusade against drugs in the 1980s, which became the dominant U.S. policy. One could argue that Reagan's war on drugs targeted the offering of drugs, more specifically, production and transport to the United States, and Argentina has never been at center stage for this.

Another reason why the war on drugs did not make its way onto Argentina's political agenda was its explicitly military dimension. In addition to suspicions that the war on drugs was nothing more than a new "role" for the Latin American military designed by Washington when its strategy shifted from supporting military coups to engagement with democracy in the region, for Argentina any military involvement in internal affairs meant a violation of the National Defense Law (23.554), which strictly limits the role of the armed forces to external threats. Even in the 1990s, during Menem's unconditional alignment with the United States, and despite two successive attempts from Washington and the temptation in Buenos Aires to accept the extension of the alignment to drug policies, public opinion in Argentina was against any move that might generate military involvement within the national borders.

It is not clear whether the reluctance of Argentina to assume a role in the war on drugs is why the country moved toward postprohibition; perhaps antiprohibition has deeper social motivations related to the rejection of repressive policies in general, considering the traumatic experience of the country during successive military regimes. However, though antiprohibition sentiment is widely accepted and supported, the fight against drug trafficking in Argentina is still limited to the prosecution of consumers and small distributors, which might be an obvious paradox. One of the reasons is that until 2009, when prosecution for personal use of drugs was declared unconstitutional, police and security forces were enforcing following Laws 20.771 (1974) and 23.737 (1989). According to Corda, "the implementation of the law falls upon actors of minor importance and easy to arrest and appears to be linked to the increasing incarceration of the population in vulnerable positions, particularly women and strangers."[30]

Marcelo Sain pushes the criticism even further by asserting the failure of drug-control policies based on prohibitionist perspectives and the persistence of deficient strategies dating back to the 1970s and deepened in the 1980s and 1990s. The increase and diversification of production, trafficking, sale, and consumption of drugs since 2000 has exposed this failure, which is, according to Sain, due to a lack of modernization of all state structures dealing with the issue. "Our country does not have a single police force specializing in drug-control issues, which, among other things, has produced notable institutional fragmentation, the most eloquent expression of which is the autonomy of each security force to formulate and implement its own strategies and actions against this criminal problem."[31] Sain maintains that institutional holes persist, and the fact that drug seizures do not, in general, lead to the arrest of important traffickers indicates the high level of corruption in police circles.

Separating addiction from trafficking is a good start; however, Argentina's uncertain position toward drug-control policies is notorious for its dual dimension: "The first is a situational precariousness as a consequence of an increase in consumption and abuse of legal and illegal drugs, and, therefore, the gradual structuring of a highly diversified and differentiated local market. The second is an institutional precariousness that is manifested in the development of drug trafficking as a criminal enterprise, also expanding and diversifying, with a very high level of state protection in the form of police corruption."[32]

Argentine society, in turn, has shown a lack of interest in the issue, as two socially accepted discourses suggest: Argentina has always been a transit country; the real problem is generated in developed countries, which fail to reduce drug consumption. "Both narratives successfully hid the fact that in Argentina, as a transit country, drug trafficking has substantially transformed, increased, diversified, became more complex, mixed with legal, social, and economic initiatives, and penetrated certain political and institutional circles, and cultural, social, economic, and structural political-institutional conditions determined or favored this process."[33]

Sain concludes that criminal groups dedicated to drug trafficking did not act autonomously, but grew from their initial embryonic form under police tutelage, when local demand was increasing and the structure of the market was forming. As the local market is still relatively small and does not favor the formation of bigger criminal groups with a solid economic base to penetrate the state or challenge it with violence, this particular police–drug dealer interaction and arrangement allows some control of the outbreak of violence inherent in the drug business.

This mechanism of control would have not been possible without the lack of governance over public security issues and their constant delegation to the police, coupled with the inefficiency of the law enforcement and security system. "All this has generated a novel form of urban marginality where common criminality proliferates and, in this context, the distribution, sale, and consumption of drugs within or outside these real 'ghettos' has become a new feature, an activity with a notorious impact on these shantytowns and their neighborhood."[34]

Sain's analysis shifts our perspective from the political economy of offer and demand to the structure of criminality. In fact, as early as 2003, when *paco* had already made its way into a crisis-shaken country, Juan Gabriel Tokatlian formulated the concept of the Triple P, standing for "policía, pandillas and políticos," or police, gangs, and politicians, to alert the authorities to the emergence of structural bases of a criminal enterprise beyond control. In an op-ed column in the Argentine newspaper *La Nación*,[35] which has been widely cited, Tokatlian argued that criminal gangs searched for liberated zones in which to operate; the police agreed to leave urban and suburban spaces under their control, sharing part of their profit and assuring that violence did spread beyond that space; and politicians simply looked the other way either because they had delegated autonomy to the police for the administration of public security or because they had granted favors that the police could provide, especially during election periods.

The lack of a social and political consensus for dealing with the situation led to the emergence and consolidation of a subculture of violence that is accepted and assimilated. Sain, who has authored two books on the police in Argentina,[36] refers to the same "crime coalition" as conceptualized by Tokatlian, although he focuses more on the failure of police reform after the return of democracy.

Drug trafficking in Argentina is best understood within the structure of the Triple P. On the one hand, Argentine society has shown a firm conviction to leave behind prohibitionist policies, which are repressive, inefficient, and a stubborn leftover from the bloody 1976–1983 dictatorship; the state's response has been to separate consumption from trafficking, adopt preventive policies, implement harm-reduction strategies, and become actively engaged in the regional and international arena in promoting the decriminalization of drugs. On the other, the historical evolution of drug trafficking has, since the 2001–2002 crisis and collapse, created a local market where drugs, both PBC and more sophisticated drugs, circulate in all sectors. This local market is the consequence of the increased transit of Andean cocaine, increased consumption, and the growth of small-scale kitchens. Drug-trafficking criminality has taken on a structural aspect with the emergence of the Triple P "crime coalition," which, on the one hand, assures containment of drug-related violence, and, on the other, perpetuates the subculture of violence, which is gradually being accepted and ignored by society.

Conclusion: The Risky Gamble of Loose Control

As Juan Cruz Vázquez says, "there is no last word or full stop for drug trafficking."[37] Today, drug trafficking is a public topic in Argentina. Of all the movies that include the issue of drugs, *Paco* (2010, directed by Diego Rafecas) is perhaps the one that, though fictional, nevertheless addresses directly the most dramatic aspect of Argentina's drug reality. While the progressive engagement of the government in preventive policies instead of repression is, overall, the right direction for a solution to the problem, the subculture of violence that the drug reality has created and is feeding persists, along with a criminal structure of Triple P that pretends to maintain drug trafficking under "loose control." For investigative journalist Mauro Federico, drug trafficking in Argentina has become dramatic since Andean cocaine ceased only to transit from the country and started to feed local networks "under the control of groups with operational capability and political protection . . . The overall picture becomes darker with policemen surprised with cocaine shipments, judges that undo international orders of capture, politicians involved in the killings of traffickers, street fights between different gangs, and lack of proper financial controls in dirty money laundering cases."[38] Yet perhaps the most troubling part of his investigation is the increasing preference of Colombian traffickers for Argentina as their residence because of the many advantages of the country as a transit route to Europe: "Little risk for extradition, higher prices, fewer risks of interception than the risk of shipments to North America, and no conflict with powerful Mexican cartels," according to a member of Colombia's Secret Service.[39] In fact, since the mid-1990s and after the dismantlement of the Medellín and Cali cartels, Colombian traffickers, their family members, including Pablo Escobar's widow,[40] have become frequent visitors to Argentina, mostly to invest drug money in the booming real estate market. As long as they did not bring any trouble, as long as Argentina maintained its reputation as the "poster child" of the Washington Consensus and the "special" relationship with the United States was not endangered, the Menem administration did not object to any flow of money. The troubles started with the post-1998 recession and the stricter control on suspicious financial flows demanded by international organizations.

After the 2001–2002 socioeconomic collapse, the presence of Colombians, Mexicans, and others involved in drugs became much more problematic. As reported by Federico, the Antidrug Association of the Argentine Republic (Asociación Antidroga de la República Argentina) has warned of a slow but firm "cartelization" of the country since 2001, with Peruvian, Bolivian, Dominican, and Paraguayan cartels silently installed in the national territory with the aim of taking total charge of the business, including distribution in the shantytowns of Greater Buenos Aires.[41]

Whether the term "cartelization" reflects an objective reality still needs to be discussed, but drug-related violence involving Colombian and Mexican citizens has made the news in Argentina more frequently since the shooting of two former right-wing paramilitaries in the parking garage of the Unicenter shopping mall on July 24, 2008. They were executed by Jairo "Mojarro" Saldarriaga, who killed them by order of his boss, Daniel "El Loco" Barrera Barrera. Mojarro, in turn, was killed on April 17, 2012, by order of his own boss, who, apparently, suspected that he had betrayed him and handed police a shipment of 500 kilos of cocaine. According to press reports, Mojarro traveled in Argentina under the auspices of a local operator who had a relationship with Juan Galvis Ramírez, assassinated on February 23, 2009, in San Fernando (Province of Buenos Aires). Mojarro's lawyer declared that he came to Argentina with his wife because he feared for his life in Colombia and was living under his real name, though it is known that he frequently visited the country using a false passport with the name Carlos Brausin García. Two Colombian drug dealers—Luis Calceido Velandia, alias "Don Lucho," and Ignacio "Nacho" Álvarez Meyendoff—

were arrested on April 12, 2010, and April 24, 2011, respectively, in the upper-class neighborhoods of Palermo and Puerto Madero in Buenos Aires and extradited to the United States at Washington's demand. The brother of the latter, Fernando Álvarez Meyendoff, seen in the Palermo district of Buenos Aires, is also on the U.S. list of wanted traffickers. All three men have connections with El Loco.

The last episode of the Colombian saga is the so-called Operativo Luis XV on Good Friday, April 6, 2012, a police operation in the Nordelta district, with thirty arrested, half of them Colombians, including a former wife of El Loco now married to an Argentine.[42]

At first glance, Colombian drug traffickers come to Argentina looking for a new life. This explains why they mostly live in upper-class neighborhoods. Their killing might be more related to revenge than to ongoing business. Yet it is naïve to think that, once in place, if local conditions are propitious, they will resist the temptation to go back into the drug business. What is true for Colombians might also be true for Mexicans and others. The question, therefore, is what will happen to the loose control on the drug trafficking created by the Triple P structure? Will there be stronger transborder relations that will end up challenging the status quo and trying either to penetrate the state or to wage a war?

Of course, there is always the hope for better institutionalization of the struggle against drug trafficking and the implementation of structural reforms of criminal intelligence, police, and other security forces. The struggle against drug trafficking is the necessary complement to the Argentine state's progressive approach to the addiction problem. It is actively engaged internationally with regard to decriminalization of consumption and the development of harm-reduction strategies, not under the illusion that the problem will have a final solution anytime soon, but for the sake of closing the social fracture that drug trafficking has created between the poor and marginalized sectors devastated by *paco*, the subculture of violence, and the middle and upper classes, where drugs has become part of their entertainment.

Notes

1. Thanks to Uriel Kuzniecki and Antonella Guidoccio for their assistance.
2. Juan Gabriel Tokatlian and Ivan Briscoe, "Conclusion: Illicit Drugs and New Paradigm: Towards a Post-Prohibitionist Debate," in *Drugs and Prohibition: An Old War, a New Debate*, ed. Juan Gabriel Tokatlian (Buenos Aires: Libros del Zorzal, 2010).

3. Emilio Ruchansky, "Un pensamiento propio," *Página/12* (March 11, 2012): 18–19.

4. United Nations Office on Drugs and Crime (UNODC), *World Drug Report, 2011* (New York, 2011), http://www.unodc.org/documents/data-and-analysis/WDR2011/World _Drug_Report_2011_ebook.pdf.

5. Ibid.

6. Raúl Arcomano, "Un *revival* de la lucha antidrogas," *Miradas al Sur* (March 11, 2012): 29. All translations are ours unless otherwise noted.

7. Juan Cruz Vázquez, *La sombra del narcotráfico: Una amenaza global* (Buenos Aires: Capital Intelectual, 2011), 22–26.

8. Ibid., 13.

9. For our theoretical perspective we have considered the following authors and texts: Mónica Serrano, "Transnational Organized Crime and International Security: Business as Usual?" in *Transnational Organized Crime and International Security: Business as Usual?* ed. Mats Berdal and Mónica Serrano (Boulder, Colo.: Lynne Rienner, 2002), 13–36; Richard Friman and Peter Andreas, "Introduction: International Relations and the Illicit Global Economy," in *The Illicit Global Economy and State Power*, ed. H. Richard Friman and Peter Andreas (New York: Rowman & Littlefield, 1999), 1–23; Diego Gambetta, *La mafia siciliana: El negocio de la protección privada* (Mexico City: Fondo de Cultura Económica, 2007), 25–39.

10. INTERPOL, "Drugs," http://www.interpol.int/Crime-areas/Drugs/Drugs.

11. Moisés Naím, "The Five Wars of Globalization," *Foreign Policy,* January 1, 2003, http://www.foreignpolicy.com/articles/2003/01/01/five_wars_of_globalization.

12. INTERPOL, "Organized Crime," http://www.interpol.int/Crime-areas/Organized -crime/Organized-crime.

13. United Nations, "The UN Convention against Transnational Organized Crime," Articles 1 and 2, http://www.uncjin.org/Documents/Conventions/dcatoc/final_documents _2/convention_spa.pdf.

14. J. G. Tokatlian, "Anotaciones en torno del crimen organizado, la seguridad nacional y la política internacional en relación con el tema de las drogas psicoactivas: Una aproximación conceptual a partir de la experiencia de Colombia," working paper, Departamento de Humanidades, Universidad de San Andrés, 1999.

15. The successive reports from which this chapter takes quotations are retrieved from the U.S. State Department's website, http://www.state.gov, in the section that deals with the topic. The reports were last accessed on February 22, 2012.

16. See the geopolitical map tracing the presence of criminality in Latin America: "Atlas géopolitique d'Amérique Latine," *Diplomatie: Affaires Stratégiques et Relations Internationals*, no. 43 (March–April 2010): 56.

17. Claudio Gutiérrez de la Cárcova, "Situación del narcotráfico en la Argentina, como manifestación del crimen organizado transnacional," Série de Artículos y Testimonios, Consejo Argentino de Relaciones Internacionales, no. 68 (2010), http://www.cari.org.ar/ pdf/at68.pdf.

18. Ibid., 2.

19. Jorge A. Hogalde, "Gendarmería Nacional Argentina en el control del tráfico ilícito de drogas," in *Las nuevas amenazas a la seguridad* (Buenos Aires: Consejo Argentino para las Relaciones Internacionales y Escuela Nacional de Inteligencia, 2002).

20. For a mapping of illicit flows of drugs in the Southern Cone (Argentina, Uruguay, Paraguay, and Chile), see Khatchik DerGhougassian (with the assistance of Paula Varone), "El crimen organizado en el Cono Sur: Un mapeo de las transacciones ilícitas en Argentina, Uruguay, Paraguay y Chile," in *Seguridad regional en América Latina y el Caribe: Anuario 2009,* ed. Hans Mathieu and Paula Rodríguez Arredondo (Bogotá: Friedrich Ebert Stiftung–Colombia, Programa de Cooperación en Seguridad Regional, 2009), 316–329.

21. Glen Evans, "El crimen organizado y el conocimiento accionable: La necesidad de entender antes de actuar," in *Prejuicio, crimen y castigo: El desafío de la seguridad sostentable,* ed. Enrique del Percio (Buenos Aires: Editorial Sudamericana, 2010), 104–106.

22. Gutiérrez de la Cárcova, "Situación del narcotráfio," 2.

23. According to the 2010 UNODC report, Argentina in 2008 reported the existence of twenty clandestine laboratories; see *Informe mundial sobre las drogas, 2010,* 164, http://www.unodc.org/documents/data-and-analysis/WDR2010/Informe_Mundial_sobre_las_Drogas_2010.pdf. A March 2011 document from SEDRONAR reveals that from 2000 to 2006, seventy-eight centers for cocaine production and two for ecstasy production were discovered, fifty-three of them in the province of Buenos Aires, eight in the federal capital, six in the province of Salta, five in the province of Santa Fe, and the rest distributed throughout the provinces of Córdoba, Tucumán, Entre Ríos, and Jujuy; see SEDRONAR, *Centros de procesamiento ilícito de estupefacientes en Argentina—Un análisis a partir de los casos judicializados,* March 2011, 15–16, http://www.sedronar.gov.ar/images/novedades/biblioteca/centros%20de%20procesamiento%20il%C3%ADcito.pdf.

24. Diego Fleitas, "Incremento del Tráfico y consumo de drogas en Argentina 1990–2008," March 2010, http://www.portaldeseguridad.org/mostrar-articulo.aspx?id=229.

25. Victoria Ranguni, Diana Rossi, and Alejandro Corda, "Informe pasta de base de cocaína, Argentina 2005–2006," Intercambios Asociación Civil, http://www.tni.org/sites/www.tni.org/archives/docs/200702282203562424.pdf.

26. Transnational Institute, "El paco bajo la lupa—El mercado de la pasta base de cocaína en el Cono Sur," *Drogas y Conflicto—Documentos de Debate,* no. 14 (2010): 12, http://www.tni.org/sites/www.tni.org/files/download/200612281211405043.pdf.

27. Ibid., 14.

28. Ana Lía Kornblit, Ana Clara Caramotti, and Pablo Francisco Di Leo, "Periodización del consumo de drogas," Sociedad Argentina de Salud Integral del Adolescente, http://www.sasia.org.ar/sites/www.sasia.org.ar/files/Modulo_2.pdf.

29. The facts are summarized from "Ochenta y cuatro años de tratamiento criminal a las personas que consumen drogas," prepared by Intercambios Asociación Civil for the VII National Conference on Drug Policies, Buenos Aires, October 4–5, 2010.

30. Raúl Alejandro Corda, "Encarcelamientos por delitos relacionados con estupefacientes en Argentina," in *Sistemas sobrecargados: Leyes de drogas y cárceles en América Latina,* ed. Pien Metaal and Coletta Youngers (Washington, D.C.: Transnational Institute and Washington Office on Latin America, 2010), 19.

31. Marcelo Sain, "La problemática del narcotráfico en la Argentina," Foro de Seguridad, 2008, http://www.psa.gov.ar/index.php/articulos_interes.htmel?file=tl_files/Docs/01_informacion_institucional/Discurso+1.pdf.

32. Marcelo Sain, "El fracaso del control de las drogas ilegales en Argentina," *Nueva Sociedad,* no. 222 (2009): 141.

33. Ibid., 142.

34. Marcelo Sain, "Un estado fallido ante las nuevas problemáticas delictivas: El caso argentino," Universidad de Belgrano, Documento de Trabajo, no. 119 (2004), 9.

35. J. G. Tokatlian, "El nefasto poder de la triple p," *La Nación*, October 15, 2003.

36. Marcelo Sain, *Política, policía y delito: La red bonaerense* (Buenos Aires: Capital Intelectual, 2004); idem, *El leviatán azul: Policía y política en Argentina* (Buenos Aires: Siglo Veintiuno, 2008).

37. Vázquez, *La sombra del narcotráfico*, 99.

38. Mauro Federico, *País narco: Tráfico de drogas en Argentina: Del tránsito a la producción propia* (Buenos Aires: Editorial Sudamericana, 2011), 10.

39. Ibid., 66.

40. On November 15, 1999, the Antiterrorist Unit of the federal police arrested María Isabel Santos Caballero and her son in the middle–upper class neighborhood of Núñez in Buenos Aires. Her real name, as it was later revealed, was Victoria Eugenia Henao Vallejo, the widow of the late Medellín boss, Pablo Escobar Gaviria, killed in 1993. The widow and her son had been living in Argentina since 1995 with false documents and with the full knowledge of the government of Carlos Saúl Menem. She later was absolved of all charges of money laundering and continues living in Argentina. The Argentine press considers the "shocking" revelation that she was living in Argentina a turning point, as Colombian traffickers heading to Argentina in search of permanent residency became news and subjects of investigation.

41. Federico, *País narco*, 135–136.

42. Virginia Messi, "El desembarco de los narcos colombianos en la Argentina," *Clarín*, no. 22 (2012): 54–55.

III

REGIONAL AND INTERNATIONAL DRUG-CONTROL POLICIES

18

The Role of the Inter-American Drug Abuse Control Commission

Confronting the Problem of Illegal Drugs in the Americas

BETTY HORWITZ

Illegal drugs are one of the most salient and multifaceted threats to the Americas.[1] Illegal-drug consumption, particularly in the United States, creates demand and fuels criminality. Drug production and trade, in turn, exploit the weaknesses in the capacity of Latin American states, provoking instability and terrible violence.

To date, efforts to eradicate these phenomena have been less than successful. This illegal industry has been able to adapt to new obstacles erected by government authorities, to keep up with demand, to transcend borders, and to affect fragile Latin American democratic states. By failing to control all of their territories, Latin American authorities have allowed illegal-drug traffickers to become an existential threat that undermines fragile national institutions and the fabric of the societies that take traffickers in.[2]

In order to eventually defeat a threat of this nature and scope, a very long term cooperative approach needs to be adopted. But is a multilateral approach to the problem of illegal drugs in the Americas possible? Are U.S. and Latin American authorities developing a cooperative approach? And if they are, is it working?

In this era of globalization, the illegal-drug phenomenon is the most evident manifestation of transnational crime in the Americas. Yet while some countries, like Colombia and Mexico, are committed to a frontal fight to confront this threat, other countries, such as Brazil and Peru, are less determined. More important, still other countries, such as Ecuador and Bolivia, are engaged only in speculative debate, ignoring the growing influence of illegality in their own societies.[3]

As a consequence, the United States has opted to support bilateral agreements, thus undermining many coalition-building approaches, particularly if they provide a platform for leaders such as the late Hugo Chávez of Venezuela. The "balloon" effect of drug production and trade present the U.S. and Latin American governments with the need to address crimes that adversely affect their societies but that only partly take place on their soil.[4]

This chapter takes the position that, in addition to bilateral agreements, the United States and Latin America are looking for ways to use multilateral organisms to confront one of the most salient threats to the Americas—the illegal-drug phenomenon—and it offers as an example of multilateral cooperation the role of the Inter-American Drug Abuse Control Commission (Comisión Interamericana para el Control del Abuso de Drogas, CICAD).[5]

CICAD is the semiautonomous unit of the Organization of American States (OAS) created in 1986 to develop and promote a coherent antidrug policy in the hemisphere. This chapter argues that CICAD is a very useful mechanism able to confront many of the challenges posed by the illegal-drug industry. CICAD is viewed in Washington and throughout the region as an important but still embryonic policy instrument for combating illegal-drug production, trafficking, and consumption, due to its capacity to develop a comprehensive and multilateral approach to tackling the multifaceted character of this phenomenon.

This chapter also contends that the only way to fully understand such a complex security issue is to adopt an analytically comprehensive and nuanced approach that combines elements of the different theoretical traditions. In so doing, particular concepts drawn from each theoretical approach can be utilized to develop a holistic theoretical model that better explains this complex phenomenon, which threatens all the countries in the Americas in different ways and degrees while quickly adapting to the international context.

Neorealists contend that states are the principal actors in an environment that lacks an international authority capable of enforcing agreements.[6] So when confronting the threat of illegal-drug consumption, production, and trade, national security forces will strive to maintain control of their territories while avoiding being bound by multilateral instruments. Nevertheless, the illegal-drug phenomenon is inherently transnational and does not stay within national borders or respect a state's sovereignty.[7] Multilateral approaches and international mechanisms can help local government authorities in weaker states, particularly when they find themselves at risk of being co-opted by illegal groups, to achieve relative gains more efficiently.

So far, the relative-gains calculation has not routinely taken place between states in the Americas. Often, this calculation occurs between weak states and illegal groups.[8]

The neoliberal institutionalist point of view holds that to confront such a complex phenomenon efficiently, first and foremost, the basic problem of coordination needs to be properly addressed. This means that some coordinating mechanism or mechanisms need to be accepted and used by all parties involved.[9]

An international mechanism such as CICAD can provide a focal point that facilitates communication between local authorities while promoting the legal protocols and joint actions of local security forces.[10] But to be able to work via international mechanisms, both U.S. and Latin American elites need to, first, perceive, identify, and define the nature and scope of this threat in the same way. From a constructivist point of view, this means that in the current international environment, it behooves state authorities to use the growing regulative effects and authority of international organizations (IOs) to more efficiently combat the unorthodox threat that illegal drugs represent.[11]

The authority of IOs can be used by political authorities not only to coordinate policies but also to persuade other elite groups and political actors to do what they otherwise would not do: define the illegal-drug phenomenon as a common security policy priority that requires the linking of national interests, security forces, and drug policies. More important, Latin American authorities will accept U.S. leadership only if all parties involved, including the United States, show that they are committed to operating within the limits set by IOs.[12] Always relying on powerful states, multilateral instruments such as CICAD can endorse and reinforce the redefinition of the totality of the illegal-drug phenomenon as an existential threat to the hemisphere and promote the need to use CICAD's mechanisms, such as the Multilateral Evaluation Mechanism (MEM), as focal points for long-term cooperation.[13]

Yet even with the growing evidence of the imminent threat that this phenomenon represents to Latin America's institutions and societies and with available cooperative mechanisms such as CICAD, the goals of long-term coordination, cooperation, and definition of illegal drugs as an impending hemispheric security threat remain elusive. Following the terrorist attacks of September 11, 2001, the Bush administration systematically subordinated the "war on drugs" to the global "war on terrorism." George W. Bush rhetorically supported CICAD's cooperative efforts during his two terms in office (2001–2009). He did not, however, entirely abandon the war on drugs and the certification process, earlier programs passed by Congress.

In turn, the Obama administration has acknowledged that the war on drugs metaphor fails to capture the complexity of the problem and fails to provide a proper comprehensive response. The 2010 National Drug Control Strategy, for example, seems to be geared toward defining the drug issue less as a criminal matter and more as a health threat to the fabric of U.S. society. Yet its support for international cooperation to confront the threat that the illegality of the drug problem represents to the hemisphere as a whole is unclear.[14]

To understand adequately the complex and multilayered issue of illegal drugs, it is essential to recognize three factors: first, the fundamentally asymmetrical relationship among states in the hemisphere and therefore the utility of international mechanisms such as CICAD for both the United States and Latin American states to best achieve their strategic advantage; second, the importance of cooperation and coordination by means of international mechanisms and regimes (states in the Americas can best capture potential gains by providing focal points through CICAD, making cooperative outcomes possible); third, CICAD can be used to persuade U.S. and Latin American political elites to confront the illegality of this phenomenon in a way that they otherwise would not do—by linking national policies and, to some degree, security forces.[15]

Long before 2008, Bush and his government had ceased to perceive the illegal-drug problem to be an existential threat to the United States. In contrast, most Latin American governments and societies had increasingly come to perceive it to be exactly such a threat to them.[16] As of 2012, at the end of the first Obama administration, the key question was still whether U.S. and Latin American views on the nature of this threat could eventually converge, and, if so, whether the United States would be willing and able to set the regional agenda unilaterally, cooperatively, or via a combination. In other words, is a multilateral approach to the illegal-drug problem in the Americas possible? Are U.S. and Latin American authorities capable of and willing to develop a cooperative approach? Can CICAD solve the inter-American cooperation problem?

Since 2000, if not before, Latin American governments have realized that illegal drugs have become an existential threat that can only be dealt with in conjunction with their neighbors. U.S. authorities, in turn, have come to realize that the traditional U.S. unilateral approach, based on the certification process, and the war on drugs have not yielded the full cooperation and positive results they expected.[17] The United States is still seeking a cooperative approach, but the kind of cooperation it aims for oscillates between limited multilateral policies in which its authority is not compromised, and the pursuit of bilateral strategies, in which the U.S. government maintains control. This disconnect leaves the future of a multilateral drug policy in doubt.

The main purpose of IOs is to construct and constrain the actions of weaker and stronger states.[18] But in the Americas, the precise role and authority of IOs and institutions has not been fully determined. This chapter contends that a successful approach to the problem of illegal drugs will work only when both the United States and Latin America identify and define this issue in its entirety in the same way—as a common security threat important enough to take absolute priority on the regional security agenda—and defer to international mechanisms such as CICAD as active agents of change. A successful drug policy requires a persistent, continuing, long-term multilateral effort. Therefore, the role played by CICAD is particularly important because the success or failure of a hemispheric drug strategy depends mostly on the development of an antidrug regime in which the United States and Latin American states have a stake, take responsibility, and share the burden.

To explore these issues, this chapter first considers the different policies that the United States, as the regional hegemon, has adopted to try to control and, eventually, to eradicate the production, trade, and use of illegal drugs in the Americas. To understand why this approach failed, this chapter examines the response to and limited cooperation of Latin American states with these policies. Then it analyzes the change in the U.S. approach toward cooperation and focuses on the extent to which CICAD—an interstate mechanism that represents a concerted effort to act cooperatively, share responsibility, and encompass all aspects of the drug problem—participates in and influences the regional illegal-drug agenda and serves as a focal point for cooperation. CICAD has been described briefly elsewhere as one of many interstate mechanisms for developing and coordinating some multilateral efforts dealing with the illegal-drug threat in the Americas.[19] This chapter, however, focuses on this semiautonomous interstate mechanism and examines where and how the multilateral approach encouraged by CICAD is succeeding and bearing fruit, what remains to be done, and where it is failing.

This chapter pays particular attention to the efforts of the MEM, which serves as an effective tool for long-term cooperation and progress evaluation and a successful source for recommendations. It considers in detail MEM's efforts pertaining to institutional strengthening through the development of an international framework, uniform national drug strategies, drug observatories, and standardization of data in a common data bank.

The Drug Problem in the Americas: From U.S. Neglect to Unilateralism, 1900–1986

The threat of illicit-drug production, consumption, and trade is not new. Neither is the constant disagreement between the United States and Latin America on the nature and scope of the threat to their countries individually and to the continent as a whole. The beginning of the pervasive contemporary use of drugs can be traced back to the beginning of the twentieth century and their wide and uncontrolled use in medicine. This contributed to the creation of a legitimate society of users, compelling U.S. authorities to create a national and international institutional framework to regulate drug use. Yet while succeeding in curbing domestic use, the U.S. Congress failed to convince the international community of the global nature of the narcotics threat, leaving Congress with unilateral policies as the only alternative. The 1914 Harrison Narcotics Act (amended in 1919) was the United States' first unilateral attempt to control the inflow and use of narcotics. In conjunction with a sustained social stigma imposed on drug use, the act seemed to help curb U.S. dependence on narcotics. Nevertheless, after World War II, this positive trend was reversed. With the onset of the Cold War and the Korean and Vietnam Wars, U.S. authorities lowered their guard while Americans began to focus on issues such as racism and changing social mores and ignored drug addiction. By the 1960s, the illegal-drug problem had leaped into the mainstream of community life.

The policies of Latin American governments exacerbated the problem when political elites supported the U.S. Cold War efforts and ignored the growing penetration of illegal drugs into their own countries. So between the 1960s and the 1980s, while illegal-drug consumption in the United States was exploding, production and trafficking in Latin America grew exponentially. By the beginning of the 1980s, U.S. authorities had begun to recognize the "drug problem" as an imminent threat to the nation's security and social fabric. But ignoring the danger to them, Latin American governments declared the issue to be exclusively a "Yankee problem."[20]

In response to growing domestic drug use and the lack of regional cooperation, President Richard Nixon adopted unilateral hard-line policies by first imposing federal interdiction initiatives to stop the illicit-drug supply by using the U.S. Coast Guard and Customs and second by creating, in 1973, the Drug Enforcement Administration (DEA) to directly attack the sources of supply by linking drug-control assistance to aid provisions for the military, the police, or counterinsurgency forces. By linking the destruction of illegal-drug crops to military assistance, the United States ended up providing aid to repressive Latin American regimes. In 1982, President Ronald Reagan declared a full-scale war on drugs, imposing, by 1986, the certification mechanism.[21]

Together with the 1980 neoliberal market reforms, these unilateral U.S. policies contributed to the constant eroding of the capacity of Latin American civilian governments and fostered the corruption of their militaries, which were starved of resources and training and yet were still charged with controlling their national territory during democratic transitions.

Both the United States and Latin American states would pay a high price for this oversight. By taking advantage of greater room to maneuver, groups linked to drug trafficking seized the opportunity to commit resources and engage subversive groups, such as Peru's Shining Path (Sendero Luminoso) and Colombia's Revolutionary Armed Forces (Fuerzas Armadas Revolucionarias de Colombia, FARC), forging alliances in regional strongholds and successfully maintaining an active presence in democratizing societies with a weak institutional presence. As a result, by the mid-1980s, drug trafficking had become one of the fastest-growing industries in Latin America and could no longer be considered solely a "Yankee problem."[22]

Recognizing the limited effect of the unilateral policies, President George H. W. Bush launched a cooperative effort: the U.S. Antidrug Abuse Act of 1988. Significant U.S. economic assistance and political support were allotted to Latin American states that were seen, at the very least, to be cooperating with U.S. efforts to combat the drug trade.[23] Still, the United States continued to sponsor unilateral policies that ended up adversely affecting Latin American economies while missing an opportunity to develop coordinated drug policies.

Both U.S. and Latin American authorities failed to understand the complex nature and great capacity for mobility and adaptation (the "balloon" effect) of the illegal-drug phenomenon. Moreover, Latin American resentment was exacerbated by the failure to consider the immediate benefits that the illegal-drug industry brings to local economies while burdening local and federal governments.[24]

Drug Summitry and the Establishment of CICAD, 1986–1996

During the 1980s, Washington started to frame the illegal-drug threat as a shared concern. So in September of 1989, the administration of George H. W. Bush inaugurated a new strategy, the Andean Initiative, which called for a substantial increase in narcotics-related funding for military and economic assistance, law enforcement, and drug-enforcement administration activities in Colombia, Peru, and Bolivia.[25] This shift in priorities came at the same time as other cooperative efforts, such as the 1986 Inter-American Program of Action in Rio de Janeiro, and the establishment of an institutional interstate mechanism, CICAD, set the stage for an embryonic antidrug regime.[26]

Thanks to Washington's backing, a regional framework continued to develop with the 1990–1991 Declaration and Program of Action of Ixtapa, the Inter-American Program of Quito: Comprehensive Education to Prevent Drug Abuse, the participation of President Bush in the Cartagena I, San Antonio, and Cartagena II summits, and the adoption of the 1996–1997 Antidrug Strategy in the Hemisphere.[27] These strategies and programs attempted to frame the illegal-drug phenomenon in its totality and, for the first time, as a shared threat. Most important, this common security strategy included a concrete cooperative mechanism, CICAD.[28]

The Evolution of CICAD, 1996–2007

Initially, CICAD was a technical agency composed of eleven members elected by the OAS General Assembly. It examined the drugs phenomenon in the context of socioeconomic development, environmental protection, and human rights. During the Second Summit of the Americas, in 1998, and following the Miami Plan of Action, however, CICAD's role and authority grew when all OAS members joined, appointed their principal representatives, and charged CICAD with assessing their efforts and progress in combating illegal-drug supply and demand. CICAD receives support from its members, yet it functions as a semiautonomous entity because it also receives support from other sources, such as the Inter-American Development Bank, the United Nations, and the European Commission.[29]

CICAD adopted a comprehensive drug policy program that embraced four main goals: (1) the strengthening of national antidrug plans; (2) the upgrading, prevention, and treatment of drug-addiction programs; (3) the reduction of drug production and the improvement of law enforcement;

and (4) the creation of specific policies to control money laundering and the illegal misuse of chemicals for drug production. In addition, CICAD was charged with restricting supply through economic assistance and introducing alternative development programs and training initiatives for police, customs officers, and employees of the port, treasury, and justice systems.[30]

To evaluate the illegal-drug phenomenon in its totality and provide a point of departure, CICAD established a framework for coordination (focal points) through governmental expert groups (GEGs) elected from among member states' officials at the beginning of each evaluation round; these GEGs can oversee the evaluation of any country except their own.

The GEGs established three model regulations that provided a normative convergence and an initial cooperative policy framework: (1) the 1990 Model Regulations to Control Chemical Precursors and Chemical Substances, Machines, and Materials; (2) the 1992 Model Regulations Concerning Laundering Offenses Connected to Illicit Drug Trafficking and Related Offenses; and (3) the 1998 Model Regulations for the Control of the International Movement of Firearms. During the year 1999–2000, databases like the Inter-American Telecommunications Network for Drug Control/National Commissions and, subsequently, the Inter-American Drug Use Data System (Sistema Interamericano de Datos Uniformes sobre el Consumo de Drogas, SIDUC) started supplying OAS members with more accurate and uniform information on the true nature and scope of the use and illegal trafficking of narcotics.[31]

Since 2004, new substances of abuse, such as synthetic, designer, and prescription drugs, and new aspects, like money laundering, firearms trafficking, maritime cooperation, port security, community policing, drug-related youth and gang violence, alternative sentencing for minor drug offenses, and, the newest, transnational organized crime, have been brought to the attention of national authorities and identified as immediate security threats. In so doing, CICAD has been instrumental in increasing the awareness of the scope and reach of the illegal-drug phenomenon, both of which are firmly tied to one another and to other serious socioeconomic and criminal challenges and, thus, cannot be effectively targeted in isolation.

In 2006, CICAD was incorporated, together with the Inter-American Committee against Terrorism (Comité Interamericano contra el Terrorismo, CICTE), the Department of Public Security, and other related areas, into the Secretariat for Multidimensional Security. As a result of this reorganization, CICAD now oversees the Multilateral Evaluation Mechanism

(MEM) and activities concerned with money laundering, demand reduction, educational development and research, supply reduction and alternative development, the Inter-American Observatory on Drugs (Observatorio Interamericano sobre Drogas, OID), and institution building, placing CICAD as a unique focal point for cooperation.[32]

CICAD and the Multilateral Evaluation Mechanism, 1996–2007

The MEM, an instrument of CICAD mandated by the heads of state at the Second Summit of the Americas in 1998, was designed to measure the progress of actions taken by OAS members against the illegal-drug industry.[33] The MEM is designed to identify specific issues and possible solutions to be implemented by regional and state institutions.[34]

Since its inception, this evaluation process has been carried out through the elaboration and publication of national and hemispheric reports, beginning with the first MEM Hemispheric Evaluation in 1999–2000, which served as the baseline. It was conducted through a questionnaire containing indicators that originated in the first thirty-four national reports—one for each OAS member—and corresponded to the priorities of the Antidrug Strategy in the Hemisphere.[35] Each country must present a document prepared by its government on the country's drug problem.[36] Refining the process through the various rounds, new indicators have been added and others eliminated. For example, in the second evaluation round, corruption-related issues that included information on the displacement of illicit-drug crops and transnational organized crime were added. In the fourth round, a new indicator on the use of the Internet to sell pharmaceuticals and other drugs was introduced.

To be measured, the MEM indicators have been classified into five main categories: (1) national plans and strategies; (2) prevention and treatment; (3) reduction of drug production; (4) law enforcement measures; and (5) the cost of the drug problem. Before the start of each round, these indicators and categories undergo a comprehensive review by the Intergovernmental Working Groups (IGWGs).[37] The results of the final analysis of these indicators are presented by the MEM through the hemispheric reports, which divide the results under National Antidrug Strategy/Institutional Strengthening, Demand Reduction, Supply Reduction, Control Measures, Hemispheric Cooperation, and Recommendations.[38]

The MEM's Evaluations and Recommendations for the Development of an International Antidrug Framework and National Antidrug Strategies

An examination of five evaluation rounds shows that great attention has been paid to the signing and ratifying of UN and inter-American conventions pertaining directly to drug trafficking and related issues, such as arms trafficking, money laundering, corruption, guerrilla groups, and organized crime. The MEM has tried to persuade national elite groups and political actors to define the illegal-drug phenomenon as a common security priority that requires the linking of national interests, security forces, and drug policies through a process of signing, ratification, and accession that has, in fact, shown progress, even if at a slow pace. By the end of the fifth evaluation round of the MEM,[39] twenty-one member states had signed, ratified, or acceded to all of the UN Conventions considered relevant to the MEM framework. Six of these entered reservations about specific instruments, while twelve countries had not signed some conventions or protocols related to the Convention against Transnational Organized Crime.

With regard to the Inter-American Conventions, twenty-nine out of the thirty-three countries have evaluated signed, ratified, or acceded to these conventions. Albeit very slowly, this area reflects a significant achievement of the MEM process as member states keep ratifying or acceding to conventions that support antidrug initiatives. Nevertheless, the UN Convention against Organized Crime, ratified by thirty-one states, and the UN Convention against Corruption, ratified by twenty-six member states, still need to be ratified by all.

Regarding the Inter-American Convention on Mutual Assistance in Criminal Matters, three countries—Uruguay, Costa Rica, and the Dominican Republic—have signed but not ratified the instrument, and Barbados, Belize, Haiti and St. Vincent, and Grenadine have not even started ratification. Member states have made significant but slow progress in becoming party to these instruments that advance an antidrugs regime, even if more progress is needed. For instance it is important to note that although the Inter-American Convention against the Illicit Manufacturing and Trafficking in Firearms, Ammunition, Explosives and Other Related Materials (Convención Interamericana contra la Fabricación y el Tráfico Ilícito de Armas de Fuego, Municiones, Explosivos y Otros Materiales Relacionados, CIFTA) has been ratified, St. Vincent and the Grenadines, Jamaica, and, more important, Canada and the United States have yet to sign. President

Obama's support for the ratification of CIFTA by the U.S. Senate during the
2009 Summit of the Americas, for example, unleashed an outcry among
groups that oppose gun control.[40]

The MEM hemispheric reports have recognized organized crime as an
existential threat. To date, twenty-nine countries, including the United
States, have completed the process of ratification of and accession to the
Optional Protocol Related to the Inter-American Convention on Mutual
Assistance on Criminal Matters.[41] Support for this protocol, however, is
weak among states that really need it, such as Mexico, Brazil, and Venezuela. Moreover, Guatemala, Panama, the Bahamas, and the United States
have signed and ratified this instrument with reservations. Making matters
worse, the United States prefers bilateral strategies, such as Plan Colombia
or the Mérida Initiative, in which U.S. authorities maintain control.

The U.S. and Latin American governments have recognized that the
success of a hemispheric drug policy depends on the effectiveness of each
national drug strategy. Therefore, one important goal established since the
first MEM round, in 1999, has been a greater harmonization among the
existing national legal frameworks. Latin American governments are increasingly relying on national commissions on drugs, gradually adopting
uniform national antidrug strategies, establishing national antidrug authorities, and creating observatories or centralized offices with more accurate
information systems.[42] In addition, the OID is assisting Latin American
authorities in the development of interstate drug-information systems and
national observatories. When the 2005–2006 hemispheric report was published, all OAS member states were participating, at least in some capacity,
in the Uniform Drug Supply Control Statistical System (Comisión Inter-
institucional contra Crímenes y Delitos de Alta Tecnología, CICDAT) and
SIDUC, signaling a growing coordination of information among states in
the region. The number of countries with a national antidrug commission
or authority, however, decreased, from thirty-three during the 2005–2006
fourth evaluation round, to thirty-one during the 2007–2009 evaluation
round. In addition, by 2009, only five countries, down from nine in 2006,
had established centralized offices for observation.[43]

An examination of the International Antidrug Framework and the national antidrug strategies shows that the United States appears to acknowledge that the drug problem requires cooperation; Latin American states
seem to recognize the need to disregard some of their distrust of the United
States. There is some evidence that all American states acknowledge the

need for a limited effort toward an international framework. There is also evidence of Latin American authorities giving access to CICAD and OIDs, and an acknowledgement of the need to abide by many MEM recommendations. Furthermore, OAS member states are complying, albeit slowly, by ratifying instruments, coordinating local legal frameworks, and promoting the standardization of data and methodologies through SIDUC and CICDAT.

But there is also evidence of a lack of sufficient resources, which is a serious obstacle for national antidrug plans. This slow progress in the national, regional, and international spheres leaves state actors at a serious disadvantage vis-à-vis organized crime actors, who manage always to stay ahead of local military and police forces and justice systems. The mere transnational nature and adaptive capacity of organized crime calls for a cooperative response, which involves a mixture of multilateral norm development, improved response capacity, policing and intelligence cooperation, and the development and connecting of international mechanisms, all of which have been undermined by the trauma of September 11, 2001, and the 2008 financial debacle. The resistance to ratifying CIFTA and the Optional Protocol Related to the Inter-American Convention on Mutual Assistance on Criminal Matters, especially by countries such as Canada and the United States, underscores this situation.

The important distinction of the "drug problem" as either a shared concern (United States) or a common existential threat (Latin America) will have important repercussions on the kind of national and multilateral policies pursued. U.S. authorities have proven hesitant to surrender control and share it with states where narcotics-related corruption and organized crime are increasingly permeating the police, judiciary, and every level of government. Latin American authorities are establishing common ground through national antidrug authorities, national drug observatories, standardized, accurate information systems, and centralized offices, all of which are insufficient. Moreover, to maintain the strategic advantage, U.S. authorities are choosing bilateral agreements in which they exercise control, disregarding the importance of U.S. society's role as the most reliable consumer and provider of illegal arms, all of which keep nourishing the illegal-drug trade. These initiatives also avoid dealing with the poverty that drives many people into the drug trade. Most important, these initiatives certainly fail to address the corruption in government circles, police forces, and judiciaries all over Latin America and also in the United States.

The MEM's Evaluations and Recommendations on Demand Reduction

Since 1999–2000, the MEM has assigned the largest number of recommendations to this particular area, showing that Latin American drug use, from alcohol and tobacco to marijuana, cocaine, and pharmaceuticals, is increasing at an alarming rate. Yet at the same time, Latin American authorities have demonstrated a lack of understanding and political will to confront this threat fully, opting instead to avoid difficult decisions and reverting to defining the drug problem as a U.S. liability and responsibility. For example, the MEM Assistance Projects Report and the MEM Achievements Report present a full account of the assigned and incomplete recommendations to countries. But the data in the reports cannot pinpoint which recommendations were completed and how important they actually are. Moreover, these reports avoid giving any indication of the consequences, if any, of uncompleted recommendations. The fourth and fifth evaluation reports concentrate on education without any concrete facts or conclusions.[44]

The modest progress is hindered by Latin American authorities' and social elites' lack of resources, motivation, determination, and, most important, accountability. The United States has not performed any better. Therefore, it is unlikely that, at least in the foreseeable future, U.S. authorities will be willing to submit their authority to, and share responsibility with, multilateral regional institutions falling prey to corrupt and authoritarian Latin American officials.[45]

Still, U.S. authorities are now attempting to achieve a modicum of cooperation. The Obama administration seems to be somewhat receptive to some MEM recommendations in certain areas, especially if they define consumption as a common threat to public health. But cooperation can be risky, and U.S. authorities will hesitate to compromise strategic resources, opting, instead, for bilateral instruments they can control.[46]

The MEM's Evaluations and Recommendations on Supply Reduction

Between 1999 and 2007, the supply-reduction area enjoyed a good deal of support from the United States and a high degree of compliance by Latin American authorities. In 2007, the Supply Reduction and Control Training Program organized thirty-seven programs for nearly 1,000 law enforcement and customs officers from several Latin American countries. CICAD also completed its eight-year support for the Andean Counter-Drug Intelligence School (Escuela Regional de la Comunidad Americana de Inteligencia Antidrogas) and the Latin American and Caribbean Community of Intelligence Police (Comunidad Latinoamérica y del Caribe de Inteligencia Policial). Moreover, CICAD expert groups are increasingly identifying new areas of concern, particularly pharmaceuticals and Internet communication.[47]

More important, the evaluations of the supply side have touched on two important policies: alternative development programs, and regulatory frameworks. Countries have shown a good measure of compliance with recommendations concerning alternative development programs, which Latin American authorities need. The 2007–2009 fifth evaluation round showed a slight decline in coca cultivation. But a closer look reveals that even if the general trend may be down, the total cultivation in hectares went up, from 167,553 hectares in 2008 to 158,825 hectares in 2009, with an increase in production in Bolivia and Peru. This evaluation also showed that the number of illicit-drug laboratories destroyed went from 37,324 in 2006 to 37,900 in 2009. Yet although all countries have ratified treaties and conventions such as the 1988 U.N. Convention against Illicit Traffic in Narcotic and Psychotropic Substances, seizures of pharmaceutical products and chemical substances are on the rise.[48]

There are considerable differences and gaps between U.S. and Latin American regulatory frameworks. Many Latin American countries find it difficult to establish and adhere to uniform national regulations and to enforce compliance in the policing of pharmaceutical products. This issue, in particular, is very problematic, especially when it comes to the definition of what constitutes the illegal use of pharmaceuticals, making compliance with international constraints difficult. This is why the 2005–2006 MEM Hemispheric Evaluation Recommendations focused on the challenge of developing uniform national legal and institutional structures for the control of pharmaceutical products and chemical substances.[49] These recommendations strove to refine the issue of illegal use of chemicals and pharmaceuticals to better protect licit commercial activities. Still, the goal of defining pharmaceuticals as a potential security threat that requires regional coordination and cooperation remains elusive.

CICAD and the MEM's Recommendations and Progress Reports

The different rounds of MEM evaluation clearly show that drug trafficking continues to be intertwined with many other illegal activities, making it difficult for one institution like CICAD to act as a focal point to tackle the problem in its entirety.[50] The MEM reports give an account of the recommendations in progress, accomplished, and not yet carried out, without contributing to a full evaluation of the quality and importance of these recommendations. CICAD members are encouraged to produce progress reports that in fact do not actually evaluate in depth the real status of the drug problem in each country; hence they fail to expose the shortcomings of government institutions implementing national drug plans and drug legislation or supporting their criminal justice systems. They also fail to examine recommendations and provide a guide for their implementation.[51]

CICAD: A Critical Juncture, Today and Beyond

This chapter has examined the role and importance of CICAD within the whole of U.S. and Latin American drug strategies by exploring where and how the multilateral approach encouraged by CICAD is succeeding and bearing fruit, what remains to be done, and where is it failing. This chapter has paid particular attention to the U.S. and Latin American foreign policy shift regarding the illegal-drug threat that took place during the second half of the 1980s and the 1990s, when authorities in the United States felt secure and confident enough to seek the cooperation of its neighbors and begin to confront the illegal-drug threat by relinquishing some of its authority to CICAD. Through CICAD, the United States has proven to be willing to support some multilateral efforts and yield some of its authority, however modest the amount, on issues where its immediate existence, national security, and strategic advantage are not at stake. Latin American authorities, in turn, have demonstrated that they can set aside their traditional distrust of the United States.

This chapter uses the different theoretical perspectives in international relations—realism, neoliberal institutionalism, and constructivism—to provide an analytically comprehensive approach. This theoretical model recognizes the utility of international mechanisms such as CICAD for both the United States and the Latin American states to best achieve their strategic advantage (contingent realism), and to achieve cooperation and coordination to better capture potential gains through CICAD's focal points (neoliberal institutionalism). More important, this chapter recognizes the importance of normative convergence between U.S. and Latin American political elites, to confront the illegality of drug trafficking in a way that they otherwise would not do: by linking national policies and, to some degree, security forces (constructivism).

As Ikenberry argues, since 1945, the balance of power has increasingly been played out through established institutions that bind powerful and weaker states to achieve a long-term satisfactory distribution of gains.[52] In this sense, when defining and confronting the drug problem, CICAD, a component of the Inter-American System, has aimed at modifying the exercise of power in the region by taming the existing asymmetries between Washington and Latin America. CICAD is in a position to solve the inter-American cooperation problem by helping Washington exercise its power with restraint, and by helping Latin American governments achieve relative gains more efficiently. CICAD can channel Latin American actions and restrain Washington's use of power, dampening, as a result, Latin American fears of U.S. domination or abandonment.

CICAD's Evolution and Contributions

As part of the antidrug strategy in the hemisphere, CICAD has managed to establish common ground for a long-term coordination and cooperation process. It has become an effective tool for promoting drug education by supporting local programs for illegal-use prevention and establishing education programs for governments and law enforcement officials, judges, and lawmakers. Moreover, CICAD has, with some success, encouraged Latin American government officials to accept the criticism coming from the drug observatories, to adopt a more serious approach toward domestic drug consumption, and to strive to develop uniform and effective national drug strategies.

OAS member states have regularly produced and published national evaluation progress reports as a result of the MEM evaluation rounds, calling attention to the utility of interstate mechanisms that can be used as focal points to tackle complex problems. CICAD's limited authority has striven to persuade the United States and most Latin American authorities to endorse a common definition of the illegal-drug phenomenon as an imminent threat. As of 2009, CICAD had been instrumental in the development of a regional institutional framework and the creation of an embryonic antidrug regime by promoting the signing and ratifying of UN and inter-American conventions related directly to drug trafficking, goals it continues to pursue.[53] CICAD has made a real contribution by persuading Latin American political and social elites to accept external criticism. Latin American governments have accepted the external intervention of the GEGs, the MEM evaluations and recommendations, and the participation of OIDs in domestic drug strategies and national drug commissions. More important, CICAD has succeeded in its efforts to standardize data and methodologies, making a real contribution to the cooperative drug effort by developing a common and standardized data bank through CICDAT and SIDUC. Yet, although this progress has been promising, it has encountered real and serious obstacles. In May of 2013, the secretary general of the OAS, Miguel Insulza, issued a stark criticism of the drug policies acknowledging the failure of the Hemispheric Drug Strategy and its 2011–2015 plan of action. Especially as a result of the disengagement of Washington after September 11, 2001, Latin American leaders seem to have taken the initiative and responsibility for the illegal-drug phenomenon in its entirety. The "Analytical Report" and "Scenarios Report" published by the OAS seem to indicate at the very least that Latin America's leaders are willing to take the first steps toward new strategies and policies to confront this threat cooperatively. Whether or not CICAD will be used as a tool for these new strategies is an open question.

CICAD's Shortcomings and Challenges

CICAD's progress has been quite modest to date. Standardized data banks, domestic and comparative studies, national and regional evaluations and recommendations, and the creation of an embryonic antidrug regime are important, particularly as a first step in a long, sustainable antidrug campaign. CICAD has made a real contribution by persuading Latin American authorities to work together in tackling specific aspects of the illegal-drug phenomenon and by providing focal points for standardizing information and national strategies, promoting education, and so on, but this process is far from complete.

Through 2009, OAS member states had implemented CICAD's recommendations only on a voluntary basis. In practice, CICAD has never possessed the authority to make hard decisions or impose sanctions when countries such as Ecuador, Bolivia, and Venezuela choose to ignore its recommendations. Governments can, and often do, disregard CICAD's authority while making a mockery of MEM's recommendations by not providing reliable data and serious evaluations.

More important, CICAD lacks the authority to call for concerted multilateral actions in countries where drug cartels are seriously eroding the legitimacy of governmental institutions at every level. For CICAD's multilateral approach not to become irrelevant in the easily foreseeable future, the stronger governments in the region, such as the United States, Canada, Mexico, and Brazil, will have to take major steps to make CICAD more effective by bestowing on it the authority to sanction noncompliant governments and government officials. CICAD needs to establish a period of review for uncompleted recommendations and then be able to issue warnings, and if warnings are not heeded and proper steps are not taken, it needs the authority and U.S. backing to impose meaningful sanctions.

Equally important, U.S. and Latin American leaders have to provide CICAD with the necessary technical and financial support to assist domestic security forces and government officials who are willing to confront narcotics-related corruption. CICAD could become a vestigial organization that exists with the sole purpose of producing data and nothing more if its members keep producing shallow reports as their final goal.[54]

These obstacles, if not properly addressed, may convert CICAD into a progressively irrelevant institution. Its current budgetary situation already reflects its limited capabilities to oblige its member states to cooperate fully.[55] Moreover, CICAD will most certainly become irrelevant if the United States continues to choose bilateral arrangements.

CICAD is a miniscule part of the Inter-American System, which, in its protracted history of aiming at cooperation and integration, has developed a wide range of regional institutions with diverging interests, unrelated development institutions, inarticulate development priorities, and a chronic lack of funding. This lack of a clear, integrated design has always complicated any effort toward full coordination and cooperation. The United States and the Latin American states have yet to fully define and agree on strong-enough reasons to oblige them to relinquish their authority to IOs and achieve full cooperation. CICAD, as part of this system, suffers from these maladies, including diverging interests, lack of funding, and the persistence of a multilateral stance with an emphasis on executive sovereignty, limiting the collective action and intervention Latin American states are willing to endorse.[56]

Since the creation of CICAD, the economic and social costs of this lack of action have driven drug trafficking–related crimes to the forefront of politics. More than promises, government authorities need to implement concrete actions, such as confronting and eradicating the deep-seated corruption at all levels of government and implementing thorough reforms of justice systems and security forces. To date, CICAD has been unable to persuade or force member states to do so, which brings us to the central problem. Before CICAD can endorse the redefinition of the totality of the illegal-drug phenomenon as an existential threat to the hemisphere and thus serve its purpose by identifying focal coordinating points, the United States and Latin American states have to define the illegal-drug problem in the same way, and they have not yet done so. For the United States, the illegal-drug trade represents a serious security concern that requires coordination, while Latin American governments perceive it to be an existential threat. Furthermore, Latin American governments contend that every hemispheric strategy so far has focused primarily on U.S. security priorities while ignoring the security problematic that Latin American societies face. This is why their cooperation with CICAD or any interstate effort will always be limited in scope since multilateralism and cooperation in the Americas have always been politicized and contested issues. How to engage Latin American states to seek and maintain stability through a legitimate order remains an elusive goal for Washington.

To be effective, common drug strategies in the Americas have required the support of U.S. administrations. Furthermore, every important cooperative strategy in place today, be it unilateral (such as the 1986 Certification Mechanism), multilateral (such as the 1996 Anti-Drug Strategy in the Hemisphere), or bilateral (such as Plan Colombia), has been backed by Washington. Therefore, even when the United States has been perceived as losing ground in many areas, when it comes to security issues, Washington still has the power to choose the conditions under which a hemispheric cooperative stance is possible. By any of those strategies, Washington will aim to achieve cooperative policies through mechanisms such as CICAD and respond to its neighbors' concerns only when it can, first and foremost, achieve its strategic goals efficiently by providing focal points in specific areas, such as information dissemination, drug observation, or legal reform, that make U.S.-preferred cooperative outcomes possible.

Washington has come to realize that its traditional unilateral approach has not yielded the results it had hoped for. Nevertheless, the U.S. government will not cede any of its authority to CICAD as long as U.S. authorities do not believe it capable of imposing genuine sanctions on Latin American states that continue to fall prey to narcotics-related corruption. CICAD has potential, but to be truly effective, it requires the full confidence and support of Washington and the full confidence and cooperation of a significant majority of Latin American governments. OAS members need to accept and support CICAD's authority to coerce and sanction delinquent member states, such as Venezuela, that decide not to cooperate. Without such backing, the future of this effort to institute a multilateral front to face the illegal-drug threat will remain uncertain.[57]

The CICAD-inspired antidrug regime in the Americas is at a critical juncture. The Obama administration seemed to be disavowing the war on drugs and leaning toward multilateralism and cooperation in the region, but it has yet to define a policy of, for example, bestowing on CICAD the authority necessary to assist public officials who are willing to confront narcotics-related corruption in their localities. If this happens, then CICAD's multilateral stance will gradually strengthen. CICAD is still an important institution serving U.S. and Latin American authorities searching for ways to identify the drug threat in the same way, as a common security threat. But the real problem is whether the different views of the nature of the threat can ever truly converge, that is, whether all states in the Americas can, in the near future, define the drug problem not just as a security issue (U.S.) but as an existential threat (Latin America), and whether CICAD will be given the power to assert its authority to implement an effective follow-up method and a true sanction system.

Notes

1. This is a revised and updated version of Betty Horwitz, "The Role of the Inter-American Drug Abuse Control Commission (CICAD): Confronting the Problem of Illegal Drugs in the Americas," *Latin American Politics and Society* 52, no. 2 (2010): 139–165. Also see idem, "Collective Security in the Western Hemisphere," in *The Transformation of the Organization of American States: A Multilateral Framework for Regional Governance* (London: Anthem Press 2011), 73–111.

2. An existential threat is a security issue that justifies the use of extraordinary measures, legitimating the mobilization of the state and, more specifically, the use of force. Existential threats and vulnerabilities can vary greatly in quality and can arise in military and nonmilitary areas. For more details, see Barry Buzan, Ole Wæver, and Jaap de Wilde, *Security: A New Framework for Analysis* (Boulder, Colo.: Lynne Rienner, 1998), 1–5.

3. For more information, see Fernando Cepeda Ulloa, "International Cooperation and the War on Drugs," in *Drug-Trafficking in the Americas*, ed. Bruce M. Bagley and William O. Walker III (Miami: University of Miami, North-South Center Press, 1996), 513–520.

4. Camilo Granada, "The OAS and Transnational Organized Crime in the Americas," in *Transnational Organized Crime and International Security: Business as Usual?* ed. Mats R. Berdal and Mónica Serrano (Boulder, Colo.: Lynne Rienner, 2002), 95–102.

5. From this point on, the term "Latin America" will encompass both Latin American and Caribbean states.

6. John J. Mersheimer, *The Tragedy of Great Power Politics* (New York: W. W. Norton, 2001), 555; Kenneth N. Waltz, *Theory of International Politics* (New York: McGraw-Hill,

1979), 251; idem, "Reductionist and Systemic Theories," in *Neorealism and Its Critics*, ed. Robert O. Keohane (New York: Columbia University Press, 1986), 46–69.

7. Realism predicts that under certain conditions, adversaries can best achieve their security goals through cooperative policies.

8. Charles L. Glazer, "Realists as Optimists: Cooperation and Self-Help," *International Security* 19, no. 3 (Winter 1995–1996): 50–90.

9. Robert O. Keohane, *After Hegemony: Cooperation and Discord in the World Political Economy* (Princeton: Princeton University Press, 2005), 290; Bruce M. Bagley and Juan G. Tokatlian, "Dope and Dogma: Explaining the Failure of U.S.–Latin American Drug Policies," in *The United States and Latin America in the 1990s: Beyond the Cold War*, ed. Jonathan Hartlyn, Lars Schoultz, and Augusto Vargas (Chapel Hill: University of North Carolina Press, 1992), 214–234.

10. Robert O. Keohane and Lisa L. Martin, "The Promise of Institutionalist Theory," *International Security* 20, no. 1 (1995): 39–51.

11. For more information on the constructivist definition of a common threat, see Alexander Wendt, *Social Theory of International Politics* (Cambridge: Cambridge University Press, 1999), 266–278. For a detailed explanation of a way to foster cooperation to confront a common problem, see Michael Barnett and Martha Finnemore, *Rules of the World: International Organizations in Global Politics* (Ithaca, N.Y.: Cornell University Press, 2004).

12. John G. Ikenberry, *Institutions, Strategic Restraint, and the Rebuilding of Order after Major Wars* (Princeton: Princeton University Press, 2001).

13. Barnett and Finnemore, *Rules of the World*, 20–29, 156–168.

14. For detailed information on U.S. drug policy, see "2011 Drug Control Strategy," in National Drug Control Policy, 2011, accessed February 24, 2012, http://www.whitehouse.gov/ondcp/2011-national-drug-control-strategy.

15. The asymmetrical relations in the hemisphere and the utility of CICAD are explained by contingent realism. The importance of strengthening cooperation and coordination by providing focal points like CICAD is explained by neoliberal institutionalism. CICAD as a persuasion instrument is explained by constructivism.

16. Interestingly, defining the precise nature of the drug problem and its identification, as either an existential or just a security threat, is precisely a constructivist issue that, as of today, is still not completely resolved.

17. For the failure of an antidrug regime, see Bagley and Tokatlian, "Dope and Dogma," 219–235.

18. Ikenberry, *Institutions*.

19. For additional descriptions of CICAD, see Dimitri Vlassis, "The UN Convention against Transnational Organized Crime," in *Transnational Organized Crime and International Security: Business as Usual?* ed. Mats R. Berdal and Mónica Serrano (Boulder, Colo.: Lynne Rienner, 2002), 96–99. For cooperation via international organisms, see Carolyn M. Shaw, *Cooperation, Conflict and Consensus in the Organization of American States* (New York: Palgrave Macmillan), 171–173. For information on the U.S.-led war on drugs, see Coletta A. Youngers and Eileen Rosin, "The U.S. 'War on Drugs': Its impact in Latin America and the Caribbean," in *Drugs and Democracy in Latin America: The Impact of U.S. Policy*, ed. Coletta A. Youngers and Eileen Rosin (Boulder, Colo.: Lynne Rienner, 2005), 1–13. See also Richard E. Feinberg and Paul Haslam, "Problems of Coordination: The OAS and

the IDB. The Inter-American System: An Overview," in *Governing the Americas: Assessing Multilateral Institutions,* ed. Gordon Mace, Jean Philippe Therien, and Paul Haslam (Boulder, Colo.: Lynne Rienner, 2007), 62–64.

20. For a detailed history of the drug problem in the Americas, see David F. Musto, *The American Disease: Origins of Narcotic Control* (New York: Oxford University Press, 1999); James A. Icardi, *The War on Drugs III: The Continuing Saga of the Mysteries and Miseries of Intoxication, Addiction, Crime and Public Policy* (Boston: Allyn & Bacon, 2002); Ted Galen Carpenter, *Bad Neighbor Policy: Washington's Futile War on Drugs in Latin America* (New York: Palgrave Macmillan, 2003).

21. For more, see Bruce M. Bagley, *Myths of Militarization: The Role of the Military in the War on Drugs in the Americas* (Miami: University of Miami, North-South Center, 1991), 13; idem, "After San Antonio," in *Drug-Trafficking in the Americas,* ed. Bruce M. Bagley and William O. Walker III (Miami: University of Miami, North-South Center Press, 1996), 612; William O. Walker III, "The Bush Administration's Andean Drug Strategy in Historical Perspective," in *Drug-Trafficking in the Americas,* ed. Bruce M. Bagley and William O. Walker III (Miami: University of Miami, North-South Center Press, 1996), 1–22.

22. For more information, see Carpenter, *Bad Neighbor Policy.*

23. Eduardo A. Gamarra, "U.S.-Bolivia Counternarcotics Efforts during the Paz Zamora Administration," in *Drug Trafficking in the Americas,* ed. Bruce M. Bagley and William O. Walker III (Miami: University of Miami, North-South Center Press, 1996), 217–256; Raphael Perl, "Congress, International Narcotics Policy, and the Anti-Drug Abuse Act of 1988," *Journal of Interamerican Studies and World Affairs* 30, nos. 2/3, Special Issue (1988): 19–51.

24. For more, see Bagley and Tokatlian, "Dope and Dogma," 231; Carpenter, *Bad Neighbor Policy,* 91–114; Youngers and Rosin, "The U.S. 'War on Drugs,'" 5–11.

25. For more information, see Bruce M. Bagley, "Globalization and Organized Crime in Latin America and the Caribbean," in *Organized Crime in Latin America and the Caribbean,* ed. Luis Guillermo Solís and Francisco Rojas Aravena (San José, C.R.: Facultad Latinoamericana de Ciencias Sociales [FLACSO]), 2009), 39–46.

26. The Bush administration also needed to defuse the condemnations of the 1989 military intervention of Panama. See Bagley, *Myths of Militarization*; Walker, "The Bush Administration's Drugs Strategy."

27. For more information on the development of the multilateral stance, see the OAS resolutions and the reports produced by CICAD, "Inter-American Program of Action of Rio de Janeiro against the Illicit Use and Production of Narcotic Drugs and Psychotropic Substances and Traffic Therein," 1987, OAS, AG/Res.699(XIV–0/84); idem, Secretariat of Legal Affairs, Anti-Drugs Strategy in the Hemisphere, 1996, AG/RES.1458 (XXVII–O/97), http://www.oas.org/juridico/english/ga-res97/Eres1458.htm); CICAD, "Anti-Drugs Strategy in the Hemisphere," OAS, 1996, CICAD/Doc.965/98add.

28. Carpenter, *Bad Neighbor Policy,* 50–52.

29. According to its mission statement, CICAD was instituted as an autonomous OAS entity performing under the guidance and objectives of the antidrug declarations and strategies. CICAD's core mission is to strengthen the human and institutional capabilities and harness the collective energy of its member states to reduce the production, trafficking, and use and abuse of drugs in the Americas. For more information, see "About CICAD,

Mission Statement," OAS, 2009, http://www.cicad.oas.org/EN/AboutCICAD.asp. In 2007, CICAD received U.S.$7,704,474 in cash and $722,195 in kind. In its 2008 report to the OAS General Assembly, CICAD reported funding from two sources: the regular fund from the OAS, which provided U.S.$1,989,544, or 23.53 percent of its revenue, and external donations (from OAS member states, permanent observers, project partners, and international organizations), which provided U.S.$6,450,275, or 76.47 percent of the total revenue. For more information, see "Annual Report of the Inter-American Drug Control Commission (CICAD) to the General Assembly of the Organization of American States at Its Thirty-Eighth Regular Session," OAS, May, 2008, OAS/Ser.L/XIV.2.43, CICAD/doc.1656/08rev.1, http://www.cicad.oas.org/EN/basicdocuments/CICADAchievements.asp, 25.

30. CICAD, "Anti-Drugs Strategy in the Hemisphere."

31. For more information, see Granada, "The OAS," 95–102.

32. CICAD also works with the United Nations Office of Drugs and Crime (UNODC) to coordinate and underwrite population surveys and comparative analyses of substance-abuse trends. Together with the Inter-American Development Bank, or Banco Intera-mericano de Desarrollo, CICAD trains judges and prosecutors. CICAD has assisted the UNODC in its ten-year evaluation process by means of the MEM hemispheric reports as a complementary source of information about illicit-crop cultivation, demand reduction, and the use of amphetamine-type stimulants and their precursors; see "Annual Report of the Inter-American Drug Control Commission," 1.

33. For more information on the development of the role of CICAD and the MEM, see the OAS resolutions and CICAD and MEM reports in OAS, "Anti-Drugs Strategy," 1996; CICAD, "Final Report: Sixth Meeting of the Intergovernmental Working Group on the Multilateral Evaluation Mechanism," OAS, IWG-MEM Provisional Version, Item Three on the Agenda, 1999, OAS/Ser.L./XIV.2.26, CICAD/doc.1026/99; "Annual Report of the Inter-American Drug Abuse Control Commission (CICAD) to the General Assembly of the Organization at Its Thirtieth Regular Session," OAS, 1999, OAS/Ser.L/XIV.2.26, CICAD/doc.1023/99 rev.3.7–9.

34. For more information on the development of the role of CICAD and the MEM, see the following CICAD and MEM reports: "Annual Report of the Inter-American Drug Abuse Control Commission (CICAD) to the General Assembly of the Organization at Its Thirtieth Regular Session," OAS, 1999; "Annual Report of the Inter-American Drug Control Abuse Commission," CICAD, OAS, 2000, OAS/Ser.L/XIV.2.26, CICAD/doc.1023/99rev.3; "Annual Report for the Inter-American Drug Abuse Control Commission (CICAD) to the General Assembly of the Organization at Its Thirty-First Regular Session," OAS, 2001, OAS/Ser.L/XIV.2.28, CICAD/doc.1079/00 rev.1; "Final Report: Seventh Meeting of the Intergovernmental Working Group of the Multilateral Evaluation Mechanism," IWG-MEM, 2001, OAS/Ser.L./XIV.4.7, CICAD/MEM/doc.13/01 rev.1; "Annual Report of the Inter-American Drug Abuse Control Commission (CICAD) to the General Assembly of the Organization at Its Thirty-Second Regular Session," OAS, 2002, OAS/Ser.L/XIV.2.30, CICAD/doc.1123/01rev.1.

35. Evaluation of Progress in Drug Control, Hemispheric Report 1999–2000," OAS, 2000, accessed February 25, 2012, http://cicad.oas.org/Main/Template.asp?File=/Main/AboutCICAD/about_eng.asp; "Evaluation of Progress in Drug Control, Hemispheric Re-

port 2001–2002," OAS, 2002, accessed February 25, 2012, http://www.cicad.oas.org/MEM/ENG/Reports/Progress_2001-2002/Hemispheric%20eng.pdf.

36. "Hemispheric Report, Evaluation of Progress in Drug Control, MEM, Hemispheric Report, 2005–2006," OAS, 2008, accessed February 25, 2012, 4–5, http://www.cicad.oas.org/MEM/ENG/Reports/Fourth%20Round%20Full/Hemispheric%20-%204th%20Round%20-%20ENG.pdf.

37. "Annual Report of the Inter-American Drug Control Commission (CICAD) to the General Assembly of the Organization of American States at Its Thirty-Eighth Regular Session," 5.

38. Mats Berdal and Mónica Serrano, eds., *Transnational Organized Crime and International Security: Business as Usual?* (Boulder, Colo.: Lynne Rienner, 2002), 98; MEM, "Questionnaire Second Evaluation Round 2001–2002," OAS, accessed February 25, 2012, http://www.cicad.oas.org/MEM/ENG/Questionnaires/Second%20Round/Questionnaire%20-%20Junio%202001.pdf.

39. MEM, "Evaluation Progress in Drug Control, Fifth Evaluation Round," OAS, 2011, accessed February 25, 2012, 7–9, http://www.cicad.oas.org/mem/reports/5/Full_Eval/Informe%20Hemisferico%20-%205ta%20Ronda%20-%20ENG.pdf.

40. For detailed information on the research, see Betty Horwitz, *The Transformation of the Organization of American States: A Multilateral Framework for Regional Governance* (London: Anthem Press, 2011); "Informe CIFTA 2001–2002," OAS, 2008, May 5, 2008, http://search.oas.org/en/default.aspx?k=Informe+CIFTA+2001-2002&s=All+Sites; "Inter-American Convention against the Illicit Manufacturing of and Trafficking in Firearms, Ammunition, Explosives and Other Related Materials, Signatories and Ratifications," OAS, 2010, July 20, 2010, accessed February 1, 2012, http://www.oas.org/juridico/english/treaties/a-63.html. See also MEM Hemispheric Reports, 2008 and 2011.

41. "Optional Protocol Related to the Inter-American Convention on Assistance in Criminal Matters," Department of International Law, 1992, accessed February 25, 2012, http://www.oas.org/juridico/english/treaties/a-59.html. See also MEM, "Hemispheric Evaluation," 2011.

42. See Horwitz, *The Transformation*, 150–180. See also "Hemispheric Report, Evaluation of Progress in Drug Control, MEM, Hemispheric Report, 2005–2006," 79–78.

43. See "Uniform Drug Supply Control Statistical System," Inter-American Observatory on Drugs, CICAD/OAS, 2007, accessed February 25, 2012, http://www.cicad.oas.org/oid/caribbean/2007/CICDAT.pdf. See also MEM Hemispheric Reports, 2008 and 2011.

44. "Hemispheric Report, Evaluation of Progress in Drug Control, 2005–2006," CICAD/OAS, 2008, OAS/Ser.L/XIV.6.1 Rev.2 MEM/INF.2006; "Hemispheric Report, Evaluation of Progress in Drug Control, 2007–2009," CICAD OAS, 2011, OAS/Ser.L/XIV.2.49 CICAD/doc.1862/11rev.1.

45. See Horwitz, *The Transformation*, 150–180.

46. Glazer, "Realists as Optimists."

47. See "Annual Report of the Inter-American Drug Control Commission (CICAD) to the General Assembly of the Organization of American States at Its Thirty-Eighth Regular Session," 9–12.

48. See MEM, "Hemispheric Report 2008," 27–36, and idem, "Hemispheric Report 2011," 20–30, for more on recent trends and the balloon effect. See also Bruce M. Bagley, "Drug Trafficking and Organized Crime in Latin America and the Caribbean"; chapter 10 in this volume.

49. "The Multilateral Evaluation Mechanism (MEM) Achievements, 1997–2007," CICAD/OAS, http://www.cicad.oas.org/MEM/ENG/Documents/MEM%20Achievements%202007_English.pdf, 81.

50. Ibid., 11–16.

51. See "Hemispheric Report, 2011," 40–48.

52. For a full explanation of how institutions participated in establishing the final power structure of the international system, particularly after World War II, see John G. Ikenberry, *Institutions, Strategic Restraint, and the Rebuilding of Order after Major Wars* (Princeton, N.J.: Princeton University Press, 2001).

53. *Hemispheric Drug Strategy, Plan of Action 2011–2015, with an Introduction by OAS Secretary General José Miguel Insulza* (Washington, D.C.: CICAD, Secretariat for Multinational Security, OAS, 2010); www.cicad.oas.org/Main/AboutCICAD/BasicDocument/DrugStrategy.pdf.

54. For the obstacles to the Democratic Charter, see Feinberg and Haslam, "Problems of Coordination," 51–70.

55. See "Annual Report of the Inter-American Drug Control Commission (CICAD) to the General Assembly of the Organization of American States at Its Thirty-Eighth Regular Session," 32–33.

56. For detailed information on regional governance and the democratic regime in Latin America, see Andrew C. Cooper and Thomas Legler, *Intervention without Intervening? The OAS Defense and Promotion of Democracy in the Americas* (New York: Palgrave Macmillan, 2006), 151–152.

57. See "Annual Report of the Inter-American Drug Control Commission (CICAD) to the General Assembly of the Organization of American States at Its Thirty-Eighth Regular Session," 37.

19

The Strategies of the European Union against Drug Trafficking

ROBERTO DOMÍNGUEZ

Studying drug trafficking entails complex analytical challenges for various reasons. Two dimensions epitomize the intricacy of this phenomenon. The first is the entangled interaction between the rationale of the groups profiting from illegal activities and the vitality and adaptability of the global drug market. In the view of the United Nations Office on Drugs and Crime (UNODC), strategies to combat transnational criminal groups "will not stop the illicit activities if the dynamics of the market remain unaddressed."[1] Second, it is quite difficult to comprehend the continual transformations of drug trafficking. Regardless of the region or country that participates in illegal trafficking, its nature results in data on clandestine markets that are limited and hardly reflective of the various dimensions of the problem.[2]

In spite of these methodological challenges, the social cost of illegal-drug trafficking is tangible and obliges policymakers and scholars to produce more effective ways to deal with and investigate the problem. In addition, globalization and global interconnections have produced more complex criminal networks, not only in the Western Hemisphere, but also in the transatlantic area. As indicated in the introduction to this book, the trafficking of cocaine is the main drug linkage between Latin America and Europe.[3]

While the majority of the heroin consumed in Europe comes from Afghanistan, cocaine, in contrast, is produced only in three countries of the Western Hemisphere (Colombia, Peru, and Bolivia). Its consumption in Europe exploded exponentially during the first decade of the twenty-first century. As a result of the "partial victories" of the U.S. strategies against drug trafficking and the changing trends in consumption worldwide, it is of the utmost importance to monitor the interrelationship between national and regional strategies. From the prohibitionist strategies of the United Nations (UN) and the Organization of American States (OAS), to the tolerant approaches of Portugal or the Netherlands, to the regional strategies of the European Union (EU), the collective problem of the use and trafficking of drugs will be more effectively approached only when transatlantic strategies coordinate the resources and actions of regional organizations and individual countries.

With these general caveats in mind, this chapter focuses on the European continent and assesses the capacity of the EU to address the evolving threats produced from drug trafficking. Since drug trafficking has been added to the EU's agenda, a process of further coordination and cooperation among EU member states is resulting in the implementation of several instruments to collectively forge action. While this process has already started, it is at an incipient stage because the process of harmonizing approaches and national drug strategies is a relatively recent effort, only since 2000.

In order to explore the argument posed, the first section reviews the composition of the drug market in the EU, followed by an overview of EU strategies designed to address the challenge of drug trafficking. The third section evaluates the cooperation of the EU with other, nonmember countries. The fourth segment of the chapter looks at the varieties of national strategies and points out some of their differences and transformations.

The Illegal-Drug Market in the European Union

According to the UNODC,[4] about 230 million people, or 5 percent of the world's adult population, are estimated to have used an illicit drug at least once in 2010, while the number of problem drug users is about 27 million, which is 0.6 percent of the adult population. Globally, the two most widely used illicit drugs remain cannabis (global annual prevalence ranging from 2.6 to 5.0 percent of the adult population) and amphetamine-type stimulants (ATs), excluding ecstasy (0.3–1.2 percent). However, data regarding the production of such substances are scarce.[5] Data available for comparable countries in other parts of the world demonstrate that the consumption of cannabis, cocaine, and amphetamines in the EU is significantly lower than in the United States. The same is true for the number of reported HIV infections related to intravenous drug use.[6] In 2006, the total number of people in the European Union who were using drugs—or had at some time used them—was estimated at 70 million for cannabis, at least 12 million for cocaine, 9.5 million for ecstasy, and 11 million for amphetamines, while at least half a million people were known to be receiving treatment for heroin addiction.[7]

A closer examination of the illegal-drug market in Europe reveals not only preferences of consumers, but also how different countries and regions participate in the production and transit of drugs. In the case of marijuana, or cannabis, the production of cannabis resin is assumed to be very small in Europe, yet the region is the world's biggest market for cannabis resin, with North Africa long Europe's predominant supplier. Most of the North African cannabis resin consumed in Europe traditionally comes from Morocco, but recent data show that that the country's relative importance as a supplier is decreasing as a result of the increasing production of it in Afghanistan.[8]

Just after cannabis products (herbal cannabis and cannabis resin), ATs are the most popular type of illicit substances in terms of consumption in the EU. However, the production of ATs displays a completely different trend. Moreover, based on the findings of the Organised Crime Threat Assessment (OCTA) 2011 report,[9] it is clear that organized crime groups are involved in the production and distribution of synthetic drugs, which makes them a major concern in terms of public order. Despite a significant rise in the dismantling of clandestine amphetamine laboratories, amphetamine seizures reported in Europe continued their downward trend in 2011, reaching their lowest level since 2002 (5.4 tons). There are signs, however, of a recovery in the European ecstasy market, with seizures of ecstasy-group substances more than doubling (from 595 kilograms in 2009 to 1.3 tons in 2010). The drug's availability and use appeal increasingly to users in United States, while there has also been an increase in ecstasy seizures in Oceania and Southeast Asia.[10]

While the consumption of cocaine has stabilized in Europe since 2009, the number of consumers in Europe has doubled, from 2 million in 1998 to 4.1 million in 2007–2008.[11] The transited product is cultivated in the Andean region and trafficked from West Africa to Europe. The number of metric tons being transported from this region has increased over 60 percent since 1998—from 97 metric tons in 1998 to 153 metric tons in 2004—which represents approximately 80 percent of the cocaine destined for non-U.S. markets in 2005. In 2006, wholesale cocaine prices in the European Union ranged between U.S.$38,000 and $77,000 per kilogram, compared to U.S.$9,000 to $40,000 per kilogram in the United States. Nonetheless, the UNODC calculates coca farmers receive less than one percent of the value of cocaine sales in Europe.

The Andean region has drug-trafficking organizations in several countries. Colombia remains the main source of cocaine found in Europe, but direct shipments from Peru and the Plurinational State of Bolivia have become more frequent. Colombian trafficking groups are more active in Spain than in any other European country, but they also have established drug-trafficking operations in the Netherlands, another important European gateway country for cocaine. Between 2001 and 2004, the Netherlands was second only to Spain in the quantity of cocaine seized, over 21 metric tons.[12] Colombian trafficking groups have established ties with African criminal organizations in countries such as Ghana, Nigeria, Guinea, Guinea Bissau, Senegal, and Togo. Together, they take advantage of the weak governments and high levels of corruption in those nations in order to smuggle drugs to Europe. Kenya and South Africa are also transit points for South American cocaine en route to Europe.[13]

After the 2010 opium crop failure in Afghanistan, a heroin shortage was observed in some European countries through 2011. Although large quantities of heroin continue to be trafficked along the Balkan route, leading from Afghanistan to western and central Europe via southeastern Europe, declining seizures were reported in most of the countries in those regions in 2010. Europe accounts for 26 percent of the global consumption of heroin, which represents 87 tons and U.S.$20 billion.[14] The main consumer of heroin is the United Kingdom (21 percent of global consumption), followed by Italy (20 percent) and France (11 percent).

EU Approach and Institutions

Since 1980, the international community has debated the most effective approaches to dealing with the consumption of drugs. While states are still the main actors in the implementation of drug policy, they and regional organizations have identified the main challenges derived from drug trafficking and developed general consensuses and similar doctrinal approaches. For instance, the UNODC has emphasized two main strategies: first, an integrated approach; and, second, rebalancing drug-control policy through alternative development, prevention, treatment, and the protection of fundamental human rights.[15] The 2010 U.S. Drug Strategy considers demand to be the main drug-related problem and sees drug abuse as a public health issue;[16] the OAS describes drug addiction as a chronic, relapsing disease; and the EU provides a comprehensive approach to the consumption of drugs.[17]

One of the salient characteristics of policymaking processes in Europe is the interrelationship between the regional and the national levels of decision-making structures. The integration process began to develop an internal market starting in the 1960s, which has provided free circulation of people and goods. The integration process, however, also requires authorities to address transnational illegal activities occurring as a result of open borders. The challenge for the EU is how to reconcile the free transit of legal goods and contain the spread of local unlawful activities. In this regard, the actions of the EU and its member states have gradually focused on effective cooperation in order to address drug trafficking. The European Commission has explained the necessity of regional policy coordination as follows: "If one Member State bans new psychoactive substances, traders open shops in Member States where the law is more permissive. Uncoordinated clampdowns may force traffickers to move drug production sites to neighboring countries or to shift trafficking routes, but these measures cannot disrupt trafficking sustainably."[18]

Policy and institutional development in the area of drug policy can be traced back to the European Committee to Combat Drugs (CELAD) in 1989, which was the first working group to bring together the national coordinators in this field. Since the creation of the ECCD, the EU has continued to adopt antidrug policies. Two European plans to combat drugs were adopted in 1990 and 1992. The EU Action Plan to Combat Drugs 1995–1999 was followed by the EU Drugs Strategy 2000–2004 and the EU Drugs Strategy 2005–2012.

The EU's current approach is based on the EU Drugs Strategy (EUDS) 2013–2020, which designed a European model for drug policy based on a balanced approach to reducing both supply and demand. The EUDS employs a combination of approaches to tackling drugs, together referred to as the "balanced approach." The Strategy has two policy areas—supply reduction and demand reduction—and three crosscutting themes—coordination, international cooperation, and information, research, and evaluation.

The 2005–2012 Strategy provides the framework for two consecutive Action Plans (2005–2008 and 2009–2012). The Action Plans have been able to gradually coordinate approaches and advance a tangible collective agenda. For example, the EU Action Plan to Combat Drugs (2000–2004) outlined methods and policies for dealing with the problem of drug control. In the view of Caroline Chatwin,[19] this document attempted to reconcile the lib-

eral drug policy positions of the Netherlands and the conservative policies of Sweden in order to advance harmonization and cooperation in the
fight against drugs in Europe.[20] The EU Drugs Action Plan for 2009–2012
made a significant contribution by setting specific and measureable objectives and actions in areas of coordination (4 objectives, 9 actions); demand
reduction (5 objectives, 13 actions); supply reduction (5 objectives, 20 actions); international cooperation (4 objectives, 17 actions); information, research, and evaluation (3 objectives, 9 actions). Additionally, the EU Drugs
Action Plan for 2009–2012 proposes wide-ranging measures to strengthen
European cooperation to curb the adverse consequences of drug use and
to cut drug-related crime.

Another important document is the European Pact to Combat International Drug Trafficking—Disrupting Cocaine and Heroin Routes, adopted by the Council of the European Union on June 3, 2010.[21] This pact
proposed three main commitments: (1) the disruption of cocaine routes by
deepening the exchange of regional information (including establishing information exchange centers in Ghana and Senegal), support from Europol,
and technical assistance for transit countries; (2) the disruption of heroin
routes by developing a common approach within the EU and coordinating cooperation with non-EU countries; and (3) countering the proceeds
of crime by increasing criminal seizures and targeting money laundering
operations.

In October 2011, the Council of the European Union published the
European Pact against Synthetic Drugs, which aims to improve coordination between the various initiatives launched to clamp down on drug
trafficking. The pact includes four major areas: (1) countering production
of synthetic drugs; (2) countering trafficking in synthetic drugs and precursors; (3) tackling new psychoactive substances; and (4) training for law
enforcement services in detecting, examining, and dismantling clandestine
laboratories.[22]

The integration process has developed regional or community policies
in most areas of European policymaking, with different levels of intrusion
into the sovereignty of states. While monetary policy is for all intents and
purposes in the hands of the European Central Bank, the external relations
of the EU are still dominated by the national states. Policing and health
institutions involved in counternarcotics policymaking are mostly in the
hands of the states, but there is also a regional approach that contributes to
enhanced cooperation. In this light, the European Commission plays a significant role because it has competence in public health, precursor control,

money laundering, development aid, close cooperation between member states' foreign policy, justice, and home affairs, and partnerships with other international organizations.

As drug-trafficking concerns have been incorporated into the regional agenda, several European agencies have either been created or have become more involved in anti–drug trafficking policies. During the first half of 1995, the European Monitoring Centre for Drugs and Drug Addiction (EMCDDA) was established in Lisbon. It is a decentralized agency and is the repository of reliable, robust data on the drugs situation in Europe and responses to it.[23]

Closely linked to the EMCDDA, the European Information Network on Drugs and Drug Addiction (Réseau Européen d'Information sur les Drogues et les Toxicomanies, REITOX) was created in 1993. REITOX is a computer network at the heart of the collection and exchange of drug information and documentation in Europe and stores national statistics on drugs from each EU member state.

The regulation governing the EMCDDA's work requires each EU member state to establish or designate one national focal point, which has the duty to pursue three core functions: (1) data collection and monitoring; (2) analysis and interpretation of data collected; and (3) reporting and dissemination of the results at the national level.[24] As part of this process of sharing data gathered by similar or harmonized methodologies, in 2011, the EMCDDA made the first step in jointly developing, with the European Commission, indicators on drug markets, drug-related crime, and drug-supply reduction.

The European Union's Judicial Cooperation Unit (Eurojust) and the European law enforcement agency (Europol) are two pillars of the EU's fight against drug trafficking. Eurojust has stimulated the coordination of investigations and prosecutions in the member states, established a legal database with an overview of available legal instruments on drug trafficking, and strengthened cooperation between Europol, EMCDDA, and the European Agency for the Management of Operational Cooperation at the External Borders of the Member States of the European Union in matters of drug trafficking. Since 2004, Eurojust has dealt with more cases of drug trafficking than any other type of crime. In 2013, 239 drug-trafficking cases were opened, which made drug trafficking the most common type of crime in Eurojust's caseload, representing 16.8 percent of the total. The number of cases decreased slightly compared with 2010 (254), although the number of coordination meetings held in drug-trafficking cases increased from 39 in

2010 to 50 in 2011. Seven Joint Investigation teams on drug-trafficking cases were initiated in 2011 compared with only three in 2010.[25]

Around a third of operational support provided by Europol to national law enforcement agencies was related to illicit-drug trafficking in 2010. As the European Union's law enforcement agency, Europol's mission is to support member states in preventing and combating all forms of serious international crime and terrorism. Its role is to help achieve a safer Europe for the benefit of EU citizens by supporting EU law enforcement authorities through the exchange and analysis of criminal intelligence.

International Cooperation

The globalization of the trafficking of illegal drugs calls for effective international actions. The EU has developed several mechanism centered on five basic policies. The first is the political dialogue with strategic partners or regions, such as the United States, Russia, Latin America, and the Caribbean. The second is Drug Action Plans involving other regions of the world, currently, Latin America, the Caribbean, Central Asia, and the western Balkan countries. The third is international agreements and cooperative efforts to prevent the diversion of chemical precursors needed for the manufacture of illicit drugs for legitimate uses. Within these rubrics, the EU has signed precursor agreements with the United States, the Andean countries, Chile, Mexico, and Turkey. The fourth is preferential trade arrangements, such as the Generalized System of Preferences (GSP)–Drugs regime for preferential access to products from the Andean and Central American countries and Pakistan to the EU market. The fifth and final is the financing of antidrug projects.

With regard to heroin routes, the EU's long-term objective is to set up a system of "filters" between the main source of opiates and heroin—Afghanistan—and Western Europe. To achieve this objective, a number of technical assistance programs and initiatives have been put in place either directly by programs earmarked to fight drugs or by complementary initiatives to reinforce customs and border control in the newly independent states (NIs) in the Balkans and Central and Eastern Europe. Three drug action programs, or filters, have been implemented in the NIs, namely, the Central Asia Drug Action Program, the South Caucasus Action Drug Program, and the Belarus, Ukraine, Moldova Action Drug Program. These three umbrella programs seek a coherent approach in all three regions by using the same methodology, experts, and practices; at the same time, they adjust each individual program to match the particular circumstances of each region. Moreover, these programs are developed in accordance with the program model developed by the Programme of Community Aid to the Countries of Central and Eastern Europe (Phare) in Bulgaria and Romania in cooperation with the UNDCP from 1997 until 2001.

There is an Action Plan on Drugs between the EU and the Balkan states, which was adopted by the Council in June 2003 and provides a political framework for supporting actions against drugs in the region. The 2000–2006 Community Assistance for Reconstruction, Development and Stabilization Program (CARDS) was intended to provide community assistance to the countries of southeastern Europe with a view to their participation in the stabilization and association process with the European Union.[26] The CARDS budget for the 2000–2006 period totaled 4.65 billion euros.

The Andean community is a strategic area as a source of illegal drugs. The European Commission has financed the Anti-Illicit Drugs Program in the Andean Community (Programa Anti-Drogas Ilícitas en la Comunidad Andina, PRADICAN), which is the first comprehensive cooperation project on drugs within the programming period of 2007–2013. Endowed with a total budget of 4 million euros, one of the main goals of this project is the establishment of a network between national observatories of drug trafficking. Other goals are developing regional activities to control precursors in the Andean Community and improving drug-related analysis of the countries of the Andean Community. In April 2007, in line with the principle of shared responsibility that governs EU-CAN relations in this area, the European Commission signed the Regional Strategy for Cooperation with the Andean Community, allocating 50 million euros under the financing instrument for development cooperation for the period 2007–2013 to assist the Andean countries in their difficult fight against illicit drugs. As the violent confrontations between the Mexican government and drug cartels in Mexico have resulted in more than 50,000 casualties since 2006, the EU hosted the first High Level Dialogue on Security and Law Enforcement between the European Union and Mexico in 2011 in Brussels.[27]

The United States is a significant partner of the EU and its member states in counternarcotics initiatives for a variety of reasons. The United States is not only one of the main consumers of drugs but also a significant actor in intelligence gathering and technology innovation applied to interdiction and global military action. With sixty employees stationed in eleven European countries,[28] the U.S. Drug Enforcement Administration (DEA) is one of the most important agencies when dealing with drug trafficking.

An important mechanism for facilitating the partnerships between the United States and Europe is the twice-yearly U.S.-EU Bilateral Drug Exchange. These meetings provide a forum for learning about the implementation of drug policies and explore ways to improve coordination on key international issues, such as drug trafficking in the Caribbean and West Africa, international aid and development assistance, law enforcement training, and demand-reduction programs for developing nations that are grappling with drug-related challenges. One area in which the United States and Europe have been expanding cooperation is driving under the influence of illicit substances. Since the publication of its initial National Drug Control Strategy in May 2010, the U.S. Office of National Drug Control Policy (ONDCP) has sought to increase the focus on the serious consequences for health and safety caused by drugged driving, both at home and around the world. As part of this international effort, the United States and the EU worked together to organize a panel discussion on drugged driving at the 2010 UNODC Narcotics and Drugs meeting. At the 2011 Commission on Narcotic Drugs meetings, the United States and the EU collaborated on a resolution calling for additional global research on drugged driving.[29]

The cooperation between the European governments and the United States has produced tangible results in international operations. Among other examples, Operation Twin Oceans was conducted with the cooperation of law enforcement agencies in Colombia, Panama, Brazil, Argentina, Venezuela, Spain, and Great Britain. This three-year-long investigation, which culminated in 2006, resulted in over 100 arrests and the seizure of over forty-seven metric tons of cocaine and nearly U.S.$70 million in assets. Another example is "Operation White Dollar," conducted jointly by Britain's Serious Organized Crime Agency and the DEA, in which a variety of agencies and countries participated: the U.S. Internal Revenue Service, Colombia, Canada, and the New York City Police Department. This investigation resulted in the indictment of thirty-four individuals, the forfeiture to the United States of U.S.$20 million in laundered funds, and the issuance of seizure warrants for more than U.S.$1 million in additional laundered funds. In the case of non-EU members, the DEA helped coordinate an international cocaine investigation from Uruguay to the Ukraine in 2005, which resulted in the arrest of eight persons.

National Drug Policies

National approaches to and policies for regulating the use of drugs and combating derived criminal activities remain the cornerstone of the policy-making process at the regional level. As explained in the previous sections, the European Union has been a vehicle for the harmonization of strategies and methodologies to deal more effectively with the problems associated with the trafficking of drugs. Global agreements also influence national drug strategies. The 1988 United Nations Convention against Illicit Traffic of Drugs, Article 3 (2), states the following: "Subject to its constitutional principles and the basic concepts of its legal system, each Party shall adopt such measures as may be necessary to establish as a criminal offence under its domestic law, when committed intentionally, the possession, purchase or cultivation of narcotic drugs or psychotropic substances for personal consumption contrary to the provisions of the 1961 Convention, the 1961 Convention as amended or the 1971 Convention."

Against this background of global and regional legal influences, European countries have maintained some latitude by adopting several forms of decriminalization and depenalization. While each one of the twenty-eight EU countries develops and implements different policies for penalizing the cultivation, possession, and consumption of drugs, three have consistently acted as models for policies dealing with drugs: the Netherlands as a liberal model; Sweden as a restrictive model; and Portugal as a model of a new decriminalization perspective.

The Dutch drugs policy has received abundant attention worldwide and has been often described as too liberal and too tolerant.[30] Based on Chatwin's analysis,[31] two elements feature in the Dutch model. The first is adherence to the principle of drug consumption as a social and health problem, which has led to policies such as needle exchanges, the free testing of ecstasy pills for purity, reception rooms where users can take drugs without making a nuisance of themselves on the streets, and methadone programs, in which those addicted to heroin can receive free methadone in an attempt to control their addiction. The Netherlands, along with Britain, is also one of the first countries to become involved in trials of marijuana treatment for patients with multiple sclerosis.

The second major strand of the Dutch drug policy is the principle of the separation of markets. By permitting the establishment of coffee shops that sell cannabis and marijuana in a controlled, semilegal environment, the Dutch have separated the markets for "soft" and "hard" drugs. The sale of drugs in coffee shops is tolerated in parts of the Netherlands as long as the shops themselves adhere to a set of carefully laid down rules. The Dutch Opium Act punishes possession, commercial distribution, production, import, and export of all illicit drugs. Drug *use*, however, is not an offense. The act distinguishes between hard drugs (e.g., heroin, cocaine, ecstasy), which have "unacceptable" risks, and soft drugs (cannabis products). One of the main aims of this policy is to separate the markets for soft and hard drugs so that soft-drug users are less likely to come into contact with hard drugs. Trafficking in hard drugs is prosecuted vigorously. The Netherlands has a wide variety of demand-reduction and harm-reduction programs. Although coffee shops themselves are legal, they are dependent on an illegal market to supply them, and this creates a paradoxical situation.[32]

More recently, drug policy in the Netherlands has evolved to face changes in the drug market and in the perceptions of Dutch citizens. For instance, in July 2008, the justice and interior minister established a task force to combat the criminal organizations behind cannabis plantations. In June 2011, the cabinet approved measures to reduce drug-related nuisance and drug tourism. The cabinet proposed that coffee shops become private clubs for the local market and accessible only to Dutch citizens on display of a Dutch ID. The legislation passed, although the rollout was slow. In 2012, new, tougher, legislation passed requiring a Dutch ID for cannabis purchases, although the mayor of Amsterdam agreed to allow tourists to use the 220 coffee shops in the city.

Sweden has developed a different model. Swedish drug policy is regarded as restrictive, and there is a consensus that production, trafficking, and abuse of drugs must not be tolerated. This consensus and low levels of drug use have been explained as a result of a combination of causes: reduced income inequality; low unemployment; policies emphasizing drug problems as risks to Swedish values; a geographical position out of the main drug routes; increases in the drug-control budget; and a health-conscious culture less prone to large-scale use of drugs.[33] Some examples of this restrictive strategy include treatment based on complete abstention; forced treatment programs; illegality of drug consumption; and the use of urine and blood tests to detect those suspected of drug use. Drug-related legislation is strictly enforced, and discussions regarding the medical value of cannabis are almost nonexistent. Swedish legislation strictly adheres to, and even surpasses, the requirements set out in the three United Nations drug conventions.[34] At the regional level, when Sweden entered the EU in 1995, it paralyzed the general trend toward liberalism in several EU countries.[35]

In short, the main aim of current Swedish drug policy can be identified as a bid to entirely free society of illegal drugs and the problems they cause.

Portugal decriminalized the use and possession of all illicit drugs in July 2001. Preliminary assessments indicate that decriminalization did not lead to major increases in drug use.[36] Central to the Portuguese policy of decriminalization is the role of commissions, managed by the Ministry of Health, in the dissuasion of drug abuse. These bodies assess the situation of drug users and have the power to provide support or impose sanctions. While no other country has yet adopted this model, a committee set up by the Norwegian government has suggested the development of similar interdisciplinary tribunals.[37] In the view of Glenn Greenwald, although postdecriminalization usage rates have remained roughly the same or even decreased slightly when compared to other states, drug-related pathologies such as sexually transmitted diseases have decreased dramatically in Portugal.[38] In spite of this, Portugal can serve as a model for Latin American countries considering decriminalizing drugs.

While these three European models are unique, most of the countries in the region have combined elements from each of them and, in fact, have created their own drug policies according to their specific circumstances. Three types of changes in penalties have been implemented in Europe. I will provide an overview of the current trends in penalization of drug users (using the 2011 annual report of the EMCDDA as a starting point). The first trend is changing the status of drug-related offense from criminal to noncriminal. These changes have taken place in Portugal, Luxembourg, and Belgium. In Luxembourg in May 2001, maximum penalties for personal possession of all drugs other than cannabis were reduced; in Belgium, the possession of a small amount of cannabis for personal use, without aggravating circumstances, was reduced to a police fine in 2003. Policy changes toward decriminalization have also occurred in Estonia (2002) and Slovenia (2005).

The second trend is maintaining the legal status of drug-related offenses but changing the way drugs are categorized. In Romania (in 2004), the law divided illegal substances into high-risk and low-risk categories and lowered the penalties for the latter. In Bulgaria (2006), penalties for both categories were reduced; in the Czech Republic (2010), the new penal code applied less severe punishments for cannabis than for other drugs. In the United Kingdom (2004), the penalty for cannabis was reduced after its reclassification from a Class B drug to a Class C, but in 2009, it was reclassified again to Class B and penalties were increased.

The third trend is changing the penalties for personal possession without addressing the legal status of the drug. Penalties were reduced in Finland (2001), Greece (2003), Denmark (2004), and France (2007).[39]

Conclusion

This chapter has developed the argument that, unlike in other regions, drug-trafficking policies in Europe are better understood when the outcomes of two levels of decision making are analyzed. The first is the regional level, at which the integration process has gradually included more policy domains in its agenda. From the perspective of the neofunctional school of integration studies, a spillover process has been taking place in Europe. What started as integration limited to the area of coal and steel has gradually included new policy domains, and today drug-trafficking policies are part of that agenda.

The second level refers to member states. Today, states are still in charge of designing and implementing their own drug policies, but as a result of EU membership, some areas of drug policy are affected by the coordination of EU institutions.

In the context of the debates and preparation of the EU Drug Strategy 2013–2020, RAND Europe elaborated a report for the European Commission Directorate General for Justice in which six main areas are posed:[40]

(1) The strategy document itself. The document is considered a logical and coherent document, but its comprehensiveness (158 actions) may come across as a wish list and affect the ability to prioritize actions.

(2) On-demand reduction. The report concurs that achievements are consistent with the objectives of the strategy, but there is a need to consider drug use in a broader policy framework of addiction and licit drugs.

(3) Demand reduction. The assessment is that there are a few visible indications that the supply side is moving in the desired direction, and there remains a serious limitation to measuring effectiveness of the supply-reduction initiatives.

(4) Coordination. The report indicates that this area has been relatively effective in contributing to a more collaborative and informed drafting of national drug policies.

(5) International cooperation. The report recognizes several successes,

particularly with regard to the EU's "speaking with one voice" in international cooperation mechanisms and enhancing the capacity of coordination in the making of policy aimed at nonmember countries.

(6) Information, research, and evaluation. While there has been notable progress, there are some disparities in quality and availability of data.

The understanding of the global market for illegal drugs involves a variety of actors and regions;. therefore, effective strategies must pursue international cooperation as a tool to reinforce national actions against illegal drugs. In the case of Europe, international or regional cooperation is part of the domestic agenda of the EU's member states because the Union has embarked on regional coordination and, where possible, the harmonization of policies and strategies. The EU Drug Strategy 2013–2020 builds on its existing international reputation in this field and continues to promote a balanced approach. The EU Drugs Strategy has helped raise the international profile of an EU model for drug policy employing a balanced approach.

Notes

1. United Nations Office on Drugs and Crime (UNODC), *The Globalization of Crime: A Transnational Organized Crime Threat Assessment* (New York, 2010), v.

2. Francisco E. Thoumi, *Illegal Drugs, Economy, and Society in the Andes* (Washington, D.C.: Woodrow Wilson Center Press and Johns Hopkins University Press, 2003).

3. See the introduction in this volume.

4. UNODC, *World Drug Report, 2012* (New York, 2012).

5. Ibid., v.

6. Council of the European Union, "EU Action Plan on Drugs 2009–2012," MEMO/08/571, Brussels, September 18, 2008.

7. European Monitoring Centre for Drugs and Drug Addiction (EMCDDA), *Annual Report 2007* (Luxembourg: Publications Office of the European Union, 2008).

8. UNODC, *World Drug Report, 2012*, 3.

9. European Police Office, *Europol's 2011 Organised Crime Threat Assessment (OCTA)* (The Hague, 2011).

10. UNODC, *World Drug Report, 2012*, 2.

11. UNODC, *The Globalization of Crime*, 95–108.

12. Michael A. Braun, "Chief of Operations Drug Enforcement Administration before the House Judiciary Committee, Subcommittee on Crime, Terrorism, and Homeland Security, and House International Relations Committee, Subcommittee on Western Hemisphere," September 21, 2006, http://www.justice.gov/dea/pr/speeches-testimony/2006t/ct092106p.html.

13. Ibid.

14. UNODC, *World Drug Report, 2012*, 1–2.

15. Ibid., v.

16. White House, *National Drug Control Strategy 2012* (Washington, D.C.: ONDCP, 2012).

17. Organization of American States (OAS), *Hemispheric Drug Strategy*, Washington, D.C., approved May 3, 2009, http://www.cicad.oas.org/apps/Document.aspx?Id=953.

18. European Commission, "Communication from the Commission to the European Parliament and the Council, towards a Stronger European Response to Drugs," Brussels, XXX COM (2011) 689/2, http://ec.europa.eu/justice/anti-drugs/files/com2011-6892_en.pdf.

19. Caroline Chatwin, "Drug Policy Developments within the European Union: The Destabilizing Effects of Dutch and Swedish Drug Policies," *British Journal of Criminology* 43 (2003): 567–582.

20. Ibid.

21. Council of the European Union, "European Pact to Combat International Drug Trafficking—Disrupting Cocaine and Heroin Routes," 3018th Justice and Home Affairs Council Meeting, Luxembourg, June 3, 2010, http://www.consilium.europa.eu/uedocs/cms_data/docs/pressdata/en/jha/114889.pdf.

22. Council of the European Union, "European Pact against Synthetic Drugs," 3121st Justice and Home Affairs Council Meeting, Luxembourg, October 27–28, 2011.

23. European Monitoring Centre for Drugs and Drug Addiction, *2011: A Year in Review* (Lisbon: Publications Office of the European Union, 2011). For download, http://www.emcdda.europa.eu/publications/general-report-of-activities/2011-highlights.

24. EMCDDA, *The Reitox Network: Frequently Asked Questions* (Lisbon, February 2012).

25. European Union's Judicial Cooperation Unit (Eurojust), *Annual Report 2011* (The Hague, 2011), 30.

26. The participant countries in this program are Albania, Bosnia and Herzegovina, Croatia, the Federal Republic of Yugoslavia, and the Former Yugoslav Republic of Macedonia.

27. European Commission, "The European Union and Mexico Hold a First High Level Dialogue on Security and Law Enforcement," press release, July 15, 2011.

28. Braun, "Chief of Operations."

29. White House, "Europe/European Partners," ONDCP, http://www.whitehouse.gov/ondcp/europe.

30. H.F.L. Garretsen, "The Dutch and Their Drugs: The End of an Era? Reflections on Dutch Policies towards Tobacco, Alcohol and Illegal Drugs," *Drugs: Education, Prevention and Policy* 17 (October 2010): 485–495.

31. Chatwin, "Drug Policy Developments."

32. Ibid.

33. UNODC, *Sweden's Successful Drug Policy: A Review of the Evidence* (New York, 2007).

34. Gérald Lafrenière, "National Drug Policy: Sweden," presentation prepared for the

Senate Special Committee on Illegal Drugs, Library of the Canadian Parliament, April 18, 2002, http://www.parl.gc.ca/content/sen/committee/371/ille/library/gerald-e.htm.

35. Chatwin, "Drug Policy Developments."

36. Caitlin Elizabeth Hughes and Alex Stevens, "What Can We Learn from the Portuguese Decriminalization of Illicit Drugs?" *British Journal of Criminology* 50 (2010): 999–1022.

37. EMCDDA, *Annual Report 2011: The State of the Drugs Problems in Europe* (Lisbon: Publications Office of the European Union, 2012).

38. Glenn Greenwald, *Drug Decriminalization in Portugal: Lessons for Creating Fair and Successful Drug Policies* (Washington, D.C.: Cato Institute, 2009).

39. EMCDDA, *The Reitox Network*, 22–24.

40. Deirdre May Culley, Jirka Taylor, Jennifer Rubin, Stijn Hoorens, Emma Disley, and Lila Rabinovich, *Assessment of the Implementation of the EU Drugs Strategy 2005–2012 and Its Action Plans* (Santa Monica, Calif.: RAND–Europe–European Communities, 2012).

20

Analytical Conclusions

The Search for Alternative Drug Policies
in the Americas

BRUCE M. BAGLEY AND JONATHAN D. ROSEN

This volume has analyzed the major overall trends in drug trafficking and organized crime in the Americas during the twenty-first century. This concluding chapter will analyze the lessons from the "war on drugs." Washington has not succeeded in the war on drugs, and the drug war has spread the problem around the globe as more and more countries have been contaminated as a result of drug trafficking and organized crime. Many academics and policymakers have been criticizing the war on drugs for decades and have provided alternatives; however, Washington has failed to learn from history and has continued to implement the same strategies over and over again despite the fact that such policies have not been effective. If the United States persists in the same wrongheaded and inflexible policies, it is highly probable that the Americas will witness increases in cultivation in new territories and spillover effects as not only cultivation but also trafficking routes expand into neighboring countries. In addition, violence will likely increase as drug-trafficking organizations battle for control of territory and routes. Current trends also indicate that the consumption of drugs will continue to increase, providing drug-trafficking organizations incentives to increase the production and trafficking of illicit substances.

One of the major lessons from the war on drugs is what is referred to by scholars and policy experts as the "balloon" effect. The balloon effect is when governments attempt to combat drug cultivation or trafficking in one country, causing it to "balloon out" to other regions. The balloon effect can be proven empirically by analyzing past trends and statistical evidence not only in terms of production but also in terms of trafficking. For scholars and policy analysts studying drug trafficking, the balloon effect is as close to a law as social scientists will ever witness. The "partial victories" in the war on drugs have resulted in coca cultivation shifting from Peru and Bolivia to Colombia.[1] Peru and Bolivia were the major coca cultivators in the world until the mid-1980s. Successful interdiction efforts, however, shifted coca cultivation to Colombia. From 2000 to 2013, Colombia surpassed Peru and Bolivia and became the number-one cultivator of coca in the world as well as the leading producer and trafficker of cocaine.[2] In 2013, Peru surpassed Colombia as the leading coca cultivator.[3]

The Globalization of Consumption

One of the major lessons in this volume is the globalization of drug consumption. Sentiments exist in Latin America that if the "gringos" to the north did not consume such large amounts of drugs, then the countries of the Americas would not have problems with drug trafficking. The laws of supply and demand demonstrate that drug traffickers will continue to operate as long as they have a market.

The United States, which is the number-one cocaine-consuming country in the world, has not been an equal partner in the drug war, and Washington has not done enough to curb demand in the United States. Instead, the United States has focused on reducing supply, arguing that a drug problem exists because countries such as Colombia cultivate, produce, and traffic these noxious substances.

Indeed, Washington must do more to reduce the demand for drugs within the country. It is impossible to obtain a definitive number for the amount of money that Americans spend on drugs annually, but research indicates that U.S. consumers alone spend approximately $150 billion on drugs. In addition, an astounding $37 billion of the $150 billion is spent on cocaine.[4] It would be wrong, however, to assume that countries in the Americas would not have a drug problem if people residing in the United States did not consume drugs. As a result of globalization, we have witnessed an ever-increasing demand for drugs around the world. The consumption of drugs is no longer "an American disease," as David Musto suggests, but has become a worldwide phenomenon.[5] Cocaine consumption has expanded rapidly throughout the developing world, particularly in Latin America. In 2010, Latin Americans consumed an estimated 200 metric tons of cocaine. The European countries also continue to consume large quantities of drugs, particularly cocaine.

Research also indicates that the Europeans pay twice as much per kilo, gram, ounce, and metric ton as American consumers. The cocaine-consuming population in Europe accounts for an estimated 29 percent of the total supply (440 metric tons) of cocaine available.[6]

In sum, the globalization of drug consumption is a major new trend. While globalization has many positive aspects and can help facilitate transactions between countries, organized criminal networks and drug traffickers also benefit from improvements in technology and the impact of globalization.

Militarization

One other major strategy implemented in the war on drugs has been the militarization of the drug war. Washington has supported countries with training, equipment, and financial resources to help them combat drug trafficking through military efforts. With regard to Mexico, Laurie Freeman and Jorge Luis Sierra declare, "The United States was an eager participant in the militarization of Mexico's counterdrug policy, prompting and supporting it every step of the way. U.S. officials encouraged Mexico to use the military to fight drugs for two basic reasons. First, the military was seen as the only institution with the manpower, resources, and equipment to counter the threat of well-armed and wealthy traffickers. Second, by 1986 Mexican law enforcement agencies had been thoroughly discredited by their links to drug traffickers, and the U.S. government saw the military as a less corrupt counterpart."[7] Militarization has not been effective and has resulted in the drug-production and drug-trafficking routes shifting to other regions. The military is not capable of resolving the underlying issues in the war on drugs, such as demand, weak institutions, and high levels of corruption.

U.S. leaders have failed to realize that the number-one objective of drug traffickers is to earn money. For instance, former secretary of state Hillary Clinton argued that Mexico needed to implement the same counterinsurgency strategies as those used to fight the drug war in Colombia.[8] This is a fundamental misconception of the problem, as drug traffickers use terrorism as a tactic to scare and intimidate rivals and civilians; however, drug traffickers in Mexico have an entirely different political objective from that of terrorist organizations such as al-Qaeda. Using the military to kill major leaders, or capos, does nothing to reduce the demand for illegal drugs.

In addition, the militarization of the war on drugs has had major legal and human rights ramifications. By definition, the military is designed to protect countries from external threats as opposed to internal enemies. Latin American countries, in particular, have a long history of military involvement in politics and internal policing, which by definition is the role of the police forces. As Isacson notes, the law in the United States clearly prohibits the military from intervening in domestic politics and affairs. However, Washington has continued to support the militarization of the war on drugs throughout the Americas. The use of the military has hindered the democratic consolidation of many countries. In addition, the military has participated in major human rights abuses. In sum, the military as an institution is not capable of addressing the demand side and has hindered institutional strengthening in countries throughout the region.

The "Cockroach" Effect

The next major lesson is the fragmentation of criminal networks and cartels, which is referred to as the "cockroach" effect. The U.S.-led war on drugs has resulted in a fragmentation of criminal drug-trafficking organizations in a manner akin to turning on the lights in a kitchen and witnessing the cockroaches disperse. The effect "refers specifically to the displacement of criminal networks from one city/state/region to another within a given country or from one country to another in search of safer havens and more pliable state authorities."[9] Colombia, for instance, experienced extreme levels of violence during the days of the Medellín cartel, led by Pablo Escobar, and the Cali cartel. The United States implemented what is referred to as the "kingpin strategy"; under the auspices of this strategy, Washington assisted the Colombian government in arresting and killing the major leaders, or capos, of the drug cartels operating within the country.[10] The logic was that capturing and killing the leaders of the organizations would be akin to cutting off the head of a snake. It was thought that, just like a snake without a head, a drug cartel without its leader could not function and would collapse.[11]

The victories against the major cartels in Colombia, however, were short-lived, as these provided a vacuum in which smaller organizations could operate. While Colombia does not have large top-down organizations, as in the past, the smaller organizations still traffic drugs and have seized control of the markets left behind with the collapse of the major cartels. The vacuum created by the collapse of the cartels resulted in the strengthening of the Revolutionary Armed Forces of Colombia (Fuerzas Armadas Revolucionarias de Colombia, FARC) as well as the paramilitaries in Colombia. The smaller organizations presented many challenges for law enforcement officials, as they became much harder to locate and dismantle.

The cockroach effect also has occurred in Colombia due to the Uribe administration's demobilization of the paramilitary organizations. As a result, Colombia has witnessed the emergence of criminal bands, often referred to as *bandas criminales*, as former paramilitary officers have demobilized and joined the new criminal networks. The paramilitaries, in essence, have switched teams and are applying their skills to the lucrative drug-trafficking business. The emergence and strengthening of such criminal networks present various challenges for the Colombian government and law enforcement.[12]

Like Colombia, Mexico has experienced a fragmentation of organized criminal networks into smaller, more nimble organizations that participate in drug trafficking and other forms of organized crime. In 2000, Mexico had two dominant cartels, the Juárez cartel and the Tijuana cartel, run by two families. Former Mexican president Vicente Fox sought to combat the cartels in both cities. As a result of his efforts, Mexico witnessed the emergence of at least five new major drug-trafficking organizations that were much smaller in size and easier to operate.

As in Colombia, the smaller and "leaner" cartels present major challenges for the notoriously corrupt Mexican police as well as the army. In 2006, Mexico had six major cartels. By 2010, the number of cartels operating within the country had doubled in number, demonstrating the increasing trend toward fragmentation.

Asymmetrical Relationships

This volume also addresses the cost of conducting the war on drugs. The burdens can be described as asymmetrical and illegitimate because countries throughout Latin America and the Caribbean have been required to sacrifice a great deal in terms of both blood and treasure. The United States has made relatively nominal contributions and has not endured the hardships experienced by many countries throughout the Americas.

Several important factors help explain why the relationship has been asymmetrical and the Latin American countries have endured a great deal of the burden. Since the United States has been the number-one consumer of drugs in the world for several decades, sentiments existed among Latin American leaders that the United States, therefore, should have to develop a solution to the drug problem. Bagley and Tokatlian state that "while at the political-diplomatic level such an approach may have appeared plausible and defensible, at the strategic level it proved to be a serious (and ultimately costly) mistake, as it excluded Latin America almost entirely from the search for positive answers to the drug question."[13]

Such actions provided the United States with the opportunity to set the agenda and develop policies that would address drug trafficking. The United States had a different construction of the problem,[14] or diagnosis, as well as proposed solutions. Washington believed that the issue that needed to be addressed was the supply of drugs from other countries. Therefore, the United States focused on supply-side strategies and did not consider the opinions of the leaders of the Latin American countries.

As the hegemonic power, the United States has often had the belief that it has the right and responsibility to intervene in "backward" nations, as Adrián Bonilla notes.[15] Beginning in the 1980s, the United States successfully established an antidrug regime throughout the Americas and used its power to coerce the less powerful countries to comply. The governments in the Americas did not have an equal voice, and Washington pressured them to abide by the rules and agenda it had designed. Said differently, "these efforts failed because Washington did not establish a legitimate, credible, and symmetrical framework capable of coping with the multiple problems presented by international drug production, smuggling, and use."[16]

In sum, the asymmetrical burdens placed on governments throughout the Americas have taken a toll, costing a tremendous amount in not only economic cost but also human lives. The unequal partnership and relatively nominal contributions of the United States have resulted in decreases in Washington's legitimacy and soft power throughout the region.[17]

Strengthening Institutions and Consolidating Democracy

Drug traffickers have continually shifted back and forth between the Americas—evidence of the balloon effect—in order to avoid detection. Weak states, particularly in the Caribbean and Central America, have become fertile territory for drug trafficking and organized crime. In Central America, Guatemala and Honduras, in particular, have been greatly impacted by the drug war, and drug cartels from other countries, such as Mexico, have moved into these territories.

Countries with institutions that are extremely weak are vulnerable to organized crime. It is crucial for governments throughout Latin America and the Caribbean to strive to consolidate effective democratic governments that can administer justice and implement the rule of law. Countries characterized by an ineffective and corrupt justice system suffer from major forms of paralysis. Many countries do not have the capacity to prosecute lawbreakers and have abysmal records in this regard, and impunity remains a major issue in 2014. Institutions must be strengthened throughout the region to help combat organized crime.

A final point is that countries hindered by weak state apparatuses do not have the capability to control their territory. Ultimately, consolidating democracy, improving the administration of justice, and strengthening institutions throughout the region are crucial for countries in order to combat drug trafficking and organized criminal networks. Countries with weak institutions and democracies are prone to corruption and bribery and are breeding grounds for organized criminal networks and activity. Combating organized crime in the absence of strong institutions and a functioning judicial system is quite difficult, if not nearly impossible.

Education, Prevention, and Treatment

A growing consensus exists within the United States and many parts of Latin America and the Caribbean that the United States would be best served by paying greater attention to domestic programs designed to reduce demand through education, prevention, rehabilitation, treatment, and community policing.

The United States has not been an equal partner in the war on drugs and remains the number-one consumer of drugs in the global market. Washington cannot afford to continue ignoring the demand side and focus only on stopping the supply of drugs entering the country. Research indicates that education and prevention, when done correctly, are effective and can help reduce the demand for drugs. Harm-reduction policies must be implemented in order to help addicts curb their appetite for drugs and provide them with the educational tools and skills necessary to become productive members of society.[18] A tremendous amount of research has been conducted regarding drug abuse, but Washington has failed to heed the lessons and implement appropriate measures to help address the demand side of the problem.[19]

Prison Reform

Another crucial aspect that the United States must address is prison reform. The United States could avoid huge costs in the prison system by routing minors and nonviolent drug offenders into alternative systems for treatment and training. Washington cannot afford to continue jailing and systematically ruining the lives of millions of Americans. Convicted felons, for instance, are denied access by the federal government to public housing. In addition, these individuals are shunned by the community and their families. Employers, especially, are hesitant to hire someone with a criminal record. States, such as Florida, deny felons access to student loans, prohibiting them from improving themselves through education. Therefore, it becomes a rational choice for young convicted felons to return to the streets and participate in drug trafficking and other forms of illegal activity.

The United States must address the problems of the prison system and stop incarcerating millions of people. Harm-reduction programs aimed at treatment and training must be implemented to avoid the significant costs and help troubled youth find the help required to reduce their chances of returning to the prison system and enable them to become productive and successful members of society.[20]

Rejection of the U.S. War on Drugs

The final conclusion reached in this volume is that a global rejection of the U.S.-led war on drugs has occurred. Growing consensus exists that there is a crucial and pressing need for the United States to find alternatives to its current prohibitionist and repressive models. Many Latin American and Caribbean governments are experimenting and can be expected to continue to experiment with legalization of personal dosages and other variations in the imprisonment of users and jail time for peasant growers. Various Latin American leaders have been quite vocal in their rejection of the U.S.-led war on drugs. The 2013 Organization of American States (OAS) meeting held in Guatemala resulted in the publication of reports that called for alternatives to the current prohibitionist models. The fact that this key institution has recognized that the U.S.-led war on drugs has been ineffective and too costly and, most important, must change is a critical moment in the history of the drug war.[21]

In sum, various leading Latin American officials have argued for a new drug policy paradigm. Some presidents, such as Juan Manuel Santos of

Colombia, recognizing the consequences of the current prohibitionist policies, have stated that they are open to legalization debates.[22] Such rhetoric marks the beginning of the breakdown of the prohibitionist regime.

Some countries have moved beyond discourse and changed their drug laws. Uruguay, for instance, has legalized marijuana, while many other countries have decriminalized drug usage because the socioeconomic costs have been too high.[23] In the United States, Colorado and Washington have legalized marijuana.

Various arguments exist for legalization of, particularly, blander drugs, such as marijuana. Many libertarians, for instance, believe that all drugs should be legalized as people should have the liberty to decide what to consume. In addition, libertarians believe that the government should not intervene in the personal lives of individuals. Others, however, advocate for the legalization of all drugs and argue that the government should tax and regulate them. This money could be used for treatment, education, and rehabilitation. On the other hand, some people are in favor of partial legalization, as it is difficult to make the case to legalize very dangerous drugs such as heroin or cocaine.

While debates exist regarding what drugs should be legalized and what the role of the government is, the argument remains pretty clear: the legalization of drugs will help take some of the profits out of the black market.[24] Clearly, the legalization of marijuana in two U.S. states will not destroy the markets of the drug cartels in Mexico, but it has been estimated by experts that it will decrease their profits by several billion dollars a year.[25] In sum, the key point is that the tides are slowly beginning to change and the policies have been altered.

If the United States expects to continue to exercise global leadership, Washington must recognize the costs and failures of its counterproductive policies since the 1970s. Ted Galen Carpenter states that "Washington's supply-side campaign against drugs has not worked, is not working, and given economic realities, will not work. This is not to suggest that the influence of the drug trade is a benign one or that Latin American countries would not be better off if the trafficking organizations were less powerful. The exaggerated importance that the drug trade has acquired is an economic distortion caused by foolish policies adopted in Washington and the drug-source countries themselves. Immediate steps can and should be taken to eliminate that distortion."[26] After recognizing the failures of such policies, Washington must adapt to the problems, complaints, and growing frictions that have emerged as a result of the war on drugs. Washington must understand that youths need to be educated about drugs. This does not happen, especially in countries that adopt highly repressive models and in countries that do not have the economic resources to implement such programs. A long-term strategy would be one that addresses issues of social inclusion, especially of youth, providing them with education, jobs, and health care, and strengthening institutions and the ability of countries to implement the rule of law.

Although it is impossible to calculate the exact amount of money that Washington has spent, some scholars estimate that the United States has allocated over a trillion dollars to the war on drugs.[27] Although the data are lacking, it is quite possible that the rest of the world has spent another trillion dollars. After over two trillion dollars spent, it is time for the United States to recognize that the same failed policies have been too costly and cannot continue.

In conclusion, the U.S.-led war on drugs has been a failure and has helped spread organized crime throughout the region. Mexico, for instance, has suffered more than 70,000 deaths since former president Felipe Calderón (2006–2012) launched an extensive drug war with the support of Washington.[28] Violence continues in Mexico as drug traffickers fight for control of territory and is likely to continue for the foreseeable future. Mexico, however, is only one example, and this volume has highlighted the impact of the war on drugs throughout the region.

The international community has witnessed a rejection of the U.S.-led war on drugs by major leaders, civilians, and policymakers because the costs of the drug war have been extremely high, and drug trafficking and organized crime have had major consequences for society as well as regional security. One of the watershed moments was the OAS report in 2013 as well as the legalization and decriminalization of certain drugs, particularly marijuana, in various countries.[29] More must be done to strengthen institutions and address the underlying problems as opposed to continuing the same failed supply-side strategies. If policies do not continue to change, we can expect more bloodshed and violence as drug traffickers continue to fight rivals for control of territory and markets.

Notes

1. See Bruce M. Bagley, *Drug Trafficking and Organized Crime in the Americas: Major Trends in the Twenty-First Century* (Washington, D.C.: Woodrow Wilson Center, 2012).
2. After the Peru-Colombia "air bridge" that transported paste, or base, from Peru's

Alto Huallaga to Colombia in small airplanes was disrupted by Peruvian president Fujimori's adoption of a shoot-down policy in 1993–1994, the subsequent termination of the cocaine flights out of Peru during the Fujimori dictatorship in the mid- to late 1990s, and the launching of Plan Dignidad in 1998 (with U.S. government funding) by the newly installed Banzer government in Bolivia, the epicenter of illegal coca cultivation shifted from eastern Peru and Bolivia to southeastern Colombia; see Paul Gootenberg, *Andean Cocaine: The Making of a Global Drug* (Chapel Hill: University of North Carolina Press, 2008), 291–324; Patrick L. Clawson and Rensselaer W. Lee III, *The Andean Cocaine Industry* (New York: St. Martin's Griffin, 1998), 16–21; Francisco E. Thoumi, *Illegal Drugs, Economy, and Society in the Andes* (Baltimore: Johns Hopkins University Press, 2003), 7 and passim. See also United Nations Office on Drugs and Crime (UNODC), "Coca Cultivation in the Andean Region: Survey of Bolivia, Colombia and Peru" (New York, 2006).

3. Adriana Leon and Chris Kraul, "Peru Passes Colombia in Coca Growth, Raising Enforcement Concerns," *Los Angeles Times,* September 27, 2013.

4. See Bagley, *Drug Trafficking and Organized Crime*; UNODC, *The Globalization of Crime: A Transnational Organized Crime Threat Assessment* (New York, 2010), 5–6; idem, *World Drug Report, 2011* (New York, 2011), 8.

5. See David F. Musto, *The American Disease: Origins of Narcotic Control*, 3rd ed. (New York: Oxford University Press, 1999, first published in 1973 by Yale University Press).

6. See Bagley, *Drug Trafficking and Organized Crime*; UNODC, *World Drug Report, 2010* (New York, 2010), 16; idem, *The Globalization of Crime*, v–vi, 82. The consumption of cocaine decreased in the United States to 1.9 percent of the population using cocaine in 2009 from 2.5 percent in 2006; see UNODC, *World Drug Report, 2011*, 93.

7. Laurie Freeman and Jorge Luis Sierra, "Mexico: The Militarization Trap," in *Drugs and Democracy in Latin America: The Impact of U.S. Policy*, ed. Coletta A. Youngers and Eileen Rosin (Boulder, Colo.: Lynne Rienner, 2005), 277.

8. Patrick Corcoran, "Counterinsurgency Is Not the Answer for Mexico," *Insight Crime,* September 26, 2011, http://www.insightcrime.org/news-analysis/counterinsurgency-is-not-the-answer-for-mexico.

9. See Bagley, *Drug Trafficking and Organized Crime*, 24–25.

10. Russell Crandall, *Driven by Drugs: U.S. Policy toward Colombia* (Boulder, Colo.: Lynne Rienner, 2002), 193.

11. Ibid.

12. See Bagley, *Drug Trafficking and Organized Crime*. For more on Colombia, see chapter 8 in this volume; see also chapter 7 in this volume.

13. Bruce M. Bagley and Juan G. Tokatlian, "Dope and Dogma: Explaining the Failure of U.S.–Latin American Drug Policies," in *The United States and Latin America in the 1990s: Beyond the Cold War*, ed. Jonathan Hartlyn, Lars Schoultz, and Augusto Varas (Chapel Hill: University of North Carolina Press, 1992), 223.

14. This is a constructivist issue. For more on constructivism, see Barry Buzan, Ole Wæver, and Jaap de Wilde, *Security: A New Framework for Analysis* (Boulder, Colo.: Lynne Rienner, 1998).

15. Adrián Bonilla, "U.S. Andean Policy, the Colombian Conflict, and Security in Ecuador," in *Addicted to Failure: U.S. Security Policy in Latin America and the Andean Region* (Lanham, Md.: Rowman & Littlefield, 2006), 129.

16. Bagley and Tokatlian, "Dope and Dogma," 232.

17. Joseph S. Nye Jr., *Soft Power: The Means to Success in World Politics* (New York: Public Affairs), 191.

18. See chapters 6 and 9 in this volume.

19. Ethan Nadelmann, "Addicted to Failure," *Foreign Policy*, no. 137 (July–August 2003): 94; Bruce M. Bagley, "U.S. Foreign Policy and the War on Drugs: Analysis of a Policy Failure," *Journal of Interamerican Studies and World Affairs* 30, nos. 2 and 3, Special Issue: Assessing the Americas' War on Drugs (Summer–Autumn, 1988): 189–212.

20. See chapter 6 in this volume; Michelle Alexander, *The New Jim Crow: Mass Incarceration in the Age of Colorblindness* (New York: New Press), 290.

21. *Report of the Drug Problem in the Americas: Terms of Reference, 2012–2013* (Panama City: OAS, 2013). For a link to the report, see http://www.countthecosts.org/sites/default/files/CICAD-Marketing-Document-ENG.pdf. See also *The Drug Problem in the Americas, 2013* (Panama City: OAS, 2013). For a link to the report, see http://www.oas.org/documents/eng/press/Introduction_and_Analytical_Report.pdf.

22. "Colombian President Calls for Global Rethink on Drugs," *The Observer*, November 12, 2011, accessed August 22, 2012, http://www.guardian.co.uk/world/2011/nov/13/colombia-juan-santos-call-to-legalise-drugs; "Presidente Santos consideraría legalizar el consumo de droga," *Caracol*, February 13, 2011, accessed August 22, 2012, http://www.caracol.com.co/noticias/actualidad/presidente-santos-consideraria-legalizar-el-consumo-de-droga/20110213/nota/1425320.aspx; "U.S.-Colombia Trade Deal to Take Effect in May," CNN, April 2012, accessed August 22, 2012, http://articles.cnn.com/2012-04-15/americas/world_americas_summit-of-the-americas_1_legalization-drug-war-drug-issue?_s=PM:AMERICAS."

23. Malena Castaldi and Felipe Llambias, "Uruguay Becomes First Country to Legalize Marijuana Trade," Reuters, December 10, 2013, accessed February 2014, http://www.reuters.com/article/2013/12/11/us-uruguay-marijuana-vote-idUSBRE9BA01520131211.

24. Geoffrey Ramsey, "Study: U.S. Marijuana Legalization Could Cut Cartel Profits by 30%," Insight Crime, November 2012, accessed 2014, http://www.insightcrime.org/news-analysis/study-legalization-cut-cartel-profits-by-30.

25. See http://www.insightcrime.org/news-analysis/study-legalization-cut-cartel-profits-by-30.

26. Ted Galen Carpenter, *Bad Neighbor Policy: Washington's Futile War on Drugs in Latin America* (New York: Palgrave Macmillan, 2003), 231.

27. "Forty Years of Failure," Drug Policy Alliance, http://www.drugpolicy.org/new-solutions-drug-policy/forty-years-failure.

28. Jan-Albert Hootsen, "How the Sinaloa Cartel Won Mexico's Drug War," *Global Post*, February 28, 2013, accessed 2014, http://www.globalpost.com/dispatch/news/regions/americas/mexico/130227/sinaloa-cartel-mexico-drug-war-US-global-economy-conflict-zones. For more on the drug war in Mexico, see Ted Galen Carpenter, *The Fire Next Door: Mexico's Drug Violence and the Danger to America* (Washington, D.C.: Cato Institute, 2012).

29. *Report of the Drug Problem in the Americas: Terms of Reference, 2012–2013* (Panama City: OAS, 2013). For a link to the report, see http://www.countthecosts.org/sites/default/files/CICAD-Marketing-Document-ENG.pdf.

CONTRIBUTORS

Sigrid Arzt was the technical secretary of Mexico's National Security Council during President Felipe Calderón's administration, where she served as the chairperson of a council of the highest-ranking federal officials in the area of national security. Dr. Arzt has been a public policy scholar at the Woodrow Wilson International Center for Scholars in Washington, D.C. Until 2006, she also served as codirector of a Mexico City nonprofit association, Democracy, Human Rights, and Security, which she founded in 2003.

Bruce M. Bagley is professor and former associate dean of the Graduate School of International Studies at the University of Miami. His research interests are in U.S.–Latin American relations, with an emphasis on drug trafficking and security issues. Recent among his many publications are *The International Relations of Latin America*, coauthored with Betty Horwitz, and *La desmovilización de los paramilitares en Colombia: Entre el escepticismo y la esperanza*, coedited with Elvira María Restrepo.

Jeanene McCoy Bengoa works at the Comprehensive Drug Research Center, University of Miami Miller School of Medicine.

Oscar Bernal is the director of the Master of Public Health Program, Universidad de los Andes, Schools of Medicine and Government, Bogotá.

Lilian Bobea is a sociologist who teaches at Bentley University in Waltham, Massachusetts, and a faculty member at the Facultad Latinoamericana de Ciencias Sociales, Dominican Republic. Dr. Bobea specializes in security and defense issues, civil-military relations, and violence and citizen security in Latin America and the Caribbean and was a consultant for the Dominican government's Democratic Security Plan from 2005 to 2007. As an SSRC/OSI Fellow, she is currently conducting comparative research on organized violence in Puerto Rico and the Dominican Republic. She has an extensive publication record of academic and policy-oriented essays on regional security, organized crime, drug trafficking, and violence in the Caribbean.

Marten W. Brienen currently teaches in the Political Science Department at Oklahoma State University. Previously, he served as the director of academic programs in Latin American Studies at the University of Miami. His recent publications include *Prisons in the Americas in the 21st Century: Human Dumping Ground*, coedited with Jonathan D. Rosen; and "Warisata y la renovación de la educación rural indigenal boliviana, 1932–1948," in *Campesinos y escolares: La construcción de la escuela en el campo latinoamericano (siglos XIX y XX)*, ed. Alicia Civera, Juan Alfonseca, and Carlos Escalante.

Carolina Cepeda is a political science PhD candidate at the Universidad de los Andes, Bogotá. Her research is focused on social movements against neoliberalism in Latin America and recent social demonstrations around the world.

Daniel H. Ciccarone is professor of family and community medicine at the Department of Family and Community Medicine at the University of California, San Francisco. He has been providing community-based primary care in San Francisco for seventeen years and directs a number of research projects, utilizing both quantitative and qualitative methodologies, which aim to deepen our understanding of HIV risk taking among socially marginalized groups. Recently, he has published, with G. Unick, D. Rosenblum, and S. Mars, "The Relationship between U.S. Heroin Market Dynamics and Heroin-Related Overdose, 1992–2008" in *Addiction*; and with D. Rosenblum, F. M. Castrillo, P. Bourgois, S. Mars, G. Karandinos, and G. J. Unick, "Urban Segregation and the U.S. Heroin Market: A Quantitative Model of Anthropological Hypotheses from an Inner-City Drug Market" in *International Journal of Drug Policy*.

Khatchik DerGhougassian is professor at the Universidad de San Andrés in Argentina. He specializes in international security, the Middle East, Latin America, and the proliferation of arms throughout the world. His recent publications include two edited volumes—*La defensa en el siglo XXI: Argentina y la seguridad regional* and *El derrumbe del negacionismo*—and "The Armenian Genocide on the International Agenda: The Case for Diplomatic Engagement" in *Haigazian Armenological Review*.

Roberto Domínguez is associate professor in the Government Department at Suffolk University and associate editor of the journal *European Security*. He was a postdoctoral Jean Monnet Fellow at the European University Institute, Florence, 2012–2013. His most recent publications include *The OSCE: Soft Security for a Hard World* and "Obstacles to Security Cooperation in North America," in *North American Integration*, ed. Gaspare Genna and David Mayer-Foulkes.

Zelde Espinel Ben-Amy is currently a resident physician in psychiatry at the University of Miami Department of Psychiatry and Behavioral Sciences/Jackson Memorial Hospital, Miami. She has completed her psychiatry residency training at Clínica Montserrat, Universidad El Bosque, Bogotá, and she is a licensed psychiatrist in Colombia. For six years she served as codirector, Center for Disaster and Extreme Event Preparedness, University of Miami Miller School of Medicine. Her current research focuses on research in Colombia dealing with mental health interventions for conflict-affected populations and drug abuse/HIV interventions for heroin users.

Glen Evans has conducted research on organized crime in the tri-border area of Argentina, Brazil, and Paraguay. Currently he is researching the status and operations of the criminal intelligence system in Argentina while pursuing a master's degree in public security at the Institute of the Federal Police. He is an executive officer and partner at Protección Inteligente, a company specializing in providing consulting and security services and lectures on complex crimes, organized crime, and criminal intelligence in several renowned academic institutions in Argentina.

Betty Horwitz earned a PhD in international studies in 2007 from the University of Miami. She is the author of *The Transformation of the Organization of American States: A Multilateral Framework for Regional Governance* and "The Role of the Inter-American Drug Abuse Control Commission (CICAD): Confronting the Problem of Illegal Drugs in the Americas" in *Latin American Politics and Society*. She is working with Bruce M. Bagley on a textbook on international relations in Latin America.

Adam Isacson joined the Washington Office on Latin America (WOLA) in 2010, after fourteen years working on Latin American and Caribbean security issues with the Center for International Policy (CIP). At WOLA, his Regional Security Policy Program monitors security trends and U.S. military assistance to the Western Hemisphere. He has published and cowritten dozens of reports and articles, testified before Congress several times, and led several congressional delegations. Before WOLA and CIP, he worked for the Arias Foundation for Peace and Human Progress in San José, Costa Rica.

Alberto Lozano-Vázquez is research professor in the Institute of International Studies at the Universidad del Mar, Huatulco, Mexico. From 1998 to 2008, he worked in both the private sector (international trade) and the public sector (education) in Mexico. He is currently a PhD candidate in international relations and comparative politics at the Universidad del Mar, and his research is focused on the U.S.-Mexico bilateral relationship in terms of regional security and transnational threats.

Duane C. McBride is the chair of the Behavioral Sciences Department and director of the Institute for the Prevention of Addiction, Andrews University, Berrien Springs, Michigan. His areas of expertise are criminology and drug abuse, and he has been published in the *American Journal of Psychiatry*, *Journal of Drug Issues*, *Journal of Health and Social Behavior*, *Criminology*, *Journal of Criminal Justice*, *International Journal of Criminology and Penology*, *Youth and Society*, *Human Organization*, *Addictive Diseases: An International Journal*, *British Journal of Addiction*, *Chemical Dependencies: Behavioral and Biomedical Issues*, and *Bulletin of the New York Academy of Medicine*.

Clyde McCoy is director of the Comprehensive Drug Research Center and chair emeritus, Department of Epidemiology and Public Health at the University of Miami Miller School of Medicine. Dr. McCoy's recent publications include "Institutionalization of Drug Abuse Research in Academia—One Professor's View" in *Journal of Drug Issues*, and, with M. Comerford and L. R. Metsch, "Employment among Chronic Drug Users at Baseline and 6-Month Follow-up" in *Substance Use and Misuse*.

J. Bryan Page is professor in the Department of Anthropology at the University of Miami. Research on people who engage in socially disapproved behaviors has dominated his professional activity since 1973. Dr. Page coauthored two books with Merrill Singer: *Comprehending Drug Use: Ethnographic Research at the Social Margins* and *The Social Value of Drug Addicts: Uses of the Useless*.

Jorge Rebolledo Flores has been a professor of international relations at the Universidad del Mar, Huatulco, Mexico. In addition, he has worked in government, specifically, public security, in Mexico City. He also has worked as a consultant for the Washington Office on Latin America. Currently, he teaches at the Colegio de Veracruz in Mexico.

Elvira María Restrepo is research assistant professor at the University of Miami. Her current research interests include comparative studies in justice, crime, and conflict at the level of individual case studies and of aggregated statistics. She published *The Colombian Criminal Justice in Crisis: Fear and Distrust* and has research papers published in a variety of international peer-reviewed journals. From 2003 to 2007, she was assistant professor in the Economics Department at the Universidad de los Andes (Bogotá), and she has been a member of the Centro de Estudios sobre Desarrollo Económico (Universidad de los Andes) and Fedesarrollo (an economics think tank).

Rocío A. Rivera Barradas has worked for the Mexican government at the Ministry of Foreign Affairs and the Ministry of Finance and Public Credit. Her research interests are related to organized crime, regional security, immigration, the U.S.-Mexico bilateral relationship, the domestic roots of U.S. foreign policy, the role of state and local authorities in international relations, and U.S. foreign policy toward Latin America. She is a PhD candidate at the University of Miami.

Francisco Rojas Aravena is rector of the Universidad para la Paz. From 2004 to 2012, Dr. Rojas Aravena was the secretary general of the Facultad Latinoamericana de Ciencias Sociales. His most recent publications are "Cooperación y seguridad internacional en las Américas," "Argentina, Brasil y Chile: Integración y seguridad," and "Globalización, América Latina y diplomacia de Cumbres."

Jonathan D. Rosen is research professor at the Institute of International Studies at the Universidad del Mar, Huatulco, Mexico. Recent publications include *The Losing War: Plan Colombia and Beyond* and, coedited with Marten Brienen, *Prisons in the Americas in the 21st Century: Human Dumping Ground*.

James M. Shultz is founder and director of the Center for Disaster and Extreme Event Preparedness; codirector of the Miami Center for Public Health Preparedness, Department of Epidemiology and Public Health; and senior fellow of the Comprehensive Drug Research Center, University of Miami Miller School of Medicine. He is also associate professor in the Master of Public Health Program, Universidad de los Andes, Bogotá, and adjunct professor for emergency management, teaching online courses for multiple universities. Dr. Shultz has written books in the area of disaster behavioral health, and he is the primary developer of the trauma signature analysis approach for providing evidence-based guidance on mental health and psychosocial support response during disasters. Dr. Shultz' current international research focuses on disaster and conflict-affected populations, including the overlap of trauma exposure and substance abuse.

Arlene B. Tickner is professor of international relations in the Department of Political Science at the Universidad de los Andes in Bogotá. Her research deals with relations between the United States and Colombia, Latin American security, Colombian foreign policy, and the sociology of knowledge. Her recent works include *Claiming the International* and *Thinking International Relations Differently*, both coedited with David Blaney.

Juan Gabriel Tokatlian is director of the Department of Political Science and International Relations at the Universidad Torcuato Di Tella, Argentina. He lived for eighteen years in Colombia (1981–1998), where he was cofounder (1982) and director (1987–1994) of the Center for International Studies of the Universidad de los Andes (Bogotá). He has published books, essays, and op-eds on Colombian and Argentine foreign policy, U.S.–Latin American relations, the contemporary international system, and drug trafficking, terrorism, and organized crime.

Yulia Vorobyeva is a PhD candidate in international studies at the University of Miami. Her research interests include drug trafficking and organized crime, with special focus on Latin America and Russia, civil-military relations, security studies, and U.S.–Latin American relations.

Marcelo Rocha e Silva Zorovich was resident fellow at the Center for Hemispheric Policy at the University of Miami in the fall of 2011. He has worked as a professor of international relations and international business at the Escola Superior de Propaganda e Marketing, São Paulo. He is pursuing a doctorate in international studies at the University of Miami.

INDEX